HANDBOOK OF SOFTWARE AGING AND REJUVENATION

Fundamentals, Methods, Applications, and Future Directions

Other World Scientific Titles by the Author

Recent Advances in Stochastic Operations Research
ISBN: 978-981-256-704-8

Recent Advances in Stochastic Operations Research II
ISBN: 978-981-279-166-5

HANDBOOK OF SOFTWARE AGING AND REJUVENATION

Fundamentals, Methods, Applications, and Future Directions

Editors

Tadashi Dohi
Hiroshima University, Japan

Kishor Trivedi
Duke University, USA

Alberto Avritzer
eSulabSolutions, Inc., USA

World Scientific

NEW JERSEY • LONDON • SINGAPORE • BEIJING • SHANGHAI • HONG KONG • TAIPEI • CHENNAI • TOKYO

Published by

World Scientific Publishing Co. Pte. Ltd.
5 Toh Tuck Link, Singapore 596224
USA office: 27 Warren Street, Suite 401-402, Hackensack, NJ 07601
UK office: 57 Shelton Street, Covent Garden, London WC2H 9HE

Library of Congress Control Number: 2020931572

British Library Cataloguing-in-Publication Data
A catalogue record for this book is available from the British Library.

HANDBOOK OF SOFTWARE AGING AND REJUVENATION
Fundamentals, Methods, Applications, and Future Directions

ISBN 978-981-121-456-1 (hardcover)
ISBN 978-981-121-457-8 (ebook for institutions)
ISBN 978-981-121-458-5 (ebook for individuals)

For any available supplementary material, please visit
https://www.worldscientific.com/worldscibooks/10.1142/11673#t=suppl

Desk Editor: Nur Izdihar Binte Ismail

Typeset by Stallion Press
Email: enquiries@stallionpress.com

Preface

Since the publication of the first paper on software aging and rejuvenation in 1995, considerable research has been devoted to this topic and the ideas that have been generated by this research have been implemented in a large number of systems. There are a few relatively simple ideas that are nearly universally applicable to all software-based systems and that can improve software reliability, availability and performance with a small overhead. We believe that the techniques of which we speak are applied on a very wide scale without necessarily using the nomenclature that we use here. It is hoped that the publication of this monograph will at once spur further research. Those practitioners that are not currently applying these simple ideas may become interested in using them. Those practitioners that are already using some form of rejuvenation may be able to improve upon that current approach based on the ideas in this monograph.

We are indebted to all the authors of the chapters in this monograph and the reviewers of the chapters. We are also indebted to the WoSAR family consisting of the aficionados of the annual Workshops on Software Aging and Rejuvenation. We are extremely happy to announce that the Huang *et al.* paper mentioned above has been selected for the prestigious Jean Claude Laprie award for 2019.

Tadashi Dohi
Alberto Avritzer
Kishor Trivedi

Contents

Preface v

List of Authors xi

Part I: Fundamentals **1**

1. **Software Aging and Rejuvenation: A Genesis** **3**
   Alberto Avritzer, Domenico Cotroneo, Yennun Huang and Kishor Trivedi

2. **Fundamentals of Software Aging** **21**
   Domenico Cotroneo, Rivalino Matias Jr. and Roberto Natella

3. **Software Rejuvenation: Key Concepts and Granularity** **41**
   Vasilis P. Koutras and Agapios N. Platis

Part II: Data-driven Approach **71**

4. **Measurements for Software Aging** **73**
   Roberto Pietrantuono, Javier Alonso and Kalyan Vaidyanathan

Part III: Model-driven Approach 91

5. **Markov Chains and Petri Nets** 93

Fumio Machida and Paulo R. M. Maciel

6. **Analysis of Queueing Models for Rejuvenation** 127

Hiroyuki Okamura and Tadashi Dohi

7. **Black-Box Models for Restart, Reboot and Rejuvenation** 155

Katinka Wolter, Tommi Pesu, Aad van Moorsel and William J. Knottenbelt

Part IV: Applications 195

8. **Using Software Aging Monitoring and Rejuvenation for the Assessment of High-Availability Systems** 197

Alberto Avritzer, Michael Grottke and Daniel Sadoc Menasché

9. **Application to Operating Systems** 229

Kenji Kono, Kenichi Kourai and Hiroshi Yamada

10. **Aging in Virtualized Environments** 261

Roberto Pietrantuono, Domenico Cotroneo and Stefano Russo

11. **Experimental Tools for Software Aging Analysis** 285

Roberto Natella and Artur Andrzejak

12. **Implementation of Micro-rejuvenation with Cooperative Stack Leasing** 327

Sandip HomChaudhuri

Part V: Future Directions and Appendix **353**

13. Future Directions for Software Aging and Rejuvenation Research **355**

Alberto Avritzer, Roberto Pietrantuono and Kishor Trivedi

Appendix: Stochastic Modeling Techniques in Software Aging and Rejuvenation Phenomena **363**

Andrea Bobbio, Antonio Puliafito, Marco Scarpa and Miklós Telek

List of Authors

Javier Alonso: Chapter 4
Artur Andrzejak: Chapter 11
Alberto Avritzer: Chapter 1, Chapter 8, Chapter 13
Andrea Bobbio: Appendix
Domenico Cotroneo: Chapter 1, Chapter 2, Chapter 10
Tadashi Dohi: Chapter 6
Michael Grottke: Chapter 8
Sandip HomChaudhuri: Chapter 12
Yennun Huang: Chapter 1
William J. Knottenbelt: Chapter 7
Kenji Kono: Chapter 9
Kenichi Kourai: Chapter 9
Vasilis P. Koutras: Chapter 3
Daniel Sadoc Menasché: Chapter 8
Fumio Machida: Chapter 5
Paulo R. M. Maciel: Chapter 5
Rivalino Matias Jr.: Chapter 2
Aad van Moorsel: Chapter 7
Roberto Natella: Chapter 2, Chapter 11
Hiroyuki Okamura: Chapter 6
Tommi Pesu: Chapter 7
Agapios N. Platis: Chapter 3
Roberto Pietrantuono: Chapter 4, Chapter 10, Chapter 13
Antonio Puliafito: Appendix
Stefano Russo: Chapter 10
Marco Scarpa: Appendix
Miklós Telek: Appendix

Kishor Trivedi: Chapter 1, Chapter 13
Kalyan Vaidyanathan: Chapter 4
Katinka Wolter: Chapter 7
Hiroshi Yamada: Chapter 9

Part I

Fundamentals

Part I of this Handbook describes the fundamentals of Software Aging and Rejuvenation.

Chapter 1, Software Aging and Rejuvenation: A Genesis, contains the historical perspective and presents the pioneering research that was performed at AT&T, Duke University and the University of Naples.

Chapter 2, Fundamentals of Software Aging, presents the fundamental concepts and definitions, such as the definitions of aging-related bugs, aging-related failure, and the aging effect. Examples of software aging in real-world systems are also provided.

Chapter 3, Software Rejuvenation: Key Concepts and Granularity, focuses on the classification of rejuvenation strategies based on granularity. Granularity concerns the level at which aging is detected and the level at which rejuvenation is applied to counteract aging.

Chapter 1

Software Aging and Rejuvenation: A Genesis

Alberto Avritzer*, Domenico Cotroneo†, Yennun Huang‡ and Kishor Trivedi§

eSulabSolutions, Inc., Princeton, USA
Università degli Studi di Napoli Federico II, Italy
Academia Sinica, Taipei
Duke University, USA
* *beto@esulabsolutions.com*
† *cotroneo@unina.it*
‡ *yennunhuang@gmail.com*
§ *ktrivedi@duke.edu*

Software aging and rejuvenation originated at AT&T Bell Labs. A significant amount of research on the topic also took place at Duke University and Università degli Studi di Napoli Federico II. We present here a historical perspective on this topic as viewed from these three places.

1.1. Introduction

Software aging and rejuvenation originated at AT&T Bell Labs. A significant amount of research on the topic also took place at Duke University and Università degli Studi di Napoli Federico II. We present here a historical perspective on this topic as viewed from these three places.

1.2. Software Aging and Rejuvenation at AT&T

1.2.1. *Software Innovation for Preventing Network Outages*

In the early 1990s, AT&T embarked on a broad software program with the objective of stimulating business growth by providing new software-based services. One of the key obstacles to the deployment of these new software-based services was the realization that as software moved to the network core, it would be required to be very reliable. In AT&T business requirements terminology [1], software was required to be “pure” or “fault-free”. These business requirements drove significant investment in the innovation of the network operating systems software development processes. Specifically, these investments were based on the realization that software was bug-prone, and would incur significant reliability degradation as more complex requirements were implemented. Another reason AT&T software could not be “bug-free” or “pure” was because its software development process started employing many commercial off-the-shelf software (COTS) components to build its telecommunication services [2]. Lawrence Bernstein, who was Operating Systems Vice President of AT&T Network Systems and Executive Director of Bell Labs [1] at the time, was a software reliability visionary and supported several software reliability research innovation initiatives that were applied to quantitatively assess and improve the reliability of the network operating systems software. Among these software reliability initiatives was the development of a set of fault-tolerant and software rejuvenation software libraries, which was led by Chandra Kintala [2]. In this section, we provide a brief overview of several breakthrough innovations in the software aging and software rejuvenation research [3–5] that resulted from software reliability initiatives conducted by AT&T Bell Labs in the early 1990s.

1.2.2. *Software Aging in Telecommunications Systems*

The software reliability initiatives implemented at AT&T Bell Labs in the early 1990s led to the development of quantitative approaches to estimate the software reliability of network operating systems during the testing phase, i.e., before they were deployed to the production environments. As a result of the application of these methods, it was empirically discovered that software availability degradation could be attributed to a phenomenon called software aging [3–6]. That is, long-running software exhibits an increasing failure rate. Even though there is no physical degradation, software “appears to age” due to error accumulation or depletion of operating system resources. In addition, it was shown that the effects of the software aging phenomenon could be overcome in a proactive manner when the software was restored to full capacity [3–6]. The software capacity restoration approach [6] by means of a restart or reboot as a preventive maintenance technique was named software rejuvenation [4]. Note that there is no change made to the software but the environment and its related resources are cleaned up, yet the technique remains known as software rejuvenation.

These telecommunication software systems operated in several telecommunication domains as, for example, the Billing Data Collector [4], the Speech Synthesis [4], the Switch Adjunct Operating System [6], and the Telecom Provisioning and Alarm System [5].

1.2.3. *Software Rejuvenation Approaches in Telecommunications Systems*

In the seminal paper [4], software rejuvenation strategies for client-server systems and for long-running computation-intensive applications were introduced. For client-server applications, it was shown that periodic rejuvenation at idle times (e.g., weekends) increased the server availability. This paper [4] was the first to introduce the term "software rejuvenation" in the context of software availability.

For long-running computationally intensive applications, a periodic rollback using checkpointing was shown to increase the probability of successful application completion. The proposed strategy considered the software rejuvenation costs, and the software failure costs, in terms of the downtime associated with crash failures and software rejuvenation operations. The output of this strategy consisted of the computation of a constant period for rejuvenation. As a result, the production system would be periodically rolled back to an earlier checkpointed state, where the system would be restored to full capacity.

In [5], a software rejuvenation strategy that was based on monitoring the software aging rate and real-time traffic demands was used to determine the best time to perform software rejuvenation. The real-time traffic data was monitored and compared to historic traffic data. The combination of all these factors was used to determine, in real-time, when to perform software rejuvenation. The main assumption used in the development of this rejuvenation strategy was that the failure cost at time t was dependent on the system state at time t, which was defined as the system traffic at time t and the amount of capacity degradation at time t. In [5], it was shown that the average time to perform software rejuvenation combined with the system state at time t were important factors that needed to be taken into consideration when deciding when to execute the software rejuvenation routine.

1.2.4. *Markov Models of Software Aging and Rejuvenation*

In [6], a continuous-time Markov-chain-based approach for the generation and execution of load tests was introduced. The system state at time t

was defined to be the set of calls active at time t. The application of the Markov-chain-based testing approach to an adjunct telecommunication switch revealed capacity degradation as a function of test time, which could be resolved through software rejuvenation [6]. In [3] the approach introduced in [6] was extended to include the estimation of the software reliability of smoothly degrading systems, also referred to as aging systems [4]. A tolerance function was added to each Markov chain state to account for the impact of software aging on the measured performance of the telecommunication system at the associated state. Therefore, the reliability of the telecommunication system, after the application of the Markov-chain-based testing approach, was computed with respect to the operational profile as the sum of the fraction of operations completed in each of the measured Markov chain states, weighted by the steady-state probability of the associated state [3]. An independence assumption was introduced to allow for the decomposition of the steady-state solution of the Markov chain into the product of the solution of the component states. This decomposition enabled the application of a depth-first search algorithm (DFS) to generate the most likely states of the underlying Markov chain, without having to solve for the large Markov chain [3]. The application of the approach to the reliability estimation of several large telecommunication systems was also reported in [3] and [7].

In the seminal paper [4], a Markov chain model was introduced to support the assessment of how software rejuvenation approaches could be used to mitigate application downtime due to crash failures. Crash failures are responsible for the costs associated with unscheduled downtime. As the application availability is impacted by software rejuvenation, the model takes into account the cost associated with carrying out software rejuvenation. In the proposed model, the cost of software rejuvenation is assumed to be a fraction of the cost associated with these crash failures. A simple 3-state Markov model is used to compute software availability without rejuvenation, where the software can be found in each one of the following 3 states: 1) a highly robust state, S_0, 2) a failure-probable state, S_P, or, 3) a failed state, S_F. A 4-state Markov model was proposed for the computation of software availability with software rejuvenation. In the Markov model with software rejuvenation a decision is modeled at the failure-probable state, S_P, where the model could transition to the failure state S_F or to the software rejuvenation state S_R. The authors have concluded that for the software rejuvenation approach to be useful, the total downtime cost of software rejuvenation, i.e., the cost of being in states S_F and S_R must be less than the cost of being in S_F, for a system without rejuvenation. Details of this model are presented in Chapter 5 of this book, written by Fumio Machida and Paulo Maciel.

In the following sections, the presentation of the detailed models and measurements of software aging and rejuvenation that were developed at Duke University are presented.

1.3. Software Aging and Rejuvenation at Duke University

1.3.1. *Analytic Models*

Sachin Garg, a Ph.D. student in Kishor Trivedi's lab at Duke, brought the seminal paper [4] to his attention in the summer of 1995. First, we decided to consider relaxing the distributional assumptions made in the homogeneous continuous-time Markov chain used for optimal scheduling in their paper.

Referring to Fig. 1 in [4] (which also appears as Fig. 5.2 in Chapter 5 of this book, by Machida and Maciel), they considered the failure-probable state S_P, as an observable state. Thus, in the traditional language of preventive maintenance literature, in their Fig. 2 (which also appears as Fig. 5.3 in Chapter 5 by Machida and Maciel), they considered condition-based or inspection-based preventive maintenance (rejuvenation in this case). We can alternatively consider the transition to the failure state S_F from the robust state S_0 via the failure-probable state S_P as merely an artifice so that the overall time to failure is hypo-exponentially distributed [8, 9]. Since the hypo-exponential distribution has a failure rate that is increasing with age, we know that, in general, in such a case, preventive maintenance could be useful. In this case, we can consider the state S_P as not observable and hence the rejuvenation trigger clock should start on entry to state S_0. This is traditionally known as time-based rejuvenation wherein the optimal time to trigger rejuvenation can be studied. It makes sense that the time to trigger rejuvenation should be deterministic (or generally distributed). This eventually led to a paper published in ISSRE 1995 [10]. Because of the existence of a generally distributed timed transition (rejuvenation trigger) that is concurrent with the transition from S_0 to S_P as well as the time from S_P to S_F, the resulting stochastic process is not a semi-Markov process but a Markov regenerative process. Thus the Fig. 2 of [4] morphs into a Markov Regenerative Stochastic Petri Net (MRSPN) (see Fig. 1 in [10]). This MRSPN [11] model is also presented as Fig. 5.13 in Chapter 5 of this book by Machida and Maciel). Another direction of extension was to consider the completion time of a program in the presence of checkpointing and rejuvenation [12]. The models in [4] and [10] do not capture the performance degradation effect of software aging. In [13] a Markov Decision Process (MDP) was used to model the performance degradation aspect of software aging. In [14], a queueing model with Poisson job arrivals, age-dependent (degrading) service rate, and age-dependent (increasing) failure rate was introduced and optimal scheduling studied. The resulting model becomes a non-homogeneous Markov chain. This model represents the behavior of the system when it is in a working state. The other two states of the higher-level model are failed (and undergoing reactive repair) or rejuvenation where proactive repair is ongoing. Such a 3-state semi-Markov model is often used in several other papers [15, 16] and is used for determining the optimal rejuvenation schedule. This paper and its extensions are discussed in detail in Chapter 6 by Okamura and Dohi in this book. Antonio Puliafito and Miklós Telek were visiting Duke at that time and worked with Sachin Garg and Kishor Trivedi on the two papers [13, 14].

Noting that all research on software aging and rejuvenation was thus far on single boxes, Steve Hunter of IBM, a former student from Trivedi's group, approached us to consider modeling software aging and rejuvenation phenomena for a cluster. We ended up with a nice stochastic reward net model of an IBM Cluster [17] that showed the effectiveness of rejuvenation on cluster availability. This subsequently led to the implementation of rejuvenation in IBM's X-series [18]. When Tadashi Dohi was on a sabbatical leave to Duke and when Katerina Goseva-Popstojanova was a postdoctoral associate at Duke, we extended the original 4-state CTMC model from [4] into a semi-Markov model where all transition times are allowed to be generally distributed [19]. This model was embellished to compute the optimal rejuvenation schedule directly from data without the intermediate step of fitting the inter-failure data to some distributions [20, 21]. Further details of these models are given in Chapter 5 of this book by Machida and Maciel. With another graduate student in Trivedi's group (Yujuan Bao), we enhanced the M/M/1 queuing model so that the arrivals correspond to memory requests. The memory request sizes were assumed to be random. From the resulting non-homogeneous Markov chain with an absorbing state, it was possible to show that the time taken to reach the absorbing state (corresponding to the rate of exhaustion of memory) has an increasing failure rate [22]. Yun Liu, another Ph.D. student in Trivedi's group, worked with Motorola engineers to develop a stochastic reward net model of a cable modem termination system [23]. When Dharmaraja Selvamuthu was a postdoctoral associate in Trivedi's lab, an inspection-based rejuvenation using MRGP was developed [24].

A comprehensive stochastic reward net performability model of a clustered system with rejuvenation under workload variations was developed in [25]. This was done with two Ph.D. students, Dazhi Wang and Wei Xie, in Trivedi's lab. The model was more comprehensive than [17, 23] in that it included a performance submodel, it allowed for a deterministic rejuvenation trigger interval and workload was varied by explicitly modeling peak and off-peak periods. The resulting model was cast as a DSPN (Deterministic and Stochastic Petri Net) by first approximating the rejuvenation trigger interval as a set of Erlang stages and keeping the deterministic transitions between peak and off-peak periods. The DSPN was solved by the method of subordinated Markov chains.

Software aging can take place at different granularities and correspondingly, rejuvenation ought to take place at different granularities. A possible list of granularities is given in [26]. A semi-Markov model of a two-level rejuvenation policy was published in the RESS journal in 2006 by Wei Xie (a Ph.D. student in Trivedi's group) and Y. Hong (a visiting Professor from the Chinese Academy of Sciences) [27]. Two-level rejuvenation has been further refined by a remote student of Trivedi's group at Beihang University (Ning Gaorong) [28]. In that paper, the diagnostic inaccuracy of state identification by monitoring was included and experiments were conducted to compare the effectiveness of two-level rejuvenation over one-level rejuvenation. A two-level rejuvenation model of the Android Smartphone has just been published as a collaboration between Duke University and Beihang University [29]. Optimal rejuvenation trigger intervals were obtained and experiments conducted to show the effectiveness of the two-level rejuvenation strategy.

When Michael Grottke was an assistant research professor in Trivedi's group, we published a paper with Alberto Avritzer on the slowdown effect of software aging on user response times and its mitigation via rejuvenation [30]. An important paper on the classification of software bugs into Bohrbugs, Mandelbugs and aging-related bugs together with their mitigations was published in 2007 during Michael Grottke's sojourn at Duke [31].

When Fumio Machida was a visiting scientist at Duke, a performability model of a virtualized system was developed [32]. In this model, VM (Virtual Machine) migration was also incorporated besides two concrete levels of rejuvenation: VM (Virtual Machine) rejuvenation and VMM (Virtual Machine Monitor) rejuvenation. This was a stochastic reward net model and was done jointly with Dong Seong Kim, a research associate in Trivedi's lab. All the models described above considered system measures such as availability or total cost. An interesting model developed during Fumio Machida's visit to Duke studied the completion of an individual job on a virtualized server subject to software aging and rejuvenation [33]. This model was based on research done for Victor Nicola's thesis at Duke in the 1980s [34, 35] and as such he kindly agreed to work with us on the paper.

1.3.2. *Monitoring*

In 1996, we felt that it was important to collect data from real systems and experimentally validate the software aging phenomenon. For this purpose, Sachin Garg was sent as a summer intern to Lucent Bell Labs. He worked in Chandra Kintala's group to develop a system of periodic monitoring of OS resources. We eventually completed the project at Duke and investigated methods of analyzing the enormous amount of data collected. The collected data successfully demonstrated the existence of the phenomenon of software aging. We note here that there is no physical deterioration in the software but the software system behaves as if its failure rate increases with execution time. Thus software "appears" to age. This eventually led to the paper published in ISSRE 1998 [36]. The paper provides details of the monitoring tool that was built, the data collected and the methods of statistical analysis used on the data. Details of the monitoring tool developed are given in Chapter 11 of this book, written by Natella and Andrzejak. Statistical techniques used included seasonal Kendall tests to detect increasing or decreasing trends in the measured data and Sen's non-parametric method [37] to estimate the time to resource exhaustion [36]. More details can also be found in Chapter 4 of this book written by Vaidyanathan, Alonso, and Pietrantuono.

It is intuitively clear that the rate at which various OS resources get depleted will depend on the workload being processed. Thus using Sen's slope and making a linear extrapolation is not cognizant of the workload variations in the system. The next Ph.D. student at Duke working on this topic, Kalyan Vaidyanathan, developed a semi-Markov reward model to keep track of different workload states and thence predict the time to resource exhaustion. This research was initially presented at ISSRE 1999 [38] and later published in IEEE TDSC [16]. It is interesting to note that the semi-Markov model states, sojourn time distributions, transition probabilities and reward rates were all derived from the measured data. More recently, Harish Sukhwani, a Ph.D. student in Trivedi's lab, developed a monitoring tool for software aging in the IBM cloud controller [39].

1.3.3. *Experimental Methods*

Experiments to study the phenomenon of software aging were started as an M.S. thesis project at Duke by Lei Li. For that research project, the experiments were conducted on the Apache Web server with an artificial workload being generated using httperf. A monitoring tool called procmon was developed. Non-parametric statistical techniques as well as parametric time-series methods were used to analyze the data. Their research findings were first presented in a conference paper [40] and a refined version of the paper was published in a journal [41] when Michael Grottke was a postdoctoral associate at Duke. A paper surveying various statistical methods of analyzing software aging data was published when Gunter Hoffman was a postdoctoral associate at Duke [42].

A significant line of experiments was started with the Ph.D. thesis of Rivalino Matias, Jr. that effectively used Accelerated Life Testing (ALT) and Accelerated Degradation Testing (ADT) in the context of software aging. ALT and ADT methods are well-known in hardware reliability but their use in the context of software was pioneered by this dissertation. Subsequently, Rivalino spent several years at Duke as a postdoctoral associate producing several important papers on experiments on software aging using ALT and ADT [43, 44]. Such experimental methods were also used during the visit of Jing Zhao to Duke [45–47].

A set of experiments was conducted to compare the performance and dependability overheads of different rejuvenation techniques when Javier Alonso Lopez was a postdoctoral research associate at Duke [48]. Besides the investigation of overheads, this paper also divided rejuvenation scheduling methods into time-based and inspection-based. The latter were further divided into threshold-based and prediction-based methods. The paper also laid out various levels of granularity for carrying out rejuvenation: starting from the physical node-level, the VMM level, and the VM level all the way to application and application component level restart (reboots).

Experimental methods were used by Javier Alonso Lopez, Antonio Bovenzi (a visiting student from the University of Naples) and Hiroshi Yamada (a visiting scientist from Tokyo University of Agriculture and Technology) at Duke University to investigate fast OS reboot techniques applicable to software rejuvenation [49]. When Paulo Maciel was on a sabbatical leave to Duke, an experimental study of software aging and rejuvenation in the Eucalyptus cloud computing infrastructure was conducted [50].

1.3.4. *Failure Data Analysis*

In 2007, when Michael Grottke was an assistant research professor at Duke, we approached Allen Nikora of JPL to acquire problem reports of NASA satellite data for the purpose of bug classification, following the characterization that had been developed in our previous work [51–53]. Together, we successfully applied for a project funded by NASA's Office of Safety and Mission Assurance, in the course of which we analyzed onboard software problem reports from eighteen NASA missions [54].

Subsequently, with our colleagues from the University of Naples, we carried out a similar analysis of Bugzilla reports for open source software including Linux and MySql [55]. More recently, with our colleagues from Beihang University, we have carried out a more extensive analysis of Linux Bugzilla reports [56] as well as problem reports from Android [57]. Yet another more recent development is the development of methods to predict the aging-related bug-proneness of software modules based on data from previous versions [58].

1.3.5. *Implementation*

Based on our study of rejuvenation in a cluster [17], IBM decided to implement rejuvenation in the IBM Director of X-series servers. Kalyan Vaidyanathan worked with Rick Harper and Steve Hunter (among others) of IBM to prototype the implementation. Statistical techniques to detect the occurrence of aging and to estimate time to resource exhaustion were developed so that rejuvenation could be automatically performed. The details of this effort are described in the IBM JRD paper [18].

In a paper with Javier Alonso Lopez, Antonio Bovenzi and Jinghui Li (of Huawei), we investigated the use of software rejuvenation in the IT and Telco industries [59]. It was found that the software rejuvenation solutions most often used were either time-based rejuvenation or threshold-values based rejuvenation. At the same time most of the patents are on a predictive approach to rejuvenation.

1.4. Software Aging Research at Università degli Studi di Napoli Federico II

From 2004, the DESSERT[a] group at the Federico II University of Naples started to work on software aging. Considerable attention has been devoted

[a]Dependable Systems and Software Engineering Research Team, www.dessert.unina.it

to the empirical analysis of software aging, based on direct measurements from real-world systems. Measurement-based studies provide detailed information about the aging phenomenon in real systems, which is useful to better understand the nature and the extent of software aging and to raise awareness of potential issues. A widely-used approach is adopting time-series analysis on monitored resources. Time series are typically analyzed by first using trend tests to accept/reject the hypothesis of no trend in data (e.g., Mann-Kendall, t-student, Seasonal Kendall tests), and using techniques to estimate such trends and possible seasonality in data (e.g, multiple linear regression, regression smoothing, Sen's slope estimate procedure, autoregressive models). Researchers from Naples adopted these techniques to study the relationship of the software aging phenomenon with workload in real-world complex systems, including the Linux Kernel [60] and the Java Virtual Machine [61, 62]. Domenico Cotroneo, Roberto Natella, Salvatore Orlando and Stefano Russo demonstrated the presence of aging in the Linux operating system and Java virtual machine. In both studies, resource usage information has been related with the observed aging trends by means of multiple linear regression and principal components analysis; these relationships were exploited to find out kernel/JVM subsystems responsible for aging phenomena. From the experimental analysis, it results that aging sources actually exist in the Linux kernel and Java Virtual Machines; they manifested as a statistically significant aging trend of memory consumption in all our experiments. In both studies, the analysis of workload parameters is used to provide indications on potential sources of software aging, by highlighting the subsystems whose parameters are correlated to the experienced aging trends. The resulting methodology is illustrated in [63].

Another important contribution from the DESSERT group is the relationship between software aging and software metrics. Indeed, traditional studies on software aging are focused on predicting the aging effects by monitoring and analytically modeling resource consumption at runtime. Domenico Cotroneo, Roberto Natella and Roberto Pietrantuono, from the DESSERT group, intended to explore if the static features of the software, as derived by its source code, have a potential relationship with software aging, by investigating what kind of relationship exists between software aging and several static features of the software. The results have been published in [60, 64].

Researchers at the Federico II University of Naples have also made important contributions to the study of software aging in mobile devices. In the context of the Android operating system, different user apps may have a different impact on software aging, as they may trigger different services of the Android OS; or different Android configurations (e.g., vendors or versions) may exhibit different software aging effects. However, considering all of the possible combinations of workloads and configurations leads to an extremely large number of long-running experiments, which would take an unfeasible amount of time to complete. In order to determine the most influential factors (e.g., workload, device vendor, OS version, etc.) and assess their impact on the software aging trend, the researchers adopted the Design of Experiments (DoE) approach and derived the methodology on the basis of a preliminary study [65]. A set of factors (i.e., the parameters of a test) and their possible values (called levels in the DoE) were used to design a test plan for the Android OS. First, they identified the feasible combinations of Android devices and Android versions, since they could not install all the versions on all the devices. Then, they defined a blocked, full-factorial design with regards to the other factors. Moreover, they introduced response variables to quantify the impact of a test on the target device in terms of software aging, and correlated the factors with the response variable to identify the most influential ones. Both user-perceived response variables and system-related response variables were considered, which respectively reflect the responsiveness of the device as perceived by the user, and the depletion of system resources that may cause aging-related failures.

The results of the empirical analysis of software aging on Android devices show that: i) tested devices experienced a noticeable performance degradation (in terms of low responsiveness of the system) after a few hours of stress testing; ii) software aging issues can be attributed to specific processes inside the Android OS, including the System Server, the System UI and the Surface Flinger, which exhibit inflated memory consumption; and iii) performance degradation trends are correlated with resource utilization metrics from the kernel, such as process PSS size and pages merged by KSM, and with the time spent on garbage collection.

Acknowledgments

We would like to thank Javier Alonso Lopez, Michael Grottke and Rivalino Matias, Jr. for reading the chapter and providing comments that improved it.

References

1. L. Bernstein. (1993). Innovative technologies for preventing network outages. *AT&T Technical Journal*, **72**(4), 4–10,

2. Y. Huang and C. M. R. Kintala. (1993). Software implemented fault tolerance technologies and experience. In *Proceedings of the 23rd Annual International Symposium on Fault-Tolerant Computing, Toulouse, France, June 22–24*, pp. 2–9.
3. A. Avritzer and E. J. Weyuker. (1994). Estimating the software reliability of smoothly degrading systems. In *Proceedings of the 5th IEEE International Symposium on Software Reliability Engineering, ISSRE 1994, Monterey, CA, USA, November 6–9*, pp. 168–177. doi: 10.1109/ISSRE.1994.341370. URL https://doi.org/10.1109/ISSRE.1994.341370.
4. Y. Huang, C. Kintala, N. Kolettis, and N. Dudley Fulton. (1995). Software rejuvenation: Analysis, module and applications. In *Proceedings of the 25th International Symposium on Fault-Tolerant Computing, Pasadena, CA, USA, June 27–30*, pp. 381–390. ISBN 0-8186-7079-7. doi: 10.1109/FTCS.1995.466961.
5. A. Avritzer and E. J. Weyuker. (1997). Monitoring smoothly degrading systems for increased dependability. *Empirical Software Engineering*, **2**(1), 59–77, doi: 10.1023/A:1009794200077. URL https://doi.org/10.1023/A:1009794200077.
6. A. Avritzer and B. Larson. (1993). Load testing software using deterministic state testing. In *Proceedings of the 1993 International Symposium on Software Testing and Analysis, ISSTA 1993, Cambridge, MA, USA, June 28–30*, pp. 82–88, doi: 10.1145/154183.154244. URL https://doi.org/10.1145/154183.154244.
7. A. Avritzer and E. J. Weyuker. (1995). The automatic generation of load test suites and the assessment of the resulting software. *IEEE Transactions on Software Engineering*, **21**(9), 705–716, ISSN 0098-5589. doi: 10.1109/32.464549.
8. K. S. Trivedi. (2016). *Probability and Statistics with Reliability, Queuing, and Computer Science Applications* (2nd ed.). New York, USA: John Wiley & Sons.
9. K. Trivedi and A. Bobbio. (2017). *Reliability and Availability Engineering: Modeling, Analysis, and Applications*. Cambridge, UK: Cambridge University Press.
10. S. Garg, A. Puliafito, M. Telek, and K. S. Trivedi. (1995). Analysis of software rejuvenation using Markov Regenerative Stochastic Petri Net. In *Proceedings of the 6th IEEE International Symposium on Software Reliability Engineering*, Toulouse, France, October 24–27, pp. 180–187. doi: 10.1109/ISSRE.1995.497656.
11. H. Choi, V. G. Kulkarni, and K. S. Trivedi. (1994). Markov Regenerative Stochastic Petri Nets. *Performance Evaluation*, **20**, 337–357.
12. S. Garg, Y. Huang, C. Kintala, and K. S. Trivedi. (1996). Minimizing completion time of a program by checkpointing and rejuvenation. In *1996 ACM SIGMETRICS International Conference on Measurement and Modeling of Computer Systems, SIGMETRICS '96, Philadelphia, PA, USA, May 23–26*, pp. 252–261. ISBN 0-89791-793-6. doi: http://doi.acm.org/10.1145/233013.233050.
13. A. Pfening, S. Garg, A. Puliafito, M. Telek, and K. S. Trivedi. (1996). Optimal software rejuvenation for tolerating soft failures. *Performance Evaluation*, **27–28**, 491–506. ISSN 0166-5316. doi: 10.1016/0166-5316(96)00038-7.
14. S. Garg, A. Puliafito, M. Telek, and K. S. Trivedi. (1998). Analysis of preventive maintenance in transactions based software systems. *IEEE Transactions on Computers*, **47**(1), 96–107. ISSN 0018-9340. doi: 10.1109/12.656092.
15. Y. Bao, X. Sun, and K. S. Trivedi. (2005). A workload-based analysis of software aging, and rejuvenation. *IEEE Transactions on Reliability*, **54**(3), 541–548. ISSN 0018-9529. doi: 10.1109/TR.2005.853442.
16. K. Vaidyanathan and K. S. Trivedi. (2005). A comprehensive model for software rejuvenation. *IEEE Transactions on Dependable and Secure Computing*, **2**(2), 124–137,

17. K. Vaidyanathan, R. E. Harper, S. W. Hunter, and K. S. Trivedi. (2001). Analysis and implementation of software rejuvenation in cluster systems. *SIGMETRICS Performance Evaluation Review*, **29**, 62–71. ISSN 0163-5999. doi: http://doi.acm.org/10.1145/384268.378434.
18. V. Castelli, R. E. Harper, P. Heidelberger, S. W. Hunter, K. S. Trivedi, K. Vaidyanathan, and W. P. Zeggert. (2001). Proactive management of software aging, *IBM Journal of Research and Development*, **45**(2), 311–332. ISSN 0018-8646. doi: 10.1147/rd.452.0311.
19. T. Dohi, K. Goseva-Popstojanova, and K. S. Trivedi. (2000). Analysis of software cost models with rejuvenation. In *Proceedings of the Fifth IEEE International Symposium on High Assurance Systems Engineering, HASE 2000*, 25–34. doi: 10.1109/HASE.2000.895436.
20. T. Dohi, K. Goseva-Popstojanova, and K. S. Trivedi. (2000). Statistical non-parametric algorithms to estimate the optimal software rejuvenation schedule. In *Proceedings of the 7th Pacific Rim International Symposium on Dependable Computing, Los Angeles, CA, USA, December 18–20*, pp. 77–84. doi: 10.1109/PRDC.2000.897287.
21. T. Dohi, K. Goseva-Popstojanova, and K. S. Trivedi. (2001). Estimating software rejuvenation schedules in high-assurance systems. *The Computer Journal*, **44**(6), 473–485. ISSN 0010-4620. doi: http://10.1093/comjnl/44.6.473.
22. Y. Bao, X. Sun, and K. S. Trivedi. (2003). Adaptive software rejuvenation: Degradation model and rejuvenation scheme. In *Proceedings of the 2003 International Conference on Dependable Systems and Networks, San Francisco, CA, USA, June 22–25*, pp. 241–248. doi: 10.1109/DSN.2003.1209934.
23. Y. Liu, K. S. Trivedi, Y. Ma, J. J. Han, and H. Levendel. (2002). Modeling and analysis of software rejuvenation in cable modem termination systems. In *Proceedings of the 13th International Symposium on Software Reliability Engineering (ISSRE 2002), Annapolis, MD, USA, 12–15 November*, pp. 159–170,
24. K. Vaidyanathan, S. Dharmaraja, and K. S. Trivedi. Analysis of inspection-based preventive maintenance in operational software systems. In *Proceedings of the 21st Symposium on Reliable Distributed Systems (SRDS 2002), Osaka, Japan*, October 13–16, pp. 286–295.
25. D. Wang, W. Xie, and K. S. Trivedi. (2007). Performability analysis of clustered systems with rejuvenation under varying workload. *Performance Evaluation*, **64**(3), 247–265.
26. J. Alonso, R. Matias, E. Vicente, A. Maria, and K. S. Trivedi. (2013). A comparative experimental study of software rejuvenation overhead. *Performance Evaluation*, **70**(3), 231–250.
27. W. Xie, Y. Hong, and K. S. Trivedi. (2005). Analysis of a two-level software rejuvenation policy. *Reliability Engineering and System Safety*, **87**(1), 13–22.
28. G. Ning, J. Zhao, Y. Lou, J. Alonso, R. Matias, K. S. Trivedi, B. B. Yin, and K. Y. Cai. (2016). Optimization of two-granularity software rejuvenation policy based on the Markov regenerative process. *IEEE Transactions on Reliability*, **65**(4), 1630–1646.
29. Y. Qiao, Z. Zheng, Y. Fang, F. Qin, K. S. Trivedi, and K. Y. Cai. (2018). Two-level rejuvenation for Android smartphones and its optimization. *IEEE Transactions on Reliability*, **68**(2), 633–652.
30. A. Avritzer, A. Bondi, M. Grottke, K. S. Trivedi, and E. J. Weyuker. (2006). Performance assurance via software rejuvenation: Monitoring, statistics and algorithms. In *Proceedings of the International Conference on Dependable Systems and Networks, 2006*, Philadelphia, PA, USA, June 25–28, pp. 435–444. doi: 10.1109/DSN.2006.58.

31. M. Grottke and K. S. Trivedi. (2007). Fighting bugs: Remove, retry, replicate, and rejuvenate. *IEEE Computer*, **40**(2), 107–109.
32. F. Machida, D. S. Kim, and K. S. Trivedi. (2013). Modeling and analysis of software rejuvenation in a server virtualized system with live VM migration. *Performance Evaluation*, **70**(3), 212–230.
33. F. Machida, V. F. Nicola, and K. S. Trivedi (2014). Job completion time on a virtualized server with software rejuvenation. *ACM Journal on Emerging Technologies in Computing Systems*, **10**(1), 10:1–10:26.
34. V. G. Kulkarni, V. F. Nicola, and K. S. Trivedi. (1986). On modelling the performance and reliability of multimode computer systems. *Journal of Systems and Software*, **6**(1–2), 175–182.
35. V. Kulkarni, V. Nicola, and K. Trivedi. (1987). The completion time of a job on a multi-mode system. *Advances in Applied Probability*, **19**, 932–954.
36. S. Garg, A. van Moorsel, K. Vaidyanathan, and K. S. Trivedi. (1998). A methodology for detection and estimation of software aging. In *Proceedings of the 9th IEEE International Symposium on Software Reliability Engineering, Paderborn, Germany, Novermber 4–7*, pp. 283–292. doi: 10.1109/ISSRE.1998.730892.
37. P. K. Sen. (1968). Estimates of the regression coefficient based on Kendall's Tau. *Journal of the American Statistical Association*, **63**, 1379–1389.
38. K. Vaidyanathan and K. S. Trivedi. (1999). A measurement-based model for estimation of resource exhaustion in operational software systems. In *Proceedings of the 10th IEEE International Symposium on Software Reliability Engineering, Boca Raton, FL, USA, November 1–4*, pp. 84–93, doi: 10.1109/ISSRE.1999.809313.
39. H. Sukhwani, R. Matias, K. S. Trivedi, and A. Rindos. (2017). Monitoring and mitigating software aging on IBM cloud controller system. In *Proceedings of the 28th IEEE International Symposium on Software Reliability Engineering Workshops, ISSRE Workshops, Toulouse, France, October 23–26*, pp. 266–272.
40. L. Lei, K. Vaidyanathan, and K. S. Trivedi. (2002). An approach for estimation of software aging in a web server. In *Proceedings of the 2002 International Symposium on Empirical Software Engineering (ISESE) Nara, Japan, October 3–4*, pp. 91–100.
41. M. Grottke, L. Lei, K. Vaidyanathan, and K. Trivedi. (2006). Analysis of software aging in a web server. *IEEE Transactions on Reliability*, **55**(3), 411–420.
42. G. Hoffmann, K. Trivedi, and M. Malek. (2007). A best practice guide to resource forecasting for computing systems. *IEEE Transactions on Reliability*, **56**(4), 615–628. ISSN 0018-9529. doi: 10.1109/TR.2007.909764.
43. R. Matias, P. A. Barbetta, K. S. Trivedi, and P. J. F. (2010). Filho, Accelerated degradation tests applied to software aging experiments. *IEEE Transactions on Reliability*, **59**(1), 102–114.
44. R. Matias, K. Trivedi, and P. Maciel. (2010). Using accelerated life tests to estimate time to software aging failure. In *Proceedings of the 21st IEEE International Symposium on Software Reliability Engineering (ISSRE), San Jose, CA, USA, November 1–4*, pp. 211–219. doi: 10.1109/ISSRE.2010.42.
45. J. Zhao, K. S. Trivedi, M. Grottke, J. Alonso, and Y. Wang. (2014). Ensuring the performance of apache HTTP server affected by aging. *IEEE Transactions on Dependable and Secure Computing*, **11**(2), 130–141.
46. J. Zhao, Y. Wang, G. Ning, K. S. Trivedi, R. Matias Jr., and K. Cai. (2013). A comprehensive approach to optimal software rejuvenation. *Performance Evaluation*, **70**(11), 917–933.

47. J. Zhao, Y. Jin, K. S. Trivedi, R. Matias Jr., and Y. Wang. (2014). Software rejuvenation scheduling using accelerated life testing. *ACM Journal on Emerging Technologies in Computing Systems*, **10**(1), 9:1–9:23.
48. J. Alonso, M. Rivalino, E. Vicente, A. Maria, and K. Trivedi. (2013). A comparative experimental study of software rejuvenation overhead. *Performance Evaluation*, **70**(3), 231–250.
49. A. Bovenzi, J. Alonso, H. Yamada, S. Russo, and K. Trivedi. (2013). Towards fast OS rejuvenation: An experimental evaluation of fast OS reboot techniques. In *Proceedings of the 24th IEEE International Symposium on Software Reliability Engineering (ISSRE), Pasadena, CA, USA, November 4–7*, pp. 61–70.
50. J. Araujo, R. Matos, V. Alves, P. Maciel, F. Vieira de Souza, R. Matias, and K. S. Trivedi. (2014). Software aging in the eucalyptus cloud computing infrastructure: Characterization and rejuvenation. *ACM Journal on Emerging Technologies in Computing Systems*, **10**(1), 11:1–11:22. ISSN 1550-4832.
51. M. Grottke and K. Trivedi. (2005). Software faults, software aging and software rejuvenation. *The Journal of Reliability Engineering Association of Japan*, **27**(7), 425–438.
52. M. Grottke and K. S. Trivedi. (2007). Fighting bugs: Remove, retry, replicate, and rejuvenate. *Computer*, **40**(2), 107–109. ISSN 0018-9162.
53. M. Grottke and K. Trivedi. (2005). Classification of software faults. In *Supplemental Proceedings of the Sixteenth International IEEE Symposium on Software Reliability Engineering Chicago, IL, USA, November 8–11*, pp. 4.19–4.20,
54. M. Grottke, A. Nikora, and K. Trivedi. (2010). An empirical investigation of fault types in space mission system software. In *Proceedings of the 2010 IEEE/IFIP International Conference on Dependable Systems and Networks, Chicago, IL, USA, June 28–July 1*, pp. 447–456.
55. D. Cotroneo, M. Grottke, R. Natella, R. Pietrantuono, and K. S. Trivedi. (2013). Fault triggers in open-source software: An experience report. In *Proceedings of the 24th IEEE International Symposium on Software Reliability Engineering, ISSRE 2013, Pasadena, CA, USA, November 4–7*, pp. 178–187.
56. G. Xiao, Z. Zheng, B. Yin, K. S. Trivedi, X. Du, and K. Cai. (2017). Experience report: Fault triggers in linux operating system: From evolution perspective. In *Proceedings of the 28th IEEE International Symposium on Software Reliability Engineering, ISSRE 2017, Toulouse, France, October 23–26*, pp. 101–111,
57. F. Qin, Z. Zheng, X. Li, Y. Qiao, and K. S. Trivedi. (2017). An empirical investigation of fault triggers in Android operating system. In *Proceedings of the 22nd IEEE Pacific Rim International Symposium on Dependable Computing, PRDC 2017, Christchurch, New Zealand, January 22–25*, pp. 135–144. doi: 10.1109/PRDC.2017.27. URL https://doi.org/10.1109/PRDC.2017.27.
58. F. Qin, Z. Zheng, Y. Qiao, and K. S. Trivedi (2018). Studying aging-related bug prediction using cross-project models. *IEEE Transactions on Reliability*. 1–20.
59. J. Alonso, A. Bovenzi, J. Li, Y. Wang, S. Russo, and K. S. Trivedi. (2012). Software rejuvenation: Do IT & telco industries use it? In *Proceedings of the 23rd IEEE International Symposium on Software Reliability Engineering Workshops, ISSRE Workshops, Dallas, TX, USA, November 27–30*, pp. 299–304.
60. D. Cotroneo, R. Natella, R. Pietrantuono, and S. Russo. (2010). Software aging analysis of the Linux operating system. In *Proceedings of the 21st IEEE International Symposium on Software Reliability Engineering (ISSRE), San Jose, CA, USA, November 1–4*, pp. 71–80. doi: 10.1109/ISSRE.2010.24.

61. D. Cotroneo, S. Orlando, and S. Russo. (2007). Characterizing aging phenomena of the Java Virtual Machine. In *Proceedings of the 26th IEEE International Symposium on Reliable Distributed Systems, Beijing, China, October 10–12*, pp. 127–136. doi: 10.1109/SRDS.2007.22.
62. D. Cotroneo, S. Orlando, R. Pietrantuono, and S. Russo. (2013). A measurement-based ageing analysis of the JVM. *Software Testing, Verification and Reliability,* **23**(3), 199–239.
63. A. Bovenzi, D. Cotroneo, R. Pietrantuono, and S. Russo. (2011). Workload characterization for software aging analysis. In *Proceedings of the 22nd IEEE International Symposium on Software Reliability Engineering (ISSRE), Hiroshima, Japan, Nov 14–17*, pp. 240–249.
64. D. Cotroneo, R. Natella, and R. Pietrantuono. (2012). Predicting aging-related bugs using software complexity metrics.. *Performance Evaluation*, **70**(3), 163–178.
65. D. Cotroneo, F. Fucci, A. K. Iannillo, R. Natella, and R. Pietrantuono. (2016). Software aging analysis of the Android mobile OS. In *Proceedings of the 27th IEEE International Symposium on Software Reliability Engineering (ISSRE) Ottawa, ON, Canada, October 23–27*, pp. 478–489. doi: 10.1109/ISSRE.2016.25.

Chapter 2

Fundamentals of Software Aging

Domenico Cotroneo*,‡, Rivalino Matias Jr.†,§ and Roberto Natella*,¶

*Università degli Studi di Napoli Federico II, Italy
†Universidade Federal de Uberlândia, Brazil
‡cotroneo@unina.it
§rivalino@ufu.br
¶roberto.natella@unina.it

Software aging consists in the increase of the failure rate or in the performance degradation of a system as it executes, which can be due to the accumulation of errors in the system state and to the consumption of resources such as physical memory. Software aging represents a real issue in long running applications, such as servers or telecom systems. This chapter provides fundamental concepts and definitions related to software aging. In particular, the concepts of aging-related bugs, aging-related failure, and aging effects are discussed in order to pave the way for the rest of the book. Examples of software aging in real-world systems are also discussed to motivate the reader to understand the potential impact of this phenomenon. At the end of this chapter, software aging research is contextualized in the wider field of performance engineering research and, in particular, in the field of software testing and monitoring.

2.1. Introduction

The *software aging* phenomenon results in the increase of the failure rate or performance degradation of a system as it executes, which can be due to the accumulation of errors in the system state and to the consumption of resources such as physical memory [1, 2]. Practitioners have known of this phenomenon for a long time. Early evidence of software aging had already been found in the 1960s: the Safeguard military system was affected by hangs occurring once error reporting buffers were full [3]. As software has grown in size and complexity, software aging has been observed in an increasing number of long-running systems, including telecommunication switching and billing software [1, 4], and it led to the well-known accident of the Patriot anti-missile system that caused the loss of human lives [5]. Software aging can be attributed to elusive *software bugs*: studies in the early 1990s by Lawrence Bernestein on telecommunication systems [6] pointed out the high incidence of bugs that, when triggered, do not immediately cause a software failure, but manifest themselves as memory leakage, unreleased file locks, data corruption and numerical error accumulation, causing the performance of the system to slowly degrade and to eventually fail. Often, such bugs are too subtle or too costly to be removed during development. Research at the AT&T Bell laboratories on fault-tolerant software then identified *Software Rejuvenation* as a cost-effective solution to counteract Software Aging [1, 3, 7, 8]. Software Rejuvenation is a *proactive* approach for preventing performance degradation and failures due to Software Aging: it consists in the occasional or periodical clean-up of aging effects (which can be achieved by a simple software restart, or by more complex techniques), in order to postpone failures and to restore performance. Software Rejuvenation represented a novel form of preventive software maintenance compared to other forms of preventive software maintenance existing at that time [9], which were focused on the installation of updates in order to prevent field failures [10] or on re-engineering a software program in order to cope with its obsolescence [11]. Since the early studies on Software Aging and Software Rejuvenation by the AT&T Bell laboratories in the 1990s, many efforts have been devoted to characterizing the software aging phenomenon and to devising cost-effective rejuvenation strategies. After two decades, a significant body of knowledge has been established and an international community of researchers in the area of Software Aging and Rejuvenation (SAR) has grown. It thus becomes important to look at what has been done, in order to identify what has still to be accomplished to make industry practitioners aware of the Software Aging problem and which are the future challenges for researchers of the SAR community, as well as to foster the adoption of Software Rejuvenation approaches. The aim of this chapter is to provide an overall picture of the state-of-the-art in Software Aging and Rejuvenation. We survey relevant studies with respect to the approaches that have been used to forecast software aging phenomena and to plan rejuvenation, the kind of systems and aging symptoms that have been studied, and the techniques that have been proposed to rejuvenate complex software systems.

2.2. Basic Concepts

In general terms, the Software Aging phenomenon is the *increase in the failure rate* and/or *decrease in the performance* of a long-running software system. In turn, it is due to the activation and propagation of the so-called **Aging-Related Bugs** (ARBs), a particular class of software faults that manifest their effect only after a long period of execution. The activation of these bugs does not immediately cause a failure of the system: considering the conceptual *fault-error-failure* chain proposed in [12], the peculiarity of ARBs is that their activation/propagation depends on *the amount and type of work the system has been doing*, and/or that *they lead to* ***error accumulation****, which causes the system to gradually shift from a correct state to a failure-prone one.* After a long enough execution time has elapsed, or after a significant number of errors has been accumulated, ARBs lead to **aging-related failures** (e.g., an operation that allocates memory fails, causing the crash of a process). Error accumulation usually takes the form of bad resource management that leads to resource exhaustion, such as memory leaks, unterminated threads, and unreleased file locks: in such cases, the expected time to aging-related failure is referred to as **time to (resource) exhaustion** (TTE). Moreover, error accumulation is influenced by the amount and type of work performed by the system, which is referred to as the **workload**.

Aging effects are the results of error accumulation, in terms of leaked resources or corrupted states; these effects can be detected by means of **aging indicators**, that is, system variables that can be directly measured and that can be related to Software Aging phenomena. Examples of aging indicators are data about the resource usage of the operating system, such as free physical memory, used swap space, and file and process table size. In [13], an experiment was performed by monitoring OS resource usage in a LAN of UNIX workstations using a distributed SNMP monitoring tool, in order to identify software aging trends. Figure 2.1 shows the consumption of real memory and file tables across 53 days. Since aging phenomena may not be evident simply by visual inspection of data, trend detection techniques are usually adopted to detect the onset of software aging. In Fig. 2.1, a trend is detected in the *smoothing* of observed data by *robust locally weighted regression*, which provides visual cues that there is a gradual decrease of free memory and an increase of file table size. To make conclusive statements regarding the presence or absence of software aging trends with statistical confidence, the use of statistical techniques is required: examples of techniques that have usually been adopted are the *seasonal Kendall* and the *Mann-Kendall tests for trends*, for testing the hypothesis that there is an upward or a downward trend in the observed data, and the *Sen slope procedure* to estimate the slope of a trend line.

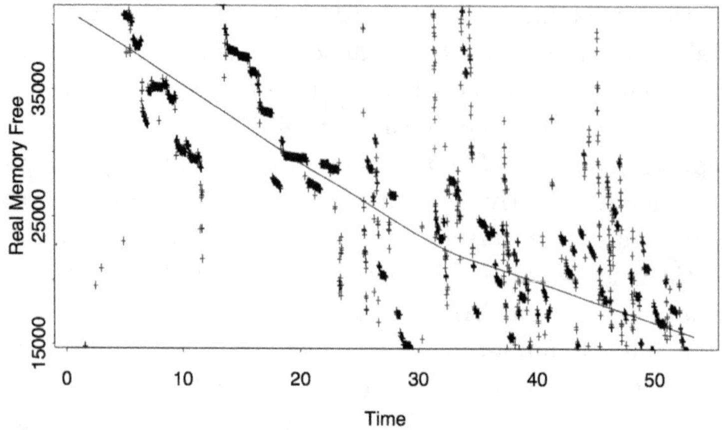

(a) Free memory

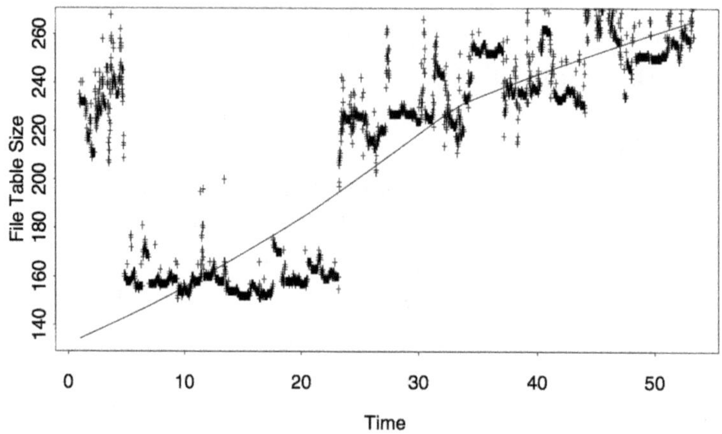

(b) File table size

Fig. 2.1. Trend analysis of resource consumption in a UNIX system [13] © IEEE.

Using the computed slope, it is possible to estimate the expected TTE of a given resource.

Resource leaking and other aging effects can be due to aging-related bugs in application software, in the libraries that the application is using or in the application execution environment (e.g., the operating system). However, fixing these bugs is not always feasible, since bugs could be in third-party or reused code. Developers might lack access to the source code and/or expertise on their internals; moreover, it can be very difficult to identify these bugs in complex software applications. Software rejuvenation is a cost-effective approach to removing aging effects and avoiding aging-related failures, which does not require one to know the location of aging-related bugs, or even the very fact of their existence. Software rejuvenation was defined in [1] as the *preemptive rollback of continuously running applications to prevent failures in the future.* Since an application may be unavailable during rejuvenation, rejuvenation can increase the downtime and incur some costs (e.g., costs due to the loss of business). However, these costs can be minimized by scheduling rejuvenation during the most idle times of an application. Instead, it is likely that the costs of downtime will be high if the downtime is unscheduled, as happens during a failure. Rejuvenation can avoid, or at least postpone, aging-related failures, therefore it can reduce the overall downtime and related costs.

For this reason, the most important problem in the SAR field is to plan *when* to perform rejuvenation during execution (**rejuvenation schedule**) in order to improve availability and reduce costs. An example is represented by the simple model based on continuous-time Markov chains that was introduced in [1] to analyze software rejuvenation (Fig. 2.2). In this model, after starting, the application stays in the "highly robust state" S_0, in which the probability of aging-related failures is negligible since the application has not aged. After some time (at a rate r_2 much lower than the others), the application will go into a failure-probable state S_P (e.g., some resources have been leaked and are close to being exhausted); in this state, the application can fail with rate λ and go to the failed state S_F, and will be repaired at a rate r_1. If the system performs rejuvenation, it will go from state S_P to S_R at rate r_4, and then to the robust state S_0 at rate r_3. This model allows one to compute the expected downtime (both scheduled and unscheduled) and its costs; in turn, it allows one to analyze whether, and under which conditions, software rejuvenation is beneficial to availability. For instance, if the cost of rejuvenation is small and the failure rate is

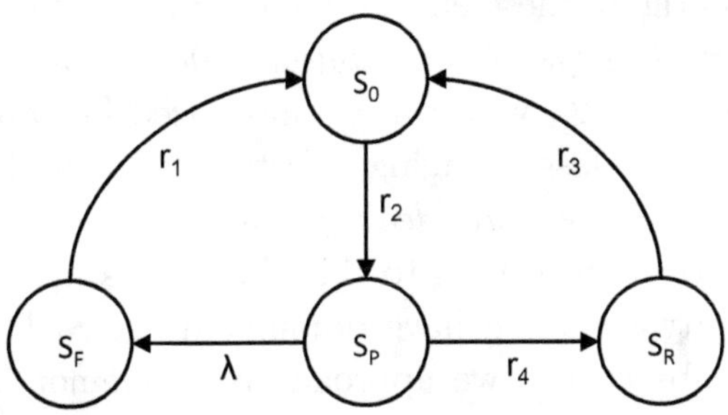

Fig. 2.2. Probabilistic state transition model for a system with rejuvenation.

large, rejuvenation should be performed as soon as the application goes into a failure-probable state. However, several other models, which will be discussed in the following sections, have been proposed in the SAR literature.

A simple way to perform software rejuvenation is to restart the application. Restarting can involve queuing the incoming messages temporarily, cleaning up the in-memory data structures, or respawning the processes at the initial state or at a previously checkpointed state. Moreover, rejuvenation can be performed at different levels, ranging from restarting an individual component to rebooting the whole node in which the application is running. The definition of **rejuvenation techniques** (i.e., *how* to perform rejuvenation) able to reduce the likelihood of aging failures and to keep rejuvenation costs low is another important problem of SAR that will be analyzed in the following sections of this chapter.

2.3. Software Aging Effects

As described in the previous sections, *software aging* is the name given to the phenomenon observed in numerous software systems and characterized by the progressive degradation of software's performance and/or reliability. It is very important to note that the cause of software aging-related failures are the *aging effects*, whose accumulation inside of the running software's internal state is the primary reason for the progressive degradation of the software dependability [2]; once a software system suffers from software aging it is affected by its effects. Hence, software aging effects are a core concept to be considered when studying software aging.

In [14], the authors found that in the first twenty years of SAR research, the major topics investigated in this field were related to detecting, characterizing, and modeling software aging effects, as well as techniques and strategies to mitigate these effects. Well-known classes of software aging effects are *resource leakage*, *fragmentation*, *numerical error accrual*, and *data corruption buildup* [2], which are summarized in Table 2.1. According to [14], the dominant class of aging effects investigated and reported in the literature has been *resource leakage*, and memory was the top most investigated resource with respect to this class. This means that studies on memory-related software aging have dominated the SAR literature so far. In the next two subsections, we approach both memory-related and non-memory related software aging effects, providing conceptual and practical explanations about these two categories of aging effects.

Table 2.1. Classes of aging effects [2].

Basic Class	Extension	Examples
Resource leakage	(1) OS specific (2) App specific	— Unreleased: • *Memory*(1, 2) • *File descriptors*(1, 2) • *Socket handles*(1) — Unterminated: • *Processes*(1) • *Threads*(1, 2)
Fragmentation	(1) OS specific (2) App specific	— Physical memory (1) — File system (1) — Database indices (2)
Numerical error accrual	(1) OS specific (2) App specific	— Round-off (1, 2)
Data corruption accrual	(1) OS specific (2) App specific	— File system (1) — Database files (2)

OS — Operating System App — Application process.

2.3.1. *Memory-related Aging Effects*

The noticeably high interest of researchers in investigating software aging effects related to main memory has produced an extensive body of knowledge within the SAR community. For the readers interested in learning more about these studies, we recommend (as a starting point) the literature reviews presented in [14–16]. In general, the studies in this area have identified two main classes of software aging effects related to memory: *memory leakage* and *memory fragmentation*. The former is the most investigated aging effect in SAR research and this prevalence can be hypothesized by some observable facts. Firstly, this aging effect is caused by software faults (*defects*) that are ubiquitous across different categories of software products, especially in server systems, which make them more exposed and more likely to be detected. Note that server systems have been extensively investigated in software aging literature. For example, the majority of the first empirical studies in SAR reported memory leaks in web servers, specifically on the Apache *httpd* software. In addition to being pervasive, the effects of memory leaks once detected are not difficult to measure and communicate. It seems a consequence of the above-mentioned facts that many studies across the years have adopted similar experimental approaches, i.e., using software systems previously investigated and with already proofed memory leaks, such as the Apache web server, to conduct their studies. Importantly, nowadays memory leakage is still a pervasive problem that affects real systems with high-impact consequences to the industry (e.g., [17] and [18]).

2.3.1.1. *Memory leakage*

A memory leak occurs once a portion of memory (also known as a *chunk*), dynamically allocated during a program execution, becomes unneeded at a certain point during runtime, and instead of being released (freed) it is simply not deallocated, which makes that portion of memory unavailable for any future use during the program execution. One of the main causes of memory leaks is the loss of reference to the allocated *chunk*, resulting in an orphan *chunk* [19]. The cumulative effects of repeated memory leaks during a program's execution may vary from a small or modest waste of memory to the whole system crashing due to main memory exhaustion. The observable effect of cumulative memory leaks in a program's process is the monotonic increasing of its size in virtual memory during its running operation. Note that the size of a process, in any OS, is limited by architectural limits, which cause the forced termination of processes that grow beyond these limits. For example, in [20] the authors show that Eucalyptus's administrative processes suffering from memory leaks were abruptly terminated by the 32-bit Linux kernel used in the experiments, as they reached a size larger than the 3 gigabytes that is the maximal process size allowed for that OS kernel type. Another observable side effect of memory leakage inside running programs is the degradation of the whole system's main memory availability, which may cause failures in other processes trying to allocate memory dynamically. The entire system's performance could degrade or crash due to virtual memory *thrashing* [21] and related problems.

Note that different factors interfere with the degree of impact caused by memory leaks in a system, such as the length of the program execution time, the rate and size of the leakage, and the amount of memory available for the program along with its execution. The aging effects caused by memory leaks end at the moment the program execution terminates; at this moment the total amount of memory (used and leaked) assigned to the program's process returns to the operating system; that is why long-running processes are more affected by these aging effects than processes that execute for short periods of time. This explains why server and embedded software systems are very often cited in the SAR literature. In these systems, the effects of memory leaks are more evident and easier to observe.

Memory leaks can be observed in different software layers. For example, they can occur in the user space (user programs and libraries) and in the kernel space (OS subsystems and device drivers). In virtualized computing systems, they can be observed inside a virtual machine (in user and kernel spaces) and also outside (in the hypervisor space). Firmware code in embedded systems may suffer from memory leaks as well, which poses a challenge these days due to the pervasiveness of these systems in people's lives. For each above-mentioned layer, an appropriate approach can be applied to deal with the aging effects. For example, memory leaks inside the OS kernel affect the entire system and not only a given application process, and their effects remain until the OS restarts/reboots. On the other hand, memory leaks inside a process can be mitigated by simply restarting that specific process with no need of a system reboot [22]. In Chapter 3 the way to mitigate the aging effects in different system layers is presented.

2.3.1.2. *Memory fragmentation*

Memory leaks are primarily caused by software faults, such as the unbalanced use of *allocation* and *deallocation* routines that result in unreleased yet unneeded memory *chunks*. On the other hand, memory fragmentation [23] is mostly a consequence of the software execution dynamics [16]. In general, it also occurs in both user and kernel/hypervisor spaces. In the former, the memory region used for dynamic memory allocations gets fragmented. This happens inside the process's *heap* in which dynamic allocations take place [19]. As memory *chunks* of varying sizes are allocated and deallocated, following different allocation/deallocation patterns, the *heap* address space can get fragmented, depending on the data structures and management strategies implemented by the memory allocator code linked to the program through standard libraries [24]. In order to illustrate how it works, in [19] the authors provide a didactic example of programming code that induces *heap* fragmentation during program execution. They performed experiments and monitored the program execution using a system call tracer that recorded all system calls made by the program's process. They show that when the program code requested (*mallocing*) an 8-kilobyte memory *chunk*, the *sbrk()* system call was made although there were 65,440 free bytes in the *heap*. It is important to highlight that in spite of the total free memory in the *heap* being larger than the 8-kilobyte *chunk* requested, more memory was necessary and requested by the OS kernel in order to increase the size of the *heap* area. This only occurred because the *heap* was not able to provide the 8-kilobyte *chunk* requested due to having its available space fragmented, and therefore had to be enlarged to meet that request. This is a very practical example of what happens when an application process accumulates memory fragmentation effects. In practical terms, the process grows in memory, with effects similar to those of memory leaks, and also suffers from loss of performance due to the frequent process and OS interactions that request additional memory. These mechanics and effects of memory fragmentation can be observed also in kernel space, given that kernel subsystems and device drivers also allocate and deallocate memory of varying sizes dynamically. The resulting effects are the same as those in user space, i.e., waste of memory causing higher memory resource consumption and loss of performance. The difference is that in kernel space the effects of memory fragmentation affect the whole system and in user space these are limited to the aged process. Memory fragmentation in kernel space also requires an OS reboot before it can be removed, but in user space a process restart suffices.

2.3.2. *Non-Memory-Related Aging Effects*

Very few studies (e.g., [15] and [25]) in SAR literature have discussed non-memory-related aging effects. In this section, we provide an introductory discussion on these types of aging effects, emphasizing the *resource leakage* class.

In general, aging effects caused by *resource leakage* other than memory (Section 3.1) are related to software objects created and managed by the operating system to provide servicing functionalities to the user-space processes. For example, *file descriptors* and *socket handles* are software objects that represent internal resources managed by the OS and used by running programs. An application process that opens a file needs a *file descriptor* to perform I/O operations on the opened file. The *file descriptor* is an object (data structure) dynamically allocated in kernel space and handled by OS kernel routines, which are activated by system calls invoked by user-space processes; likewise are the *socket handles* with respect to inter-processes communication. Both types of the above-mentioned objects are servicing resources provided on demand by the OS to running programs. The leakage of these resources is a consequence of software faults activated during the program execution, and they may produce varying effects. They are different from memory leakage in that their effects do not cause the increasing of the process's size, which makes their detection less evident than the detection of memory leaks. Another example of resource leakage commonly found in real systems is related to processes/threads. The next two subsections describe in detail these four types of non-memory software aging effects.

2.3.2.1. *Leakage of processes/threads*

A *process* is an abstraction created by the OS kernel to execute a program that is a file containing static executable instructions and data. Multiple processes can be created from the same program execution. All processes are created single-threaded, i.e., they have only one execution control flow. A *thread* can be understood as an execution context that can run a set of instructions within a process. A single-threaded process can become multithreaded by dynamically spawning new threads in runtime, like a process can spawn multiple child processes on demand. Like *file descriptors* and *socket handles*, objects, processes and threads are implemented through data structures within the OS kernel, respectively, Process Control Block (PCB) and Thread Control Block (TCB) data structures. PCB/TCB data structures are used to store particular state information about the process/thread execution contexts. The size and format of these structures are different across operating systems, which makes the accumulative effects of their leakage different. The effect of PCB/TCB leakage manifests mainly within the kernel address space and its main consequence is the exhaustion of the number of process/thread entries, which are limited resources. Operating systems limit the number of processes that can be created by a user, as well as the number of threads that can be created by a process. Hence, the successive leakage of these structures can cause the exhaustion of these resources within the kernel space. Thread leakage usually causes the increase of process size in virtual memory, but it is not always the case. Differently, process leakage does not increase the system memory consumption significantly; although PCBs require a certain amount of memory to be created, most of time their limit is reached before there is a significant increase in the system memory usage, hence, differently from memory leaks, these effects are more difficult to observe by measuring the process size or even the used/free memory. Despite these aging effects manifesting differently, their dynamics are the same for thread and process leakage, that is, the cumulative effects of the successive activation of software faults deteriorates the internal states of the processes or system (OS kernel). An example of the aging effects caused by process leakage is illustrated in Fig. 2.3.

In Fig. 2.3, we can see an excerpt of the *ps* command output, in which every line corresponds to a process executing in a Linux OS system, and the

USER	PID	%CPU	%MEM	VSZ	RSS	TTY	STAT	START	TIME	COMMAND
...	...									
rivalino	32154	0.0	0.0	1700	244	pts/0	S+	15:23	0:00	ProgAged01
rivalino	32155	0.0	0.0	0	0	pts/0	Z+	15:23	0:00	ProgAged01 <defunct>
rivalino	32156	0.0	0.0	0	0	pts/0	Z+	15:23	0:00	ProgAged01 <defunct>
rivalino	32157	0.0	0.0	0	0	pts/0	Z+	15:23	0:00	ProgAged01 <defunct>
rivalino	32158	0.0	0.0	0	0	pts/0	Z+	15:23	0:00	ProgAged01 <defunct>
rivalino	32159	0.0	0.0	0	0	pts/0	Z+	15:23	0:00	ProgAged01 <defunct>

Fig. 2.3. Example of process leakage.

USER	PID	%CPU	%MEM	VSZ	RSS	TTY	STAT	START	TIME	COMMAND
...	...									
rivalino	637	0.0	0.0	10124	264	pts/0	Tl	16:30	0:00	ProgAged01
rivalino	638	0.0	0.0	18316	268	pts/0	Tl	16:30	0:00	ProgAged02
rivalino	639	0.0	0.0	26508	268	pts/0	Tl	16:30	0:00	ProgAged03
rivalino	640	0.0	0.0	34700	268	pts/0	Tl	16:30	0:00	ProgAged04
rivalino	641	0.0	0.0	42892	264	pts/0	Tl	16:30	0:00	ProgAged05

Fig. 2.4. Example of thread leakage.

columns contain different state information stored in the process's control block (PCB). ProgAged01 (PID 32154) is an active process and the other five processes (32155 to 32159) are its child processes that were leaked. It can be seen that the size of the leaked processes in virtual memory (column VSZ) and in resident memory (column RSS) are both zero bytes, which means the leaked processes do not occupy user-space memory. Note that any OS limits the maximal number of processes per user. Hence, in a scenario of process leakage, once a user reaches this maximal number of processes she can't create new processes, which prevents the system from being used for any purpose productively.

Figure 2.4 contains a similar output to Fig. 2.3, however, it shows evidence of thread leakage. All processes (ProgAged01 to ProgAged05) are multithreaded and are created from the same program execution. The only difference between them is that each of them leaked a given number of threads (ProgAged01 leaked one thread, ProgAged02 leaked two threads, and so forth). This is different from what has been shown in Fig. 2.3; in this case the leaked threads occupy virtual memory (VSZ), but not resident memory (RSS). Note that there are different approaches to implementing multithreading and some of them show similar behavior in terms of process and thread leakage with respect to memory usage. Also, the amount of memory increase per thread is highly dependent on the thread creation approach. This means that a process's size is not always a good aging indicator for thread leakage as common sense might seem to dictate. This is even the conclusion suggested by the case of Fig. 2.4, but it is not the true one. Detecting the aging effects in both process and thread leakage is not a trivial task. Considering the specific case of thread leakage, how does one know if a given thread has been leaked? A memory *chunk* with an unknown reference can be considered leaked for sure, but no similar "signature" (*aging indicator*) is available for detecting a leaked thread.

2.3.2.2. *Leakage of file descriptors/socket handles*

The same rationale related to aging effects in processes/threads applies to files/sockets. An opened file or opened socket requires data structures (*file descriptor/socket handle*) to be kept within the kernel space in order to allow these resources to be used by the processes that own them. Leaking these resources means that opened files/sockets become unused and are still allocated (not closed), which makes their related data structures occupy memory in kernel space and also reduces the number of their available entries. Given that the OS also limits these resources per process, their successive leaking causes the exhaustion of the availability of these resources, preventing processes from opening or creating new files or communication sockets. A practical example is shown in Fig. 2.5. ProcAgedf0 leaked no file descriptor, while ProcAgedf1 leaked one, and so forth.

We can see that the number of file descriptors leaked does not increase the process's size, either in virtual memory or resident memory. The software performance (e.g., response time) is also not affected by aging effects of this type. The same question posed regarding thread leakage detection applies in this case, i.e., how does one know if a given file descriptor has been leaked? As in the case of threads, so far there is no well-known *aging indicator* to

USER	PID	%CPU	%MEM	VSZ	RSS	TTY	STAT	START	TIME	COMMAND
...	...									
rivalino	4043	0.0	0.0	1700	244	pts/2	T	19:45	0:00	ProcAgedfd0
rivalino	4044	0.0	0.0	1700	240	pts/2	T	19:45	0:00	ProcAgedfd1
rivalino	4045	0.0	0.0	1700	244	pts/2	T	19:45	0:00	ProcAgedfd2
rivalino	4046	0.0	0.0	1700	240	pts/2	T	19:45	0:00	ProcAgedfd3
rivalino	4047	0.0	0.0	1700	244	pts/2	T	19:45	0:00	ProcAgedfd4
rivalino	4048	0.0	0.0	1700	240	pts/2	T	19:45	0:00	ProcAgedfd5

Fig. 2.5. Example of file descriptor leakage.

USER	PID	%CPU	%MEM	VSZ	RSS	TTY	STAT	START	TIME	COMMAND
...	...									
rivalino	6085	0.0	0.0	1696	240	pts/0	S	22:00	0:00	ProcAgedsck0
rivalino	6086	0.0	0.0	1696	240	pts/0	S	22:00	0:00	ProcAgedsck1
rivalino	6087	0.0	0.0	1696	240	pts/0	S	22:00	0:00	ProcAgedsck2
rivalino	6088	0.0	0.0	1696	240	pts/0	S	22:00	0:00	ProcAgedsck3
rivalino	6089	0.0	0.0	1696	240	pts/0	S	22:00	0:00	ProcAgedsck4
rivalino	6090	0.0	0.0	1696	240	pts/0	S	22:00	0:00	ProcAgedsck5

Fig. 2.6. Example of socket handle leakage.

identify file descriptor leakage. The same applies to socket handle leakage. Figure 2.6 follows the same setup as Fig. 2.5 with respect to socket handles. ProcAgedsck0 leaked no socket handles, while ProcAgesck1 leaked one, and so forth. It can be seen from Fig. 2.6 that there is no effect of socket leakage on the processes's size; the same applies to any other technical-oriented or user-oriented quality metrics usually considered in SAR literature, except that once the application process reaches the number of allowed opened sockets, it will fail when attempting to create new sockets.

2.4. Software Aging in the Performance Engineering Panorama

Software aging can be viewed as part of the more general field of *performance engineering* of software systems. Performance is a key non-functional requirement (explicit or implicit) for many software systems. As the term 'performance engineering' suggests, this requirement should be taken into account across the software development lifecycle, from specification to verification.

There is much evidence in the scientific literature about software systems that suffer from performance-related failures. Performance testing aims at evaluating how the system will perform in the field and/or at identifying performance problems before deployment. The literature related to performance testing, which is sometimes mingled with load or stress testing, considers performance in terms of throughput, average stimulus-response time, or some combination of the two [26], and proposes techniques to test a system against requirements which could be the average or minimum/maximum of these measures. However, most of the performance testing studies do not deal with long-running scenarios, i.e., to find out if and how the performance degrades with time. This gap has been addressed by experimental research on software aging.

Different facets of performance testing have been studied in the past. The most common approach is to test the system against some performance requirement, with either the objective of assessing the expected runtime performance (i.e., under the estimated operational workload), and tuning the system before release, or of finding performance flaws to be corrected. Very closely related areas are *load* testing and *stress* testing. Although there are different definitions in the literature, it usually happens that when the workload used for testing is the nominal or operational one, the practice is also referred to as load testing, whereas, when it is particularly intensive or devoted to unveiling some undesired behavior, it is named stress testing [27]. In general, there is overlap between performance, stress and load testing areas, and there is not a clear taxonomy.

For stress testing, test cases must be processing-intensive, and many techniques exploit models of the system under test (SUT) to identify the most stressful workload for the system's requirements: in [28] the SUT is modeled as a constraint programming problem and a test case that violates the constraints is sought; in [29–31] search-based techniques based on genetic algorithms are used to generate test cases stressing the performance upper-bound limit; in [32] a PID (Proportional–Integral–Derivative) controller is used to the same end.

The performance testing of stateful systems gave rise to state-aware techniques. The approach in [33] generates a stateful synthetic workload according to the operational profile: it extracts the chronological order of a single user's requests and generates test cases according to the logic of the session-based request and of the think-time of users. The field of performance prediction contributed to the development of software aging theory. Some important examples are reported in the following. Liu *et al.* propose in [34] a hybrid approach based on empirical testing and a queueing network model to predict the performance of component-based applications. They point out the importance of isolating performance issues due to business logic from the ones due to the underlying middleware infrastructure (i.e., the container), and to the operating environment (e.g., hardware, OS, and DBMS). In [35] the authors combine performance testing and simulation models to predict the performance problems of an e-commerce application consisting of a front-end web application, a middle-tier application server, and a back-end database.

Several authors addressed load and stress testing as they apply to other goals: in [36] load testing is used to assess the dependability of the system, i.e., as operational testing; load testing can also be done as a comparison between two or more versions e.g. in [37], where no performance specifications were explicitly defined, or as a form of regression testing. Finally, load testing is also used as a form of functional testing aimed at detecting scalability problems or *load-sensitive faults*: these are faults that manifest only under a (heavy) load or over a long period of time [38]. The latter category has an intersection with the above-mentioned aging bugs, and is indirectly related to *performance degradation* testing. There are fewer works on this specific type of performance testing. In [39] the authors introduce the problem of smoothly degraded systems in which the accumulation of errors, due to memory leaks, leads to progressive performance degradation in terms of users and packet loss. Most of the literature on performance degradation refers to the operational phase, and falls under the umbrella of *software aging* studies. These address techniques and strategies for the best assessment of runtime degradation (in terms of resource depletion, throughput loss, or response time), and for the optimal schedule of rejuvenation actions as preventive maintenance.

References

1. Y. Huang, C. Kintala, N. Kolettis, and N. Fulton (1995). Software rejuvenation: analysis, module and applications. In *Proceedings of the 25th International Symposium on Fault-Tolerant Computing, Pasadena, California, USA, June 27–30*, pp. 381–391. doi: 10.1109/FTCS.1995.466961.
2. M. Grottke, R. Matias, and K. Trivedi. (2008). The fundamentals of software aging. In *Proceedings of the 2008 IEEE International Conference on Software Reliability Engineering Workshops, Seattle, Washington, USA, November 11–14*, pp. 1–6. doi: 10.1109/ISSREW.2008.5355512.
3. L. Bernstein and C. Kintala. (2004). Software rejuvenation. *CrossTalk*, **17**(8), 23–26.
4. A. Avritzer and E. Weyuker. (1997). Monitoring smoothly degrading systems for increased dependability. *Empirical Software Engineering*, **2**(1), 59–77.
5. E. Marshall. (1992). Fatal error: How Patriot overlooked a Scud. *Science*, **255**(5050), 1347–1347.
6. L. Bernstein. (1993). Innovative technologies for preventing network outages. *AT&T Technical Journal*, **72**(4), 4–10.
7. Y. Huang and C. Kintala. (1993). Software implemented fault tolerance: Technologies and experience. In *Proceedings of the 23rd International Symposium on Fault-Tolerant Computing, Toulouse, France, June 22–24*, pp. 2–9.
8. Y.-M. Wang, Y. Huang, K.-P. Vo, P.-Y. Chung, and C. Kintala. (1995). Checkpointing and its applications. In *Proceedings of the 25th International Symposium on Fault-Tolerant Computing, Pasadena, California, USA, June 27–30*, pp. 22–31. doi: 10.1109/FTCS.1995.466999.
9. M. Kajko-Mattsson. (2001). Can we learn anything from hardware preventive maintenance? In *Proceedings of the 7th International Conference on Engineering of Complex Computer Systems, Skövde, Sweden, June 11–13*, pp. 106–111.

10. E. Adams. (1984). Optimizing preventive service of software products. *IBM Journal of Research and Development*, **28**(1), 2–14.
11. D. Parnas. (1994). Software aging. In *Proceedings of the 16th International Conference on Software Engineering, Sorrento, Italy, May 16–21*, pp. 279–287.
12. A. Avizienis, J. Laprie, B. Randell, and C. Landwehr. (2004). Basic concepts and taxonomy of dependable and secure computing. *IEEE Transactions on Dependable and Secure Computing*, **1**(1), 11–33.
13. S. Garg, A. van Moorsel, K. Vaidyanathan, and K. Trivedi. (1998). A methodology for detection and estimation of software aging. In *Proceedings of the 9th International Symposium on Software Reliability Engineering, Paderborn, Germany, November 4–7*, pp. 283–292. doi: 10.1109/ISSRE.1998.730892.
14. N. A. Valentim, A. Macedo, and R. Matias. (2016). A systematic mapping review of the first 20 years of software aging and rejuvenation research. In *Proceedings of the 2016 IEEE 27th International Symposium on Software Reliability Engineering Workshops (ISSREW), Ottawa, Ontario, Canada, October 23–27*, pp. 57–63. doi: 10.1109/ISSREW.2016.42.
15. A. Bovenzi, D. Cotroneo, R. Pietrantuono, and S. Russo. (2012). On the aging effects due to concurrency bugs: A case study on MySQL. In *Proceedings of the 2012 IEEE 23rd International Symposium on Software Reliability Engineering, Dallas, Texas, USA, November 27–30*, pp. 211–220. doi: 10.1109/ISSRE.2012.50.
16. G. O. D. Sena and R. Matias. (2018). A systematic mapping review of memory leak detection techniques. In *Proceedings of the 2018 IEEE 29th International Symposium on Software Reliability Engineering Workshops (ISSREW), Memphis, Tennessee, USA, October 15–18*, pp. 264–270.
17. B. Butler. (November 1, 2012). Amazon cites cause of recent outage, issues refunds. URL https://www.networkworld.com/article/2161153/amazon-cites-cause-of-recent-outage--issues-refunds.html. Accessed 2019-11-30.
18. H. Sukhwani, R. Matias, K. S. Trivedi, and A. Rindos. (2017). Monitoring and mitigating software aging on IBM cloud controller system. In *Proceedings of the 2017 IEEE 28th International Symposium on Software Reliability Engineering Workshops (ISSREW), Toulouse, France, October 23–26*, pp. 266–272. doi: 10.1109/ISSREW.2017.65.
19. A. Macêdo, T. B. Ferreira, and R. Matias. (2010). The mechanics of memory-related software aging. In *Proceedings of the 2010 IEEE Second International Workshop on Software Aging and Rejuvenation, San Jose, California, USA, November 2*, pp. 1–5. doi: 10.1109/WOSAR.2010.5722097.
20. J. Araujo, R. Matos, V. Alves, P. Maciel, F. V. d. Souza, R. Matias, and K. S. Trivedi. (2014). Software aging in the eucalyptus cloud computing infrastructure: Characterization and rejuvenation. *Journal of Emerging Technologies in Computing Systems*, **10**(1), 11:1–11:22. ISSN 1550-4832. doi: 10.1145/2539122. URL http://doi.acm.org/10.1145/2539122.
21. P. J. Denning. (1968). Thrashing: Its causes and prevention. In *Proceedings of the AFIPS Fall Joint Computing Conference 1968, San Francisco, California, USA, December 9–11*, pp. 915–922. doi: 10.1145/1476589.1476705. URL http://doi.acm.org/10.1145/1476589.1476705.
22. J. Alonso, R. Matias, E. Vicente, A. Maria, and K. S. Trivedi. (2013). A comparative experimental study of software rejuvenation overhead. *Performance Evaluation*, **70**(3), 231–250. ISSN 0166-5316. doi: https://doi.org/10.1016/j.peva.2012.09.002. URL http://www.sciencedirect.com/science/article/pii/S0166531612000922. Special Issue on Software Aging and Rejuvenation.

23. M. S. Johnstone and P. R. Wilson. (1998). The memory fragmentation problem: Solved? In *Proceedings of the 1st International Symposium on Memory Management (ISMM), Vancouver, British Columbia, Canada, October 17–19*, pp. 26–36. ISBN 1-58113-114-3. doi: 10.1145/286860.286864. URL http://doi.acm.org/10.1145/286860.286864.
24. U. Vahalia. (1996). *UNIX Internals: The New Frontiers*. New Jersey, USA: Prentice Hall Press. ISBN 0-13-101908-2.
25. D. Cotroneo and R. Natella. (2012). Monitoring of aging software systems affected by integer overflows. In *Proceedings of the 2012 IEEE 23rd International Symposium on Software Reliability Engineering Workshops, Dallas, Texas, USA, November 27–30*, pp. 265–270. doi: 10.1109/ISSREW.2012.91.
26. E. J. Weyuker and F. I. Vokolos. (2000). Experience with performance testing of software systems: Issues, an approach, and case study. *IEEE Transactions on Software Engineering*, **26**(12), 1147–1156.
27. Z. M. Jiang. (2013). *Automated Analysis of Load Testing Results* (PhD thesis, Queen's University, Kingston, Ontario, Canada). URL http://hdl.handle.net/1974/7775.
28. S. Di Alesio, S. Nejati, L. Briand, and A. Gotlieb. (2013). Stress testing of task deadlines: A constraint programming approach. In *Proceedings of the 24th IEEE International Symposium on Software Reliability Engineering, Pasadena, California, USA, November 4–7*, pp. 158–167.
29. L. Briand, Y. Labiche, and M. Shousha. (2006). Using genetic algorithms for early schedulability analysis and stress testing in real-time systems. *Genetic Programming and Evolvable Machines*, **7**(2), 145–170. ISSN 1389-2576. doi: 10.1007/s10710-006-9003-9. URL http://dx.doi.org/10.1007/s10710-006-9003-9.
30. V. Garousi. (2010). A genetic algorithm-based stress test requirements generator tool and its empirical evaluation. *IEEE Transactions on Software Engineering*, **36**(6), 778–797. ISSN 0098-5589. doi: 10.1109/TSE.2010.5.
31. R. Nilsson, J. Offutt, and J. Mellin. (2006). Test case generation for mutation-based testing of timeliness. In *Proceedings of the Second Workshop on Model Based Testing (MBT 2006), Vienna, Austria, March 25–26*, pp. 97–114. doi: http://dx.doi.org/10.1016/j.entcs.2006.10.010. URL http://www.sciencedirect.com/science/article/pii/S1571066106005081.
32. M. Bayan and J. A. W. Cangussu. (2008). Automatic feedback, control-based, stress and load testing. In *Proceedings of the 2008 ACM Symposium on Applied Computing (SAC '08), Fortaleza, Ceara, Brazil, March 16–20*, pp. 661–666. ISBN 978-1-59593-753-7. doi: 10.1145/1363686.1363847. URL http://doi.acm.org/10.1145/1363686.1363847.
33. D. Krishnamurthy, J. Rolia, and S. Majumdar. (2006). A synthetic workload generation technique for stress testing session-based systems. *IEEE Transactions on Software Engineering*, **32**(11), 868–882. ISSN 0098-5589. doi: 10.1109/TSE.2006.106.
34. Y. Liu, I. Gorton, A. Liu, N. Jiang, and S. Chen. (2002). Designing a test suite for empirically-based middleware performance prediction. In *Proceedings of the Fortieth International Conference on TOOLS Pacific: Objects for internet, mobile and embedded applications, Sydney, Australia, February 18–21*, pp. 123–130.
35. A. Avritzer and E. J. Weyuker. (2004). The role of modeling in the performance testing of e-commerce applications. *IEEE Transactions on Software Engineering*, **30**(12), 1072–1083. ISSN 0098-5589. doi: 10.1109/TSE.2004.107.
36. A. Avritzer and E. Weyuker. (1995). The automatic generation of load test suites and the assessment of the resulting software. *IEEE Transactions on Software Engineering*, **21**(9), 705–716. ISSN 0098-5589. doi: 10.1109/32.464549.

37. S. Ghaith. (2013). Analysis of performance regression testing data by transaction profiles. In *Proceedings of the 2013 International Symposium on Software Testing and Analysis (ISSTA 2013), Lugano, Switzerland, July 15–20*, pp. 370–373. ISBN 978-1-4503-2159-4. doi: 10.1145/2483760.2492399. URL http://doi.acm.org/10.1145/2483760.2492399.
38. C.-S. D. Yang and L. L. Pollock. (1996). Towards a structural load testing tool. In *Proceedings of the 1996 ACM SIGSOFT International Symposium on Software Testing and Analysis (ISSTA '96), San Diego, California, USA, January 8–10*, pp. 201–208. ISBN 0-89791-787-1. doi: 10.1145/229000.226318. URL http://doi.acm.org/10.1145/229000.226318.
39. A. Avritzer and E. J. Weyuker. (1997). Monitoring smoothly degrading systems for increased dependability. *Empirical Software Engineering*, **2**, 59–77. ISSN 1382-3256. URL http://dx.doi.org/10.1023/A:1009794200077. 10.1023/A:1009794200077.

Chapter 3

Software Rejuvenation: Key Concepts and Granularity

Vasilis P. Koutras* and Agapios N. Platis†

University of the Aegean, Chios 82100, Greece

**v.koutras@fme.aegean.gr*

†*platis@aegean.gr*

Software aging is a phenomenon that causes system performance degradation and eventual failures. Software rejuvenation is a proactive software fault management technique that provides an effective way to preventively counteract such issues. Software rejuvenation is the concept of periodically stopping the running software, cleaning its internal state through garbage collection, defragmentation, flushing operating system kernel tables and reinitializing internal data structures, and restarting it. In this chapter, key software rejuvenation concepts and approaches are briefly presented. The chapter focuses on the classification of rejuvenation strategies based on granularity. Granularity concerns the level at which aging is detected and the level at which rejuvenation is applied to counteract aging. Besides granularity definitions, the chapter classifies most of the existing rejuvenation literature with respect to the granularity level.

3.1. Introduction

Prior to the mid-90s, the way to deal with software aging involved actions like restarting an application or rebooting a computer system after a failure. Such methods are reactive, i.e., they are normally initiated subsequent to the occurrence of a failure incident. Clearly, it is preferable to avoid such disruptive failure incidents in the first place. A proactive restart or reboot could, instead, be performed in the case of systems where the software failure rate tends to increase with time. In order to prevent increasing and unbounded resource consumption, data corruption, and numerical error accumulation, such proactive actions can be used [1]. In view of the non-deterministic nature of aging-related failures, it is imperative to take into account that a failure occurrence time is random.

In order to mitigate the effects of software aging, the concept of software rejuvenation was proposed in [2] and was defined as the periodic preemptive rollback of continuously running applications to prevent (or postpone) software failures in the future. In practice, software rejuvenation can be described as the concept of periodically stopping the running software, cleaning its internal state and restarting it [3]. Cleaning the internal state of software might involve garbage collection, defragmentation, flushing operating system kernel tables and reinitializing internal data structures [1, 4]. In other words, software rejuvenation is a preventive and proactive maintenance technique applied to software systems. It can be considered as a cost-effective approach to proactively schedule a clean-up of the software system before the occurrence of aging-related failures. Software rejuvenation does not aim to remove software bugs but instead it aims to "refresh" software by removing accumulated errors and releasing system resources [5].

The main advantage of software rejuvenation lies in its proactive nature, since it is designed to eliminate error accumulation and release software system resources. Potential error conditions are minimized and thus failures with unexpected consequences may be avoided or postponed. By rejuvenating an application/system or operating system (OS), it is possible to avoid future occurrences of software failure altogether or to extend the time taken for the system or application to fail, a fact that contributes to the system's reliability. On the other hand, software rejuvenation can also maximize the fraction of time during which the system is providing service to its users and hence can increase its availability. Despite its advantages in removing aging effects and preventing software from future failures, rejuvenation obviously involves an overhead since the running software is stopped so that its internal state can be cleaned. Although this can be considered as a major drawback, in its defense, one can claim that rejuvenation involves scheduled downtime as opposed to possible higher downtime caused by unplanned outages due to failures that can be disruptive. However, in the relevant literature an intense effort is dedicated to reducing [1, 6, 7] or even eliminating the downtime and the corresponding cost due to rejuvenation [8–10]. This is the major reason for deciding properly on when and how to implement rejuvenation.

Various approaches have been proposed in the relevant literature attempting to answer the above-mentioned questions. In general, these approaches can be classified into two main groups: the data-driven (also known as measurement-based) approaches and the model-driven approaches.

The data-driven approach consists in periodically monitoring (inspecting) software system attributes in order to detect the signs of software aging and enable proactive actions like rejuvenation to prevent failures. Data-driven approaches for software aging and rejuvenation can be found in [6] and [11–24]. It is worth mentioning that in data-driven approaches, one can consider three different approaches to determining the rejuvenation schedule based on the state of the system to be rejuvenated [25]. In the first approach, a threshold is pre-defined by the system designer for every metric aging indicator [8, 26]. In the second approach, prediction methods (machine learning [27, 28], statistical approaches [9], structural models [29]) are adopted to estimate the time to resource exhaustion or the failure time due to aging, and based on these predicted times, the rejuvenation schedule is decided on. Finally, combining both approaches using prediction methods to determine the rejuvenation threshold has also gained some research attention [30]. In the model-driven approach, analytic models are used to determine the rejuvenation trigger interval (i.e., the number of hours before rejuvenation is next performed) that will best improve software system performance. This is called the optimal rejuvenation policy (schedule). Many analytic models can be found in the literature in [2, 12, 15, 21] and [31–36]. They are also reviewed in detail in Chapter 6 of this book and the background material on these models is provided in Appendix A.1 of the book.

Besides the above-mentioned classification that is based on the techniques used for detecting aging and thereafter scheduling software rejuvenation, there is another classification of rejuvenation strategies. This classification is based on the granularity of the rejuvenation. The granularity defines the location of aging effects and the part of the system that will benefit from rejuvenation. Thus, granularity concerns the level at which aging effects are detected and at which rejuvenation should be employed to counteract the aging. The literature defines four fundamental granularity levels: ***physical node level***, ***virtualization level***, ***operating system (OS) level*** and ***application level*** [5, 25, 36].

Most research efforts to date have considered rejuvenation on a single- granularity level. Nevertheless, multi-granularity rejuvenation was proposed in the early phase of software rejuvenation literature [1] and has been applied later in [35]. In [37], an experimental study of various rejuvenation techniques for application level, OS level, virtualization level and physical node level is presented for the purpose of comparing the cost of these rejuvenation strategies. Moreover, in [25], an experimental study of four-granularity rejuvenation strategies (application level, OS level, virtual machine level, and physical machine level) is presented, and in [38] a theoretical analysis on multi-granularity rejuvenation is provided.

However, using multi-granularity rejuvenation in real-life systems is not an easy task due to the issues like [5]:

- identifying the granularity level that is affected by aging
- modeling the multi-granularity software system, taking into account potential dependencies
- proving, either experimentally or theoretically, that a multi-granularity rejuvenation strategy is more effective than single-granularity level rejuvenation.

Concerning the first issue, when detecting aging effects in a software system, generally, there is not enough information to identify the location of the aging effects. In this case, single-granularity rejuvenation, implemented by rebooting the OS, may be the best solution. However, when the relevant aging granularity can be identified in a certain level, the single-granularity rejuvenation strategy at that level is the most appropriate strategy to adopt. On the other hand, multi-granularity rejuvenation strategies could be beneficial for a software system in various cases. For example, in cases in which the aging phenomena are identified in multiple levels, multi-granularity rejuvenation is the appropriate method to adopt. Or, for instance, when the aging effects accumulate inside the OS kernel, or when they are due to the interaction between the application software and OS, application software rejuvenation can be incapable of mitigating aging impacts and rejuvenation at the OS level is required [38]. In such cases, when a multi-granularity rejuvenation actually incorporates two (or more) single-granularity rejuvenation levels, the software system can be benefited in terms of performance, availability and/or cost. However, taking into account that rejuvenation strategies of different granularity deal with different aging impacts and obviously incur different costs, it is of prior importance to select the appropriate strategy in terms of system performance, availability and/or cost [38]. In practice a trade-off needs to be made between the aforementioned measures prior to deciding on either single or multi-granularity rejuvenation strategies [5, 35, 176, 178].

The aim of this chapter, apart from referring to the key concepts of software rejuvenation, is to focus on the rejuvenation granularity level. For this purpose, first, definitions and explanations for single and multi-granularity software rejuvenation strategies are provided. Next, key research studies adopting both approaches are presented.

The remainder of this chapter is organized as follows: In Section 3.2, the single-granularity rejuvenation approach is defined and analyzed and research papers dealing with this level are listed and classified. In Section 3.3, the multi-granularity level approach is presented along with the corresponding software rejuvenation literature, while in Section 3.4 the concept of failed rejuvenation as well as the corresponding literature is presented. The chapter concludes with a short discussion in Section 3.5.

3.2. Single-granularity Rejuvenation

The single-granularity rejuvenation is the most common one and it is discussed in the majority of research papers on software aging and rejuvenation. Key research papers are classified in the following section, with respect to the single-granularity level considered, as defined in Section 3.1.

3.2.1. *Physical Node Level Granularity*

The physical node or physical machine reboot is the most common rejuvenation approach. This approach is based on stopping the node/machine where the software system is running and restarting it. In this scenario, the machine is physically restarted instead of rebooting the OS. Such an approach is a baseline used for comparison with other less drastic approaches. Note that rejuvenation at such granularity usually incurs the highest cost [25, 38].

In [29] the authors use Stochastic Reward Nets (SRNs) to model and analyze cluster systems under node-level software rejuvenation. In particular, a time-based rejuvenation policy is employed and the optimal rejuvenation interval with respect to availability and cost is determined. Moreover, they introduce a rejuvenation policy based on prediction which can significantly increase system availability as well as reduce downtime cost. Node-level preventive maintenance is also the case in [7], where a model-based approach to accenting the effects of on-board preventive maintenance on reliability for a spacecraft which performs a long-life deep-space mission is presented, and the optimal interval between maintenance is determined. Time-based node-level rejuvenation policies that can improve the performability measures of a cluster system are discussed as well in [39]. Standard, delayed and mixed rejuvenation policies are designed to improve the cluster's performability under varying workloads by utilizing deterministic and stochastic Petri nets

(DSPNs), and the effects of these policies on a system's performance are examined.

3.2.2. *Virtualization Level Granularity*

Recently, virtualization technology has often been adopted to reduce the IT infrastructure costs. In particular, virtualized computing platforms have been used for deploying long-running applications in data centers. The virtualized environment is composed of different layers such as physical hardware, hypervisors (Virtual Machine Monitor — VMM), virtual machines (VM), operating systems and applications running on the operating system. Aging phenomena are manifested in these layers. These phenomena can be counteracted by triggering software rejuvenation on VMs and/or on VMMs (which can host multiple VMs). Rejuvenation in the virtualization level granularity aims to mitigate potential aging in the virtualized environment when a guest OS-level rejuvenation or reboot cannot remove it [141]. Based on the layer that rejuvenation is applied to, virtualization granularity can be partitioned into three sub-categories: VM rejuvenation granularity, VMM rejuvenation granularity and VM & VMM rejuvenation granularity. Various research papers adopt the aforementioned approaches to mitigate aging effects by rejuvenation.

The idea behind VM rejuvenation lies in holding multiple replicas of the application that experiences software aging in a single physical server configuration, and triggering rejuvenation of each one when aging indications are detected [142]. VM rejuvenation policies for counteracting software aging can be found in [142–151].

A VMM is a software module and is naturally subject to software aging, and potential failures can have serious effects on the running VMs. These effects range from service interruption to data or session loss. Software degradation can lead the VMM to a failure-probable state or even to a total failure state. When a failure is detected (e.g. by inspection of memory usage), the status of all the running VMs is saved (if possible) and the VMM is restored. After VMM repair, the VMs can be reactivated. To avoid VMM failures, rejuvenation actions can be triggered as soon as the VMM enters a failure-probable state. On this occasion, the running VMs are suspended in a safe way and the VMM is rebooted [152]. VMM software rejuvenation techniques can be implemented in three different approaches. In the first approach, called cold-VM rejuvenation, all the VMs built on the VMM are shut down, regardless of their running states, before the rejuvenation for the VMM is performed. The process of rebooting the VMM includes VMM shutdown, hardware reset, VMM restarting, and service stopping and restarting. In the second approach, called warm-VM rejuvenation, instead of stopping all the VM hosts, VMs are resumed or suspended before the VMM rejuvenation. Since the jobs running on the VMs are stored in memory, in practice jobs are not canceled by the rejuvenation although the job completion time increases. Note that the service downtime in this case is less than the cold-VM rejuvenation service downtime, since the time to "unfreeze" suspended VMs is considerably less than the time needed to reboot them. In the third approach, called migrate-VM rejuvenation, another VMM in the same environment with the original VMM is required. Live migration, which can move running VMs from one VMM to another VMM before rejuvenation without service downtime, takes place. Given that VMM rejuvenation is completed, the migrated VMs are moved back to the rejuvenated VMM [153]. Although VMM rejuvenation is suggested as an alternative solution for mitigating aging effects, it may incur considerable downtime compared to conventional rejuvenation in common software components, since hosted VMs running on a VMM might become unavailable during the VMM rejuvenation. This feature ought to be considered when deciding on the appropriate rejuvenation technique to be adopted [154]. Nevertheless, VMM rejuvenation has gained a lot of research effort in the past years and as a result, a considerable number of research papers can be found in this area [152–168].

The above-mentioned rejuvenation approaches in the virtualization granularity can only rejuvenate VMM or VMs. However, in the relevant literature software rejuvenation approaches that can be applied to both VMM and VMs are also studied in [169–174].

3.2.3. *OS-Level Granularity*

Rejuvenation at OS granularity is at a lower (finer) level than rejuvenation at application-level granularity. In cases in which the aging errors are accumulating in the OS kernel or even caused by the interaction of application software with the OS, application-level rejuvenation strategies are ineffective in counteracting aging phenomena. In these cases, OS-level rejuvenation is required. This rejuvenation granularity is more complex than the application granularity since it lies beneath the application-level granularity; when aging errors accumulate inside the operating system kernel or even when they are caused by the interaction between the OS and the application software, application software granularity becomes ineffective and OS-level rejuvenation needs to be performed [38]. Generally, OS rejuvenation granularity can be further divided into two sub-categories: OS Reboot and OS Fast Reboot [37].

In OS Reboot, the system is rebooted by enabling the typical reboot mechanism of the OS, which includes reloading the firmware, re-executing the power-on self-test routines, reloading and restarting the OS kernel code, restarting the basic OS services and then restarting the application [25, 37]. OS Reboot level rejuvenation is adopted in [132–136]. In the OS Fast Reboot approach, the OS kernel is replaced, at runtime, refreshing the internal state; likewise in the OS Reboot, but without the delay caused by the hardware initialization related routines [37]. OS Fast Reboot is also used as a single-granularity rejuvenation strategy at the OS level in the relevant literature [37, 137–140].

3.2.4. *Application-Level Granularity*

Application-level rejuvenation manages to mitigate the impacts of software aging at application software level by stopping and restarting an aged application. It is a preventive application restart to remove specific aging effects related to the application level. Application-level rejuvenation incurs service downtime and consequently overhead cost. Nevertheless, this overhead is sufficiently lower than the overhead of node-level rejuvenation, since stopping and restarting an application lasts a shorter time and costs less than stopping and rebooting the entire node [5, 25, 37, 38]. This technique has been widely used to counteract aging effects in various general and special purpose systems that are presented hereinafter.

The model proposed in [2] (thereafter called the *basic model*) is the first software rejuvenation model where single-granularity rejuvenation is applied at the application level. Software aging does not cause the application to fail immediately after its initiation; there is a certain time period that elapses before an application ages and therefore becomes failure-prone. The running application initially is in a robust state. The sojourn time in this state is called the base longevity interval and when this time elapses, the application becomes failure-probable and reaches a failure-probable state. Given that the application is in this state, a software failure may occur, or software rejuvenation can be proactively triggered in order to avoid a failure. After a failure, the repair procedure is initiated immediately to restore the application in its robust state. In cases in which rejuvenation is performed, after recovering from rejuvenation, the application enters the robust state. With this model, the steady-state probability distribution can be derived, given that the system is intended to run continuously. The total expected downtime and the total expected downtime cost in an interval of L time units are evaluated with respect to the rejuvenation interval. The optimal rejuvenation schedule is derived with respect to the above-mentioned measures.

Based on this basic model, application-level rejuvenation strategies are extensively studied in the relevant literature. In [40], deterministic intervals between successive application-level rejuvenations are considered. The behavior of a system similar to this is represented through a Markov regenerative stochastic Petri net model in [2]. Steady-state as well as transient conditions are derived and closed-form analytical solutions for the steady-state expected downtime and cost are provided. The optimal time to perform rejuvenation in the robust state is evaluated with respect to software unavailability. This work is further extended in [41] by applying the phase expansion technique. In [15] and [32] the application-level rejuvenation model of [2] is extended using a semi-Markov process aiming to obtain the rejuvenation policies that optimize steady-state availability and the expected cost per unit time correspondingly; furthermore statistical non-parametric algorithms are provided for estimating the optimal rejuvenation schedules, while [33] extends the work in [32] by introducing a non-parametric predictive inference approach to estimate an optimal software rejuvenation schedule which minimizes the expected total software cost per unit time. The basic model in application-level rejuvenation strategies is further extended [34, 42, 43] where the optimal rejuvenation policies in terms of reward rates and interval reliability correspondingly are derived. Extensions of the single-granularity application-level rejuvenation strategy of [34] can be found in [44–46], while [45] and [46] are further extended in [47–49] correspondingly. In [50] and [51], the basic model is adopted, and the opportunity-based rejuvenation policy is introduced using a semi-Markov process. Furthermore, in [3], the basic model is used for a high-assurance software system with fault-tolerance and preventive rejuvenation. Its stochastic behavior is analyzed, and the asymptotic availability is evaluated quantitatively. In [52], the authors proposed a software rejuvenation model considering attacks or failures and use stochastic Petri nets to derive the optimal rejuvenation policy that maximizes system availability. In [53] the authors consider the basic application-level model and maximize the level of reliability for continuous and safety-critical systems, taking into account transient faults caused by software aging effects as well as network transmission faults. In [54], the concept of omitting the recovery time from the rejuvenation and/or the repair procedure is introduced for the application-level rejuvenation model when the recovery time is too short as it can be negligible. In [55], application-level rejuvenation for improving maritime software operation according to the safety and minimum cost requirements for applications on board a ship is presented. In [56] a more theoretical view of the basic application-level rejuvenation model is provided.

Besides the model introduced in [2], operational software degradation has also been studied as a multistage process using single-granularity rejuvenation models at the application level. This concept was firstly introduced in [57], where the authors use a Markov process to model a system's evolution in time and derive rejuvenation schedules that optimize the total expected operational cost per unit time using a dynamic programming approach. This work is further extended in [58–61]. Single-granularity rejuvenation strategies at the application level have also been used to model and examine how and when rejuvenation should be implemented and its impact on various dependability and performance measures in cluster systems [62–68], in distributed environments such as grid and cloud environments [69–78], in fault-tolerant systems with redundancies [79–81], in transaction-based systems [82, 83] and in queuing model-based applications [84–89], in billing telecommunication applications and in VoIP applications [90–95], in security applications [96–99], in degradation models [100–102] as well as in modeling the allocation/de-allocation of system resources when rejuvenation is implemented [103–105]. Finally, various other application-level rejuvenation strategies can be further found in the relevant literature [9, 107–129].

3.2.4.1. *Application component level granularity*

Instead of application-level rejuvenation, downtime and overhead cost can be also reduced by adopting an application component rejuvenation strategy. Instead of restarting the entire aged application, parts of it can be restarted. This approach can be considered as single-granularity rejuvenation at the application component level [25]. Although this approach requires re-engineering the application, hence reducing its cost-effectiveness, it has been also considered in the relevant literature.

In [8], the authors present a software solution to achieve highly available and responsive application servers that provide grid services. They use techniques like virtualization, primary-back-up schemes, and system surveillance schemes as well as software rejuvenation at the application component level. The proposed methodology is experimentally evaluated using a package of grid middleware. In [130], a software rejuvenation scheduling problem in a distributed software system composed of a number of processes that can communicate with message exchanging is considered. To prevent failures, which are expressed as process deadlock, occasional software rejuvenation (garbage collection and re-scheduling of transmitted messages) is executed based on rejuvenation scheduling algorithms that aim to minimize the expected total time of computation. In [131], the authors describe enabling component level rejuvenation by adopting the Recursive Restartability (RR) technique to improve the MTTF of a software system.

3.3. Multi-granularity Rejuvenation

3.3.1. *Two-level Rejuvenation Policies*

Although most of the research papers in software rejuvenation consider only one of the above-mentioned single-granularity rejuvenation strategies, there is a lot of research in two-granularity rejuvenation approaches too. Two-granularity rejuvenation can be considered similar to maintenance approaches where minimal and major maintenance actions are triggered [175]. Thus, the two-granularity rejuvenation strategies, usually called two-level rejuvenation strategies, incorporate two single-granularity rejuvenation levels: *Level 1* or *partial* rejuvenation and *Level 2* or *full* rejuvenation.

The first level is the application granularity rejuvenation level. In the relevant literature, this level can be also referred to as *Level 1* rejuvenation or as *partial* rejuvenation. It is applied in order to mitigate the impacts of software aging at the application level. It includes stopping the running application, saving any necessary data and then restarting it. Partial rejuvenation is useful for removing volatile in-memory application-specific aging effects [5]. The impact of partial rejuvenation on other applications running on the same OS is assumed to be minimal [35].

The second level, also called *Level 2* or *full* rejuvenation, is the OS granularity rejuvenation level. Its effects are more complex than partial rejuvenation since it affects all applications running on the OS, and obviously needs more time to be accomplished. Full rejuvenation needs to be triggered when the aging effects are due to the OS kernel, or when there exists an interaction between the application software and the OS, since in such cases application granularity rejuvenation is rather ineffective [5, 35].

Two-level software rejuvenation was firstly introduced in [1], where the authors present some techniques developed for detecting aging due to resource exhaustion and for estimating the remaining time until the available resources reach a critical level. Once available resources reach this level, software rejuvenation actions are triggered either at the application level or at the OS level. Their purpose is to evaluate various rejuvenation policies for optimizing the availability of a cluster system. In [35], a semi-Markov process is used to model two-level software rejuvenation (partial-Level 1 and full-Level 2 rejuvenation). The aim is to maximize system asymptotic availability. The authors provide a closed-form solution for the asymptotic availability with respect to the rejuvenation interval and the probability of selecting partial rejuvenation. In [176], the authors deal with the dependency between the application components and the application server platform, and propose a two-level rejuvenation strategy. The availability and maintenance cost functions are obtained and through evaluation experiments, the authors have come up with the result that compared with the traditional rejuvenation policy, the two-level policy can further increase the availability of the application server and reduce the maintenance cost. A model incorporating application level and system level rejuvenation is presented in [177], where the advantage of the proposed two-level rejuvenation over conventional rejuvenation policies is shown in terms of downtime, availability and reliability. In [178], partial and full rejuvenations in a redundant computer system with imperfect switch are modeled via a semi-Markov process. The aim is to determine the optimal rejuvenation policies that maximize system asymptotic availability. The proposed model with partial and full rejuvenation actions has proven to be more efficient in terms of asymptotic availability than the corresponding model with single-granularity rejuvenation. A software system experiencing gradual performance degradation is considered in [179], where partial and full rejuvenation actions are triggered to counteract the degradation since the system is supposed to provide service continuously, independently of resource degradation. A semi-Markov process is adopted to model the system's evolution in time, though a Markov reward model is also used for examining the impact of the load on system performance. The efficiency of the proposed approach is indicated in terms of availability, reliability and maintainability. Partial and full rejuvenation with reconfiguration are proposed in [180], where a Markov model is used to describe the system's evolution in time. Two-level rejuvenation with reconfiguration manages to improve system availability. Moreover in [181] and [182], the performance of time warp-based parallel discrete event simulation (PDES) systems is improved by adopting partial and full rejuvenation schemes. The work in these papers indicates that rejuvenation in a time warp simulation should be performed either partially or fully, since only full rejuvenation is not efficient in managing the progress of processes equally. The P^2-resource model is extended by adopting partial and full rejuvenation policies in [183]. The optimal interleaving between partial and full rejuvenations that maximizes the average resource performance is derived based on a linear search algorithm. The study presented in [184] considers a software/hardware system under the assumption that failures can occur at both levels. Maintenance policies for improving hardware degradation are considered, though multi-level rejuvenation is proposed for the software. The efficiency of the proposed model is shown in terms of system downtime cost and availability. A two-granularity rejuvenation strategy is proposed in [5] to improve a computing system's performance when it suffers from aging phenomena. Rejuvenation at the application level as well as at the OS level is applied and a Markov regenerative process model is used. The authors obtain the degradation rate of the application software and operating system from fault injection experiments, as well the availability and the overall loss probability along with the corresponding optimal inspection time intervals. Through the experimental results it is shown that the two-granularity software rejuvenation approach is much more effective than traditional single-level software rejuvenation in terms of the aforementioned measures. Availability and performance improvements made by considering adaptive two-granularity rejuvenation strategies is the case in [185], though in [186] the schedulability of a hard real-time task set on a resource which experiences performance degradation over time with a known pattern with both partial and full periodic rejuvenations as countermeasures is examined.

Finally, note that rejuvenation strategies in virtualization level granularity which discuss both VM-level rejuvenation and VMM-level rejuvenation can be categorized as multi-granularity level rejuvenation approaches (two-level), depending on the classification criteria [154, 169–174].

3.3.2. *Other Multi-level Rejuvenation Policies*

Although the idea of higher-level rejuvenation strategies has not gained a lot of research attention, mostly due to modeling and analysis complexity, a few approaches in three-level or four-level rejuvenation appear in the relevant literature.

In [38], the authors study multi-granularity software rejuvenation policies using a Markov model. Four granularity levels are considered: Application software (AS) level, operating system (OS) level, virtual machine (VM) level, and physical machine (PM) level. The level of granularity to be carried out is determined by monitor and analysis equipment which periodically inspects the whole computer system and collects system data. The measures of interest are the asymptotic availability and the cost, which are estimated using the collected data.

In [196], an active/standby cluster system in which PCs are connected in a loosely-coupled fashion is examined and software rejuvenation is incorporated to improve the performance of the system. A three-level software rejuvenation policy for this system is proposed. In Level 1, the stoppage of the cluster system does not have any effect on the running applications. All the necessary data are saved and after a restart the service runs as a healthy state. In Level 2, the stoppage of the cluster system has some impact on applications and actions running on the cluster system, but this impact is supposed to be minimal. In Level 3, the cluster system and all the applications built on it are stopped. The main objective of Level 3 rejuvenation consists in restarting the cluster system to recover all its free memory. All the applications of the same cluster system are equally affected in this case. A model for this three-level rejuvenation system is proposed and the steady-state probability distribution is computed to estimate the system availability and downtime cost.

Finally in [197], a reliability analysis of an embedded cluster system is carried out by incorporating software rejuvenation to counteract aging. A Markov model is developed by assuming four levels of software rejuvenation: three partial rejuvenation actions with different impacts on the system state and a full rejuvenation action. The asymptotic probability distribution of the system is derived and furthermore the availability, the MTTF and the downtime cost are evaluated.

3.4. Failed Rejuvenation

It is worth mentioning that based on some of the aforementioned multi-granularity rejuvenation models, a new concept for rejuvenation was also introduced. This concept concerns the cases when rejuvenation actions may not be properly completed or when a rejuvenation action may be performed improperly. Such a scenario is defined as *failed rejuvenation*, which indicates an abnormal function during the rejuvenation process. The case of failed rejuvenation may be extremely rare, but it may occur under certain conditions and circumstances, as for example when garbage collection problems due to too large applications or applications with severe real-time constraints occur. When a failed rejuvenation, either partial or full, occurs, the system enters a failure state. Failed rejuvenation on two-granularity rejuvenation models has lately attracted considerable research attention [187–194]. However, the concept of a failed rejuvenation action can be also considered in single-granularity rejuvenation models as in [195], where single-granularity rejuvenation can be perfect with probability p or imperfect with probability 1-p. In the case of imperfect rejuvenation, the modeled system returns to its failure-prone state.

3.5. Discussion

Software rejuvenation strategies have been widely used for more than 20 years to mitigate the effects of aging related to fault accumulation which can lead a software system to performance degradation and eventually to total failure. Software rejuvenation tends to be a rather established approach for improving software systems' dependability and performance. Key rejuvenation concepts have been repeatedly reported in the relevant literature as well as in this chapter. However, the concept of rejuvenation granularity can be considered as rather new, although it has been reported a long time ago in the literature. The purpose of this chapter is to organize rejuvenation granularity definitions as well as to classify the majority of the existing literature on rejuvenation in one of the granularity categories mentioned above. To this extent, the classification of the research effort in software rejuvenation with respect to granularities is given in Table 3.1.

Based on the software rejuvenation literature, it seems that the multi-granularity rejuvenation strategies tend to provide improved dependability

Table 3.1. Classification of software rejuvenation articles with respect to rejuvenation granularity.

Single-granularity Rejuvenation				Multi-granularity Rejuvenation	
Node Level	Application Level	OS Level	Virtualization Level	Two-level Rejuvenation	Higher-level Rejuvenation
[7], [29], [39]	[2], [8], [15], [32–34], [39–131]	[25], [37], [38], [132–140]	[141–174]	[1], [5], [35], [176–195]	[196], [197]

and performance for software systems when used. Consequently, due to the fact that multi-granularity rejuvenation manages to counteract aging phenomena in more software system layers, it can be considered as the future of software rejuvenation schemes. However, issues like identifying the granularity level affected by aging, modeling the multi-granularity software system, considering several granularities which may reveal dependencies, and proving, either experimentally or theoretically, that a multi-granularity rejuvenation strategy is more effective than single-granularity level rejuvenation, should be carefully taken into account in the future in order to design efficient multi-granularity schemes.

Another important issue on software rejuvenation implementation is that system virtualization techniques are getting more and more popular and easy to adopt, hence are gaining significant interest in the enterprise and personal computing spaces. Software rejuvenation design should take advantage of the growth of virtualization techniques for mitigating aging-related effects for software systems. This project is not too difficult to carry out, since, as mentioned, there is already a state-of-the-art in the area consisting of a lot of research papers that have been using rejuvenation implementation in virtualized environments.

References

1. V. Castelli, R. E. Harper, S. W. Hunter, K. S. Trivedi, K. Vaidyanathan, and W. P. Zeggert. (2001). Proactive management of software aging. *IBM Journal of Research and Development*, **45**(2), 311–332.
2. Y. Huang, C. Kintala, N. Kolettis, and N. Fulton. (1995). Software rejuvenation: analysis, module and applications. In *Proceedings of the 25th International Symposium on Fault-Tolerant Computing (FTCS '95), Pasadena, California, USA, June 27–30*, pp. 381–390.
3. K. Rinsaka and T. Dohi. (2005). Behavioral analysis of fault-tolerant software system with rejuvenation. *IEICE Transactions on Information and Systems*, **E88-D**(12), 2681–2690.
4. K. S. Trivedi, K. Vaidyanathan, and K. Goseva-Popstojanova. (2000). Modeling and analysis of software aging and rejuvenation. In *Proceedings of the 33rd Annual Simulation Symposium (SS 2000), Washington, DC, USA, April 16–20*, pp. 270–279.
5. G. Ning, J. Zhao, Y. Lou, J. Alonso, R. Matias Jr., and Kishor S. Trivedi. (2016). Optimization of two-granularity software rejuvenation policy based on the Markov regenerative process. *IEEE Transactions on Reliability*, **65**(4), 1630–1646.
6. M. Grottke, L. Li, K. Vaidyanathan, and K. S. Trivedi. (2006). Analysis of software aging in a web server. *IEEE Transactions on Reliability*, **55**(3), 411–420.
7. A. T. Tai, H. Hecht, S. N. Chau, and L. Alkalaj. (1997). On-board preventive maintenance: analysis of effectiveness and optimal duty period. In *Proceedings of*

the 3rd Workshop on Object-Oriented Real-Time Dependable Systems (WORDS '97), Newport Beach, California, USA, February 5–7, pp. 40–47.

8. J. Alonso, L. Silva, A. Andrzejak, P. Silva, and J. Torres. (2007). High-available grid services through the use of virtualized clustering. In *Proceedings of the IEEE/ACM 8th International Conference on Grid Computing (GRID '07) Austin, Texas, USA, September 19–21*, pp. 34–41.
9. R. Matias and P. J. F. Filho. (2006). An experimental study on software aging and rejuvenation in web servers. In *Proceedings of the 30th Annual International Computer Software and Applications Conference, Chicago, Illinois, USA, September 17–21*, pp. 189–196.
10. L. M. Silva, J. Alonso, P. Silva, J. Torres, and A. Andrzejak. (2007). Using virtualization to improve software rejuvenation. In *Proceedings of the Sixth IEEE International Symposium on Network Computing and Applications (NCA 2007), Cambridge, Massachusetts, USA, July 12–14*, pp. 33–44.
11. A. Bobbio and M. Sereno. (1998). Fine grained software rejuvenation models. In *Proceedings of the IEEE International Symposium on Computer Performance and Dependability (IPDS '98), Durham, North Carolina, USA*, pp. 4–12.
12. S. Garg, A. Puliafito, M. Telek, and K. S. Trivedi. (1998). Analysis of preventive maintenance in transactions-based software systems. *IEEE Transactions on Computers*, **47**, 96–107.
13. L. Li, K. Vaidyanathan, and K. S. Trivedi. (2002). An approach for estimation of software aging in a Web server. In *Proceedings of the International Symposium in Empirical Software Engineering, Nara, Japan, October 3–4*, pp. 91–100.
14. K. Vaidyanathan and K. S. Trivedi. (1999). A measurement-based model for estimation of resource exhaustion in operational software systems. In *Proceedings of the 10th IEEE International Symposium on Software Reliability Engineering, Boca Raton, Florida, USA, November 1–4*, pp. 84–93.
15. T. Dohi, K. G. Popstojanova, and K. S. Trivedi. (2000). Statistical non-parametric algorithms to estimate the optimal software rejuvenation schedule. In *Proceedings of the Pacific Rim International Symposium on Dependable Computing, Los Angeles, California, USA, December 18–20*, pp. 77–84.
16. Y. Bao, X. Sun, and K. S. Trivedi. (2005). A workload-based analysis of software aging, and rejuvenation. *IEEE Transactions on Reliability*, **54**(3), 102–114.
17. Y. Hong, D. Chen, L. Li, and K. S. Trivedi. (2002). Closed loop design for software rejuvenation. *Presented at the Workshop on Self-Healing, Adaptive, and Self-Managed Systems, New York City, New York, USA, June 23.*
18. W. Qin and Q. Wang. (2005). Feedback performance control for computer systems: An LPV approach, In *Proceedings of the American Control Conference, Portland, Oregon, USA, June 8–10*, pp. 4760–4765.
19. A. Bobbio, A. Sereno, and C. Anglano. (2001). Fine grained software degradation models for optimal rejuvenation policies. *Performance Evaluation*, **46**, 45–62.
20. S. Garg, Y. Huang, C. Kintala, and K. S. Trivedi. (1995). Time and load based software rejuvenation: Policy, evaluation and optimality. In *Proceedings of the 1st Fault-Tolerant Symposium, Madras, India, December*, pp. 22–25.
21. S. Garg, A. Van Moorsel, K. Vaidyanathan, and K. S. Trivedi. (1998). A methodology for detection and estimation of software aging. In *Proceedings of the 9th International Symposium on Software Reliability Engineering, Paderborn, Germany, November 4–7*, pp. 283–292.

22. M. Shereshevsky, J. Crowell, B. Cukic, V. Gandikota, and Y. Liu. (2003). Software aging and multifractality of memory resources. In *Proceedings of the 2003 International Conference on Dependable Systems and Networks, San Francisco, California, USA, June 22–25*, pp. 721–730.
23. Y. Jia, X. Chen, and K.-Y. Cai. (2006). Chaotic analysis of software aging in a web server. In *Proceedings of the 2nd International Workshop on Service-Oriented Systems Engineering, Shanghai, China, October 25–26*, pp. 117–120.
24. K. Xue, L. Su, Y. Jia, and K.-Y. Cai. (2009). A neural network approach to forecasting computing-resource exhaustion with workload. In *Proceedings of the 9th International Conference on Quality Software, Jeju, Korea, August 22–25*, pp. 315–324.
25. J. Alonso, R. Matias, E. Vicente, A. Maria, and K. S. Trivedi. (2013). A comparative experimental study of software rejuvenation overhead. *Performance Evaluation*, **70**(3), 231–25.
26. L. Silva, J. Alonso, and J. Torres. (2009). Using virtualization to improve software rejuvenation. *IEEE Transactions on Computers*, **58**(11), 1525–1538.
27. A. Andrzejak and L. Silva. (2008). Using machine learning for non-intrusive modeling and prediction of software aging. In *Proceedings of the IEEE/IFIP Network Operations & Management Symposium (NOMS 2008), Salvador, Bahia, Brazil, April 7–11*, pp. 7–11.
28. J. Alonso, J. Torres, J. Berral, and R. Gavalda. (2010). Adaptive on-line software aging prediction based on machine learning. In *Proceedings of the IEEE/IFIP International Conference on Dependable Systems and Networks (DSN 2010)*, pp. 507–516.
29. K. Vaidyanathan, R. E. Harper, S. W. Hunter, and K. S. Trivedi. (2001). Analysis and implementation of software rejuvenation in cluster systems. In *Proceedings of the 2001 ACM SIGMETRICS International Conference on Measurement and Modeling of Computer Systems (SIGMETRICS '01). Cambridge, Massachusetts, USA, June 16–20*, pp. 62–71.
30. R. Matos, J. Araujo, P. Maciel, F. Vieira de Souza, R. Matias, and K. Trivedi. (2012). Software rejuvenation in eucalyptus cloud computing infrastructure: A hybrid method based on multiple thresholds and time series prediction. *International Transactions on Systems Science and Applications*, **8**, 1–16.
31. K. Vaidyanathan and K. S. Trivedi. (2005). A comprehensive model for software rejuvenation. *IEEE Transactions on Dependable and Secure Computing*, **2**(2), 124–137.
32. T. Dohi, K. G. Popstojanova, and K. S. Trivedi. (2000). Analysis of software cost models with rejuvenation. In *Proceedings of the International Symposium on High Assurance Systems Engineering, Albuquerque, New Mexico, USA, November 15–17*, pp. 25–34.
33. K. Rinsaka and T. Dohi. (2017). An adaptive cost-based software rejuvenation scheme with nonparametric predictive inference approach. *Journal of the Operations Research Society of Japan*, **60**(4), 461–478.
34. T. Dohi, K. G. Popstojanova, and K. S. Trivedi. (2001). Estimating software rejuvenation schedules in high assurance systems. *The Computer Journal*, **44**, 473–485.
35. W. Xie, Y. Hong, and K. S. Trivedi. (2005). Analysis of a two-level software rejuvenation policy. *Reliability Engineering and System Safety*, **87**, 13–22.
36. T. Dohi, K. Goševa-Popstojanova, and K. S. Trivedi. (2000). Analysis of software cost models with rejuvenation. In *Proceedings of the 5th IEEE International Symposium*

on High Assurance Systems Engineering, Albuquerque, New Mexico, USA, November 15–17, pp. 25–34.

37. J. Alonso, R. Matias, E. Vicente, A. M. Carvalho, and K. Trivedi. (2011). A comparative evaluation of software rejuvenation strategies, In *Proceedings of the 2011 IEEE 3rd International Workshop on Software Aging and Rejuvenation, Hiroshima, Japan, November 29–December 2*, pp. 26–31.
38. G. Ning, K. S. Trivedi, H. Hu, and K.-Y. Cai. (2011). Multi-granularity software rejuvenation policy based on continuous time Markov chain. In *Proceedings of the IEEE 3rd Int. Workshop on Software Aging and Rejuvenation, Hiroshima, Japan, November 29–December 2*, pp. 32–37.
39. D. Wang, W. Xie, and K. S. Trivedi. (2007). Performability analysis of clustered systems with rejuvenation under varying workload. *Performance Evaluation*, **64**(3), 247–265.
40. S. Garg, A. Puliafito, and K. S. Trivedi. (1995). Analysis of software rejuvenation using Markov regenerative stochastic Petri net. In *Proceedings of the 6th International Symposium on Software Reliability Engineering*, pp. 180–187.
41. H. Okamura and T. Dohi. (2016). A phase expansion approach for transient analysis of software rejuvenation model. In *Proceedings of the 2016 IEEE International Symposium on Software Reliability Engineering Workshops (ISSREW), Ottawa, Ontario, Canada, October 23–27*, pp. 98–103.
42. H. Suzuki, T. Dohi, N. Kaio, and K. S. Trivedi. (2003). Maximizing interval reliability in operational software system with rejuvenation. In *Proceedings of the 14th International Symposium on Software Reliability Engineering (ISSRE 2003), Denver, Colorado, USA, November 17–20*, pp. 479–490.
43. T. Dohi, H. Okamura, and K. S. Trivedi. (2012). Optimizing software rejuvenation policies under interval reliability criteria. In *Proceedings of the 9th International Conference on Ubiquitous Intelligence and Computing and 9th International Conference on Autonomic and Trusted Computing, Fukuoka, Japan, September 4–7*, pp. 478–485.
44. K. Rinsaka and T. Dohi. (2016). Toward high assurance software systems with adaptive fault management. *Software Quality Journal*, **24**(1), 65–85.
45. K. Rinsaka and T. Dohi. (2007). A faster estimation algorithm for periodic preventive rejuvenation schedule maximizing system availability. In *Proceedings of the International Service Availability Symposium (ISAS 2007), Durham, New Hampshire, USA, May 21–22*, pp. 94–109.
46. K. Iwamoto, T. Dohi, H. Okamura, and N. Kaio. (2006). Discrete-time cost analysis for a telecommunication billing application with rejuvenation. *Computers & Mathematics with Applications*, **51**(2), 335–344.
47. X. He, W. Wei, and X. Gui. (2008). The software rejuvenation model with pre-start technology. In *Proceedings of the International Symposium on Information Processing, Moscow, Russia, May 23–25*, pp. 723–727.
48. K. Rinsaka, W. E. Wong, and T. Dohi. (2016). NPI-based adaptive software rejuvenation schedule under random censoring. In *Proceedings of the 2016 IEEE International Symposium on Software Reliability Engineering Workshops (ISSREW), Ottawa, Ontario, Canada, October 23–27*, pp. 91–97.
49. K. Iwamoto, T. Dohi, and N. Kaio. (2010). Estimating periodic software rejuvenation schedules under discrete-time operation circumstance. *IEICE Transactions on Information and Systems*, **E91.D**(1), 23–31.

50. H. Okamura and T. Dohi. (2012). Optimization of opportunity-based software rejuvenation policy. In *Proceedings of the 2012 IEEE 23rd International Symposium on Software Reliability Engineering Workshops, Dallas, Texas, USA, November 27–30*, pp. 283–286.
51. H. Okamura and T. Dohi. (2013). Optimal trigger time of software rejuvenation under probabilistic opportunities. *IEICE Transactions on Information and Systems*, **E96D**, 1933–1940.
52. H. Meng, X. Hei, Y. Li, Y. Du, and G. Xie. (2015). A rejuvenation model for software system under normal attack. In *Proceedings of the 2015 IEEE Trustcom/BigDataSE/ISPA, Helsinki, Finland, August 20–22*, pp. 1160–1164.
53. C. Guo, H. Wu, X. Hua, S. Ren, and J. M. Nogiec. (2015). Maximize system reliability for long lasting and continuous applications. In Rocha A., Correia A., Costanzo S., and Reis L. (eds.), *New Contributions in Information Systems and Technologies*. Advances in Intelligent Systems and Computing, vol 353. Cham, Switzerland: Springer.
54. V. Koutras and A. Platis. (2016). User-perceived availability of a software rejuvenation model with recovery time omission. *Quality and Reliability Engineering International*, **32**, 1521–1533.
55. V. P. Koutras, E. Mennis, N. Nikitakos, and A. N. Platis. (2005). Software rejuvenation in maritime applications. In Kołowrocki, K. (ed.). *Advances in Safety and Reliability*. London, UK: Taylor & Francis Group.
56. H. Xu. (2011). Modelling and well-posed analysis for software system with rejuvenation. *Mathematical and Computer Modelling of Dynamical Systems*, **17**(6), 583–600.
57. H. Eto and T. Dohi. (2005). Optimality of control-limit type of software rejuvenation policy. In *Proceedings of the 11th International Conference on Parallel and Distributed Systems (ICPADS'05), Fukuoka, Japan, July 20–22*, pp. 483–487.
58. H. Eto and T. Dohi. Penkler D. (2006). Analysis of a service degradation model with preventive rejuvenation. In *Proceedings of the 3rd International Service Availability Symposium, Helsinki, Finland, May 15–16*, pp. 17–29.
59. H. Eto and T. Dohi. (2006). Determining the optimal software rejuvenation schedule via semi-Markov decision process. *Journal of Computer Science*, **2**(6), 528–534.
60. H. Okamura and T. Dohi. (2011). Application of reinforcement learning to software rejuvenation. In *Proceedings of the 2011 Tenth International Symposium on Autonomous Decentralized Systems, Tokyo, Japan, March 23–27*, pp. 647–652.
61. T. Dohi and H. Okamura. (2016). Dynamic software availability model with rejuvenation. *Journal of the Operations Research Society of Japan*, **59** (4), 270–290.
62. K. Vaidyanathan, R. E. Harper, S. W. Hunter, and K. S. Trivedi. (2001). Analysis and implementation of software rejuvenation in cluster systems. In *Proceedings of the 2001 ACM SIGMETRICS International Conference on Measurement and Modeling of Computer Systems, Cambridge, Massachusetts, USA, June 16–20*, pp. 62–71.
63. Y. Liu, K. S. Trivedi, Y. Ma, J. J. Han, and H. Levendel. (2002). Modeling and analysis of software rejuvenation in cable modem termination systems. In *Proceedings of the 13th International Symposium on Software Reliability Engineering, Annapolis, Maryland, USA, November 12–15*, pp. 159–170.
64. W. Xie, Y. Hong, and K. S. Trivedi. (2004). Software rejuvenation policies for cluster systems under varying workload. In *Proceedings of the 10th IEEE Pacific Rim International Symposium on Dependable Computing, Papeete, Tahiti, March 3–5*, pp. 122–129.

65. Y. Liu, Y. Ma, J. L. Han, H. Levendel, and K. S. Trivedi. (2005). A proactive approach towards always-on availability in broadband cable networks. *Computer Communications*, **28**, 51–64.
66. V. P. Koutras and A. N. Platis. (2006). Applying software rejuvenation in a two node cluster system for high availability. In *Proceedings of the 2006 International Conference on Dependability of Computer Systems, Szklarska Poreba, Poland, May 25–27*, pp. 175–182.
67. A. Avritzer, A. Bondi, and E. J. Weyuker. (2007). Ensuring system performance for cluster and single server systems. *Journal of Systems and Software*, **80**(4), 441–454.
68. Q. Yong, M. Haining, H. Di, and C. Ying. (2008). A study on software rejuvenation application server cluster in two-dimension state space using Markov process. *Information Technology Journal*, **7**(1), pp. 98–104.
69. J. Alonso, L. Silva, A. Andrzejak, P. Silva, and J. Torres. (2008). High-available grid services through the use of virtualized clustering. In *Proceedings of the 8th IEEE/ACM International Conference on Grid Computing, Austin, Texas, USA, September 19–21*, pp. 34–41.
70. V. P. Koutras, A. N. Platis, and G. A. Gravvanis. (2007). In *Proceedings of the European Safety and Reliability Conference 2007, Stavanger, Norway, June 25–27*, pp. 1723–1730.
71. V. P. Koutras, A. N. Platis, and G. A. Gravvanis. (2007). Software rejuvenation on a grid computing environment for higher availability based on approximate inverse preconditioning. In *Proceedings of the 8th Hellenic European Research on Computer Mathematics & its Applications Conference (HERCMA 2007), Athens, Greece, September 20–22*, pp. 69–86.
72. V. P. Koutras, A. N. Platis, and G. A. Gravvanis. (2010). Availability and performance on a grid computing environment with software rejuvenation based on approximate inverse preconditioning. *HERMIS: The International Journal of Computer Mathematics and its Applications*, **11**, 69–86.
73. V. P. Koutras, S. Malefaki, and A. N. Platis. (2011). A Monte Carlo simulation based dependability analysis of a non-Markovian grid computing environment with software rejuvenation. In *Proceedings of the 20th European Safety and Reliability Conference, Troyes, France, September 18–22*, pp. 1959–1966.
74. V. P. Koutras, S. Malefaki, and A. N. Platis. (2014). Rejuvenation effects on the grid environment performance with response time delays using Monte Carlo simulation. *Simulation Modelling Practice and Theory*, **40**, pp. 176–191.
75. H. Meng, X. Zhang, L. Zhu, L. Wang, and Z. Yang. (2017). Optimizing software rejuvenation policy based on CDM for cloud system. In *Proceedings of the 12th IEEE Conference on Industrial Electronics and Applications (ICIEA 2017), Siem Reap, Cambodia, June 18–20*, pp. 1850–1854.
76. J. Rahme and H. Xu. (2017). Preventive maintenance for cloud-based software systems subject to non-constant failure rates. In *Proceedings of the 2017 IEEE SmartWorld Congress, San Francisco, California, USA, August 4–8*, pp. 1–6.
77. A. T. Tai, K. S. Tso, W. H. Sanders, and S. N. Chau. (2005). A performability-oriented software rejuvenation framework for distributed applications. In *Proceedings of the 2005 International Conference on Dependable Systems and Networks (DSN'05), Yokohama, Japan, June 28–July 1*, pp. 570–579.
78. J. Araujo, R. Matos, V. Alves, P. Maciel, F. Vieira de Souza, R. Matias Jr., and K. S. Trivedi. (2014). Software aging in the eucalyptus cloud computing infrastructure:

Characterization and rejuvenation. *ACM Journal on Emerging Technologies in Computing Systems (JETC)*, **10**(1), 1–22.

79. J. Braun, J. Mottok, C. Miedl, D. Geyer, and M. Minas. (2012). Increasing the reliability of single and multi-core systems with software rejuvenation and coded processing. In *Proceedings of Automotive — Safety & Security, 2012, Karlsruhe, Germany, 14–15 November 2012*, pp. 163–178.
80. D. S. Kim, S. M. Lee, J.-H. Jung, T. H. Kim, S. Lee, and J. S. Park. (2012). Reliability and availability analysis for an on-board computer in a satellite system using standby redundancy and rejuvenation. *Journal of Mechanical Science and Technology*, **26**(7), 2059–2063.
81. S. Malefaki, V. P. Koutras, and A. N. Platis. (2012). Modeling software rejuvenation on a redundant system using Monte Carlo simulation. In *Proceedings of the 2012 IEEE 23rd International Symposium on Software Reliability Engineering Workshops (ISSREW), Dallas, Texas, USA, November 27–30*, pp. 277–282.
82. H. Okamura and T. Dohi. (2013). Dynamic software rejuvenation policies in a transaction-based system under Markovian arrival processes. *Performance Evaluation*, **70**(3), 197–211.
83. J. Zheng, H. Okamura, L. Li, and T. Dohi. (2017). A comprehensive evaluation of software rejuvenation policies for transaction systems with Markovian arrivals. *IEEE Transactions on Reliability*, **66**(4), 1157–1177.
84. A. Pfening, S. Garg, A. Puliafito, M. Telek, and K. S. Trivedi. (1996). Optimal software rejuvenation for tolerating soft failures. *Performance Evaluation*, **27–28**, 491–506.
85. H. Okamura, S. Miyahara, and T. Dohi. (2005). Effect of preventive rejuvenation in communication network system with burst arrival. In *Proceedings of the 2005 International Symposium on Autonomous Decentralized Systems (ISADS 2005), Chengdu, China, April 4–8*, pp. 151–158.
86. H. Okamura and T. Dohi. (2010). Performance-aware software rejuvenation strategies in a queueing system. In *Proceedings of the 2010 IEEE Second International Workshop on Software Aging and Rejuvenation, San Jose, California, USA, November 2*, pp. 1–6.
87. J. Zhao, K. S. Trivedi, M. Grottke, J. Alonso, and Y. Wang. (2014). Ensuring the performance of Apache HTTP Server affected by aging. *IEEE Transactions on Dependable and Secure Computing*, **11**(2), 130–141.
88. F. Machida and N. Miyoshi. (2015). An optimal stopping problem for software rejuvenation in a job processing system. In *Proceedings of the 2015 IEEE International Symposium on Software Reliability Engineering Workshops (ISSREW), Gaithersburg, Maryland, USA, November 2–5*, pp. 139–143.
89. F. Machida and N. Miyoshi. (2017). Analysis of an optimal stopping problem for software rejuvenation in a deteriorating job processing system. *Reliability Engineering & System Safety*, **168**, 128–135.
90. T. Dohi, K. Iwamoto, H. Okamura, and N. Kaio. (2002). Discrete availability models to rejuvenate a telecommunication billing application. In *Proceedings of the 7th IEEE International Symposium on High Assurance Systems Engineering, Tokyo, Japan, October 23–25*, pp. 159–166.
91. K. Iwamoto, T. Dohi, H. Okamura, and N. Kaio. (2006). Discrete-time cost analysis for a telecommunication billing application with rejuvenation. *Computers & Mathematics with Applications*, **51**(2), 335–344.

92. V. P. Koutras and A. N. Platis. (2006). Optimal rejuvenation policy for increasing VoIP service reliability. In Soares, C. G. (ed.). *Advances in Safety and Reliability*, **3**. London, UK: Taylor & Francis.
93. V. P. Koutras and A. N. Platis. (2007). VoIP availability and service reliability through software rejuvenation policies. In *Proceedings of the 2nd International Conference on Dependability of Computer Systems (DepCoS-RELCOMEX '07), Szklarska, Poland, June 14–16*, pp. 262–269.
94. V. P. Koutras, C. S. Salagaras, and A. N. Platis. (2009). Software rejuvenation for higher levels of VoIP availability and mean time to failure. In *Proceedings of the 4th International Conference on Dependability of Computer Systems (DepCoS-RELCOMEX '09), Brunow, Poland, June 30–July 2*, pp. 99–106.
95. V. Gupta and S. Dharmaraja. (2011). Semi-Markov modeling of dependability of VoIP network in the presence of resource degradation and security attacks. *Reliability Engineering & System Safety*, **96**(12), 1627–1636.
96. K. M. M. Aung and J. S. Park. (2004). Software rejuvenation approach to security engineering. In Laganá A., Gavrilova M. L., Kumar V., Mun Y., Tan C. J. K., and Gervasi, O. (eds). *Computational Science and Its Applications — ICCSA 2004*. Lecture Notes in Computer Science, **3046**. Berlin/Heidelberg, Germany: Springer.
97. K. M. M. Aung, K. Park, and J. S. Park. (2005). A rejuvenation methodology of cluster recovery. In *Proceedings of the IEEE International Symposium on Cluster Computing and the Grid 2005 (CCGrid 2005), Cardiff, Wales, UK, May 9–12*, pp. 90–95.
98. A. N. Platis and V. P. Koutras. (2010). Software rejuvenation on a PKI infrastructure. In *Proceedings of the 21st Annual International Symposium on Software Reliability Engineering (ISSRE 2010) and the 2nd Workshop on Software Aging and Rejuvenation (WoSAR 2010), San Jose, California, USA, November 1–4*, pp. 1–6.
99. E. Yuan, S. Malek, B. Schmerl, D. Garlan, and J. Gennari. (2013). Architecture-based self-protecting software systems. In *Proceedings of the 9th International ACM Sigsoft Conference on Quality of Software Architectures (QoSA '13), Vancouver, British Columbia, Canada, June 17–21*, pp. 33–42.
100. A. Bobbio, M. Sereno, and C. Anglano. (2011). Fine grained software degradation models for optimal rejuvenation policies. *Performance Evaluation*, **46**(1), 45–62.
101. G. Levitin, L. Xing, and H. Ben-Haim. (2018). Optimizing software rejuvenation policy for real time tasks. *Reliability Engineering & System Safety*, **176**, 202–208.
102. Y. Bao, X. Sun, and K. S. Trivedi. (2003). Adaptive software rejuvenation: Degradation model and rejuvenation scheme. In *Proceedings of the 2003 International Conference on Dependable Systems and Networks, San Francisco, California, USA, June 22–25*, pp. 241–248.
103. V. P. Koutras and A. Platis. (2005). Optimizing the amount of free resources on a computer system using software rejuvenation. In Kołowrocki K. (ed.). *Advances in Safety and Reliability*. London, UK: Taylor & Francis Group.
104. V. P. Koutras, A. N. Platis, and G. A. Gravvanis. (2007). On the optimization of free resources using non-homogeneous Markov chain software rejuvenation model. *Reliability Engineering and System Safety*, **92**(12), 1724–1732.
105. V. P. Koutras, A. N. Platis, and G. A. Gravvanis. (2013). Software rejuvenation and resource reservation policies for optimizing server resource availability using cyclic non-homogeneous Markov chains. *Applied Stochastic Models in Business and Industry*, **29**(1), 61–78.

106. S. Garg, Y. Huang, C. Kintala, and K. S. Trivedi. (1996). Minimizing completion time of a program by checkpointing and rejuvenation. In *Proceedings of the 1996 ACM SIGMETRICS Conference, Philadelphia, Pennsylvania, USA, May 23–26*, pp. 252–261.
107. A. T. Tai, S. N. Chau, L. Alkalaj, and H. Hecht. (1997). On-board preventive maintenance: analysis of effectiveness and optimal duty period. In *Proceedings of the Third International Workshop on Object-Oriented Real-Time Dependable Systems, Newport Beach, California, USA, February 5–7*, pp. 40–47.
108. V. Castelli, R. E. Harper, P. Heidelberger, S. W. Hunter, K. S. Trivedi, K. Vaidyanathan, and W. P. Zeggert. (2001). Proactive management of software aging. *IBM Journal of Research & Development*, **45**(2), 311–332.
109. A. Avritzer, A. Bondi, M. Grottke, K. S. Trivedi, and E. J. Weyuker. (2006). Performance assurance via software rejuvenation: Monitoring, statistics and algorithms. In *Proceedings of the International Conference on Dependable Systems and Networks (DSN'06), Philadelphia, Pennsylvania, USA, June 25–28*, pp. 435–444.
110. A. Andrzejak and L. Silva. (2007). Deterministic models of software aging and optimal rejuvenation schedules. In *Proceedings of the 2007 10th IFIP/IEEE International Symposium on Integrated Network Management, Munich, Germany, May 21–25*, pp. 159–168.
111. P. K. Saravakos, G. A. Gravvanis, V. P. Koutras, and A. N. Platis. (2009). A comprehensive approach to software aging and rejuvenation on a single node software system. In *Proceedings of the 9th Hellenic European Research on Computer Mathematics & its Applications Conference (HERCMA 2009), Athens, Greece, September 24–26*.
112. P. Reinecke and K. Wolter. (2010). A simulation study on the effectiveness of restart and rejuvenation to mitigate the effects of software ageing. In *Proceedings of the 2010 IEEE Second International Workshop on Software Aging and Rejuvenation, San Jose, California, USA, November 2*, pp. 1–6.
113. O. Laadan and S. E. Hallyn. (2010). Linux-CR: Transparent application checkpoint-restart in Linux. In *Proceedings of the 12th Annual Ottawa Linux Symposium (OLS), Ottawa, Ontario, Canada, July 13–16*.
114. L. Jiang and G. Xu. (2011). Apply time and measurement-based software rejuvenation to improve system availability. In Wu, Y. (eds.). *Advances in Computer, Communication, Control and Automation.* Lecture Notes in Electrical Engineering, **121**. Berlin/Heidelberg, Germany: Springer.
115. E. C. Andrade, F. Machida, D. Kim, and K. S. Trivedi. (2011). Modeling and analyzing server system with rejuvenation through SysML and stochastic reward nets. In *Proceedings of the 2011 Sixth International Conference on Availability, Reliability and Security, Vienna, Austria, August 22–26*, pp. 161–168.
116. J. Zhao, Y. B. Wang, G. R. Ning, K. S. Trivedi, R. Matias, and K.-Y. Cai. (2013). A comprehensive approach to optimal software rejuvenation. *Performance Evaluation*, **70**(11), 917–933.
117. M. Haining, H. Xinhong, and L. Jianjun. (2013). Analytical modeling of periodically inspected software rejuvenation policy. *Information Technology Journal*, **12**, 1227–1232.
118. Q. Li, K. Zhu, Y. Cheng, and J. Zhang. (2013). Constrained elements-based software rejuvenation policy in embedded environment. *Journal of Computational Information Systems*, **9**(16), 6391–6398.

119. J. Zhao, Y. Jin, K. S. Trivedi, R. Matias Jr., and Y. Wang. (2014). Software rejuvenation scheduling using accelerated life testing. *Journal of Emerging Technologies in Computing Systems*, **10**(1), Article 9, 23 pages.
120. H. Santos, J. F. Pimentel, V. T. Da Silva, and L. Murta. (2015). Software rejuvenation via a multi-agent approach. *Journal of Systems and Software*, **104**, 41–59.
121. H. Meng, J. Liu, and X. Hei. (2015). Modeling and optimizing periodically inspected software rejuvenation policy based on geometric sequences. *Reliability Engineering & System Safety*, **133**, 184–191.
122. H. Okamura, J. Guan, C. Luo, and T. Dohi. (2015). Quantifying resiliency of virtualized system with software rejuvenation. *IEICE Transactions on Fundamentals of Electronics, Communications and Computer Sciences*, **E98A**(10), 2051–2059.
123. M. Haining, H. Xinhong, and Z. Jiulong. (2016). Software aging and rejuvenation in a J2EE application server. *Quality And Reliability Engineering International*, **32**, 89–97.
124. V. Nagaraju, V. V. Basavaraj, and L. Fiondella. (2016). Software rejuvenation of a fault-tolerant server subject to correlated failure. In *Proceedings of the Annual Reliability and Maintainability Symposium (RAMS), Tucson, Arizona, USA, January 25–28*, pp. 1–6.
125. H. Meng, Y. Wang, H. Wang, F. Wang, and J. Liu. (2017). Optimal control method for runtime system maintenance. In *Proceedings of the 29th Chinese Control And Decision Conference (CCDC), Chongqing, China, May 28–30*, pp. 3272–3275.
126. W. Dang and J. Zeng. (2017). Software system rejuvenation modeling based on sequential inspection periods and state multi control limits. *Communications in Computer and Information Science*, **728**, 350–364.
127. Y. Jumonji and H. Yamada. (2017). Efficient software rejuvenation of in-memory key-value storages. In *Proceedings of the IEEE International Symposium on Software Reliability Engineering Workshops (ISSREW), Toulouse, France, October 23–26*, pp. 280–285.
128. M. Ficco, R. Pietrantuono, and S. Russo. (2018). Aging-related performance anomalies in the apache storm stream processing system, *Future Generation Computer Systems*, **86**, 975–994.
129. W. Dang and J. Zeng. (2018). Optimization of software rejuvenation policy based on state-control-limit. *International Journal of Performability Engineering*, **14**(2), 210–222.
130. H. Eto and T. Dohi. (2006). Optimal rejuvenation scheduling of distributed computation based on dynamic programming. *Journal of Computer Science*, **2**(6), 505–512.
131. G. Candea, J. Cutler, A. Fox, R. Doshi, P. Garg, and R. Gowda. (2002). Reducing recovery time in a small recursively restartable system. In *Proceedings of the International Conference on Dependable Systems and Networks, Washington, DC, USA, June 23–26*, pp. 605–614.
132. M. Swift, S. Martin, H. M. Leyland, and S. J. Eggers. (2002). Nooks: an architecture for reliable device drivers. In *Proceedings of the Tenth ACM SIGOPS European Workshop, Saint-Emilion, France, September 22–25*, pp. 102–107.
133. M. M. Swift, M. Annamalai, B. N. Bershad, and H. M. Levy. (2004). Recovering device drivers. In *Proceedings of the 6th Symposium on Operating Systems Design and Implementation, San Francisco, California, USA, December 6–8*, pp. 1–15.
134. S. Sundararaman, S. Subramanian, A. Rajimwale, A. C. Arpaci-Dusseau, R. H. Arpaci-Dusseau, and M. M. Swift. (2010). Membrane: Operating system support for restartable file systems. *Transactions on Storage*, **6**(3), Article 11, 30 pages.

135. J. N. Herder, H. Bos, B. Gras, P. Homburg, and A. S. Tanenbaum. (2006). Reorganizing UNIX for reliability. In Jesshope C., Egan C. (eds.). *Advances in Computer Systems Architecture. Lecture Notes in Computer Science*, **4186**. Berlin/Heidelberg, Germany: Springer.
136. J. N. Herder, H. Bos, B. Gras, P. Homburg, and A. S. Tanenbaum. (2007). Failure resilience for device drivers. In *Proceedings of the 37th Annual IEEE/IFIP International Conference on Dependable Systems and Networks (DSN'07), Edinburgh, Scotland, UK, June 25–28*, pp. 41–50.
137. K. Kourai. (2010). CacheMind: Fast performance recovery using a virtual machine monitor. In *Proceedings of the 2010 International Conference on Dependable Systems and Networks Workshops (DSN-W), Chicago, Illinois, USA, June 28–July 1*, pp. 86–92.
138. K. Yamakita, H. Yamada, and K. Kono. (2011). Phase-based reboot: Reusing operating system execution phases for cheap reboot-based recovery. In *Proceedings of the IEEE/IFIP 41st International Conference on Dependable Systems & Networks (DSN), Hong Kong, China, June 27–30*, pp. 169–180.
139. A. Bovenzi, J. Alonso, H. Yamada, S. Russo, and K. S. Trivedi. (2013). Towards fast OS rejuvenation: An experimental evaluation of fast OS reboot techniques. In *Proceedings of the IEEE 24th International Symposium on Software Reliability Engineering (ISSRE), Pasadena, California, USA, November 4–7*, pp. 61–70.
140. D. Cotroneo, F. Fucci, A. K. Iannillo, R. Natella, and R. Pietrantuono. (2016). Software aging analysis of the android mobile OS. In *Proceedings of the IEEE 27th International Symposium on Software Reliability Engineering (ISSRE), Ottawa, Ontario, Canada, October 23–27*, pp. 478–489.
141. I. M. Umesh, G. N. Srinivasan, and M. Torquato. (2017). Software rejuvenation model for cloud computing platform. *International Journal of Applied Engineering Research*, **12**(19), 8332–8337.
142. T. Thein and S. Park. (2009). Availability analysis of application servers using software rejuvenation and virtualization. *Journal of Computer Science and Technology*, **24**, 339–346.
143. T. Thein, S.-D. Chi, and J. S. Park. (2008). Availability modeling and analysis on virtualized clustering with rejuvenation. *International Journal of Computer Science and Network Security*, **8**(9), 72–80.
144. L. M. Silva, J. Alonso, and J. Torres. (2009). Using virtualization to improve software rejuvenation. *IEEE Transactions on Computers*, **58**(11), 1525–1538.
145. Q. Ao, L. Zhang, S. Chen, J. Fu, and B. Liao. (2015). A fault-tolerant Java virtual machine using fast rejuvenation for soft-error-prone systems. In *Proceedings of the IEEE 17th International Conference on High Performance Computing and Communications. IEEE 7th International Symposium on Cyberspace Safety and Security*, and *IEEE 12th International Conference on Embedded Software and Systems, New York, NY, USA, August 24–26*, pp. 463–469.
146. I. M. Umesh and G. N. Srinivasan. (2016). Optimum software aging prediction and rejuvenation model for virtualized environment. *Indonesian Journal of Electrical Engineering and Computer Science*, **3**(3), 572–578.
147. A. Pellegrini, P. D. Sanzo, and D. R. Avresky. (2016). Proactive cloud management for highly heterogeneous multi-cloud infrastructures. In *Proceedings of the IEEE International Parallel and Distributed Processing Symposium Workshops, Chicago, Illinois, USA, May 23–27*, pp. 1311–1318.

148. J. Liu and J. Zhao. (2016). Providing proactive fault tolerance as a service for cloud applications. In *Proceedings of the IEEE World Congress on Services (SERVICES), San Francisco, California, USA, June 27–July 2*, pp. 126–127.
149. J. Rahme and H. Xu. (2017). Dependable and reliable cloud-based systems using multiple software spare components. In *Proceedings of the IEEE SmartWorld, Ubiquitous Intelligence & Computing, Advanced & Trusted Computed, Scalable Computing & Communications, Cloud & Big Data Computing, Internet of People and Smart City Innovation (SmartWorld/SCALCOM/UIC/ATC/CBDCom/IOP/SCI), San Francisco, California, USA, August 4–8*, pp. 1–8.
150. X. Chang, T. Wang, R. J. Rodríguez, and Z. Zhang. (2018). Modeling and analysis of high availability techniques in a virtualized system. *Computer Journal*, **61**(2), 180–198.
151. M. Escheikh, Z. Tayachi, and K. Barkaoui. (2018). Performability evaluation of server virtualized systems under bursty workload. *IFAC-PapersOnLine*, **51**(7), 45–50.
152. A. Puliafito. (2014). Software rejuvenation in cloud systems. In *Proceedings of the IEEE International Symposium on Software Reliability Engineering Workshops, Naples, Italy, November 3–6*, pp. 413–413.
153. F. Machida, D. S. Kim, and K. S. Trivedi. (2010). Modeling and analysis of software rejuvenation in a server virtualized system. In *Proceedings of the IEEE Second International Workshop on Software Aging and Rejuvenation, San Jose, California, USA, November 2*, pp. 1–6.
154. F. Machida, D. Seong Kim, and K. S. Trivedi. (2013). Modeling and analysis of software rejuvenation in a server virtualized system with live VM migration. *Performance Evaluation*, **70**(3), 212–230.
155. K. Kourai and S. Chiba. (2007). A fast rejuvenation technique for server consolidation with virtual machines. In *Proceedings of the 37th Annual IEEE/IFIP International Conference on Dependable Systems and Networks (DSN'07), Edinburgh, Scotland, UK, June 25–28*, pp. 245–255.
156. J. Araujo, R. Matos, P. Maciel, R. Matias, and I. Beicker. (2011). Experimental evaluation of software aging effects on the eucalyptus cloud computing infrastructure. In *Proceedings of the Middleware 2011 Industry Track Workshop, Lisbon, Portugal, December 12–16*, pp. 1–7.
157. K. Kourai and S. Chiba. (2011). Fast software rejuvenation of virtual machine monitors. *IEEE Transactions on Dependable and Secure Computing*, **8**(6), 839–851.
158. F. Machida, V. F. Nicola, and K. S. Trivedi. (2011). Job completion time on a virtualized server subject to software aging and rejuvenation. In *Proceedings of the IEEE Third International Workshop on Software Aging and Rejuvenation, Hiroshima, Japan, November 29–December 2*, pp. 44–49.
159. J. Alonso, I. Goiri, J. Guitart, R. Gavalda, and J. Torres. (2011). Optimal resource allocation in a virtualized software aging platform with software rejuvenation. In *Proceedings of the IEEE 22nd International Symposium on Software Reliability Engineering, Hiroshima, Japan, November 29–December 2*, pp. 250–259.
160. M. Melo, J. Araujo, R. Matos, J. Menezes, and P. Maciel. (2013). Comparative analysis of migration-based rejuvenation schedules on cloud availability. In *Proceedings of the IEEE International Conference on Systems, Man, and Cybernetics, Manchester, UK, October 13–16*, pp. 4110–4115.
161. D. Bruneo, S. Distefano, F. Longo, A. Puliafito, and M. Scarpa. (2013). Workload-based software rejuvenation in cloud systems. *IEEE Transactions on Computers*, **62**(6), 1072–1085.

162. J. Xu, X. Li, Y. Zhong, and H. Zhang. (2014). Availability modeling and analysis of a single-server virtualized system with rejuvenation. *Journal of Software*, **9**(1), 129–139.
163. C. Sudhakar, I. Shah, and T. Ramesh. (2014). Software rejuvenation in cloud systems using neural networks. In *Proceedings of the International Conference on Parallel, Distributed and Grid Computing, Solan, Himachal Pradesh, India, December 11–13*, pp. 230–233.
164. K. Kourai and H. Ooba. (2015). Zero-copy migration for lightweight software rejuvenation of virtualized systems. In *Proceedings of the 6th Asia-Pacific Workshop on Systems (APSys '15), Tokyo, Japan, July 27–28*, Article 7, 8 pages.
165. M. Torquato, P. Maciel, J. Araujo, and I. M. Umesh. (2017). An approach to investigate aging symptoms and rejuvenation effectiveness on software systems. In *Proceedings of the 12th Iberian Conference on Information Systems and Technologies (CISTI), Lisbon, Portugal, June 14–17*, pp. 1–6.
166. I. M. Umesh and G. N. Srinivasan. (2017). Dynamic software aging detection-based fault tolerant software rejuvenation model for virtualized environment. *Advances in Intelligent Systems and Computing*, **469**, 779–787.
167. M. Torquato, I. M. Umesh, and P. J. Maciel. (2018). Models for availability and power consumption evaluation of a private cloud with VMM rejuvenation enabled by VM Live Migration. *The Journal of Supercomputing*, **74**(9), 4817–4841.
168. W. Dang and J. Zeng. (2018). State-control-limit-based rejuvenation modeling of virtualized cloud server. *International Journal of Performability Engineering*, **14**(3), 473–482.
169. K. Su, H. Fu, J. Li, and D. Zhang. (2011). Software rejuvenation in virtualization environment. In *Proceedings of the 6th IEEE Joint International Information Technology and Artificial Intelligence Conference, Chongqing, China, August 20–22*, pp. 329–331.
170. L. Hana and J. Xu. (2013). Availability models for virtualized systems with rejuvenation. *Journal of Computational Information Systems*, **9**(20), 8389–8396.
171. T. A. Nguyen, D. S. Kim, and J. S. Park. (2014). A comprehensive availability modeling and analysis of a virtualized servers system using stochastic reward nets. *The Scientific World Journal*, **2014**, Article ID 165316, 18 pages.
172. H. Okamura, K. Yamamoto, and T. Dohi. (2016). Transient analysis of software rejuvenation policies in virtualized system: Phase-type expansion approach. *Quality Technology & Quantitative Management*, **11**(3), 335–351.
173. X. Changa, Z. Zhang, X. Li, and K. S. Trivedi. (2016). Model-based survivability analysis of a virtualized system. In *Proceedings of the IEEE 41st Conference on Local Computer Networks (LCN), Dubai, UAE, November 7–10*, pp. 611–614.
174. M. Escheikh, Z. Tayachi, and K. Barkaoui. (2016). Workload-dependent software aging impact on performance and energy consumption in server virtualized systems. In *Proceedings of the IEEE International Symposium on Software Reliability Engineering Workshops (ISSREW), Ottawa, Ontario, Canada, October 23–27*, pp. 111–118.
175. K. Vaidyanathan, D. Selvamuthu, and K. S. Trivedi. (2002). Analysis of inspection-based preventive maintenance in operational software systems. In *Proceedings of the 21st IEEE Symposium on Reliable Distributed Systems*, pp. 286–295.
176. Z. Tianhai, Q. Yong, S. Junyi, H. Di, Z. Xiaomel, and L. Liang. (2006). Application server aging model and multi-level rejuvenation strategy using semi-Markov process. *Wuhan University Journal of Natural Sciences*, **11**(5), 1209–1215.

177. J. You, J. Xu, X.-L. Zhao, and F.-Y. Liu. (2005). Modeling and availability analysis of nested software rejuvenation policy. In *Proceedings of the IEEE International Conference on Systems, Man and Cybernetics, Waikoloa, Hawaii, USA, October 10–12*, pp. 34–38.
178. V. P. Koutras and A. N. Platis. (2008). Semi-Markov availability modeling of a redundant system with partial and full rejuvenation actions. In *Proceedings of the 3rd International Conference on Dependability of Computer Systems (DepCoS-RELCOMEX'08), Szklarska Poreba, Poland, June 26–28*, pp. 127–134.
179. R. Vinayak and S. Dharmaraj. (2012). Semi-Markov modeling approach for deteriorating systems with preventive maintenance. *International Journal of Performability Engineering*, **8**(5), 515–526.
180. X. Du, H. Lu, and Y. Rao. (2014). Modeling and analyses of operational software system with rejuvenation and reconfiguration. In Patnaik S. and Li X. (eds.). *Advances in Intelligent Systems and Computing*, **255**. New Delhi, India: Springer.
181. S. Fukumoto and M. Ohara. (2015). Software rejuvenation schemes for time warp-based PDES. In *Proceedings of the IEEE 21st Pacific Rim International Symposium on Dependable Computing (PRDC), Zhangjiajie, China, November 18–20*, pp. 313–314.
182. M. Ohara and S. Fukumoto. (2016). An experimental implementation of software rejuvenation in time warp simulation. In *Proceedings of the IEEE International Symposium on Software Reliability Engineering Workshops (ISSREW), Ottawa, Ontario, Canada, October 23–27*, pp. 104–110.
183. C. Guo, H. Wu, X. Hua, D. Lautner, and S. Ren. (2015). Use two-level rejuvenation to combat software aging and maximize average resource performance. In *Proceedings of the IEEE 17th International Conference on High Performance Computing and Communications. IEEE 7th International Symposium on Cyberspace Safety and Security*, and *IEEE 12th International Conference on Embedded Software and Systems, New York City, New York, USA, August 24–26*, pp. 1160–1165.
184. G. Kumar, M. Kaushik, and Preeti. (2016). Maintenance policies for improving the availability of a software-hardware system. In *Proceedings of the 11th International Conference on Reliability, Maintainability and Safety (ICRMS), Hangzhou, China, October 26–28*, pp. 1–5.
185. Y. Fang, B. Yin, G. Ning, Z. Zheng, and K. Cai. (2017). A rejuvenation strategy of two-granularity software based on adaptive control. In *Proceedings of the IEEE 22nd Pacific Rim International Symposium on Dependable Computing (PRDC), Christchurch, New Zealand, January 22–25*, pp. 104–109.
186. X. Hua, C. Guo, H. Wu, D. Lautner, and S. Ren. (2017). Schedulability analysis for real-time task set on resource with performance degradation and dual-level periodic rejuvenations. *IEEE Transactions on Computers*, **66**(3), 553–559.
187. V. P. Koutras and A. N. Platis. (2008). Modeling perfect and minimal rejuvenation for client server systems with heterogeneous load. In *Proceedings of the 14th IEEE Pacific Rim International Symposium on Dependable Computing, Taipei, Taiwan, December 15–17*, pp. 95–103.
188. V. P. Koutras, A. N. Platis, and N. Limnios. (2008). Availability and reliability estimation for a system undergoing minimal, perfect and failed rejuvenation. In *Proceedings of the First International Workshop on Software Aging and Rejuvenation (WOSAR 2008), Seattle, Washington, USA, November 11–14*, pp. 1–6.

189. V. P. Koutras, A. N. Platis, and N. Limnios. (2010). Dependability measures maximum likelihood estimation for a redundant system with minimal, perfect and failed rejuvenation. In *Proceedings of the European Safety and Reliability Conference (ESREL 2010), Rhodes, Greece, September 5–9*, pp. 1553–1560.
190. V. P. Koutras and A. N. Platis. (2010). Semi-Markov performance modeling of a redundant system with partial, full and failed rejuvenation. *International Journal of Critical Computer Based Systems*, **1**, 59–85.
191. V. P. Koutras and A. N. Platis. (2011). Applying partial and full rejuvenation in different degradation levels. In *Proceedings of the 22nd annual International Symposium on Software Reliability Engineering (ISSRE 2011) — 3rd Workshop on Software Aging and Rejuvenation (WoSAR 2011), Hiroshima, Japan, November 29–December 2*, pp. 20–25.
192. V. P. Koutras. (2011). Two-level software rejuvenation model with increasing failure rate degradation. In Zamojski W., Kacprzyk J., Marzukiewicz J., Sugier J., and Walkowiak, T. (eds.). *Dependable Computer Systems*, **97**. Berlin/Heidelberg, Germany: Springer Verlag.
193. S. Malefaki, V. P. Koutras, and A. N. Platis. (2012). Modeling software rejuvenation on a redundant system using Monte Carlo simulation. In *Proceedings of the IEEE 23rd International Symposium on Software Reliability Engineering Workshops (ISSREW), Dallas, Texas, USA, November 27–30*, pp. 277–282.
194. V. P. Koutras, A. N. Platis, and N. Limnios. (2012). Performance estimation of a system under minimal, perfect and failed rejuvenation. In *Proceedings of the 11th International Probabilistic Safety Assessment and Management Conference* and *Annual European Safety and Reliability Conference 2012 (PSAM11 & ESREL12), Helsinki, Finland, June 25–29*, **3**, pp. 1859–1868.
195. G. Jacques-Silva, A. Avritzer, D. S. Menasché, A. Koziolek, L. Happe, and S. Suresh. (2015). Survivability modeling to assess deployment alternatives accounting for rejuvenation. In *Proceedings of the IEEE International Symposium on Software Reliability Engineering Workshops (ISSREW), Gaithersburg, Maryland, USA, November 2–5*, pp. 114–119.
196. J. M. Preeti. (2015). Availability analysis of software rejuvenation in active/standby cluster system. *International Journal of Industrial and Systems Engineering*, **19**(1), 75–93.
197. M. Jain, T. Manjula, and T. R. Gulati. (2016). Software rejuvenation policies for cluster system. In *Proceedings of the National Academy of Sciences. India Section A: Physical Sciences*, **86**(3), 339–346.

Part II

Data-driven Approach

Part II of this Handbook focuses on data-driven approaches for the detection of software aging.

Chapter 4, Measurements for Software Aging, covers the main methods adopted for the analysis and detection of software aging phenomena based on measurements. It discusses the methods for trend detection, estimation, and forecasting, as well as data manipulation.

Chapter 4

Measurements for Software Aging

Roberto Pietrantuono*, Javier Alonso† and Kalyan Vaidyanathan‡

Università degli Studi di Napoli Federico II, Italy
Amazon, Seattle, USA
BAE Systems, San Diego, USA
**roberto.pietrantuono@unina.it*
†jjava@amazon.com
‡kalyan.vaidyanathan@baesystems.com

Considerable attention has been devoted to the analysis of software aging based on measurements from real systems. This approach aims to infer the presence of aging trends (aging detection) and to forecast the future evolution of such trends to determine the optimal rejuvenation time through an analysis of collected data.

This chapter will cover the main methods adopted for the analysis and detection of software aging phenomena based on measurements. It will discuss the methods for trend detection, estimation, forecasting, as well as data manipulation.

These methods can be classified as *threshold-based* approaches, *statistical* approaches for time series analysis and *machine learning* approaches for aging state classification and failure prediction. Mathematical details of the discussed techniques will be described in Appendix A-2.

4.1. Introduction

A significant amount of effort has been dedicated by academia as well as industry [1] to the analysis of software aging indicators (i.e., hardware and software metrics) primarily due to the fact that the software aging phenomenon can easily be observed in a complex enough system. These indicators are used to determine the existence of the phenomenon, and once this has been determined, the remaining time to life of the system under the effect of software aging is estimated, with the ultimate aim of determining the *optimal* moment to trigger the software rejuvenation process.

Depending on the techniques applied on the measurements collected from the system to estimate the presence of software aging and the estimation of the time to failure, we can broadly classify measurement-based software rejuvenation into three major approaches: the threshold-based approach, the statistics-based approach and the machine learning based approach.

In all of these approaches, a variety of system metrics such as memory usage, CPU usage, number of system requests, response time and file descriptors used are monitored. These metrics are used to determine which parts of the system are affected by the aging phenomena, to determine the time until the system reaches an unacceptable state, and finally to estimate the optimal moment to initiate the recovery process. The above-mentioned approaches differ in the way the system metrics are treated — thereby resulting in substantial differences in terms of accuracy and limitations, and in the way prior knowledge about the system is captured.

Threshold-based approaches are based solely on applying some level of prior knowledge of the system and the metric (or metrics) that exhibit the aging effect, and determining a threshold. If an aging metric reaches the pre-determined threshold value, the rejuvenation process is triggered. These techniques are usually based on some level of expert human knowledge and/or historical data.

The second group of techniques called the statistics-based approach use traditional statistical methods and tests. Statistical approaches use techniques like trend detection or time series analysis to determine if the aging phenomena actually exist and to estimate the time to failure of the system. This approach may be further categorized depending on the actual statistical techniques applied.

Finally, machine learning approaches leverage various machine learning algorithm families to try and predict system crashes due to software aging phenomena based on the indicators generated by the system such as memory usage, file descriptors and CPU usage.

This chapter devotes one section to each of the approaches discussed above. It can be argued that some statistical techniques can also be considered part of the machine learning family of approaches or that some approaches present hybrid solutions involving techniques from two or more groups of approaches.

This level of overlap can make it hard to classify each individual technique. However, in the opinion of the authors of this chapter, this proposed classification represents the best way to understand the idiosyncrasies and pros and cons of each family. So, when the reader confronts any new (hybrid or not) solution, they would be in a good spot to analyze it and understand the implications of such a solution, even if it involves techniques from more than one method presented here.

The rest of the chapter is thus organized as follows: Section 4.2 focuses on the threshold-based approaches. Section 4.3 analyzes the statistical approaches and describes the major techniques used within this field. Section 4.4 describes the main machine learning approaches used to predict when the system is most likely to crash due to the aging phenomena. Section 4.5 assists the reader by providing a comprehensive list of metrics that have been historically linked with the aging phenomena. The main goal of this section is to provide a good repository of well-known aging metrics. Section 4.6 concludes the chapter with some final thoughts.

4.2. Threshold-Based Approaches

Threshold-based approaches define thresholds for one or more aging indicators and rejuvenation is triggered when the monitored indicators exceed these thresholds. Aging indicators used here may refer to resource consumption levels. With this approach, it can sometimes be hard to assess how to trade-off between aging-related system crashes and the triggering of superfluous rejuvenation events.

An example of this approach is presented in the work by Silva *et al.* [2], which adopts thresholds on mean response time and on quality of service indicators. The authors propose a rejuvenation approach based on self-healing techniques that exploits virtualization to optimize recovery. They implemented a rejuvenation framework called *VM-Rejuv*, in which an *Aging Detector* module is designed to detect aging conditions based on the mentioned thresholds. Another work by Silva *et al.* [3] is a further example of the threshold-based approach; the paper presents an analysis of software aging in a SOAP-based server, in which a dependability benchmarking study is conducted to evaluate some SOAP-RPC implementations, focusing in particular on Apache Axis, where they detected the presence of aging by parameter monitoring.

Thresholds are also adopted by Matias *et al.* [4] to evaluate the aging effects in the Apache web server based on a controlled experiment. The memory consumed by Apache is observed together with three controllable workload parameters: page size, page type (dynamic or static) and request rate. The authors adopt thresholds on the usage of virtual memory as aging indications.

Threshold-based approaches can be combined with other approaches. For instance, a threshold could be established for some parameters for which a statistical or machine learning approach is difficult to apply (e.g., because of the characteristics of the observations such as high noise or variability), while time-series or machine learning approaches could be applied for other indicators. Such an approach has been applied on the Eucalyptus cloud computing platform: Araujo *et al.* [5] combined the threshold-based approach (with a threshold on memory utilization) with time-series analysis, implementing a rejuvenation policy in Eucalyptus by using multiple thresholds and forecasting with time series analysis models. The time-series models adopted in this work are the linear model, quadratic model, growth curve model, and S-curve trend model.

In related work, Avritzer *et al.* [6] applied the central limit theorem to customer response time samples to account for response time variability. Then, this was used to provide a mechanism to implement a trade-off between the detection of performance degradation transients and software rejuvenation events. The authors implement a series of varying buckets to store response time sample measurements that exceed the response time threshold. If a sample measurement was found to be less than the response time threshold, that would be used to cancel a previous sample that exceeded the response time threshold. The central limit theorem is used to show that even for a small number of samples, the response time distribution approaches a symmetric distribution over the mean response time [7]. If a given bucket sample storage has an overflow condition, the system declares the detection of performance degradation, creating a new bucket for sample storage, but not triggering a software rejuvenation event. Therefore, the system designers had the ability to postpone software rejuvenation, if the performance degradation was found to be related to a transient load increase. In contrast, if several buckets showed the overflow condition in sequence, the software aging detection mechanism would have an increased level of certainty that the detected performance degradation was not transient and that software rejuvenation would be beneficial.

4.3. Statistical Approaches

A widely used technique for the measurement-based approach is time series analysis. Variables potentially related to software aging, such as system resource consumption or user-perceived performance indicators, are monitored periodically over time, and the resulting time series data are analyzed to assess the presence of aging phenomena. A time series analysis for aging assessment addresses two main problems: 1) detecting the presence of a degradation trend, and, if such a degradation trend is present, 2) quantitatively estimating the extent of the degradation and its characteristics (e.g., seasonality in data). The problems are approached using *statistical trend detection* and *trend estimation* techniques, respectively. Trend detection applies statistical hypothesis testing to determine whether the values within a time series (i.e., a series of observations of a random variable) generally increase (or decrease) over a long period of time. The statistical test is used to make conclusive statements about the presence or absence of software aging trends with a desired statistical confidence. Trend estimation allows one to quantitatively characterize the long-term component of a time series.

The most used *trend detection* techniques in software aging research are, by far, the Mann-Kendall test and the seasonal Kendall test. They are hypothesis tests (for non-periodic and periodic time series, respectively) that are used to accept/reject the hypothesis of no trend in data. Being non-parametric tests, they do not make assumptions regarding the distribution of data and are more robust to outliers than parametric tests; on the other hand, they are generally conservative, in other words, some actual trend could be missed. The Mann-Kendall (and seasonal Kendall) test is usually applied in conjunction with Sen's (and the seasonal Sen's) trend estimation procedure for *trend estimation.* Sen's procedure is also a non-parametric linear regression technique (also insensitive to outliers) that fits a linear model and computes the rate at which the samples increase over time by simply estimating the slope as the median of all slopes between paired values [8, 9]. The combination of the Mann-Kendall test and Sen's estimator is a widely used approach and it has been reported in several papers from the reviewed aging research literature [10–13].

One of the first measurement-based analyses applying the Mann-Kendall test and Sen's procedure was by Garg *et al.* [10] Until then, observations of software aging had been mainly anecdotal. Instead of collecting metrics on failure events (which most research on software reliability relies on), the main idea behind this work was to periodically monitor and store data on the attributes of a software system that are indicative of the "health" of the system.

Using the SNMP (Simple Network Management Protocol) framework, a distributed resource monitoring tool was designed and developed. The goal was to monitor the health of Unix (Solaris) workstations at the OS level. The objects (or metrics) that were monitored fell broadly into seven categories — host details (that are constant), timestamps, OS resources, process states, file system resources, network resources and I/O resources. The SNMP agent ran on each monitored workstation while the monitoring station ran the SNMP manager and acted as a central data repository. Eight workstations were monitored for approximately two months with the frequency of data collection set to fifteen minutes.

Some of the questions that the authors attempted to answer were (a) is aging present (b) how do the metrics behave over time (c) can observed failures be related to specific metric values and (d) can software aging be quantified? Linear and periodic dependency analysis (autocorrelation and harmonic analysis) and trend detection and estimation techniques (the seasonal Kendall test) were used to answer these questions. Daily and weekly dependencies were observed in many of the monitored variables. Smoothing techniques (non-parametric local weighted regression) and trend detection (the seasonal Kendall test) were applied to the time-series data to detect global trends that pointed to evidence of software aging.

The major contributions of this paper were aging quantification and the estimations of time to failure due to aging. The quantification aspect was addressed by calculating a slope metric using Sen's non-parametric method for each metric and the corresponding time to failure estimation was performed using a simple linear projection, given the minimum/maximum of the metric of interest.

The above work was extended by Vaidyanathan and Trivedi [14], where a measurement-based model was proposed to estimate resource exhaustion times based on time as well as system workload state. The same setup as [10] was used to monitor and collect Unix data. Statistical clustering techniques were employed to identify different workload states and a semi-Markov state space model was developed. This approach can also be understood as a machine learning approach. For each of the monitored metrics of interest, a reward function was computed based on the exhaustion rate of these metrics (resources) at each of the identified workload states. The expected accumulated reward was used an indicator of the resource usage trend and estimates of failure times were computed using this. This work clearly demonstrated the relation between system workload and resource exhaustion and supports prior studies that showed that workload does affect system reliability/availability. Not only were the system workload dynamics captured in the model but also the effect of workload on resource usage was quantified by means of reward rates or slopes in the model. In doing this, the software aging phenomenon was validated with respect to resource exhaustion. This workload-based model was further expanded in [15] by feeding the results to a higher level availability model that accounts for failure followed by reactive as well as proactive recovery. Optimal rejuvenation schedules are derived that minimize downtime cost and maximize availability.

Grottke *et al.* [11] have analyzed the performance degradation in the Apache Web Server by sampling the web server's response time to predefined HTTP requests at fixed intervals, using a similar procedure as the one adopted by Garg *et al.* They have also analyzed the seasonal patterns, where trend analysis accounts for the possible presence of seasonal variation in data.

More recently, Zheng *et al.* [16] proposed an alternative to the conventional (seasonal) Mann-Kendall test and Sen's procedure. The authors point out a few areas where improvements can be made to the Mann-Kendall test and Sen's trend estimator (e.g., suitability for linear trends only, sensitivity to noise and computational complexity) and propose to use a modified version of the Cox-Stuart test for trend detection and the iterative Hodrick-Prescott Filter for (linear and non-linear) trend estimation. The Cox-Stuart test is based on the sign test between pairs of a series of observations (a modified version is proposed for periodic time series). The Hodrick-Prescott filter does not presume the structure of the trend (e.g., linear trend); it solves a "penalized" spline model, fitting the raw time series to be a more smoothened representation, by using a smooth parameter that penalizes the variability of the trend component, thus controlling the trade-off between the goodness of fit and smoothness (the larger its value, the smoother the trend component). This test is also insensitive to periodicity.

Together with the conventional Mann-Kendall test for trend detection, Li *et al.* [17] used time-series ARMA/ARX models for trend estimation on the Apache Web Server to estimate the resource exhaustion. Compared with the linear regression and extended linear regression models, the ARX model incurs higher initial overhead, but once the model parameters are established, these parameters can be used for prediction without the need for frequent model re-calibration.

ARIMA (Autoregressive Integrated Moving Average) and Holt-Winters (Triple Exponential Smoothing) models have been used by Magalhaes and Silva [18], wherein the authors develop a framework for detection of performance anomalies caused by aging, which is targeted to web and component-based applications. In particular, the framework monitors application/system parameters, used to determine the correlation between the application response time and the input workload, in turn used to train machine learning (ML) algorithms. At run-time, parameters collected by monitoring are estimated by the ARIMA and Holt-Winters algorithms, and the estimations are classified by the trained ML algorithms to determine if the application may experience performance anomalies.

Time-series analysis has also been adopted to study the relationship between software aging and workload in complex systems, including the Linux Kernel code [19] and the Java Virtual Machine [20]. In both cases, the analysis of workload parameters is used to provide indications of potential sources of software aging, by highlighting the subsystems whose parameters are correlated to the experienced aging trends. In the latter, parametric trend detection was used for aging detection, specifically the conventional *t-student* test. Then, Principal Component Analysis (PCA) followed by multiple linear regression was also used to remove first-order correlation among predictors and then to provide linear estimates of aging trends, so as to reduce the problem of multicollinearity. Clustering is also preliminarily exploited to separate out different workload states possibly exhibiting different trends.

In the work by Bovenzi *et al.* [21] the authors adopt a Design of Experiment (DoE) technique that is used to assess the presence of aging under different workload configurations in several applications, such as the James mail server, a middleware for an air traffic control system, the Apache web server, and the MySQL DBMS. A series of controlled long-running experiments are planned and executed, and the resulting time series are analyzed by the conventional Mann-Kendall test and Sen's procedure followed by the Analysis of Variance (ANOVA) to assess the impact of various workload factors on software aging. The impact of concurrency bugs on aging is also assessed using this technique.

Non-linear time-series analyses are used by Araujo *et al.* [5]. Four different time-series models have been used to schedule software rejuvenation: 1) the linear model, 2) the quadratic model, 3) the exponential growth model, and, 4) the model of the Pearl-Reed logistic. They have been adopted to predict memory consumption trends on the Eucalyptus cloud computing framework. One further paper considering nonlinear models is by Jia *et al.* [22] in which aging is studied in the Apache server by constructing a dynamic model to describe the software aging process following the method of nonlinear dynamic inversion. The software aging process is shown to be nonlinear and chaotic.

In the best practice guide by Hoffmann *et al.* [23], multivariate nonlinear models (support vector machines, radials, and universal basis functions) have been compared with multivariate linear models. The former ones have shown better performance than linear models in the benchmarking case studies.

Finally, Chen *et al.* [24] propose a new aging metric based on Multidimensional Multi-scale Entropy (MMSE) for trend analysis and aging-related failure prediction. PCA is leveraged to select variables from an initial set of multiple aging indicators. Using a normalized time series of the selected indicators, the MMSE metric is computed, where a greater entropy is demonstrated to relate to a more severe aging phenomenon.

4.4. Machine Learning Approaches

As stated in the previous section, there are several works that use time series approaches as a first step in the area of machine learning. If we consider software aging phenomena as a result of two factors (the system resource presenting the aging bug, and time), time series approaches could be considered ideal. However, these approaches are drastically limited by the need to have previous knowledge about the resource that is affected by the aging phenomena and the affected performance metric (e.g., response time, throughput). This represents an increasingly higher barrier to adopting time series approaches with the increasing complexity of the systems and the interdependency between resources at different system layers.

In this scenario machine learning approaches come into play. Machine learning approaches are a more sophisticated form of data analysis, which adopts machine learning algorithms (e.g., classifiers and regressors) to identify trends (e.g., estimating time to failure) and to classify a system state as robust or failure-prone.

Pattern recognition methods have been used by Cassidy *et al.* [25] to predict software aging in shared memory pool latch contention in large OLTP servers. The approach applies non-linear, non-parametric regression to a large set of system variables, and analyzes the residual error between the predicted and the actual system values using a sequential probability ratio test, in order to predict the onset of software aging effects. The obtained results have shown that these methods could be used to detect significant deviations from "standard" behavior with a 2-hour early warning.

We subdivide the machine learning approaches into two major families based on the type of machine learning algorithm used: regression approaches and classification approaches.

The former approach is focused on trying to predict the time to exhaustion (TTE) of the system resource or resources due to aging phenomena. The later approach is focused on determining the state of the system (i.e., stable vs non-stable state).

There are several published papers within the domain of predicting the time to crash due to software aging. For example, Alonso *et al.* [26] compare different regression algorithm families (i.e., regression trees, linear regression and hybrids). The authors focus on comparing these algorithms within the different scenarios and multiple aging phenomena involved. The conclusion arrived at by the authors was that the aging phenomena was better modeled by a hybrid model (i.e., MP5) between Decision Trees and Linear Regression, since the aging phenomena caused by resource exhaustion due to bugs in the software (i.e., memory leaks or threads unreleased after use) can be modeled by linear piecewise models capturing different aging slopes or speeds. In addition to the above, three different machine learning algorithms (a naive Bayes classifier, decision trees and a neural network model) have been also used in combination with time-series models to predict aging in web applications [18].

They automatically built the models relating several system variables (e.g., the number of connections and throughput) to aging trends, based on the observation that software aging trends can be approximated using a piecewise linear model. The models were trained using data samples collected in preliminary experiments, and were used to predict the TTE of system resources in conditions different than the ones observed during the training phase.

An example of the application of machine learning classifier algorithms is presented by Alonso *et al.* [27]. The paper compares a large set of families (i.e., random forest, decision trees, LDA/QDA, Naive Bayes, Support Vector Machines and K-nearest neighbors) to predict state in the context of a three-tier J2EE system.

Andrzejak and Silva [28] compare four classification algorithms: J48 (a decision tree based algorithm), Naïve Bayes, Support Vector Machines (i.e., SMO) and ZeroR (The 0/R classifier). The authors compare these four algorithms in software aging scenarios caused by only one metric with a constant software aging injection rate. The experimental evaluation suggested that all these four main families of classification techniques perform similarly, even though SMO presents better overall results.

An approach not exactly falling within this area but still related to it is to use reinforcement learning for aging estimation. Eto, Dohi and Ma [29] used reinforcement learning to estimate the optimal rejuvenation schedule adaptively, i.e., by considering runtime data to update the estimation. Thus, their estimation technique does not require a complete knowledge of system failure (degradation) time distribution in the operational phase, even if the underlying software state transition is governed by models, i.e., by CTMCs or SMPs. This is an example of a *hybrid* approach, wherein a measurement-based approach is used in conjunction with a model-based one [30].

4.5. Relevant Software Aging Metrics: Beyond Memory Leaks

Aging indicators are an important area of study for measurement-based approaches. The correct identification of metrics representing the aging of the system is of paramount importance in order to have a clear assessment of the system health's state. Aging indicators can refer to both *resource usage* and to *performance*. The following classes of aging indicators are commonly used in measurement-based aging analysis techniques:

- **Memory consumption**: metrics related to memory consumption are by far the most commonly used metrics for monitoring resource depletion. Empirical evidence showed that free memory exhibits the shortest Time to Exhaustion (TTE) among system resources [10] and that memory management defects are a significant cause of aging failures [31] and of software failures in general [32]. Therefore, several measurement-based studies analyze aging phenomena affecting free memory by measuring the amount of *free physical memory* and *swap space* [11, 14, 33], and applying time series and statistical models to these variables.
- **Performance degradation**: Measurement-based techniques often refer to *performance degradation* in software systems affected by aging, which is the other symptom (aside from resource depletion) caused by aging. Performance degradation is indeed related to memory usage: for instance, the consumption of physical memory increases the time required by memory allocation procedures and garbage collection mechanisms, since their computational complexity is a function of the number of memory areas that have been allocated [20, 34, 35]. But performance degradation can be also due to other, more complex and hard-to-reproduce, aging causes such as fragmentation or concurrency management [21, 36]. Common indicators are response time, latency, throughput, transaction rate or, less commonly, the number of SLA (Service Level Agreement) violations. In the presence of this kind of phenomena, software rejuvenation can be triggered when the quality of service (e.g., in terms of response time or throughput) is below a given threshold.

- **Other resource consumption**: Software aging can impact several other resource types. Besides memory-related resources (e.g., physical memory, virtual memory, swap space, cache memory), the reviewed literature also addressed the following other types of resources:

  — filesystem-related resources, such as stream descriptors and file handles [10, 37, 38]
  — storage, whose space may be consumed by bad management [39]
  — network-related resources, such as socket descriptors [37]
  — concurrency-related resources, such as locks, threads and processes [10, 21, 38]
  — application-specific resources, such as DBMS shared pool latches [25] and OSGi references [40].

  In many cases, the approach is not constrained to a specific resource, but is focused on detecting incorrect API usage and incorrect exception handlers that may cause a resource leakage. For instance, in the work by Zhang *et al.*, the authors present an approach that dynamically mines resource usage patterns by monitoring API calls, and provides an experimental evaluation of open source programs based on the Java I/O and concurrency APIs [38]. A frequent kind of resource leak in Java programs is represented by sockets and file handles, due to faulty exception handlers that do not release these resources [37, 38]. Other resources can also be affected by software aging depending on the kind of system, such as free disk space in DBMS [39]. In some cases, a wider set of resources can be analyzed. The above-mentioned example by Garg *et al.* applies time series analysis on a network of UNIX workstations monitored on several resources (related to virtual memory, the OS kernel, the file system, the disk, and the network), noticing a statistically significant trend in the process table size and in the file table size (although their time-to-exhaustion was lower than that of free memory). Other resources include CPU utilization, power consumption, and the number of threads/processes. In cloud systems, indicators can be measured at any layer of the virtualization technology stack, e.g., at the application or the OS level within the VM layer, at the VM layer to probe the state and the resource consumption of the VMs (e.g., for load balancing, scaling, VM migration and rejuvenation decisions), as well as at the VMM layer. Besides system resources, other indicators of interest are related to VMs, for instance, the number of VM new allocations/releases, the time to start/stop VMs, or to the time to migration.

A recent field in which software rejuvenation is being studied is related to **security attacks** [41, 42], that is, attempts by malicious users to access unauthorized resources, to cause their gradual leakage or to make the system unavailable. In fact, security attacks may take place and gradually compromise a system over a long period of time (e.g., password theft through brute force guessing, or flood attacks that trigger software aging phenomena), which can be mitigated by periodically rejuvenating a system, such as by changing cryptographic keys, by restarting compromised processes, and by randomizing the location of data and instructions in memory [43–48]. Currently, the aging rate is assumed at design time [43, 49] or is based on imperfect attack/intrusion detectors that could raise false alarms and miss attacks [50, 51].

Other aging indicators may be aimed at capturing effects like the *accumulation of numerical errors* [52] and *memory fragmentation* [52, 53]. These kinds of aging effects are not necessarily caused by bugs in the software, but are related to the nature of floating-point arithmetic and memory allocation algorithms respectively.

4.6. Conclusions

This chapter described the main approaches to dealing with software aging based on *measurements*. Unlike model-based approaches, measurement-based techniques rely on observations from real systems, with the goal of *detecting* whether the system is in a failure-prone state due to software aging, *forecasting* the time-to-aging-failure, and *planning* software rejuvenation accordingly.

The advantage of such solutions lies in the possibility of gathering accurate and detailed information about the aging state of the system under analysis, and the use of real data to estimate metrics and model parameters.

However, while the techniques described in this chapter can be applied to any system for which monitoring is possible, it is also true that the gathered observations from one system are difficult to generalize. A good example of this difficulty is that of trained machine learning models, which may work accurately only for the system that was used to generate the training data.

Moreover, at design time there are no data available to determine the potential sources of possible aging behaviors — a real system is needed in order for data to be collected. This requires a tuning of the technique used based on the system to be analyzed, which considers the indicators that are more likely related to the aging phenomena of that specific system — hence more explanatory of aging behaviors — and that can be monitored with acceptable overhead.

Due to the underlying limitations of the measurement-based approaches, it is natural to combine measurement-based approaches with model-based approaches. Real data can be used to estimate the parameters for the models. So, combining both approaches increases our capabilities to study the effect of the software aging on a given system in much more detail than is possible with simple observations.

In the future, we expect the impact of the measurement-based aging analysis technique to increase in the SAR literature. We expect to see an increased use of machine learning techniques because they represent a hybrid between model-based and measurement-based approaches.

Indeed, as systems become more and more complex, several indicators will need to be analyzed to detect software aging. Moreover, it will become increasingly difficult to distinguish between software aging and the expected fluctuations of the system performance, because of inter-relations among multiple parameters [6, 7].

All these call for more complex statistical techniques able to analyze the cause-effect relations (and not only correlations) among multiple indicators and to spot those critical patterns relevant for aging identification in complex systems. This is a challenge of great importance due to the increasing impact of aging problems in complex systems.

References

1. J. Alonso, A. Bovenzi, J. Li, Y. Wang, S. Russo, and K. Trivedi. (2013). Software rejuvenation: Do IT and telco industries use it? In *Proceedings of the 2012 IEEE 23rd International Symposium on Software Reliability Engineering Workshops (ISSREW), Dallas, Texas, USA, November 27–30*, pp. 299–304. doi: 10.1109/ISSREW.2012.96.
2. L. Silva, J. Alonso, and J. Torres. (2009). Using virtualization to improve software rejuvenation. *IEEE Transactions on Computers*, **58**(11), 1525–1538.
3. L. Silva, H. Madeira, and J. Silva. (2006). Software aging and rejuvenation in a SOAP-based server. In *Proceedings of the 5th IEEE International Symposium on Network Computing and Applications (NCA 2006), Cambridge, Massachusetts, USA, July 24–26*, pp. 56–65.
4. R. Matias Jr. and P. Filho. (2006). An experimental study on software aging and rejuvenation in web servers. In *Proceedings of the 30th Annual International Computer Software and Applications Conference (COMPSAC'06), Chicago, Illinois, USA, September 17–21*, pp. 189–196.
5. J. Araujo, R. Matos, P. Maciel, F. Vieira, R. Matias, and K. Trivedi. (2011). Software rejuvenation in eucalyptus cloud computing infrastructure: A method based on time series forecasting and multiple thresholds. In *Third International Workshop on Software Aging and Rejuvenation (WoSAR), Hiroshima, Japan, November 29–December 2*, pp. 38–43.

6. A. Avritzer, A. Bondi, and E. J. Weyuker. Ensuring stable performance for systems that degrade. In *Proceedings of the 5th International Workshop on Software and Performance (WOSP '05), Palma, Illes Balears, Spain, July 12–14*, pp. 43–51. ISBN 1-59593-087-6. doi: 10.1145/1071021.1071026.
7. A. Avritzer, A. Bondi, M. Grottke, K. S. Trivedi, and E. J. Weyuker. (2006). Performance assurance via software rejuvenation: Monitoring, statistics and algorithms. In *International Conference on Dependable Systems and Networks (DSN'06), Philadelphia, Pennsylvania, USA, June 25–28*, pp. 435–444. doi: 10.1109/DSN.2006.58.
8. P. K. Sen. (1968). Estimates of the regression coefficient based on Kendall's Tau. *Journal of the American Statistical Association*, **63**(324), 1379–1389. ISSN 01621459.
9. H. Theil. (1992). A rank invariant method of linear and polynomial regression analysis. In Raj, B. and Koerts, J. (eds.). *Henri Theil's Contributions to Economics and Econometrics: Econometric Theory and Methodology*. Dordrecht, Netherlands: Springer. ISBN 978-94-011-2546-8. doi: 10.1007/978-94-011-2546-8_20.
10. S. Garg, A. van Moorsel, K. Vaidyanathan, and K. Trivedi. (1988). A methodology for detection and estimation of software aging. In *Proceedings of the Ninth International Symposium on Software Reliability Engineering, Paderborn, Germany, November 4–7*, pp. 283–292. doi: 10.1109/ISSRE.1998.730892.
11. M. Grottke, L. Li, K. Vaidyanathan, and K. Trivedi. (2006). Analysis of software aging in a web server. *IEEE Transactions on Reliability*, **55**(3), 411–420. ISSN 0018-9529. doi: 10.1109/TR.2006.879609.
12. A. Bovenzi, D. Cotroneo, R. Pietrantuono, and S. Russo. (2011). Workload characterization for software aging analysis. In *Proceedings of the 22nd International Symposium on Software Reliability Engineering (ISSRE), Tokyo, Japan, November 14–17*, pp. 240–249.
13. K. S. Trivedi, K. Vaidyanathan, and K. Goseva-Popstojanova. (2000). Modeling and analysis of software aging and rejuvenation. In *Proceedings of the 33rd Annual Simulation Symposium (SS 2000), Washington, DC, USA, April 16–20*, pp. 270–279.
14. K. Vaidyanathan and K. Trivedi. (1999). A measurement-based model for estimation of resource exhaustion in operational software systems. In *Proceedings of the 10th International Symposium on Software Reliability Engineering, Boca Raton, Florida, USA, November 1–4*, pp. 84–93. doi: 10.1109/ISSRE.1999.809313.
15. K. Vaidyanathan and K. Trivedi. (2005). A comprehensive model for software rejuvenation. *IEEE Transactions on Dependable and Secure Computing*, **2**(2), 124–137.
16. P. Zheng, Y. Qi, Y. Zhou, P. Chen, J. Zhan, and M. R. T. Lyu. (2014). An automatic framework for detecting and characterizing performance degradation of software systems. *IEEE Transactions on Reliability*, **63**(4), 927–943. ISSN 0018-9529. doi: 10.1109/TR.2014.2338255.
17. L. Li, K. Vaidyanathan, and K. Trivedi. (2002). An approach for estimation of software aging in a web server. In *Proceedings of the 2002 International Symposium on Empirical Software Engineering, Nara, Japan, October 3–4*, pp. 91–102. doi: 10.1109/ISESE.2002.1166929.
18. J. Magalhaes and L. Silva. (2010). Prediction of performance anomalies in web-applications based-on software aging scenarios. In *Proceedings of the Second International Workshop on Software Aging and Rejuvenation (WoSAR), San Jose, California, USA, November 2*, pp. 1–7. doi: 10.1109/WOSAR.2010.5722095.
19. D. Cotroneo, R. Natella, R. Pietrantuono, and S. Russo. (2010). Software aging analysis of the Linux operating system. In *Proceedings of the 21st International*

Symposium on Software Reliability Engineering (ISSRE) San Jose, California, USA, November 1–4, pp. 71–80. doi: 10.1109/ISSRE.2010.24.

20. D. Cotroneo, S. Orlando, R. Pietrantuono, and S. Russo. (2013). A measurement-based ageing analysis of the JVM. *Software Testing, Verification and Reliability*, **23**(3), 199–239.
21. A. Bovenzi, D. Cotroneo, R. Pietrantuono, and S. Russo. (2012). On the aging effects due to concurrency bugs: A case study on MySQL. In *Proceedings of the 2012 IEEE 23rd International Symposium on Software Reliability Engineering, Dallas, Texas, USA, November 27–30*, pp. 211–220. doi: 10.1109/ISSRE.2012.50.
22. Y.-F. Jia, L. Zhao, and K.-Y. Cai. (2008). A nonlinear approach to modeling of software aging in a web server. In *Proceedings of the 15th Asia-Pacific Software Engineering Conference, Beijing, China, December 3–5*, pp. 77–84. doi: 10.1109/APSEC.2008.38.
23. G. Hoffmann, K. Trivedi, and M. Malek. (2007). A best practice guide to resource forecasting for computing systems. *IEEE Transactions on Reliability*, **56**(4), 615–628. ISSN 0018-9529. doi: 10.1109/TR.2007.909764.
24. P. Chen, Y. Qi, X. Li, D. Hou, and M. Lyu. (2017). Arf-predictor: Effective prediction of aging-related failure using entropy. *IEEE Transactions on Dependable and Secure Computing*, **15**(4), 675–693. ISSN 1545-5971. doi: 10.1109/TDSC.2016.2604381.
25. K. Cassidy, K. Gross, and A. Malekpour. (2002). Advanced pattern recognition for detection of complex software aging phenomena in online transaction processing servers. In *Proceedings of the International Conference of Dependable Systems and Networks, Bethesda, Maryland, USA, June 23–26*, pp. 478–482. doi: 10.1109/DSN.2002.1028933.
26. J. Alonso, J. Torres, J. Berral, and R. Gavalda. (2010). Adaptive on-line software aging prediction based on machine learning. In *Proceedings of the International Conference on Dependable Systems and Networks (DSN), Chicago, Illinois, USA, June 28–July 1*, pp. 507–516. doi: 10.1109/DSN.2010.5544275.
27. J. Alonso, L. Belanche, and D. Avresky. (2011). Predicting software anomalies using machine learning techniques. In *Proceedings of the 10th IEEE International Symposium on Network Computing and Applications (NCA), Cambridge, Massachusetts, USA, August 25–27*, pp. 163–170.
28. A. Andrzejak and L. Silva. (2008). Using machine learning for non-intrusive modeling and prediction of software aging. In *Proceedings of the IEEE Network Operations and Management Symposium, Salvador, Bahia, Brazil, April 7–11*, pp. 25–32.
29. H. Eto, T. Dohi, and J. Ma. (2008). Simulation-based optimization approach for software cost model with rejuvenation, In Rong C., Jaatun M. G., Sandnes F. E., Yang L. T., Ma J. (eds.). *Autonomic and Trusted Computing*. ATC 2008. Lecture Notes in Computer Science, vol 5060. Berlin/Heidelberg, Germany: Springer.
30. D. Cotroneo, R. Natella, R. Pietrantuono, and S. Russo. (2014). A survey of software aging and rejuvenation studies. *Journal of Emerging Technologies in Computing Systems*, **10**(1), 8:1–8:34. ISSN 1550-4832. doi: 10.1145/2539117.
31. D. Cotroneo, R. Natella, and R. Pietrantuono. (2012). Predicting aging-related bugs using software complexity metrics. *Performance Evaluation*, **70**(3), 163–178.
32. M. Sullivan and R. Chillarege. (1991). Software defects and their impact on system availability — a study of field failures in operating systems. In *Proceedings of the Twenty-First International Symposium on Fault-Tolerant Computing (FTCS-21), Montreal, Quebec, Canada, June 25–27*, pp. 2–9.
33. M. Ficco, R. Pietrantuono, and S. Russo. (2017). Aging-related performance anomalies in the Apache Storm stream processing system. *Future Generation Computer Systems*, **86**, 975–994.

34. G. Carrozza, D. Cotroneo, R. Natella, A. Pecchia, and S. Russo. (2010). Memory leak analysis of mission-critical middleware. *Journal of Systems and Software*, **83**(9), 1556–1567.
35. T. Ferreira, R. Matias, A. Macedo, and L. Araujo. (2011). An experimental study on memory allocators in multicore and multithreaded applications. In *Proceedings of the 12th International Conference on Parallel and Distributed Computing, Applications and Technologies (PDCAT), Gwangju, Korea, October 20–22*, pp. 92–98. doi: 10.1109/PDCAT.2011.18.
36. D. G. Cavezza, R. Pietrantuono, J. Alonso, S. Russo, and K. S. Trivedi. (2014). Reproducibility of environment-dependent software failures: An experience report. In *Proceedings of the 2014 IEEE 25th International Symposium on Software Reliability Engineering, Naples, Italy, November 3–6*, pp. 267–276. doi: 10.1109/ISSRE.2014.19.
37. W. Weimer. (2006). Exception-handling bugs in Java and a language extension to avoid them. In Dony C., Knudsen J. L., Romanovsky A., Tripathi A. (eds.) *Advanced Topics in Exception Handling Techniques.* Lecture Notes in Computer Science, vol. 4119. Berlin/Heidelberg, Germany: Springer.
38. H. Zhang, G. Wu, K. Chow, Z. Yu, and X. Xing. (2011). Detecting resource leaks through dynamical mining of resource usage patterns. In *Proceedings of the 41st IEEE/IFIP International Conference on Dependable Systems and Networks Workshops (DSN-W) Hong Kong, China, June 27–30*, pp. 265–270.
39. A. Bobbio, M. Sereno, and C. Anglano. (2001). Fine grained software degradation models for optimal rejuvenation policies. *Performance Evaluation*, **46**(1), 45–62.
40. K. Gama and D. Donsez. (2008). Service coroner: A diagnostic tool for locating OSGi stale references. In *Proceedings of the 34th Euromicro Conference on Software Engineering and Advanced Applications, Parma, Italy, September 3–5*, pp. 108–115.
41. A. Avritzer, R. G. Cole, and E. J. Weyuker. (2010). Methods and opportunities for rejuvenation in aging distributed software systems. *Journal of Systems and Software*, **83**(9), 1568–1578. ISSN 0164-1212. doi: https://doi.org/10.1016/j.jss.2010.05.026.
42. A. Avritzer, R. G. Cole, and E. J. Weyuker. (2007). Using performance signatures and software rejuvenation for worm mitigation in tactical manets. In *Proceedings of the 6th International Workshop on Software and Performance (WOSP '07), Buenos Aires, Argentina, February 5–8*, pp. 172–180. ISBN 1-59593-297-6. doi: 10.1145/1216993.1217023.
43. P. Sousa, A. Bessani, M. Correia, N. Neves, and P. Verissimo. (2010). Highly available intrusion-tolerant services with proactive-reactive recovery. *IEEE Transactions on Parallel and Distributed Systems*, **21**(4), 452–465. ISSN 1045-9219. doi: 10.1109/TPDS.2009.83.
44. A. Tai, K. Tso, W. Sanders, and S. Chau. (2005). A performability-oriented software rejuvenation framework for distributed applications. In *Proceedings of the 2005 International Conference on Dependable Systems and Networks, Yokohoma, Japan, June 28–July 1*, pp. 570–579. doi: 10.1109/DSN.2005.12.
45. A. Valdes, M. Almgren, S. Cheung, Y. Deswarte, B. Dutertre, J. Levy, H. Saidi, V. Stavridou, and T. Uribe. (2003). An architecture for an adaptive intrusion-tolerant server. In Christianson B., Crispo B., Malcolm J. A., and Roe M. (eds.). *Security Protocols.* Security Protocols 2002. Lecture Notes in Computer Science, vol 2845. Berlin/Heidelberg, Germany: Springer.
46. B. Cox, D. Evans, A. Filipi, J. Rowanhill, W. Hu, J. Davidson, J. Knight, A. Nguyen-Tuong, and J. Hiser. (2006). N-variant systems: A secretless framework for security through diversity. In *Proceedings of the 15th Conference on USENIX Security*

Symposium, Vancouver, British Columbia, Canada, July 31–August 4, Volume 15, p. 9. USENIX Association, (2006).
47. Y. Huang, D. Arsenault, and A. Sood. (2006). SCIT-dNS: Critical infrastructure protection through secure DNS server dynamic updates. *Journal of High Speed Networks*, **15**(1), 5–19.
48. T. Roeder and F. Schneider. (2010). Proactive obfuscation. *ACM Transactions on Computer Systems (TOCS)*, **28**(2), 4.
49. Q. Nguyen and A. Sood. (2009). Quantitative approach to tuning of a time-based intrusion-tolerant system architecture. In *Proceedings of the 3rd Workshop on Recent Advances in Intrusion-Tolerant Systems, Lisbon, Portugal, June 29–July 2*, pp. 132–139.
50. K. Aung, K. Park, and J. Park. (2005). A model of ITS using cold standby cluster. In Fox E. A., Neuhold E. J., Premsmit P., and Wuwongse V. (eds.). *Digital Libraries: Implementing Strategies and Sharing Experiences*. ICADL 2005. Lecture Notes in Computer Science, vol 3815. Berlin/Heidelberg, Germany: Springer.
51. A. Nagarajan and A. Sood. (2010). SCIT and IDS architectures for reduced data exfiltration. In *Proceedings of the International Conference on Dependable Systems and Networks Workshops (DSN-W), Chicago, Illinois, USA, June 28–July 1*, pp. 164–169.
52. M. Grottke, R. Matias, and K. Trivedi. (2008). The fundamentals of software aging. In *Proceedings of the IEEE International Symposium on Software Reliability Engineering Workshops, Seattle, Washington, USA, November 11–14*, pp. 1–6.
53. A. Macedo, T. Ferreira, and R. Matias. (2010). The mechanics of memory-related software aging. In *Proceedings of the 2010 IEEE Second International Workshop on Software Aging and Rejuvenation (WoSAR), San Jose, California, USA, November 2*, pp. 1–5. doi: 10.1109/WOSAR.2010.5722097.

Part III

Model-driven Approach

Part III of this Handbook focuses on the model-driven approaches.

Chapter 5, Markov Chains and Petri Nets, contains an introduction of Markov and Petri net models for analyzing the dynamics of software aging and rejuvenation. Starting from the original rejuvenation model presented by Huang *et al.* which was based on a continuous-time Markov chain, this chapter presents a variety of Markov and semi-Markov models that have been used for representing different rejuvenation policies, techniques, and systems. The earliest study in this realm was that on Markov regenerative stochastic Petri nets presented by Garg *et al.* Further complex systems are analyzed by modeling with fluid stochastic Petri nets, stochastic reward nets, deterministic and stochastic Petri nets, and hierarchical models. The history of the evolution of these models is also reviewed in this chapter.

Chapter 6, Analysis of Queueing Models for Rejuvenation, describes the mathematical analysis of queueing models for rejuvenation. In particular, the chapter describes the early queueing model for rejuvenation in Garg *et al.* and variations of Garg *et al.*'s model in detail. The chapter also presents a generalized queueing model defined by a quasi-birth-and-death process.

Chapter 7, Models for Restart, Reboot and Rejuvenation provides a survey of model-based assessment and optimization of restart, reboot and rejuvenation strategies, for 'black-box' models.

Chapter 5

Markov Chains and Petri Nets

Fumio Machida*,‡ and Paulo R. M. Maciel†,§

** University of Tsukuba, Japan*
† Universidade Federal de Pernambuco, Brazil
‡ machida@cs.tsukuba.ac.jp
§ prmm@cin.ufpe.br

This chapter is dedicated to the introduction of Markov and Petri net models for analyzing the dynamics of software aging and rejuvenation that have been studied for the last quarter of the century. Starting from the original rejuvenation model presented by Huang *et al.* which was based on a continuous time Markov chain, a wide variety of Markov and semi-Markov models have been used to represent different rejuvenation policies, techniques, and systems. The semi-Markov model allows the incorporation of a deterministic trigger of software rejuvenation in the state-space model. Using the solution technique of the semi-Markov model, it is possible to derive the optimal interval to trigger software rejuvenation. Another important evolution of the Markov model for software rejuvenation can be seen in the models based on stochastic Petri nets and their variants, which are suitable for modeling more complex and large-scale systems. The earliest study in this realm was that of the Markov regenerative stochastic Petri nets presented by Garg *et al.* Further complex systems are analyzed by modeling with fluid stochastic Petri nets, stochastic reward nets, deterministic stochastic Petri nets, and hierarchical models. The history of the evolution of these models is also reviewed in this chapter.

5.1. Introduction

As has been discussed in the previous chapters, software rejuvenation is known to be an effective countermeasure to software aging, since the downtime cost incurred by software rejuvenation is usually smaller than the reactive system recovery cost caused by system failure as a consequence of aging. However, it is not trivial to determine when to trigger software rejuvenation because the process of software aging and associated degradation cannot usually be characterized as a deterministic process but involves uncertainties. The effectiveness of software rejuvenation depends upon various random variables such as the time to software aging, the time to failure, the time to recovery, the time to carry out rejuvenation and the associated costs. To deal with such processes, Markov and related state space models are used as a powerful mathematical approach to abstract the dynamics of systems and to analyze the relations of those factors contributing to system availability and performance. In this chapter, we will review the modeling approach based on Markov and related models to characterize the behavior of software aging and the rejuvenation of systems. The content of this chapter is divided into two sections; the section for Markov chains and semi-Markov processes and the section for Petri nets. Since the contents of both these sections are rooted in the fundamental model studied by Huang, Kintala, Kolettis, and Fulton [1], we first revisit their original Markov model. Figure 5.1 shows a historical overview of modeling studies covered in this chapter.

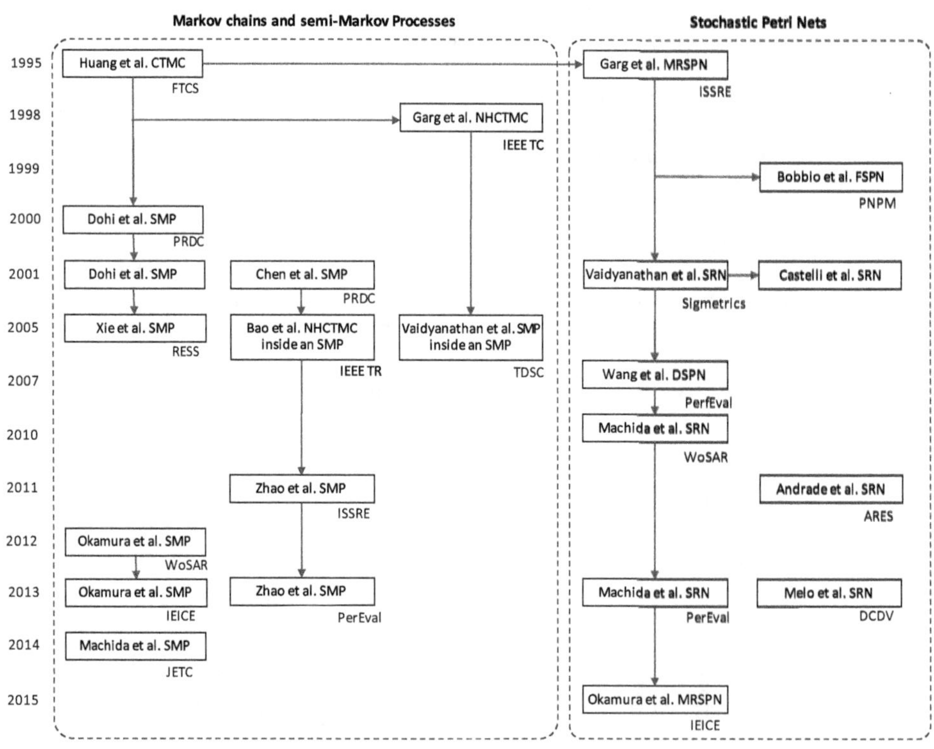

Fig. 5.1. A brief history of Markov chains and stochastic Petri nets applied to software aging and rejuvenation.

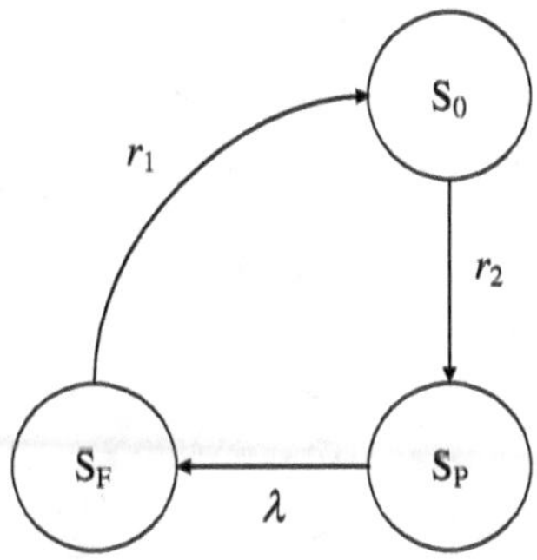

Fig. 5.2. CTMC representing a system with software aging [1].

5.2. Markov Chains and Semi-Markov Processes

The first application of the Markov model to the analysis of the dynamics of software aging and rejuvenation was presented by Huang, Kintala, Kolettis, and Fulton [1]. The authors proposed a continuous-time Markov chain (CTMC) to represent and analyze a software system with software aging (see Fig. 5.2).

The system first starts in a highly robust state S_0 and then goes into a failure-probable state S_P due to software aging. Subsequently, the system goes into failure state S_F, and it goes back to state S_0 after (reactive) recovery. The times to occurrence of all events are assumed to be exponentially distributed, hence such behavior may be represented by a homogeneous CTMC. The state transition rates when leaving states S_0, S_P and S_F are r_2, λ, and r_1, respectively. Note that if we remove the recovery transition out of state S_F, then the time to absorption distribution starting from state S_0 follows a hypo-exponential distribution which is known to be an increasing failure rate (IFR) distribution [23]. This is important since preventive maintenance makes sense only for a system with an IFR time to failure distribution. They could have chosen an IFR Weibull distribution, but they chose the hypo-exponential distribution presumably because the model retains the simplicity of a homogeneous CTMC. The solution of the CTMC of Fig. 5.2 yields the steady-state probability of state S_F, which represents the steady-state unavailability of the system. Huang *et al.* introduce an additional state S_R for carrying out software rejuvenation as shown in Fig. 5.3.

The system goes into state S_R from state S_P when software rejuvenation is applied, and then returns to state S_0 after its completion. The rates of transition to state S_R and state S_0 are specified by r_4 and r_3, respectively.

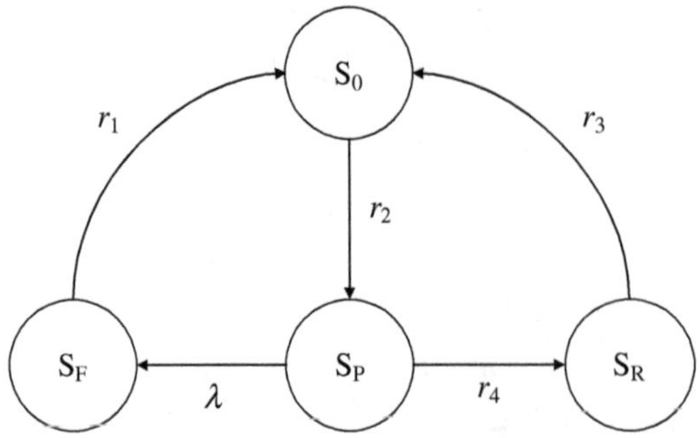

Fig. 5.3. CTMC representing a system with software aging and rejuvenation [1].

The sum of the steady-state probabilities for state S_F and state S_R can compute the steady-state unavailability of the system, that is

$$U = \frac{\frac{\lambda}{r_1} + \frac{r_4}{r_3}}{1 + \frac{\lambda}{r_1} + \frac{\lambda}{r_2} + \frac{r_4}{r_2} + \frac{r_4}{r_3}}.$$

To examine the unavailability as the rejuvenation trigger r_4 changes, we take the derivative of the above expression

$$\frac{dU}{dr_4} = \frac{\lambda}{r_1 r_2 r_3} \times \frac{1}{\left(1 + \frac{\lambda}{r_1} + \frac{\lambda}{r_2} + \frac{r_4}{r_2} + \frac{r_4}{r_3}\right)^2} \times \left[r_1\left(1 + \frac{r_2}{\lambda}\right) - r_3\right].$$

Since the denominator in the derivative is always positive, the sign of the derivative is determined by the sign of the term $[r_1(1 + r_2/\lambda) - r_3]$. When $r_3 > r_1(1+r_2/\lambda)$, the derivative is negative, implying that the unavailability always decreases as r_4 increases. Thus, to minimize the unavailability, the rejuvenation should be performed as soon as the system enters state S_P, i.e., $r_4 = \infty$. On the other hand, when $r_3 \leq r_1(1 + r_2/\lambda)$, the derivative is positive or equal to 0, implying that the unavailability always increases or does not change as r_4 increases. In this case, the unavailability is minimized at $r_4 = 0$ implying that rejuvenation (preventive maintenance) should never be carried out. As a result, the effectiveness of rejuvenation regarding system unavailability does not depend on the rejuvenation rate r_4, but it is determined by the threshold condition $r_3 > r_1(1 + r_2/\lambda)$. This is the first analytical result obtained through a Markov model for software rejuvenation.

The previous CTMC model was generalized to a continuous-time semi-Markov process (SMP) by Dohi, Popstojanova, and Trivedi [2, 3]. As already mentioned, in a homogeneous CTMC, all the transition time distributions

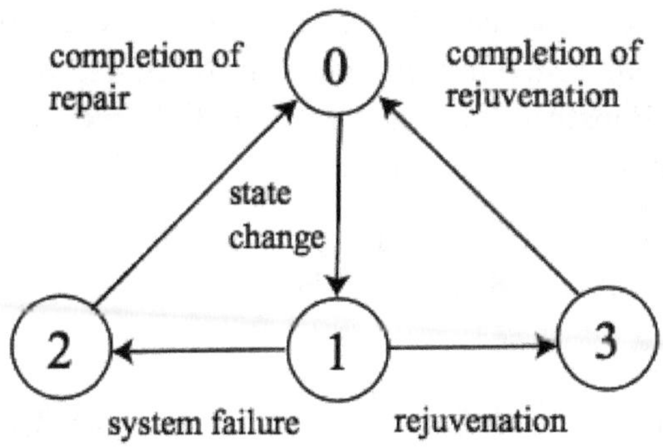

Fig. 5.4. SMP with four states to represent software aging and rejuvenation [2].

are exponential. SMP allows us to assign general distributions to state transitions and thus to extend the model capability. For example, when we consider time-based software rejuvenation, the time to trigger rejuvenation could be deterministic rather than exponentially distributed. Figure 5.4 shows the SMP with four states to represent the dynamics of software aging and rejuvenation. Although the state definitions are inherited from the original CTMC model in [1], the state transition times are assumed to be generally distributed, and all the states are considered as regeneration points. Let $F_f(t)$ and $F_r(t)$ be the distribution functions for failure time and the time to trigger software rejuvenation from the failure-probable state (depicted as state 1).

In time-based software rejuvenation, $F_r(t)$ can be defined as a unit step function as below:

$$F_r(t) = \mathrm{u}(t - t_0) = \begin{cases} 1, & \text{if } t \geq t_0 \\ 0, & \text{otherwise,} \end{cases}$$

where t_0 represents the fixed time to trigger software rejuvenation. Assume that μ_0, μ_a and μ_c represent the finite mean time to reach the failure-probable state from the robust state (state 0 in Fig. 5.4), the mean time to repair, and the mean time to complete rejuvenation, respectively. The steady-state availability of the system is given by the sum of the steady-state probabilities of the robust state and the failure-probable state and it can be derived by using the standard solution technique for SMP (See Appendix A.1 for details):

$$A(t_0) = \frac{\mu_0 + \int_0^{t_0} (1 - F_f(t))dt}{\mu_0 + \mu_a F_f(t_0) + \mu_c(1 - F_f(t_0)) + \int_0^{t_0} (1 - F_f(t))dt} = \frac{S(t_0)}{T(t_0)}.$$

Since the steady-state availability of the system is the function of t_0, we can find the optimal rejuvenation schedule t_0^* that maximizes the system availability. Dohi, Popstojanova, and Trivedi [3] derive the following theorem for this optimal rejuvenation schedule.

Theorem: Suppose that the failure time distribution is strictly IFR (increasing failure rate) and $\mu_a > \mu_c$ holds. Define the following nonlinear function:

$$q_A(t_0) = T(t_0) - \{(\mu_a - \mu_c)r_f(t_0) + 1\}S(t_0),$$

where

$$r_f(t) = \frac{1}{1 - F_f(t)} \frac{dF_f(t)}{dt}.$$

(i) If $q_A(0) > 0$ and $q_A(\infty) < 0$, meaning that $dA(t_0)/dt_0|_{t_0=0} > 0$ and $dA(t_0)/dt_0|_{t_0=\infty} < 0$, then there exists a finite and unique optimal software rejuvenation schedule $t_0^*(0 < t_0^* < \infty)$ satisfying $q_A(t_0^*) = 0$, and the corresponding maximum steady-state availability is given by:

$$A(t_0^*) = \frac{1}{(\mu_a - \mu_c)r_f(t_0^*) + 1}.$$

(ii) If $q_A(0) \leq 0$, meaning that $dA(t_0)/dt_0|_{t_0=0} \leq 0$, then the optimal software rejuvenation schedule is $t_0^* = 0$, and the corresponding maximum steady-state availability is $A(0) = \mu_0/(\mu_0 + \mu_c)$.

(iii) If $q_A(\infty) \geq 0$, meaning that $dA(t_0)/dt_0|_{t_0=\infty} \geq$, then the optimal rejuvenation schedule is $t_0^* \to \infty$, and the maximum steady-state availability is $A(\infty) = (\mu_0 + \lambda_f)/(\mu_0 + \mu_a + \lambda_f)$ where λ_f is the finite mean of $F_f(t)$. In other words, in this case, rejuvenation is not to be triggered at all.

Since it is quite natural to assume IFR for software aging phenomena, most likely there exists an optimal software rejuvenation schedule in practice. This result provides further research motivations to investigate the optimal software rejuvenation in different contexts and various types of systems.

Xie, Hong, and Trivedi [4] exploited an SMP to analyze a two-level software rejuvenation policy. The SMP shown in Fig. 5.4 only considers the single-level rejuvenation in which all the applications running on the system become unavailable by system-level rejuvenation. However, it is not always necessary to restart the entire system to recover from an aging

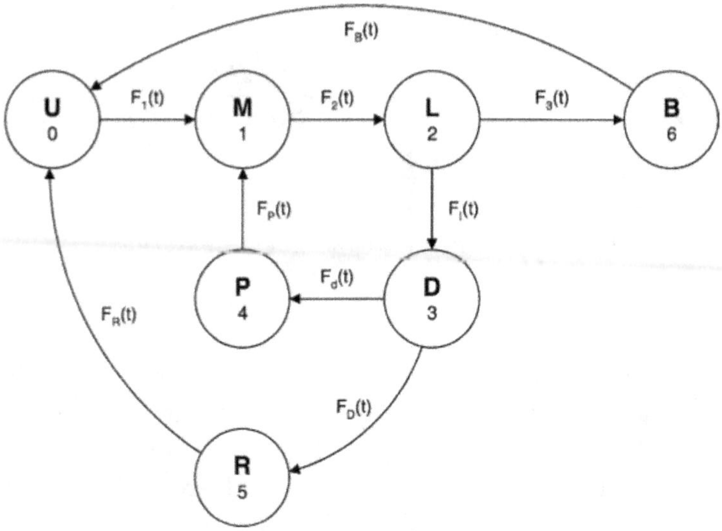

Fig. 5.5. SMP model for two-level software rejuvenation [4].

state of a specific application (refer to Chapter 3). A two-level rejuvenation approach distinguishes service-level partial rejuvenation from the system-level full rejuvenation. In the service-level partial rejuvenation, service will save any necessary data before carrying out rejuvenation, and the operation is resumed in a more efficient state after the completion of rejuvenation. The behavior of the system is modeled by an SMP as depicted in Fig. 5.5.

Starting from the robust state U, the system enters the medium-efficient state M and subsequently goes into the low-efficient state L according to the progress of software aging. From state L, the system may fail, which corresponds to the transition to the reactive reboot state B, or perform rejuvenation at the decision state D. It is assumed that the transition time from state L to state B is distributed as $F_3(t)$. In case partial rejuvenation is chosen, the system enters the partial rejuvenation state P from state D and moves to the state M upon the completion of partial rejuvenation. Otherwise, the system goes to full rejuvenation state R and returns to state U upon the completion of full rejuvenation. Although this SMP model is somewhat more complex than the model in Fig. 5.4, the standard two-stage solution method is still viable, and the steady-state availability of the system is obtained by the sum of the steady-state probabilities of states U, M, and L which are denoted as π_0, π_1 and π_2, respectively. Therefore, the steady-state availability is a function of the time to trigger software rejuvenation (r), and the probability of choosing partial rejuvenation (p). The steady-state availability is given by

$$A(r,p) = \pi_0 + \pi_1 + \pi_2 = \frac{S(r,p)}{S(r,p) + V(r,p)},$$

where

$$S(r,p) = (1 - p + pF_3(r))t_0 + t_1 + \int_0^r (1 - F_3(t))dt,$$
$$V(r,p) = (p - pF_3(r))t_4 + (1 - p - F_3(r) + pF_3(r))t_5 + F_3(r)t_6,$$

and $t_i (i = 0, 1, 4, 5, 6)$ are the mean sojourn times for state i. The optimal values of r and p, which maximize the steady-state availability, can be analyzed by taking the first-order partial derivative of $A(r,p)$ with respect to r and p. By enumerating all (r,p) pairs that are at boundaries and/or in which the first order partial derivatives are zero, it is shown that the maximum availability is achieved at either $p = 0$ or 1, considering the failure rate is either an IFR, a decreasing failure rate (DFR) or a constant failure rate (CFR), and $t_6 > t_5 > t_4$ holds. Note that the model is reduced into the SMP model depicted in Fig. 5.4, when $p = 0$, i.e., there is no partial rejuvenation.

The SMP model was also adopted for analyzing optimal preventive maintenance by Chen and Trivedi [5]. The model is not limited to software aging and rejuvenation, but it is generally applicable to any preventive maintenance technique. Figure 5.6 shows the three-state SMP model representing a preventive maintenance system.

State 0 represents a robust state in which the system is up. State 1 is the state where the system is under preventive maintenance and is unavailable. State 2 is the down state in which the system is forced to undergo the repair process. Let $F_0(t)$, $F_1(t)$, $F_2(t)$ and $F_3(t)$ be the general distribution functions for the times to preventive maintenance, to complete the preventive

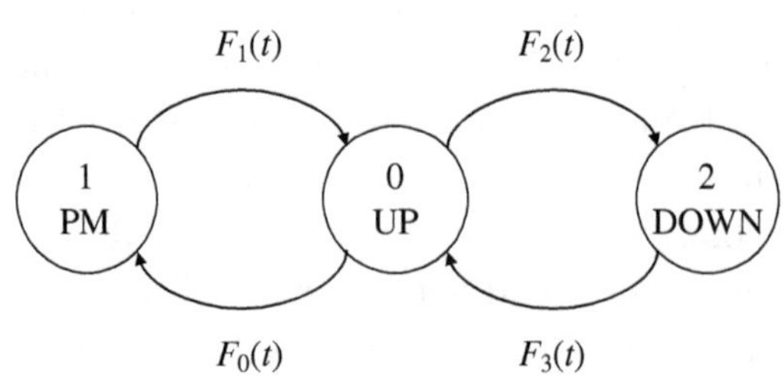

Fig. 5.6. SMP model representing a preventive maintenance system [5].

maintenance, to failure, and to recovery from failure, respectively. The expected sojourn times h_i in state i are given by

$$h_0 = \int_0^\infty (1 - F_0(t))(1 - F_2(t))dt,$$

$$h_1 = \int_0^\infty (1 - F_1(t))dt,$$

$$h_2 = \int_0^\infty (1 - F_3(t))dt.$$

The steady-state availability of the system as a function of the time to maintenance t_0 is given by

$$A(t_0) = \frac{h_0}{h_0 + (1 - F_2(t_0))h_1 + F_2(t_0)h_2}.$$

Similar to the theorem presented before, there exists a unique optimal time to trigger preventive maintenance when $h_1 < h_2$ holds and $F_2(t)$ is IFR. Assuming a hypo-exponential distribution for $F_2(t)$, the optimal time to maintenance (TTM) is derived through numerical experiments as shown in Fig. 5.7. In this experiment, the mean sojourn time for state 1 is assumed to

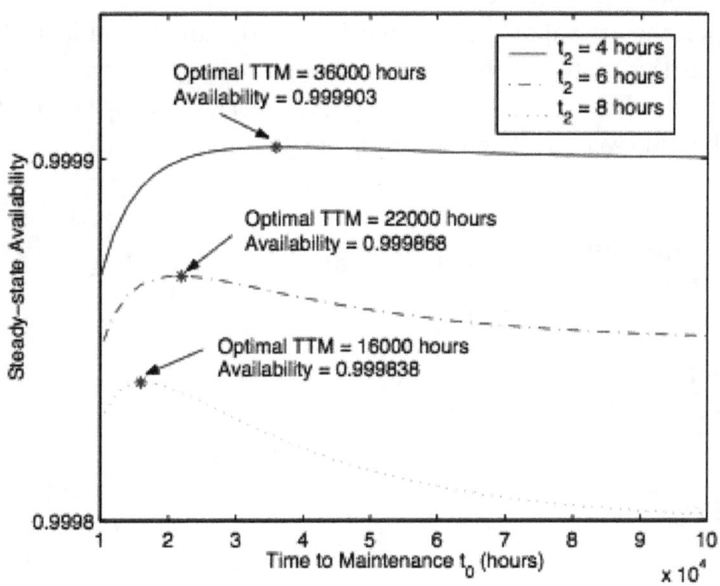

Fig. 5.7. Steady-state availability vs. time to maintenance under different repair times [5].

be 1 hour and the parameters of the 2-stage hypo-exponential distribution are chosen as $(\lambda_1, \lambda_2) = (0.00004, 0.000067)$.

The three-state SMP model is considered as a reduced version of time-based software rejuvenation and also the simplest version to date, and hence it is used as a reference building block to create further comprehensive models [6, 8, 10, 11].

Bao, Sun, and Trivedi [6] utilized the SMP model to build a hierarchical model for analyzing software aging and rejuvenation in software systems suffering from performance degradation caused by memory leaks. The hierarchical model consists of a non-homogeneous Markov chain, which is used to represent the performance degradation process, and an SMP used to represent software rejuvenation. The three-state SMP is used as a top level of the hierarchical model, and its failure rate is computed in a lower-level non-homogeneous Markov chain. Figure 5.8 shows the components of the hierarchical model.

In the lower-level performance degradation model, the state labeled $k(k \geq 0)$ represents the system state, where k-independent application processes each hold a portion of memory resource. The resource requests are independent of each other and arrive from a Poisson source with rate λ. A request is granted when sufficient memory is available; otherwise the system fails, which is represented by a transition to the sink state. The coefficient $\xi[k, l(t)]$ is the conditional probability that the system fails in state k upon the arrival of a new request while the amount of leaked resource at time t in the system is $l(t)$. The holding memory at state k is released at the rate μ_k. Let $\pi(t) = [\pi_0(t), \pi_1(t), \ldots, \pi_n(t), \pi_{sink}(t)]$ be the transient state probability vector. The instantaneous failure rate of the system can be

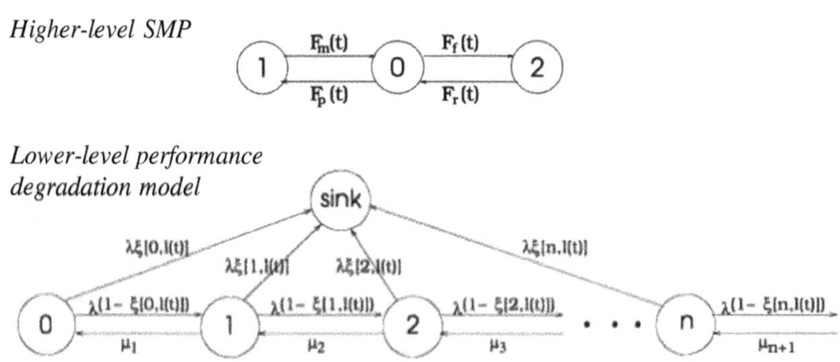

Fig. 5.8. A hierarchical model for software aging and rejuvenation [6].

expressed as

$$h(t) = \frac{\frac{d\pi_{\text{sink}}(t,l(t))}{dt}}{1 - \pi_{\text{sink}}(t, l(t))} = \frac{\lambda \sum_k \xi[k, l(t)]\pi_k(t, l(t))}{\sum_k \pi_k(t, l(t))}.$$

This failure rate is applied for the higher-level SMP to characterize the distribution function for system failure $F_f(t)$. In the SMP, software rejuvenation is performed at the fixed time interval τ, and hence the distribution function for the time to trigger software rejuvenation is given by $F_p(t) = \mathrm{u}(t - \tau)$, which is the unit step function at τ. By the analytical result in [5], the steady-state system availability is given by

$$A(\tau) = \frac{h_0}{h_0 + (1 - F_f(\tau))h_1 + F_f(\tau)h_2},$$

where $F_f(\tau) = \pi_{\text{sink}}(\tau)$ and

$$h_0 = \tau(1 - \pi_{\text{sink}}(\tau)) + \lambda \int_0^{\tau} t \sum_k \xi[k, l(t)]\pi_k(t)dt,$$

$$h_1 = \int_0^{\infty} (1 - F_m(t))dt,$$

$$h_2 = \int_0^{\infty} (1 - F_r(t))dt$$

When resource leaks exist, the failure rate increases monotonically [6], and hence the analysis of steady-state system availability as the function of τ will yield the optimum software rejuvenation schedule.

While a non-homogeneous Markov chain is used to represent memory leaking in the above case, Garg, Puliafito, Telek, and Trivedi [7] used a non-homogeneous CTMC to represent the states of the transaction process in a transaction-based software system. Depending on the severity of software aging, the software failure rate and service time performance could be affected. Let $\mu(\cdot)$ and $\rho(\cdot)$ be the general functions for transaction service rate and system failure rate, respectively. These functions could directly depend on the time (i.e., $\mu(t), \rho(t)$), or can be the functions of instantaneous load on the system, or mean accumulated work done by the software system in a given time interval, or a combination of the three. In any case, the transaction processing state can be captured by a non-homogeneous CTMC as shown in Fig. 5.9. A transaction arrives from a Poisson source with rate λ, and it is processed at service rate $\mu(\cdot)$ which depends on aging state. The process is

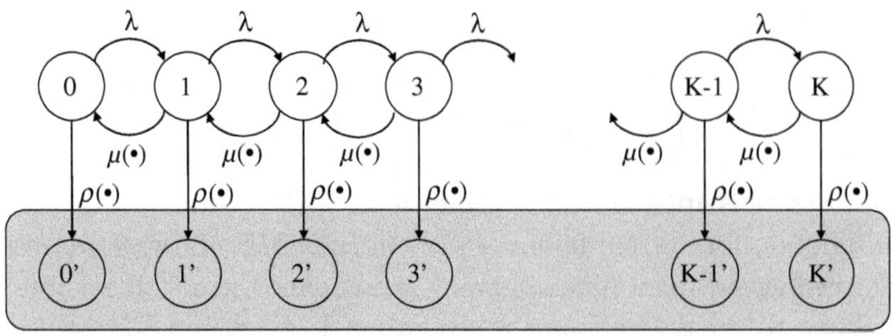

Fig. 5.9. Nonhomogeneous CMTC for transaction processing system with software aging [7].

Table 5.1. Statistics for workload clusters [8].

Cluster No.	Cluster Centroid				% of Data Points
	cpuContextSwitch	sysCall	pageOut	pageIn	
1	45054.00	136913.00	3.44	319.56	2.67
2	21177.36	38859.81	0.32	60.78	9.06
3	15734.65	54056.27	0.27	14.45	6.55
4	37825.76	40912.18	0.91	12.21	11.77
5	11013.22	38682.46	0.03	10.43	42.87
6	67290.83	37246.76	7.58	19.88	4.93
7	10003.94	32067.20	0.01	9.61	21.23
8	197934.42	67822.48	415.71	184.38	0.93

terminated when the system encounters a failure or rejuvenation is triggered following a specific policy. By tracking the number of transactions in the system, the impact of rejuvenation on the probability of the transaction losses and the expected response time can be computed.

Hierarchical models can be used to combine the analytical model with statistical models constructed from real observations of system workloads. Vaidyanathan and Trivedi [8] presented a comprehensive model for software rejuvenation in which a lower-level semi-Markov reward model is constructed from workload and resource usage data collected from a UNIX operating system, and a higher-level SMP is used to analyze the availability of the system. The statistical model captures the dynamics of resource usage, and the model estimates the time to resource exhaustion. The estimated time to resource exhaustion is then applied to the SMP model for system availability analysis. In order to build a semi-Markov reward model from real monitoring data, Vaidyanathan and Trivedi [8] use a clustering method and obtain eight different clusters of data points as shown in Table 5.1.

The columns *cpuContextSwitch*, *sysCall*, *pageOut*, and *pageIn* are the chosen variables from the measured data to characterize the workload, and their cluster centroids are summarized in the table.

Assuming each cluster represents a workload state of the system, the transition probability from state i to state j can be estimated from the sample data by

$$p_{ij} = \frac{\textit{observed no. of transitions from state } i \textit{ to state } j}{\textit{total observed no. of transitions from state } i}.$$

On the other hand, the sojourn time distribution for each state is fitted with either 2-stage hyper-exponential or 2-stage hypo-exponential distributions. While the transition probability matrix $P = (p_{ij})$ and the sojourn time distributions can characterize the SMP with respect to workload state transitions, the resource usage in each state is incorporated by assigning a reward to the state. The estimated slopes for *usedSwapSpace* and *realMemoryFree* are assigned as reward rates to the states, and they are used to compute the estimated time to resource exhaustion. In the higher-level SMP, the distribution function of time to failure is approximated by a 2-stage Erlang distribution, whose mean value is given by the estimated time to resource exhaustion. Since an Erlang distribution is an IFR distribution, the optimal software rejuvenation schedule can be obtained by the analysis of the SMP.

Although the analysis of optimal software rejuvenation schedules depends on the distribution function of the time to system failure, in practice such a distribution is not easy to acquire due to the lack of failure data. The accelerated life test (ALT) for software aging [9] provides a powerful solution to this issue by estimating the lifetime distribution from the lifetime data obtained under accelerated stresses. Zhao, Jin, Trivedi and Matias Jr. [10] first applied ALT to web application systems into which memory leak faults have been injected and the failure time distribution is fitted to the Inverse Power Law (IPL) Weibull distribution and IPL lognormal distribution. The IPL Weibull distribution is given by

$$f(t,s) = \beta k s^w (k s^w t)^{\beta-1} e^{-(k s^w t)^\beta},$$

where β is the shape parameter of Weibull distribution, k and w are IPL model parameters, and s is the stress level of ALT. β, k, and w can be estimated through the maximum likelihood method. For example, Table 5.2 presents the estimated values of β, k, and w with a 90% confidence interval (CI) [11].

Table 5.2. IPL-Weibull parameter [11].

Parameter	ML Estimate	90% CI Lower	90% CI Upper
β	17.3682	13.7767	21.8959
k	9E-6	8E-6	1.1E-5
w	0.9796	0.9397	1.0195

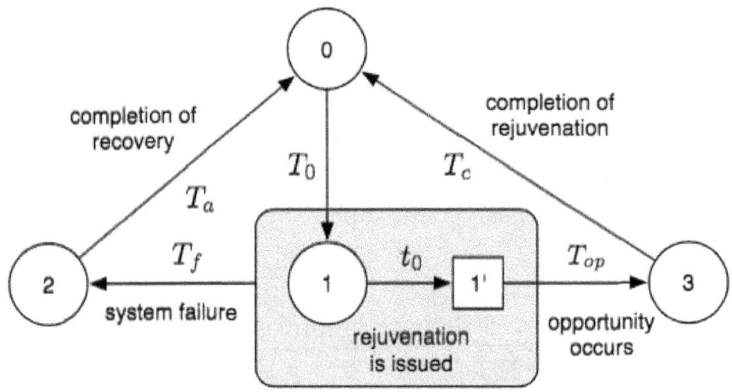

Fig. 5.10. State transition diagram for opportunity-based rejuvenation model [13].

The estimated IPL Weibull distribution is then used as the failure time distribution in the three-state SMP model (Fig. 5.6), and the optimal software rejuvenation schedule can be obtained through the analysis of the SMP.

Based on the SMP model presented in [2], Okamura and Dohi [12] extended the original model to consider the opportunity time-triggered rejuvenation policy, where software rejuvenation is performed at the first opportunity after the scheduled trigger time of rejuvenation. The policy is proposed to address the problem of time-based software rejuvenation in which software rejuvenation is performed without considering the operational condition of the software. In practice, the application may not be stopped depending on the software's operational state. The chance to perform rejuvenation after the scheduled rejuvenation time is called opportunity. In order to incorporate such an opportunity waiting condition, the original SMP model [2] is extended as shown in Fig. 5.10.

In addition to the four states in the original model, the failure-probable state, in which one is waiting for an opportunity, is inserted as state 1'. The system can fail from either state 1 or state 1', but the rejuvenation will be performed only after state 1' is visited. The top represents the duration of the wait for the first rejuvenation opportunity occurrence from state 1' and its distribution function has a dependency on time to trigger rejuvenation t_0, which can be expressed as $F_{op}(s; t_0)$. When we assume that the opportunity will occur following a renewal process, which is independent of the system behavior, $F_{op}(s; t_0)$ is given by

$$F_{op}(s; t_0) = \frac{1}{E[Y]} \int_0^s (1 - G(t))dt,$$

where Y is the random variable representing the time interval between the consecutive occurrence of opportunities with the distribution function $G(t)$. $F_{op}(s; t_0)$ is essentially the equilibrium distribution in the renewal process theory [14]. In this case, it is proved that the optimal trigger time of rejuvenation exists if the failure time distribution is IFR [13]. Similarly, Okamura and Dohi [13] have shown that this is the sufficient condition for the existence of the optimal trigger time under the opportunity time-triggered rejuvenation policy, where the opportunity process follows an independent Markovian arrival process.

Machida, Nicola, and Trivedi [15] introduced an SMP to model software aging and rejuvenation in a server-virtualized system and analyze the completion time of the job running on the system. Job completion time, in general, is another essential performance measure of the software system, while many previous studies focus on steady-state system availability or downtime costs. In order to compute the job completion time, the progress of job execution on the system needs to be tracked along with the state transitions of the system. In [15], the system state transition is modeled by an SMP and the distribution of job completion time on the system is computed through the framework presented by Kulkarni, Nicola, and Trivedi [16]. Figure 5.11 shows the SMP model for a virtualized server with Cold-VM rejuvenation in which the execution of the VM is stopped and the running job needs to restart from its beginning after VMM rejuvenation.

The VMM failure in State 3, the VM failure in State 4, and the VMM rejuvenation in State 5 are categorized as preemptive-repeat (*prt*) states, which are represented as shaded circles. When the system enters a *prt* state, all the intermediate results of job execution are lost, and the job needs to be restarted from the beginning. As a result of the analysis using the framework, the job completion time distribution is derived in the form of

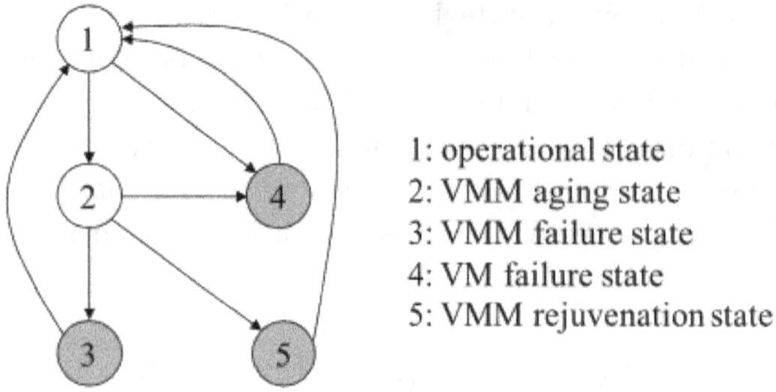

Fig. 5.11. SMP model for a virtualized server with Cold-VM rejuvenation [15].

the Laplace-Stieltjes transform (LST).

$$F^{\sim}(s) = \int_0^{\infty} e^{-st} dF(t),$$

where $F(t), t > 0$ is the original distribution function of the job completion time. For the Cold-VM rejuvenation case, the LST of the job completion time is given by

$$F^{\sim}_{cold}(s) = \sum_{k=1}^{5} L^{\sim}_{k}(s, x) \cdot \pi_k,$$

$$L^{\sim}_{i}(s, x) = \begin{cases} M^{\sim}_{i}(s, x), & i = 1, 2 \\ Y^{\sim}_{i}(s) M^{\sim}_{1}(s, x), & i = 3, 4, 5, \end{cases}$$

where π_k is the steady-state probability that the system is in state k, $M^{\sim}_{i}(s, x)$ is the LST of the job completion time conditioned by starting upon entry to state i, and $Y^{\sim}_{i}(s)$ is the LST of the remaining time in state i. The approximate original distribution can be obtained by the numerical inversion technique (e.g., [45]).

Figure 5.12 shows numerical examples, in which the software exhibits a better job completion time performance after Cold-VM rejuvenation than without rejuvenation (i.e., when VMM aging occurs). The job completion time performance of the software is even better with Warm-VM rejuvenation. In Warm-VM rejuvenation, the job running on the VM is suspended during VMM rejuvenation, and its execution state is resumed after the completion of the rejuvenation. Hence, State 5 in the Warm-VM rejuvenation case is changed to the preemptive-resume (*prs*) state instead of the *prt* state. It has been shown that the effectiveness of Cold-VM rejuvenation in terms of

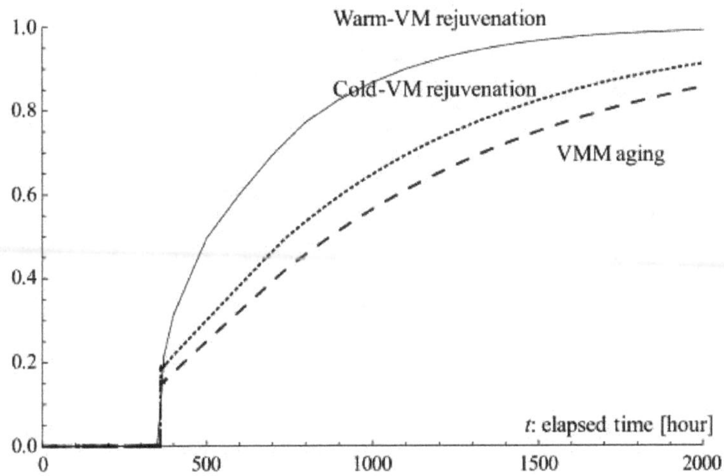

Fig. 5.12. Job completion time distribution obtained through numerical inversion of LST.

job completion time performance is dominated by the level of performance degradation rather than the hazard rate function of VMM failure [15].

5.3. Stochastic Petri Nets

Markov models allow us to characterize the fundamental behavior of software aging and rejuvenation as presented in the literature. The analytic solutions of such models give solid theoretical results such as the condition where a finite and unique optimal rejuvenation schedule exists. However, as the scale of software systems grows, the needed size of state spaces expands exponentially; thus the scalability issue of Markov models arises. Markov chains do not readily model complex large-scale systems, and the solution to large-scale Markov chains often requires formidable efforts. An alternative to dealing with the scalability issues is to employ higher-level representation of stochastic processes.

Petri nets (PNs) [38] are a family of formalisms very well suited for modeling several system types, since concurrency, synchronization, and communication mechanisms as well as deterministic and probabilistic delays are naturally represented. Molloy [35], Florin and Natkin [39] independently proposed stochastic Petri nets (SPNs) [35–37] as a stochastic extension of the untimed Petri net model. Such a model allows the association of stochastic delays to transitions. Since then, many extensions have been proposed to the basic SPN models [36, 37]. In the following, we will review the applications of SPN to model software aging and rejuvenation for complex systems.

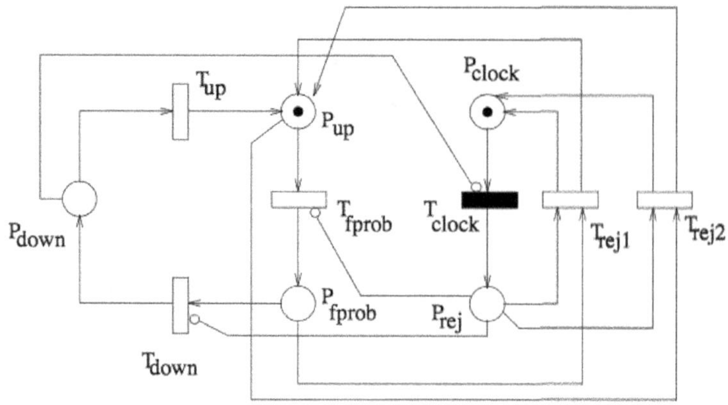

Fig. 5.13. MRSPN model for software rejuvenation [17].

The initial attempt to apply SPN to model software rejuvenation systems was carried out by Garg, Puliafito, Telek, and Trivedi [17]. In order to deal with the deterministic transition for a rejuvenation trigger, a Markov regenerative stochastic Petri net (MRSPN), which allows immediate and generally-distributed firing time, was used. Although the underlying stochastic process of the MRSPN is not a CTMC, it falls into the class of Markov regenerative processes (MRGPs) that can be analyzed by Markov renewal theory. Figure 5.13 shows the MRSPN for the time-based software rejuvenation system.

The places P_{up}, P_{fprob}, and P_{down} represent the robust, failure-probable and down local states of the system, respectively. Meanwhile, the transitions T_{fprob}, T_{down}, and T_{up} represent the state transitions to P_{fprob}, P_{down}, and P_{up}, whose transition rates are exponentially distributed. Time-based software rejuvenation is represented by the deterministic transition T_{clock} depicted as a filled rectangular. A token in P_{clock} is removed when the fixed time interval passes, and subsequently, a token is deposited in the place P_{rej}, representing the rejuvenation state. From MRSPN in Fig. 5.13, the reachability graph can be obtained as shown in Fig. 5.14, where the label of each state indicates the net markings in (P_{up}, P_{fprob}, P_{down}, P_{clock}, P_{rej}). For example, (10010) means that one token is separately stored in places P_{up} and P_{clock}, which represents the upstate.

Since the reachability graph has a non-regenerative marking that is labeled (01010), the graph is essentially an MRGP. By solving the MRGP, we can obtain the steady-state probability of each marking. The steady-state availability of the system can be computed by the sum of steady-state

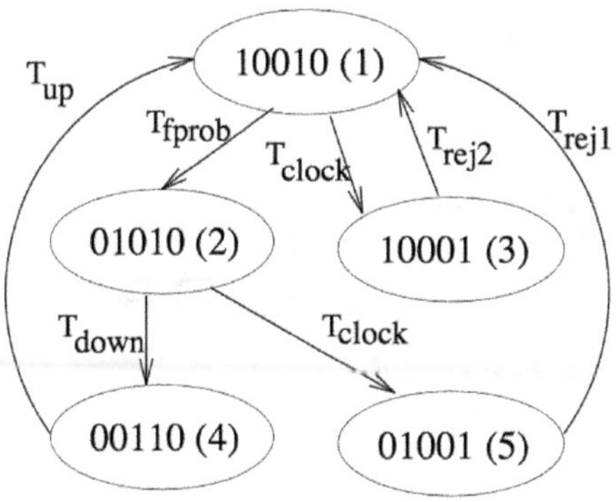

Fig. 5.14. Reachability graph for the MRSPN model [17].

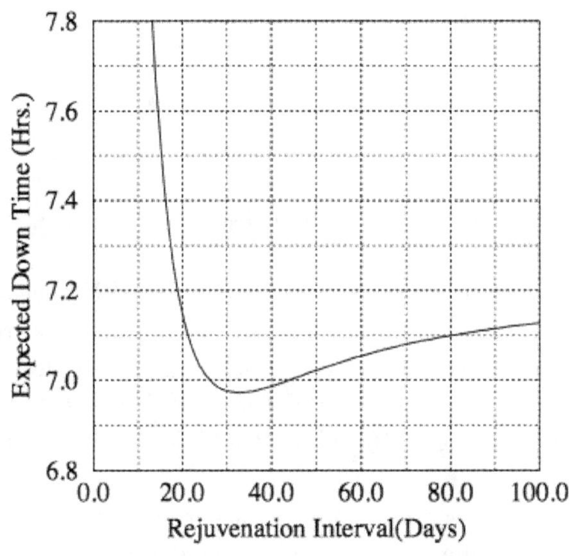

Fig. 5.15. Steady-state expected downtime versus rejuvenation interval [17].

probabilities for the markings (10010) and (01010). A numerical experiment shows an optimal rejuvenation interval to trigger software rejuvenation that minimizes the expected downtime (see Fig. 5.15).

It is worth noting that this time-based software rejuvenation model can be reduced into a three-state SMP model, but the better expressiveness that originates from SPN opens up further exploration of comprehensive modeling for complex and large-scale systems.

Bobbio *et al.* [18] introduced fluid stochastic Petri nets (FSPNs) to model the dynamics of aging software systems with checkpointing, software

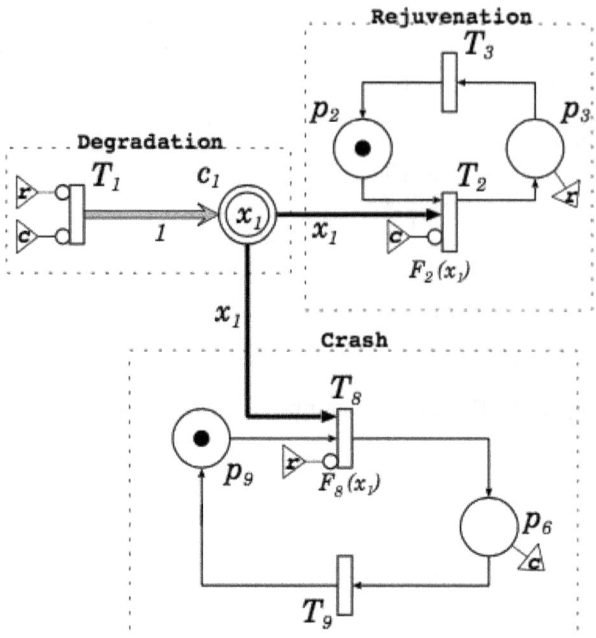

Fig. 5.16. FSPN model for a software rejuvenation system [18].

rejuvenation, and self-restoration. FSPN extends SPN such that the model can capture the continuous flow of transitions. Since software aging can be regarded as an error accumulation process, it can be modeled by a continuous flow to the continuous state. By FSPN, the behavior of software rejuvenation can be represented as Fig. 5.16, which could be a component of the whole system.

The subnet-labeled degradation consists of transition T_1 and continuous place c_1, whose marking x_1 represents the degradation level. Transition T_1 pumps fluid in place c_1 and represents the increase of the system degradation level unless there are tokens in p_3 or p_6. In the subnet-labeled rejuvenation, the transitions T_2 and T_3 represent the trigger and completion of rejuvenation, respectively. The firing rate $F_2(x_1)$ depends on the fluid level in c_1. Alternatively, the subnet-labeled crash represents the system failure and reactive recovery process. Transition T_8 and T_9 correspond to the system failure and reactive recovery transitions, respectively. The firing rate $F_8(x_1)$ also depends on the fluid level in c_1. Those subnets are further integrated with the subnets of workload, checkpointing and self-restoration [18].

So far, we have reviewed the system rejuvenation for a single instance of a software process. When multiple instances of software executions are

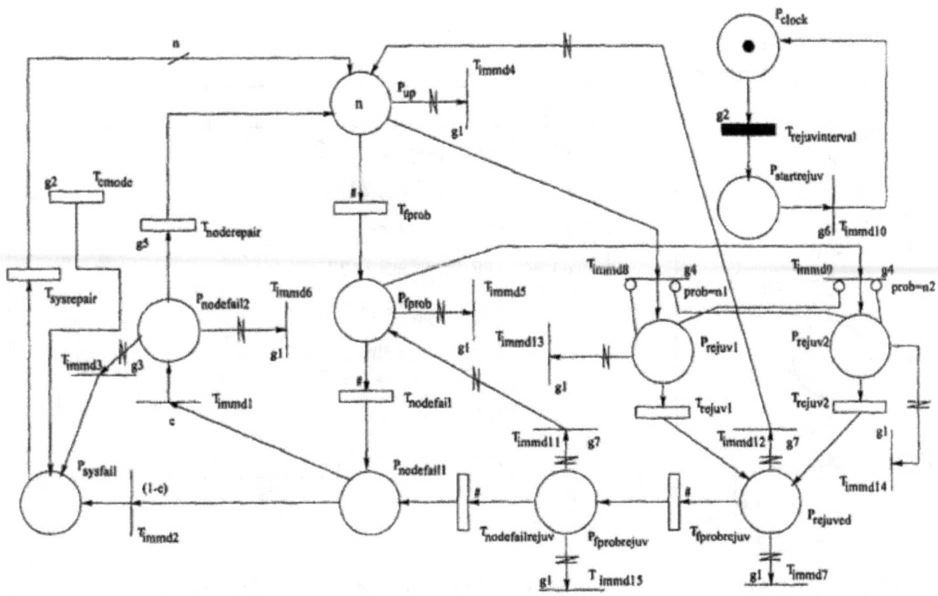

Fig. 5.17. SRN for cluster system employing time-based rejuvenation [19, 20].

independently subject to aging and forced to perform rejuvenation, the state-space becomes huge. Vaidyanathan, Harper, Hunter, and Trivedi [19] modeled and analyzed software rejuvenation in cluster systems by using stochastic reward nets (SRNs), which introduce reward assignment to SPN. In an SRN, every tangible marking can be associated with a reward rate. It can be shown that an SRN is mapped into a Markov Reward model and thus that a variety of reward-based measures can be specified and calculated by the SRN. The software rejuvenation model for the cluster systems consisting of n nodes is presented in Fig. 5.17.

At the beginning, all the n nodes are in the robust state, which is represented by tokens in place P_{up}. As time goes by, each node eventually transits to a failure-probable state (place P_{fprob}) and subsequently fails (place $P_{nodeFail}$). A node can be successfully repaired with probability c or fail to be repaired with a probability (1-c), leading to a system failure (all n nodes are down). Time-based rejuvenation is represented by the deterministic transition $T_{rejinterval}$, which fires every d time units. Its firing stores a token in place $P_{startrejuv}$. If there are tokens in places P_{up} or P_{fprob}, immediate transitions T_{immd8} and T_{immd9} are enabled respectively. All the clustered nodes are rejuvenated in a sequence. After a node has been rejuvenated, it goes back to the robust state, represented by tokens in place $P_{rejuved}$.

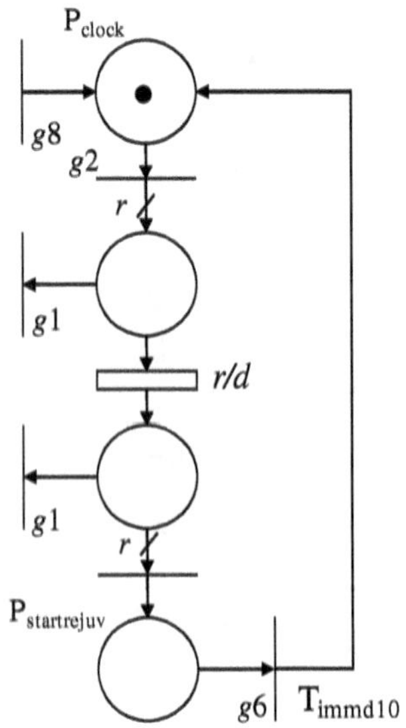

Guard	Function
g1	$(\#P_{sysfail} == 1)\ ?\ 1 : 0$
g2	$(\#P_{sysfail}\ != 1)\ ?\ 1 : 0$
g3	$(\#P_{nodefail2} + \#P_{rejuv1} + \#P_{rejuv2} == a)\ ?\ 1 : 0$
g4	$(\#P_{startrejuv} == 1)\ ?\ 1 : 0$
g5	$(\#P_{startrejuv}\ != 1)\ ?\ 1 : 0$
g6	$(\#P_{nodefail2} + \#P_{rejuved} + \#P_{fprobrejuv} == n \mid\mid \#P_{sysfail} == 1 \mid\mid \#P_{nodefail2} == a\text{-}1)\ ?\ 1 : 0$
g7	$(\#P_{clock} == 1)\ ?\ 1 : 0$
g8	$(\#P_{sysfail}\ != 1)\ ?\ 1 : 0$

Fig. 5.18. R-Stage Erlang approximation of deterministic transition and guard functions.

Table 5.3. Reward functions [19].

Unavailability	$(\#P_{sysfail} == 1)\ ?\ 1 : 0$
Cost	$\#P_{rejuv} * cost_{rejuv} + \#P_{nodefail2} * cost_{nodefail} + \#P_{sysfail} + cost_{sysfail}$

The rejuvenation of the cluster completes when all n nodes are rejuvenated when the immediate transition T_{immd10} becomes enabled. An r-stage Erlang distribution can approximate the deterministic transition in the clock subnet. Each stage of the Erlang distribution is exponentially distributed with mean d/r. The approximated SRN with the associated guard functions are shown in Fig. 5.18.

The reward functions to evaluate the effects of cluster rejuvenation are given in Table 5.3.

The expected unavailability is computed as the expected number of tokens in place $P_{sysfail}$, while the expected cost can be computed as the sum of the costs due to rejuvenation, node failures, and system failures. With these measures, the optimal rejuvenation interval can be obtained by using the tool Stochastic Petri Net Package (SPNP) [21].

For cluster systems offering web application services the good performance as well as the availability of the service is important. Performability measures can be useful for the quantification of such services. The rejuvenation impact on the performability of a cluster system was analyzed by Wang, Xie, and Trivedi [22] by taking into account workload intensity and fluctuation.

They adopted deterministic and stochastic Petri nets (DSPNs) [42] to model the cluster systems under the diverse workload and different rejuvenation policies. DSPN is a class of MRSPN such that each transition in the model is either exponentially distributed or deterministic, besides adopting immediate transitions. While the cluster system is modeled by an SRN similar to the one in [19], the DSPN model introduces an additional subnet for workload status as shown in Fig. 5.19. A token is deposited in either $\mathrm{P}_{\mathrm{peak}}$ or $\mathrm{P}_{\mathrm{offpeak}}$, which represents the peak period or off-peak period, respectively. Transitions $\mathrm{T}_{\mathrm{peak}}$ and $\mathrm{T}_{\mathrm{offpeak}}$ fire in a deterministic time interval, and thus the entire model becomes a DSPN. Depending on the workload status, request arrival rates are different, and also impact the failure rate of a server. To analyze the performability, the performance of a cluster system is modeled as an $M/M/i/m+i$ queue (see Fig. 5.20), where i is the number of servers in the system, and m is the maximum queue length.

The parameter values are determined by the corresponding marking of the DSPN model. For marking c of the DSPN model, $i(c)$ is computed as the sum of the number of tokens in P_{up}, $\mathrm{P}_{\mathrm{rejuved}}$, $\mathrm{P}_{\mathrm{fprone}}$, and $\mathrm{P}_{\mathrm{fpronerej}}$.

$$i(c) = \#\mathrm{P}_{\mathrm{up}}(c) + \#\mathrm{P}_{\mathrm{rejuved}}(c) + \#\mathrm{P}_{\mathrm{fprone}}(c) + \#\mathrm{P}_{\mathrm{fpronerej}}(c).$$

Request arrival rate $\lambda(c)$ changes depending on the workload state as

$$\lambda(c) = \begin{cases} \lambda_{\mathrm{peak}}, & \text{if } \#P_{\mathrm{peak}}(c) = 1 \\ \lambda_{\mathrm{offpeak}}, & \text{if } \#P_{\mathrm{offpeak}}(c) = 1. \end{cases}$$

Let μ_{up} and μ_{fp} denote the service rates for up servers and failure-prone servers, respectively. The equivalent service rate μ for the marking c of the DSPN is computed as

$$\mu(c) = \frac{\mu_{\mathrm{up}}(\#P_{\mathrm{up}}(c) + \#P_{\mathrm{rejuved}}(c)) + \mu_{\mathrm{fp}}(\#P_{\mathrm{fprone}}(c) + \#P_{\mathrm{fpronerej}}(c))}{i}.$$

The blocking probability and system throughput can be computed from the $M/M/i/m+i$ model [23]. Specifically, the blocking probability is

$$P_b(c) = \frac{\lambda(c)^{m+i}}{i^m \cdot i! \cdot \mu(c)^{m+i}} \cdot \frac{1}{\sum_{k=0}^{i} \frac{\lambda(c)^k}{k! \cdot \mu(c)^k} + \sum_{k=i+1}^{i+m} \frac{\lambda(c)^k}{i^{k-i} \cdot i! \cdot \mu(c)^k}},$$

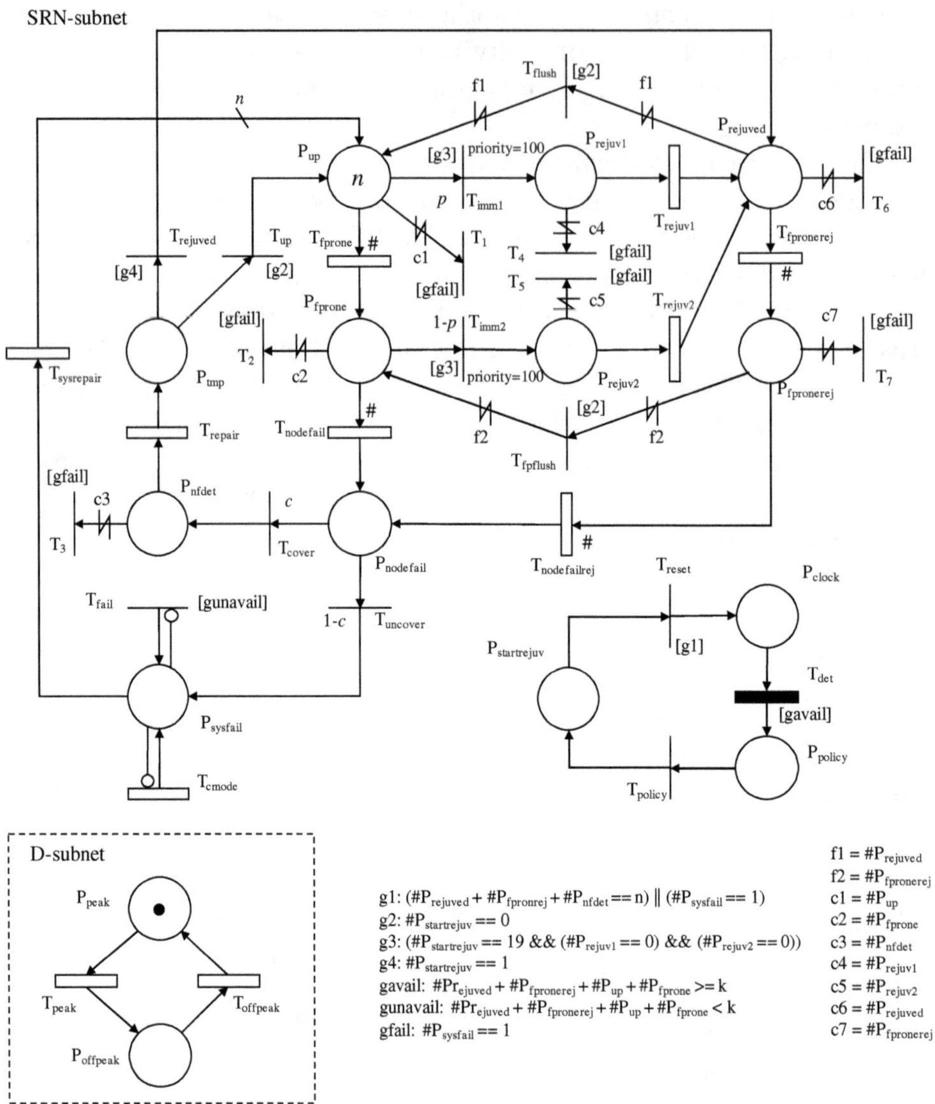

Fig. 5.19. DSPN for cluster rejuvenation system with periodic workload changes [22].

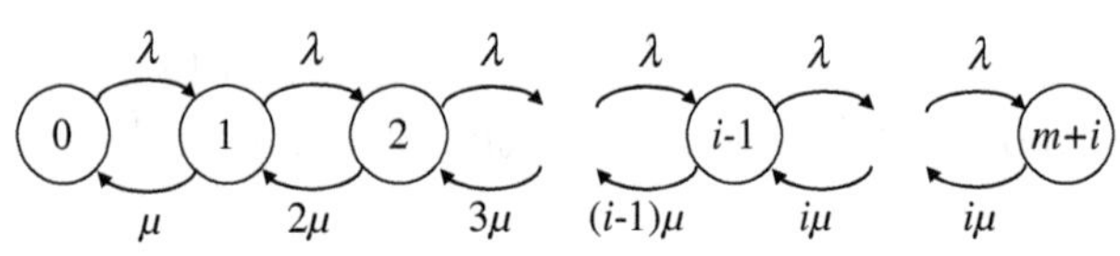

Fig. 5.20. A $M/M/i/m+i$ queue.

thus the throughput is given by $T_{\text{put}}(c) = \lambda(c) \cdot (1 - P_b(c))$. The results of these numerical experiments imply the following general policy for rejuvenation scheduling. If the rejuvenation is scheduled early in the peak period, the best rejuvenation policy is to perform rejuvenation immediately. Such a strategy can reduce the job blocking probability, and increase the system throughput. Otherwise, it should be delayed until the next off-peak period begins [22].

Nowadays, server virtualization has become a popular way to build server systems with virtual machines (VMs). Since a VM is essentially instantiated as a software process on top of server visualization software, both the VM and virtualization software can entail a risk of software aging. Machida, Kim, and Trivedi [24, 25] investigated the software aging and rejuvenation techniques for server virtualized systems and modeled the system behavior using an SRN. By leveraging the modularity of SRN formalism, three different rejuvenation methodologies are modeled simultaneously; namely Cold-VM rejuvenation, Warm-VM rejuvenation, and Migrate-VM rejuvenation. Figure 5.21 shows an SRN model for a server virtualized system with Cold-VM rejuvenation.

The model consists of four subnets; (a) a Virtual Machine Monitor (VMM) model, (b) a VMM clock model, (c) a VM model and (d) a VM clock model. The VMM model represents the software aging and rejuvenation process of a host server with a VMM. VMM software rejuvenation is triggered by the timer represented by the VMM clock model. The VM model represents the state transition of a VM running on the host. The execution of the VM will stop when the underlying VMM goes for rejuvenation or fails. Meanwhile, the VM also has a risk of software aging, and software rejuvenation is applied by following the clock represented by the VM clock model. Thus, system availability is affected by the two rejuvenation parameters; the VM rejuvenation trigger interval and the VMM rejuvenation trigger interval. As a numerical example in Fig. 5.22 shows, there exists the optimal combination of those parameters, which maximizes the steady-state availability of the VM.

In Cold-VM rejuvenation, the VM running on the host is also stopped at the VMM rejuvenation, and it can be restarted after the VMM rejuvenation. On the other hand, in Warm-VM rejuvenation, the VM is suspended before the VMM rejuvenation is triggered, and its execution is resumed at the completion of the VMM rejuvenation. It is intuitive that Warm-VM rejuvenation is better for the high-availability of the VM. However, numerical experiments with a sensitivity analysis on the rejuvenation trigger interval of

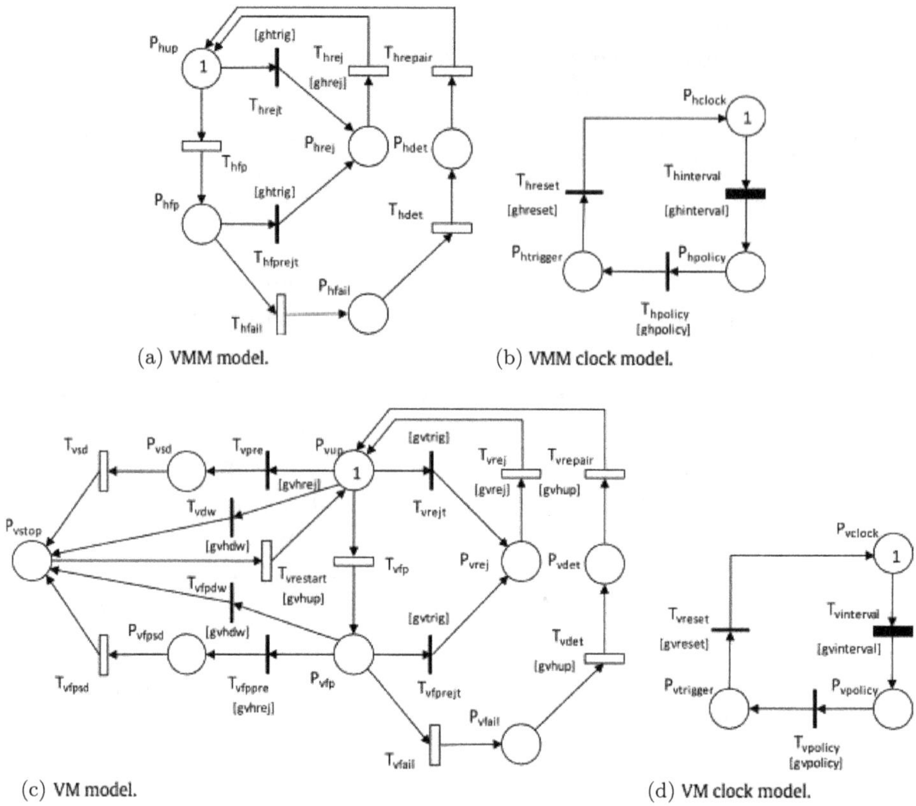

(a) VMM model. (b) VMM clock model.

(c) VM model. (d) VM clock model.

Fig. 5.21. SRN model for a server virtualized system with Cold-VM rejuvenation [25].

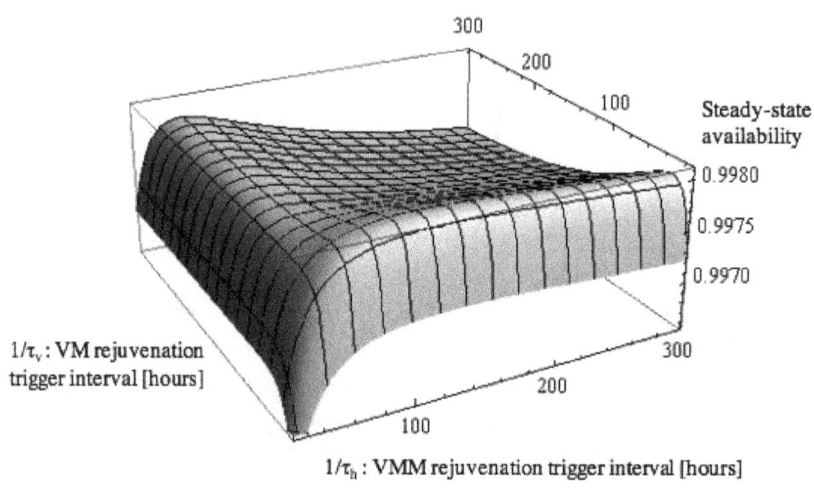

Fig. 5.22. Steady-state availability of the system with Cold-VM rejuvenation.

the VM reveal that the Cold-VM rejuvenation technique achieves higher VM availability when the interval is long. The effectiveness of VMM rejuvenation with live VM migration is also extensively studied in Machida, Kim, and Trivedi [25].

Melo, Maciel, Araujo, Matos, and Araujo [26] also considered the combination of live VM migration and VMM rejuvenation in a cloud computing environment. The model is composed of three sub-models: a) the ManagementServer Model, b) the Clock Model and c) the System Model. The ManagementServer Model is a simple availability model, which represents the behavior of the Management Server of the cloud. Times to failure and repair for this sub-model (MS_fail and MS_repair, respectively) are retrieved from a reliability block diagram (RBD) model depicted in Fig. 5.23(b).

The transition Trigger in Clock Model fires after an established deterministic time, and deposits a token in the place ReadyToMigrate. The ResetClock transition has a guard function enabling the transition only when the migration process is over. The System Model represents the main events related to the Main Node, the Standby Node, and the VM. The place MN_UP represents that the Main Node and its VM are running correctly. From

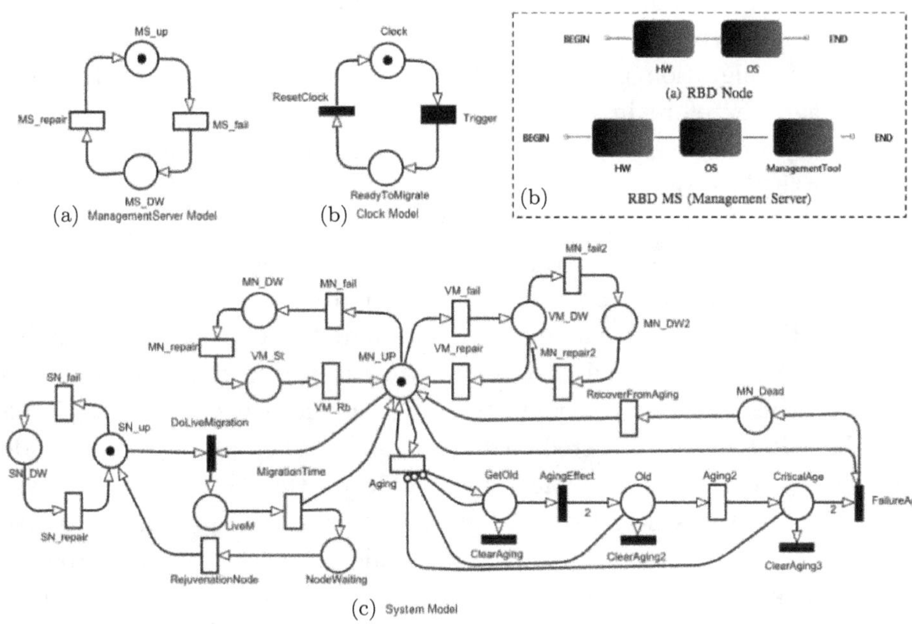

Fig. 5.23. A hierarchical model for a virtualized system with live VM migration.

this point, several transitions can be fired. MN_fail fires when an internal (non-aging) failure occurs on the Main Node. As the VM depends on the node, the system fails when this transition is fired. A two-step process leads to the recovery. First, the Main Node is repaired, in an attempt to solve this problem. After that, the VM needs to be restarted until the system becomes operational again. The time values for the transitions MN_fail and MN_repair are retrieved from the RBD model depicted in Fig. 5.23(a). Another possibility when the system is running correctly is VM failure. In the model, this is represented by firing the transition VM_fail, which deposits one token in the VM_DW place. This place represents that the VM is failed. At this point, two events are possible. Either the VM is repaired, so the system returns to operating state, or the Main Node also fails. If the second possibility occurs, first the problem on the Main Node is solved, thus allowing the repair of the VM. In any case, the system only goes up when both (the VM and Main Node) are working. A 3-phase Erlang sub-net is used to model the VMM aging phenomenon so that the model can represent an increasing failure rate. The transitions Aging and Aging2 represent the phases of the sub-net. The transitions ClearAging, ClearAging2, and ClearAging3 represent events, which clear the VMM aging. The model considers that these events occur when the Main Node or the VM fails, since the particular repair actions involve rejuvenation actions, and there is no reason to accumulate aging when the VM is not working. When a live migration is performed, the VM is moved to a fresh VMM environment, therefore justifying the removal of aging effects. If none of these events occur, the VMM achieves a critical age, which leads to failure (transition FailureAging fires). After that, the node reaches an inactive state (MN_Dead) where it needs recovery from aging effects (transition RecoverFromAging), so the system returns to an upstate. When there is a token in SN_up, the spare machine is up and can receive a VM by live migration. However, if SN_fail is fired, the Standby Node reaches an inactive state and needs to be repaired to return to the active state (SN_repair is fired). The time values for the transitions SN_fail and SN_repair are retrieved from the RBD model depicted in Fig. 5.23(a). When the Standby Node fails, the system can fail if the Main Node or the Management Server also fails. The transition DoLiveMigration represents the start of a live migration event. MainNode and StandbyNode must be running correctly, and the clock controls the time to migrate (token in place ReadyToMigrate of Clock Model). When both conditions are satisfied, DoLiveMigration fires and a token is stored on the LiveM place. Live Migration moves the VM to another host with a very small downtime, which is represented in the model by the MigrationTime transition. Thus, while a token remains on the LiveM place, the system is down. After the end of live migration, the source node will undergo a rejuvenation process, the Standby Node takes the role of Main Node, and the system is up again. Therefore, in this model, the VM live migration is used to avoid an extended downtime during the rejuvenation action. The primary goal is to keep a spare machine with clear aging status ready to receive the migrated VM. The RejuvenationNode transition represents the process of rejuvenation. When the node is under the rejuvenation process, no migration is allowed. Those models are used to analyze the steady-state availability of the system, where Mercury [40, 41] or SHARPE [27] and TimeNET [28] are used to evaluate the RBD and SPN, respectively.

Okamura, Guan, Duo, and Dohi [29] analyzed the resiliency of a virtualized system with Cold-VM rejuvenation and Warm-VM rejuvenation. Resiliency is defined as the persistence of service delivery that can justifiably be trusted when facing changes [30, 31]. In order to quantitatively evaluate the resiliency of a virtualized system, the SRN models in [25] are transformed into an approximated CTMC by PH-expansion. As a result of the numerical study, it is shown that the time duration of change is insensitive to the system availability, and the system with Cold-VM rejuvenation is more robust for the change than the system with Warm-VM rejuvenation [29].

Another high-level representation of a system is given by semi-formal specification languages, such as the Unified Modeling Language (UML) [43], and the Systems Modeling Language (SysML) [44]. Although SRN helps the specification process when compared with CTMC, there is still a considerable gap between the capabilities of system engineers and the skills required to specify SRNs correctly. Andrade, Machida, Kim, and Trivedi [33] proposed an automated transformation method from a SysML model to an SRN and applied the proposed method to analyze a system with software rejuvenation. In SysML, a state transition diagram can be used to represent state transitions of a system component (such as software aging, failure, and recovery). On the other hand, system operations such as monitoring, failure detection, and rejuvenation are described by an activity diagram. Figure 5.24 shows an example of a state machine diagram for a server process and an activity diagram representing a server maintenance operation.

According to the defined translation rules, those diagrams are transformed into the corresponding SRNs as shown in Fig. 5.25.

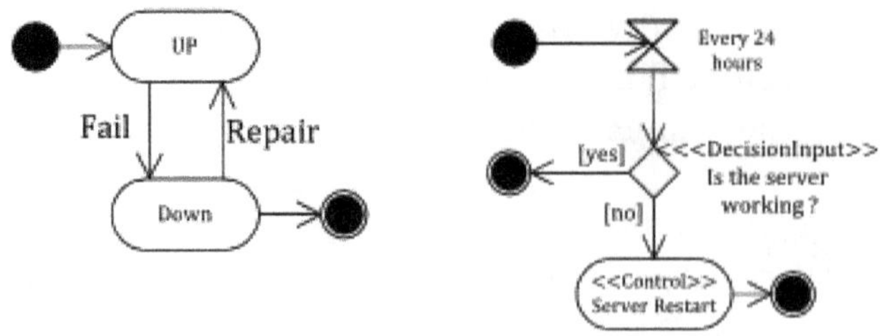

State machine diagram for a server process

Activity diagram for a server maintenance operation

Fig. 5.24. State machine diagram and activity diagram for software maintenance [33].

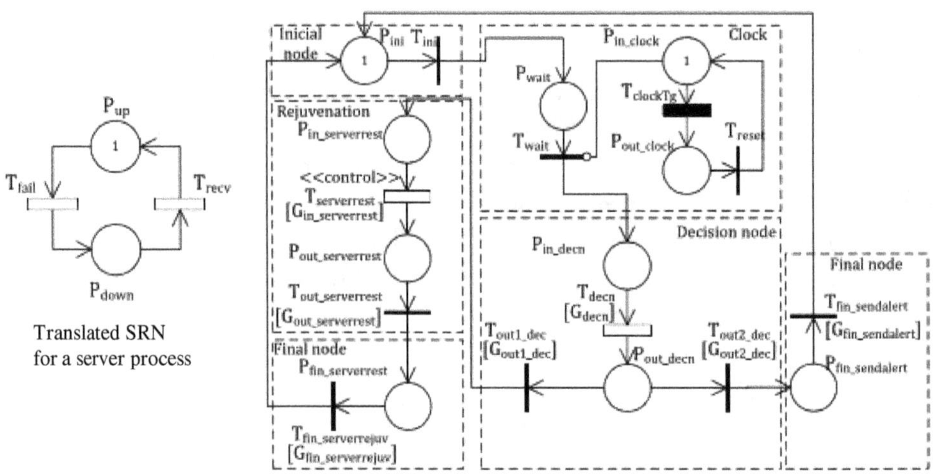

Translated SRN for a server maintenance operation

Fig. 5.25. Translated SRNs for server processes and server maintenance operations [33].

The SRN subnets transformed by SysML diagrams are integrated adopting the technique presented in [32]. The generated SRN models for condition-based rejuvenation and time-based rejuvenation were validated with the corresponding conventional models studied in [1] and [17], respectively.

5.4. Summary and Future Directions

In this chapter, we have reviewed the evolution of state-space models for software rejuvenation that originated from the CTMC presented by Huang *et al.* [1]. Two main streams, which continue from the original to the recent studies on software rejuvenation are outlined: 1) the extension of Markov models and 2) the utilization of higher-level representation. The former thread includes the approach with SMP, which can relax the assumption of exponential distribution in Markov models and allows the analysis of the optimal rejuvenation schedule in a time-based software rejuvenation scheme. Hierarchical models provide a powerful solution to integrate the rejuvenation model with a comprehensive model for the software aging process. On the other hand, the latter thread often resorts to the expressive power of SPN that can be transformed into equivalent Markov chains in order to capture more complex and more extensive systems. SPN-based models are usually applied to software rejuvenation in fault-tolerant systems, cluster systems, and server virtualized systems. Reward assignments to SPN allow computing system availability and other performance measures.

In future, these two threads of studies will continue to develop in a complementary manner. CTMC, SMP, and other Markovian models will be used to assess the fundamental effectiveness of the novel rejuvenation technique or another countermeasure to software aging such as software life-extension [34]. On the other hand, as the size and the complexity of ICT systems continuously increase, SPN and other higher-level representations of rejuvenation models should be used to capture the system dynamics and analyze the impact of software rejuvenation in larger-scale systems. Software-defined networks (SDNs) and network function virtualization (NFV), IoT systems, edge, and fog computing might be the next challenges as they are highly software-intensive systems.

References

1. Y. Huang, C. Kintala, N. Kolettis, and N. D. Fulton. (1995). Software rejuvenation: Analysis, module, and applications. In *Proceedings of the International Symposium on Fault-Tolerant Computing (FTCS 1995), Pasadena, California, USA, June 27–30*, pp. 381–390.
2. T. Dohi, K. Goševa-Popstojanova, and K. S. Trivedi. (2000). Statistical non-parametric algorithms to estimate the optimal software rejuvenation schedule. In *Proceedings of the Pacific Rim International Symposium on Dependable Computing (PRDC), Los Angeles, California, USA, December 18–20*, pp. 77–84.
3. T. Dohi, K. Goševa-Popstojanova, and K. S. Trivedi. (2001). Estimating software rejuvenation schedules in high assurance systems, *Computer Journal*, **44**(6), 473–482.
4. W. Xie, Y. Hong, and K. S. Trivedi. (2005). Analysis of a two-level software rejuvenation policy. *Reliability Engineering and System Safety*, **87**, 13–22.
5. D. Chen and K. S. Trivedi. (2001). Analysis of periodic preventive maintenance with general system failure distribution. In *Proceedings of the Pacific Rim International*

Symposium on Dependable Computing (PRDC), Seoul, Korea, December 17–19, pp. 103–107.
6. Y. Bao, X. Sun, and K. S. Trivedi. (2005). A workload-based analysis of software aging and rejuvenation. *IEEE Transactions on Reliability*, **54**(3), 541–548.
7. S. Garg, S. Pfening, A. Puliafito, M. Telek, and K. S. Trivedi. (1998). Analysis of preventive maintenance in transactions based software systems. *IEEE Transactions on Computers*, **47**, 96–107.
8. K. Vaidyanathan and K. S. Trivedi. (2005). A comprehensive model for software rejuvenation. *IEEE Transactions on Dependable and Secure Computing*, **2**(2), 124–137.
9. R. Matias Jr., K. S. Trivedi, and P. R. M. Maciel. (2010). Using accelerated life tests to estimate time to software aging failure. In *Proceedings of the International Symposium of Software Reliability Engineering (ISSRE), San Jose, California, USA, November 1–4*, pp. 211–219.
10. J. Zhao, Y. Jin, K. S. Trivedi, and R. Matias Jr. (2011). Injecting memory leaks to accelerate software failures. In *Proceedings of the International Symposium on Software Reliability Engineering (ISSRE), Hiroshima, Japan, November 29–December 2*, pp. 260–269.
11. J. Zhao, Y. Wang, G. Ning, K. S. Trivedi, R. Matias Jr., and K. Y. Cai. (2013). A comprehensive approach to optimal software rejuvenation. *Performance Evaluation*, **70**(11), 917–933.
12. H. Okamura and T. Dohi. (2012). Optimization of opportunity-based software rejuvenation policy. In *Proceedings of the International Workshop on Software Aging and Rejuvenation, (WoSAR), Dallas, Texas, USA, November 27–30*, pp. 283–286.
13. H. Okamura and T. Dohi. (2013). Optimal trigger time of software rejuvenation under probabilistic opportunities. *IEICE Transactions on Information and Systems*, **96**(9), 1933–1940.
14. S. M. Ross. (2000). *Introduction to Probability Models* (7th ed.). London, UK: Academic Press.
15. F. Machida, V. F. Nicola, and K. S. Trivedi. (2014). Job completion time on a virtualized server with software rejuvenation. *ACM Journal on Emerging Technologies in Computing Systems*, **10**(1), 10.
16. V. G. Kulkarni, V. V. Nicola, and K. S. Trivedi. (1987). The completion time of a job on multimode systems. *Advances in Applied Probability*, **19**, 932–954.
17. S. Garg, A. Puliafito, M. Telek, and K. S. Trivedi. (1995). Analysis of software rejuvenation using Markov regenerative stochastic Petri nets. In *Proceedings of the International Symposium on Software Reliability Engineering (ISSRE), Toulouse, France, October 24–27*, pp. 180–187.
18. A. Bobbio, S. Garg, M. Gribaudo, A. Horvath, M. Sereno, and M. Telek. (1999). Modeling software systems with rejuvenation, restoration and checkpointing through fluid stochastic Petri nets. In *Proceedings of the International Workshop on Petri Nets and Performance Models (PNPM), Zaragoza, Spain, September 8–10*, pp. 82–91.
19. K. Vaidyanathan, R. E. Harper, S. W. Hunter, and K. S. Trivedi. (2001). Analysis and implementation of software rejuvenation in cluster systems. In *Proceedings of the International Conference on Measurement and Modeling of Computer Systems (SIGMETRICS), Cambridge, Massachusetts, USA, June 16–20*, pp. 62–71.
20. V. Castelli, R. E. Harper, P. Heidelberger, S. W. Hunter, K. S. Trivedi, K. Vaidyanathan, and W. P. Zeggert. (2001). Proactive management of software aging. *IBM Journal of Research and Development*, **45**(2), 311–332.

21. G. Ciardo, A. Blakemore, P. F. Chimento, J. K. Muppala, and K. S. Trivedi. (1993). Automated generation and analysis of Markov reward models using stochastic reward nets. *Linear Algebra, Markov Chains and Queuing Models*, **48**, 145–191.
22. D. Wang, W. Xie, and K. S. Trivedi. (2007). Performability analysis of clustered systems with rejuvenation under varying workload. *Performance Evaluation*, **64**(3), 247–265.
23. K. S. Trivedi. (2001). *Probability and Statistics with Reliability, Queuing, and Computer Science Applications*. Chichester, UK: John Wiley & Sons.
24. F. Machida, D. Kim, and K. S. Trivedi. (2010). Modeling and analysis of software rejuvenation in a server virtualized system. In *Proceedings of the International Workshop on Software Aging and Rejuvenation (WoSAR 2010), San Jose, California, USA, November 2*, pp. 1–6.
25. F. Machida, D. Kim, and K. S. Trivedi. (2013). Modeling and analysis of software rejuvenation in a server virtualized system with live VM migration. *Performance Evaluation*, **70**(3), 212–230.
26. M. Melo, P. Maciel, J. Araujo, R. Matos, and C. Araujo. (2013). Availability study on cloud computing environments: Live migration as a rejuvenation mechanism. In *Proceedings of the International Workshop on Dependability of Clouds, Data Centers and Virtual Machine Technology (DCDV), Budapest, Hungary, June 24–27*, pp. 1–6.
27. K. S. Trivedi and R. Sahner. (2009). SHARPE at the age of twenty-two. *SIGMETRICS Performance Evaluation Review*, **36**(4), 52–57.
28. R. German, C. Kelling, A. Zimmermann, and G. Hommel. (1995). TimeNET: a toolkit for evaluating non-Markovian stochastic Petri nets. *Performance Evaluation*, **24**(1–2), 69–87.
29. H. Okamura, J. Guan, C. Luo, and T. Dohi. (2015). Quantifying resiliency of virtualized system with software rejuvenation. *IEICE Transactions on Fundamentals of Electronics, Communications and Computer Sciences*, **98**(10), 2051–2059.
30. J. C. Laprie. (2008). From dependability to resilience. In *Proceedings of 38th IEEE/IFIP International Conference On Dependable Systems and Networks (DSN), Anchorage, Alaska, USA, June 24–27*, pp. G8–G9.
31. R. Ghosh, D. Kim, and K. S. Trivedi. (2013). System resiliency quantification using non-state-space and state-space analytic models. *Reliability Engineering and System Safety*, **116**, 109–125.
32. F. Machida, E. Andrade, D. Kim, and K. S. Trivedi. (2011). Candy: component-based availability modeling framework for cloud service management using SysML. In *Proceedings of the International Symposium on Reliable and Distributed Systems (SRDS), Madrid, Spain, October 4–7*, pp. 209–218.
33. E. Andrade, F. Machida, D. Kim, and K. Trivedi. (2011). Modeling and analyzing server system with rejuvenation through SysML and stochastic reward nets. In *Proceedings of the International Conference on Availability, Reliability and Security (ARES), Vienna, Austria, August 22–26*, pp. 22–26.
34. F. Machida, J. Xiang, K. Tadano, and Y. Maeno. (2017). Lifetime extension of software execution subject to aging. *IEEE Transactions on Reliability*, **66**(1), 123–134.
35. M. K. Molloy. (1982). Performance analysis using stochastic Petri nets. *IEEE Transactions on Computers*, **31**(9), 913–917.
36. M. Marsan, G. Conte, and G. Balbo. (1984). A class of generalized stochastic Petri nets for the performance evaluation of multiprocessor systems. *ACM Transactions on Computer Systems*, **2**(2), 93–122.

37. R. German. (2000). *Performance Analysis of Communication Systems with non-Markovian Stochastic Petri Nets.* New York City, NY, USA: John Wiley & Sons.
38. T. Murata. (1989). Petri nets: Properties, analysis and applications. In *Proceedings of the IEEE*, **77**(4), 541–580.
39. G. Florin and S. Natkin. (1982). Evaluation based upon stochastic Petri nets of the maximum throughput of a full duplex protocol. In Pagnoni A. and Rozenberg G. (eds.). *Application and Theory of Petri Nets.* Berlin/Heidelberg, Germany: Springer-Verlag.
40. D. Oliveira, A. Brinkmann, and P. Maciel. (2017). Advanced stochastic Petri net modeling with the Mercury scripting language. In *Proceedings of the EAI International Conference on Performance Evaluation Methodologies and Tools (ValueTools), Venice, Italy, December 5–7*, pp. 192–197.
41. P. Maciel, R. Matos, B. Silva, J. Figueiredo, D. Oliveira, I. Fé, R. Maciel, and J. Dantas. (2017). Mercury: performance and dependability evaluation of systems with exponential, expolynomial and general distributions. In *Proceedings of the IEEE Pacific Rim International Symposium on Dependable Computing (PRDC), Christchurch, New Zealand, January 22–25*, pp. 50–57.
42. M. A. Marsan and G. Chiola. (1986). On Petri nets with deterministic and exponentially distributed firing times. In *Proceedings of the 7th European Workshop on Applications and Theory of Petri Nets, Oxford, UK, June*, pp. 132–145.
43. J. Rumbaugh, I. Jacobson, and G. Booch. (2004). *Unified Modeling Language Reference Manual* (2nd ed.). Boston, Massachusetts, USA: Addison-Wesley.
44. S. Friedenthal, A. Moore, and R. Steiner. (2014). *A Practical Guide to SysML: The Systems Modeling Language.* Burlington, Massachusetts, USA: Morgan Kaufmann.
45. F. Durbin. (1974). Numerical inversion of Laplace transforms: an efficient improvement to Durbner and Abate's method. *Computer Journal*, **17**(4), 371–376.

Chapter 6

Analysis of Queueing Models for Rejuvenation

Hiroyuki Okamura* and Tadashi Dohi†

Hiroshima University, Higashi-Hiroshima, Japan
* *okamu@hiroshima-u.ac.jp*
† *dohi@hiroshima-u.ac.jp*

This chapter introduces the mathematical analysis of queueing models for rejuvenation. In particular, we describe the earliest queueing model for rejuvenation [6] and variations of Garg *et al.*'s model in detail. Also, we present a generalized queueing model defined by a quasi-birth-and-death process. This framework can represent many existing queueing models for rejuvenation mathematically.

6.1. Introduction

Software rejuvenation is regarded as one of the fault avoidance techniques against software aging. Typically software rejuvenation can be done by restarting processes, system reboot and garbage collection (see Chapter 3). Since specific hardware equipment is not required in order for rejuvenation to be performed, software rejuvenation is considered as a low-cost fault avoidance technique. In the design of software rejuvenation operation in a system, there are two main issues; (i) how to detect the degraded states of the system, and (ii) when to start the rejuvenation operation in the system. The first issue is a kind of statistical problem. The measurement-based approach and its associated statistical approach are important when addressing this issue. On the other hand, the second issue is related to the overhead of software rejuvenation, as frequent execution of rejuvenation negatively affects the system performance. To counteract this issue, the model-based approach can be used to determine the optimal rejuvenation timing in terms of several performance indices.

Huang *et al.* [8] first discussed a random rejuvenation policy based on a simple CTMC (continuous-time Markov chain) model. In Huang *et al.* [8], the system is modeled with four states; normal, failure-probable, failure and rejuvenation. The model is used to investigate the effect of rejuvenation on the system performance. Garg *et al.* [6] also introduced the queueing model for a transaction system with software aging. The transaction system is fundamental for server-type applications such as Web servers, and a queueing model is well defined to represent the dynamic behavior of transaction systems. Garg *et al.* [6] considered an $M/M_t/1/K$ queueing model in which the service rate is degraded with elapsed time. The essential difference between the queueing model by Garg *et al.* [6] and Huang *et al.*'s model is twofold: the condition of rejuvenation execution timing and the performance measure.

In general, we prefer to perform the rejuvenation when the system becomes idle so as to minimize the rejuvenation overhead. Since the queueing model can represent the dormant period of the system, we can discuss the more precise rejuvenation policy in the queueing models rather than in the simple state-based models. Also, since the queue models can represent the service process for each transaction, it is possible to measure the system indices such as loss probability of transaction and throughput. In fact, Garg *et al.* [6] discussed a rejuvenation policy that considered the dormancy of the system and derived the loss probability of a transaction and the response time as performance indices.

This chapter introduces queueing models to determine the timing of software rejuvenation for transaction systems. In particular, we focus on the mathematical analysis of queueing models for rejuvenation to derive the performance indices. In Section 6.2, we introduce a brief survey of the queueing models for rejuvenation. Section 6.3 summarizes the rejuvenation policies in the queueing models for rejuvenation. In Section 6.4, we describe Garg *et al.*'s model and its mathematical analysis in detail. Section 6.5 shows variations of Garg *et al.*'s model and their mathematical analysis. Also, in Section 6.6, we mention one of the most generalized queueing models, which is based on a quasi-birth-and-death process. Finally we remark upon the direction to be taken in the future in Section 6.7.

6.2. Queueing Models for Rejuvenation

Queueing models have been used for several purposes in software rejuvenation research. The most popular and fundamental purpose is to derive the performance measures related to the service process. Garg *et al.* [6] and variations of Garg *et al.*'s model derived the loss probability of transactions and the mean response time as well as the system availability. Wang *et al.* [24] also derived the blocking probability and the throughput of the queueing model for rejuvenation described by the DSPN (deterministic and stochastic Petri net). Machida *et al.* [9] discussed the stochastic model for the rejuvenation of the virtualized system with the GSPN (generalized stochastic Petri net). In Machida *et al.* [9], the expected number of transactions lost was studied by combining the GSPN-based availability model with an $M/M/1/n$ queueing model.

Another purpose of introducing the queueing model is to represent the real computational situation. Since the queue architecture is widely implemented in computer systems, it is natural to use the queueing model to represent the dynamic behavior of a system. In fact, Avritzer *et al.* [2] used the queueing model to represent the degraded system behavior in simulation.

Queueing models can also be used to discuss the optimality of rejuvenation policy. As mentioned later, since the work of Garg *et al.* [7], the time-triggered policy has been used as one of the most popular rejuvenation policies. However, we do not know whether the time-triggered policy is the best or not among all the possible policies, i.e., it is necessary to discuss the optimality of policy. The Markov decision process (MDP) is a powerful tool to discuss the optimality of policy. In the context of the MDP, the action is determined based on observable states. Since the software aging is related to the load of the system, it is natural for the MDP to use the queueing process of the workload. Pfening *et al.* [17], Okamura and Dohi [11] and Machida and Miyoshi [10] used the queueing models for rejuvenation in the context of the MDP.

6.3. Rejuvenation Policies

Rejuvenation policies are generally categorized into time-triggered and condition-triggered policies. The time-triggered software rejuvenation policy was first introduced by Garg *et al.* [7] as a controllable policy for software rejuvenation. Under the time-triggered policy, the system performs the rejuvenation by monitoring an accumulated operation time. Compared to the other policies, the time-triggered policy is a simpler method to implement the rejuvenation. Garg *et al.* [7] extended Huang *et al.*'s CTMC model to the MRGP (Markov regenerative process) model by considering the periodic time-triggered policy. Also, Dohi *et al.* [5] discussed the semi-Markov models and proposed statistically non-parametric algorithms to determine the optimal rejuvenation policy under the time-triggered rejuvenation policy.

The condition-triggered policy is an alternative scheme for controllable rejuvenation policies. In general, the condition-triggered policy utilizes observable system attributes rather than the accumulated operation time. Since system performance degradations and system failures are associated with the system workloads as well as the operation time and/or the processing time, it is useful to consider a rejuvenation scheme that monitors indicators of the system workload, such as the number of processed transactions and the maximum load in the past. Okamura *et al.* [16] considered the simplest workload-based policy where the rejuvenation is triggered when the number of processed transactions exceeds a threshold. Vaidyanathan and Trivedi [23] presented a model in which the system workload is estimated from observed system attributes. Essentially, this approach is regarded as the estimation of the level of system degradation from the system attributes. Bruneo *et al.* [4] considered virtualized systems under the workload-based rejuvenation policy. Their policy is to change the rejuvenation timing by the number of activated virtual machines. In Bruneo *et al.* [4], they evaluated the performance in the cases where requests arrive at the system according to a Poisson process and an MMPP (Markov modulated Poisson process). As a result, the workload-based policy outperformed the time-based policy under the assumption that the failure time distribution also depends on the number of activated virtual machines. The policies in Vaidyanathan and Trivedi [23] and Bruneo *et al.* [4] concentrate on the internal conditions of the system, e.g., the attributes and the number of activated virtual machines.

For a transaction system, Garg *et al.* [6] presented a queueing model with homogeneous Poisson arrivals and service degradation. This queueing model was based on the stochastic model. They discussed the system performance indices of the queueing model, such as system availability, loss probability of transaction and mean response time under the time-based policies. In addition, Garg *et al.* [6] discussed an execution policy of rejuvenation in which the system executes rejuvenation when the number of transactions becomes zero after the accumulated operation time exceeds a threshold. Okamura *et al.* analyzed several queueing models with workload-based policies [12, 16], resume scheme [13], multiple servers [14], and burst arrival [15]. Also, Salfner and Wolter [20] compared the time-triggered policies proposed by Garg *et al.* [6] with an additional time-triggered policy in which the system allows no more arrivals to the queue after the accumulated operation time exceeds a threshold. In Okamura and Dohi [11], the authors presented an MDP for the transaction system with MMPP arrivals, and analyzed the optimality of software rejuvenation policy. As the most general model, a quasi-birth-and-death model was discussed by Zheng *et al.* [25].

6.4. Transaction System Model

6.4.1. *Model Description*

In this section, we introduce the queueing model with rejuvenation by Garg *et al.* [6].

Consider a single server type of software system. Suppose that the buffer is empty at time $t = 0$ and that transactions arrive at the system in accordance with a homogeneous Poisson process with rate λ (>0). Each transaction is processed by a single server under the FCFS (first come first serve) discipline. The service rate is expressed by $\mu(\cdot)$ (>0) which depends on some metrics such as an accumulated operation time to model the system performance degradation. The capacity of the system is given by K ($\geq$1). If the server is busy (processing a transaction), new transactions wait in the buffer for the process to be finished. If a transaction arrives at the system when it is at full capacity, the transaction is lost. The service is exhaustive, i.e., the server continuously processes the transactions in the system if there are any transactions. The server is idle when there is no transaction in the system, i.e., the system waits for the next arrival of transactions. The system behavior is described by an $M/M_t/1/K$ queueing system, which is an inhomogeneous type of queueing system because the service rate depends on the time. Furthermore, Garg *et al.* [6] considered the system failure. Concretely, let $\rho(\cdot)$ be a failure rate which also depends on some information. Once the system failure occurs, the recovery (repair) operation starts immediately. All the transactions in the system are lost when the recovery operation starts. The time for the recovery operation is given by a random variable Y_f with a finite mean $\mathrm{E}[Y_f] < \infty$. Since the service and failure rate functions $\mu(t)$ and $\rho(t)$ can represent the software aging phenomenon, they are assumed to be decreasing and increasing functions, respectively, and become as good as new after the recovery operation. The software rejuvenation is preventive maintenance against system performance degradation and system failure. The system will issue the rejuvenation command under a certain policy. Let Y_r be the time duration of the rejuvenation operation, and let its mean be given by $\mathrm{E}[Y_r]$. Similar to what occurs after the recovery operation, the service and failure rates of systems become as good as new after the rejuvenation operation. Also we assume $\mathrm{E}[Y_r] < \mathrm{E}[Y_f]$.

Garg *et al.* [6] considered the following two software rejuvenation strategies based on the accumulated operation time. They are called T-policy in this chapter.

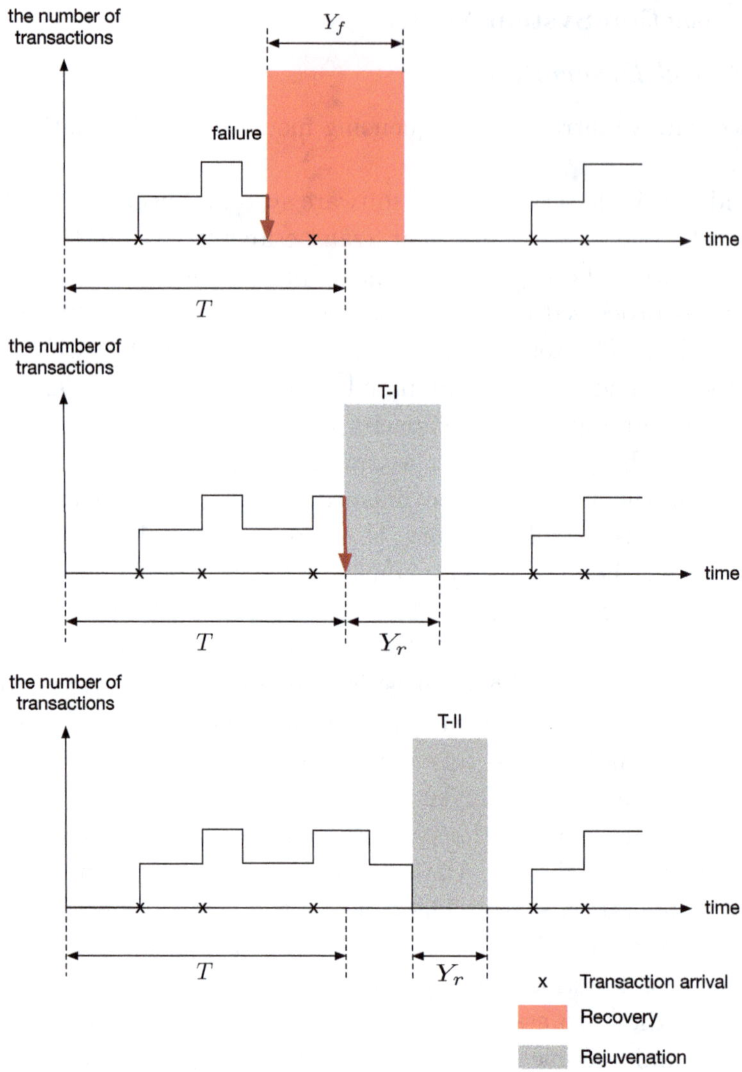

Fig. 6.1. The possible behavior of a transaction system with time-triggered rejuvenation.

- T-policy I (T-I) [6]: Rejuvenate the system when the accumulated operation time becomes T (>0). Before starting the rejuvenation, all the transactions in the system are cancelled and discarded.
- T-policy II (T-II) [6]: Rejuvenate the system at the beginning of the first idle period after the accumulated operation time becomes T (>0).

Figure 6.1 depicts the possible behaviors of a transaction system under T-I and T-II, respectively.

6.4.2. *Measures*

In Garg *et al.* [6], there are three dependability measures: steady-state availability, loss probability of transactions and mean response time on transactions. The basic idea of the stochastic analysis is to generate a 3-state model for rejuvenation from the original queueing model by using the embedded Markov chain technique or the renewal reward process. In this chapter, we discuss the renewal reward process. Consider the following three states for the transaction system:

State A: System is normally operated.
State B: System is failed and recovered.
State C: System is rejuvenated.

The system state can be represented by a discrete-time Markov chain (DTMC) when we focus on time instances of entry points of the above three states. The DTMC and the time instances are called an embedded Markov chain and embedded points, respectively.

Let P_{AB} and P_{AC} denote the transition probabilities from State A to State B and from State A to State C, respectively. Taking account of $P_{AC} = 1 - P_{AB}$, the transition probability matrix is given by

$$\boldsymbol{P} = \begin{pmatrix} 0 & P_{AB} & P_{AC} \\ 1 & 0 & 0 \\ 1 & 0 & 0 \end{pmatrix} \tag{6.1}$$

Let $\boldsymbol{\pi} = (\pi_A, \pi_B, \pi_C)$ be the steady-state probability vector for the DTMC. We have

$$\pi_A = \frac{1}{2}, \quad \pi_B = \frac{P_{AB}}{2}, \quad \pi_C = \frac{P_{AC}}{2}. \tag{6.2}$$

The dependability measures are obtained based on these stationary probabilities and some rewards between two successive embedded points. In fact, the original paper derived the dependability measures based on the embedded Markov chain. However, in this case, the system state always returns State A via State B or State C. Hence we introduce the renewal reward approach [19] to derive the dependability measures. Based on the renewal reward approach, the performance measure in the steady state can be obtained by the expected reward rate over one cycle, where the cycle is defined by the time duration between two successive starting points of State A.

(i) Steady-state availability

The steady-state availability is given by a time fraction of the sojourn time of State A over one cycle. Let U be the sojourn time of State A in one cycle. The steady-state availability is given by

$$A_{ss} = \frac{\mathrm{E}[U]}{\mathrm{E}[U] + P_{AB}\mathrm{E}[Y_f] + P_{AC}\mathrm{E}[Y_r]}, \tag{6.3}$$

where the expected time length of one cycle is given by $\mathrm{E}[U] + P_{AB}\mathrm{E}[Y_f] + P_{AC}\mathrm{E}[Y_r]$.

When we apply the embedded Markov chain approach, the steady-state availability is given by a time fraction of the sojourn time of State A over the time period between two successive embedded points. Let X be the time length of two embedded points. Since the system is available only in State A, the steady-state availability is given by

$$A_{ss} = \frac{\pi_A \mathrm{E}[X|A]}{\pi_A \mathrm{E}[X|A] + \pi_B \mathrm{E}[X|B] + \pi_C \mathrm{E}[X|C]}, \tag{6.4}$$

where $\mathrm{E}[X|A]$, $\mathrm{E}[X|B]$ and $\mathrm{E}[X|C]$ are the expected times of two successive embedded points provided that the beginning of each state is State A, B and C, respectively. The expected time lengths of State A, B and C are $\mathrm{E}[X|A] = \mathrm{E}[U]$, $\mathrm{E}[X|B] = \mathrm{E}[Y_f]$ and $\mathrm{E}[X|C] = \mathrm{E}[Y_r]$. By substituting π_A, π_B and π_C into the above equation, we rewrite the steady-state availability as follows:

$$A_{ss} = \frac{\frac{1}{2}\mathrm{E}[U]}{\frac{1}{2}\mathrm{E}[U] + \frac{P_{AB}}{2}\mathrm{E}[Y_f] + \frac{P_{AC}}{2}\mathrm{E}[Y_r]} = \frac{\mathrm{E}[U]}{\mathrm{E}[U] + P_{AB}\mathrm{E}[Y_f] + P_{AC}\mathrm{E}[Y_r]}. \tag{6.5}$$

Note that the formulation of the renewal reward approach can be obtained by multiplying 2 by both the numerator and denominator of the formulation of the embedded Markov chain approach in Garg *et al.*'s [6] model.

(ii) Loss probability of transactions

The loss probability of transactions is given by the fraction of the number of lost transactions over the total number of transactions during one cycle. Since the arrival process follows a homogeneous Poisson process, the total number of transactions that arrive during one cycle becomes $\lambda(\mathrm{E}[U] + P_{AB}\mathrm{E}[Y_f] + P_{AC}\mathrm{E}[Y_r])$. In Garg *et al.*'s [6] queueing model, these are the cases where the transactions are lost:

(a) A transaction arrives during the recovery operation.
(b) A transaction arrives during the rejuvenation operation.
(c) A transaction arrives when the system capacity is full.
(d) The system failure occurs.
(e) The software rejuvenation starts under T-I.

The expected number of lost transactions by (a), (b) and (c) in one cycle becomes $\lambda(\mathrm{E}[U_K] + P_{AB}\mathrm{E}[Y_f] + P_{AC}\mathrm{E}[Y_r])$, where $\mathrm{E}[U_n]$ is the sojourn time when the number of transactions is n in State A. When $\mathrm{E}[N_l]$ is the expected number of lost transactions by (d) and (e) in one cycle, the loss probability of transactions is given by

$$P_{loss} = \frac{\mathrm{E}[N_l] + \lambda(\mathrm{E}[U_K] + P_{AB}\mathrm{E}[Y_f] + P_{AC}\mathrm{E}[Y_r])}{\lambda(\mathrm{E}[U] + P_{AB}\mathrm{E}[Y_f] + P_{AC}\mathrm{E}[Y_r])}. \tag{6.6}$$

(iii) Mean response time

The mean response time is derived by a fraction of the total processing time of the accepted transactions over the total number of accepted transactions in one cycle. The expected number of accepted transactions E_s in one cycle becomes

$$E_s = \lambda(\mathrm{E}[U] - \mathrm{E}[U_K]) - \mathrm{E}[N_l]. \tag{6.7}$$

Let W_s be the expected total processing time for the accepted transactions. Then the mean response time for a transaction is given by

$$T_{res} = \frac{W_s}{E_s}, \tag{6.8}$$

On the other hand, it is difficult to obtain the analytically closed form of the expected total processing time for transactions W_s. Define W as the expected total processing time for all the transactions that arrive at the system. Then we have $W = \sum_{n=0}^{K} n\mathrm{E}[U_n]$. Then W is strictly larger than W_s, i.e., $W_s < W$. Hence, we obtain an upper bound of the mean response time as follows:

$$T_{res} < \frac{W}{E_s} = \overline{T}_{res}. \tag{6.9}$$

6.4.3. *Analysis*

To obtain the three measures; the steady-state availability, the loss probability of transactions and the upper bound of the mean response time, we should compute P_{AB}, $\mathrm{E}[U]$, $\mathrm{E}[U_n]$ and $\mathrm{E}[N_l]$, and they can be computed by the analysis of non-homogeneous Markov chains (NHMCs). We define the following probabilities:

$p_n(t)$: The probability that n transactions are in the system at time t.
$p_{n'}(t)$: The probability that the system fails up to timc t and that n transactions are in the system at an instance of failure.

where $n = 0, \ldots, K$. These probabilities are computed from the difference-differential equations that depend on rejuvenation policies.

T-I

In this case, we consider only the time period from $t = 0$ to T, because the software rejuvenation runs if the accumulated operation time attains T without failure. The difference-differential equations (Kolmogorov's forward equation) during $0 < t \leq T$ are

$$\frac{dp_0(t)}{dt} = \mu(\cdot)p_1(t) - (\lambda + \rho(\cdot))p_0(t), \tag{6.10}$$

$$\frac{dp_n(t)}{dt} = \lambda p_{n-1}(t) + \mu(\cdot)p_{n+1}(t) - (\lambda + \mu(\cdot) + \rho(\cdot))p_n(t), \quad n=1,\ldots,K-1, \tag{6.11}$$

$$\frac{dp_K(t)}{dt} = \lambda p_{K-1}(t) - (\mu(\cdot) + \rho(\cdot))p_K(t), \tag{6.12}$$

$$\frac{dp_{n'}(t)}{dt} = \rho(\cdot)p_n(t), \quad n = 0, \ldots, K. \tag{6.13}$$

Figure 6.2 shows a state diagram under T-I. The states $0'$ through K' are absorbing states. Let $L(t)$ be a functional of $p_n(t)$, e.g.,

$$L(t) = \int_0^t \sum_{n=0}^{K} c_n p_n(\tau)d\tau, \tag{6.14}$$

where c_n is an arbitrary constant. If the service and failure rate functions depend on $L(t)$, i.e., $\mu(L(t))$ and $\rho(L(t))$, then we add the following

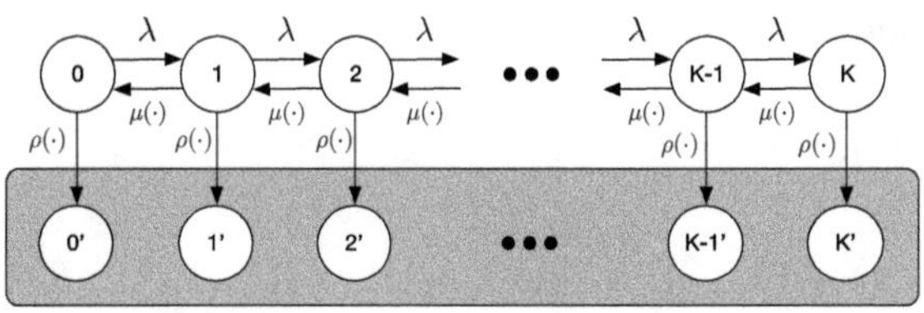

Fig. 6.2. State transition diagram of Garg *et al.*'s model for $0 < t \leq T$.

additional equation to the above difference-differential equations;

$$\frac{d}{dt}L(t) = \sum_{n=0}^{K} c_n p_n(t). \tag{6.15}$$

The difference-differential equations can be solved by the ordinary numerical approaches such as the Runge-Kutta method with the initial values

$$p_0(0) = 1, \quad p_n(0) = 0, \quad n = 1, \ldots, K, \quad p_{n'}(0) = 0, \quad n = 0, \ldots, K. \tag{6.16}$$

After solving the difference-differential equations, we obtain the following values under T-I:

$$P_{AB} = \sum_{n=0}^{K} p_{n'}(T), \tag{6.17}$$

$$\mathrm{E}[U] = \int_0^T \sum_{n=0}^{K} p_n(t)dt, \tag{6.18}$$

$$\mathrm{E}[U_n] = \int_0^T p_n(t)dt, \tag{6.19}$$

$$\mathrm{E}[N_l] = \sum_{n=0}^{K} n(p_{n'}(T) + p_n(T)). \tag{6.20}$$

T-II

The dynamic behavior of the system under T-II is exactly the same as that under T-I during $0 < t \leq T$. The difference-differential equations change after $t > T$ as follows.

$$\frac{dp_0(t)}{dt} = \mu(\cdot)p_1(t), \tag{6.21}$$

$$\frac{dp_1(t)}{dt} = \mu(\cdot)p_2(t) - (\lambda + \mu(\cdot) + \rho(\cdot))p_1(t), \quad n = 1, \ldots, K-1, \tag{6.22}$$

$$\frac{dp_n(t)}{dt} = \lambda p_{n-1}(t) + \mu(\cdot)p_{n+1}(t) - (\lambda + \mu(\cdot) + \rho(\cdot))p_n(t), \; n = 2, \ldots, K-1, \tag{6.23}$$

$$\frac{dp_K(t)}{dt} = \lambda p_{K-1}(t) - (\mu(\cdot) + \rho(\cdot))p_K(t), \tag{6.24}$$

$$\frac{dp_{n'}(t)}{dt} = \rho(\cdot)p_n(t), \quad n = 0, \ldots, K. \tag{6.25}$$

Figure 6.3 shows a state diagram under T-II. In this case, the state 0 becomes an absorbing state because the system runs until the number of transactions becomes zero. Eventually, the system goes to the absorbing states $0'$ through K' or the alternative absorbing state 0. The difference-differential equations are solved on $T < t < \infty$ where the initial probabilities $p_n(T)$ and $p_{n'}(T)$ are given from the solutions of difference-differential equations for T-I. Also, it should be noted that $p_{0'}(t) = p_{0'}(T)$ for $T < t < \infty$, because the system does not go to the state $0'$ for $T < t < \infty$ as shown in Fig. 6.3. The probability and expected values under T-II are given by

$$P_{AB} = \sum_{n=0}^{K} p_{n'}(\infty), \tag{6.26}$$

$$\mathrm{E}[U] = \int_0^T p_0(t)dt + \int_0^\infty \sum_{n=1}^{K} p_n(t)dt, \tag{6.27}$$

$$\mathrm{E}[U_n] = \int_0^\infty p_n(t)dt, \quad n = 1, \ldots, K \tag{6.28}$$

$$\mathrm{E}[N_l] = \sum_{n=0}^{K} np_{n'}(\infty). \tag{6.29}$$

6.5. Variations of Garg *et al.*'s Model

Based on the earlier work of Garg *et al.*'s [6] queueing model, there are several versions of queueing models with rejuvenation. In this section, we

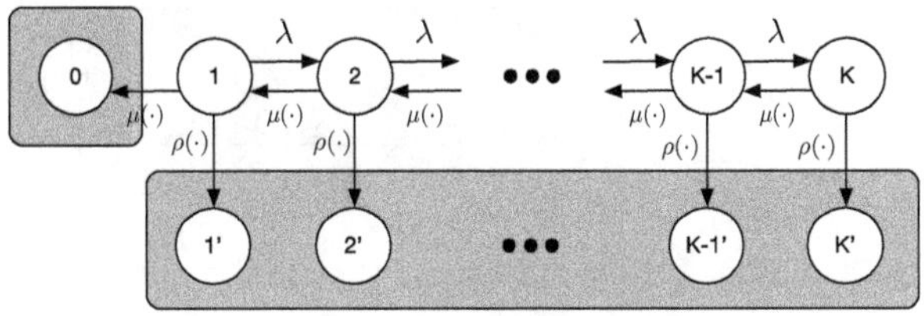

Fig. 6.3. State transition diagram of Garg *et al.*'s model under T-II for $T < t < \infty$.

introduce the variations of queueing models that are in the same framework of Garg *et al.*'s [6] queueing model.

N-policy

Okamura *et al.* [12, 16] proposed the rejuvenation policies based on the number of processed transactions called N-policy. Concretely, they considered the following two policies according to the original T-I and T-II policies.

- N-policy I (N-I): Rejuvenates the system when N ($\geq$1) transactions are processed. Before starting the rejuvenation, all the transactions in the system are cancelled and discarded.
- N-policy II (N-II): Rejuvenates the system at the beginning of the first idle period after N ($\geq$1) transactions are processed.

We define the following states

(n, i): The state where n transactions are in the system and i transactions have been processed.

n': The state where the failure occurs when n transactions are in the system.

Figure 6.4 depicts the state transition diagram under N-I. In the diagram, the states surrounded by the dotted line are subject to transitions with the same destinations as the transitions from the dotted line. In order to keep the information on the number of processed transactions, the state (n, i) transitions to the state $(n - 1, i + 1)$. Let $p_{n,i}(t)$ be the state probability for (n, i) at time t, which is obtained by solving the difference-differential equations according to Fig. 6.4 with the initial conditions $p_{0,0}(0) = 1$ and $p_{n,i}(0) = 0$ ($n \neq 0$, $i \neq 0$). Using $p_{n,i}(t)$, we obtain the following values

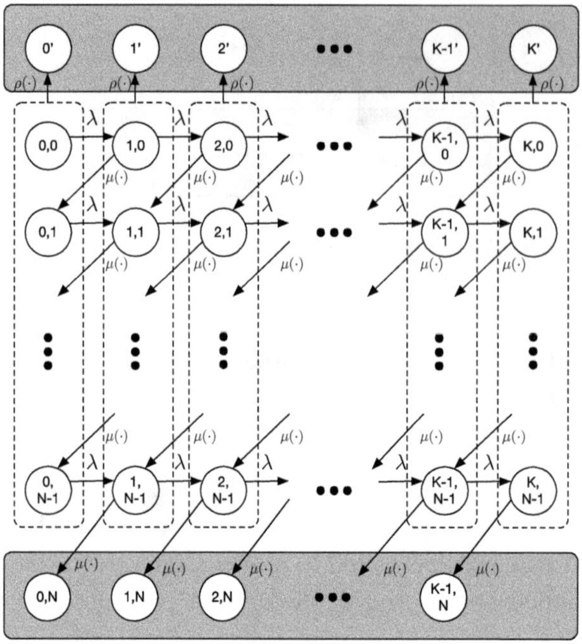

Fig. 6.4. State transition diagram under N-I.

under N-I:

$$P_{AB} = \sum_{n=0}^{K} p_{n'}(\infty), \tag{6.30}$$

$$\mathrm{E}[U] = \int_0^\infty \sum_{n=0}^{K} \sum_{i=0}^{N-1} p_{n,i}(t)dt, \tag{6.31}$$

$$\mathrm{E}[U_n] = \int_0^\infty \sum_{i=0}^{N-1} p_{n,i}(t)dt, \quad n = 1, \ldots K, \tag{6.32}$$

$$\mathrm{E}[N_l] = \sum_{n=0}^{K} np_{n'}(\infty) + \sum_{n=0}^{K-1} np_{n,N}(\infty). \tag{6.33}$$

Figure 6.5 shows the state transition diagram under N-II. The main difference from N-I is that the absorbing state is only the state where the number of transactions becomes 0 after N transactions have been processed.

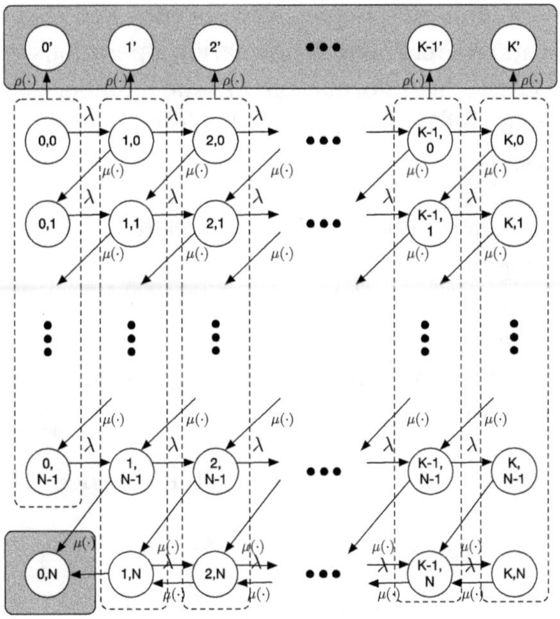

Fig. 6.5. State transition diagram under N-II.

After computing the state probabilities, we have

$$P_{AB} = \sum_{n=0}^{K} p_{n'}(\infty) = 1 - p_{0,N}(\infty), \tag{6.34}$$

$$\mathrm{E}[U] = \int_0^\infty \sum_{n=0}^{K}\sum_{i=0}^{N-1} p_{n,i}(t)dt + \sum_{n=1}^{K} p_{n,N}(t)dt, \tag{6.35}$$

$$\mathrm{E}[U_n] = \int_0^\infty \sum_{i=0}^{N} p_{n,i}(t)dt, \quad n = 1, \dots K, \tag{6.36}$$

$$\mathrm{E}[N_l] = \sum_{n=0}^{K} n p_{n'}(\infty). \tag{6.37}$$

Resume policy

The paper [13] revisited Garg *et al.*'s [6] model under T-I with a resume scheme. Concretely, it is assumed that the system keeps the transactions even if either system failure or rejuvenation occurs, and that the transactions arriving during the recovery and rejuvenation operations are stored in the system. In this case, the information on the number of transactions at embedded points should be kept. Thus the states of embedded DTMC are changed as follows.

State A_n: System is normally operated and there are n transactions at the beginning of this state.
State B_n: System is failed and recovered and there are n transactions at the beginning of this state.
State C_n: System is rejuvenated and there are n transactions at the beginning of this state.

Then the transition probability matrix of embedded Markov chains is expressed by

$$\boldsymbol{P} = \begin{pmatrix} \boldsymbol{O} & \boldsymbol{P}_{AB} & \boldsymbol{P}_{AC} \\ \boldsymbol{P}_{BA} & \boldsymbol{O} & \boldsymbol{O} \\ \boldsymbol{P}_{CA} & \boldsymbol{O} & \boldsymbol{O} \end{pmatrix}, \tag{6.38}$$

where $\boldsymbol{P}_{AB}$, $\boldsymbol{P}_{AC}$, $\boldsymbol{P}_{BA}$ and $\boldsymbol{P}_{CA}$ are $(K+1)$-by-$(K+1)$ matrices.

By applying the Markov renewal reward process, we consider the probability vector at the beginning of State A satisfying the following linear equation:

$$\boldsymbol{\pi}_A = \boldsymbol{\pi}_A(\boldsymbol{P}_{AB}\boldsymbol{P}_{BA} + \boldsymbol{P}_{AC}\boldsymbol{P}_{CA}), \quad \boldsymbol{\pi}_A\boldsymbol{1} = 1, \tag{6.39}$$

where $\boldsymbol{1}$ is a column vector whose elements are 1.

We define $\boldsymbol{Q}$ as the following $(K+1)$-by-$(K+1)$ matrix

$$\boldsymbol{Q} = \begin{pmatrix} -\lambda & \lambda & & \\ & \ddots & \ddots & \\ & & -\lambda & \lambda \\ & & & 0 \end{pmatrix}. \tag{6.40}$$

Then $\boldsymbol{P}_{BA}$ and $\boldsymbol{P}_{CA}$ are given by

$$\boldsymbol{P}_{BA} = \int_0^\infty \exp(\boldsymbol{Q}t)dF_f(t), \quad \boldsymbol{P}_{CA} = \int_0^\infty \exp(\boldsymbol{Q}t)dF_r(t), \tag{6.41}$$

where $F_f(t)$ and $F_r(t)$ are the cumulative distribution functions (c.d.f.s) of Y_f and Y_r.

By using the conditional expectation, three measures are reformulated as

$$A_{ss} = \frac{\boldsymbol{\pi}_A \boldsymbol{u}_A}{\boldsymbol{\pi}_A \boldsymbol{u}_A + \boldsymbol{\pi}_A \boldsymbol{P}_{AB} \mathbf{1} \mathrm{E}[Y_f] + \boldsymbol{\pi}_A \boldsymbol{P}_{AC} \mathbf{1} \mathrm{E}[Y_r]}, \tag{6.42}$$

$$P_{loss} = \frac{\lambda(\boldsymbol{\pi}_A \boldsymbol{u}_A(K) + \boldsymbol{\pi}_A \boldsymbol{P}_{AB} \boldsymbol{u}_B(K) + \boldsymbol{\pi}_A \boldsymbol{P}_{AC} \boldsymbol{u}_C(K))}{\lambda(\boldsymbol{\pi}_A \boldsymbol{u}_A + \boldsymbol{\pi}_A \boldsymbol{P}_{AB} \mathbf{1} \mathrm{E}[Y_f] + \boldsymbol{\pi}_A \boldsymbol{P}_{AC} \mathbf{1} \mathrm{E}[Y_r])}, \tag{6.43}$$

$$T_{res} = \frac{\sum_{n=1}^{K} n(\boldsymbol{\pi}_A \boldsymbol{u}_A(n) + \boldsymbol{\pi}_A \boldsymbol{P}_{AB} \boldsymbol{u}_B(n) + \boldsymbol{\pi}_A \boldsymbol{P}_{AC} \boldsymbol{u}_C(n))}{\lambda \sum_{n=0}^{K-1} (\boldsymbol{\pi}_A \boldsymbol{u}_A(n) + \boldsymbol{\pi}_A \boldsymbol{P}_{AB} \boldsymbol{u}_B(n) + \boldsymbol{\pi}_A \boldsymbol{P}_{AC} \boldsymbol{u}_C(n))}, \tag{6.44}$$

where $\boldsymbol{u}_x(n)$ denotes a column vector whose i-th entry represents the expected sojourn time in which the number of transactions is n in State x provided that there are i transactions in the system at the beginning of State x. Note that $\boldsymbol{u}_A = \sum_{n=0}^{K} \boldsymbol{u}_A(n)$. Also, from the cumulative reward argument [18], $\boldsymbol{u}_B(n)$ and $\boldsymbol{u}_C(n)$ are

$$\boldsymbol{u}_B(n) = \int_0^\infty \int_0^t \exp(\boldsymbol{Q}s) ds dF_f(t) \mathbf{1}_n, \quad \boldsymbol{u}_C(n) = \int_0^\infty \int_0^t \exp(\boldsymbol{Q}s) ds dF_r(t) \mathbf{1}_n. \tag{6.45}$$

In the above, $\mathbf{1}_n$ is a column vector where only the n-th element is 1 and the others are 0. The other values of $\boldsymbol{P}_{AB}$, $\boldsymbol{P}_{AC}$, and $\boldsymbol{u}_A(n)$ are obtained from the difference-differential equations by Eqs. (6.10)–(6.13). Concretely, the (i, j)-elements of $\boldsymbol{P}_{AB}$ and $\boldsymbol{P}_{AC}$ are $p_{j'}(T)$ and $p_j(T)$, respectively, which are the solutions of difference-differential equations with the initial conditions; $p_i(0) = 1$ and $p_j(0) = 0$ for $j \neq i$. Also, the i-th element of $\boldsymbol{u}_A(n)$ is given by

$$[\boldsymbol{u}_A(n)]_i = \int_0^T p_n(t) dt, \tag{6.46}$$

provided that the initial conditions remain true; $p_i(0) = 1$ and $p_j(0) = 0$ for $j \neq i$. This value can also be computed by the difference-differential equations.

Multiple server

The queueing model is extended to the case of a multiple server system [14] i.e., an $M/M_t/m/K$ queueing system. Based on the system architecture of parallel processing with a hot standby system, the service and failure rates when s servers are active become $s\mu(\cdot)$ and $s\rho(\cdot)$. Also, it is assumed that the recovery operation of the failed server is immediately and concurrently started. For simplification, the recovery time for one server follows an

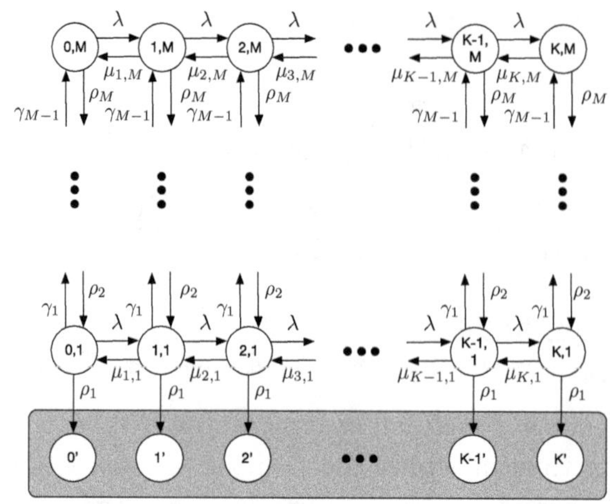

Fig. 6.6. State transition diagram for a multiple server system under T-I.

exponential distribution with mean $1/\gamma_f$. The system failure is defined by the event that all the servers are failed.

We define the following states

(n, s): The state where n transactions are in the system and s servers are active.

n': The state where the failure occurs when n transactions are in the system.

Figure 6.6 shows the state transitions for a multiple server system under T-I. In the figure, $\mu_{n,s}$, ρ_s and γ_s are the service rate, failure rate and repair (recovery) rate when the number of transactions is n and s servers are active. They are given by

$$\mu_{n,s} = \min(n, s)\mu(\cdot), \quad \rho_s = s\rho(\cdot), \quad \gamma_s = (M - s)\gamma_f. \tag{6.47}$$

Let $p_{n,s}(t)$ and $p_{n'}(t)$ be the state probabilities for the states (n, s) and n', respectively, which are computed by solving the difference-differential equations numerically according to Fig. 6.6. Then we have the following values for a multiple server system under T-I:

$$P_{AB} = \sum_{n=0}^{K} p_{n'}(T), \tag{6.48}$$

$$\mathrm{E}[U] = \int_0^T \sum_{n=0}^{K} \sum_{s=1}^{M} p_{n,s}(t)dt, \tag{6.49}$$

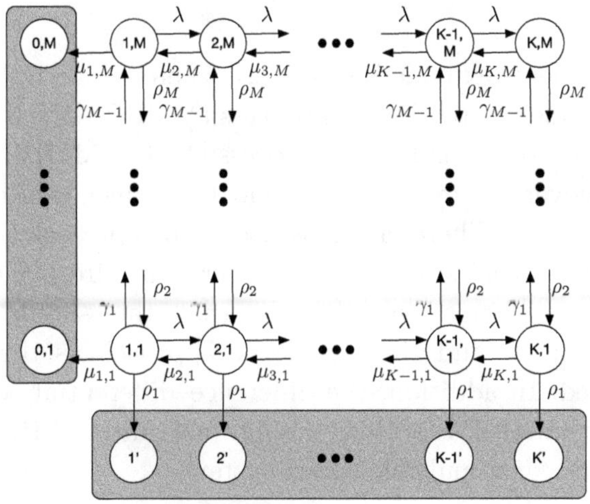

Fig. 6.7. State transition diagram for a multiple server system under T-II for $T < t < \infty$.

$$\mathrm{E}[U_n] = \int_0^T \sum_{s=1}^{M} p_{n,s}(t)dt, \quad n = 1, \dots K, \tag{6.50}$$

$$\mathrm{E}[N_l] = \sum_{n=0}^{K} n(p_{n'}(T) + \sum_{s=1}^{M} p_{n,s}(T)). \tag{6.51}$$

Under T-II, we need the difference-differential equations according to Fig. 6.7 for $T < t < \infty$, and their initial condition is given by the solutions of difference-differential equations under T-I. Also, note that $p_{0'}(t) = p_{0'}(T)$ for $T < t < \infty$. Analogous to the analysis of T-II in Garg *et al.*'s [6] model, we obtain the following values for a multiple server system under T-II.

$$P_{AB} = \sum_{n=0}^{K} p_{n'}(\infty), \tag{6.52}$$

$$\mathrm{E}[U] = \int_0^T \sum_{s=1}^{M} p_{0,s}(t)dt + \int_0^\infty \sum_{n=1}^{K} \sum_{s=1}^{M} p_{n,s}(t)dt, \tag{6.53}$$

$$\mathrm{E}[U_n] = \int_0^\infty \sum_{s=1}^{M} p_{n,s}(t)dt, \quad n = 1, \dots K, \tag{6.54}$$

$$\mathrm{E}[N_l] = \sum_{n=0}^{K} np_{n'}(T). \tag{6.55}$$

Burst arrival

The queueing model is extended to the case where the arrival process follows a 2-state Markov modulated Poisson process (MMPP) [15]. The MMPP is an extension of a homogeneous Poisson process [3]. The MMPP has an internal state which is governed by a CTMC and its arrival rate depends on the current internal state. Therefore, it is useful to represent the burst arrival by changing the internal state. On the other hand, from the mathematical point of view, the information on the internal state should be kept at the beginning of State A, and thus the same approach as the resume policy should be applied. In addition, the difference–differential equations should be extended so that they represent the internal states of the arrival process with N-policy and/or a multiple server system.

Block policy

Salfner and Wolter [20] proposed another time-triggered policy in which the system blocks arrivals after T under T-II. Although the model was described by a stochastic Petri net in the original paper, it can also be represented by the framework of Garg *et al.*'s [6] model. The difference-differential equations during $T < t < \infty$ change as follows.

$$\frac{dp_0(t)}{dt} = \mu(\cdot)p_1(t), \tag{6.56}$$

$$\frac{dp_n(t)}{dt} = -(\mu(\cdot) + \rho(\cdot))p_n(t) + \mu(\cdot)p_{n+1}(t), \quad n = 1, \ldots, K-1, \tag{6.57}$$

$$\frac{dp_K(t)}{dt} = -(\mu(\cdot) + \rho(\cdot))p_K(t), \tag{6.58}$$

$$\frac{dp_{n'}(t)}{dt} = \rho(\cdot)p_n(t), \quad n = 0, \ldots, K. \tag{6.59}$$

Also, the expected number of lost transactions after T should be added in order to compute the loss probability of transactions. Since the expected number of lost transactions after T equals the number of arrivals after T when there is at least one transaction, it is given by

$$\lambda \int_T^{\infty} \sum_{n=1}^{K} p_n(t)dt. \tag{6.60}$$

6.6. A Generalized Transaction Model

Garg *et al.*'s [6] model works well to represent the degradation of software systems even if the degradation depends on some rewards such as accumulation of execution time. However, from the mathematical point of view, the analysis of Garg *et al.*'s [6] model is not easy, because the difference-differential equations should be solved as the NHMC analysis. Zheng *et al.* [25] presented a quasi-birth-and-death (QBD) model by representing the degradation process as a CTMC. This is also regarded as an approximation model of Garg *et al.*'s [6] model with the phase-type expansion [22], and requires only the Markov regenerative process (MRGP) analysis which is systematically solved compared to the NHMC analysis. In this section, we introduce the QBD model for software aging and rejuvenation. It is noted that this generalized model can involve the existing queueing model [24] mathematically.

Suppose that the arrival stream to the system follows a Markovian arrival process (MAP). The MAP is an extension of the Poisson process and MMPP. Let $N(t)$ be the cumulative number of arrivals following a MAP before time t. When the underlying CTMC is given by $J(t)$ on the state space $\{1, 2, \ldots, m\}$, the MAP is represented by the two-dimensional point process $(N(t), J(t))$ which is a CTMC with the following infinitesimal generator:

$$\boldsymbol{Q}_{\text{MAP}} = \begin{pmatrix} \boldsymbol{D}_0 & \boldsymbol{D}_1 & & \\ & \boldsymbol{D}_0 & \boldsymbol{D}_1 & \\ & & \ddots & \ddots \end{pmatrix}, \tag{6.61}$$

where $\boldsymbol{D}_0$ is an m-by-m infinitesimal generator without the occurrence of arrivals and $\boldsymbol{D}_1$ is an m-by-m transition rate matrix when an arrival occurs. Also, the state of $J(t)$ is a phase of the MAP, which corresponds to the internal state of the arrival process.

Consider a transaction system with the finite capacity $K(\geq 1)$. The service rate for each transaction is assumed to depend on the degradation level. For instance, we suppose that there are n degradation levels. Let μ_k, $k = 1, \ldots, n$, be the service rate when the degradation level of the system is k. When $\mu_1 > \cdots > \mu_n$, the degradation level 1 indicates the normal condition of the system and the degradation level n corresponds to the most degraded system condition. In addition, the system degradation is also dominated by a CTMC with an n-by-n infinitesimal generator $\boldsymbol{G}$. The (i, j)-element of $\boldsymbol{G}$ indicates a transition rate from the degradation level i to j.

The behavior of the transaction system can be represented by $(X(t), J(t), D(t))$ where $X(t)$ is the number of transactions in the system, $J(t)$ is the phase process of the arrival stream and $D(t)$ is the process of the degradation levels. The stochastic process $(X(t), J(t), D(t))$ is described as a CTMC with the following block matrix:

$$\boldsymbol{Q}_{\mathrm{QBD}} = \underbrace{\begin{pmatrix} \boldsymbol{B}_{00} & \boldsymbol{B}_{01} & & & & \\ \boldsymbol{B}_{10} & \boldsymbol{A}_1 & \boldsymbol{A}_2 & & & \\ & \boldsymbol{A}_0 & \boldsymbol{A}_1 & \boldsymbol{A}_2 & & \\ & & \ddots & \ddots & \ddots & \\ & & & \boldsymbol{A}_0 & \boldsymbol{A}_1 & \boldsymbol{A}_2 \\ & & & & \boldsymbol{A}_0 & \boldsymbol{A}_1 + \boldsymbol{A}_2 \end{pmatrix}}_{(K+1) \times (K+1) \text{ blocks}}. \tag{6.62}$$

The CTMC having the above block structure is called the QBD process. In the above equation, the matrices are given by

$$\boldsymbol{B}_{00} = \boldsymbol{D}_0 \oplus (\boldsymbol{S}_0 + \boldsymbol{S}_1), \tag{6.63}$$

$$\boldsymbol{B}_{01} = \boldsymbol{A}_2 = \boldsymbol{D}_1 \otimes \boldsymbol{I}_n, \tag{6.64}$$

$$\boldsymbol{B}_{10} = \boldsymbol{A}_0 = \boldsymbol{I}_m \otimes \boldsymbol{S}_1, \tag{6.65}$$

$$\boldsymbol{A}_1 = \boldsymbol{D}_0 \oplus \boldsymbol{S}_0. \tag{6.66}$$

where $\otimes$ and $\oplus$ are the Kronecker product and sum, and $\boldsymbol{I}_k$ is an identity matrix with size k. Also $\boldsymbol{S}_0$ and $\boldsymbol{S}_1$ are infinitesimal generators that represent the service process. When the system degradation follows the scenario mentioned above, we have

$$\boldsymbol{S}_0 = \boldsymbol{G} - \boldsymbol{S}_1, \quad \boldsymbol{S}_1 = \begin{pmatrix} \mu_1 & & & \\ & \mu_2 & & \\ & & \ddots & \\ & & & \mu_n \end{pmatrix}. \tag{6.67}$$

If the degradation level of the system does not change when the system is idle, the infinitesimal generators are given by

$$\boldsymbol{B}_{00} = \boldsymbol{D}_0 \otimes \boldsymbol{I}_n, \tag{6.68}$$

$$\boldsymbol{B}_{01} = \boldsymbol{A}_2 = \boldsymbol{D}_1 \otimes \boldsymbol{I}_n, \tag{6.69}$$

$$\boldsymbol{B}_{10} = \boldsymbol{A}_0 = \boldsymbol{I}_m \otimes \boldsymbol{S}_1, \tag{6.70}$$

$$\boldsymbol{A}_1 = \boldsymbol{D}_0 \oplus \boldsymbol{S}_0. \tag{6.71}$$

The representation of Eq. (6.62) is flexible so that all the models presented in Section 6.5 could be involved. Since the MMPP is a subclass of the MAP, the model involves the MMPP case. If the matrices $\boldsymbol{A}_0$, $\boldsymbol{A}_1$ and $\boldsymbol{A}_2$ are changed to the level-dependent representations, i.e., $\boldsymbol{A}_{0,l}$, $\boldsymbol{A}_{1,l}$ and $\boldsymbol{A}_{2,l}$ where l is the number of transactions, we can obtain the QBD process for the multiple server system. It should be noted that the performance analysis of the QBD model depends only on the rejuvenation policy, and does not depend on the system configurations such as the arrival, service and degradation processes.

In Zheng *et al.* [25], based on the QBD model, the performance measures under T-I, T-II, N-I and N-II are derived. In addition, the following wait-time policy has been proposed.

- T-policy III (T-III): Rejuvenate the system when no transaction arrives in the duration t_0 ($\geq$0) of an idle period after the accumulated operation time T (>0).
- N-policy III (N-III): Rejuvenate the system when no transaction arrives in the duration t_0 ($\geq$0) of an idle period after N ($\geq$1) transactions are processed.

Figure 6.8 shows a possible sample path of the QBD model with T-III. The wait time t_0 works to detect whether the internal state of the arrival stream is a low arrival state or not.

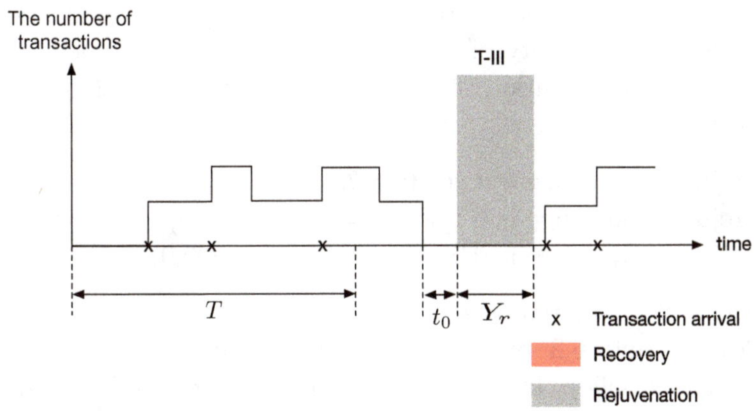

Fig. 6.8. The possible behavior of a transaction system under T-III.

Finally, we illustrate the application example of the QBD model to the real system which was introduced in Zheng *et al.* [25]. The parameters of the arrival stream were estimated from the access log (1.2E+6 sec.) of an Apache web server for two weeks as follows.

$$\boldsymbol{D}_0 = \begin{pmatrix} -1.093\text{E-3} & 2.092\text{E-4} \\ 0.2771 & -100.6 \end{pmatrix}, \tag{6.72}$$

$$\boldsymbol{D}_1 = \begin{pmatrix} 2.673\text{E-5} & 8.567\text{E-4} \\ 1.605 & 98.73 \end{pmatrix}. \tag{6.73}$$

The size of the MAP has been determined by the Akaike information criterion [1]. From the estimated parameters, it can be found that there exist two states with high and low arrival rates in the example of a real system. The average arrival rate and inter-arrival time of the estimated MAP are 0.058 (1/sec) and 17.34 (sec), respectively. On the other hand, the parameters of the service process are also estimated from the processing data of an Apache web sever in a closed experimental network:

$$\boldsymbol{G} = \begin{pmatrix} -7.904\text{E-4} & 7.904\text{E-4} & 0 \\ 8.066\text{E-3} & -8.077\text{E-3} & 1.035\text{E-5} \\ 0 & 0 & 0 \end{pmatrix}, \tag{6.74}$$

$$\boldsymbol{S}_1 = \begin{pmatrix} 2176.982 & & \\ & 46.631 & \\ & & 0.058 \end{pmatrix}. \tag{6.75}$$

Note that the service rate process was assumed to have 3 states and the last state corresponds to the event occurrence of the time-out of the request in the experiment. The service rate of the last state is set as 0.058 (1/sec), so that the traffic intensity of the transaction system becomes 1. We also assume that the rejuvenation time R follows the gamma distribution under the following three cases:

- mean rejuvenation time is 1 sec (a = 2.0, b = 2.0),
- mean rejuvenation time is 0.1 sec (a = 2.0, b = 20.0),
- mean rejuvenation time is 0.01 sec (a = 2.0, b = 200.0).

The capacity of the system is set as $K = 10$.

Tables 6.1 and 6.2 present the optimal rejuvenation timing under T-policy and N-policy. In Table 6.1, T-III outperforms T-I and T-II in terms of both loss probability of transaction and mean response time. The presented rejuvenation scheme with wait time is effective. Similarly,

Table 6.1. Optimal rejuvenation timing under T-policy.

$\mathrm{E}[R]$ [sec]	Policy	T^* [sec]	t_0^* [sec]	P_{loss}	$\bar{T}_{res}$ [msec]
	T-I	107.10	—	2.167E-2	3.52
1	T-II	106.73	—	2.156E-2	3.72
	T-III	77.09	0.20	1.760E-2	2.95
	T-I	27.36	—	7.622E-3	1.41
0.1	T-II	27.31	—	7.658E-3	1.47
	T-III	9.08	0.20	2.938E-3	0.84
	T-I	8.38	—	2.553E-3	0.78
0.01	T-II	8.20	—	2.608E-3	0.81
	T-III	0.51	0.51	4.799E-4	0.54

Table 6.2. Optimal rejuvenation timing under N-policy.

$\mathrm{E}[R]$ [sec]	Policy	N^*	t_0^* [sec]	P_{loss}	$\bar{T}_{res}$ [msec]
	N-I	948	—	1.092E-1	829.13
1	N-II	935	—	1.083E-1	824.12
	N-III	0	73.27	1.774E-2	2.97
	N-I	468	—	7.557E-2	455.80
0.1	N-II	472	—	7.588E-2	464.43
	N-III	0	9.21	2.943E-3	0.84
	N-I	213	—	5.636E-2	255.04
0.01	N-II	239	—	5.833E-2	281.81
	N-III	0	1.02	4.800E-4	0.54

in Table 6.2, N-III outperforms N-I and N-II in terms of both loss probability of transaction and mean response time. In particular, the performance of N-I and N-II becomes worse. Finally, by comparing T-III and N-III, T-III outperforms N-III for all the cases.

6.7. Summary and Future Direction

In this chapter, we have introduced the queueing models for software aging and rejuvenation. Generally, queueing models are appropriate to represent the dynamic behavior of transaction systems, and thus they are widely applied to estimate the system performance of communication, production and other computer-aided systems with the model-based approach. In the area of software aging and rejuvenation, based on the queueing model presented by Garg *et al.* [6] with NHMC analysis, a generalized model with the QBD process has been developed. The advantage of queueing models is the ability to represent the system's busy and idle states. Since software rejuvenation is a kind of maintenance, it is preferred for the rejuvenation to be executed when the system is idle. From this point of view, the queueing model is essential to discuss when the software rejuvenation is executed.

On the other hand, the weakness of the queueing model is the applicability to a real system. In the last section, although we have presented the application example to the real system, this is based on an off-line estimation. For the real applications of software aging and rejuvenation, since the system configuration dynamically changes, on-line estimation is more appropriate. Therefore, in future, it is important to combine on-line estimation such as machine learning techniques and the model-based approach. One of the possible solutions is a Markov decision process and its related reinforcement learning algorithm [21]. For example, one of the lessons from the queueing model for rejuvenation is that it is important to check if the system is busy, not just to check if system degradation has occurred, in order to decide the execution timing of rejuvenation. This lesson is directly and immediately transferred to the on-line rejuvenation control.

References

1. H. Akaike. (1974). A new look at the statistical model identification. *IEEE Transactions on Automatic Control*, **19**(6), 716–723.
2. A. Avritzer, A. Bondi, M. Grottke, E. J. Weyuker, and K. S. Trivedi. (2006). Performance assurance via software rejuvenation: Monitoring, statistics and algorithms. In *Proceedings of International Conference on Dependable Systems and Networks (DSN 2006), Philadelphia, Pennsylvania, USA, June 25–28*, pp. 435–444.
3. G. Bolch, S. Greiner, H. de Meer, and K. S. Trivedi. (2006). *Queueing Networks and Markov Chains: Modeling and Performance Evaluation with Computer Science Applications* (2nd ed.). New York City, NY, USA: John Wiley & Sons.
4. D. Bruneo, S. Distefano, F. Longo, and A. Puliafito. (2013). Workload-based software rejuvenation in cloud systems. *IEEE Transactions on Computers*, **62**(6), 1072–1085.
5. T. Dohi, K. Goševa-Popstojanova, and K. S. Trivedi. (2001). Estimating software rejuvenation schedule in high assurance systems. *The Computer Journal*, **47**, 473–485.
6. S. Garg, S. Pfening, A. Puliafito, M. Telek, and K. S. Trivedi. (1998). Analysis of preventive maintenance in transactions based software systems. *IEEE Transactions on Computers*, **47**(1), 96–107.

7. S. Garg, M. Telek, A. Puliafito, and K. S. Trivedi. (1995). Analysis of software rejuvenation using Markov regenerative stochastic Petri net. In *Proceedings of the 6th International Symposium on Software Reliability Engineering (ISSRE'95), Toulouse, France, October 24–27*, pp. 24–27.
8. Y. Huang, C. Kintala, N. Kolettis, and N. D. Fulton. (1995). Software rejuvenation: Analysis, module and applications. In *Proceedings of the 25th International Symposium on Fault-Tolerant Computing, Pasadena, California, USA, June 27–30*, pp. 381–390.
9. F. Machida, D. S. Kim, and K. S. Trivedi. (2013). Modeling and analysis of software rejuvenation in a server virtualized system with live VM migration. *Performance Evaluation*, **70**(3), 212–230.
10. F. Machida and N. Miyoshi. (2017). Analysis of an optimal stopping problem for software rejuvenation in a deteriorating job processing system. *Reliability Engineering and System Safety*, **168**(C), 128–135.
11. H. Okamura and T. Dohi. (2013). Dynamic software rejuvenation policies in a transaction-based system under Markovian arrival processes. *Performance Evaluation*, **70**(3), 197–211.
12. H. Okamura, S. Miyahara, and T. Dohi. (2001a). Refined non-homogeneous Markovian models for a single-server type of software system with rejuvenation. *Revue Francaise d'Automatique, Informatique et Recherche Operationnelle (Recherche Operationnelle/Operations Research)*, **36**(2), 129–148.
13. H. Okamura, S. Miyahara, and T. Dohi. (2002). Dependability analysis of a client/server software system with rejuvenation. In *Proceedings of the 13th International Symposium on Software Reliability Engineering (ISSRE'02), Annapolis, Maryland, USA, November 12–15*, pp. 171–180.
14. H. Okamura, S. Miyahara, and T. Dohi. (2003). Dependability analysis of a transaction-based multi server system with rejuvenation. *IEICE Transactions on Fundamentals of Electronics, Communications and Computer Sciences (A)*, **E86-A**(8), 2081–2090.
15. H. Okamura, S. Miyahara, and T. Dohi. (2005). Rejuvenating communication network system with burst arrival. *IEICE Transactions on Communications (B)*, **E88-B**(12), 4498–4506.
16. H. Okamura, S. Miyahara, T. Dohi, and S. Osaki. (2001b). Performance evaluation of workload-based software rejuvenation scheme. *IEICE Transactions on Information and Systems (D)*, **E84-D**(10), 1368–1375.
17. S. Pfening, S. Garg, A. Puliafito, M. Telek, and K. S. Trivedi. (1996). Optimal rejuvenation for tolerating soft failure. *Performance Evaluation*, **27/28**(4), 491–506.
18. A. Reibman and K. S. Trivedi. (1989). Transient analysis of cumulative measures of Markov model behavior. *Stochastic Models*, **5**(4), 683–710.
19. S. M. Ross. (1970). *Applied Probability Models with Optimization Applications.* San Francisco, California, USA: Holden-Day.
20. F. Salfner and K. Wolter. (2010). Analysis of service availability for time-triggered rejuvenation policies. *Journal of Systems and Software*, **83**, 1579–1590.
21. R. S. Sutton and A. G. Barto. (1998). *Reinforcement Learning: An Introduction.* Cambridge, Massachusetts, USA: MIT Press.
22. K. S. Trivedi and A. Bobbio. (2017). *Reliability and Availability Engineering: Modeling, Analysis, and Applications.* Cambridge, UK: Cambridge University Press.
23. K. Vaidyanathan and K. S. Trivedi. (2005). A comprehensive model for software rejuvenation. *IEEE Transactions on Dependable and Secure Computing*, **2**(2), 124–137.

24. D. Wang, W. Xie, and K. S. Trivedi. (2007). Performability analysis of clustered systems with rejuvenation under varying workload. *Performance Evaluation*, **64**(3), 247–265.
25. J. Zheng, H. Okamura, L. Li, and T. Dohi. (2017). A comprehensive evaluation of software rejuvenation policies for transaction systems with Markovian arrivals. *IEEE Transactions on Reliability*, **66**(4), 1157–1177.

Chapter 7

Black-Box Models for Restart, Reboot and Rejuvenation

Katinka Wolter*,§, Tommi Pesu†,¶, Aad van Moorsel‡,‖ and William J. Knottenbelt†,**

*Free University Berlin, Germany
†Imperial College London, UK
‡Newcastle University, UK
§katinka.wolter@fu-berlin.de
¶tommi.pesu13@imperial.ac.uk
‖aad.vanmoorsel@ncl.ac.uk
**w.knottenbelt@imperial.ac.uk

This chapter discusses black-box models for retries, where no distinction is made between the purpose of the retry. Retries can be used as restart, to improve user-observed performance, as reboot, for fault-tolerance, or as rejuvenation, to treat the aging of the system. The chapter derives stochastic models and shows the results we obtained for optimising moments of the user-observed job completion time as well as the probability of meeting a deadline. The second part of the chapter provides a review of the literature in this area of the past decade. The chapter closes with a discussion of open problems.

7.1. Introduction

This chapter provides a survey for the model-based assessment and optimization of restart, reboot and rejuvenation strategies for 'black-box' models. That is, the models contain no representation of the structure of the system. Instead, we consider situations in which one only has available the probability distribution function of the time it takes to complete a task (i.e., the completion time distribution). This is both relevant if the specifics of a system are not known, or if the system is exceedingly complex, such as in the case of jobs executed over the Internet. In our discussion, we abstract away the specific technique (reboot, rejuvenation, etc.) and elements such as the aging of software or failures are not explicitly identified, but are only represented through their impact on the completion time distribution of a task.

The approach behind this chapter is as follows. We base the chapter on the Habilitation thesis of Wolter [90], which provides an overview of the state of the art up to 2007 in a high level of detail. The first part of this chapter is a much abridged version of the information available in Wolter [90], summarising the main insights gained, with the most basic derivations of the results included. The main addition since Wolter [90] is the section on the total time taken for test transforms in Section 7.4.1. The second part is a systematic overview of the research trends since 2007. It complements the basic theory in the first part with an overview of the many research activities in the field, thus providing ample illustration of the rich area of research to which the theory discussed in this chapter applies. Based on the material presented, this chapter can serve as a textbook, presenting a complete but concise review of black-box models for restart, reboot and rejuvenation, as well as the latest trends in system research that make use of and expand on these models.

The chapter is organised as follows. First, we discuss, in Section 7.2, metrics to assess restart, namely (1) moments of completion time and (2) the probability of exceeding a deadline. We also illustrate results for these metrics for basic completion time distributions, including exponential, hyper- and hypo-exponential distributions, as well as heavy tail distributions. Section 7.3 then derives expressions for the measures of interest, that is, for the moments of completion time and for the probability of meeting a deadline, respectively. Based on these expressions, Section 7.4 studies the optimal restart time for both these metrics, again subdivided into optimizing moments and deadline probabilities, respectively. Section 7.5 identifies the way restart approaches have been implemented in practice, and also when the completion time distributions are not known, either because not enough data has been collected or because a reliable estimate of the distribution is too impractical to obtain. Section 7.6 provides a survey of literature published since 2007, identifying trends and new insights. Finally, Section 7.7 discusses open issues in the theory and practice of the black-box modeling of restarts.

7.2. Metrics to Assess the Benefits of Restarts

At first glance, a restart may seem a counter-intuitive approach to improve performance: how could it be beneficial to restart a task completely from scratch? Nevertheless, most of us use the technique when browsing the web: if a web page takes too long to load, we click the reload button. From individual experience we know this is often the best approach to download a page if it 'hangs'. Krishnamurthy and Rexford [46] explain why and how this works: clicking the reload button 'overrules' the TCP retransmission timer (a restart mechanism in its own right), resulting in an earlier renewed download attempt.

Restarts appear in many shapes and forms, and are sometimes called by a different name more appropriate for the specific field, such as a reboot, rejuvenation, reload, etc. In our treatise, the term restart may apply to any job, for any kind of system. The completion of a task corresponds to either a result being returned, in the case of a computation, or a completion message being returned, in case of, for instance, a database transaction. If a job or transaction does not complete within a certain time, it is re-issued. That is, we conduct a restart. Several variants exist. For instance, in some cases the old instance can be aborted, in others it cannot. Similarly, in some restart scenarios a task is restarted in an exactly identical configuration or parameterisation, while in other scenarios the restarted task may have a new set of parameters, perhaps even a new work requirement.

The models we discuss in this chapter are valid under two assumptions: (1) we assume that the restart of a task terminates the previous attempt. This is for instance the case when we click the reload button in a web browser: the connection with the server is terminated and a new download attempt is issued [46]. And, (2) we assume that successive tries are statistically independent and identically distributed. This assumption has been found realistic in a measurement study of HTTP GET [65] as well as for the use case of downloading web pages [52].

In mathematical terms, the problem formulation is then as follows. Let the random variable T denote the completion time of a job, with probability distribution $F(t), t \in [0, \infty)$, and probability density function $f(t), t \in [0, \infty)$. For convenience, but without loss of generality,[a] we assume that $F(t)$ is a continuous probability distribution function defined over the domain $[0, \infty)$, so that $F(t) > 0$ if $t > 0$. Assume τ is a restart time,[b] and introduce the random variable T_τ to denote the completion time when an unbounded number of retries is allowed. That is, a retry takes place periodically, every τ time units, until the deadline has passed (if a deadline is set). We write $f_\tau(t)$ and $F_\tau(t)$ for the density and distribution of T_τ, respectively.

[a] At the cost of more notation, and with a proper discussion for special cases, the results in this section also apply to distributions defined over finite domains, as well as to defective distributions and distributions with jumps.

[b] At times we also refer to τ as the as restart *interval*.

Moments of Expected Completion Time

The first metrics of interest are the moments of completion time $\mathrm{E}[T_\tau^n]$, for $n = 1, 2, \ldots$. Under the assumption of independent identically distributed completion times of successive tries, for the first moment, one would conduct the first restart at time τ if and only if:

$$\mathrm{E}[T] < \mathrm{E}[T - \tau | T > \tau]. \tag{7.1}$$

Intuitively, this says that the expected completion time $\mathrm{E}[T]$ when starting anew must be less than $\mathrm{E}[T - \tau|T > \tau]$, the expected remaining completion time when not restarting. Equation (7.1) only considers the first restart, but in Section 7.3.1 we will show that Eq. (7.1) is a necessary and sufficient condition for *any* number of repeated restarts to be beneficial as well, a result that is not necessarily obvious at first hand.

Similarly, we can articulate when restarts are beneficial if one is concerned about improving higher moments of completion time $\mathrm{E}[T^n]$:

$$\mathrm{E}[T^n] < \mathrm{E}[(T - \tau)^n | T > \tau]. \tag{7.2}$$

We will see in Section 7.3.1 that for higher moments we cannot conclude from Eq. (7.2) that repeated restarts will also be beneficial.

Probability of Meeting Deadlines

The second type of metrics of interest is individual points of the completion time distribution, that is, the probability of meeting deadlines. One can reason about the completion time distribution with restarts as Bernoulli trials. At each interval between restarts there is a probability $F(\tau)$ that the completion 'succeeds.' Hence, if the deadline d is a multiple of the restart time τ, we can relate the probability of missing the deadline without and with restarts through:

$$1 - F_\tau(d) = (1 - F(\tau))^{\frac{d}{\tau}}. \tag{7.3}$$

Then the probability of meeting the deadline under restarts is

$$F_\tau(d) = 1 - (1 - F(\tau))^{\frac{d}{\tau}}, \tag{7.4}$$

and restarts only make sense if the probability of meeting the deadline is higher with restarts than without:

$$F_\tau(d) > F(d). \tag{7.5}$$

7.2.1. *Example Distributions*

It is useful to explore for which completion time distributions $F(t)$ the above conditions hold. We explore the exponential distribution and its variants, which all possess exponential tails, as well as the Pareto distribution, which is an example of a heavy-tail distribution. We will see that distributions with heavy tails always benefit from restarts, while for distributions with exponential tails the situation is more diverse. Considering the three prototypical cases of exponentially decaying distributions [32], restarts are beneficial (eventually) for hyper-exponential distributions, not beneficial for hypo-exponential distributions, including the Erlang distribution, and immaterial for the exponential distribution.

Exponential Completion Time Distribution

For exponentially-distributed task completion time we obtain:

$$\begin{aligned} \mathrm{E}[T] &= \int_0^\infty t\lambda \cdot e^{-\lambda t}\, dt = \frac{1}{\lambda} \\ \mathrm{E}[T-\tau | T > \tau] &= \frac{1}{1-F(\tau)} \int_\tau^\infty (t-\tau) f(t)\, dt \\ &= \int_\tau^\infty (t-\tau)\lambda \cdot e^{-\lambda(t-\tau)}\, dt = \frac{1}{\lambda} \end{aligned}$$

So, for the exponential distribution a restart is not beneficial, but does not do any harm either.

For exponentially-distributed task completion time the condition in Eq. (7.5) is easily proven to be an equality, i.e.,

$$F_\tau(d) = F(d)$$

In other words, the probability of meeting the deadline is equal whether or not one restarts an exponentially-distributed job. Hence, for exponential job completion time a restart neither helps nor hurts.

Hyper-Exponential Completion Time Distribution

Hyper-exponential distributions contain choices between exponentials, and the choices imply that hyper-exponential distributions are characterized by a coefficient of variation that is larger than 1. The hyper-exponential distribution belongs to a class of distributions that take values from different random variables with different probabilities, that is, with probability p_1 it is distributed as X_1, with probability p_2 it is distributed as X_2, etc. Intuitively, it then is beneficial to perform a restart when time passes and it becomes likely one drew one of the slower distributions. Restarting provides a chance to draw one of the faster distributions instead.

For illustration, consider a hyper-exponential distribution with N choices, each with probability p_i and parameters λ_i for the i-th choice, then we have that, by definition, the density and distribution function are

$$f(t) = \sum_{i=1}^{N} p_i \lambda_i e^{-\lambda_i t}$$

$$F(t) = 1 - \sum_{i=1}^{N} p_i e^{-\lambda_i t},$$

and for the expected completion time without and with restarts, we have

$$\mathrm{E}\left[T\right] = \sum_{i=1}^{N} \frac{p_i}{\lambda_i} \tag{7.6}$$

$$\mathrm{E}\left[T - \tau | T > \tau\right] = \frac{\sum_{i=1}^{N} \frac{p_i}{\lambda_i} e^{-\lambda_i \tau}}{\sum_{i=1}^{N} p_i e^{-\lambda_i \tau}}. \tag{7.7}$$

Now, let us consider restarts when the restart time τ becomes increasingly large. Let $\lambda_k = \min_{i=1}^{N} \lambda_i$ be the slowest among the N exponentially-distributed completion times. Then, for $\tau \to \infty$, dividing the numerator and denominator of Eq. (7.7) by $e^{-\lambda_k \tau}$, we obtain:

$$\lim_{\tau \to \infty} \mathrm{E}\left[T - \tau | T > \tau\right] = \frac{1}{\lambda_k}. \tag{7.8}$$

Assuming that $p_i > 0$ for all i and that not all rates λ_i are equal, it follows that $\frac{1}{\lambda_k} > \mathrm{E}\left[T\right]$. Restarts therefore become beneficial in hyper-exponential distributions as time increases.

Hypo-Exponential Completion Time Distribution

Hypo-exponentials contain stages of exponentially-distributed time, and have a coefficient of variance less than 1. A special case is the Erlang distribution, in which all stages have the same rate. Breaking up an exponentially-distributed time into stages decreases the variance of the overall completion time. For hypo-exponential distributions we can show that Condition (7.5) never holds. For instance, assume an Erlang distribution, and let the restart interval τ and the deadline d relate as $\tau = \alpha d$, $0 < \alpha < 1$. Then:

$$1 - F(d) > (1 - F(\tau))^{\frac{d}{\tau}} \Leftrightarrow \quad (1 + \lambda d)^{\alpha} > 1 + \alpha\lambda d$$

Assume that $\lambda d > 0$ (neither a deadline nor an event rate less or equal to zero makes much sense), and for $0 < \alpha < 1$ we have

$$(1 + \lambda d)^{\alpha} < 1 + \alpha\lambda d, \tag{7.9}$$

which means that a restart is never beneficial for a completion time distribution of the hypo-exponential type, no matter what deadline is set or what the parameters of the distribution are. This can be understood intuitively, since multiple subtasks need to be completed sequentially to finish service, and none of the individual subtasks benefit from restart (because the subtasks are exponentially-distributed). If one were to restart after some completed subtasks, one would return to the initial subtask, which is never beneficial.

Heavy Tails: Pareto Completion Time Distribution

The Pareto distribution is an example of a heavy-tailed distribution, that is, a distribution that does not exponentially decay to 0 for large t, but that decays in polynomial manner. Heavy-tailed distributions commonly arise when studying Internet applications, see for instance Krishnamurthy and Rexford [46]. They describe a situation in which most tasks are quick, but a few take particularly long. The Pareto distribution has density

$$f(t) = \frac{a \cdot b^a}{t^{a+1}}, \quad \text{for } t > b.$$

For $a \neq 1$, the expected completion time with and without restart evaluates to

$$\begin{aligned} \mathrm{E}[T] &= \frac{a \cdot b}{a - 1} \\ \mathrm{E}[T - \tau | T > \tau] &= \int_{\tau}^{\infty} (t - \tau)\frac{b}{(t - \tau)^2}\, dt \\ &= [b \ln(t - \tau)]_{\tau}^{\infty} = \infty. \end{aligned}$$

Having waited a period τ, the expected completion time does not converge, therefore it is always useful to restart a task with Pareto distributed completion time. Pareto distributed tasks typically do not take particularly long, but if they do, they should be aborted and restarted.

7.3. Expressions for Completion Time under Restarts

In this section we present expressions for the moments of completion time under restarts, as well as for the probability of missing the deadline. For the moments of completion time, we distinguish two cases. First, we discuss in Section 7.3.1 unbounded restarts, in which restarts take place repeatedly with fixed length restart intervals. Then we consider in Section 7.3.2 the case in which restart intervals may not be all of equal length, and can be finite in number. Section 7.3.3 discusses expressions for the probability of missing the deadline, possibly with restart intervals of unequal length.

7.3.1. *Moments of Completion Time: Unbounded Number of Restarts*

Let us first study the completion time distribution under an unbounded number of restarts, that is, the restarts will repeat after a period τ again and again, until the task completes. We use the notation introduced in Section 7.2 and introduce an overhead cost c, expressed as the number of time-units it takes to conduct a restart. We find that $F_\tau(t)$, the completion time under restarts, relates to that without restarts as:

$$1 - F_\tau(t) = \begin{cases} (1 - F(\tau))^k (1 - F(t - k(\tau + c))) \\ \quad \text{if } \; k(\tau + c) \leq t < k(\tau + c) + \tau \\ (1 - F(\tau))^{k+1} \\ \quad \text{if } \; k(\tau + c) + \tau \leq t < (k+1)(\tau + c) \end{cases} \tag{7.10}$$

for $k = 0, 1, 2, \ldots$. Note that the second line in Eq. (7.10) represents the period of time of length c for the restart to take place. For the density we obtain also for any integer value $k = 0, 1, 2, \ldots$:

$$f_\tau(t) = \begin{cases} (1 - F(\tau))^k f(t - k(\tau + c)) \\ \quad \text{if } \; k(\tau + c) \leq t < k(\tau + c) + \tau \\ 0 \\ \quad \text{if } \; k(\tau + c) + \tau \leq t < (k+1)(\tau + c) \end{cases} \tag{7.11}$$

Example. It is worth visualising the density of T_τ, see Figs. 7.1 and 7.2, for a mixed hyper/hypo-exponentially distributed T. Figure 7.1 is the 'original' density of the hyper/hypo-exponential distribution and Fig. 7.2 the density f_τ under restarts for that same hyper/hypo-exponential. The parameters of the hyper/hypo-exponential random variable are as follows. It draws with

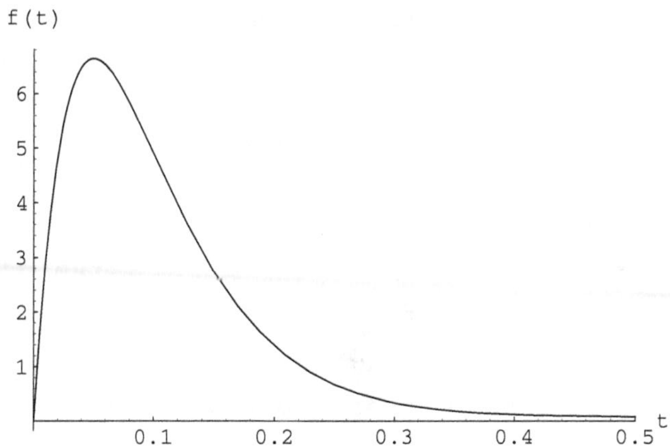

Fig. 7.1. The probability density function f of the example hyper/hypo-exponential distribution. (Optimal restart times are 0.25 for single restarts and 0.19 for an unbounded number of restarts.)

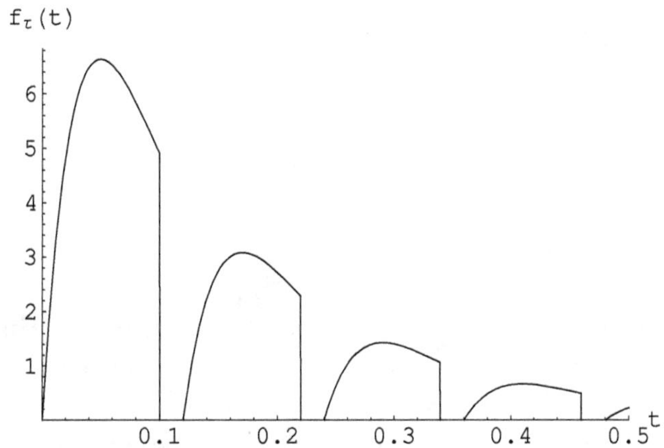

Fig. 7.2. The probability density f_τ of completion time with an unbounded number of restarts (for the example the hyper/hypo-exponential distribution, with restart time $\tau = 0.1$ and cost $c = 0.02$).

probability $p = 0.9$ from an Erlang distribution with two phases and mean 0.1 and with probability $p = 0.1$ from an Erlang distribution with two phases and mean 1.0. We also assume the restart time $\tau = 0.1$, and the cost $c = 0.02$. We will see later that for a single restart, the optimal restart time is 0.25, while for an unbounded number of repeated restarts, the optimal restart time is 0.19. The expected completion time decreases for a single restart from 0.190 to 0.136, and for unbounded restarts to 0.127.

For the expression of moments of completion time, we need the partial moments $M_n(\tau)$ at τ of the completion time, which are defined as:

$$M_n(\tau) = \int_0^{\tau} t^n f(t)dt = \int_0^{\tau} t^n f_\tau(t)dt. \tag{7.12}$$

The equality of partial moments of T and T_τ follows from the fact that their respective densities are identical between 0 and τ (see Eq. (7.11) for $k = 0$).

Theorem 7.1. *The moments* $E[T_\tau^n] = \int_0^\infty t^n f_\tau(t)dt$, $n = 1, 2, \ldots,$ *of the completion time with unbounded number of restarts, restart interval length* $\tau > 0$, *and time* c *consumed by a restart, can be expressed as*:

$$E[T_\tau^n] = \frac{M_n(\tau)}{F(\tau)} + \frac{1-F(\tau)}{F(\tau)} \sum_{l=0}^{n-1} \binom{n}{l} (\tau + c)^{n-l} E\left[T_\tau^l\right], \tag{7.13}$$

where $E\left[T_\tau^0\right] = 1$.

Proof. The derivation is particularly elegant if one exploits the recursive structure of Eq. (7.11), but we refer to van Moorsel and Wolter [82] for the details. □

For example, the expected completion time is given by:

$$\mathrm{E}\left[T_\tau\right] = \frac{M_1(\tau)}{F(\tau)} + \frac{1-F(\tau)}{F(\tau)}(\tau + c). \tag{7.14}$$

The expression for the variance can be found in Maurer and Huberman [52]. The result for the first moment is indeed as it should be: Eq. (7.14) must account for the interval in which the task completes, as well as for the times the job fails to complete. The first term in Eq. (7.14) is the expected download time conditioned on success within a restart interval. The second term represents the expected number of intervals in which the download does not complete.

Figure 7.3 shows the relative gain using restarts versus the restart interval length, for the first three moments, where we use identical interval lengths for all restarts, which we will later see is not always optimal. Notice that the gain increases rather dramatically with the order of the moment. Also, notice the wide range of restart times which perform well, which suggests that rough estimates may often suffice to set a restart time. An important engineering rule we deduce from Fig. 7.3 for distributions such as in our example is not to make the restart time too small, since the completion time will then quickly tend to infinity. In general, it is safer to make the restart time too large than too small.

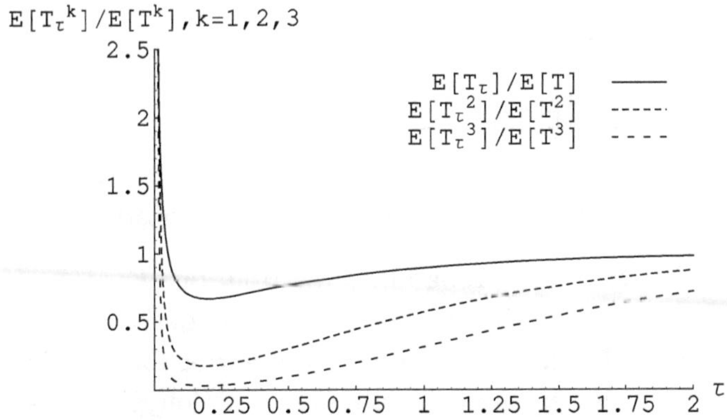

Fig. 7.3. Restart time versus the normalised difference between unbounded restarts and no restarts, for the first three moments.

As a corollary of Theorem 7.1 we state a fundamental result, which was also observed by Chen *et al.* [14] for failure detectors.

Corollary 7.1. *Under unbounded restarts, the expectation (as well as higher moments) of the completion time* T_τ *with restart time* $\tau > 0$ *(for which* $F(\tau) > 0$*), is* always *finite, even if the moments of the original completion time are not.*

This is an important observation, stressing the value of restarts for situations in which there is a strictly positive probability that a task can fail and not complete at all (thus making the moments of completion time infinite).

7.3.2. *Moments of Completion Time: Finite Number of Restarts, Restart with Non-Identical Intervals*

There may be cases in which one is interested in a *finite* number of restarts, or in non-identical restart intervals. For example, in the mixed hyper/hypo-exponential example, too low a restart time is very detrimental for the completion time if there is no bound on the number of restarts. For such distributions it may be wise to limit the number of restarts, or increase the period between restarts with the restart count, to avoid getting stuck with too short a restart time.

For our discussion it is convenient to label the restarts as shown in Fig. 7.4. We assume the total number of restarts is K, and the restart intervals have length $\tau_1, \tau_2, \ldots, \tau_{K-1}, \tau_K$, respectively. The k-th interval starts at time s_k. So, we get $s_1 = 0$, $s_2 = \tau_1 + c$, $s_3 = \tau_1 + c + \tau_2 + c$, etc., until $s_K = \sum_{k=1}^{K} \tau_k + Kc$. The completion time with K restarts is represented by the random variable $T_{\tau_1,\ldots,\tau_K}$.

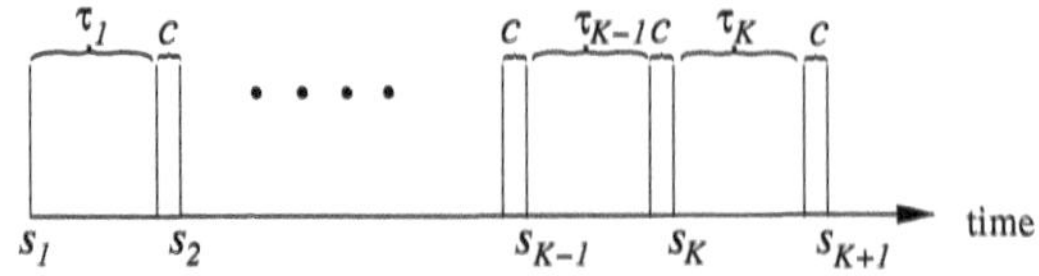

Fig. 7.4. Labeling restarts, total of K restarts.

The completion time probability distribution $F_{\tau_1,\ldots,\tau_K}$ and density $f_{\tau_1,\ldots,\tau_K}$ for the scenario with K restarts can be derived in the same way as Eqs. (7.10) and (7.11). If we introduce $\tau_{K+1} = \infty$ for notational purposes we can define the density and distribution function piece-wise over every restart interval:

$$1 - F_{\tau_1,\ldots,\tau_K}(t) = \begin{cases} \prod_{i=1}^{k-1}(1 - F(\tau_i))(1 - F(t - s_k)) \\ \quad \text{if } s_k \leq t < s_k + \tau, k = 1, \ldots, K+1 \\ \prod_{i=1}^{k}(1 - F(\tau_i)) \\ \quad \text{if } s_k + \tau_k \leq t < s_{k+1}, k = 1, 2, \ldots, K \end{cases}$$

$$f_{\tau_1,\ldots,\tau_K}(t) = \begin{cases} \prod_{i=1}^{k-1}(1 - F(\tau_i))f(t - s_k) \\ \quad \text{if } s_k \leq t < s_k + \tau, k = 1, \ldots, K+1 \\ 0 \\ \quad \text{if } s_k + \tau_k \leq t < s_{k-1}, k = 1, 2, \ldots, K \end{cases} \tag{7.15}$$

We express the moments in the following theorem, where the moments of the completion time with K restarts are formulated with one restart less.

Theorem 7.2. *The moments* $E\left[T^n_{\tau_1,\ldots,\tau_K}\right] = \int_0^\infty t^n f_{\tau_K,\ldots,\tau_1}(t)dt$, $n = 1, 2, \ldots,$ *of the completion time with K restarts, restart interval lengths $\tau_1, \tau_2, \ldots, \tau_K$, and time c consumed by each restart, can be expressed as:*

$$E\left[T^n_{\tau_1,\ldots,\tau_K}\right] = M_n(\tau_1) + (1 - F(\tau_1)) \sum_{l=0}^{n} \binom{n}{l} (\tau_1 + c)^{n-l} E\left[T^l_{\tau_2,\ldots,\tau_K}\right], \tag{7.16}$$

where $E\left[T^0_{\tau_2,\ldots,\tau_K}\right] = 1$.

We again refer to van Moorsel and Wolter [82] for the proof, and van Moorsel and Wolter [81] for the algorithmic implications (Theorem 7.2 allows for efficient numerical calculations of the moments of completion time under restarts). As an illustration, we get for the first moment:

$$\mathrm{E}\left[T_{\tau_1,\ldots,\tau_K}\right] = M_1(\tau_1) + (1 - F(\tau_1))(\tau_1 + c + \mathrm{E}\left[T_{\tau_2,\ldots,\tau_K}\right]). \tag{7.17}$$

7.3.3. *Expressions for Probability of Meeting Deadlines*

As we have seen before, assuming the deadline d is a multiple of the restart time τ, we can relate the probability of missing the deadline without and with restart through:

$$1 - F_\tau(d) = (1 - F(\tau))^{\frac{d}{\tau}}. \tag{7.18}$$

In the general case, the restart intervals $\tau_1, \ldots, \tau_n$, assuming n intervals, may not be identical. If furthermore d is not exactly reached by the last interval, then the remaining time after the last interval until the deadline is $d - \sum_{i=1}^{n} \tau_i$. The probability of missing the deadline then becomes:

$$1 - F_\tau(d) = \begin{cases} \prod_{i=1}^{k}(1 - F(\tau_i)) \cdot \left(1 - F\left(d - \sum_{i=1}^{k}(\tau_i + c)\right)\right) \\ \quad \text{if } \sum_{i=1}^{k}(\tau_i + c) \leq d < \sum_{i=1}^{k+1}\tau_i + kc \\ \prod_{i=1}^{k+1}(1 - F(\tau_i)) \\ \quad \text{if } \sum_{i=1}^{k+1}\tau_i + kc \leq t < \sum_{i=1}^{k+1}(\tau_i + c). \end{cases} \tag{7.19}$$

7.4. Optimization of Restart Strategies

In this section we find optimal restart times. We distinguish the first moment of completion time (Section 7.4.1), higher moments (Section 7.4.2) and deadline probabilities (Section 7.4.3). Each of these categories has different optima, both in terms of the actual time out values, as well as in terms of generic strategies. The optimal restart strategy also depends on how many restarts are allowed, and whether all restart intervals have equal length.

Throughout this section we will use the hazard rate, defined as:

$$h(t) = \frac{f(t)}{1 - F(t)}. \tag{7.20}$$

The hazard rate at moment t can be interpreted as the intensity of completion at that moment. Intuitively, to complete a task quickly, one wants to have a high hazard rate. As a consequence, a decaying hazard rate suggests restart is beneficial, while an increasing hazard rate indicates one should not restart. The fact that the exponential distribution has a constant hazard rate, $h(t) = \lambda$, implies that task completion is not impacted by restarts.

7.4.1. *Optimal Restart Times for Expected Completion Time*

Theorem 7.3. *The optimal restart time $\tau^* > 0$ that minimises the expected completion time $E[T_\tau]$ is such that:*

$$\frac{1 - F(\tau^*)}{f(\tau^*)} = E[T_{\tau^*}] + c. \tag{7.21}$$

That is, if $c = 0$, the inverse of the hazard rate at τ^* equals the expected completion time under unbounded restarts.

Proof. To obtain this result, we equate to zero the derivative with respect to τ of $\mathrm{E}[T_\tau] = \frac{M_1(\tau)}{F(\tau)} + \frac{1-F(\tau)}{F(\tau)}(\tau + c)$ (the base relation (7.14)). After some manipulation we find:

$$h^{-1}(t) = \frac{d}{d\tau}\mathrm{E}[T_\tau] = 0 \iff \frac{1 - F(\tau)}{f(\tau)} = \mathrm{E}[T_\tau] + c. \qquad \square$$

It is important to realise that Eq. (7.21) may hold for more than one restart value, including $\tau \to \infty$, and thus not only holds for the global optimum, but also for local minima and maxima. This has been addressed in Okamura and Dohi [62], which presents a number of developments that complement van Moorsel and Wolter [82], including aperiodic and probabilistic restart policies. Particularly relevant in the context of this chapter is Theorem 5 of Okamura and Dohi [62], which articulates the optimization problem in terms of the scaled Total Time on Test transform (scaled TTT transform), defined as:

$$\phi(p) = \frac{1}{\mu_F} \int_0^{F^{-1}(p)} 1 - F(t)dt, \tag{7.22}$$

where

$$\mu_F = \int_0^{F^{-1}(p)} 1 - F(t)dt.$$

Theorem 5 of Okamura and Dohi [62] shows that the restart optimization problem can be formulated in terms of the TTT transform as:

$$\min_{0 \leq p \leq 1} \left\{ \frac{c}{\mu_F} + \phi(p) \right\} \Big/ p. \tag{7.23}$$

This formulation allows for an attractive graphical interpretation of the optimization problem, for which we refer to Okamura and Dohi [62] as well as Dohi *et al.* [20]. The literature on Total Time on Test transforms goes back several decades, and presents an attractive theory that applies to a broad set of optimization problems. An attractive introduction to its use in reliability theory can be found in Bergman and Klefsjö [9], and a textbook derivation can be found in Nair *et al.* [57]. An additional advantage of the TTT transform is that it lends itself particularly well to online estimation of the optimum, as we will discuss in Section 7.7.

In van Moorsel and Wolter [82] it was shown that if a single restart improves completion time, this is a necessary and sufficient condition for any number of restarts to be useful. Moreover, if a single restart improves the mean completion time, multiple restarts perform even better, and unbounded restarts perform best. This is depicted in Fig. 7.5. The straight line is the expected completion time $\mathrm{E}[T]$ without restarts, and the curve with the highest maxima and lowest minima is $\mathrm{E}[T_\tau]$ for unbounded restarts. Note that all curves improve the completion time over the same range of restart times (roughly $t > 0.05$), and the more restarts, the better. Similarly, when the completion time increases with restarts, fewer restarts are less detrimental for the completion time.

Theorem 7.21 is for unbounded restarts, that is, the restart will be repeated every τ time units. If there is a finite number of restarts, results are different, and there is no generic result as in the above theorem. Instead, van Moorsel and Wolter [82] provide an iterative algorithm to calculate

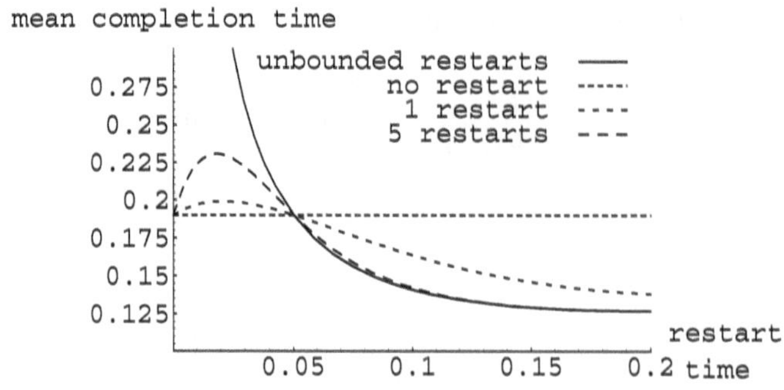

Fig. 7.5. Expected completion time for varying number of restarts.

Table 7.1. Optimal restart intervals for finite and unbounded number of restarts.

Interval Index k	Optimal Length τ_k of k-th Interval
unbounded	0.198254
1	0.198254
2	0.198254
3	0.198254
4	0.198256
5	0.198265
6	0.1983
7	0.199
8	0.200
9	0.209
10	0.249

optimal restart times. As an illustration, Table 7.1 shows the results if there are 10 restarts, for the mixed hyper/hypo-exponential distribution, with parameters as given in Fig. 7.2. For instance, for $k = 9$, the two remaining restart times will be after 0.209 and $0.209 + 0.249 = 0.458$ time units, respectively. As one sees, the optimal restart intervals have different lengths, longer if they are closer to the last restart. Conversely, the more restarts that follow, the closer the interval length is to the optimum for unbounded restarts, which is 0.198254.

7.4.2. *Optimal Restart Times for Higher Moments*

For higher moments, the situation is complicated. First of all, a restart time can be optimal for one moment but not for others, i.e. each moment has its respective optimal restart times. Furthermore, the irregular behaviour

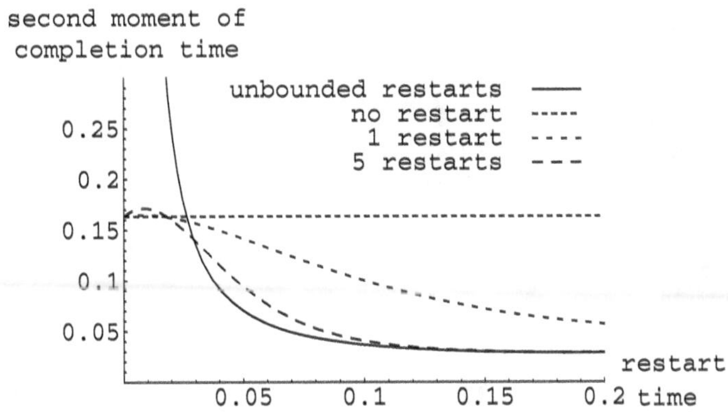

Fig. 7.6. Second moment of completion time for varying number of restarts.

for $t < 0.05$ in Fig. 7.6 shows that there exist values for which one or two restarts improve the second moment, but unbounded restarts do not. In other words, the nice property that increasing the number of restarts is increasingly beneficial once a single restart is beneficial, does not hold for higher moments. It is also typically not optimal to apply restarts at constant intervals when minimising higher moments, even if an infinite number of restarts is allowed.

As a consequence, for every situation, optimal restart times need to be computed, taking into account which moment, how many restarts and if intervals between restarts need to be identical. We refer to van Moorsel and Wolter [82] for these algorithms. Here we limit ourselves to showing optimal restart times for the case in which the completion time T has a lognormal distribution, with parameters $\mu = -2.31$ and $\sigma = 0.97$. The lognormal is a heavy-tail distribution and therefore amenable to restarts. There is no particular significance to the chosen parameter values. They happen to be the parameters of a lognormal fit for the experimental data of HTTP GET completion times [65].

We calculate $K = 15$ restart times that minimise the first, second and third moments of the completion time (T_K denotes the completion time under K restarts). These restart times (with an interpolating curve) are shown in Fig. 7.7. The figure also shows τ_∞, the optimal restart time for the first moment.

Figure 7.7 indicates that when minimising the first moment, the optimal restart time $\tau_{k|K}$ monotonically converges when k gets smaller, to a single optimum τ_∞, provided K is large enough. We also saw this in Table 7.1. The convergence behaviour for higher moments is not as straightforward, but an important observation is that if the number of restarts increases,

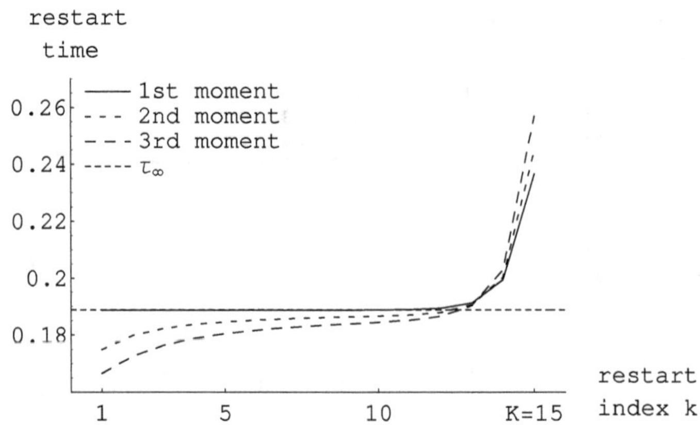

Fig. 7.7. Optimal restart times, with respect to the moments $\mathrm{E}[T_{15}]$, $\mathrm{E}[T_{15}^2]$ and $\mathrm{E}[T_{15}^3]$, respectively.

using the restart times that minimise the first moment is a useful strategy to approximate the optimal restart time for higher moments, provided K is large enough (see van Moorsel and Wolter [82] for an explanation).

7.4.3. *Optimal Restart Time for Deadline Probability*

In this section we discuss three possible strategies for restarts to meet a deadline, all based on hazard rates, and derived in van Moorsel and Wolter [80]. The first strategy is the *equihazard* strategy, which restarts at points in time with equal hazard rates. We will see that restarting at equihazard points corresponds to local extrema for the probability of making the deadline. We will then introduce the *equidistant* strategy, which is an easy-to-implement special case of the equihazard strategy, with all restart intervals of equal length. This also corresponds to local optima, but, as for the equihazard strategy, it is not guaranteed that the chosen strategy is also a global optimum. Nevertheless, for our examples, we found the equidistant strategy to give results that are globally optimal. The above two strategies are sensitive to the specified deadline, and therefore we present a third strategy, called the *rectangle = surface rule*. The rectangle = surface rule is not optimal for all deadlines, but has an attractive property, namely that it is optimal in the limit when the deadline tends to infinity.

For a single retry during the finite interval $[0, d)$, when the retry is at time τ, $\tau < d$, then the probability of completion before d is:

$$F_\tau(d) = 1 - (1 - F(\tau))(1 - F(d - \tau)). \tag{7.24}$$

By equating the derivative with respect to τ to zero, we obtain for the extrema of $F_\tau(d)$ that:

$$\frac{f(\tau)}{1-F(\tau)} = \frac{f(d-\tau)}{1-F(d-\tau)},$$

that is:

$$h(t) = h(d-t). \tag{7.25}$$

The above result says that minima and maxima for the probability that a deadline is met with restarts are found at *equihazard* restart intervals. Moreover, the *equidistant* restart intervals $\tau = \frac{d}{2}$ are a special case of equihazard intervals, and form thus also a local extremum.

Figure 7.8 shows typical behaviour if one considers a single restart. It shows results for the lognormal distribution with parameters as in Fig. 7.7 and deadline $d = 0.7$. The equidistant restart (at $\tau = 0.35$) is optimal, while the other equihazard points turn out to be minima ($\tau = 0.013$ or $\tau = 0.687$). The improvement in probability of making the deadline is from 0.977 to 0.990.

For multiple retries before the deadline similar mathematics can be applied. The restarts take place at times $\tau_1, \tau_1+\tau_2, \ldots, \sum_{n=1}^{N}\tau_n$, and we assume without loss of generality that $\sum_{n=1}^{N}\tau_n = d$. Then we obtain that an optimum with respect to all retry intervals $\tau_1, \ldots, \tau_N$ is found when:

$$h(\tau_1) = h(\tau_2) = \cdots = h(\tau_N). \tag{7.26}$$

Again, the extrema are at equihazard intervals, with the equidistant restart intervals $\tau_n = \frac{d}{N}$ as a special case.

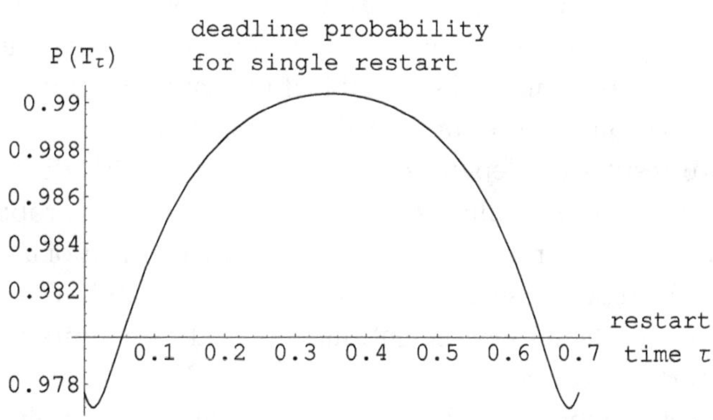

Fig. 7.8. Probability of meeting deadline $d = 0.7$ for one restart for lognormal distribution with $\mu = -2.3, \sigma = 0.97$.

Table 7.2. Equihazard restart intervals and associated probability of meeting the deadline $d = 0.7$ (for lognormal distribution with $\mu = -2.3, \sigma = 0.97$).

# Restarts	Equihazard Intervals	$P(T_{\{\tau\}} < d)$
0	—	0.978
1	0.35, 0.35	0.990
1	0.013, 0.687	0.977
2	0.23, 0.23, 0.23	0.993
2	0.019, 0.34, 0.34	0.990
2	0.013, 0.013, 0.674	0.976
3	0.175, 0.175, 0.175, 0.175	0.99374
3	0.024, 0.225, 0.225, 0.225	0.993
3	0.019, 0.019, 0.331, 0.331	0.989
3	0.013, 0.013, 0.013, 0.660	0.976
4	0.14, 0.14, 0.14, 0.14, 0.14	0.99366
⋮	⋮	⋮

Table 7.2 shows results for an increasing number of restarts, displaying all sets of equihazard intervals that are extrema. We see from the table that for this example equidistant hazard rates always outperform the other equihazard points, and that the optimum is for three equidistant restarts (and thus four intervals). In fact, the equihazard points that are not equidistant are local minima, with the probability of meeting the deadline worse than it would be without any restart.

It turns out that equidistant restarts are optimal in all experiments with lognormal distributions, as reported in van Moorsel and Wolter [80]. Although we can construct examples in which for instance two non-equidistant points outperform equidistant points, for the lognormal distribution this only seems to be possible if no restart performs even better. Unfortunately, we have no proof for this phenomenon.

The above results all depend on the deadline d, with different optimal restart times for different values of d. We now introduce a robust strategy, called the rectangle = surface strategy, that is independent of d, and optimal when $d \to \infty$. Moreover, as explained in van Moorsel and Wolter [79], there is an interesting mathematical insight, namely that for a finite deadline d the rectangle = surface strategy would be optimal if there existed such as thing as a non-integer number of restarts (it is optimal if the number of restarts before deadline d can be real-valued).

Theorem 7.4. *Let the rectangle = surface strategy restart at intervals of length τ^* with*

$$\tau h(\tau^*) = \int_0^{\tau^*} h(t)dt.$$

For $d \to \infty$, this strategy maximizes the probability of meeting the deadline d.

As a final note, because the rectangle = surface strategy is independent of the deadline and optimizes the distribution (except for the tail greater than d), it is also a likely candidate for a restart strategy for moments of completion time.

7.5. Time-Out Strategies in Practice

In this section we discuss existing applications of restarts in practical settings. The models discussed thus far provide optimal strategies if the distribution of the completion time is known, but in practice there may be considerable uncertainty about the actual completion time distribution. As a consequence, algorithms used in practice tend to build in risk mitigation, to avoid the possibility that using restarts when misjudging the completion time distribution leads to deteriorated performance. We will discuss restarts in TCP, randomized algorithms and failure detection, respectively.

7.5.1. *Congestion Control in TCP*

TCP (Transmission Control Protocol) is one of the core protocols operating the Internet, providing reliability on top of IP routing [76]. TCP acknowledges the receipt of every packet that has been sent. A sender can send only a limited number of packets while waiting for acknowledgements. If no acknowledgement arrives within a certain time called the retransmission timeout (RTO) the packet is resent. This is equivalent to a *restart*. The performance of TCP depends to a large extent on the choice of the time between retransmissions.

Several proposals for the choice of the RTO exist. Most TCP implementations today use the Jacobson-Karn algorithm [37] at their core. This algorithm adjusts the RTO continuously using

$$RTO = \beta R,$$

where β accounts for the variation in Round Trip Time (RTT) of previous packets [37] and R is an estimate of the RTT computed as

$$R_{\text{new}} = \alpha R_{\text{old}} + (1 - \alpha)M,$$

with M being the RTT estimate of the most recently acknowledged packet. The parameter α is a filter gain typically chosen as $\alpha = 0.9$. Note that both α and to an extent β are used as risk mitigation against the lack of knowledge of the actual completion time of packet transmissions. In addition to the dynamic scheme, TCP implementations typically use for the first few packet transmissions the following fixed values for their RTO timer: $3, 6, 12, 24, 48, \ldots,$ seconds. This exponential back-off scheme seems to work well, although it is unclear whether the base modulus of 3 seconds indeed leads to optimal performance.

Experiments from Reinecke *et al.* [65] demonstrate the implications of the TCP exponential back-off approach. Figure 7.9 shows data sampled for the time needed to perform connection setup [65]. The sample consists of roughly 230000 experiments connecting to approximately 200 different hosts world-wide. The horizontal lines clearly show the retries carried out by TCP after the expiration of the RTO timer. Reinecke *et al.* [65] also found out

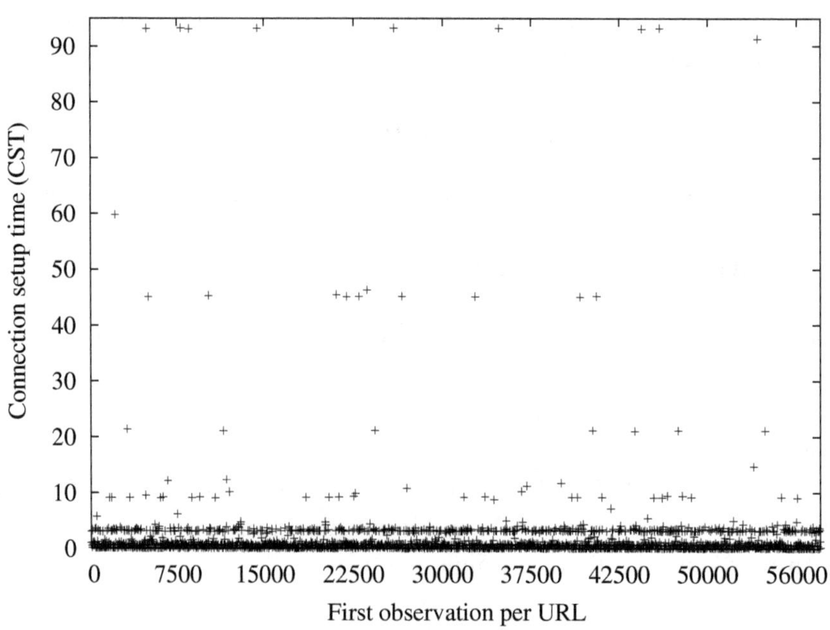

Fig. 7.9. Connection set-up times for the first connection per URL download.

that roughly 0.5% of all connections time out at least once and perform a restart.

7.5.2. *Randomised Algorithms*

The restart of algorithms may make sense if the restarted algorithm executes differently from the first time. This may happen if the algorithm draws random numbers, or allows for different execution choices during run-time. An important class are randomized algorithms, in particular Las Vegas algorithms, which always provide a correct result but have a random and sometimes very long runtime [2, 48]. Randomised Quicksort as well as theorem provers searching a state space are Las Vegas algorithms. Motwani and Raghavan [55] point out the relationship between Las Vegas and Monte Carlo algorithms.

The research in this area is interesting for our discussion of restarts. In Gomes *et al.* [30], restart times in tree search algorithms were determined experimentally and improved strategies for restart times are discussed in Guddeti and Choueiry [31]. Tree-structures that lead to heavy-tailed cost functions for search algorithms are further classified in Walsh [83].

Of particular interest is a practical approach proposed by Luby *et al.* [48]. Let an execution strategy consist of several attempts, each of length t_i and let $S_1 = (t_2, t_3, \ldots)$ be the restart strategy without the first trial. Luby *et al.* [48] show that the strategy with runs of equal length $S^* = (t, t, \ldots)$ is optimal for every probability distribution. However, in reality the completion time distribution is not known. In that case, Luby *et al.* [48] shows that the expected runtime can be bounded for all possible distributions by using the following 'universal' strategy, which boils down to a modified exponential back-off.

$$S_{\text{univ}} = (1, 1, 2, 1, 1, 2, 4, 1, 1, 2, 1, 1, 2, 4, 8, 1, \ldots). \tag{7.27}$$

Another practical angle is that if the distribution is not known, it may be that the mean completion time is. This may lead to pragmatic rules for restarts, such as aborting after twice the expected runtime.

A related application is that of distributed queries using search algorithms that have a random aspect. This has recently been studied in, e.g., Ruan *et al.* [72], and on-line algorithms have been derived to set the restart time if dependencies between successive tries can be exploited. Finally, randomised algorithms can also be run with several replicas simultaneously. As soon as one replica obtains the correct result all replicas are stopped.

Strategies for how long to run each replica and when to restart have been investigated in Luby *et al.* [48].

7.5.3. *Failure Detectors*

Fault-tolerant distributed systems are designed to provide reliable and continuous service despite the failure of some of their components. A failure detector is a basic building block of such systems and is used by a monitoring process to determine whether the monitored process is still alive. Of interest is the accuracy of failure detection and the detection time. The accuracy is defined as the probability of the suspicion being correct and the monitored system having in fact failed. The detection time is the period between the failure of the system and failure detection by the monitoring system.

A good choice of the timers in the monitoring process is essential when optimising both metrics [10, 14]. If the frequency of checking is too high or the timeout is too small then the monitored system is suspected of being down too often, while if checks are not frequent enough or the timeout is too long, detection time increases unnecessarily.

The setting of timers is slightly more complicated than the completion time problems discussed in this chapter. The conclusion that *it is impossible to create a failure detection mechanism with the best accuracy and delay together* [23] corroborates the concept of a trade-off between timeliness and fairness for the restart model as elaborated in Reinecke *et al.* [66].

7.6. Trends in the Past Decade (2007–2017)

In this section we conduct a systematic review of the literature of the past ten years. The Habilitation thesis of Wolter, on which this chapter is based, considers the literature until 2007. We review recent trends in the model-based analysis of restart, reboot and rejuvenation that have taken place after Wolter's review.

The collection of reference papers for the literature survey was obtained as follows. We searched using the following keywords on Google Scholar: 'restart', 'software rejuvenation', 'checkpointing', and 'reboot'. We went through the search results for each keyword we searched for page by page (that is, web page after web page returned by Google Scholar). For each paper, we decided whether they were on-topic, and we continued until relevant papers stopped appearing. We then did a similar exercise searching for all papers that cited the key literature belonging in this chapter, particularly

Table 7.3. Relevant literature since 2007, categorized.

Applications.
Blanchette *et al.* [12], Loshchilov *et al.* [47], Fujiwara *et al.* [26], García-Nieto and Alba [28], Dong *et al.* [22], Biere [11], Tong *et al.* [77], Kim *et al.* [43, 44], Odonoghue and Candes [63]

Implementation.
Yamakita *et al.* [92], Danilkina *et al.* [19]

Modeling & Analysis.
Reinecke and Wolter [68], Jain *et al.* [42], Rinsaka and Dohi [70], He *et al.* [33], Wang and Wolter [88], Reinecke and Wolter [67], Machida and Miyoshi [50], Okamura and Dohi [62], Salfner and Wolter [73], Wang and Wolter [86], Jain and Rani [41], Jain and Preeti [40], Jain [38], Machida *et al.* [51], Moody *et al.* [54], Wang and Wolter [85], Wang [84], Gebennini *et al.* [29], Dohi and Okamura [21], Okamura and Dohi [60], Andersson *et al.* [4], Gagliolo and Schmidhuber [27], Fourneau and Wolter [24], Machida *et al.* [49], Hsu *et al.* [35], Fourneau *et al.* [25], Okamura and Dohi [59, 61], Simeonov and Avresky [75], Andrzejak and Silva [5], Wang and Wolter [87], Wolter and Reinecke [91], Ballerini *et al.* [8], Yang *et al.* [93], Nagaraju *et al.* [56], Jain *et al.* [39], Hsu *et al.* [34], Rinsaka and Dohi [71], Pesu *et al.* [64]

Real Data.
Cotroneo *et al.* [18], Torquato *et al.* [78], Kourai and Chiba [45], Shylo *et al.* [74], Cotroneo *et al.* [15, 16], Meng *et al.* [53], Araujo *et al.* [6], Bovenzi *et al.* [13]

Survey.
Alonso *et al.* [1], Cotroneo *et al.* [17]

the author's papers on this topic. In this manner we selected 95 articles that capture the main literature relevant to this chapter over the past decade.

Table 7.3 provides all the relevant papers we considered. We classified them according to five broad categories depending on the content of the paper. The categories we used for labeling are: 'Applications', 'Implementation','Modeling & Analysis', 'Real Data' and 'Survey'. We chose these categories because we felt that research papers can almost always be placed in one of the categories, and that there is little overlap between the categories. Also at this stage, if we felt a paper was not relevant to the topic, we removed it from the list. Table 7.3, which contains the considered papers after the final sifting explained in the next paragraph, contains 63 different papers.

The 38 'Modelling & Analysis' papers from Table 7.3 were further divided into sub-categories based on the type of model used in the paper, as shown in Table 7.4. For this table, we constructed the set of labels through an iterative approach, until we felt that the categories were useful in understanding the

Table 7.4. Further categorization of papers in the 'Modelling & Analysis' category of Table 7.3.

Adaptivity Metric.
Reinecke and Wolter [67]

Blackbox Restart.
Wang and Wolter [88], Okamura and Dohi [62], Wang and Wolter [85, 86], Gagliolo and Schmidhuber [27], Fourneau *et al.* [25], Wang and Wolter [87], Wolter and Reinecke [91], Pesu *et al.* [64], Wang [84]

DNA Computing.
He *et al.* [33]

Markov Model.
Jain *et al.* [42], Jain and Rani [41], Jain [38], Jain and Preeti [40], Machida *et al.* [51], Gebennini *et al.* [29], Okamura and Dohi [60], Hsu *et al.* [35], Jain *et al.* [39]

Machine Learning.
Simeonov and Avresky [75], Andrzejak and Silva [5]

Petri and Stochastic Reward Nets.
Salfner and Wolter [73], Ballerini *et al.* [8], Yang *et al.* [93], Machida *et al.* [49]

Queueing Model.
Reinecke and Wolter [68], Machida and Miyoshi [50], Fourneau and Wolter [24]

Semi Markov Model.
Rinsaka and Dohi [70], Okamura and Dohi [59, 61], Nagaraju *et al.* [56], Hsu *et al.* [34], Rinsaka and Dohi [71], Dohi and Okamura [21]

Supervisory Control Theory.
Andersson *et al.* [4]

survey outcomes. First, we categorized the papers based on the type of model they used. Then we included other themes, such as machine learning or the application area, if these dominated the papers. We also removed a number of papers, especially in checkpointing, in which the model actually was a system model, not a model for evaluation or optimization. This resulted in a grouping of 38 papers around common themes, as shown in Table 7.4.

7.6.1. *Survey of Research of the Past Decade*

With 63 related papers published in the past decade, the area can be considered reasonably active. We subdivide between modeling and non-modeling papers, first reviewing the papers from Table 7.3 that are not in the category 'Modeling & Analysis', and then discussing the 'Modeling & Analysis' papers further categorized in Table 7.4. We note that since

Wolter's previous literature survey [90], we have come across two other related interesting literature surveys [1, 17], both focused on rejuvenation. Alonso *et al.* [1] provides a comprehensive system perspective on rejuvenation techniques, while Cotroneo *et al.* [17] provides a broad discussion on rejuvenation and software aging. Our survey is complementary to the rejuvenation surveys since we include restart techniques and particularly emphasize modeling aspects.

7.6.1.1. *Survey of modeling papers*

In this section we consider the modeling papers from Table 7.4.

Blackbox Models. Most directly relevant to this chapter are the 'Blackbox Restart' papers, in which there is no representation of system structure in the used model. A number of interesting ways of expanding on the results in this chapter have emerged in the past decade. The following papers used blackbox restart to improve mobile offloading [84–88]. The papers describe a strategy, based only on time elapsed, where several attempts are made to offload an intensive computation to a computing platform better adept at computing the problem. Local computation of the problem is only done if the offloading attempts fail. Okamura and Dohi [62] optimise the restart interval with the help of empirical data. Compared to van Moorsel and Wolter [82], it relaxes the assumption of equidistant restart intervals and derives a solution with the help of Laplace Transforms. Gagliolo and Schmidhuber [27] study the k-armed bandit problem to decide how much information to gain about the service time distribution in order to determine an optimal policy. In other work, the metrics of interest are more complex than in this chapter. Fourneau *et al.* [25] and Wolter and Reinecke [91] investigate how system performance is affected when multiple users in the system use restart to improve their own performance, a topic we touch on in Section 7.7. Pesu *et al.* [64] have a case study on how the performance of a split–merge system can be improved with respect to task response time, subtask dispersion and energy consumption.

Markov Models. Markov models have been used by a number of authors. As we have seen, Markov models are limited in that exponential delays cannot represent aging, however, states can be used to represent levels of degradation. For instance, Jain *et al.* [42] derive various performance metrics for the machine repair problem with reboot and imperfect coverage under the care of a single unreliable server. Jain *et al.* [42] and Jain and Rani [41], Jain and Preeti [40] and Jain [38] derive results for the availability characteristics of a repairable system where time-to-failure, time-to-repair and time-to-delay are all exponentially distributed. Hsu *et al.* [35] compute the steady state probabilities of a system with switching failure, reboot delay and repair pressure. Jain *et al.* [39] present a model for restart policies in cluster systems. The paper derives various performance indicators such as the availability, mean time to failure and downtime cost. Machida *et al.* [51] present a rejuvenation strategy where both the virtual machine and the virtual machine monitor are rejuvenated at the same time to minimise downtime. A different use of states is seen in Gebennini *et al.* [29], which obtains an analytic model for the communication between two machines with a finite buffer. When the buffer becomes full the machine is forced to remain idle until the buffer becomes empty. Okamura and Dohi [60] introduce a Markov Decision Process for rejuvenation that models the trade-off between system performance and power efficiency.

Semi-Markov Models. The research in this category all expands on the semi–Markov model first presented by Dohi *et al.* [20]. Dohi and Okamura [21] use a semi–Markov decision process and reinforcement learning to derive an optimal software rejuvenation policy to maximise the steady-state system availability, whereas Rinsaka and Dohi [70] develop a fast estimation algorithm for the optimal periodic rejuvenation schedule. Okamura and Dohi [59, 61] present an opportunity-based software rejuvenation technique, which can only rejuvenate during given periods in time and Okamura and Dohi [59] investigate optimal rejuvenation policies when system failures are correlated. Hsu *et al.* [34] expand the semi–Markov decision process to take into account the unreliablility of the rejuvenation process and Rinsaka and Dohi [71] present a statistically non-parametric adaptive algorithm to estimate the optimal preventive rejuvenation schedule.

Queueing Models. A few papers studied the effects of restart using queuing models to analyze delays or blocking probabilities. Reinecke and Wolter [68] is a study of the effect of client-side restart and server-side rejuvenation policies on system and service availability. Machida and Miyoshi [50] provide analysis of the optimal stopping problem for software rejuvenation in a deteriorating job processing system and Fourneau and Wolter [24] contains a theoretical investigation into a network of queues with multiples classes of customers and restart signals.

Petri and Stochastic Reward Nets. To represent more complex system structure and behaviour, Petri nets and their variants are shown to be particularly intuitive in a number of recent papers. Ballerini *et al.* [8]

describes a model for a phased-mission system with software rejuvenation. It analyses the impact of software rejuvenation on the success probability and completion time distribution of the mission. An investigation of the effects of the frequency of rejuvenation on system utilization and service availability can be found in Salfner and Wolter [73]. Yang *et al.* [93] investigate software rejuvenation policies in cluster computing systems where dependency exists between nodes, with the use of stochastic reward nets. Machida *et al.* [49] also use stochastic reward nets in a study on three different types of rejuvenation policies in virtual machines.

Machine Learning and Other Developments. Machine learning approaches have also been pioneered in recent years, see also Section 7.6.1.2. To inform proactive restarts, Simeonov and Avresky [75] use machine learning to detect anomalies which cause crashes and Andrzejak and Silva [5] use machine learning to determine the software degradation levels of a system. Three other papers have a strong modeling flavor and do not fit any of the above categories. Reinecke and Wolter [67] use adaptivity metrics to determine the optimal restart rate. He *et al.* [33] study restarts in the context of DNA computing. Andersson *et al.* [4] present a method for restarting manufacturing systems with the help of safe states to make sure production goals and specifications are fulfilled during restarts. The paper uses supervisory control theory to model the system.

7.6.1.2. *Survey of non-modeling papers*

Regarding the non-modeling papers we discuss three categories, namely applications, implementations and the use of real-life system data. Note that, concerning the other categories in Table 7.3, the 'Modeling & Analysis' papers were discussed in Section 7.6.1.1, while the survey papers were discussed at the start of this section.

Applications. The most common application of system restart among the papers we reviewed is to improve the performance of various search problem algorithms. Examples of such problems include SAT solvers [11, 12], optimisation algorithms [28, 47, 63], statistics regarding random walks [26, 43, 44, 77] and flow shop scheduling [22]. Shylo *et al.* [74] performed a study on optimising restarts in Las Vegas algorithms, also using real data (see next paragraph).

Implementation. Yamakita *et al.* [92] implemented a phased-reboot of Xen 3.4.1 running para-virtualized Linux 2.6.18, where the aim is to reduce downtime of recovery-based rebooting. Their experiments showed that downtime was 34.3 to 93.6% shorter compared to a normal reboot. Danilkina *et al.* [19] have created a project called Sfera, which provides a simulation framework for restart algorithms in Service-Oriented Systems.

Real Data. Multiple papers describe experiments performed on real systems, where they analyse whether the system suffers from software aging. Some of the systems studied include Android [15], operating systems [13, 16], the Java virtual machine [18, 53], and cloud computing systems [6, 45, 78].

7.6.2. *Main Conclusions from the 2007–2017 Survey*

A dominant trend in our literature review of the decade 2007–2017 is the emphasis in the field on real world applications. The recent literature exhibits a multitude of use cases for system restart in the real world, as witnessed by the examples in the black box model, implementation and application papers.

In addition to restart being helpful in a large number of use cases, there are many ways to decide when the optimal time to restart is. Many of the Markov model, semi-Markov model, queueing model, Petri and stochastic reward net model papers slightly vary the underlying modeling environment and cover different metrics, which can be used to assess the efficiency of the system. They then introduce restart policies, which provide good results for the respective metrics and models.

A category of papers that stood out in the literature review were papers that try to estimate the amount of degradation of the system, so as to predict future errors in computation before they occur. Examples of such papers are found among the machine learning and real data papers.

7.7. Open Problems

Future work in utilising black-box models of restart, such as those discussed in this chapter, are manifold. Ideally, the research should lead us to real-time adaptive schemes for restarts, based on continuous data collection, as we will discuss in Section 7.7.1. Within this setting, the network effect still requires further study (Section 7.7.2), since current analysis tends to ignore that if all parties or nodes change restart times, it leads to changes in overall system behaviour that may be suboptimal. There are interesting research challenges associated with understanding the implications of and mitigating for the lack of data or changing characteristics of completion time distributions, see Section 7.7.3. That is, what are the theoretical results for minimising the risk associated with restart strategies, such as the ones analyzed in this chapter? Finally, there are known pragmatic approaches, such as exponential back-off, whose properties should be analysed in more detail, as we discuss in Section 7.7.4. These practical algorithms aim to reduce the risk of restarts by backing off, but their theoretical properties are not as well understood.

7.7.1. *Towards Online Restart for Self-Management of Systems*

Online restart mechanisms require up-to-date knowledge of system characteristics, such as the response time distribution. The literature has seen some attempts in this direction, using different approaches, based on estimating either (1) completion time distributions, (2) hazard rates, or (3) total time to test.

Completion Time Distributions. Especially for the problem of optimising the mean completion time, experimentally obtaining the completion time distribution is the most obvious approach to use for online adaptation. Normally, the histogram of observations is used as the estimator, for example in the work at HTTP level in Reinecke *et al.* [65, 69]. These approaches can be included in a software module like the proxy server in Reinecke *et al.* [65], to be executed in real-time. One of the challenges is that characteristics of distributions may change over time, and future work could enhance the adaptation mechanisms using methods such as online dynamic histograms to adjust the estimate of the measured distribution, trying to capture changes as soon as possible after they occur [7, 94].

Hazard Rates. To optimize the probability of meeting deadlines, the hazard rate plays an important role (see Section 7.4), and an alternative to collecting completion time distribution is to attempt to estimate the hazard rate. Estimating the hazard rate is not a straightforward task, since it needs numerical computation of the derivative, either of the cumulative hazard rate or the cumulative distribution function.

In Wolter [89] we use the rectangle = surface rule from Section 7.4.3, a simple rule and therefore a likely candidate for run-time deployment. The optimal restart time does not exist in all cases but restart is applicable to a system if (and only if) the rule finds an optimal restart time. So, our simple rule actually serves a two-fold purpose: it enables us to decide whether restart will be beneficial in the given situation, and if so, it provides us with the optimal restart time.

The research in Wolter [89] identifies a number of interesting informal insights to be explored further. The smallest data sets were usually sufficient for a reasonably good estimate of the optimal restart time. The optimal restart time will always be placed at the end of the bulk of observed completion time and some few hundred observations are enough to get a notion of 'bulk' and 'end of the bulk'. Furthermore, small samples seem to overestimate the optimal restart time, which does the resulting completion time much less harm than underestimation. All these engineering insights deserve further attention.

Total Time On Test. The total time on test transform discussed in Section 7.4.1 is particularly interesting for online restart optimization. The intuition behind the total time on test transform is as follows [58]. Say there are N copies with equally distributed survival time and that we observe them until all N fail (one can also see this as the test time, or completion time). Then the TTT transform at $p = \frac{i}{N}$ equals the sum of the time each of the N copies has been alive until the i-th failure [9, 58]. As a consequence, we can construct the TTT transform directly from the data, and the optimal restart time for the first moment of completion time can then be derived as discussed in Section 7.4.1. The application of TTT transforms to the online optimisation of restarts, such as suggested by Dohi *et al.* [20]. Okamura and Dohi [62] deserves further attention from researchers.

7.7.2. *The Network Effect*

Arguably, if all nodes in a network apply restarts this will impact the overall performance of the network, possibly making it more congested, with response times dropping as a consequence. (In networks, round-trip response times should be considered the completion times.) Therefore, an interesting area of study is the network effect, such as is considered in Huberman and Maurer [36].

Restarts can also be studied in other contexts where individual restarts impact the performance for multiple players in the system. As an example, Ananthanarayanan *et al.* [3] present arguments for the use of service restarts in speeding up job completion in server farms. The application papers in Section 7.6 provide various other examples of real-life applications of restarts, and it would be a topic of considerable research interest to identify fundamental insights and rules for restarts in these varied settings.

7.7.3. *Mitigation of the Risk of the Uncertainty of Completion Time Distribution*

One of the challenges is to understand and mitigate the risk that comes from the uncertainty about the completion time distribution. In most situations, as long as a transaction processing system operates well, sufficient data can be sampled in a reasonably short time. However, data collection becomes prohibitively expensive if the optimal completion time is dependent on rare events, whether these are performance metrics that are difficult to obtain and rarely seen, or failures that rarely happen.

As we remarked earlier, underestimating the optimal restart time is dangerous, since it would potentially end up in a very poor performance caused by repeated unnecessary restarts. A conservative strategy is to choose a relatively large restart time, as an engineering rule. A different way of phrasing this is that one can aim to identify a *failed* completion by trying to distinguish the outliers from the bulk of observed completion times.

We can generalize this observation. Restarts often become viable if a failure happens, but one cannot always observe the failure. Our black box models do not represent failures in the model, but if a system lends itself to one being able to observe or infer a failure, then one could include this state change in the model. In future work one may try to combine restarts with methods that aim at detecting transient or permanent failures efficiently. This could improve the heuristics that trigger a restart.

7.7.4. *Performance and Risk Properties of Back-Off Strategies*

The intervals between successive restart can be increasingly extended, which is also known as a back-off strategy. Back-off can sometimes avoid performance problems caused by network overload, but it can also introduce unnecessary delays and hence reduce system performance. The literature in this area goes back to communication networks with shared bandwidth such as early radio networks or Ethernet. More recently, Luby *et al.* [48] presented a universal strategy for backing up that performs well in the optimization of Las Vegas algorithms. However, the proposed strategy is not necessarily optimal, and it would be of great interest to identify the theoretical properties of back-off strategies.

References

1. J. Alonso, R. Matias, E. Vicente, A. Maria, and K. S. Trivedi. (2013). A comparative experimental study of software rejuvenation overhead. *Performance Evaluation*, **70**(3), 231–250.
2. H. Alt, L. Guibas, K. Mehlhorn, R. Karp, and A. Wigderson. (1996). A method for obtaining randomized algorithms with small tail probabilities. *Algorithmica*, **16**(4–5), 543–547.
3. G. Ananthanarayanan, A. Ghodsi, S. Shenker, and I. Stoica. (2012). Why let resources idle? Aggressive cloning of jobs with Dolly. *Memory*, **40**(60), 80.
4. K. Andersson, B. Lennartson, P. Falkman, and M. Fabian. (2011). Generation of restart states for manufacturing cell controllers. *Control Engineering Practice*, **19**(9), 1014–1022.
5. A. Andrzejak and L. Silva. (2008). Using machine learning for non-intrusive modeling and prediction of software aging. In *Proceedings of the Network Operations and Management Symposium 2008 (NOMS 2008), Salvador, Bahia, Brazil, April 7–11*, pp. 25–32.
6. J. Araujo, R. Matos, P. Maciel, F. Vieira, R. Matias, and K. S. Trivedi. (2011). Software rejuvenation in eucalyptus cloud computing infrastructure: A method based on time series forecasting and multiple thresholds. In *Proceedings of the 2011 IEEE Third International Workshop on Software Aging and Rejuvenation (WoSAR), Hiroshima, Japan, November 29–December 2*, pp. 38–43.
7. B. Babcock, S. Babu, M. Datar, R. Motwani, and J. Widom. (2002). Models and issues in data stream systems. In *Proceedings of the Twenty-First ACM SIGMOD-SIGACT-SIGART Symposium on Principles of Database Systems, Madison, Wisconsin, USA, June 3–6*, pp. 1–16.
8. S. Ballerini, L. Carnevali, M. Paolieri, K. Tadano, and F. Machida. (2013). Software rejuvenation impacts on a phased-mission system for Mars exploration. In *Proceedings of the 2013 IEEE International Symposium on Software Reliability Engineering Workshops (ISSREW), Pasadena, California, USA, November 4–7*, pp. 275–280.
9. B. Bergman and B. Klefsjö. (1984). The total time on test concept and its use in reliability theory. *Operations Research*, **32**(3), 596–606.
10. M. Bertier, O. Marin, and P. Sens. (2002). Implementation and performance evaluation of an adaptable failure detector. In *Proceedings of the 2002 International Conference on Dependable Systems and Networks (DSN '02), Bethesda, Maryland, USA, June 23–26*, pp. 354–363.
11. A. Biere. (2008). Adaptive restart strategies for conflict driven SAT solvers. In *Proceedings of the International Conference on Theory and Applications of Satisfiability Testing, Guangzhou, China, May 12–15*, pp. 28–33.
12. J. C. Blanchette, M. Fleury, and C. Weidenbach. (2016). A verified SAT solver framework with learn, forget, restart, and incrementality. In *Proceedings of the International Joint Conference on Automated Reasoning, Coimbra, Portugal, June 27–July 2*, pp. 25–44.
13. A. Bovenzi, J. Alonso, H. Yamada, S. Russo, and K. S. Trivedi. (2013). Towards fast OS rejuvenation: An experimental evaluation of fast OS reboot techniques. In *Proceedings of the 2013 IEEE 24th International Symposium on Software Reliability Engineering (ISSRE), Pasadena, California, USA, November 4–7*, pp. 61–70.

14. W. Chen, S. Toueg, and M. K. Aguilera. (2000). On the quality of service of failure detectors. In *Proceedings of the International Conference on Dependable Systems and Networks (DSN 2000), New York City, NY, USA, June 25–28*, pp. 191–200.
15. D. Cotroneo, F. Fucci, A. K. Iannillo, R. Natella, and R. Pietrantuono. (2016). Software aging analysis of the Android mobile OS. In *Proceedings of the 2016 IEEE 27th International Symposium on Software Reliability Engineering (ISSRE), Ottawa, Ontario, Canada, October 23–27*, pp. 478–489.
16. D. Cotroneo, R. Natella, R. Pietrantuono, and S. Russo. (2010). Software aging analysis of the Linux operating system. In *Proceedings of the 2010 IEEE 21st International Symposium on Software Reliability Engineering (ISSRE), San Jose, California, USA, November 1–4*, pp. 71–80.
17. D. Cotroneo, R. Natella, R. Pietrantuono, and S. Russo. (2014). A survey of software aging and rejuvenation studies. *ACM Journal on Emerging Technologies in Computing Systems*, **10**(1), Article No. 8.
18. D. Cotroneo, S. Orlando, R. Pietrantuono, and S. Russo. (2013). A measurement-based ageing analysis of the JVM. *Software Testing, Verification and Reliability*, **23**(3), 199–239.
19. A. Danilkina, P. Reinecke, and K. Wolter. (2013). SFERA: A simulation framework for the performance evaluation of restart algorithms in service-oriented systems. *Electronic Notes in Theoretical Computer Science*, **291**, 3–14.
20. T. Dohi, K. Goševa-Popstojanova, and K. S. Trivedi. (2001). Estimating software rejuvenation schedules in high-assurance systems. *The Computer Journal*, **44**(6), 473–485.
21. T. Dohi and H. Okamura. (2016). Dynamic software availability model with rejuvenation. *Journal of the Operations Research Society of Japan*, **59**(4), 270–290.
22. X. Dong, P. Chen, H. Huang, and M. Nowak. (2013). A multi-restart iterated local search algorithm for the permutation flow shop problem minimizing total flow time. *Computers & Operations Research*, **40**(2), 627–632.
23. L. Falai and A. Bondavalli. (2005). Experimental evaluation of the QoS of failure detectors on wide area network. In *Proceedings of the 2005 International Conference on Dependable Systems and Networks (DSN '05), Yokohama, Japan, June 28–July 1*, pp. 624–633. doi:http://dx.doi.org/10.1109/DSN.2005.47.
24. J.-M. Fourneau and K. Wolter. (2015). Mixed networks with multiple classes of customers and restart. In *Proceedings of the International Conference on Analytical and Stochastic Modeling Techniques and Applications, Albena, Bulgaria, May 26–29*, pp. 73–86.
25. J.-M. Fourneau, K. Wolter, P. Reinecke, T. Krauß, and A. Danilkina. (2013). Multiple class G-networks with restart. In *Proceedings of the 4th ACM/SPEC International Conference on Performance Engineering, Prague, Czech Republic, April 21–24*, pp. 39–50.
26. Y. Fujiwara, M. Nakatsuji, M. Onizuka, and M. Kitsuregawa. (2012). Fast and exact top-k search for random walk with restart. *Proceedings of the VLDB Endowment*, **5**(5), 442–453.
27. M. Gagliolo and J. Schmidhuber. (2007). Learning restart strategies. In *Proceedings of the International Joint Conferences on Artificial Intelligence, Hyderabad, India, January 6–12*, pp. 792–797.
28. J. García-Nieto and E. Alba. (2011). Restart particle swarm optimization with velocity modulation: A scalability test. *Soft Computing*, **15**(11), 2221–2232.

29. E. Gebennini, A. Grassi, C. Fantuzzi, S. B. Gershwin, and I. C. Schick. (2013). Discrete time model for two-machine one-buffer transfer lines with restart policy. *Annals of Operations Research*, **209**(1), 41–65.
30. C. P. Gomes, B. Selman, and H. Kautz. (1998). Boosting combinatorial search through randomization. In *Proceedings of the Fifteenth National Conference on Artificial Intelligence (AAAI'98), Madison, Wisconsin, USA, July 26–30*, pp. 431–437.
31. V. P. Guddeti and B. Y. Choueiry. (2004). An Empirical Study of a New Restart Strategy for Randomized Backtrack Search. In *Proceedings of the Workshop on CSP Techniques with Immediate Application (CP'04), Toronto, Canada, September 27*, pp. 66–82.
32. B. R. Haverkort. (1998). *Performance of Computer Communication Systems: A Model-Based Approach.* Chichester, UK: John Wiley & Sons.
33. Y.-Z. He, J.-J. Xiong, and W. Zhan. (2016). A research on software rejuvenation policy based on DNA computing. In *Proceedings of the 2016 International Conference on Artificial Intelligence and Computer Science (AICS 2016), Guilin, China, December 23–25*, pp. 1–7.
34. Y.-L. Hsu, J.-C. Ke, and T.-H. Liu. (2011). Standby system with general repair, reboot delay, switching failure and unreliable repair facility — a statistical standpoint. *Mathematics and Computers in Simulation*, **81**(11), 2400–2413.
35. Y.-L Hsu, J.-C. Ke, T.-H. Liu, and C. H. Wu. (2014). Modeling of multi-server repair problem with switching failure and reboot delay and related profit analysis. *Computers & Industrial Engineering*, **69**, 21–28.
36. B. A. Huberman and S. M. Maurer (1999). Restart strategies and internet congestion. In *Proceedings of Computing in Economics and Finance, Chestnut Hill, Massachusetts, USA, June 24–26*, p. 522.
37. V. Jacobson. (1988). Congestion avoidance and control. In *Proceedings of the ACM Symposium on Communications Architectures and Protocols, Stanford, CA, USA, August 16–18*, pp. 314–329.
38. M. Jain. (2013). Availability prediction of imperfect fault coverage system with reboot and common cause failure. *International Journal of Operational Research*, **17**(3), 374–397.
39. M. Jain, T. Manjula, and T. Gulati. (2016). Software rejuvenation policies for cluster system. *Proceedings of the National Academy of Sciences, India Section A: Physical Sciences*, **86**(3), 339–346.
40. M. Jain and Preeti. (2014). Availability analysis of software rejuvenation in active/standby cluster system. *International Journal of Industrial and Systems Engineering*, **19**(1), 75–93.
41. M. Jain and S. Rani. (2013). Availability analysis for repairable system with warm standby, switching failure and reboot delay. *International Journal of Mathematics in Operational Research*, **5**(1), 19–39.
42. M. Jain, C. Shekhar, and V. Rani. (2014). N-policy for a multi-component machining system with imperfect coverage, reboot and unreliable server. *Production & Manufacturing Research*, **2**(1), 457–476.
43. T. H. Kim, K. M. Lee, and S. U. Lee. (2008). Generative image segmentation using random walks with restart. In *Proceedings of the European Conference on Computer Vision, Marseilles, France, October 12–18*, pp. 264–275.
44. T. H. Kim, K. M. Lee, and S. U. Lee. (2009). Edge-preserving colorization using data-driven random walks with restart. In *Proceedings of the 2009 16th IEEE International Conference on Image Processing (ICIP), Cairo, Egypt, November 7–10*, pp. 1661–1664.

45. K. Kourai and S. Chiba. (2011). Fast software rejuvenation of virtual machine monitors. *IEEE Transactions on Dependable and Secure Computing*, **8**(6), 839–851.
46. B. Krishnamurthy and J. Rexford. (2001). *Web Protocols and Practice.* Boston, Massachusetts, USA: Addison-Wesley.
47. I. Loshchilov, M. Schoenauer, and M. Sebag. (2012). Alternative restart strategies for CMA-ES. In *Proceedings of the International Conference on Parallel Problem Solving from Nature, Taormina, Italy, September 1–5*, pp. 296–305.
48. M. Luby, A. Sinclair, and D. Zuckerman. (1993). Optimal speedup of Las Vegas algorithms. In *Proceedings of the Israel Symposium on Theory of Computing Systems, Natanya, Israel, June 7–9*, pp. 128–133.
49. F. Machida, D. S. Kim, and K. S. Trivedi. (2010). Modeling and analysis of software rejuvenation in a server virtualized system. In *Proceedings of the 2010 IEEE Second International Workshop on Software Aging and Rejuvenation (WoSAR), San Jose, California, USA, November 2*, pp. 1–6.
50. F. Machida and N. Miyoshi. (2017). Analysis of an optimal stopping problem for software rejuvenation in a deteriorating job processing system. *Reliability Engineering & System Safety*, **168**, 128–135.
51. F. Machida, J. Xiang, K. Tadano, and Y. Maeno. (2012). Combined server rejuvenation in a virtualized data center. In *Proceedings of the 2012 9th International Conference on Ubiquitous Intelligence & Computing and 9th International Conference on Autonomic & Trusted Computing (UIC/ATC), Fukuoka, Japan, September 4–7*, pp. 486–493.
52. S. M. Maurer and B. A. Huberman. (2001). Restart strategies and Internet congestion. *Journal of Economic Dynamics and Control*, **25**, 641–654.
53. H. Meng, X. Hei, J. Zhang, J. Liu, and L. Sui. (2016). Software aging and rejuvenation in a J2EE application server. *Quality and Reliability Engineering International*, **32**(1), 89–97.
54. A. Moody, G. Bronevetsky, K. Mohror, and B. R. D. Supinski. (2010). Design, modeling, and evaluation of a scalable multi-level checkpointing system. In *Proceedings of the 2010 ACM/IEEE International Conference for High Performance Computing, Networking, Storage and Analysis, New Orleans, Louisiana, USA, November 13–19*, pp. 1–11.
55. R. Motwani and P. Raghavan. (1995). *Randomized Algorithms.* New York City, New York, USA: Cambridge University Press.
56. V. Nagaraju, V. V. Basavaraj, and L. Fiondella. (2016). Software rejuvenation of a fault-tolerant server subject to correlated failure. In *Proceedings of the 2016 Annual Reliability and Maintainability Symposium (RAMS), Tucson, Arizona, USA, January 25–28*, pp. 1–6.
57. N. U. Nair, P. Sankaran, and N. Balakrishnan. (2010). *Quantile-Based Reliability Analysis.* Statistics for Industry and Technology. Basel, Switzerland: Birkhäuser.
58. A. A. Neath and F. J. Samaniego. (1992). On the total time of test transform of an IFRA distribution. *Statistics and Probability Letters*, **14**, 289–291.
59. H. Okamura and T. Dohi. (2012). Optimization of opportunity-based software rejuvenation policy. In *Proceedings of the 2012 IEEE 23rd International Symposium on Software Reliability Engineering Workshops (ISSREW), Dallas, Texas, USA, November 27–30*, pp. 283–286.
60. H. Okamura and T. Dohi. (2013a). Dynamic software rejuvenation policies in a transaction-based system under Markovian arrival processes. *Performance Evaluation*, **70**(3), 197–211.

61. H. Okamura and T. Dohi. (2013b). Optimal trigger time of software rejuvenation under probabilistic opportunities. *IEICE Transactions on Information and Systems*, **96**(9), 1933–1940.
62. H. Okamura and T. Dohi. (2016). Analysis of optimal restart policies for software systems. *Journal of Japan Industrial Management Association*, **66**(4E), 416–425.
63. B. O'Donoghue and E. Candes. (2015). Adaptive restart for accelerated gradient schemes. *Foundations of Computational Mathematics*, **15**(3), 715–732.
64. T. Pesu, J. Kettunen, K. Wolter, and W. J. Knottenbelt. (2017). Three-way optimisation of response time, subtask dispersion and energy consumption in split–merge systems. In *Proceedings of the 11th International Conference on Performance Evaluation Methodologies and Tools (ValueTools), Venice, Italy, December 5–7*, pp. 244–251.
65. P. Reinecke, A. van Moorsel, and K. Wolter. (2004). A measurement study of the interplay between application level restart and transport protocol. In *Proceedings of the International Service Availability Symposium (ISAS), Munich, Germany, May 13–14*, pp. 86–100.
66. P. Reinecke, A. P. A. van Moorsel, and K. Wolter. (2006a). Experimental analysis of the correlation of HTTP GET invocations. In *Proceedings of the 3rd European Performance Engineering Workshop, Budapest, Hungary, June 21–22*, pp. 226–237.
67. P. Reinecke and K. Wolter. (2008). Adaptivity metric and performance for restart strategies in web services reliable messaging. In *Proceedings of the 7th International Workshop on Software and Performance, Princeton, New Jersey, USA, June 23–26*, pp. 201–212.
68. P. Reinecke and K. Wolter. (2010). A simulation study on the effectiveness of restart and rejuvenation to mitigate the effects of software ageing. In *Proceedings of the 2010 IEEE Second International Workshop on Software Aging and Rejuvenation (WoSAR), San Jose, California, USA, November 2*, pp. 1–6.
69. P. Reinecke, K. Wolter, and A. P. van Moorsel. (2006b). The fast and the fair: A fault-injection-driven comparison of restart oracles for reliable web services. In *Proceedings of the International Conference on Quantitative Evaluation of Systems (QEST), Riverside, California, USA, September 11–14*, pp. 375–384.
70. K. Rinsaka and T. Dohi. (2007). A faster estimation algorithm for periodic preventive rejuvenation schedule maximizing system availability. In *Proceedings of the International Service Availability Symposium, Durham, New Hampshire, USA, May 21–22*, pp. 94–109.
71. K. Rinsaka and T. Dohi. (2016). Toward high assurance software systems with adaptive fault management. *Software Quality Journal*, **24**(1), 65–85.
72. Y. Ruah, E. Horvitz, and H. Kautz. (2002). Restart policies with dependence among runs: A dynamic programming approach. In *Proceedings of the Eighth International Conference on Principles and Practice of Constraint Programming, Ithaca, New York, USA, September 9–13*, pp. 573–586.
73. F. Salfner and K. Wolter. (2010). Analysis of service availability for time-triggered rejuvenation policies. *Journal of Systems and Software*, **83**(9), 1579–1590.
74. O. V. Shylo, T. Middelkoop, and P. M. Pardalos. (2011). Restart strategies in optimization: Parallel and serial cases. *Parallel Computing*, **37**(1), 60–68.
75. D. Simeonov and D. Avresky. (2009). Proactive software rejuvenation based on machine learning techniques. In *Proceedings of the International Conference on Cloud Computing, Bangalore, India, September 21–25*, pp. 186–200.

76. A. S. Tanenbaum. (1996). *Computer Networks.* Upper Saddle River, New Jersey, USA: Prentice Hall PTR.
77. H. Tong, C. Faloutsos, and J.-Y. Pan. (2008). Random walk with restart: Fast solutions and applications. *Knowledge and Information Systems*, **14**(3), 327–346.
78. M. Torquato, P. Maciel, J. Araujo, and I. Umesh. (2017). An approach to investigate aging symptoms and rejuvenation effectiveness on software systems. In *Proceedings of the 2017 12th Iberian Conference on Information Systems and Technologies (CISTI), Lisbon, Portugal, June 14–17*, pp. 1–6.
79. A. van Moorsel and K. Wolter. (2004a). Analysis and algorithms for restart. In *Proceedings of the 1st International Conference on the Quantitative Evaluation of Systems (QEST), Enschede, The Netherlands, September 27–30*, pp. 195–204.
80. A. van Moorsel and K. Wolter. (2004b). Making deadlines through restart. In *Proceedings of the 12th GI/ITG Conference on Measuring, Modelling and Evaluation of Computer and Communication Systems (MMB 04), Dresden, Germany, September 12–15*, pp. 155–160.
81. A. van Moorsel and K. Wolter. (2004c). Optimal restart times for moments of completion time. *IEE Proceedings — Software*, **151**(5), 219–223.
82. A. P. A. van Moorsel and K. Wolter. (2006). Analysis of restart mechanisms in software systems. *IEEE Transactions on Software Engineering*, **32**(8), 547–558.
83. T. Walsh. (1999). Search in a small world. In *Proceedings of the International Joint Conference on AI (IJCAI), Stockholm, Sweden, July 31–August 6*, pp. 1172–1177.
84. Q. Wang. (2015). *Restart in Mobile Offloading* (PhD thesis, Freie Universität Berlin, Germany).
85. Q. Wang and K. Wolter. (2014). Detection and analysis of performance deterioration in mobile offloading system. In *Proceedings of the 2014 IEEE International Symposium on Software Reliability Engineering Workshops (ISSREW), Naples, Italy, November 3–6*, pp. 420–425.
86. Q. Wang and K. Wolter. (2015a). Automated adaptive restart for accelerating task completion in cloud offloading systems. In *Proceedings of the 2015 IEEE International Conference on Autonomic Computing (ICAC), Grenoble, France, July 7–10*, pp. 157–158.
87. Q. Wang and K. Wolter. (2015b). Reducing task completion time in mobile offloading systems through online adaptive local restart. In *Proceedings of the 6th ACM/SPEC International Conference on Performance Engineering, Austin, Texas, USA, January 31–February 4*, pp. 3–13.
88. Q. Wang and K. Wolter. (2016). Accelerating task completion in mobile offloading systems through adaptive restart. *Software & Systems Modeling*, **17**(2), 397–413.
89. K. Wolter. (2005). Self-management of systems through automatic restart. In Babaoglu O., Jelasity M., Montresor A., Fetzer C., and Leonardi S. (eds.). *Self-Star Properties in Complex Information Systems.* Berlin/Heidelberg, Germany: Springer-Verlag.
90. K. Wolter. (2010). *Stochastic Models for Fault Tolerance: Restart, Rejuvenation and Checkpointing.* Berlin/Heidelberg, Germany: Springer-Verlag.
91. K. Wolter and P. Reinecke. (2008). Restart in competitive environments. In *Proceedings of the 24th UK Performance Engineering Workshop, London, UK, July 3–4*, p. 18.
92. K. Yamakita, H. Yamada, and K. Kono. (2011). Phase-based reboot: Reusing operating system execution phases for cheap reboot-based recovery. In *Proceedings of the 2011 IEEE/IFIP 41st International Conference on Dependable Systems & Networks (DSN), Hong Kong, China, June 27–30*, pp. 169–180.

93. M. Yang, G. Min, W. Yang, and Z. Li. (2014). Software rejuvenation in cluster computing systems with dependency between nodes. *Computing*, **96**(6), 503–526.
94. Q. Zhang and W. Wang. (2007). A fast algorithm for approximate quantiles in high speed data streams. In *Proceedings of the 19th International Conference on Scientific and Statistical Database Management (SSBDM'07), Banff, Canada, July 9–11*, pp. 29–29.

Part IV

Applications

Part IV of this Handbook focuses on the practical applications of software aging and rejuvenation.

Chapter 8, Using Software Aging Monitoring and Rejuvenation for the Assessment of High-Availability Systems, presents the application of an agile devops methodology leveraging a failure model that incorporates aging-related failures. This agile devops methodology has been developed to integrate the failure reporting from production (i.e., ticket history), the Markov chain design, the performance test case design, the performance test case execution, the performance check and the decision to release the software.

Chapter 9, Application to Operating Systems, presented the application of software aging to operating systems. The presented investigation on the Linux bug-fix patches reveals that Linux can cause typical aging errors such as memory leaks. The chapter introduces rejuvenation techniques tailored for operating systems.

Chapter 10, Aging in Virtualized Environments, discusses the main existing approaches to study the aging phenomena in virtualized environments, and the corresponding rejuvenation techniques. It targets those contexts where virtual machines are massively adopted — such as cloud computing platforms — as well as relevant virtualization technologies.

Chapter 11, Experimental Tools for Software Aging and Analysis, presents a pool of popular tools for detecting software aging, which have been chosen from the scientific literature and from industry. The chapter considers tools both for C/C++ and Java software, and analyze their internals, use cases, the aging symptoms that they address, and relevant applications in real case studies.

Chapter 12, Implementation of Micro-Rejuvenation with Cooperative Stack Leasing, focuses on micro-rejuvenation approaches to deal with system failures triggered by stack overflow, a condition where the contents of a stack frame of one thread spills and overwrites one or more locations of the adjacent stack belonging to another thread.

Chapter 8

Using Software Aging Monitoring and Rejuvenation for the Assessment of High-Availability Systems

Alberto Avritzer*, Michael Grottke†,‡ and Daniel Sadoc Menasché§

eSulabSolutions, Inc., Princeton, USA
GfK SE and Friedrich-Alexander-Universität, Germany
Federal University of Rio de Janeiro (UFRJ), Brazil
**beto@esulabsolutions.com*
†Michael.Grottke@gfk.com
‡Michael.Grottke@fau.de
§sadoc@dcc.ufrj.br

Background: In this chapter, we present the application of software aging monitoring and software rejuvenation for the assessment of high-availability systems. In high-availability systems, the metric of interest is the transient performability during system recovery, also referred to as "survivability". A survivability assessment requires the definition of the failure model. In addition, extensive testing using loads and configurations that are able to model the conditions customers encounter in production is required.

Aim: We describe the application of an agile devops methodology leveraging a failure model that incorporates aging-related failures. This agile devops methodology has been developed to integrate the failure reporting from production (i.e., ticket history), the Markov chain design, the performance test case design, the performance test case execution, the performance check and the decision to release the software.

Applicability domain: The domain of applicability of this study is mission-critical systems that employ high-availability strategies, such as software component hosting supporting open-source development, media streaming hardware and software supporting high-volume media processing, and online banking. Continuous integration, testing and operations is a key part of building software in the new devops paradigm.

Method: Our method involves the following steps, which embrace development and operations. Each step is based on its predecessor output: 1) an analysis of ticket history generated by *operations*; 2) a Markov chain design derived from ticket history; 3) a performance test case design based on Markov chain analysis; 4) a performance test case execution for each software version; 5) a Markov chain parameterization based on test case results; 6) an evaluation of performance metrics of interest using the parameterized Markov chain; 7) performance checks and 8) a new software release delivered to *operations*. The *development* team receives feedback on performance issues and bugs, and provides new releases for performance checking and testing.

Results: We present extensive measurements from a large industrial system, as well as a list of test cases identified from the high-availability Markov chain. These test cases were executed using the industrial system under study in this research, and the obtained test results are presented. These results were used in the Markov model parameterization.

Lessons learned: Several high-availability strategies, such as automated load balancing and software rejuvenation, require that failures be detected in an efficient manner. We have found that high-availability strategies implemented for fast failure recovery also need to focus on implementing strategies for fast failure detection, as in our experiments failure recovery rates were dominated by the failure detection time. We believe that this finding can be used to help high-availability system architects select which software aging and rejuvenation features to add to their high-availability designs.

8.1. Introduction

In this chapter, we report on an approach to integrate software aging monitoring and software rejuvenation into an overall system model that is used to assess the survivability of a high-availability system. The importance of software aging and rejuvenation integration is reflected in the overall Markov model design, which impacts the survivability metric estimation.

The handbook chapters on *Markov Chains and Petri Nets* as well as *Models for Restart, Reboot and Rejuvenation* contain overviews of the models that have been proposed to abstract software aging and rejuvenation system mechanisms. In this chapter, we present an example of an application of software aging and rejuvenation modeling to the performance assessment of a high-availability system. In addition, we have integrated our approach into a modern devops organization in which the barriers between development and operations teams have been removed to enable shorter software release cycles and feedback loops from operations to development.

We have analyzed over 100 customer issues related to performance and reliability, and have derived a failure classification that contains the most important failure types observed by customers. The failures we observed were consistent with failures reported in the literature for similar types of systems [1]. By doing so, we have created a failure classification that represents the types of failures that we expect to occur in the field for the project under study. These issues need to be addressed by the high-availability software solution. The failure classification was used to create a Markov chain that represents the high-availability system states that can be entered as a consequence of failure occurrences and the failure recovery process. The Markov chain also contains the transitions between states and the associated transition rates. In addition, a performance reward is assigned to each state. These rewards capture the sustained throughput that is delivered by the high-availability system throughout the failure recovery process. The Markov model is used to generate test cases for high-availability assessment. The test results are used to parameterize the model and enable the computation of a survivability metric, such as expected throughput from failure to recovery.

Figure 8.1 illustrates a general devops ecosystem which leverages Markov chain models. The boxes marked in bold are the focus of this chapter. Note that there are two loops in the figure. The outer loop, which is connected by solid thick arrows, corresponds to the set of activities that are executed to support the software release lifecycle. It accounts for the history of tickets issued by final users, where some of these tickets may correspond to software failures that shall be taken into account for the Markov model design. The Markov model design impacts the performance test case design and execution. The inner loop, which is connected by dashed arrows, relates to the development of internal software versions based on the results of performance testing and corresponding bugs found during the execution of test cases. The devops methodology described in Fig. 8.1 shows

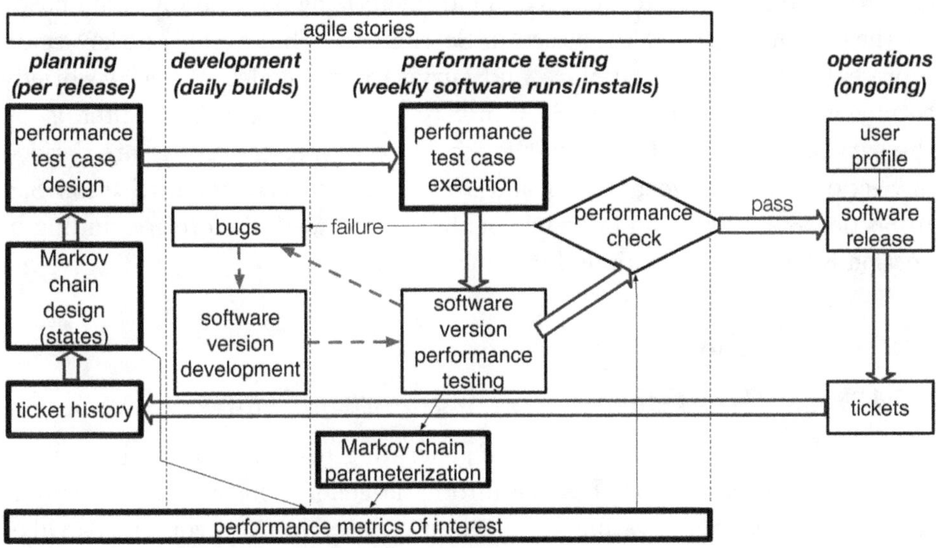

Fig. 8.1. Devops methodology leveraging Markov chain models.

how continuous performance testing is integrated into the agile process. The production ticket history analysis is used to help define the Markov chain and the performance tests.

We have developed or re-used open-source scripts to automate most of the performance testing execution and analysis. One script is used to instantiate Amazon Web Services (AWS) instances to run automated testing. Another script is used for the automated analysis of the test results to provide pass/fail assessment based on CPU, memory, and I/O usage.

In summary, this chapter's main contributions are:

- The presentation of the application of an agile devops methodology that leverages a failure model incorporating aging-related failures;
- A description of an approach for performance test case generation that can be used for the assessment of high-availability systems;
- The extension of previous research on survivability analysis for the assessment of high-availability systems.

The outline of the chapter is as follows. In Section 8.2, we give some background information on aging-related failures, as well as the Markov-chain-based test case generation approach. Section 8.3 shows the architecture of the high-availability system under study. In Section 8.4, we present the empirical strategy followed, consisting of ticket history analysis, failure classification and the structural design of the resulting Markov chain. Empirical results were obtained in our test environment by designing and executing performance test cases and parameterizing our Markov chain based on the outcomes; this is discussed in Section 8.5. The overall Markov chain represents an integrated failure and survivability model. While we briefly comment on its solution in Section 8.6, the focus of this chapter is on the survivability model component, for which numerical results are derived in Section 8.7. Rejuvenation events are taken into account in Section 8.8. In Section 8.9 we give an overview of the related work, before concluding in Section 8.10 with suggestions for future research.

8.2. Background

8.2.1. *Test Case Generation Using Markov Chains*

Test case generation is the process of generating test suites to verify a given system. In a seminal work on the automatic generation of load test suites, the deterministic state testing approach introduced by Avritzer and Weyuker relied on the Markovian property, or memoryless assumption: all information required to assess behavior in a Markovian state depends only on the state description and not on the path taken to reach the state [2]. Therefore, if a system can be accurately modeled as a Markov chain, the system can be effectively tested by deterministically driving the system to each of the states of interest in the Markov chain and assessing pass/fail criteria for each state.

It was shown by Avritzer and Weyuker that testing telecommunication systems using deterministic state testing is a cost-effective way to uncover rare resource-allocation-related failures and to provide a measure of system probability state coverage [2]. Several test case generation approaches were designed for the performance testing of telecommunication systems. Then, Avritzer *et al.* extended that work by including resource usage and resource failure analysis [3]. The approach employed performability modeling and transient Markov chain analysis to provide a time-dependent software reliability estimation.

In this chapter we further extend the approaches presented in the aforementioned works in the following ways. First, while Avritzer and Weyuker defined Markovian states as a function of the number of operations (e.g., call types) being used by the system at a given time, in this chapter we define the Markov states based on the resource failure type and the associated mechanism used for failure recovery. Second, we assign performance rewards to each state. Third, the state probabilities and rewards are used to compute performance metrics throughout the failure recovery process as, for example, instantaneous relative throughput during the failure recovery process.

The test case generation approach for testing high-availability systems introduced in this chapter is composed of a failure classification based on field data, and the design of a Markov model that represents the high-availability system failure and recovery processes. This recovery process consists of both a manual recovery process to address failures that cannot be automatically recovered and that require manual recovery, and an automated part which implements the automated recovery of the high-availability system.

Each state in the high-availability Markov chain is a candidate test case that can be used for system performance and survivability assessment. Therefore, the scope of performance testing can be reduced by focusing on a subset of the high-availability Markov chain.

Figure 8.2 presents a classification of instantaneous and cumulative metrics that can be derived from a high-availability Markov chain, such as the one presented in Section 8.4. There, we will explain the modeling approach used to develop the Markov chain for our system under study.

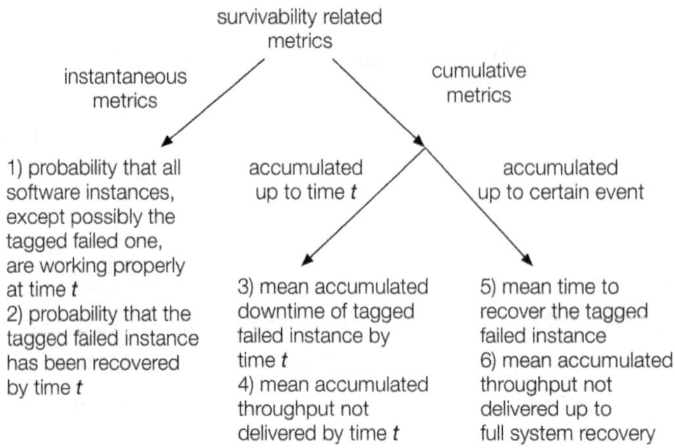

Fig. 8.2. Tree encompassing metrics of interest.

8.2.2. *Modeling Software Aging and Failure Recovery*

Beginning with the seminal paper by Huang *et al.* [4], Markov chains have frequently been used to model systems experiencing software aging. From a highly-robust state, in which the system is safe from immediate failures, the aging phenomenon makes the system enter a failure-probable state as time progresses; from this state, the system can finally transition into the failure state, or software rejuvenation may be triggered. Instead, Suzuki *et al.* [5] used a semi-Markov model consisting of three states only: an up state, a crash state, and a rejuvenation state. In this model, the system does not need to have experienced a certain degree of aging before rejuvenation can be initiated. Many papers on software rejuvenation, such as Vaidyanathan and Trivedi [6], have made use of this three-state model structure. Grottke and Schleich [7] employed the same kind of model for the operational phase, but they explicitly accounted for failures caused by both aging-related and non-aging-related bugs. Adding a second model for the testing phase, they were able to investigate the effects of software testing on the availability attainable during operations. Based on these models, Grottke and Schleich [8] explored cost optimality in testing and rejuvenating for software systems that can age.

While the last two papers mentioned accounted for the possibility of removing software faults during the testing phase, all the papers discussed so far focused on rejuvenation as an amenable technique for improving availability during operations. However, the software faults responsible for the software aging phenomenon, known as aging-related bugs, are a special type of Mandelbugs [9, 10]. The behavior of such a Mandelbug may appear non-deterministic, because the same set of input data seems to make it cause a failure at some times, but not at others. This is due to the complexity of its activation or error propagation, for example, the influence of indirect factors, such as the timing of inputs and operations. While this makes Mandelbugs more difficult to debug, on the positive side this allows one to recover a system that failed because of a Mandelbug without fixing the fault in the code [11]. For example, a mere restart or reboot may be sufficient to ensure that the failed operation works without any problems. Grottke *et al.* [12] used a semi-Markov model to investigate the recovery of systems from failures caused by Mandelbugs, examining the influence of model parameters on the mean time to recovery and the steady-state system unavailability.

In this chapter, we propose a Markov model accounting for aging and non-aging-related failures. Both complete failures and partial failures are considered. The focus of our analysis is on failure recovery. In contrast to Grottke *et al.* [12], we also carry out transient analyses of the recovery behavior.

8.3. System Architecture Overview

The system architecture under study is shown in Fig. 8.3 and consists of a load balancer, several hosts and a shared blobstore.

The load balancer is responsible for receiving http requests and routing them to the online hosts. In addition, the load balancer is also responsible

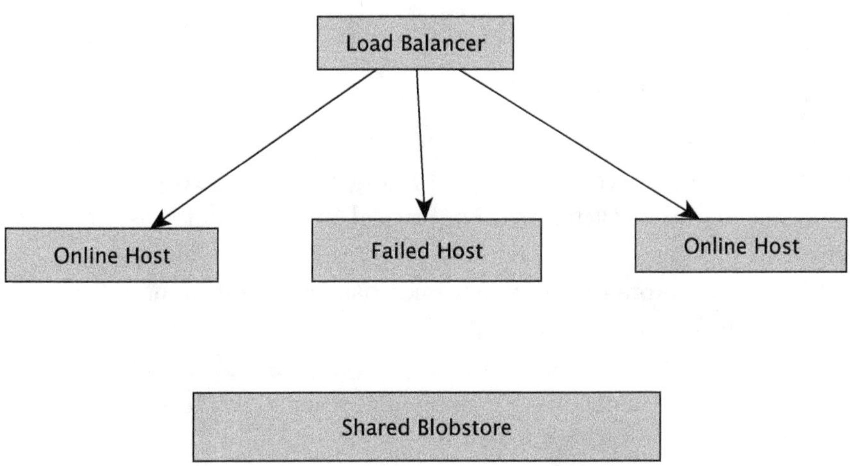

Fig. 8.3. System architecture under study.

for the periodic monitoring of the hosts to determine their health status. If a host fails to respond to the health status request for a pre-determined number of times, it is put into an unhealthy state.

All hosts have the same processing capability and are network-connected to the load balancer and to the shared blobstore.

The shared blobstore is connected to the hosts using a Network File System (NFS).

In this study, we have provisioned all these components using the AWS cloud environment.

The software architecture includes high-availability features that enable the online hosts to continue to operate correctly even when some of the hosts have failed.

8.4. Empirical Strategy

Our empirical strategy is based on tasks that are implemented in the planning, development and performance testing stages of the devops methodology shown in Fig. 8.1.

By analyzing the history of failure tickets collected during operations, we first classify the failures observed. This failure classification is then used for deriving the structure of a Markov chain representing the failure and recovery behavior of the system.

Empirical results are generated as a result of performance test execution and are presented in Section 8.5.

In the remainder of this section we describe the activities performed in the planning stage of our empirical strategy.

8.4.1. *Ticket History Analysis*

One of the objectives of this research is to develop a test case generation and execution approach for a new system under development. This is a new release of an existing mission-critical system that has been widely deployed in industry. While the new system has a new architecture, it will be deployed to a large existing customer base and will be used in the same domain as the existing system. For the existing system, we had at our disposal a large database containing several years of customer issues. In addition, issues are tagged as *performance* when they have been perceived by customer support personnel as being performance-affecting. Therefore, the *performance* category used in the ticket failure analysis is customer-perceived and not related to the *survivability* performance metric used in the Markov model. Each customer report issue contains several pages of problem identification and problem resolution. The analysis of these ticket reports was performed manually by reading several pages of reports for each ticket and assigning to each ticket a failure category. Therefore, a practical approach for ticket filtering needed to be employed, concentrating on the issues reported by the largest customers. This was seen as a reasonable approach, as the largest customers also have the largest system deployments and largest usage rates. Using this approach, we were able to reduce the number of *performance*-tagged issues from hundreds to tens of issues. In the next subsection, we present the failure classification resulting from this analysis.

8.4.2. *Failure Classification*

The approach we used for performance-tagged failure classification consisted of the following steps:

- Identification of the customer community having the largest deployments;
- Classification of the performance-tagged issues by failure type and performance root cause;
- Aggregation of the performance-tagged issues by root cause;
- Generation of the performance issue profile based on the root cause aggregation.

We identified the following failure types as reported by customers: outage due to performance, performance degradation due to high I/O, slow response, timeouts, system crash, disk full, high load, number of items exceeded, system unstable, capacity issues, and outage due to high load. As these failure types were extracted from the ticket reports, there was the need to determine the failure root causes and to group the tickets into consistent categories. The root causes of these performance issues were: insufficient memory, system misconfigurations, NFS, network, Lightweight Directory Access Protocol (LDAP), database, and file system.

The final consistent categories that were developed based on the root cause analysis performance/failure categories are as follows:

- *Resource exhaustion*: CPU, memory, disk, network;
- *Misconfiguration*: this involved the incorrect system usage or installation;
- *Metadata accumulation*: threads, databases, memory;
- *Slow performance*: a need for performance improvement in a specific area was identified;

- *Concurrency*: excessive locking, deadlock, database corruption;
- *Bottleneck resource*: single thread, LDAP;
- *System hung*: waiting for timeout, too many threads, shutdown failed;
- *Recoverable performance issues*: memory fragmentation, timeouts, I/O, caching.

These categories were used to define the structure of the Markov chain design as described in the next subsection.

8.4.3. *Structural Markov Chain Design*

In this section, we construct a Markov model representing the failure behavior of the system, including the measures taken to prevent future failure occurrences, as well as system recovery following a failure.

From the failure classification in Section 8.4.2, it is clear that the existing system has sometimes encountered issues that left it in a degraded performance mode. Avižienis *et al.* [13] refer to the occurrence of such a problem as a "partial failure". In addition, the system also experienced "complete failures", which led to the cessation of any service. These will be referred to as "failures" in the following sections.

The failure classification also indicates that some of the problems were due to an aging behavior, as the longer the system had been running continuously, the higher the rate at which failures and partial failures occurred. An example of such a problem is one caused by not properly releasing resources after usage.

These aspects are accounted for in our Markov model, shown in Fig. 8.4. In state N, where the system is operating normally, a partial failure can occur at rate σ_n, while the system fails at rate γ_n. Also, internal error conditions (e.g., resources that are not released although no longer needed) may accumulate inside the running system, leading it into a state in which it is prone to showing an aging-related failure; this happens at rate η_1. A failure that occurs once the system is in state A may or may not be due to the aging effects. Therefore, the rate at which state F is entered is the sum of γ_n and γ_a, with the latter representing the additional failure risk caused by aging. Similarly, from the aging-failure-prone state, the occurrence rate of partial failures amounts to $\sigma_n + \sigma_a$. If such a failure is experienced, then the system switches to state PA. It should be noted that this state does not imply that the partial failure was actually due to aging. Instead, it represents the fact that both a partial failure has occurred and that the system has aged. We therefore assume that the rate at which the system fails completely is $\gamma_n + \gamma_a$,

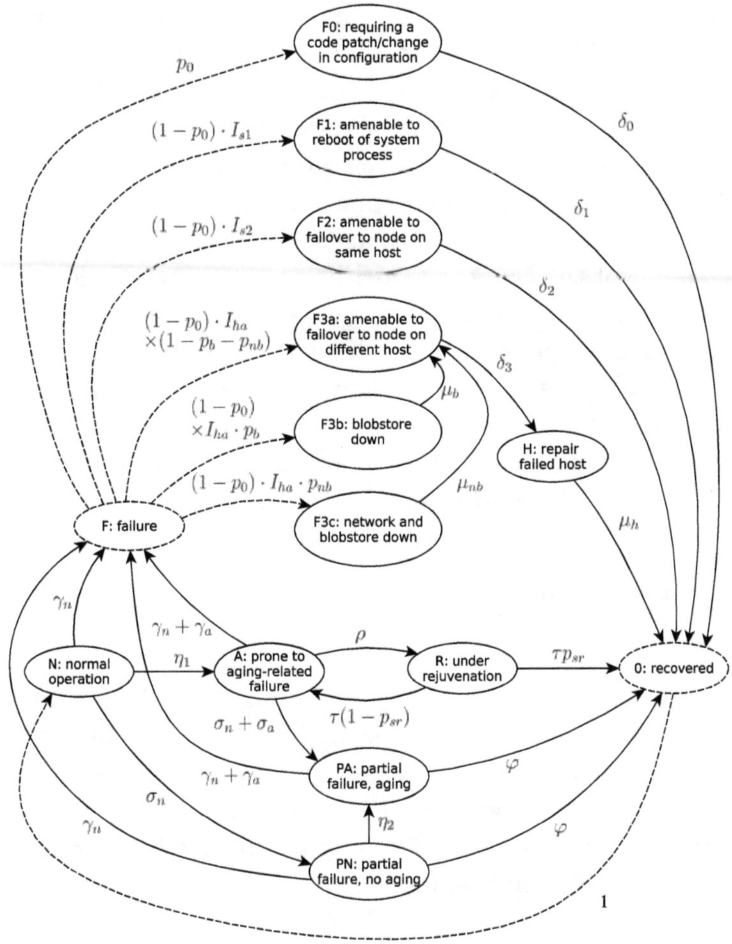

Fig. 8.4. Markov model.

like in state A. In contrast, state PN is the one attained by the system if it experienced a partial failure without any prior aging. Thus, from this state, complete failures occur at rate γ_n. Internal failure conditions may also accrue inside the partially failed system, making it prone to an aging-related failure. In this case the rate is denoted by η_2.

In the following a host represents a computer system. A node is one of several software entities that may run on a given host. A replicated node may be recovered at the same host or at a different host.

In our model the complete failure state F is a vanishing state from which the system immediately switches into a state indicating the appropriate recovery approach. The switching probabilities depend on p_0, p_b, p_{nb}, as well as the configuration variables I_{s1}, I_{s2} and I_{ha}. The coefficients at the edges leaving the states $F0$, $F1$, $F2$ and $F3a$ represent the rates for recovering the system with the respective appropriate action upon a failure, including the detection of the problem: a manual code patch or a system configuration issue (δ_0), a manual restart of the sytem process (δ_1), a manual failover to a node on the same host (δ_2), or an automated failover to a node on a different host provided that both the network and the blobstore are working (δ_3).

The creation of the Markov model by mapping production tickets into Markov states was done manually using expert knowledge. The performance engineers used their experience in the development of aging and survivability models [3, 14–16] to create the high-availability model presented in this section. As an area for further research, it would be interesting to investigate how to develop a production ticket coverage metric. Specifically, practitioners should have guidance on how to map specific tickets to a particular state.

8.5. Empirical Results

8.5.1. *Test Environment*

We have built a performance testing environment on AWS that is able to mimic large mission-critical deployments. The testbed contains two nodes that were deployed in three hosts using a one-node-per-host configuration. Each host was configured with 8 CPUs and 2 Tera-Byte SSD drives. The test environment configuration was adapted to match the requirement of each test case presented in Section 8.5.2.

8.5.2. *Performance Test Case Design*

Each Markov state represents a testing configuration, and several tests could be required to verify the correctness of each state in the Markov model. In addition, the Markov model serves as a basis for systematically reducing the number of test cases required to be executed, as the performance/reliability tester may decide to focus the performance/reliability testing on a subset of the Markov chain states. Therefore, the test cases described in this section are labeled with the Markov model state that is exercised by the test case.

The test cases that were identified from the Markov chain states are the following:

- *State $F1$ — Amenable to reboot*: This test case verifies that after a failure, a single-host-single-node system can be restored using a process reboot.

- *State F2 — Amenable to failover to node on the same host*: This test case verifies that after a failure in one node of a dual-node system that is configured in a high-availability mode, service can be restored using a failover to the second node.
- *State F3a — Amenable to automated failover to a node on a different host if network and blobstore are both working*: This test case verifies that after a system failure, a dual-host-dual-node system that is configured in a high-availability mode can be restored using a failover to the second node in the second host.
- *State F3b — Blobstore down*: This test case is used to assess the time required to manually restore a failed blobstore.
- *State F3c — Network and blobstore down*: This test case is used to assess the time required to manually restore both the network and the blobstore.
- *State R — Under rejuvenation*: This test case is used to assess the time required to remove a task that creates excessive load in one node of a dual-host-dual-node configuration.
- *State A — Prone to aging-related failure*: This test creates a prone-to-aging-related-failure condition by executing a task to smoothly increase memory usage.
- *State PA — Partial failure, aging*: This test is a continuation of the *prone-to-aging-related-failure* test. It continues to smoothly add memory to create a partial failure due to aging.
- *State PN — Partial failure, no aging*: This test creates a partial failure that is not due to aging by creating a task to generate excessive CPU load.
- *State H — Repair failed host*: This test case is used to assess the time required to manually restore a failed host in a dual-host-dual-node system.
- *State N — Normal operation*: This test case consists of starting the system in a dual-node configuration to assess the baseline throughput during normal operation.

*State F*0 was not associated with a test case as it requires, for recovery, a code patch or a system configuration change.

Each state of the Markov chain is entered with a certain probability that depends on the occurrence probability of the associated performance issue. Because, for high-availability systems, performance failures are rare events, their probability of occurrence is very difficult to assess. The

Markov-chain-based approach introduced in this chapter tackles this problem using a two-pronged approach:

(1) For each of the states of the Markov chain, test cases are generated to measure the state reward and transition rate that is activated as a reaction to the performance failures represented in the associated state;
(2) The impact of the occurrence probability of each Markov chain state on the system performability and survivability metrics is evaluated by generating plots of these metrics as a function of the occurrence probability of the performance issues of interest to the analysis. The objective of generating these plots, for each Markov chain state, is to quantitatively assess the benefit of using high-availability features, such as software rejuvenation, for failure avoidance associated with a given Markov chain state.

State rewards are introduced in Section 8.5.4.

8.5.3. *Performance Test Case Execution*

8.5.3.1. *Analysis approach*

The approach for test execution employs, as much as possible, a devops methodology that includes:

- Automation of test execution using the Apache JMeter performance testing tool;
- Automation of the creation and termination of the AWS instance that runs the JMeter load testing scripts;
- Automation of performance data collection and analysis using scripts to detect deviations of the performance signatures from the baseline.

A very important feature of a devops environment is the automated testing of new builds using a continuous integration approach. While this is fine for unit testing in continuous integration environments, performance testing environments require stable builds and significant coordination of the team to select which build should be subjected to longer performance/reliability testing runs.

8.5.3.2. *Results*

The following test results were obtained for the executed test cases. The manual recovery times are dominated by the manual detection time, θ.

The detection times reported below vary depending if the state was part of a manual recovery process or an automated recovery process.

- *State F1 — Amenable to reboot*: The manual recovery rate for a full failure that is amenable to a reboot of the failed process was estimated as $\delta_1 = \frac{1}{60s+\theta}$, because the manual process restart time was measured to be 60 seconds. The detection time, θ, was estimated to be 5 minutes for the monitored system. The total recovery time is the average time to detect the failure plus the time from manually restarting the system to the restoration of normal operation.
- *State F2 — Amenable to failover to node on same host*: Manual recovery rate for a full failure that is amenable to a failover to a node on the same host was estimated as $\delta_2 = \frac{1}{7m+\theta}$. Total recovery time was estimated as the time to detect the failure plus the time to rehome the load driver from primary to secondary port on the same host and to restart the load driver, because there is no load balancer implemented for the configuration modeling of this state.
- *State F3a — Amenable to automated failover to a node on a different host if network and blobstore are both working*: In this configuration, a load balancer is used as a front end to all requests. Therefore, no rehoming is required and the automated routing of requests to the working node is performed automatically by the load balancer once the AWS instance has consecutively failed at least the number of specified health checks. This number is known as the unhealthy threshold. We set the unhealthy threshold to 2, and the health check interval is set at 30 seconds. Therefore, since recovery is implemented as the automated routing of requests to a working node, the total recovery time is equal to the detection time, which is $\delta_3 = \frac{1}{60s}$.
- *State F3b — Blobstore down*: The manual restoration rate of a failed blobstore was measured as $\mu_b = \frac{1}{1m+\theta}$. This rate is estimated from the time required for the execution of the NFS remount required to restore access to the NFS-mounted blobstore.
- *State F3c — Network and blobstore down*: The manual restoration rate of both the network and the blobstore was estimated as $\mu_{nb} = \frac{1}{5m+\theta}$. This rate is estimated from the time required to manually restart the network interface followed by the manual restoration of the blobstore.
- *State R — Under rejuvenation*: The system recovery rate τ was estimated as $\tau = \frac{1}{45s}$.
- *State A — Prone to aging-related failure*: This test creates a prone-to-aging-related-failure condition by executing a task to smoothly increase

memory usage. This test was executed and a prone-to-aging-related state condition was created.

- *State PA — Partial failure, aging*: The system recovery rate after an aging-related partial failure due to memory issues was manually corrected was estimated as $\varphi = \frac{1}{4m16s+\theta}$. The degraded throughput in this state was measured as 18.5 requests/sec.
- *State PN — Partial failure, no aging*: The system recovery rate after a non-aging-related partial failure was manually corrected was estimated as $\varphi = \frac{1}{4m16s+\theta}$. The degraded throughput in this state was measured as 18.5 requests/sec.
- *State H — Repair failed host*: In this test, to assess the time required to manually restore a failed host in a dual-host-dual-node system, a host was brought down and back up. The system recovery rate was estimated as $\mu_h = \frac{1}{2m1s+\theta}$.
- *State N — Normal operation*: This test case assessed the baseline throughput in normal operation; it was measured as 37 requests/sec.

8.5.4. *Predicted and Measured Markov Model State Rewards*

The associated state reward is defined as the relative system throughput achieved for that state. In normal operation we expect the relative system thoughput to be 1. Table 8.1 summarizes the relative rewards predicted and measured as described in this section.

The rewards predicted based on the system design for each Markov state are the following:

- A reward rate of 1 for $F3a$, N, A, and H.
- A reward rate of 0 for R, $F0$, $F1$, $F2$, $F3b$, and $F3c$.
- The reward rates for states PA and PN are to be measured based on test cases.

In our measurements of the high-availability system, we have found that actual rewards depend on the high-availability capability of the software implementation. In our first measurement, we assessed the following rewards:

- A reward rate of 1 was measured for states N and A.
- A reward rate of 0 was measured for states H, $F0$, $F1$, $F2$, $F3a$, $F3b$, and $F3c$. For states H and $F3a$, a software fault in the high-availability code was detected that required a manual repair of the primary host to

Table 8.1. State reward summary for predicted, original and refined systems.

State	Predicted (by design)	Test 1 (original system)	Test 2 (refined system)
N	1	1	1
A	1	1	1
H	1	0	1
$F3a$	1	0	2/3
$F3b$	0	0	0
$F3c$	0	0	0
R	0	N/A	N/A
$F0$	0	0	0
$F1$	0	0	0
$F2$	0	0	0
PA	N/A	0.5	0.5
PN	N/A	0.5	0.5

enable the correct operation of the high-availability cluster (primary and secondary nodes).

- A reward rate of 0.5 was measured for states PA and PN.
- State R was not part of the experiment.

In our second measurement, we used three hosts with one node per host, and we observed the following rewards:

- A reward rate of 1 was measured for states N, A, and H. For states H and $F3a$, the software fault found in high-availability code was corrected by using a three-host environment that enabled the correct operation of the high-availability cluster (primary and secondary nodes).
- A reward rate of 0 was measured for states $F0$, $F1$, $F2$, $F3b$, and $F3c$.
- A reward rate of 2/3 was measured for state $F3a$, as two out of three hosts are up in that state.
- A reward rate of 0.5 was measured for states PA and PN.
- As before, state R was not part of the experiment.

Table 8.1 summarizes the relative performance rewards for each Markov state.

In this section, we have shown how to measure the Markov chain state transition rates, and how to define the Markov state reward rates. In the next sections, we present the evaluation of the high-availability Markov chain using different scenarios.

8.6. Integrated Failure and Survivability Model

In this section, we present the solution of the proposed Markov model and summarize the reference setup obtained through an adequate model parameterization.[a]

8.6.1. *Solution of Integrated Failure and Survivability Model*

We consider the transient solution of the proposed Markov model shown in Figure 8.4 (excluding the transition with rate 1 from state 0 to state N), with state space Ω. The cardinality of Ω is $|\Omega| = 14$. States are assumed to be indexed, and are henceforth referred to interchangeably either by their names or by their indices. The indices of states 0 and N are assumed to be 0 and 14, respectively. Let $\boldsymbol{Q}$ be the infinitesimal generator matrix of the Markov chain. Let $\pi_i(t)$ be the probability that the system is in state i at time t. We assume that $\pi_N(0) = 1$ and $\pi_i(0) = 0$ for $i \neq N$. Then, $\boldsymbol{\pi}(t)$ is the unique solution to $\frac{d\boldsymbol{\pi}(t)}{dt} = \boldsymbol{\pi}(t)\boldsymbol{Q}$,

$$\boldsymbol{\pi}(t) = \left[\sum_{n=0}^{\infty} (\boldsymbol{Q}t)^n / n! \right]_N , \tag{8.1}$$

where $[\boldsymbol{A}]_i$ refers to the row of $\boldsymbol{A}$ associated with state i, $i \in \Omega$.

In the numerical experiments that follow, we use the Matlab `expm` function to numerically evaluate Equation (8.1).

When assessing survivability-related metrics, it is also of interest to evaluate the fraction of time that the system remains in a given state (or a subset of states) before recovery. We therefore build a modified Markov chain, with infinitesimal generator $\tilde{\boldsymbol{Q}}$ given by Fig. 8.4 (including the transition with rate 1 from state 0 to state N). Let $\tilde{\boldsymbol{\pi}}$ be the steady-state solution of this Markov chain, $\boldsymbol{0} = \tilde{\boldsymbol{\pi}}\tilde{\boldsymbol{Q}}$. Let R be the recovery time, i.e., the time to reach state 0 starting from state N. Then, $E[R] = 1/\tilde{\pi}_0$. Let f_i be the fraction of time that the system remains in state i before reaching state 0,

$$f_i = \frac{\tilde{\pi}_i}{1 - \tilde{\pi}_0}.$$

[a]A reproducibility package containing data and mathlab scripts used to create the figures in this chapter can be found at https://tinyurl.com/bookrejuvenation

Let R_i be the time the system remains in state i before recovery. Then, $E[R_i]$ is given by

$$E[R_i] = f_i E[R].$$

8.6.2. *Markov Chain Parameterization*

We now describe how to parameterize the proposed Markov model using data reported by the failure tickets issued by users (Section 8.4) and empirical findings obtained with controlled experiments (Section 8.5).

The reference setup considered in our numerical experiments is presented in Table 8.2.

8.6.3. *Challenges of Integrated Model: Survivability Model Motivation*

The discussion above highlights some of the key challenges involved in an integrated analysis of failures and recovery times, some of which are listed below.

Model parameterization: The derivation of all the parameters shown in Table 8.2 is required to generate an accurate solution to the Markov chain. This is sometimes difficult, because for high-availability systems the

Table 8.2. Reference setup (time values in seconds).

Variable	Value	Variable	Value
	Failure detection time		
θ	60		
	Recovery times (obtained from controlled experiments)		
δ_0^{-1}	$4 \times 60 \times 60 = 14400$	δ_1^{-1}	$60 + \theta = 120$
δ_2^{-1}	$7 \times 60 + \theta = 480$	δ_3^{-1}	60
$\mu_{nb}{}^{-1}$	$5 \times 60 + \theta = 360$	μ_b^{-1}	$60 + \theta = 120$
μ_h^{-1}	$121 + \theta = 181$	φ^{-1}	$256 + \theta = 316$
	Monitoring, aging and rejuvenation times and probabilities (based on expert knowledge)		
ρ^{-1}	1	τ^{-1}	45
p_{sr}	1		
	Fraction of failures of given type (p_O obtained from previous literature [17] and additional parameters set so as to obtain a simple case study)		
p_O	0.457	I_{s1}	0
I_{s2}	0	I_{ha}	1
p_b	1/3	p_{nb}	1/3

failure data is usually very small. In this chapter, some of the parameters were derived from an optimization approach based on a small failure data set, comprising tickets issued by users capturing their experience with the system.

Interpretation of results: The interpretation of results obtained from combined failure and repair models requires delicate analysis. Failure rates and repair rates may have different orders of magnitude. Separating the analysis conditioned on the phase of the cycle (failure or recovery) makes the analysis easier to handle.

In the remainder of this chapter, we focus on model simplifications obtained by using a survivability approach that assesses recovery time based on failure conditioning. We present an approach to generate fast analytical solutions for subsets of the Markov model that are relevant to specific deployment configurations.

8.7. Survivability Model

In this section, we focus on the survivability model that captures how the system behaves from failure up to recovery. We incrementally simplify the Markov model presented in Figure 8.4, in order to illustrate how different parts of its state space can be used to obtain desired metrics of interest under simple setups. First, we focus on the states that characterize system behavior from failure up to repair (Section 8.7.1), and then we specialize to one specific path of such a model, referred to as the high-availability path (Section 8.7.2).

8.7.1. *Survivability Model Overview*

The survivability model is a subset of the integrated failure and survivability model in Fig. 8.4, wherein we focus on the states that characterize system behavior from failure up to repair. Figure 8.5 illustrates a simplified version of the survivability model, in which p_b and p_{nb} have been set to zero, omitting states $F3b$ and $F3c$.

Let $\pi_i(t)$ be the probability of finding the system in state i at time t if it starts in state F at $t = 0$. We refer to the outgoing rate from state i as Λ_i. Let p_i, $i \in \{F0, F1, F2, F3a\}$, denote the probability of transitioning from state F to state i. From Fig. 8.4, it can be seen that $p_1 = (1 - p_0) \cdot I_{s1}$, $p_2 = (1 - p_0) \cdot I_{s2}$, etc. Obviously, $\sum_{i \in \{F0,F1,F2,F3a\}} p_i = 1$. Note that whereas in previous sections we assumed that the residence time at state F was negligible, in what follows we separate the detection time (θ) from

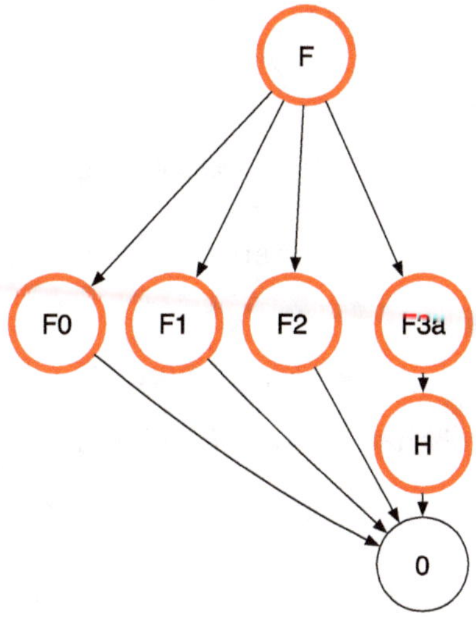

Fig. 8.5. Acyclic chain accounting for simplified survivability analysis.

Table 8.3. Reference setup (time values in seconds).

Variable	Reference Value	Variable	Reference Value
Λ_H^{-1}	121	Λ_{F3a}^{-1}	60
Λ_F^{-1}	θ, detection time, varies between 50 and 150		

the recovery times ($1/\Lambda_i$), and let the mean residence time at state F equal $\theta = 1/\Lambda_F$ (Table 8.3).

Denote by $\tilde{\pi}_H(\Lambda_F, t)$ the probability of being in state H at time t, given that the output rate from state F is Λ_F and that the system transitions from state F to state $F3a$. In Appendix 8.A.1, we present closed-form expressions for $\tilde{\pi}_H(\Lambda_F, t)$ as well as $\pi_i(t)$. Such expressions serve to illustrate how to obtain the instantaneous metrics referred to in Fig. 8.2.

Next, we illustrate how to obtain the cumulative metrics discussed in Fig. 8.2. Let m_i be the mean time at state i before reaching state 0. Then,

$$\begin{aligned} m_F &= 1/\Lambda_F, \\ m_i &= p_i/\Lambda_i, \quad i \in \{F0, F1, F2, F3a\}, \\ m_H &= p_{F3a}/\Lambda_H. \end{aligned}$$

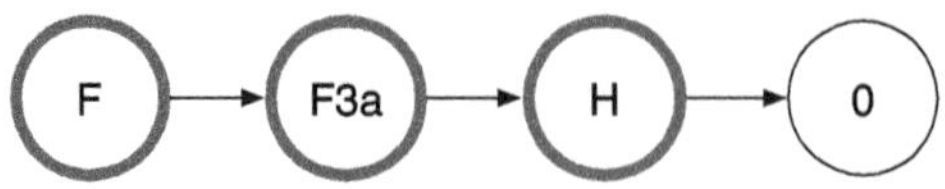

Fig. 8.6. High-availability path.

Let m be the mean time to reach state 0. It is given by

$$m = \sum_{i \in \{F, F0, F1, F2, F3a, H\}} m_i.$$

Let f_i^* be the fraction of time at state i, before reaching 0. Then,

$$f_i^* = m_i/m.$$

The equations above serve to illustrate how to obtain mean cumulative metrics. Alternatively, the distribution of cumulative metrics can be computed using techniques such as those proposed by de Souza e Silva *et al.* [18]

8.7.2. *High-Availability Path*

Figure 8.6 shows the path obtained from the Markov chain by a further simplification of the analysis, assuming that the probability of failures requiring a code patch or configuration change is zero, and focusing on a well-configured high-availability system that is amenable to failover to a node on a different host (i.e., $I_{ha} = 1, I_{s1} = I_{s2} = 0$). The transient state probabilities for this high-availability path are given in Appendix 8.A.2.

Next, we numerically illustrate some properties of the high-availability path. Table 8.3 shows the adopted reference setup. Note that we separate the detection time from the recovery time, accounted at states F and $F3a$, respectively. This is in contrast to Table 8.2, where the time at state F was assumed to be negligible and the detection time was accounted for as part of the time in the states following state F.

Figures 8.7 and 8.8 (resp., 8.9) serve to illustrate the behavior of instantaneous (resp., cumulative) survivability metrics. Such metrics correspond to the leftmost and middle branches of the tree in Fig. 8.2.

Figure 8.7 shows the transient state probabilities of full system recovery (π_0) and of the failed host recovery (π_H) obtained for the solution of this high-availability path. We see from this figure the improvements achieved when shorter detection times are possible.

Figure 8.8 shows the instantaneous reward associated with the high-availability path for the original and the refined system. The curves in

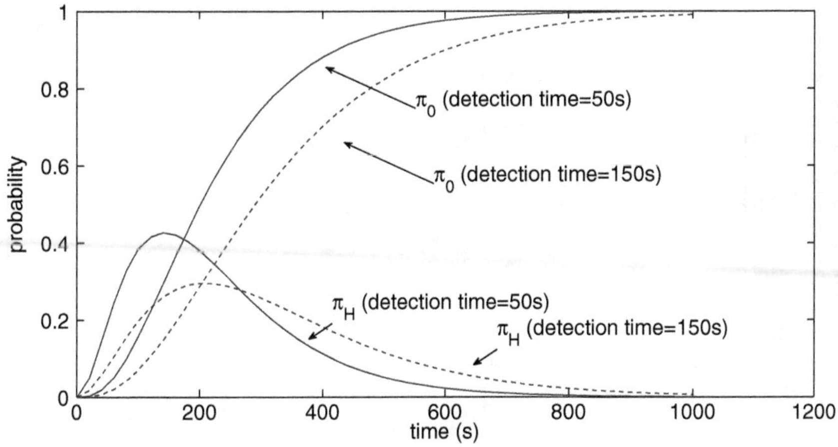

Fig. 8.7. Transient solution associated to high-availability path.

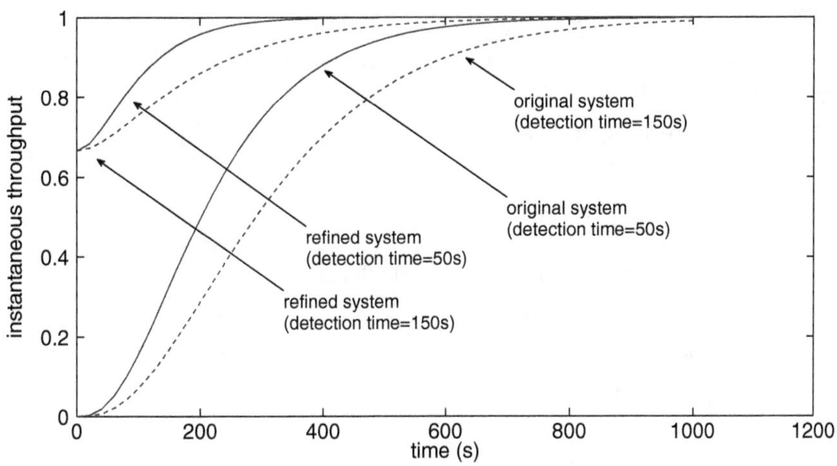

Fig. 8.8. Transient solution associated to high-availability recovery path (instantaneous reward).

Fig. 8.8 correspond to weighted averages of the ones presented in Fig. 8.7. Again, we consider detection times of 50 and 150 seconds. We note the improved instantaneous throughput obtained for the refined system, and a gain achieved when reducing the detection time.

Figure 8.9 shows the accumulated throughput, at time t after failure. Figure 8.9 is obtained from Fig. 8.8 after integration. Whereas Fig. 8.8 shows the instantaneous throughput at time t, Fig. 8.9 depicts the accumulated mean number of packets served by time t. The accumulated throughput

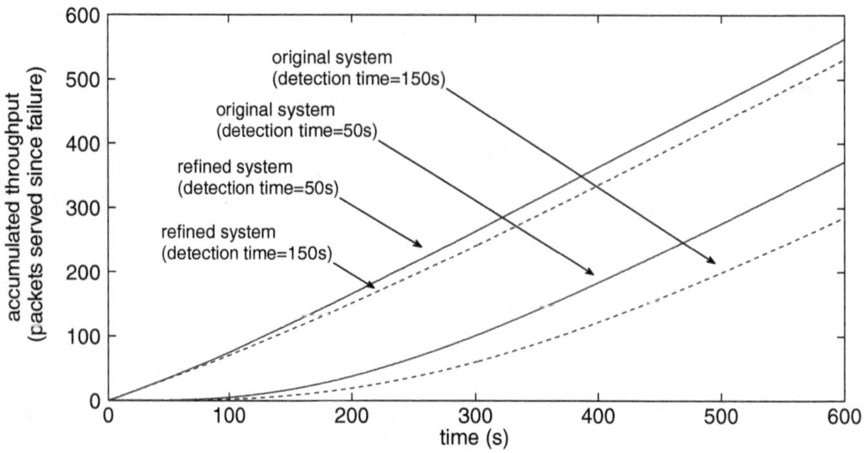

Fig. 8.9. Transient solution associated to high-availability recovery path (accumulated reward).

served by the refined system grows faster than the one associated to the original system. We note that after roughly 400 seconds, the accumulated throughput grows linearly in all the considered setups, indicating that by this time the system is fully available with high probability.

8.8. Accounting for Rejuvenation

In what follows, we take into account rejuvenation when assessing system performance, as shown in Fig. 8.10. Let ρ be the software aging detection rate; i.e., $1/\rho$ is the mean time to detect software aging. We let $\rho = 1$s and consider a detection time of 150s, i.e., $\Lambda_F^{-1} = \theta = 150$s.

Note that rejuvenation events (e.g., system reboots) may take place at different moments during the software lifecycle. Nonetheless, in our model we only explicitly capture rejuvenation events that are effective to prevent failures. Effective rejuvenation events occur after the software has become prone to an aging-related failure. The parameters are summarized in Table 8.4.

Figures 8.11, 8.12 and 8.13 illustrate transient metrics accounting for rejuvenation. We vary the probability of taking the upper (red) or lower (blue) path in Fig. 8.10.

In what follows, we assume $\gamma_N + \gamma_A \ll \rho$.

When $\gamma_N = 0$, the aging-prone state A is always reached after the system leaves its normal state N. In this case, the system does not directly fail due to non-aging-related faults.

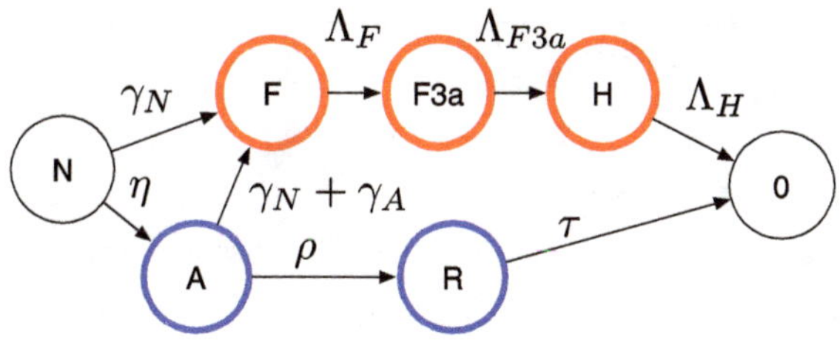

Fig. 8.10. Accounting for the rejuvenation path.

Table 8.4. Parameters used in an analysis of the impact of rejuvenation, accounting for dynamics between state A and state 0 (times measured in seconds). The normalized throughputs at states A and R are 1 and 0, respectively.

Variable	Reference Value	Variable	Reference Value
$1/\rho$	1	$1/\tau$	30
		$\gamma_N + \gamma_A \ll \rho$	

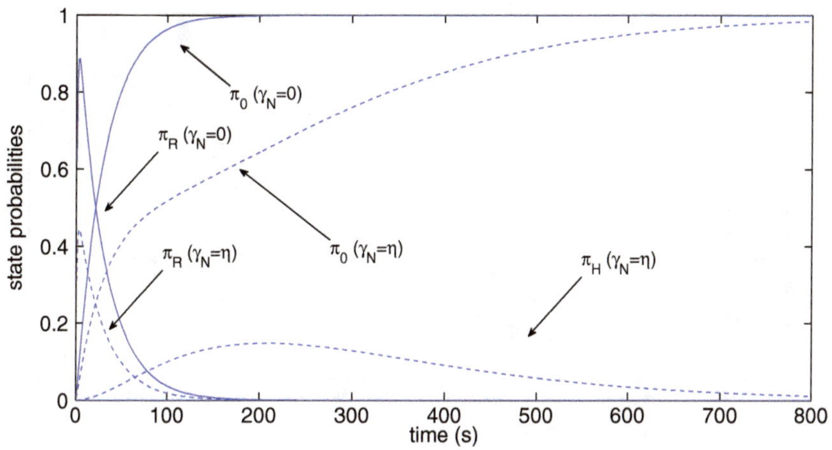

Fig. 8.11. System with rejuvenation: a transient solution associated to a high-availability path. When $\gamma_N = 0$ (resp., $\gamma_N = \eta$), rejuvenation always occurs before failure (resp., occurs before failure for half of the potential failures). Note that state H is not reachable when $\gamma_N = 0$. Probabilities associated to states F, F3a and A are not represented.

When $\gamma_N = \eta$, in half of the cases the system tends to fail due to a non-aging-related fault. In the other cases, the system enters the aging-prone state and is then either rejuvenated, or it fails before rejuvenation has been triggered.

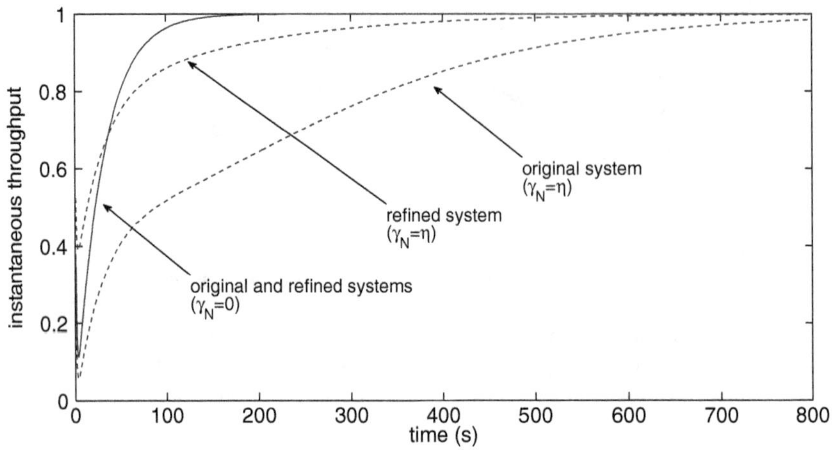

Fig. 8.12. System with rejuvenation: a transient solution associated to a high-availability recovery path (instantaneous reward). When $\gamma_N = 0$ (resp., $\gamma_N = \eta$), rejuvenation always occurs before failure (resp., occurs before failure for half of the potential failures). Note that when $\gamma_N = 0$ the original and the refined systems are indistinguishable, as they only differ in the instantaneous rewards associated to the top path in Fig. 8.10.

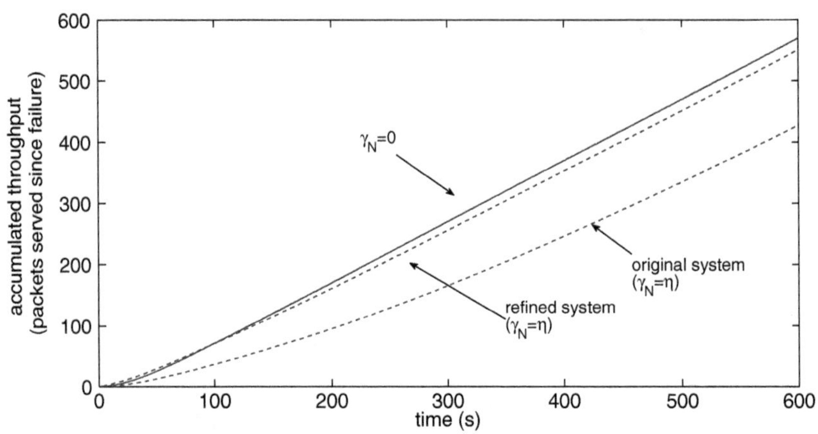

Fig. 8.13. System with rejuvenation: a transient solution associated to a high-availability recovery path (accumulated reward). Rejuvenation benefits are more pronounced in the original (non-refined) system.

Figure 8.11 indicates that state R, where the system is under rejuvenation, concentrates significant probability mass up to 100 seconds. If $\gamma_N = 0$, the system is likely recovered by time 100s (solid lines). Otherwise, it is still likely to pass through state H before fully recovering (dotted lines in Fig. 8.11). In the latter case, the behavior of the system is similar to the one previously presented in Fig. 8.7.

Figure 8.12 shows how the instantaneous reward varies as a function of time. Note that if $\gamma_N = 0$ there is no distinction between the refined and the original systems, as the Markov chain always rejuvenates before failure, and the two systems are equivalent. Finally, Fig. 8.13 illustrates how the accumulated throughput varies as a function of time. Note that rejuvenation particularly benefits the original (non-refined) system when detection time equals 150 seconds (compare the bottom dotted lines in Figs. 8.12 and 8.9).

8.9. Related Work

The use of statistical models to understand the behavior of software systems dates back to the study of the distribution of software inputs, which comprise the input domain, e.g., using Markov chains [19]. Under input domain partition testing, software inputs that lead to similar fault-revealing behavior, or similar workloads, are classified into equivalence classes, which partition the input domain. Each Markov chain state corresponds to a partition of the input domain.

Brunnert *et al.* presented a research agenda to help overcome the challenges of integrating performance engineering with devops approaches [20]. The authors proposed to do so by employing systematic measurement and model-based performance engineering. In addition, the report contained a comprehensive literature review of the topic of performance engineering for devops.

In this chapter, we extend our previous research on Markov-chain-based test case generation [2, 3] and the survivability modeling of critical infrastructures [16, 21, 22] to address the survivability assessment of mission-critical systems that employ high-availability strategies, such as software component hosting supporting open-source development, media streaming hardware and software supporting high-volume media processing, and online banking.

The assessment of failure rates based on small failure samples, as found in high-availability systems, may incur significant errors in the failure rate estimates, because the failure sample is very small [23]. Survivability modeling has been proposed as one of the techniques to help design high-availability systems, with the detailed modeling of failure recovery conditioned on the occurrence of the failure event [15, 16, 21, 22]. Therefore, survivability modeling can be used to cope with the difficulty of estimating failure rates in high-availability systems. Such difficulty is particularly challenging in critical systems, e.g., nuclear systems. Park and Jang, for instance, combined

Bayesian statistical inference with software test cases to improve software reliability model estimates in the nuclear safety domain [24].

Trivedi *et al.* described an overview of architectural approaches to achieve high availability, considering different types of faults [25]. Then, several approaches to assess the design of high-availability smart-grid power systems using survivability modeling were presented [16, 21, 22]. In particular, scenarios with a single failure and with multiple failures were taken into account [16]. The survivability modeling approach was also shown to be applicable to model a number of different domains, including water and gas infrastructures, accounting for the impact of a large storm in metropolitan areas and the assessment of worm intrusions in mission-critical systems [14, 21, 26, 27]. Grottke *et al.* developed a framework with metrics and models to help manage the response to security intrusions [14, 27]. The survivability modeling approach is instrumental to efficiently capture the impact of network neighborhoods and node quarantine behavior on the system infection probability.

In conclusion, the related work discussed above indicates that architecture modeling, performance anti-patterns, root cause analysis, performance testing and analysis, and the relationship to high-availability modeling can all benefit from the new devops continuous integration environment in order to be successful.

8.10. Conclusions

In this chapter, we have presented a novel test case generation and execution approach for the assessment of high-availability mission-critical software systems. In our new approach, we have integrated failure analysis and classification, test case generation based on Markov chains, survivability analysis, and software aging and rejuvenation modeling and analysis.

We have introduced a performance failure classification based on the analysis of a large performance failure data set, and have shown how to construct a high-availability Markov chain based on the failure classification.

We have used the failure classification, and the test case generation and execution approach to obtain the required Markov model parameters.

We have also presented extensive measurements from a large industrial system, as well as a list of test cases identified from the high-availability Markov chain. These test cases were executed using the industrial system under study in this research, and the obtained results have been presented. These results were used in the Markov model parameterization. Specifically, we have found that recovery rates were dominated by the failure detection time. This was true for both manual and automated recovery and for the aging and non-aging cases. We believe that this finding can be used to help high-availability system architects select which features to add to their high-availability designs.

We are very encouraged by these results, and we are currently planning to execute more detailed measurements of performance for each of the identified test cases based on the high-availability Markov chain states.

As topics for future research, we are planning to extend our devops performance testing environment in the following ways:

- Use the high-availability Markov chain model results to assess the benefits of adding certain architecture features (e.g., software monitoring and rejuvenation);
- Automatically track the performance-related metrics as the software system evolves;
- Completely automate our performance testing environment including both the generation and analysis of performance snapshots for the identification of performance bottlenecks, as well as the installation and configuration of the system under test using automated installation tools (e.g., Docker).

8.A.1. Solution of the Survivability Model

Given the survivability model in Fig. 8.5, we have

$$\begin{aligned}
&\tilde{\pi}_H(\Lambda_F, t) \\
&= \int_{y=0}^{t} \int_{z=0}^{t-y} \Lambda_F \exp(-\Lambda_F y) \Lambda_{F3a} \exp(-\Lambda_{F3a} z) \exp(-\Lambda_H (t-y-z)) dz dy \\
&= \frac{\Lambda_F \Lambda_{F3a}}{\Lambda_{F3a} - \Lambda_H} \left(\frac{e^{-\Lambda_{F3a} t} - e^{-\Lambda_F t}}{\Lambda_{F3a} - \Lambda_F} - \frac{e^{-\Lambda_F t} - e^{-\Lambda_H t}}{\Lambda_F - \Lambda_H} \right).
\end{aligned}$$

Thus,

$$\pi_F(t) = e^{-\Lambda_F t}.$$

For states $i \in \{F0, F1, F2, F3a\}$,

$$\pi_i(t) = p_i \cdot \frac{\Lambda_F}{\Lambda_F - \Lambda_i} \cdot (e^{-\Lambda_i t} - e^{-\Lambda_F t}).$$

Similarly, for state H,

$$\pi_H(t) = p_{F3a} \cdot \tilde{\pi}_H(\Lambda_F, t).$$

Finally,

$$\pi_0(t) = 1 - \pi_F - \sum_{i \in \{F0,F1,F2,F3a,H\}} \pi_i.$$

8.A.2. Solution of the High-Availability Path

The transient solution associated to the high-availability path shown in Fig. 8.6 is given by

$$\begin{aligned}
\pi_F(t) &= e^{-\Lambda_F t}, \\
\pi_{F3a}(t) &= \frac{\Lambda_F}{\Lambda_F - \Lambda_{F3a}} \cdot (e^{-\Lambda_{F3a} t} - e^{-\Lambda_F t}), \\
\pi_H(t) &= \tilde{\pi}_H(\Lambda_F, t), \\
\pi_0(t) &= 1 - \pi_F(t) - \pi_{F3a}(t) - \pi_H(t).
\end{aligned}$$

Acknowledgments

This work was partially supported by the Dr. Theo and Friedl Schoeller Research Center for Business and Society.

References

1. G. Jacques-Silva, A. Avritzer, D. S. Menasché, A. Koziolek, L. Happe, and S. Suresh. (2015). Survivability modeling to assess deployment alternatives accounting for rejuvenation. In *Proceedings of the 2015 IEEE International Symposium on Software Reliability Engineering Workshops (ISSREW), Gaithersburg, Maryland, USA, November 2–5*, pp. 114–119. doi: 10.1109/ISSREW.2015.7392055.
2. A. Avritzer and E. R. Weyuker. (1995). The automatic generation of load test suites and the assessment of the resulting software. *IEEE Transactions on Software Engineering*, **21**(9), 705–716. ISSN 0098-5589. doi: 10.1109/32.464549.
3. A. Avritzer, E. de Souza e Silva, R. M. Leão, and E. Weyuker. (2011). Automated generation of test cases using a performability model. *IET Software*, **5**(2), 113–119.
4. Y. Huang, C. Kintala, N. Kolettis, and N. Fulton. (1995). Software rejuvenation: Analysis, module and applications. In *Proceedings of the 25th International Symposium on Fault-Tolerant Computing, Pasadena, California, USA, June 27–30*, pp. 381–390.
5. H. Suzuki, T. Dohi, K. Goševa-Popstojanova, and K. S. Trivedi. (2002). Analysis and estimation of multi-step failure models with periodic software rejuvenation. In Artalejo J. R. and Krishnamoorthy A. (eds.). *Advances in Stochastic Modelling.* New Jersey, USA: Notable Publications Inc.
6. K. Vaidyanathan and K. S. Trivedi. (2005). A comprehensive model for software rejuvenation. *IEEE Transactions on Dependable and Secure Computing*, **2**(2), 124–137.

7. M. Grottke and B. Schleich. (2013). How does testing affect the availability of aging software systems? *Performance Evaluation*, **70**(3), 179–196.
8. M. Grottke and B. Schleich. (2012). Cost optimality in testing and rejuvenation. In *Proceedings of the 4th International IEEE Workshop on Software Aging and Rejuvenation, Dallas, Texas, USA, November 27–30*, pp. 259–264.
9. M. Grottke and K. S. Trivedi. (2005). A classification of software faults. In *Supplemental Proceedings of the 16th International IEEE Symposium on Software Reliability Engineering, Chicago, Illinois, USA, November 8–11*, pp. 4.19–4.20.
10. M. Grottke and K. S. Trivedi. (2005). Software faults, software aging and software rejuvenation. *Journal of the Reliability Engineering Association of Japan*, **27**(7), 425–438.
11. M. Grottke and K. S. Trivedi. (2007). Fighting bugs: Remove, retry, replicate, and rejuvenate. *IEEE Computer*, **40**(2), 107–109.
12. M. Grottke, D. S. Kim, M. Nambiar, R. Natella, R. Mansharamani, and K. S. Trivedi. (2016). Recovery from software failures caused by Mandelbugs. *IEEE Transactions on Reliability*, **65**(1), 70–87.
13. A. Avizienis, J.-C. Laprie, B. Randell, and C. Landwehr. (2004). Basic concepts and taxonomy of dependable and secure computing. *IEEE Transactions on Dependable and Secure Computing*, **1**(1), 11–33.
14. M. Grottke, A. Avritzer, D. S. Menasché, L. P. de Aguiar, and E. Altman. (2016). On the efficiency of sampling and countermeasures to critical-infrastructure-targeted malware campaigns. *SIGMETRICS Performance Evaluation Review*, **43**(4), 33–42. ISSN 0163-5999. doi: 10.1145/2897356.2897361.
15. P. E. Heegaard and K. S. Trivedi. (2009). Network survivability modeling. *Computer Networks*, **53**(8), 1215–1234. ISSN 1389-1286. doi: 10.1016/j.comnet.2009.02.014.
16. A. Avritzer, S. Suresh, D. S. Menasché, R. M. M. Leão, E. de Souza e Silva, M. C. Diniz, K. Trivedi, L. Happe, and A. Koziolek. (2013). Survivability models for the assessment of smart grid distribution automation network designs. In *Proceedings of the 4th ACM/SPEC International Conference on Performance Engineering (ICPE '13), Prague, Czech Republic, April 21–24*, pp. 241–252. ISBN 978-1-4503-1636-1. doi: 10.1145/2479871.2479905.
17. D. Cotroneo, M. Grottke, R. Natella, R. Pietrantuono, and K. S. Trivedi. (2013). Fault triggers in open-source software: An experience report. In *Proceedings of the 2013 IEEE 24th International Symposium on Software Reliability Engineering (ISSRE), Pasadena, California, USA, November 4–7*, pp. 178–187.
18. E. de Souza e Silva, D. R. Figueiredo, and R. M. M. Leão. (2009). The TANGRAM-II integrated modeling environment for computer systems and networks. *SIGMETRICS Performance Evaluation Review*, **36**(4), 64–69. ISSN 0163-5999. doi: http://doi.acm.org/10.1145/1530873.1530886.
19. J. A. Whittaker and M. G. Thomason. (1994). A Markov chain model for statistical software testing. *IEEE Transactions on Software Engineering*, **20**(10), 812–824.
20. A. Brunnert, A. van Hoorn, F. Willnecker, A. Danciu, W. Hasselbring, C. Heger, N. R. Herbst, P. Jamshidi, R. Jung, J. von Kistowski, A. Koziolek, J. Kroß, S. Spinner, C. Vögele, J. Walter, and A. Wert. (2015). Performance-oriented devops: A research agenda. *Computing Research Repository*, **abs/1508.04752**.
21. A. Avritzer, L. Carnevali, H. Ghasemieh, L. Happe, B. R. Haverkort, A. Koziolek, D. Menasché, A. Remke, S. S. Sarvestani, and E. Vicario. (2015). Survivability evaluation of gas, water and electricity infrastructures. *Electronic Notes in Theoretical Computer Science*, **310**, 5–25. ISSN 1571-0661. doi: http://dx.doi.org/10.1016/j.entcs.2014.12.010.

22. D. S. Menasché, A. Avritzer, S. Suresh, R. M. Leão, E. de Souza e Silva, M. Diniz, K. Trivedi, L. Happe, and A. Koziolek. (2014). Assessing survivability of smart grid distribution network designs accounting for multiple failures. *Concurrency and Computation: Practice and Experience*, **26**(12), 1949–1974. ISSN 1532-0634. doi: 10.1002/cpe.3241.
23. M. R. Lyu (ed.). (1996). *Handbook of Software Reliability Engineering*. Hightstown, New Jersey, USA: McGraw Hill. ISBN 0-07-039400-8.
24. G.-Y. Park and S. C. Jang. (2014). A software reliability estimation method to nuclear safety software. *Nuclear Engineering and Technology*, **46**(1), 55–62.
25. K. S. Trivedi, G. Ciardo, B. Dasarathy, M. Grottke, A. Rindos, and B. Vashaw. (2008). Achieving and assuring high availability. In *Proceedings of the 22nd IEEE International Symposium on Parallel and Distributed Processing, IPDPS 2008, Miami, Florida, USA, April 14–18*, pp. 1–7.
26. A. Avritzer, L. Carnevali, L. Happe, A. Koziolek, D. S. Menasché, M. Paolieri, and S. Suresh. (2014). A scalable approach to the assessment of storm impact in distributed automation power grids. In *Proceedings of the International Conference on Quantitative Evaluation of Systems, Florence, Italy, September 8–10*, pp. 345–367.
27. M. Grottke, A. Avritzer, D. S. Menasché, J. Alonso, L. Aguiar, and S. G. Alvarez. (2015). WAP: Models and metrics for the assessment of critical-infrastructure-targeted malware campaigns. In *Proceedings of the 2015 IEEE 26th International Symposium on Software Reliability Engineering (ISSRE), Washington, DC, USA, November 2–5*, pp. 330–335.

Chapter 9

Application to Operating Systems*

Kenji Kono[†,¶], Kenichi Kourai[‡,||] and Hiroshi Yamada[§,**]

[†]*Keio University, Japan*
[‡]*Kyushu Institute of Technology, Japan*
[§]*Tokyo University of Agriculture and Technology, Japan*
[¶]*kono@sslab.ics.keio.ac.jp*
[||]*kourai@ksl.ci.kyutech.ac.jp*
[**]*hiroshiy@cc.tuat.ac.jp*

Software aging in operating systems is critical because all the applications running on the operating system fail to execute when the operating system is aging. Although the operating systems are well tested and maintained, they are not aging-free. Our investigation on the Linux bug-fix patches reveals that Linux can cause typical aging errors such as memory leaks. In this chapter, we introduce rejuvenation techniques tailored for operating systems. Rejuvenating the operating system is hard because a naive reboot results in a long disruption of the applications' services and the unacceptably low performance of the services after the reboot. This is because it takes a long time to reboot the operating system and the reboot loses all the states internal to the operating system, such as file caches, to speed up user-level applications. This chapter introduces three rejuvenation techniques: 1) the phase-based reboot, which targets a quick reboot of the operating system, 2) the warm-cache reboot, which maintains the internal states of the operating system across the reboot, and 3) Dwarf, which maintains the process states across the reboot. All of these techniques rely on virtual machine monitors and thus, we also discuss the rejuvenation of the virtual machine monitors.

9.1. Software Aging and Rejuvenation in Operating Systems

High availability is important for all ranges of computer systems. High-end enterprise systems lose millions of dollars if their services are unavailable. Low-end device vendors lose their customers if their products, such as smart

*This chapter is based on the authors' papers: [8], [10], [17], and [22].

phones, are not stable. These computer systems are not mission-critical, but users expect those services and devices to be available 24/7 at cheap prices; high availability is not exclusive anymore to expensive mission-critical systems.

Operating systems are crucial for achieving the high availability of computer systems. Compared to application-level failures, kernel-level failures occur less frequently because kernels are well-maintained pieces of software. However, they have a considerable impact on the overall availability of computer systems. Even if the applications are highly available and do not cause any failures at all, a bug inside the kernel can cause severe damage to the entire software stack; no application can continue to run on the crashed kernel.

Unfortunately, modern operating systems are not bug-free. Palix *et al.* [1] report that bugs are introduced to Linux 2.6 at a higher rate than before. In addition, the average time between when a bug is introduced and when a fix is released is 1.8 years for Linux kernels. Lu *et al.* [2] report that almost 40% of Linux patches for file systems are for bug fixes. Our investigation of the change logs of Linux 2.6.24 and 2.6.25 also reveals that there are critical bugs inside the kernel core components. Kernel bugs are not the sole reason for kernel failures. Soft errors in high-density semiconductors are increasing [3], and they cause incorrect values to be read from memory or incorrect instruction results to be produced.

Bugs in the kernel can lead to software aging of the operating system. Cotroneo *et al.* [4] experimentally show that the Linux kernel can cause software aging; the memory consumption of the Linux kernel is statistically analyzed to show the aging trend. Our analysis of the Linux patches for bug fixes also supports the fact that the Linux kernel can show the aging trends. We have investigated all the patches from Linux 2.6.12 to 3.12 [5]. This investigation uses a machine-learning approach to analyze natural languages and statistically classifies the patches based on the topics mentioned in the patches. There are 426 patches classified into "memory leak", which suggests the Linux kernel can show aging trends during the production run.

For end users of computer systems, sometimes the only remedy for kernel aging is to reboot the operating system (and thus the entire software stack). For example, if a smartphone freezes or slows down due to the kernel aging, the end user reboots it in the expectation that the reboot will recover the smartphone; she does not have any skill or tools to diagnose and recover from the aging. Aside from low-end consumer devices, skillful administrators for high-end enterprise systems sometimes reboot the system to avoid or recover from failures. A Cisco Security Advisory [6] reports that their network products had a bug involving a memory leak, and the reboots were necessary to recover from it until a bug fix was released. IBM Director, a cluster management system for xSeries servers, periodically reboots (i.e., rejuvenates) the system to counteract software aging [7]. Although this chapter focuses on transient bugs in the kernel, the rejuvenation is useful for temporary hardware failures such as the overheating of certain sub-systems that forces some of the cores to be shut down or to run slower.

This chapter overviews several techniques to rejuvenate the operating system. The simplest, naive approach to rejuvenating the operating system kernel is just to reboot the kernel. However, this simple rejuvenation of the operating system poses two serious problems, which are peculiar to the operating system:

- **Long disruption of services:** It takes a long time to reboot the operating system kernel because it involves initializing hardware devices and in-kernel data structures, launching daemon processes, and finally starting the applications that serve for end-users. This long disruption, caused by the operating system reboot, is peculiar to the operating system and not acceptable in many cases.
- **Slow execution after reboot:** The execution performance of the applications slows down after the reboot. To control and speed up the execution of user-level processes, the kernel maintains a number of internal states including those used for accelerating the execution. For example, it retains file cache to speed up the access to files. After the operating system reboots, all the internal states are lost and thus the applications have to start running on the cold cache; the file cache is empty at this time and all access to the files requires access to the disks.

In this chapter, we introduce the rejuvenation techniques of the operating system. The techniques can be classified into two categories:

- **State-less Approach:** This approach disposes of in-kernel states when rejuvenating the operating system kernel. At first glance, this approach is similar to the naive approach because it does not retain any internal states across reboots. However, the state-less approach differs from the naive one in that it shortens the reboot time dramatically; the service disruption is much shorter than the naive approach. The phase-based reboot, introduced in Section 9.2.1, is the state-less approach.
- **State-retaining Approach:** This approach retains in-kernel states across reboots and addresses the second problem pointed out above. If all the states are retained, the kernel is not rejuvenated at all.

In this category, it is thus critically important to choose the internal states that should be kept across the reboots. Section 9.2.2 introduces a technique that maintains file-related caches across reboots. This technique avoids the slowdown caused by the cold file cache after the reboots. Section 9.2.3 introduces a technique that maintains process-related states across reboots. This technique shortens the time required to re-start the daemon processes and applications.

Finally, this chapter introduces a rejuvenation technique for virtual machines. Recent trends in cloud computing are based on virtualization technology in which many virtual machines are running on top of the virtual machine monitor. This situation is similar to the relationship between user-level processes and the operating system kernel; if the virtual machine monitor fails, all the virtual machines fail. The rejuvenation technique for the virtual machines is introduced in Section 9.3.

9.2. Rejuvenating the Operating System

9.2.1. *Quick Reboot*

Once we accept reboot-based recovery as a fact of life, we need to try to reduce the downtime caused by reboots as much as possible. The "phase-based" reboot shortens the downtime caused by reboot-based recovery [8]. In a phase-based reboot, a boot sequence is divided into three *phases*: 1) the hardware-initialization phase, 2) the kernel-boot phase, and 3) the daemon-startup phase. The key idea behind a phase-based reboot is that a reboot repeats the same procedure as in the previous boot and sometimes reproduces the system state such that it is identical to the previous one; we can *reuse* a system state in the previous boot if the next boot reproduces the same state. In a phase-based reboot, a system state is saved after each boot-phase is finished. When a reboot is done for recovery, our system restores the saved state to skip the boot-phases that reproduce the same states as in the previous boot.

9.2.1.1. *Execution phases*

To reduce the downtime of reboot-based recovery, the phase-based reboot skips some phases of the time-consuming boot sequence. A boot sequence can be divided into three *phases*: 1) hardware initialization, 2) kernel boot, and 3) daemon startup. Normal reboot-based recovery executes all the boot phases in order to reconstruct a consistent system state and to restart

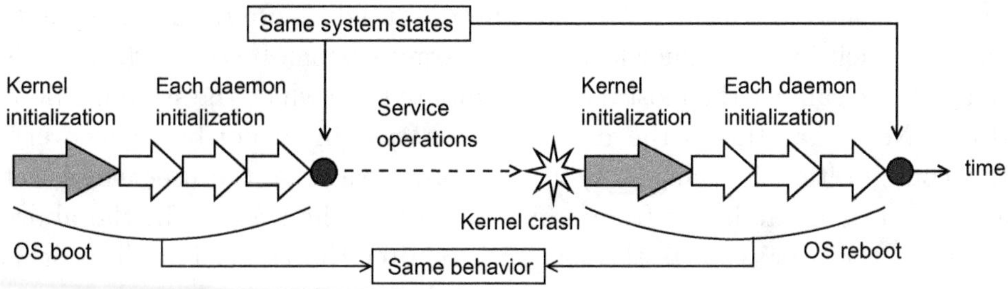

Fig. 9.1. Key idea behind the phase-based reboot. In most cases, the reboot process produces the same system state as in the previous boot.

services. The normal reboot-based recovery repeats the same boot sequence as in the previous boot. Most parts of the sequence are similar to the previous boot because the system configuration is not changed in the context of reboot-based recovery. In a reboot-based recovery, the system is *not* rebooted so as to make the configuration changes effective; the boot sequence starts from the same system configuration and is thus expected to result in the same system state as the previous boot.

As illustrated in Fig. 9.1, the system starts its services after initializing the hardware, booting the kernel, and starting up every daemon. Through these operations, a consistent system state is constructed from which we can start services. When a kernel crashes, a reboot-based recovery is attempted; the system repeats the same procedures to reconstruct the same system state from which we can restart the services. In a reboot-based recovery, no system configuration is changed in most cases. Therefore, the resulting system states are expected to be the same in the previous and current boot sequences.

The key idea behind a phase-based reboot is to save and reuse consistent system states during the reboots. If the next reboot always creates the same state as the previous one, we can simply save and restore the previous state for reboot-based recovery instead of rebooting the entire system. Unfortunately, this is an oversimplification. During service operations, an administrator may change the configuration of some daemons. In this case, we cannot reuse the system state saved in the previous boot because the different configuration may result in a different system state.

To address this reusability problem, the phase-based reboot saves system states at several points, called *restartable points*, during the boot sequence. System states saved at restartable points are called *restartable candidates*, from which the user can select the appropriate point to start the system reboot. By default, the phase-based reboot saves the candidates every time each boot-phase is finished. Administrators can add more restartable points based on their intimate knowledge of the target system. If no configuration is changed, we can use the most recent candidate from which the system reboot starts. Note that this is the most common case in reboot-based recovery. If a configuration is changed as in the above example, the user can select an appropriate candidate from which to restart the system. In the above example, the user restarts the system just after the kernel initialization is finished. To help the user select an appropriate restartable point, the phase-based reboot can determine which restartable point can be used for recovery.

9.2.1.2. *Design details*

The phase-based reboot leverages the snapshot function provided by system virtualization to restart the system at a restartable point. System virtualization is becoming commonplace in computing environments. The snapshot function enables us to save/restore a virtual machine (VM) state including CPU registers, memory, and disks at an arbitrary point. The phase-based reboot uses a snapshot taken during an OS boot to restart the VM at a restartable point. We refer to the snapshot as a *restartable image*. The phase-based reboot overwrites CPU registers and memory states preserved in the restartable image to the running VM; the phase-based reboot never rolls back the disk state to save updates of disks in the service operation.

In the phase-based reboot, we treat snapshots as restartable candidates that can be used as a restartable image. The phase-based reboot appropriately selects a snapshot from the restartable candidates and restores it. To prepare restartable candidates, we take snapshots at many points during an OS boot. Figure 9.2 shows a typical example of how restartable candidates are prepared. We can collect them by taking a snapshot when the kernel boot is complete, when every daemon has been launched, and after a log-in prompt appears. When a phase-based reboot is conducted, we pick up a snapshot from the restartable candidates that has the same state as after the normal reboot-based recovery.

The use of system virtualization allows us to prevent kernel failures inside a VM from corrupting its restartable candidates. If their contents are modified by the propagation of kernel failures, we cannot successfully restore the restartable image. Since the virtual machine monitor (VMM) isolates VMs running on it, the kernel failures are not propagated to the other VMs or the VMM, where snapshots are saved. Although commodity OSes offer a hibernation mechanism that saves their memory states to disks, the saved memory images are more easily affected by kernel failures. This is

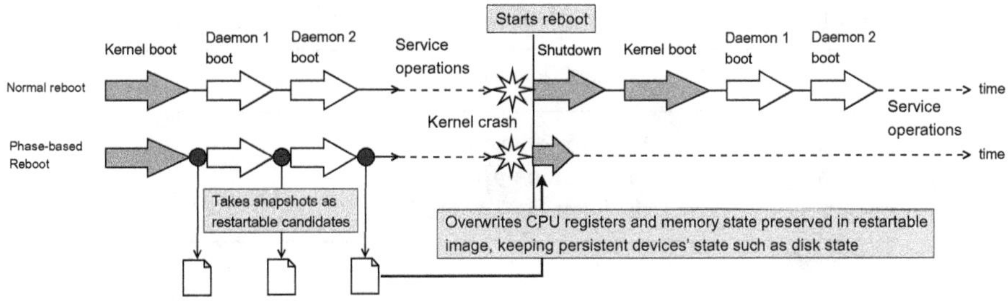

Fig. 9.2. Comparison of normal reboot and phase-based reboot.

because the hibernation mechanism saves memory images to the disk that is not isolated from the OS. This is not reasonable for saving restartable candidates.

To save and restore a system state, the phase-based reboot uses the *snapshot* functionality of virtual machines (VMs). At first glance, saving and restoring a system state is straightforward; the entire memory image of the VM is saved to and restored from a disk. However, this is time-consuming, especially when the memory size assigned to a VM is large. In the worst case, the phase-based reboot takes a longer time to reboot than a normal reboot. To avoid this situation, our mechanism avoids saving unnecessary memory pages that can be reconstructed after the memory image is restored.

Restoring a system state is much more complicated. The memory image saved to a disk contains a disk cache that may be updated after the snapshot is taken. In other words, the disk cache in the saved image may be out of date. If the saved image is simply restored, the out-of-date disk cache is also restored and regarded as up-to-date. To solve this problem, our mechanism refreshes in-memory file objects with the corresponding disk blocks after it restores the saved image.

The phase-based reboot relies on the assumption that memory images just after the system boot are healthy, following the same philosophy as the software rejuvenation. Although the system refreshed by phase-based rebooting faces the same failure soon if the restartable images already involve numerous error states, the restartable images can be created until the target system is ready to service after its boot.

9.2.1.3. *Effectiveness*

We measured the downtime of the phase-based reboot to determine how the phase-based reboot shortens the downtime of reboot-based recovery. To execute the phase-based reboot, we prepared two restartable images. The

Table 9.1. Experimental configuration of phase-based reboot.

Name	Snapshot Point	Snapshot Opt.
pr-naive	Disk is mounted	
pr w/o opt	All daemons are ready	
pr-opt	All daemons are ready	√

first was a restartable image that was taken before the guest kernel mounted the virtual disk. We refer to the phase-based reboot that is restoring this restartable image as *pr-naive*. The other was a restartable image that was taken when a log-in prompt appeared after the kernel and all the daemons were ready. We simply refer to the phase-based reboot that is restoring this restartable image as *pr-opt*. For comparison, we also measured the downtime of a normal boot and a normal reboot on the guest domain (*guest boot* and *guest reboot*). We briefly summarized the experimental configration of the phase-based reboot in Table 9.1.

To clarify how effective our optimization described in Section 9.2.1.2 was, we executed the phase-based reboot without our snapshot optimization and measured its downtime (*pr without snapshot opt*). We started measuring when each operation was triggered, and stopped when all the daemons registered in run level 3 were ready on the domain. We measured the downtime of each reboot-based recovery, varying the memory size of the guest domain.

We assumed a scenario of recovering from fail-stop failures, and compared the guest boot to pr-opt, pr-naive, and pr without snapshot opt. In this scenario, each reboot-based recovery contains a `fsck` execution; the Linux kernel conservatively runs `fsck` in the boot after the kernel is shut down without partitions being unmounted. Next, we assumed a scenario of recovering from gradually corrupting failures such as memory leaks, and we compared the guest reboot to pr-opt, pr-naive, and pr without snapshot opt. In this scenario, none of the reboot-based recoveries need a `fsck` execution because we assume the situation where the virtual disk is correctly unmounted.

Tables 9.2 and 9.3 list the average downtime of each reboot-based recovery. Table 9.2 indicates that the downtime of the phase-based reboot was shorter than that of the guest boot in many cases. For pr-opt, the downtime was 75.0% to 86.2% shorter than that of the guest boot, while the downtime of pr-naive was 34.3% to 60.6% shorter than that of the guest boot. For pr without snapshot opt, its downtime was shorter than that of the guest boot when the domain memory size was smaller than 2 GB.

Table 9.2. Average downtime of guest boot, pr without snapshot opt with fsck, phase-based reboot with fsck.

Memory Size [MB]	Guest Boot [sec]	pr w/o opt. w/fsck [sec]	pr-opt w/fsck [sec]	pr-naive w/fsck [sec]
64	18.96	3.23	2.62	7.47
128	18.50	3.96	2.68	7.81
256	18.39	5.82	2.59	7.90
512	18.45	10.29	2.77	7.69
1024	18.85	18.46	2.90	8.47
2048	19.00	38.09	3.38	9.49
4096	19.29	67.05	4.83	12.67

Table 9.3. Average downtime of guest reboot, pr without snapshot opt, phase-based reboot, pr-naive.

Memory Size [MB]	Guest Reboot [sec]	pr w/o opt. w/o fsck [sec]	pr-opt w/o fsck [sec]	pr-naive w/o fsck [sec]
64	29.01	2.42	1.87	6.51
128	28.58	3.18	1.93	6.87
256	28.27	5.01	1.84	6.98
512	28.42	9.57	2.02	6.78
1024	28.83	17.65	2.15	7.57
2048	28.92	37.17	2.63	8.56
4096	29.38	66.15	4.08	11.72

Table 9.3 lists similar results to Table 9.2, where the downtime of the phase-based reboot was shorter than that of the guest reboot in many cases. In pr-opt, the downtime was 86.1% to 93.6% shorter than that of the guest reboot. The downtime of pr-naive was 60.1% to 77.6% shorter than that of the guest reboot.

To analyze the downtime caused by the phase-based reboot, we show the breakdown of the downtime of pr without snapshot opt, pr-naive and pr-opt in Fig. 9.3. Figures 9.3(a) and (b) reveal that our snapshot optimization significantly contributed to shortening the downtime of reboot-based recovery. In pr without snapshot opt, the restore time was much longer than the other configurations, pr-naive and pr-opt. In particular, the restore times were about 37 and 66 seconds when the memory sizes of the domain were 2 and 4 GB respectively. This is because Xen's snapshot function saves and restores all the memory pages assigned to the guest domain even if the

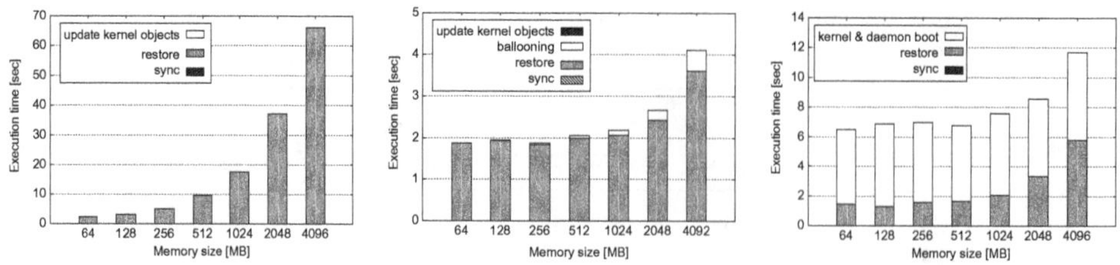

(a) pr without snapshot opt (b) pr-opt (c) pr-naive

Fig. 9.3. Breakdown of pr without snapshot opt, pr-opt, and pr-naive downtime.

pages are not used by the kernel and user processes. The restore time in the other configuration was at most 5.8 seconds.

In addition, our snapshot optimization successfully shrank the restartable images. For example, when a VM was assigned 1024 MB of memory, the optimized snapshot function saved only 99 MB as a restartable image, but Xen's snapshot function saved 1050 MB. The time for the phase-based reboot becomes longer as the memory size is bigger. This is because the Linux kernel has to manage more metadata for memory management so that we need to save a bigger memory image to the disk; there is a room for the optimization of shrinking memory images for big memory VMs. Also, as described in Section 9.2.1.2, we can shorten the downtime of the phase-based reboot by preparing RAM disks or solid-state drives to place these memory checkpoints on them.

The figure also shows that omitting the kernel and daemon boot phase is effective to shorten the downtime of reboot-based recovery (Fig. 9.3 (b) and (c)). In pr-naive, booting the kernel and daemons is the main part of its downtime since the impact of the restore operation and ballooning is relatively smaller. The phase-based reboot in pr-opt effectively shortens its downtime by omitting the launch phase. In fact, the downtime of pr-opt was 61.9% to 67.2% shorter than that of pr-naive, as exhibited in Table 9.2.

A quantitative comparision between kexec and the phase-based reboot is conducted. The results are reported in detail in the research literature [9].

9.2.2. *Maintaining the Internal States*

After the reboot of the operating system, the system performance is largely degraded for a while. One of the causes is that the cache in the operating system is lost. Particularly, losing the *page cache* largely affects performance. The operating system stores the contents of files in the main memory as the page cache when it reads them from disks. Since disks, even SSDs, are much slower than the main memory, the operating system can speed up file access by using the page cache in the main memory. When the operating system is rebooted, the contents of the main memory are erased and the page cache managed by the operating system is lost. Just after the reboot of the operating system, the execution performance of applications running on top of it degrades due to frequent cache misses.

It takes a long time to recover the same performance as before the reboot. To regain the same performance, the operating system has to re-fill the page cache. However, modern operating systems use most of their free memory as the page cache to improve performance. The size of the page cache is almost equivalent to that of the free memory, which tends to become larger because the size of memory installable on one machine is increasing due to cheaper memory modules. For example, several terabytes of memory can be used at the time of writing. Until the page cache is re-filled, the operating system has to read necessary files from slow disks and cannot recreate the speed of its pre-reboot performance.

In a virtualized environment, the performance recovery takes a longer time after the operating system in a VM is rebooted. At the time of writing, server consolidation is performed with VMs for cost efficiency. In such an environment, physical disks are often shared among VMs. Although a different physical disk may be allocated to each VM exclusively, this is usually difficult due to physical constraints or cost. In other words, one VM cannot occupy the whole disk bandwidth. Worse, disk bandwidth allocated to each VM may be limited for fairness. Since this disk sharing degrades the throughput of disk accesses, it takes a longer time to re-fill the page cache by reading files from disks.

Frequent disk accesses affect not only a rebooted VM but also all the other VMs. The conflicts of disk accesses degrade the performance of all the VMs. Just after the operating system in a VM is rebooted, it frequently accesses a physical disk. Increasing disk accesses in one VM affects the performance of disk accesses by the other VMs. For the same reason, prefetching does not work well in a virtualized environment. Prefetching is a common technique for hiding the initial cache misses particularly when the system is booted. Files are read from disks in advance before they are accessed. Prefetching issues too many requests for disk accesses during a short period because it is batch processing, not processing on-demand. This makes the performance of the other VMs worse.

To quickly recover the system performance after the reboot of the operating system, a new reboot mechanism called the *warm-cache reboot* has

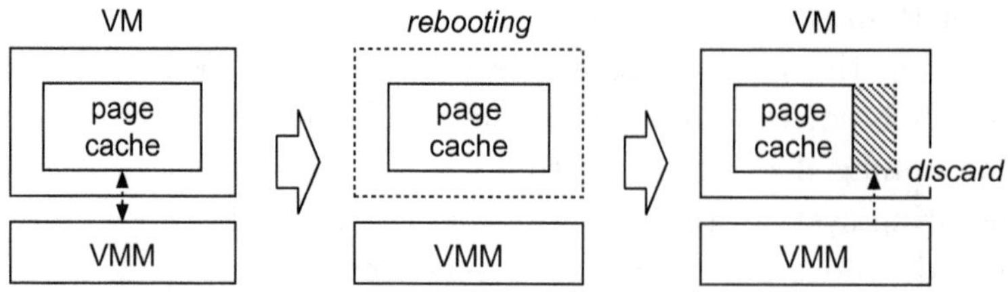

Fig. 9.4. The procedure of the warm-cache reboot.

been proposed [10]. It is achieved by combining the operating system and the underlying VMM. To use the VMM, operating systems run in VMs created by the VMM. The VMM is a useful software layer underlying operating systems to preserve the page cache through the reboot and maintain its consistency. Without the VMM, it is difficult to reuse the page cache consistently because the operating system can crash suddenly and cannot always be rebooted normally.

9.2.2.1. *Preserving the page cache*

The basic idea of the warm-cache reboot is to preserve the page cache in memory during the reboot and enable the operating system to restore it after the reboot, as illustrated in Fig. 9.4. The page cache does not need to be discarded at a reboot. The purpose of a reboot is to initialize the internal state in the operating system or to update its components such as its kernel. Even if the data structures in the operating system are changed by its update, the contents of the page cache are reusable because they are just copies of file blocks on disks. However, the operating system should not reuse corrupted page caches. In such a case, it should read file blocks from disks. The warm-cache reboot discards only corrupted page caches using the consistency mechanism described in the next section.

By reusing the page cache, the warm-cache reboot prevents performance degradation caused by cache misses just after the reboot. In other words, it recovers the system performance as well as the functionality. After the reboot, most of the files accessed are expected to exist in the page cache as long as a working set is within the size of the page cache. The workload does not largely change after the reboot because the time needed for the reboot is not very long. The files accessed for the reboot can lower the cache hit ratio after the reboot, but such accesses would just replace a very small part of the page cache in many cases.

While the operating system in a VM is rebooted by using the warm-cache reboot mechanism, the VMM preserves the contents of the memory allocated to the VM. The VMM allocates the same physical memory as before the reboot to the VM. The memory layout is the same as well. Without the VMM, it is not guaranteed that the contents of physical memory are preserved because there could be a hardware reset. A hardware reset may corrupt a part of memory, depending on the hardware [11] and its temperature [12]. When the VMM reallocates physical memory, it leaves the contents of the memory as they are. Normally, when the VMM allocates memory pages to VMs, it erases the contents for security. This is because the memory pages may include sensitive information previously used by the other VMs and the VMM. During the warm-cache reboot, reusing memory pages without erasing the contents is secure. Those pages are necessarily reused by the same operating system. Since sensitive information is kept within the same VM, information leakage to the other VMs does not occur.

A rebooted operating system reserves all the memory pages that have been used for the page cache before the reboot. Such memory pages are called *cache pages*. This reservation is performed at an early stage of booting the kernel, that is, before the kernel starts dynamic memory allocation. This prevents the cache pages from being used for other purposes and corrupted. Since the cache management in the operating system is initialized by the reboot, the VMM manages information to reuse the page cache of the operating system. When the operating system allocates a cache page, it registers the page to the VMM, with the information on the corresponding file block. When the operating system uses that page for other purposes, it unregisters the page. When the operating system is rebooted, it obtains the information on the page cache from the VMM.

9.2.2.2. *Maintaining cache consistency*

The warm-cache reboot reuses a cache page only when the page is guaranteed to be consistent. A cache page is consistent when the contents of the page are the same as those of the corresponding file block on a disk. When a file block is read from a disk to a cache page, the page is consistent. After the page is modified by file writes or destroyed by faults, it becomes inconsistent. When the cache page is written back to a disk, it becomes consistent again.

The VMM maintains the consistency of each cache page. In a virtualized environment, device accesses in the operating system running on a VM are performed via the VMM. The VMM reads data on a disk into a cache page passed from the operating system or writes data in a cache page into a disk,

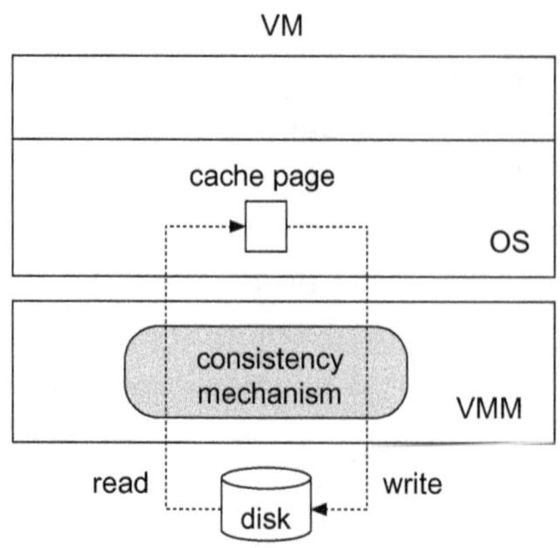

Fig. 9.5. Tracking the consistency of cache pages.

as illustrated in Fig. 9.5. When disk reads or writes are completed, the VMM makes the cache page reusable because the contents of the cache page are guaranteed to be the same as those of a file block on a disk. It is assumed that the VMM works as intended and disk reads and writes are performed correctly.

To track the cache consistency, the VMM protects cache pages in a read-only manner. When the VMM reads a file block into a cache page, it protects the page *before* that file has been read so that it can detect the modification to the cache page. While a cache page is protected, it is reusable because the cache page is guaranteed to be consistent. This memory protection also prevents a cache page from being corrupted by faults. When the operating system modifies the protected cache page, the VMM changes its protection mode to writable before that write so that the operating system can modify the cache page freely. In this state, the cache page is not reusable because the page is not consistent. When the VMM writes back the contents of the cache page into a disk, it protects the page again before that file is written. Thus, the cache page becomes reusable again.

The help of the VMM is indispensable to guarantee this cache consistency. Without the VMM, the operating system cannot read a file block on disk into protected cache pages because it cannot write data in protected memory pages. Therefore, the contents of cache pages may be corrupted *during* disk reads because the operating system has to protect cache pages *after* disk reads. If faults make the operating system unstable, the operating system may not protect the cache page correctly. Even if the page is protected correctly, the protection mode may be changed to writable by corrupting the page table. Although the operating system has to manage the reusability of cache pages, such management information may be corrupted accidentally. If that information were wrong, the warm-cache reboot would reuse inconsistent cache pages.

The above assumption for the cache consistency is strong but reasonable. If the page cache is not corrupted, it could be reused even when the contents have not yet been written back to disk. This enables the operating system to use the latest updates to files after it has been rebooted. However, it is difficult to distinguish correct modification from corruption because the correctness of modification depends on semantics. To avoid this semantic problem, the warm-cache reboot allows a cache page to be reused only after the modification to the page is written back to a disk.

9.2.2.3. *Effectiveness*

Figure 9.6 shows the changes in throughput of a web server running in a VM when the VM was rebooted at time 30 seconds. When a normal reboot was used, the throughput was degraded by 41% on average. The performance degradation lasts for 90 seconds after the web server restarts its service. During this period, the web server loses the benefit of about 3300 requests, compared with before the reboot. In contrast, when the warm-cache reboot was used, the throughput was degraded only by 5% after the reboot. In the 60 seconds after the web server was restarted, the throughput was recovered completely.

Figure 9.7 shows the ratio at which the page cache was inconsistent when the consistency mechanism in the warm-cache reboot was disabled. At

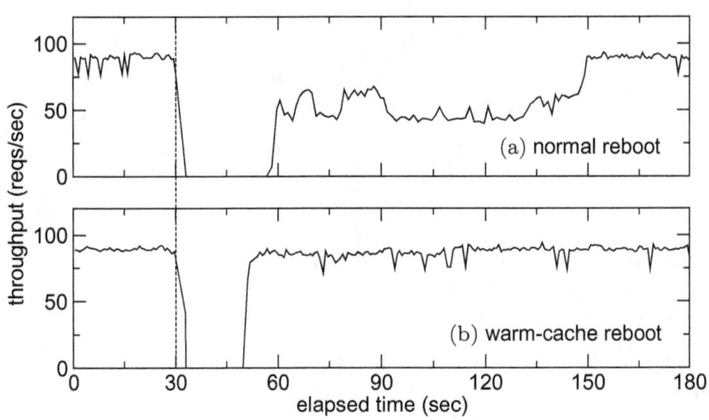

Fig. 9.6. The throughput of a web server during the rejuvenation of the operating system.

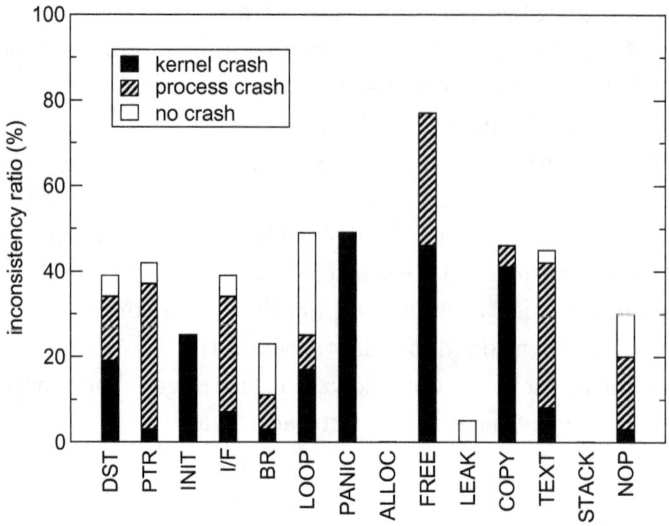

Fig. 9.7. The ratio of cache inconsistency when the consistency mechanism was disabled.

this time, the operating system managed a cache reuse without the help of the VMM. Before the reboot, faults were injected into the operating system using a fault injection tool, which was originally developed for the Rio file cache project [13]. Injected faults are listed in Table 9.4. For most fault types, the page cache was inconsistent at a high ratio. This figure also shows the breakdown of the results of this fault injection when the page cache was inconsistent. Although fault injection did not always cause a crash, the page cache became inconsistent.

When the consistency mechanism was enabled, on the other hand, the page cache was consistent for all fault types except 4% of DST. In that exceptional case, some faults were injected into the ext3 file system and flipped a random bit of the destination of an instruction to emulate assignment errors. Then the file system failed to write back cache pages to a disk. This resulted in the inconsistency between the page cache and files on the disk.

9.2.3. *Maintaining the Process States*

OS rejuvenation involves restarts of all the running processes even if their states are not stale. The service disruption caused by process restarts is a non-trivial cost especially in recent big memory applications which have a huge amount of memory compared to stateless applications such as web servers. For example, in-memory DBs, such as memcached [14], Redis [15],

Table 9.4. Injected fault types.

Type	Description
DST	flip a random bit of the destination of an instruction
PTR	flip a random bit of the address for memory reference
INIT	delete an instruction that initializes a local variable on the kernel stack
I/F	delete an instruction that reads a function parameter
BR	delete a branch instruction or a repeat prefix
LOOP	invert the termination condition for a repeat prefix or a branch instruction
PANIC	cause a kernel panic
ALLOC	return NULL at the kmalloc function
FREE	release a memory region that is still used
LEAK	not release a memory region at the kfree function
COPY	overrun the length of memory copy by one byte to four pages
TEXT	flip a random bit of a random instruction in the kernel
STACK	flip a random bit in a stack of a random process
NOP	delete a random instruction in the kernel

and VoltDB [16], typically allocate a large amount of memory and manage numerous running states such as DB block caches and key-value pairs in their own memory regions. Since restarting in-memory DBs causes them to lose running states preserved in their memory regions, it is required to restore the running states of the rejuvenated in-memory DB. The current trend of in-memory processing, including graph processing, also makes the restart cost much higher.

Dwarf [17] avoids unnecessary process restarts in OS rejuvenation. Dwarf launches the newer kernel in the background on the same physical machine and forces the kernel to inherit the running states of the stale kernel. Different from other fast OS reboot techniques [8, 18], Dwarf makes downtime as short as possible by keeping the running states of processes and concealing the newer kernel boot. Also, Dwarf is applicable to the kernel updates and thus allows us to shorten the downtime of the OS restarts for them.

9.2.3.1. *Process state inheritance*

The key idea behind Dwarf is that the fresh kernel is launched in the background on the same physical machine and the kernel is forced to inherit the running states of the stale kernel. The execution flows of OS reboot- and Dwarf-based rejuvenation are illustrated in Fig. 9.8. The traditional rejuvenation involves an OS reboot to stop the stale kernel and start the new kernel, causing downtime for the restarting applications and the kernel.

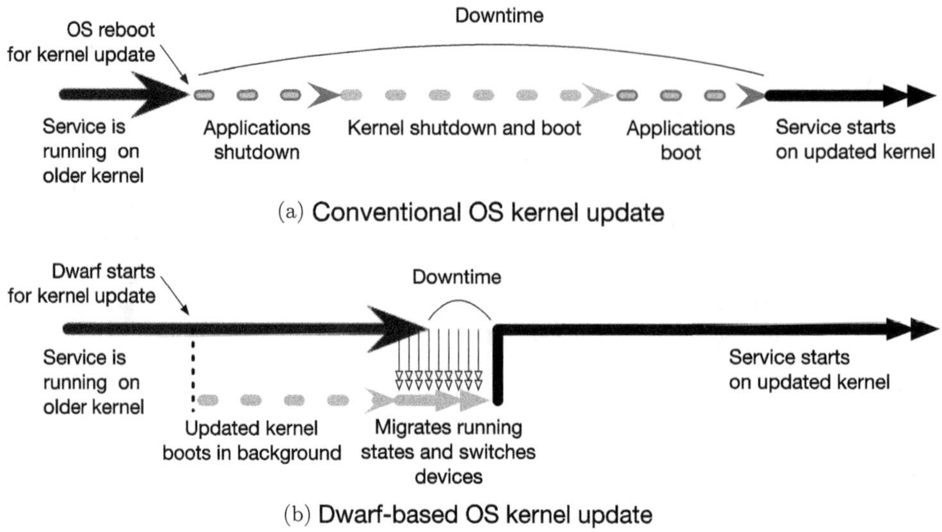

Fig. 9.8. Conventional rejuvenation and Dwarf-based rejuvenation.

On the other hand, when triggering the rejuvenation, Dwarf launches a fresh kernel while simultaneously running the applications and the stale kernel. When the fresh kernel finishes its memory initialization, Dwarf extracts the running process states and migrates them to the fresh kernel. Then, it switches the I/O devices from the stale to the fresh kernel, and then the stale one terminates.

To do so, Dwarf orchestrates the OS kernel and a thin hypervisor offering CPU and memory virtualization. The Dwarf hypervisor runs the target system on it, instantiates the kernel, and migrates the running process states from the stale kernel to the fresh kernel by using the cooperation of both kernels. To minimize the virtualization overhead, we design the Dwarf-based rejuvenation scheme to be applicable to VMs with not only virtualized I/O devices but also pass-through I/O devices. We believe that allowing various configurations of I/O devices contributes to the mitigation of a barrier to adopting Dwarf.

9.2.3.2. *Design details*

Our design goals pose three challenges as follows: 1) how do we migrate running processes with as little resource consumption as possible?, 2) how do we launch the fresh kernel in the background?, and 3) how do we effectively conduct the transfer of the running process states and the I/O device switch?

To overcome these challenges, Dwarf offers three functionalities: *zero-copy process migration*, *background boot*, and *attachment pipelining*.

It is a challenge to get Dwarf to force the fresh kernel to inherit the states of the running processes with as little resource consumption as possible. Existing process migration techniques significantly consume CPU, network, and memory resources. The basic behavior of the techniques is to extract target process states and transfer them to the destination through the network. The transfer of the process states, including memory pages in the user-space and process objects managed by the kernel-level mechanism, takes longer as the target processes consume more memory. The current trend of having an in-memory database and in-memory processing makes this situation worse. In addition, twice the amount of the memory of the target process is required for migration.

To efficiently migrate running processes to the fresh kernel, Dwarf invokes *zero-copy process migration*, called simply *zero-copy migration*, a kernel-level functionality that moves a large portion of the target process memory to the fresh kernel in a zero-copy manner. In migrating the user-space memory, the zero-copy migration only copies machine addresses of the pages instead of copying process memory. Specifically, the zero-copy migration preserves the page tables of the target processes and forces the fresh kernel to use them to map the target process pages into its memory space.

To consistently restart the running processes in the fresh kernel, the zero-copy migration also uses the selected process information that is stable and unchanged between kernel versions. From the kernel-level process objects, Dwarf extracts a part of the process context that is enough to reconstruct the corresponding process objects in the fresh kernel. Table 9.5 lists the process objects to be tracked. The targets of our Linux implementation are the process ID, the threads, the parent/child relationships, the signals, the pipes, the file descriptors, the file objects, the event polls, and the socket states.

Figure 9.9 shows the overall behavior of the zero-copy migration. Dwarf first stops the target processes at the system call boundary by sending the STOP signals and flushing the dirty buffers. It tracks process objects and stores the extracted contexts and the page tables in the Dwarf hypervisor. The fresh kernel reconstructs the process objects using the context values passed to it by the hypervisor and updates the kernel region of the restored page table. The fresh kernel restarts the processes after the restoration operations complete.

Table 9.5. Kernel-level process contexts used by zero-copy migration.

Type	Kernel Objects
Hardware context	Register values, System call arguments
Memory	Memory maps, Page states (access rights, etc.)
Directory	Root directory, Current directory
File	File descriptor table, Opened file states (path, open mode, etc.)
Network	IP address, Socket states, TCP headers
Parent/Child	Process ID, List of child processes

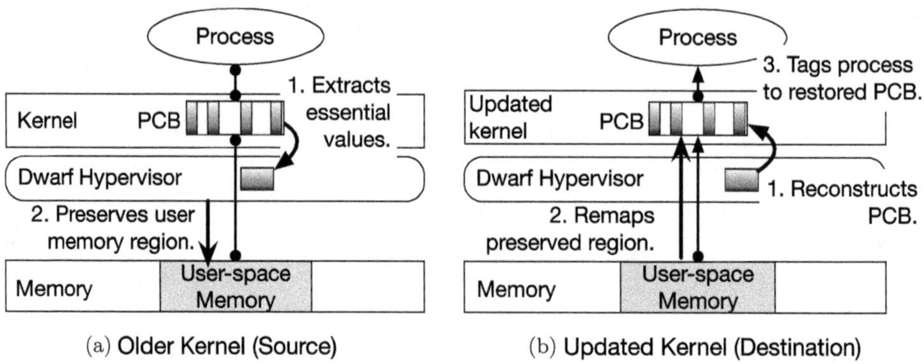

Fig. 9.9. Zero-copy process migration.

The next issue is to launch the fresh kernel in the background. To achieve the background execution of the fresh kernel, we require a mechanism to run the stale kernel and fresh kernel in parallel. Kexec [19], a kernel-level mechanism that loads the new kernel, and kexec-based systems [20], sequentially stop the stale kernel and start the fresh one so that skipping the kernel memory initialization is not possible. The launch of a new virtual machine (VM) where the fresh kernel is running allows us to run the stale kernel and fresh kernel in parallel. However, we have to prepare identical virtual devices for the new VM; thus, the same device states, such as disk contents and mac addresses, cannot be used by both the stale and fresh kernel.

Our *background boot mechanism* allows us to execute the fresh kernel in the background and to switch the I/O devices attached to the stale kernel to the fresh one. The mechanism leverages only CPU and memory virtualization. It creates a lightweight VM that is equipped with virtual CPUs and its memory, not any I/O devices. Dwarf starts the fresh kernel in the VM and finishes its initialization in the background so that the downtime excludes the kernel initialization phase.

Dwarf performs *attachment pipelining* to efficiently start the restored processes on the fresh kernel. The attachment pipelining mechanism allows us to restart the stored processes even when the attachment of all I/O devices is not yet complete. In attachment pipelining, the fresh kernel first reconstructs the memory objects of the processes restored by zero-copy migration and then starts the processes. The fresh kernel blocks processes that issue an I/O request to a device not yet attached, while the attachment pipelining mechanism attaches the kernel I/O devices one by one. It unblocks the processes after attaching the corresponding device.

9.2.3.3. *Effectiveness*

To demonstrate the effectiveness of Dwarf for real-world applications, we prepare six applications: *matmul*, *grep*, *tar*, *apache*, *MySQL*, and *memcached.* Matmul multiples two matrices whose size is 500 × 500. Grep searches for the word "linux" from the Linux-4.5.0 source tree, and tar compresses the source tree. Apache handles 40,000 requests from apachebench, each of which fetches a 10 KB html file, and MySQL runs under the Sysbench OLTP workload issuing 8 million SELECT queries. Lastly, memcached handles 100,000 SET requests generated by memslap. We conducted an OS reboot and a Dwarf-based reboot during the execution of the benchmarks and measured their downtime. We noted that the applications are simply restarted when we conduct the normal OS reboot. In that case, we measure the turnaround time of the applications across the OS reboot.

The result is shown in Fig. 9.10. The x-axis is the benchmark, and the y-axis is the downtime normalized by the OS reboot. This figure shows that Dwarf achieves much shorter downtime than the traditional OS reboot. The downtime of Dwarf is almost 8x shorter than that of the OS reboot in all the cases. The OS reboot takes slightly longer in the MySQL case because of the synchronization of more dirty buffers generated by MySQL.

We demonstrate Dwarf's beneficial behavior using our Linux 2.6 configuration with MySQL, whose buffer pool is 9 GiB, as shown in Fig. 9.11. We trigger an OS reboot and a Dwarf-based reboot in 10 seconds just after the DB cache is warm. In the OS reboot case, MySQL stops for 30 seconds while the OS kernel boots (10–40 seconds). Since MySQL's buffer pool is empty just after the fresh kernel is ready, the throughput of MySQL is significantly lower than that before the OS reboot. After MySQL warms its cache

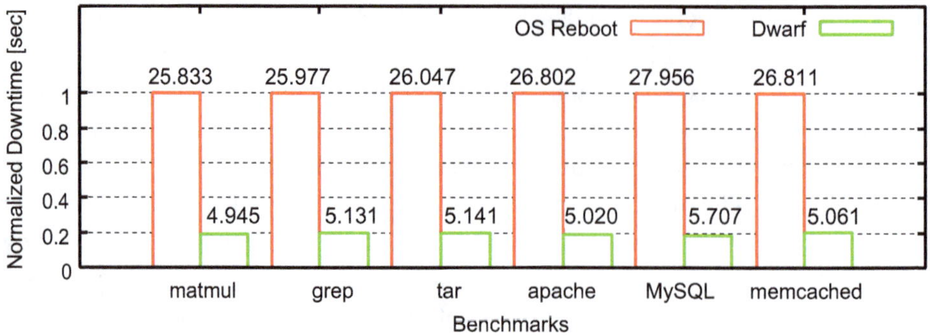

Fig. 9.10. Downtime of real-life applications using OS reboot and Dwarf.

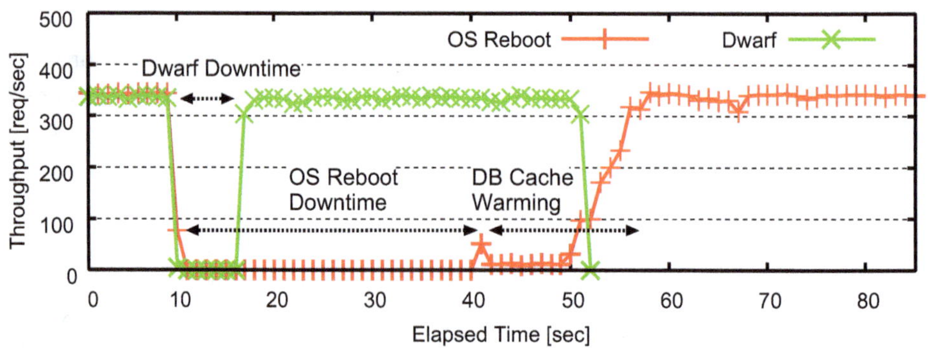

Fig. 9.11. MySQL throughput using OS reboot and Dwarf.

(40–58 seconds), its performance is restored. On the other hand, MySQL stops for only 5 seconds in the Dwarf case (10–15 seconds). Additionally, MySQL performs with almost the same throughput just after the downtime because zero-copy migration brings the buffer pool to the fresh kernel.

9.2.4. *Analysis*

Table 9.6 summarizes the properties of the rejuvenation techniques for operating systems. The phase-based reboot is state-less. Because all the in-kernel states revert to the initial one, it can cure any aging effects and thus is the most robust. But it incurs a long disruption time since all the in-kernel states must be re-constructed. The warm-cache reboot and Dwarf retains partial in-kernel state across reboots. Dwarf is the least robust because it re-uses process-related states in the kernel; if the re-used state is aging, Dwarf cannot cure it. However, Dwarf shows the shortest disruption time.

Table 9.6. The applicability of the OS-level quick reboot. (best: ++, good: +, moderate: −).

OS-level Reboot	Disruption Time	Robustness
Phase-based reboot	−	++
Warm-cache reboot	+	+
Dwarf	++	−

The warm-cache reboot comes in the middle of the phase-based reboot and Dwarf. In practice, these techniques are used like "micro-reboots". Dwarf, the warm-cache reboot, and the phase-based reboot are tried in this order.

We also note that the pipelining of complicated I/O devices such as GPUs is also challenging. Since such devices are sometimes tightly coupled with the running processes, migrating both the running process states and device states might be needed. This is out of the scope of this paper.

9.3. Rejuvenating the Virtual Machine Monitors

The software aging of virtual machine monitors (VMMs) is becoming critical because many VMs are running on top of the VMM. Since the VMM is long-running software and is not rebooted frequently, the influences due to software aging accumulate more easily. Software aging in the VMM not only leads to the performance degradation of the VMM itself but also affects all the VMs. In addition to the aging of VMMs, that of privileged VMs can also affect the other VMs. Privileged VMs are used in some VM architectures to help the VMM for VM management and the I/O processing of all VMs. The reboot of the privileged VM causes the VMM to be rebooted because the privileged VM strongly depends on the VMM. Therefore, the privileged VM is considered as part of the VMM.

For VMMs, software rejuvenation is also used to counteract software aging. A system reboot is well-known as a simple example of software rejuvenation. However, when the VMM is rejuvenated, operating systems on the VMs built on top of the VMM also have to be rebooted. Operating systems running in VMs have to be shut down to keep their integrity before the VMM terminates the VMs. Then, after the reboot of the VMM, newly created VMs have to boot the operating systems and restart all services again.

This increases the downtime of services provided by operating systems. First, many operating systems are shut down and booted in parallel when the VMM is rebooted. The time for rebooting each operating system is proportional to the number of VMs because shutting down and booting multiple operating systems in parallel causes resource contention among them. The number of VMs that can run simultaneously is increasing due to processor support of virtualization, a larger number of processor cores, and a larger amount of memory. In addition, recent servers tend to provide heavyweight services and the time taken to stop and restart services is increasing.

Second, shutting down operating systems, rebooting the VMM, and booting operating systems are performed sequentially. The in-between reboot of the VMM increases the service downtime. The reboot of the VMM includes shutting down the VMM, resetting hardware, and booting the VMM. In particular, a hardware reset involves a power-on self-test by BIOS. Examples of such self-tests include time-consuming checks of a large amount of main memory and SCSI initialization. Furthermore, the performance of operating systems in VMs degrades after they are rebooted with the VMM, as described in the previous section.

When the VMM needs rejuvenation, only the VMM should be rebooted. In other words, rebooting operating systems should be independent of rebooting the underlying VMM. Although the operating systems may be rejuvenated occasionally as well as the VMM, the timing of the rejuvenation of the operating systems does not always have to be the same as that of the rejuvenation of the VMM. If some of the operating systems do not need to be rejuvenated when the VMM is rejuvenated, rebooting these operating systems is just wasteful.

9.3.1. *Warm-VM Reboot for Fast Software Rejuvenation*

To minimize the influences of the rejuvenation of VMMs, a technique for fast rejuvenation called the *warm-VM reboot* has been proposed [21, 22]. It enables the VMM to preserve the memory images of all the VMs through its reboot and to reuse those memory images after the reboot. The warm-VM reboot consists of two mechanisms: the *on-memory suspend/resume* of VMs and the *quick reload* of the VMM. As illustrated in Fig. 9.12, the VMM suspends all VMs using the on-memory suspend mechanism before it is rebooted, reboots itself by the quick reload mechanism, and resumes all VMs using the on-memory resume mechanism after the VMM is rebooted. Using these mechanisms, the warm-VM reboot enables one to reboot only the VMM.

The on-memory suspend mechanism simply *freezes* the memory image used by a VM as it is. The memory image is preserved on memory through

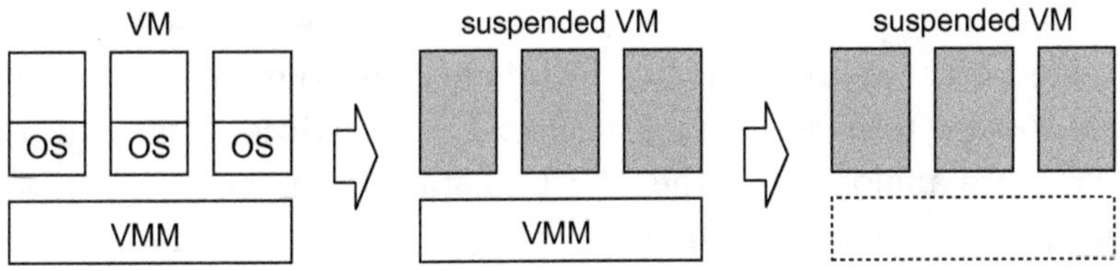

Fig. 9.12. The procedure of the warm-VM reboot.

the reboot of the VMM until the VM is resumed. This mechanism needs neither to save the image to any persistent storage such as disks nor to copy it to non-volatile memory such as flash memory. This is very efficient because the time needed for the suspend mechanism to finish working hardly depends on the size of the memory allocated to the VM. Even if the total memory size of all VMs becomes larger, the on-memory suspend mechanism can scale. At the same time, this mechanism saves the execution state of the suspended VM to the memory area that is also preserved through the reboot of the VMM.

On the other hand, the on-memory resume mechanism *unfreezes* the frozen memory image to restore the suspended VM. The frozen memory image is preserved through the reboot of the VMM by the quick reload mechanism. The on-memory resume mechanism also needs neither to read the saved image from persistent storage nor to copy it from non-volatile memory. Since the memory image of the VM, including the page cache, is restored completely, performance degradation due to cache misses is prevented even just after the reboot. At the same time, the saved execution state of the VMs is also restored. These mechanisms are analogous to the ACPI S3 state (suspend-to-RAM) in that they can suspend and resume a VM without touching its memory image in main memory.

The quick reload mechanism preserves the memory images of VMs through the reboot of the VMM and furthermore makes the reboot itself faster. Usually, rebooting the VMM needs a hardware reset to reload the VMM instance, but there is no guarantee that memory contents are preserved during a hardware reset. In addition, a hardware reset takes a long time as described in the previous section. The quick reload mechanism can bypass a hardware reset by loading a new VMM instance by software and can start the VMM instance by jumping to its entry point. Since the software mechanism can manage memory during the reboot, it is guaranteed that the memory contents are preserved. Furthermore, the quick reload mechanism prevents the frozen memory images of VMs from being corrupted while the VMM initializes itself.

Although many VMMs provide suspend/resume mechanisms, they are not suitable for the rejuvenation of VMMs because they have to use disks as persistent storage to save memory images. These traditional suspend/resume mechanisms are analogous to the ACPI S4 state (suspend to disk), so-called hibernation. These mechanisms need heavy disk accesses and they are too slow. In contrast, the on-memory suspend/resume mechanism does not need to save the memory images to persistent storage. The memory images on volatile main memory can be reused.

9.3.1.1. *Rejuvenation model and availability*

When the warm-VM reboot is used, the downtime is caused by suspending all VMs, rebooting the VMM, and resuming all VMs. The downtime $D_w(n)$ is the sum of the times needed for performing the on-memory suspend and resume of n VMs in parallel and for rebooting the VMM. In the warm-VM reboot, rebooting the VMM depends only on the number of VMs, not the memory size of VMs, because the VMM does not need to initialize the memory area reserved for suspended VMs during its reboot.

For comparison, let us consider the rejuvenation of the VMM by a normal reboot, which is called the *cold-VM reboot* in contrast to the warm-VM reboot. When the cold-VM reboot is used, the downtime is caused by shutting down all operating systems, resetting hardware, rebooting the VMM, and booting all operating systems. The downtime $D_c(n)$ is the sum of the times needed for shutting down and booting n operating systems in parallel, rebooting the VMM without preserving any VMs, and performing a hardware reset.

To define the availability of both the warm-VM reboot and the cold-VM reboot, the following rejuvenation model is considered. Usually, the rejuvenation of the VMM (VMM rejuvenation) is used with the rejuvenation of operating systems (OS rejuvenation) running in VMs. For simplicity, it is assumed that each operating system is rejuvenated by relying on the time elapsed since the last OS rejuvenation [23]. The intervals of the VMM rejuvenation and the OS rejuvenation are defined as T_{vmm} and T_{os}, respectively.

When the warm-VM reboot is used, the VMM rejuvenation can be performed independently of the OS rejuvenation. This is because the warm-VM reboot does not involve the OS rejuvenation. Figures 9.13(a) and 9.13(b) show the rejuvenation timing when $T_{vmm} > T_{os}$ and $T_{vmm} \leq T_{os}$, respectively. In contrast, when the cold-VM reboot is used, the VMM rejuvenation

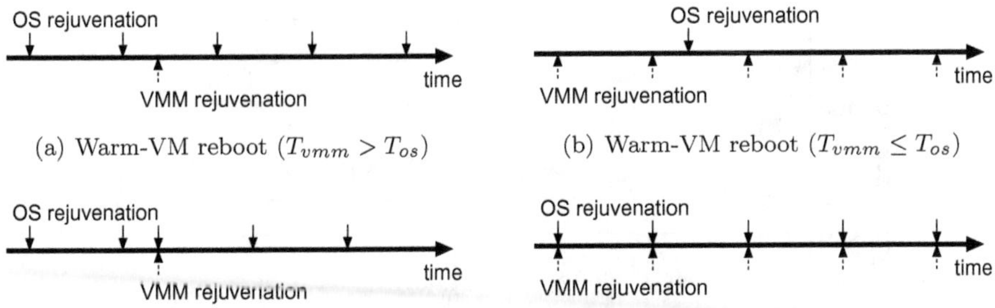

(a) Warm-VM reboot ($T_{vmm} > T_{os}$) (b) Warm-VM reboot ($T_{vmm} \leq T_{os}$)

(c) Cold-VM reboot ($T_{vmm} > T_{os}$) (d) Cold-VM reboot ($T_{vmm} \leq T_{os}$)

Fig. 9.13. The timing of the VMM and OS rejuvenation.

affects the timing of the OS rejuvenation because the VMM rejuvenation involves the OS rejuvenation. Figure 9.13(c) shows the rejuvenation timing when $T_{vmm} > T_{os}$. Since the OS rejuvenation is performed at the same time with the VMM rejuvenation, the timer for the OS rejuvenation is reset and the OS rejuvenation is rescheduled. When $T_{vmm} \leq T_{os}$, the OS rejuvenation is always performed together with the VMM rejuvenation as shown in Fig. 9.13(d). Before the timer for the OS rejuvenation reaches T_{os}, the VMM rejuvenation is performed and the timer is reset.

The availability is defined using the above rejuvenation model. First, let us consider the total downtime in T_{vmm}. In the system using the warm-VM reboot, the total downtime is $D_w(n) + N_w D_{os}$, where D_{os} is the time needed for rebooting one operating system for the OS rejuvenation. N_w is the average number of the OS rejuvenation performed in T_{vmm} and defined by $(T_{vmm} - D_w(n))/T_{os}$. Note that the timer for the OS rejuvenation is stopped during the VMM rejuvenation. Therefore, the availability A_w is defined by

$$A_w = 1 - \frac{D_w(n) + N_w D_{os}}{T_{vmm}}. \tag{9.1}$$

In the system using the cold-VM reboot, on the other hand, the total downtime in T_{vmm} is $D_c(n) + \lfloor N_c \rfloor D_{os}$, where N_c is defined by $(T_{vmm} - D_c(n))/T_{os}$. $\lfloor N_c \rfloor$ is the exact number of the OS rejuvenation solely performed in T_{vmm}. Since the timer for the OS rejuvenation is reset by the VMM rejuvenation in the cold-VM reboot, the average number of the OS rejuvenation is an integer less than N_c. Note that the OS rejuvenation performed together with the VMM rejuvenation is not counted in N_c. Its

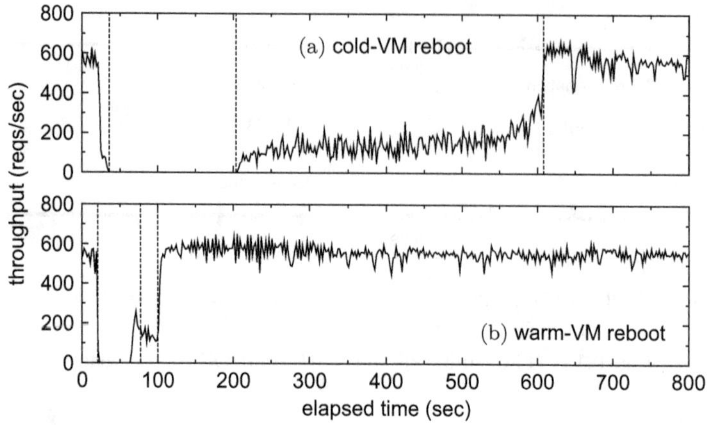

Fig. 9.14. The total throughput during the VMM rejuvenation.

downtime is included in $D_c(n)$. Therefore, the availability A_c is defined by

$$A_c = 1 - \frac{D_c(n) + \lfloor N_c \rfloor D_{os}}{T_{vmm}}. \tag{9.2}$$

9.3.1.2. *Effectiveness*

Figure 9.14 shows the changes in total throughput of the web servers in 11 VMs when the cold-VM reboot or the warm-VM reboot was used for the VMM rejuvenation. For the cold-VM reboot, the average downtime of the web servers was 219 seconds. After all the operating systems were booted again, the total throughput was largely degraded for a long time because of cache misses in all the operating systems. The performance degradation was 72% and its duration was 397 seconds. For the warm-VM reboot, in contrast, the average downtime was largely reduced to 59 seconds. After the warm-VM reboot, the total throughput still degraded until all the VMs were resumed, but its duration was only 25 seconds.

9.3.2. *Analysis*

Table 9.7 shows the applicability of the warm-VM reboot on domains and criticality. The warm-VM reboot is effective particularly for large and medium best-effort and industrial servers. The quick reload mechanism can reduce the boot time of such servers significantly by bypassing the self-test of a large amount of main memory. The on-memory suspend/resume mechanism is more effective when a VM has a larger amount of memory and runs more heavyweight services that take a longer time to be rebooted.

Table 9.7. The applicability of the warm-VM reboot. (best: ++, good: +, bad: −, worst: −−).

Domain	Best-effort	Industrial	Mission-critical
large server (many large VMs)	++	++	−
medium server (a few large VMs)	++	++	−
medium server (many small VMs)	++	++	−
small server (a few small VMs)	+	+	−

Similarly, the mechanism is more effective when a server runs more VMs. In contrast, the warm-VM reboot is relatively less effective when a server has a smaller amount of memory and runs a smaller number of VMs. For mission-critical servers, the warm-VM reboot is not sufficiently effective because it still causes non-negligible downtime by rebooting the VMM and the privileged VM.

9.4. Summary and Future Directions

Software aging in operating systems is critical because all the applications running on the operating system fail to execute under the operating system aging. This chapter introduced three techniques for rejuvenating the operating system kernel. The first approach, called the phase-based reboot, is a technique to shorten the reboot time without retaining the in-kernel data structures. The second approach, called the warm-cache reboot, retains the file cache across reboots so that the applications can start from the hot file cache. The third approach maintains process states across the reboots. Finally, this chapter introduces the rejuvenation technique for the virtual machine monitors.

The rejuvenation techniques introduced in this chapter have the following trade-off. If the service disruption time becomes shorter, the robustness of the rejuvenation is lowered. The phase-based reboot is the best in robustness but the worst in disruption time. Dwarf is the best in disruption time but the worst in robustness. The warm-cache reboot comes in the middle. These three techniques can be used as "micro-reboots" [24]; Dwarf, the warm-cache reboot, and the phase-based reboot are tried in this order.

For future directions, it is interesting to develop a technique to confine error states to in-kernel lightweight domains. Even if a fault is activated and the error propagates inside the kernel, the in-kernel lightweight domain confines the error propagation inside it. To rejuvenate the kernel, the entire kernel is not rebooted. Instead, only the erroneous domain is restarted. By doing this, it is expected that the reboot time will be shortened as well as as many as possible of the in-kernel states retained.

References

1. N. Palix, G. Thomas, S. Saha, C. Calvés, J. Lawall, and G. Muller. (2011). Faults in Linux: Ten years later. In *Proceedings of the ACM International Conference on Architectural Support for Programming Languages and Operating Systems (ASPLOS'11), Newport Beach, California, USA, March 5–7*, pp. 305–318.
2. L. Lu, A. C. Arpaci-Dusseau, R. H. Arpaci-Dusseau, and S. Lu. (2014). A study of linux file system evolution. *ACM Transactions on Storage*, **10**(1), 1–32. ISSN 15533077. doi: 10.1145/2560012.
3. R. C. Baumann. (2002). Soft errors in commercial semiconductor technology: overview and scaling trends. IEEE 2002 Reliability Physics Tutorial Notes, Reliability Fundamentals, 121.
4. D. Cotroneo, R. Natella, R. Pietrantuono, and S. Russo. (2010). Software aging analysis of the Linux operating system. In *Proceedings of the 2010 IEEE 21st International Symposium on Software Reliability Engineering (ISSRE'10), San Jose, California, USA, November 1–4*, pp. 71–80.
5. T. Yoshimura. (2016). *A Study on Faults and Error Propagation in the Linux Operating System.* (PhD thesis, Keio University, Minato, Tokyo, Japan).
6. C. S. Advisory. (2001). Cisco catalyst memory leak vulnerability. ID:13618.
7. V. Castelli, R. E. Harper, P. Heidelberger, S. W. Hunter, K. S. Trivedi, K. Vaidyanathan, and W. P. Zeggert. (2001). Proactive management of software aging. *IBM Journal of Research and Development*, **45**(2), 311–332.
8. K. Yamakita, H. Yamada, and K. Kono. (2011). Phase-based reboot: Reusing operating system execution phases for cheap reboot-based recovery. In *Proceedings of the 41st Annual IEEE/IFIP International Conference on Dependable Systems and Networks (DSN'11), Hong Kong, China, June 27–30*, pp. 169–180.
9. A. Bovenzi, J. Alonso, H. Yamada, S. Russo, and K. S. Trivedi. (2013). Towards fast OS rejuvenation: An experimental evaluation of fast OS reboot techniques. In *Proceedings of the 24th IEEE International Symposium on Software Reliability Engineering (ISSRE'13), Pasadena, California, USA, November 4–7*, pp. 61–70.
10. K. Kourai. (2011). Fast and correct performance recovery of operating systems using a virtual machine monitor. In *Proceedings of the 2011 ACM International Conference on Virtual Execution Environments, Newport Beach, California, USA, March 9–11*, pp. 99–110.
11. W. Ng and P. Chen. (2001). The design and verification of the Rio file cache. *IEEE Transactions on Computers*, **50**(4), 322–337.
12. J. Halderman, S. Schoen, N. Heninger, W. Clarkson, W. Paul, J. Calandrino, A. Feldman, J. Appelbaum, and E. Felten. (2008). Lest we remember: Cold boot attacks on encryption keys. In *Proceedings of the USENIX Security Symposium, San Jose, California, USA, July 28–August 1*, pp. 45–60.
13. P. Chen, W. Ng, S. Chandra, C. Aycock, G. Rajamani, and D. Lowell. (1996). The Rio file cache: Surviving operating system crashes. In *Proceedings of the 7th International Conference on Architectural Support for Programming Languages and Operating Systems, Cambridge, Massachusetts, USA, October 1–5*, pp. 74–83.

14. B. Fitzpatrick. (2003). Memcached — a distributed memory object caching system. Available at: http://www.memcached.org/.
15. Redis. Available at: http://redis.io/.
16. VoltDB. Available at: https://www.voltdb.com/.
17. K. Terada and H. Yamada. (2016). Dwarf: Shortening downtime of reboot-based kernel updates. In *Proceedings of the 12th European Dependable Computing Conference (EDCC'16), Gothenburg, Sweden, September 5–9*, pp. 208–217.
18. H. Yamada and K. Kono. (2013). Traveling forward in time to newer operating systems using ShadowReboot. In *Proceedings of the 9th ACM International Conference on Virtual Execution Environments (VEE'13), Houston, Texas, USA, March 16–17*, pp. 121–130.
19. Reboot linux faster using kexec. https://www.linux.com/news/reboot-linux-faster-using-kexec/
20. M. Siniavine and A. Goel. (2013). Seamless kernel updates. In *Proceedings of the 43rd Annual IEEE/IFIP International Conference on Dependable Systems and Networks (DSN'13), Budapest, Hungary, June 24–27*, pp. 1–12.
21. K. Kourai and S. Chiba. (2007). A fast rejuvenation technique for server consolidation with virtual machines. In *Proceedings of the 37th Annual IEEE/IFIP International Conference on Dependable Systems and Networks, Edinburgh, UK, June 25–28*, pp. 245–254.
22. K. Kourai and S. Chiba. (2011). Fast software rejuvenation of virtual machine monitors. *IEEE Transactions on Dependability and Security*, **8**(6), 839–851.
23. S. Garg, Y. Huang, C. Kintala, and K. Trivedi. (1995). Time and load-based software rejuvenation: Policy, evaluation and optimality. In *Proceedings of the 1st Fault-Tolerance Symposium, Madras, India, December 22–25*, pp. 22–25.
24. G. Candea, S. Kawamoto, Y. Fujiki, G. Friedman, and A. Fox. (2004). Microreboot — A Technique for Cheap Recovery. In *Proceedings of the 6th USENIX Symposium on Operating Systems Design and Implementation, Berkeley, California, USA, December 4–7*, pp. 31–44.

Chapter 10

Aging in Virtualized Environments

Roberto Pietrantuono*, Domenico Cotroneo† and Stefano Russo‡

Università degli Studi di Napoli Federico II, Italy
**roberto.pietrantuono@unina.it*
†*cotroneo@unina.it*
‡*stefano.russo@unina.it*

With virtualization technologies becoming a predominant paradigm of computing, there is a strong need to analyze long-running performance and aging issues in virtualized environments. Software aging in such environments can have a severe impact on millions of customers of business-critical applications, as well as on end-users of more critical (e.g., mission-critical) systems where virtualization is also vastly being adopted.

This chapter discusses the main existing approaches to studying the aging phenomena in virtualized environments, and the corresponding rejuvenation techniques. It targets those contexts where virtual machines are massively adopted — such as cloud computing platforms — as well as relevant virtualization technologies.

The chapter covers first model-based methods for the analysis of resource consumption and/or performance degradation, as well as for the optimal scheduling of rejuvenation in virtualized systems. Then, measurement-based approaches are discussed, where the statistical analysis of monitored health indicators is exploited to detect and forecast aging trends in the considered contexts.

10.1. Introduction

This chapter explores the main approaches to dealing with software aging analysis and with rejuvenation in virtualized environments. Virtualization is a key technology for today's IT organizations. Virtualization solutions greatly ease the build and deploy of applications, increase their runtime availability, and alleviate several manual tasks — saving people time to deliver greater value. Moreover, by reducing the number of physical machines, the infrastructure cost, the maintenance and IT staffing cost as well as the backup and recovery cost are drastically lowered. For instance, a Forrester study[a] found that Red Hat Virtualization speeds up virtualization tasks and improves performance by delivering the following results: *i)* a return on investment of 103% over 3 years; *ii)* 10% to 20% of the infrastructure developer's time saved through an increased number of virtualization tasks and increased process efficiency; *iii)* a payback period of 5.6 months.

A main advantage of virtualization is its ability to make better use of existing resources, enabling multiple systems (i.e., the operating system, system-level software and application-level software) to run on the same physical machine, sharing and dynamically acquiring/releasing the same set of resources (e.g., the CPU, memory and storage) depending on the runtime need. Systems/services making massive use of virtualization in this sense are those based on cloud computing. In this case, virtualization is implemented by means of an intermediate software layer called a hypervisor or Virtual Machine Monitor (VMM), responsible for managing the execution of virtual machines and for the interaction with the hardware resources. It works by separating virtual from physical layers. Another advantage of virtualization is the much greater portability of applications (and of entire systems) across various physical environments. Besides cloud computing, a former successful example of software virtualization technology, with a strong focus on portability, is the Java Virtual Machine (JVM).

As many enterprises employ virtualization to run their services, the problem of performance degradation and, more generally of *software aging*, becomes critical. Aging has been analyzed by researchers in several modern virtualized environments, wherein long executions lead to accumulation errors and gradual performance decrease. Conventional approaches for aging detection and estimation have been used, which can be roughly divided into model-based and measurement-based approaches. At the same time, besides aging detection and estimation, which can be used to determine if and *when* an aging failure is likely to occur, the problem of *how* to rejuvenate a virtualized system is also of interest to software aging and rejuvenation research. Indeed, rejuvenation is a key high-availability technique in this context, since the advantages given by VMs as application "containers" have led to novel and lightweight rejuvenation strategies (based on restarts, migration and failover), which are capable of guaranteeing high levels of service continuity in the presence of aging problems.

[a] "The Total Economic Impact of Red Hat Virtualization", available at: *www.redhat.com/it/engage/efficiency-of-virtualization.*

The next section introduces the general characteristics of SAR research in virtualized environments. Section 10.3 contains a survey of the model-based techniques for *aging*, while Section 10.4 reviews the measurement-based techniques. Hybrid approaches combining both types of techniques are presented in Section 10.5. Section 10.6 presents the main techniques that are used to perform rejuvenation in virtualized environments. Finally, Section 10.7 contains the chapter conclusions.

10.2. Aging Analysis and Rejuvenation for Virtualized Environments

The analysis of software aging deals usually with two main tasks, the detection and the estimation of aging trends through one or more *aging indicators*. These are related to resource exhaustion (e.g., memory, storage, operating system resources, energy), and/or to user-perceived performance (e.g., response time, latency, served transactions, throughput). These *aging indicators* characterize a degradation phenomenon that is customer-affecting and that can also be detected at the system level within the *execution environment* of the application software. In virtualized environments, the *system* level — namely, the *execution environment* — includes not only the physical machine with its operating system (OS) and low-level software, but also the virtual environment, such as the Virtual Machine (VM) on which the software is running and/or the whole virtualization technology including the Virtual Machine Monitor (VMM), the most important layer responsible for creating a VM environment for an OS and its applications. Figure 10.1 sketches a generic architecture of a virtualized environment. Virtualization can be implemented: *i)* via native VMMs, also known as *bare-metal hypervisors*, such as *Xen, VMware ESX, Oracle Vm Server*, in which there is no "host" OS but the VMM runs on and controls the hardware directly, or *ii)* via"hosted" solutions, also known as *hosted hypervisors*, like, for instance, *VMware Workstation, VirtualBox and Parallels*, in which the access to hardware is managed via the host OS. On top of the VMM, there are VMs: depending on the proactive/reactive fault tolerance strategy (including rejuvenation), there can be standby VMs, which can take over the active VMs in case of failure or upon a rejuvenation request. In a more general scheme (e.g., in virtualized data centers), there may be other physical nodes and a VM can be migrated to a different node if, for instance, the hosting node or part thereof, such as the VMM, fails or needs to be rejuvenated.

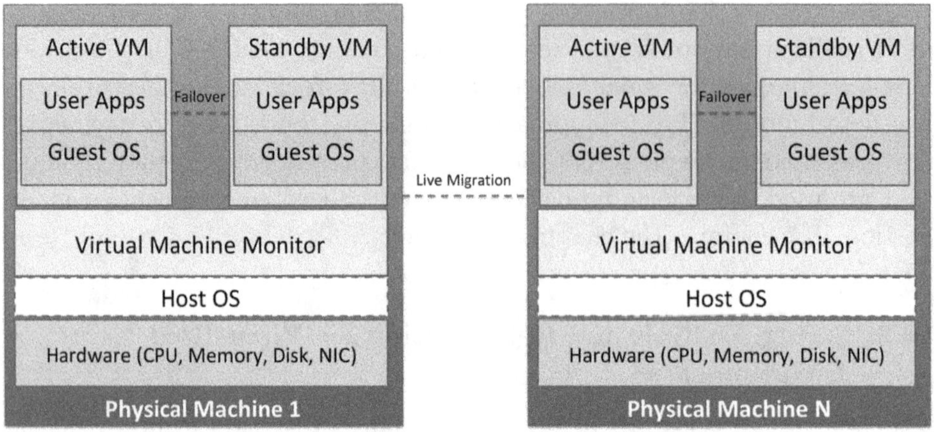

Fig. 10.1. A generic architecture of a virtualized environment.

In such a scenario, the *execution environment* is quite different from a traditional non-virtualized environment. From the SAR perspective, this affects: *i)* the choice of the most appropriate strategy for aging analysis (i.e., how to predict the most likely time of aging failure occurrence in order to figure out *when* to schedule a rejuvenation action), and *ii)* the consequent rejuvenation action to perform (i.e., *how* rejuvenation should be performed).

The ultimate goal of aging analysis — encompassing detection and estimation — is to determine the most likely time of aging failure occurrence, so as to figure out *when* to schedule a rejuvenation action. This is done either through analytical modelling — formulating the problem via stochastic models and finding the best rejuvenation time, when the system availability/survivability/performability will be maximized — or by monitoring a system's health indicators and applying statistical inference techniques on time series to forecast future trends. These approaches, also known as **model-based** and **measurement-based**, respectively, are sometimes combined into a hybrid strategy, wherein models are properly parametrized by field data. In the next sections, aging analysis and then rejuvenation techniques proposed for virtualized environments are explained.

10.3. Model-Based Analysis Techniques

Model-based aging analysis techniques for virtualized environments share the following characteristics:

- The software applications within a more or less complex virtualized environment (with one or more VMs, physical hosts, and the associated rejuvenation strategies) are most commonly modeled by Markov models, including continuous-time Markov chains (CTMCs), homogeneous and non-homogeneous, Markov regenerative processes (MRGMs), semi-Markov processes (SMPs), stochastic Petri nets (SPNs) and stochastic reward nets (SRNs), that capture the aging behaviour at different levels of abstraction (the application or virtualized environment or physical environment level) and, sometimes, the non-aging failing behavior too [1].
- Model-based aging analysis techniques do not usually refer to specific aging indicators, since the model is assumed to work regardless of which resource is being depleted or of the user-perceived metric. Even when the model refers to a specific indicator, it can easily be applied to other aging indicators. The attribute of interest is related to the final (user-perceived) metric of *availability* (or to related metrics, such as *survivability* or *performability*).
- The evaluation of alternatives is one of the objectives of model-based analyses: in most cases, model-based techniques are associated with the evaluation of alternative *rejuvenation* techniques at various levels, such as at the application level, at the VM level, at the VMM/cloud platform level, or at the node level. Indeed, exploring many such alternatives with a measurement-based approach would be too onerous. The adopted models very often encompass the rejuvenation action being performed, for which proper parameters are considered (e.g., the time/cost for rejuvenation) for the availability computation on different rejuvenation alternatives. SAR research for virtualized systems is addressed by more studies than SAR literature for generic systems, since, in virtualized environments, there are more viable options for rejuvenation.
- Model-based techniques are usually validated by means of analysis or simulation, since the collection of runtime data for all or part of the cases being modelled is expensive and may not be representative of the system being modelled.
- Models are, by their nature, applicable to many systems; their drawbacks lie in the simplifying assumptions, such as those about the underlying stochastic distributions that characterize the system. This too is not different in the case of the virtualized environment SAR research area.

An example of the model-based approach, from Chang *et al.* [2], is shown in Fig. 10.2.

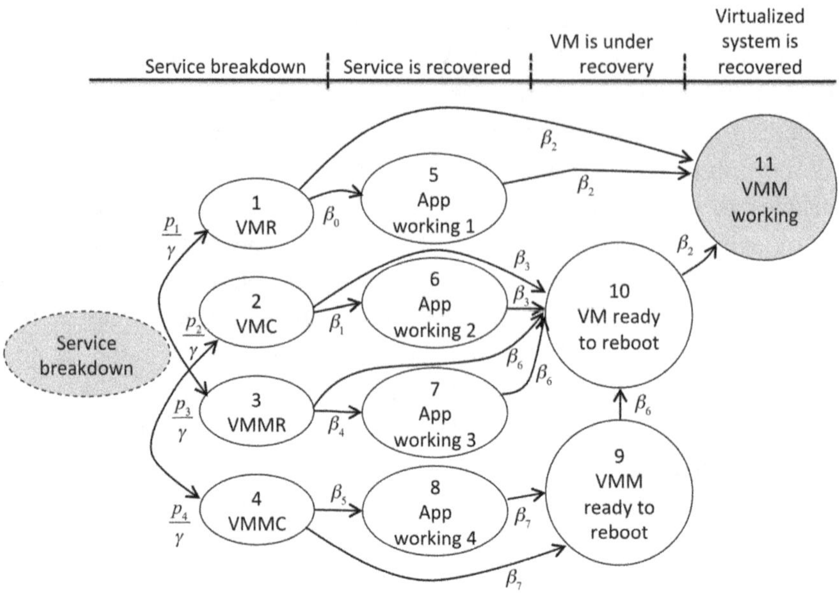

Fig. 10.2. A model of aging-related service failure/recovery in a virtualized system (from Chang *et al.* [2]).

In this CTMC model, the initial state is conditioned to be the *service breakdown*. It is assumed that no other failure occurs during the system recovery. When the service breakdown occurs due to an active VM rejuvenation or an active VM reboot caused by an aging-related bug (VMR), a standby VM on the same host is selected. The failover requires the time $1/\beta_0$; the VM restart requires $1/\beta_2$. VMC represents that the service breakdown is due to a VM crash caused by a non-aging Mandelbug. The failover takes the time $1/\beta_1$ (larger than $1/\beta_0$); the VM is repaired in the time $1/\beta_3$. After repair, the state is "VM ready to reboot", and the service is fully recovered after $1/\beta_2$. Similarly, VMMR is the service breakdown due to the VMM rejuvenation, and VMMC is the service breakdown caused by a VMM crash. Live VM migration is applied in these cases, with different time delays. In this *multi-phase CTMC model*, transient *survivability* is considered as the measure of interest, and VM/VMM rejuvenation is included as well as the bug-caused failures of these components.

Model-based approaches mostly differ from the presented example in the *type of model* adopted, the *configuration/architectural model* (e.g., single vs multiple-host), and the *attributes of interest* analyzed. Several of such works also propose rejuvenation techniques, which will be presented in Section 10.6.

In the following, a brief overview is given about the main model-based techniques proposed in the literature.

Zheng *et al.* [3] propose a *single-phase* version of the approach proposed by Chang *et al.* [2] to model again *survivability*. Silva *et al.* [4] evaluate the survivability of a cloud computing system by exploiting *Petri nets* rather than CTMCs.

Xu *et al.* [5] and Rezaei *et al.* [6] use *Stochastic Reward Nets* (SRNs) for *availability* modelling in a *single-server* virtualized system with rejuvenation applied at VMM level (by time-based policy), in combination with a measurement-based policy at VM level. SRNs for *availability* modeling are also used in the technique by Nguyen [1] which considers various failure and recovery modes of multiple VMs and VMMs, and in the one by Han and Xu [7] which considers three different rejuvenation policies (non-rejuvenation, time-based rejuvenation, and time and load-based delay rejuvenation) for single-server virtualization systems with multiple VMs on a single VMM. Similarly, Machida *et al.* [8, 9] use SRNs for cold-VM, warm-VM and VM-migration rejuvenation policies. A further example of *multiple-host multiple-VMs* availability analysis is presented by Myint and Thein [10], who designed a primary-standby server model, encompassing a load balancer VM in each node responsible for monitoring resources, and a rejuvenation agent installed on each VM. SRNs are also used in the recent works by Escheikh [11, 12] where power management *performability* analysis is performed to evaluate the impact on performance and energy consumption in virtualized systems.

The work by Thein *et al.* [13] analyzes system *availability* with the time-based rejuvenation policy under different cluster configurations, 2 VMs hosted on a single physical server and 2 VMs per a physical server in dual physical servers. The same authors further present a software rejuvenation framework named VMSR to offer high *availability* for application server systems [14], proposing again a *CTMC* to model a *single-host, multiple-VM* system in the scheme with hot standby replicas.

Machida *et al.* [15, 16] present the analysis of job completion time under aging and rejuvenation of the VMM using a *semi-Markov process*. Okamura *et al.* [17] present the transient analysis of the two main rejuvenation policies, Cold- and Warm-VM rejuvenation, by means of *Markov Regenerative Stochastic Petri Nets* (MRSPNs). Zhao *et al.* [18] formulate the problem by using a game method, representing the different goals of a service provider (who wants to maximize availability) and a maintainer (who wants to minimize cost). *Markov Renewal Processes* (MRPs) are used to determine the optimal rejuvenation schedule and compute the steady-state *availability* and *maintenance cost*. Melo *et al.* [19] present an SPN model with cloud *availability* under two migration-based rejuvenation strategies (with and without a test before migration).

Finally, some researchers propose slightly different models for aging analysis: examples include the work by Melo *et al.* [20], who formulate an *availability* model considering live migration for VMM rejuvenation based on extended *Deterministic Stochastic Petri Nets* (DSPNs) *and Reliability Block Diagrams* (RBDs), and the one by Rahme *et al.* [21, 22], who use *Dynamic Fault Trees* (DFTs) to model cloud-based software rejuvenation.

10.4. Measurement-Based Analysis Techniques

On the other side of the spectrum there are measurement-based approaches, which monitor and analyze the values of aging indicators through probes at the system level related to system resources exhaustion (e.g., memory, storage), as well as at the user level (e.g., response time, latency, throughput, violations of Service Level Agreements (SLAs)). In a virtualized setting, measurement-based techniques are characterized by the following features:

- Indicators are measured at any layer of the virtualization technology stack. Specifically, monitoring can be done at application or OS level within the VM layer, at the VM layer to probe the state and resource consumption of the VMs (e.g., for load balancing, scaling, VM migration and rejuvenation decisions), as well as at the virtualization technology layer, most often referring to the VMM component. Besides system resources (CPU, memory, storage, network), other indicators of interest are related to VMs, for instance, the number of VM new allocations/releases, the time to start/stop VMs or the time to migration. These are some of the parameters of interest to the rejuvenation technique cost assessment. These metrics are collected during execution time, and can be used to forecast future trends. Other tradeoffs involved in making a rejuvenation decision are load balancing and resource allocation. These can be static or dynamic.
- Data gathered are analyzed by one or more of the following techniques:
  - *Time Series Analysis.* It is based on trend detection and an estimation of a set of aging indicators. Tests for trend detection are used to accept/reject the hypothesis of no trend in data (e.g., Mann-Kendall, t-student, Seasonal Kendall tests). Trend estimation can exploit many models, e.g., multiple linear regression, regression smoothing, Sen's slope estimate procedure, autoregressive models, non-linear models. In

the common case of the presence of correlation among multiple aging indicators, data transformation, feature selection, or dimensionality reduction techniques are used; an example is the Principal Component Analysis (PCA) followed by regression.

A time-series analysis technique in virtualized systems is the one by Araujo *et al.* [23], who use the *linear*, *quadratic*, *exponential growth*, and the *Pearl Reed logistic* models in order to schedule software rejuvenation properly. These models have been adopted to predict memory consumption trends on the Eucalyptus cloud computing framework.

Umesh *et al.* [24] also exploit time series models to identify (and forecast) software aging patterns of the Windows active directory service.

DeCelles *et al.* [25] apply an anomaly detection technique based on *principal component analysis* (PCA) aimed at incipient faults such as software aging. Using case studies involving long-running enterprise applications, Trade6 and RuBBoS, with injected memory leaks, the performance of the PCA-based detector when using just the compressed data is almost equivalent to the case in which the raw data is completely available, but with fewer samples with a compression rate over 75%.

Cotroneo *et al.* [26] define a stress test methodology applied to the HotSpot JVM, based on Design of Experiment (DoE) for a workload-based analysis, PCA to remove first-order correlation among aging indicators at JVM level, *clustering* to identify workload states, and then *multiple regression* to relate JVM aging indicators (transformed in the PC space) to the OS memory depletion and user-perceived throughput loss.

Mohan *et al.* [27] study the effect of aging on power usage by using *linear regression* to estimate the trend. Energy consumption is also considered by Villalobos [28], who presents an IDS-based self-protection mechanism at the virtual machine level inspired by software rejuvenation concepts. A correlation between IDS accuracy, attack rate, cloud system workload, energy consumption, and response time is identified.

— *Machine Learning.* Machine learning adopts algorithms from the field of artificial intelligence (e.g., classifiers and regressors) to identify trends and classify a system state as robust or failure-prone.

One of the first works in this area is by Alonso *et al.* [29]. They analyze a three-tiered J2EE system; a machine learning approach is used to automatically build regression tree models that relate several system variables (such as number of connections and throughput) to aging trends, based on the observation that such trends can be approximated using a piecewise linear model. The models are trained using data samples collected in preliminary experiments, and then used to predict the Time To Exhaustion (TTE) of system resources under conditions different than the ones observed during the training phase.

Other techniques use classifiers, like naïve Bayes classifiers, decision trees, and Artificial Neural Networks (ANN). In particular, Sudhakar *et al.* [30] use ANN to capture non-linear relationships between resource usage statistics and the time to failure in cloud systems, to generate a prediction of the time to failure.

The works by Avresky *et al.* [31] and Di Sanzo *et al.* [32] present a framework using machine learning models to predict failures caused by the accumulation of anomalies and a proactive system scale up/scale down technique applied at client-server applications in the cloud. It predicts the remaining time to the occurrence of some unexpected event (system failure, service level agreement violation, etc.) of a VM hosting a server instance of the application. Machine learning is also used in the work by Simeonov *et al.* [33], which proposes a framework with three VMs, one VM master and two identical slaves, one active and the other in standby; the slaves send health data to the master, which predicts aging based on the machine learning algorithm running on such data.

— *Threshold-Based Approaches.* These approaches define thresholds for some aging indicators, so as to trigger rejuvenation when the monitored indicators exceed such thresholds. An examples of this approach is in the work by Silva *et al.* [34], which adopts thresholds on mean response time and on the quality of service indicators. The authors propose a rejuvenation approach based on self-healing techniques that exploits virtualization to optimize recovery. They propose a rejuvenation framework called *VM-Rejuv*, exploiting virtualization to optimize recovery, with an aging detector module detecting aging conditions based on the abovementioned thresholds.

The advantage of a measurement-based approach is that software aging forecasting can adapt to the current condition of the system, e.g., the current operational profile, which may not have been foreseen before operation, and which can accurately predict the occurrence of aging phenomena. However, this kind of approach may not be easily generalizable, since it exploits some peculiar aspect related to the nature of the considered system, e.g., the fact that some particular resource exhibits seasonal, fractal patterns, or the regularity of the phenomenon. Moreover, measurement-based approaches are not meant to estimate long-term dependability measures such as availability.

- Differently from model-based techniques, the analysis and validation of these techniques consider measurements from real systems, with the goal of identifying whether the system is in a failure-prone state due to software aging, in order to forecast the time-to-aging-failure and to plan software rejuvenation accordingly. The advantage of a measurement-based solution is the possibility of gathering accurate and detailed information about the aging state of the system. In addition, there is no need to make assumptions about model parameters, since real data is available. On the other hand, findings are very system-specific, and hard to generalize, even though the large number of systems being analyzed with these approaches is constantly increasing.

  In the context of virtualized environments, systems range from cloud applications (more often web/application servers running on the cloud) to entire platforms, the most studied one being Eucalyptus. Specifically, several authors [23, 35–38] analyze aging and propose rejuvenation in the Eucalyptus cloud computing infrastructure by using measurement-based approaches, e.g., time series forecasting. These are applied to common indicators about resource consumption, especially RAM memory and swap space exhaustion and CPU utilization by the VMs. Based on the time series analyses, a prediction-based rejuvenation is scheduled, so as to reduce the downtime by predicting the proper time to perform the rejuvenation.

  A quite different aging study on Eucalyptus is presented by Langner *et al.* [39] The authors propose a technique to detect aging problems shortly after their introduction by performing runtime comparisons of different development versions of the same software. In this case — as in the few other cases in the SAR literature where aging-related bugs are analyzed at development-time [40–42] — the detection aims at revealing aging problems before their long-term runtime manifestation.
- Besides studies on cloud computing, a relevant environment to which measurement-based methods have been applied is represented by the **Java Virtual Machine** (JVM) and its related applications (i.e., applications based on J2EE). In this case, the parameters of interest at the VM level are about the state of the JVM, which is captured by parameters like heap usage, instantiated classes, number of threads, object size, number

of allocations, number of garbage collections, number of JIT compilations, etc. Several examples of measurement-based approaches in the JVM present techniques for **leak detection**.

Haining *et al.* [43], and then Meng *et al.* [44], studied the performance of the JVM running a J2EE Application Server, looking for memory leaks associated with the garbage collection mechanism in the JVM. They use the Virtual Machine Profiler Interface (JVMPI), to collect resource usage data from the application server, including data on the JVM heap memory usage and CPU utilization, as well as the response time and throughput at client level.

In the studies by Šor *et al.* [45, 46], memory leak detection in Java applications is performed through a statistical approach based on the "age" of objects, measured as the number of garbage collection cycles (or generations) they survive. The idea is to analyze how live instances of the class are distributed over different generations, and evaluate if objects follow the "generational hypothesis", i.e., most of them become unreachable very soon after creation (in other words, they "die" young). The growth of the number of generations where class instances are present is a symptom that the application allocates some objects without then freeing them (memory leak).

Memory leaks are also analyzed by Xu *et al.* [47], who present an assertion-based technique for leak detection within the Jikes RVM, a high-performance Java virtual machine, and then apply it to real leaks in large-scale applications like Eclipse and MySQL. Xu *et al.* [48] have proposed the Self-organizing Maps (SOMs) to capture VMM behaviors from runtime measurement data. In their work, they have used the neighborhood area density of a winning neuron as an aging quantification metric. The results of two experiments injecting different resource leaks on the Xen platform show that the algorithm has a high true positive rate and a low false positive rate. Sor *et al.* [49] use machine learning for memory leak detection implemented in a commercial tool called *Plumbr*.

An additional JVM study, Cotroneo *et al.* [26], investigates throughput loss and memory consumption in the JVM Hotspot, via a James' mail server workload. Several JVM parameters are monitored through *JVMMon*, a monitoring tool developed for the purpose of aging analysis. Correlation analysis is used to identify aging JVM components. An interesting finding is that the garbage collector, which was designed to limit aging trends in Java applications, was found to suffer from aging [26].

10.5. Hybrid Analysis Techniques

An important generalization of the previous two methods for aging analysis is what are called **hybrid** approaches, proposed by some researchers as a combination of model-based and measurement-based solutions. Hybrid solutions usually adopt a stochastic model to describe the phenomenon, and determine the model parameters through measurement, that is, via observed data. Solutions of this type are not yet widely deployed, but have the potential of taking advantage of the best features found in model-based and measurement-based approaches. A typical example is the one proposed by Trivedi and Vaidyanathan [50] in which: *i)* a measurement-based semi-Markovian model for a system workload is built; *ii)* the TTE for each considered resource and state (using reward functions) is estimated, and finally *iii)* a semi-Markov availability model is provided, based on field data rather than on assumptions about system behavior.

In the context of virtualized environments, a hybrid solution is adopted by Liu *et al.* [51], which measures the trends of various resources in a cloud-based streaming system with ATM endpoints, including the CPU, storage, and network, at several layers, and uses the measured trends to parametrize a model to schedule service rejuvenation, implemented by means of the VM failover to replicas. The end result is an improvement in terms of served transactions per second.

A further hybrid strategy is proposed by Machida *et al.* [52], who present an original countermeasure to software aging different from rejuvenation, called *software life extension* — a sort of workaround in which, upon software aging detection, additional memory is allocated to the VM executing the aging-affected software. In this case, experimental data on *memcached* are used to derive a more general model using a semi-Markov process formalism.

The solution proposed by Kadirvel *et al.* [53] is applied to a system manager for a batch-based job submission system on a virtualized platform, aimed at managing and controlling virtualized resources to support remediation approaches, such as the elastic increase and decrease of resource capacity, VM migrations, and dynamic resource configuration changes. The technique combines a Petri Net-based approach to model a system manager module, suffering from health deterioration due to resource exhaustion, with the usage of feedback control theory to control resource consumption and to delay/prevent resources. Three different rejuvenation strategies are implemented and tested — process rejuvenation, VM migration and dynamic increase of resource allocation — chosen based on the planning module.

In all the mentioned classes of studies, an additional analysis factor is workload dependency. Since aging has been shown to be correlated with workload variation [54, 55] several studies accounted for its impact; two examples are the following.

Brueno *et al.* [56] present a workload-based analysis of VMM aging and rejuvenation under different policies for availability maximization, under *variable* workload conditions. They exploit dynamic reliability theory and symbolic algebraic techniques, representing the CDFs associated with the VMM events, under different workload conditions, by continuous phase type (CPH) distributions, and using the Kronecker algebra to implement the conservation of the reliability principle and the variable timer policy.

Ficco *et al.* [57] perform a workload-dependent analysis of performance degradation and memory indicators in Apache Storm, an event stream processing (ESP) application that can deploy tasks over a cloud architecture, by means of a workload-dependent time series analysis. The Mann-Kendall test and Sen's procedure, often used for aging trend detection and estimation, are used on sliced windows where the workload and the performance/memory trends are judged to be in contrast (e.g., their trends increase despite the workload decreasing).

10.6. Rejuvenation Techniques

In virtualized environments, several further alternatives are explored besides the conventional rejuvenation techniques, e.g., application/component, OS/node reboot, cluster failover. The additional layers (i.e., the VMM and VM layers) give the opportunity to set up various scenarios (e.g., multiple hosts with multiple VMs) and this, in turn, enables the development of new rejuvenation strategies exploiting, for instance, VM restarts, migration and failover, to guarantee high levels of service continuity in the presence of aging problems. Figure 10.3 outlines the common rejuvenation techniques at VMM and at VM level. Software rejuvenation can act on a virtual machine infrastructure by rejuvenating the VMM and/or its VMs. VMM rejuvenation

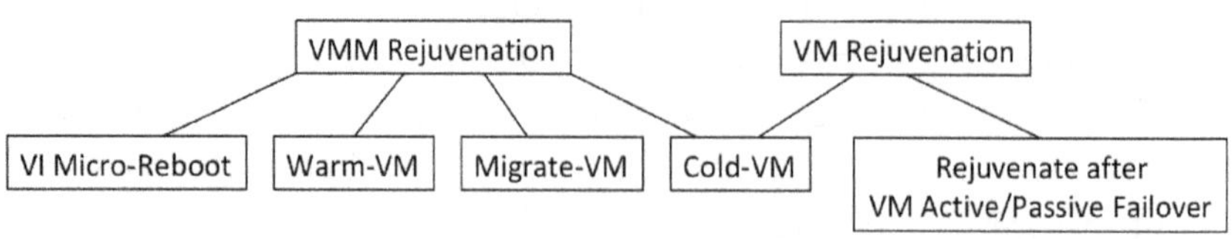

Fig. 10.3. Rejuvenation techniques.

can be performed by restarting the VMM or part thereof, and alternative strategies depend on whether rejuvenation affects only the VMM, or also the VMs running on top of the VMM [8, 9]. As for VM rejuvenation, the strategies differ in how the rejuvenation process is managed. They are explained in detail hereafter.

VMM rejuvenation can be performed by the following techniques:

- **Cold-VM rejuvenation**, in which the VMs are also restarted when the VMM is rejuvenated. Cold-VM rejuvenation simply shuts down the hosted VMs before triggering the VMM rejuvenation and restarts the VMs after the completion of VMM rejuvenation.
- **Warm-VM rejuvenation**, in which the execution state of each VM, including the OS and applications running in the VM, are stored to persistent memory, and resumed after the restart of the VMM, in order to reduce the downtime of restarting VMs and their services. In this type of rejuvenation, the software running in the VMs is not rejuvenated. This operation can be quickly performed by adopting an on-memory suspend/resume mechanism, in which the memory images of VMs are preserved in main memory during the VMM restart rather than on persistent storage, in order to avoid slow read/write operations to persistent storage. Kourai *et al.* [58, 59] propose such a variant, and show that compared with Cold-VM rejuvenation, a Warm-VM reboot improves the availability of the applications hosted on the VMs by introducing the on-memory suspend technique and the quick reload mechanism.
- **Migrate-VM rejuvenation** is a type of rejuvenation in which the downtime is further reduced by migrating a VM to another host while the VMM is being rejuvenated, in order to make it available during rejuvenation. This latter scheme does not rejuvenate VMs, and is limited by the capacity of other hosts to accept migrated VMs. Migration can further be categorized based on the type of live VM migration (*stop-and-copy* or *pre-copy*), and the type of policy with regard to returning back to the original host after VMM rejuvenation (*return-back* or *stay-on*) [9]. Specifically, the *stop-and-copy* migration stops the VM operation and copies all the memory contents to the destination server. In the *pre-copy* variant, the VM's memory is first copied to a destination server without stopping its operation, causing dirty pages in the copied memory contents; then, a stop-and-copy phase is performed, which, however, updates only the dirty pages, so considerably reducing the downtime overhead compared to that which would result from a complete stop-and-copy of the entire

VM's memory. As for the restore of the VM on the original host, a *return-back* policy foresees the migration to the original host soon after the VMM rejuvenation is completed; a *stay-on* policy allows the migrated VM to run on the other hosting server even after the completion of VMM rejuvenation on the original host.

The work by Machida *et al.* [9] uses SRNs for cold-VM rejuvenation, warm-VM rejuvenation and migration. They studied the steady-state availability of the VMs and the expected number of transactions lost, finding that Migrate-VM rejuvenation generally achieves higher steady-state availability compared to Cold- and Warm-VM rejuvenation, because of the ability to preserve the VM execution even during VMM rejuvenation.

Regarding the types of VM migration, they also found that the pre-copy approach generally achieves higher availability than the stop-and-copy approach because it minimizes the downtime caused by VM migration thanks to the pre-copy phase. For the migration back policy, the return-back policy is generally more effective than the stay-on policy because a host that just finished VMM rejuvenation is more reliable than a host that has been running for some time after the last VMM rejuvenation, i.e., the availability of the VMs running on the migrated host is affected by the uptime of the host from the last restart.

Machida *et al.* [60, 61] propose also the contemporary rejuvenation of aged VMs and the VMM in virtualized data centers; differently from the usual Cold-VM rejuvenation, this technique forces shutdown only to aged VMs which are to be rejuvenated in the near future, while the robust VMs are moved out from the host server by live VM migration before VMM rejuvenation.

Kourai *et al.* [62] present *VMBeam*, a technique that enables lightweight software rejuvenation of virtualized systems using zero-copy migration. The technique starts a new virtualized system at the same host by using nested virtualization, and then migrates all the VMs from the aged virtualized system to the clean one. VMBeam relocates the memory of the VMs on the aged virtualized system directly to the clean system, without any copy.

Melo *et al.* [19] use an SPN model under two migration-based rejuvenation strategies (with and without a test before migration).

The approach proposed by Torquato *et al.* [63] discussed in the previous section foresees a rejuvenation phase performed by means of VM Live Migration, applied on a Cloud Computing testbed which uses OpenNebula and KVM as the VMMs.

- **VI Micro reboot**. A more complex technique is to perform a very fine-grained reboot of software modules (a micro reboot), tailored for the system-level virtualization software (i.e., for the virtualization infrastructure — VI). The technique has been proposed by Le *et al.* [64], who applied a micro reboot to all the modules of the Xen virtualization software; this consists of three main components: the privileged virtual machine, the device driver virtual machine, and the virtual machine monitor. This is an instance of the more general case of micro reboot: Candea *et al.* applied a micro reboot to Java-based virtualized environments [65, 66]. The technique requires "*microrebootable*" software, in which a system can be decomposed into components that are loosely coupled, e.g., they do not share the same memory address space, and are stateless, e.g., important states are located in dedicated storage outside the application, in order to quickly restart a component without affecting the other ones — an approach suitable for modern service-based systems. The approach has been successfully implemented in a J2EE application [66] (in which individual Enterprise Java Beans can be restarted) as well as in a Java-based mission-critical system [65], consisting of a set of components running in different Java Virtual Machines. A limitation of component rejuvenation is that it can be applied only in systems made up of individually restartable components; if this is not the case, the system has to be modified based on the microreboot schema.

The best technique, or the best combination of techniques, depends on the speed of storing/migrating the state of the VMs and on the capacity of hosts, as well as on the aging rate of VMs and VMMs, therefore the rejuvenation policy should be determined according to these factors.

In order to rejuvenate VMs themselves, besides the mentioned Cold-VM rejuvenation that indirectly also rejuvenates the VM, a conventional replication approach can be applied:

- **VM Failover**: *VM Failover* techniques are based on conventional active/passive replication. The idea is to redirect, upon detection of aging in a VM, all the incoming requests to another VM, and then rejuvenate the aged VM (e.g., by restart). A VM can be rejuvenated while the other replicas are active and the workload is redirected to them, or by activating a standby (i.e., idle) replica when rejuvenation is triggered.
  For example, Silva *et al.* [34] propose a cluster failover framework for web applications based on virtualization, namely *VM-Rejuv*. The framework consists of a Load Balancer, an Active Server, and a Standby Server,

each running in a dedicated VM. The Load Balancer redirects requests to the Active Server while it is correctly working, and monitors the Active Server for aging symptoms (e.g., performance falls below a threshold). When rejuvenation is triggered, new requests are redirected to the Standby Server; the Active Server is rejuvenated only after all pending requests have been processed and session data have been migrated to the Standby Server, in order to ensure a clean restart, i.e., in order that rejuvenation does not cause the loss of session data and the failure of user requests. This framework can be implemented in a cost-effective way by using off-the-shelf application servers, monitoring, and load balancing software, at the cost of a moderate overhead.

In a virtualized environment, the management of the state transfer can also be done by exploiting the hypervisor. For instance, the work by Distler *et al.* [67] addresses the problem of stateful replica management by proposing an architecture where recovery is allowed in parallel with service execution, and which uses copy-on-write techniques for state transfer between virtual replicas of a host. Similarly, Reiser *et al.* [68] initially proposed to use hypervisor to initialize a new replica in parallel to normal system execution, and thus minimizes the time in which a proactive reboot interferes with system operation.

It is finally worth noting that the advantages of using VMs can be counterbalanced by a higher memory fragmentation induced by the virtualized environment. Alonso *et al.* [69] experimentally study the main software rejuvenation techniques, considering (i) physical node reboot, (ii) virtual machine reboot, (iii) OS reboot, (iv) fast OS reboot, (v) standalone application restart, and (vi) application rejuvenation by a hot standby server, and blame virtualization for the drastic increase in memory fragmentation, which can cause aging-related failures in long-running systems. This stresses the importance of choosing the right set of techniques to apply rejuvenation in a virtualized environment.

10.7. Conclusions

SAR techniques in virtualized environments have increasingly emerged in the last few years. More than 55% of research studies in this area were published in the last 5 years, hence it is a relatively young research area. These research studies have appeared mainly after 2007, after the widespread adoption of this kind of system. In such studies, researchers often analyze several rejuvenation policies based on virtual machine and/or virtual machine monitor reboot/rejuvenation. Such strategies are then evaluated both by model-based approaches and by measurements. The availability of cloud computing software, which can be used to experiment with such strategies without excessive costs, is favoring aging analysis in the cloud. A relevant example is represented by the studies on the Eucalyptus cloud-computing framework. From the model-based perspective, models differ from each other in the formalism adopted (e.g., CTMC, SPN, SRN, MRGP, MRP), in the configuration/architectural model (e.g., single vs multiple-host), in the attributes of interest analyzed (survivability, availability, performability), and in the rejuvenation schemes (e.g., Cold-VM, Warm-VM, Migrate-VM, VM failover). Measurement-based approaches differ from the traditional SAR approach only in the indicators being adopted: as mentioned, the *execution environment* concept is quite different from non-virtualized systems, but the techniques used (mostly, time series analysis and machine learning) are unchanged with respect to conventional SAR literature. A relevant difference is that in most of the works on SAR in the virtualized environment, researchers associate one or more rejuvenation actions to the aging evaluation task, resulting in a literature review with many more works including rejuvenation strategies with respect to the general SAR literature. Looking at the increasing trends of virtualization and cloud computing, it is easy to envision a proportionally increasing trend in the studies dealing with aging and rejuvenation in virtualized environments in the next few years. Moreover, because of the increased economical impact of availability/performability/survivability and thanks to the possibilities offered by emerging cloud-based architectures, we will likely be witness to an increase in the number of deployments of virtualized rejuvenation solutions, in each of the several layers of the virtualized environment.

References

1. T. A. Nguyen, D. S. Kim, and J. S. Park. (2014). A comprehensive availability modeling and analysis of a virtualized servers system using stochastic reward nets. *The Scientific World Journal*, **2014**, Article 165316.
2. X. Chang, Z. Zhang, X. Li, and K. S. Trivedi. (2016). Model-based survivability analysis of a virtualized system. In *Proceedings of the IEEE 41st Conference on Local Computer Networks (LCN), Dubai, UAE, November 7–10*, pp. 611–614.
3. J. Zheng, H. Okamura, and T. Dohi. (2015). Survivability analysis of VM-based intrusion tolerant systems. *IEICE Transactions on Information and Systems*, **E98.D**(12), 2082–2090.

4. B. Silva, P. R. M. Maciel, A. Zimmermann, and J. Brilhante. (2014). Survivability evaluation of disaster tolerant cloud computing systems. In *Proceedings of the Probabilistic Safety Assessment & Management Conference (PSAM 12), Honolulu, Hawaii, USA, June 22–27*, p. 453.
5. J. Xu, X. Li, Y. Zhong, and H. Zhang. (2014). Availability modeling and analysis of a single-server virtualized system with rejuvenation. *Journal of Software*, **9**(1), 129–139.
6. A. Rezaei and M. Sharifi. (2010). Rejuvenating high available virtualized systems. In *Proceedings of the 5th International Conference on Availability, Reliability, and Security (ARES), Krakow, Poland, February 15–18*, pp. 289–294.
7. L. Han and J. Xu. (2013). Availability models for virtualized systems with rejuvenation. *Journal of Computational Information Systems*, **9**(20), 8389–8396.
8. F. Machida, D. S. Kim, and K. S. Trivedi. (2010). Modeling and analysis of software rejuvenation in a server virtualized system. In *Proceedings of the Second International Workshop on Software Aging and Rejuvenation (WoSAR), San Jose, California, USA, November 2*, pp. 1–6.
9. F. Machida, D. S. Kim, and K. S. Trivedi. (2013). Modeling and analysis of software rejuvenation in a server virtualized system with live VM migration. *Performance Evaluation*, **70**(3), 212–230.
10. M. Myint and T. Thein. (2010). Availability improvement in virtualized multiple servers with software rejuvenation and virtualization. In *Proceedings of the Fourth International Conference on Secure Software Integration and Reliability Improvement (SSIRI), Singapore, June 9–11*, pp. 156–162.
11. M. Escheikh, Z. Tayachi, and K. Barkaoui. (2016). Workload-dependent software aging impact on performance and energy consumption in server virtualized systems. In *Proceedings of the IEEE International Symposium on Software Reliability Engineering Workshops (ISSREW), Ottawa, Ontario, October 23–27*, pp. 111–118.
12. M. Escheikh, K. Barkaoui, and H. Jouini. (2017). Versatile workload-aware power management performability analysis of server virtualized systems. *Journal of Systems and Software*, **125**, 365–379.
13. T. Thein, S. Chi, and J. S. Park. (2008). Availability modeling and analysis on virtualized clustering with rejuvenation. *International Journal of Computer Science and Network Security*, **8**(9), 72–80.
14. T. Thein and J. S. Park. (2009). Availability analysis of application servers using software rejuvenation and virtualization. *Journal of Computer Science and Technology*, **24**(2), 339–346.
15. F. Machida, V. F. Nicola, and K. S. Trivedi. (2011). Job completion time on a virtualized server subject to software aging and rejuvenation. In *Proceedings of the Third International Workshop on Software Aging and Rejuvenation (WoSAR), Hiroshima, Japan, November 29–December 2*, pp. 44–49.
16. F. Machida, V. F. Nicola, and K. S. Trivedi. (2014). Job completion time on a virtualized server with software rejuvenation. *ACM Journal on Emerging Technologies in Computing Systems*, **10**(1), 10:1–10:26.
17. H. Okamura, K. Yamamoto, and T. Dohi. (2014). Transient analysis of software rejuvenation policies in virtualized system: Phase-type expansion approach. *Quality Technology & Quantitative Management*, **11**(3), 335–351.
18. J. Zhao, Y.-B. Wang, G.-R. Ning, C.-H. Wang, K. S. Trivedi, K.-Y. Cai, and Z.-Y. Zhang. (2014). Software maintenance optimization based on Stackelberg game methods. In *Proceedings of the IEEE International Symposium on Software Reliability Engineering Workshops (ISSREW), Naples, Italy, November 3–6*, pp. 426–430.

19. M. Melo, J. Araujo, R. Matos, J. Menezes, and P. Maciel. (2013). Comparative analysis of migration-based rejuvenation schedules on cloud availability. In *Proceedings of the IEEE International Conference on Systems, Man, and Cybernetics (SMC), Manchester, UK, October 13–16*, pp. 4110–4115.
20. M. Melo, P. Maciel, J. Araujo, R. Matos, and C. Araujo. (2013). Availability study on cloud computing environments: Live migration as a rejuvenation mechanism. In *Proceedings of the 43rd Annual IEEE/IFIP International Conference on Dependable Systems and Networks (DSN), Budapest, Hungary, June 24–27*, pp. 1–6.
21. J. Rahme and H. Xu. (2015). A software reliability model for cloud-based software rejuvenation using dynamic fault trees. *International Journal of Software Engineering and Knowledge Engineering*, **25**(09n10), 1491–1513.
22. J. Rahme and H. Xu. (2015). Reliability-based software rejuvenation scheduling for cloud-based systems. In *Proceedings of the 27th International Conference on Software Engineering and Knowledge Engineering (SEKE), Pittsburgh, Philadelphia, USA, July 6–8*, pp. 298–303.
23. J. Araujo, R. Matos, P. Maciel, F. Vieira, R. Matias, and K. Trivedi. (2011). Software rejuvenation in eucalyptus cloud computing infrastructure: A method based on time series forecasting and multiple thresholds. In *Proceedings of the Third International Workshop on Software Aging and Rejuvenation (WoSAR), Hiroshima, Japan, November 29–December 2*, pp. 38–43.
24. I. M. Umesh and G. N. Srinivasan. (2017). Dynamic software aging detection-based fault-tolerant software rejuvenation model for virtualized environment. In Satapathy S. C., Bhateja V., and Joshi A. (eds.). *Proceedings of the International Conference on Data Engineering and Communication Technology*, Advances in Intelligent Systems and Computing, vol. 469. Singapore: Springer.
25. S. DeCelles, T. Huang, M. C. Stamm, and N. Kandasamy. (2016). Detecting incipient faults in software systems: A compressed sampling-based approach. In *Proceedings of the 9th IEEE International Conference on Cloud Computing (CLOUD), San Francisco, California, USA, June 27–July 2*, pp. 303–310.
26. D. Cotroneo, S. Orlando, R. Pietrantuono, and S. Russo. (2013). A measurement-based ageing analysis of the JVM. *Software Testing, Verification and Reliability*, **23**(3), 199–239.
27. B. R. Mohan and G. R. M. Reddy. (2015). The effect of software aging on power usage. In *Proceedings of the 9th International Conference on Intelligent Systems and Control (ISCO), Tamil Nadu, India, January 9–10*, pp. 1–3.
28. J. J. Villalobos, I. Rodero, and M. Parashar. (2014). Energy-aware autonomic framework for cloud protection and self-healing. In *Proceedings of the International Conference on Cloud and Autonomic Computing (ICCAC), London, UK, September 8–12*, pp. 3–4.
29. J. Alonso, L. Belanche, and D. Avresky. (2011). Predicting software anomalies using machine learning techniques. In *Proceedings of the 10th IEEE International Symposium on Network Computing and Applications (NCA), Cambridge, Massachusetts, USA, July 15–17*, pp. 163–170.
30. C. Sudhakar, I. Shah, and T. Ramesh. (2014). Software rejuvenation in cloud systems using neural networks. In *Proceedings of the International Conference on Parallel, Distributed and Grid Computing (PDGC), Himachal Pradesh, India, December 11–13*, pp. 230–233.

31. D. R. Avresky, P. D. Sanzo, A. Pellegrini, B. Ciciani, and L. Forte. (2015). Proactive scalability and management of resources in hybrid clouds via machine learning. In *Proceedings of the 14th International Symposium on Network Computing and Applications (NCA), Cambridge, Massachusetts, USA, October 31–November 2*, pp. 114–119.
32. P. D. Sanzo, A. Pellegrini, and D. R. Avresky. (2015). Machine learning for achieving self-* properties and seamless execution of applications in the cloud. In *Proceedings of the 2015 IEEE Fourth Symposium on Network Cloud Computing and Applications (NCCA), Munich, Germany, June 11–12*, pp. 51–58.
33. D. Simeonov and D. R. Avresky. (2010). Proactive software rejuvenation based on machine learning techniques. In Avresky D. R. *et al.* (eds.). *Cloud Computing.* Lecture Notes of the Institute for Computer Sciences, Social-Informatics and Telecommunications Engineering, vol. 34. Berlin/Heidelberg, Germany: Springer.
34. L. Silva, J. Alonso, and J. Torres. (2009). Using virtualization to improve software rejuvenation. *IEEE Transactions on Computers*, **58**(11), 1525–1538.
35. J. Araujo, R. Matos, V. Alves, P. Maciel, F. V. de Souza, R. Matias Jr., and K. S. Trivedi. (2014). Software aging in the eucalyptus cloud computing infrastructure: Characterization and rejuvenation. *ACM Journal on Emerging Technologies in Computing Systems*, **10**(1), 11:1–11:22.
36. R. Matos, J. Araujo, V. Alves, and P. Maciel. (2012). Experimental evaluation of software aging effects in the eucalyptus elastic block storage. In *Proceedings of the IEEE International Conference on Systems, Man, and Cybernetics (SMC), Seoul, Korea, October 14–17*, pp. 1103–1108.
37. J. Araujo, R. Matos, P. Maciel, and R. Matias. (2011). Software aging issues on the eucalyptus cloud computing infrastructure. In *Proceedings of the IEEE International Conference on Systems, Man, and Cybernetics (SMC), Anchorage, Alaska, USA, October 9–12*, pp. 1411–1416.
38. J. Araujo, R. Matos, P. Maciel, R. Matias, and I. Beicker. (2011). Experimental evaluation of software aging effects on the eucalyptus cloud computing infrastructure. In *Proceedings of the Middleware 2011 Industry Track Workshop, Lisbon, Portugal, December 12–16.*
39. F. Langner and A. Andrzejak. (2013). Detecting software aging in a cloud computing framework by comparing development versions. In *Proceedings of the IFIP/IEEE International Symposium on Integrated Network Management, Ghent, Belgium, May 27–31*, pp. 896–899.
40. D. Cotroneo, R. Natella, and R. Pietrantuono. (2012). Predicting aging-related bugs using software complexity metrics. *Performance Evaluation*, **70**(3), 163–178.
41. D. Cotroneo, R. Natella, and R. Pietrantuono. (2010). Is software aging related to software metrics? In *Proceedings of the Second International Workshop on Software Aging and Rejuvenation (WoSAR), San Jose, California, USA, November 2*, pp. 1–6.
42. D. Cotroneo, R. Pietrantuono, S. Russo, and K. Trivedi. (2016). How do bugs surface? A comprehensive study on the characteristics of software bugs manifestation. *Journal of Systems and Software*, **113**, 27–43.
43. M. Haining, H. Xinhong, L. Jianjun, and W. Wei. (2013). Detection and analysis of software aging in a service-oriented J2EE application server. *Information Technology Journal*, **12**(9), 1857–1862.
44. H. Meng, X. Hei, J. Zhang, J. Liu, and L. Sui. (2016). Software aging and rejuvenation in a J2EE application server. *Quality and Reliability Engineering International*, **32**(1), 89–97.

45. V. Šor, N. Salnikov-Tarnovski, and S. N. Srirama. (2011). Automated statistical approach for memory leak detection: Case studies. In Meersman R. *et al.* (eds.). *On the Move to Meaningful Internet Systems: OTM 2011*. Lecture Notes in Computer Science, vol. 7045. Berlin/Heidelberg, Germany: Springer.
46. V. Sor and S. N. Srirama. (2011). A statistical approach for identifying memory leaks in cloud applications. In *Proceedings of the International Conference on Cloud Computing and Services Science (CLOSER 2011), Noordwijkerhout, The Netherlands, May 7–9*, pp. 623–628.
47. G. Xu, M. Bond, F. Qin, and A. Rountev. (2011). Leakchaser: Helping programmers narrow down causes of memory leaks. In *Proceedings of the ACM SIGPLAN Conference on Programming Language Design and Implementation (PLDI), San Jose, California, USA, June 4–8*, pp. 270–282.
48. J. Xu, W.-W. Wu, and C.-Y. Ma. (2014). SOM-based aging detection for Virtual Machine Monitor. In *Proceedings of the IEEE Workshop on Electronics, Computer and Applications, Ottawa, Ontario, Canada, May 8–9*, pp. 782–785.
49. V. Sor, P. Oü, T. Treier, and S. N. Srirama. (2013). Improving statistical approach for memory leak detection using machine learning. In *Proceedings of the IEEE International Conference on Software Maintenance (ICSM), Eindhoven, The Netherlands, September 22–28*, pp. 544–547.
50. K. Vaidyanathan and K. Trivedi. (2005). A comprehensive model for software rejuvenation. *IEEE Transactions on Dependable and Secure Computing*, **2**(2), 124–137.
51. Y. Liu, W. Liu, J. Song, and H. He. (2015). An empirical study on implementing highly reliable stream computing systems with private cloud. *Ad Hoc Networks*, **35**(C), 37–50.
52. F. Machida, J. Xiang, K. Tadano, and Y. Maeno. (2012). Software Life-Extension: A New Countermeasure to Software Aging. In *Proceedings of the 23rd International Symposium on Software Reliability Engineering, Dallas, Texas, USA, November 27–30*, pp. 131–140.
53. S. Kadirvel and J. A. B. Fortes. (2010). Self-caring IT systems: A proof-of-concept implementation in virtualized environments. In *Proceedings of the IEEE Second International Conference on Cloud Computing Technology and Science (CloudCom), Indianapolis, Indiana, USA, November 30–December 3*, pp. 433–440.
54. A. Bovenzi, D. Cotroneo, R. Pietrantuono, and S. Russo. (2011). Workload characterization for software aging analysis. In *Proceedings of the 22nd International Symposium on Software Reliability Engineering (ISSRE), Hiroshima, Japan, November 29–December 2*, pp. 240–249.
55. A. Bovenzi, D. Cotroneo, R. Pietrantuono, and S. Russo. (2012). On the aging effects due to concurrency bugs: A case study on MySQL. In *Proceedings of the 2012 IEEE 23rd International Symposium on Software Reliability Engineering, Dallas, Texas, USA, November 27–30*, pp. 211–220.
56. D. Bruneo, S. Distefano, F. Longo, A. Puliafito, and M. Scarpa. (2013). Workload-based software rejuvenation in cloud systems. *IEEE Transactions on Computers*, **62**(6), 1072–1085.
57. M. Ficco, R. Pietrantuono, and S. Russo. (2018). Aging-related performance anomalies in the Apache Storm stream processing system. *Future Generation Computer Systems*, **86**, 975–994.
58. K. Kourai and S. Chiba. (2007). A fast rejuvenation technique for server consolidation with virtual machines. In *Proceedings of the 37th Annual IEEE/IFIP International Conference on Dependable Systems and Networks (DSN), Edinburgh, UK, June 25–28*, pp. 245–255.

59. K. Kourai and S. Chiba. (2011). Fast software rejuvenation of virtual machine monitors. *IEEE Transactions on Dependable and Secure Computing*, **8**(6), 839–851.
60. F. Machida, J. Xiang, K. Tadano, and Y. Maeno. (2012). Combined server rejuvenation in a virtualized data center. In *Proceedings of the 9th International Conference on Ubiquitous Intelligence & Computing and 9th International Conference on Autonomic & Trusted Computing (UIC/ATC), Fukuoka, Japan, September 4–7*, pp. 486–493.
61. F. Machida, D. S. Kim, J. S. Park, and K. Trivedi. (2008). Toward optimal virtual machine placement and rejuvenation scheduling in a virtualized data center. In *Proceedings of the IEEE International Conference on Software Reliability Engineering Workshops, Seattle, Washington, USA, November 11–14*, pp. 1–3.
62. K. Kourai and H. Ooba. (2015). Zero-copy migration for lightweight software rejuvenation of virtualized systems. In *Proceedings of the 6th Asia-Pacific Workshop on Systems (APSys), Tokyo, Japan, July 27–28*, pp. 7:1–7:8.
63. M. Torquato, P. Maciel, J. Araujo, and I. M. Umesh. (2017). An approach to investigate aging symptoms and rejuvenation effectiveness on software systems. In *Proceedings of the 12th Iberian Conference on Information Systems and Technologies (CISTI), Lisbon, Portugal, June 14–17*, pp. 1–6.
64. M. Le and Y. Tamir. (2012). Applying microreboot to system software. In *Proceedings of the IEEE Sixth International Conference on Software Security and Reliability (SERE), Gaithersburg, Maryland, USA, June 20–22*, pp. 11–20.
65. G. Candea, J. Cutler, A. Fox, R. Doshi, P. Garg, and R. Gowda. (2002). Reducing recovery time in a small recursively restartable system. In *Proceedings of the 2002 International Conference on Dependable Systems and Networks, Bethesda, Maryland, USA, June 23–26*, pp. 605–614. doi: 10.1109/DSN.2002.1029006.
66. G. Candea, S. Kawamoto, Y. Fujiki, G. Friedman, and A. Fox. (2004). Microreboot — a technique for cheap recovery. In *Proceedings of the Symposium on Operating Systems Design & Implementation, San Francisco, California, USA, December 6–8*, pp. 31–44.
67. T. Distler, R. Kapitza, and H. P. Reiser. (2008). Efficient state transfer for hypervisor-based proactive recovery. In *Proceedings of the 2nd Workshop on Recent Advances on Intrusion-Tolerant Systems (WRAITS), Glasgow, UK, April 1*, pp. 4:1–4:6.
68. H. P. Reiser and R. Kapitza. (2007). Hypervisor-based efficient proactive recovery. In *Proceedings of the 26th IEEE International Symposium on Reliable Distributed Systems (SRDS), Beijing, China, October 10–12*, pp. 83–92.
69. J. Alonso, R. Matias, E. Vicente, A. Maria, and K. Trivedi. (2013). A comparative experimental study of software rejuvenation overhead. *Performance Evaluation*, **70**(3), 231–250.

Chapter 11

Experimental Tools for Software Aging Analysis

Roberto Natella*,‡ and Artur Andrzejak†,§

*Università degli Studi di Napoli Federico II, Italy
†Ruprecht-Karls-University of Heidelberg, Germany
‡roberto.natella@unina.it
§artur.andrzejak@informatik.uni-heidelberg.de

Software aging analysis tools are a cornerstone for applying software rejuvenation strategies, as well as to pinpoint and to fix software aging bugs during testing. In this chapter, we review a pool of popular tools for detecting software aging, which have been chosen from the scientific literature and from industry. We consider tools both for C/C++ and Java software, and analyze their internals, use cases, the aging symptoms that they address, and their relevant applications in real case studies.

11.1. Introduction

To achieve the strict high-availability goals of critical long-running systems, the software aging and rejuvenation (SAR) solutions discussed so far need to be supported by automated tools. Therefore, a significant amount of effort in SAR research has been dedicated to designing, implementing, and experimenting with tools for the *detection of software aging* in complex software systems. There are two fundamental reasons for the importance of these tools. First, these tools are the basis for condition-based software rejuvenation in production environments. They can measure the presence of aging symptoms, such as high resource consumption and degraded performance. Moreover, jointly with aging forecasting models, they can trigger rejuvenation actions when aging symptoms point out that software aging failures are imminent. The second reason is that these tools can be used for software aging analysis in laboratory environments, for example during stress tests before releasing a product, in order to pinpoint software aging bugs (such as memory leak bugs) and to provide useful information to developers to fix them.

In this chapter, we review the most important tools that have been adopted, both by researchers and by software developers, to detect software aging. We selected a pool of representative aging detection tools from the SAR literature, including from international conferences on dependability (DSN, ISSRE, SRDS), conferences and journals on software engineering, and the WoSAR workshop, the main international event devoted to SAR research. Moreover, we complemented the pool of tools with popular commercial tools and tools from technical sources by developers, such as blogs. We included tools for native software, such as systems software written in C and C++, which monitor resource consumption at the OS level and probe software internals, such as heap allocations. In addition, we included tools for Java software, such as web and enterprise applications, which monitor performance and resource consumption at the JVM level.

The tools discussed in this chapter are summarized in Table 11.1. We classified these tools with respect to the following aspects:

- **Availability**: We point out whether the tool has been publicly distributed as *open-source* software, distributed as a *commercial product*, or presented as a *research* solution in scientific papers.
- **Target**: We distinguish between tools for C/C++ software (e.g., native applications for the UNIX or Linux OSes), and Java software (including tools targeting applications, and tools targeting the underlying JVM).
- **Lifecycle phase**: We point out whether the tool is meant to be used during the *testing* of software (i.e., before deploying the software, developers can use the tool to study software aging in a controlled environment, and to pinpoint aging bugs); or whether the tool is intended to be applied during the *operation* of the software (i.e., after deploying the software at the users' site). *Testing* tools typically provide more detailed information, but at a high computational cost (e.g., ten times or more the execution time without the tool); *Operational* tools have a moderate computational overhead (e.g., a few percentage points of CPU and memory utilization), and are designed to collect aggregate metrics about resource utilization, in order to detect the onset of software aging in production and to trigger software rejuvenation.
- **Monitored aging effects**: Most of the tools surveyed analyze the impact of software aging on *memory consumption*, and point out *memory leaks* and their originating bugs; other tools also monitored the *consumption of OS resources* (such as the file system, the networking stack, etc.) and *application performance metrics* (such as the latency and throughput of client-server applications).

Table 11.1. Overview of tools for software aging analysis.

Tool	Availability	Target	Lifecycle phase	Monitored aging effects	Monitoring technique
SNMP-based PFM [1]	Research tool	UNIX systems and applications	Operation	OS resource consumption	OS metrics polling
Valgrind/Memcheck [3, 4]	Open-source tool	C/C++ applications	Testing	Memory leaks, memory management bugs	Dynamic binary instrumentation
SystemTap [6, 7, 8, 9]	Open-source tool	Linux kernel and applications	Testing, Operation	Memory fragmentation, numerical overflows	OS program debugging mechanisms
sysmon/SRA [12]	Research tool	Server applications	Operation	Memory consumption	OS metrics polling
VM-REJUV [13, 14, 15]	Research tool	Server applications	Operation	OS resource consumption, application performance	OS metrics polling, error logs, proxy-based perf. metrics
xSeries SRA [11]	Commercial tool	Server applications	Operation	OS resource consumption	OS metrics polling
VerComp [17, 18, 19]	Research tool	Server applications	Testing	Memory leaks	OS metrics polling
DynamoRIO/Dr. Memory [24]	Open-source tool	C/C++ applications	Testing	Memory leaks, memory management bugs	Dynamic binary instrumentation
AddressSanitizer [25]	Open-source tool	C/C++ applications	Testing	Memory leaks, memory management bugs	Compile-time instrumentation
Insure++ [22]	Commercial tool	C/C++ applications	Testing	Memory leaks, memory management bugs	Compile-time instrumentation
PurifyPlus [23]	Commercial tool	C/C++ applications	Testing	Memory leaks, memory management bugs	Link-time binary instrumentation
LeakBot [32]	Research tool	Java applications	Testing	Memory leaks	Heap snapshots
plumbr [34, 35, 36]	Commercial tool	Java applications	Testing, Operation	Memory leaks, application performance	Bytecode instrumentation, JVM debug interfaces
Eclipse Memory Analyzer [38, 39, 43]	Open-source tool	Java applications	Testing	Memory leaks	Heap snapshots
JVMMon [44]	Research tool	Java Virtual Machine	Testing, Operation	Memory consumption, JVM performance	JVM debug interfaces, bytecode instrumentation
PerfBlower [48]	Research tool	Java applications	Testing, Operation	Configurable due to own DSL	JVM debug interfaces, bytecode instrumentation
YourKit [49]	Commercial tool	Java applications	Testing, Operation	Memory leaks	Heap snapshots, bytecode instrumentation, exception telemetry

- **Monitoring technique**: In the case of C/C++ software, the tools often *periodically poll the OS* to collect information about resource utilization. More advanced tools leverage program analysis techniques based on the *instrumentation* of the target application (e.g., *static instrumentation* when the application is compiled or linked, or *dynamic instrumentation* at run-time). In the case of Java software, the tools collect *snapshots of heap memory* from the JVM; and *instrument the code* and *query the JVM debug interface* to collect selected information and events from the application and from the JVM.

The rest of this chapter is divided into two parts: tools for C/C++ software (Section 11.2), and tools for Java software (Section 11.3). Each section is further divided into subsections, one per tool surveyed. For each tool, we provide overviews of how it works, and how it has been applied to analyze real software aging issues.

11.2. C and C++ Applications

11.2.1. *SNMP-Based Proactive Fault Management (PFM) Tool*

11.2.1.1. *Overview*

In an early work on software aging analysis, which influenced the design of many aging monitoring tools, Garg *et al.* [1] developed a tool for the live monitoring of UNIX workstations in a local-area network. This distributed monitoring tool collects data on OS system resource usage and system activity at regular intervals. It was based on the Simple Network Management Protocol (SNMP) standard for network management services [2], in order to inter-operate with multiple platforms.

In this protocol, a *PFM agent* runs in the background on each monitored workstation, and listens for requests from a *PFM manager*, which gathers information from all of the agents. The information exchanged between the manager and the agents follows a schema defined in the *PFM Management Information Base* (MIB). The MIB defines the objects that are used to determine the health of a UNIX workstation (see Fig. 11.1).

The "pfmMIB" is a branch of the wider object tree of an organization that defines seven categories of objects, including:

- **hostID**: General, constant information about the node (name, OS release, hardware name, etc.).

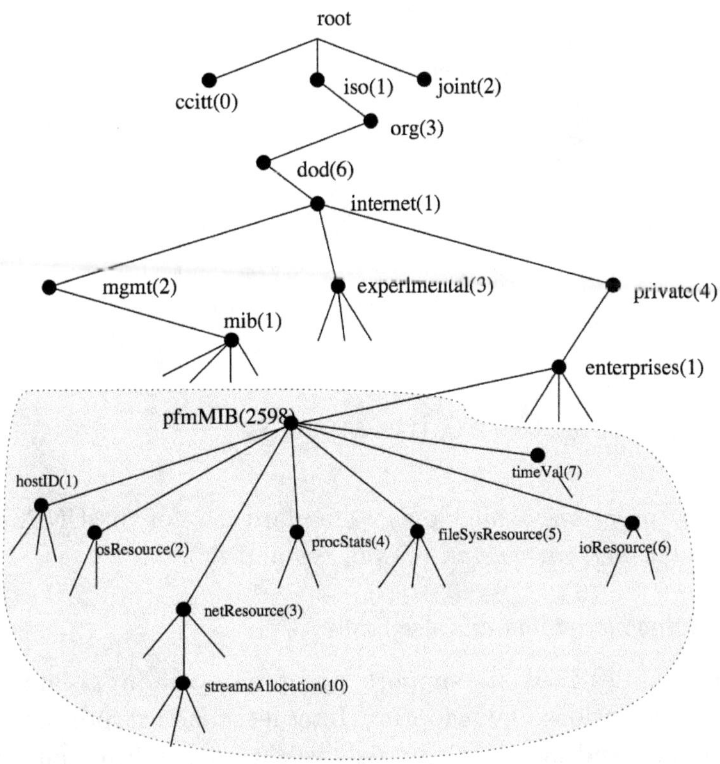

Fig. 11.1. Management Information Base (MIB) in the PFM monitoring tool.

- **osResource**: The state of key OS resources, including the swap space utilization, the file table size, the real memory free, and the number of processes.
- **netResource**: The state of network-related resources, such as queue utilization and the number of active streams.
- **procStats**: Objects with the state of processes running on the machine.
- **fileSysResource**: The state of filesystem-related resources, such as the size and the utilization of the */tmp* directory.
- **ioResource**: Objects with information about the terminal devices and disk I/O activity.
- **timeVal**: The current day and time, and the node uptime.

The PFM manager queries an agent either periodically, or on demand on behalf of the network administrator. In turn, the PFM agent executes OS commands to get the requested information (Fig. 11.2), by executing various

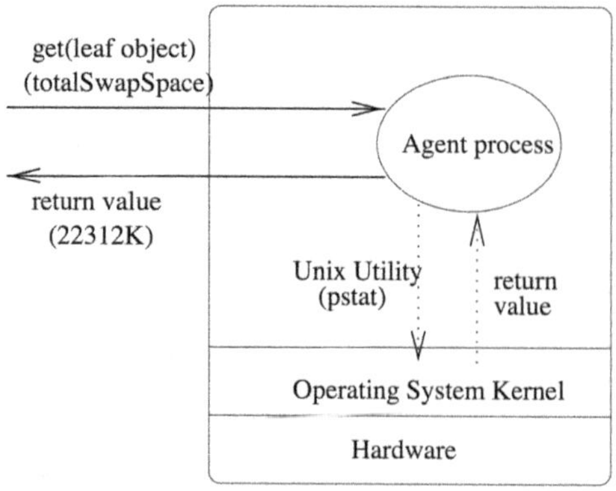

Fig. 11.2. PFM agent.

UNIX utility programs available as a standard part of the UNIX OS (such as *pstat*, *iostat*, *netstat*, *vmstat*, *nfsstat*, *top* and *df*).

11.2.1.2. *Aging symptoms and use cases*

The tool was designed to support aging analysis in a large network of UNIX workstations, by adopting Internet-standard protocols to ease interoperability, and by adopting a lightweight approach to gauge the state of these nodes. These features make this tool suitable to be deployed in the operational environment, and to detect aging effects in live systems. In particular, this kind of tool can be adopted to identify any *trend* in resource utilization, that is, a long-term increase or decrease of the values that denote a gradual resource exhaustion, which will cause aging-related failures. The aging trends can be found either by visual analysis of the data; or by applying classical time series analysis techniques on the data, such as linear and periodic dependency analysis, and trend detection and estimation. Moreover, the data collected can also provide information on the system activity, such as the system workload at the time of aging failures. For example, the workload for a UNIX system can be quantified in terms of running processes, network and storage utilization, number of interrupt requests, number of page faults, etc.

11.2.1.3. *Applications*

Garg *et al.* [1] used the SNMP-based PFM tool to analyze software aging phenomena in a network of 8 UNIX workstations at Duke University, over a period of 53 days. The values for all objects were collected every 15 minutes.

The frequency of data collection is a compromise between the accuracy of view and the overhead of collecting data. The machines experienced 12 outages, of which half could be attributed to software aging (as resources were nearing exhaustion before the failure). Figure 11.3 shows two examples of resource consumption trends that were observed using the distributed monitoring tool.

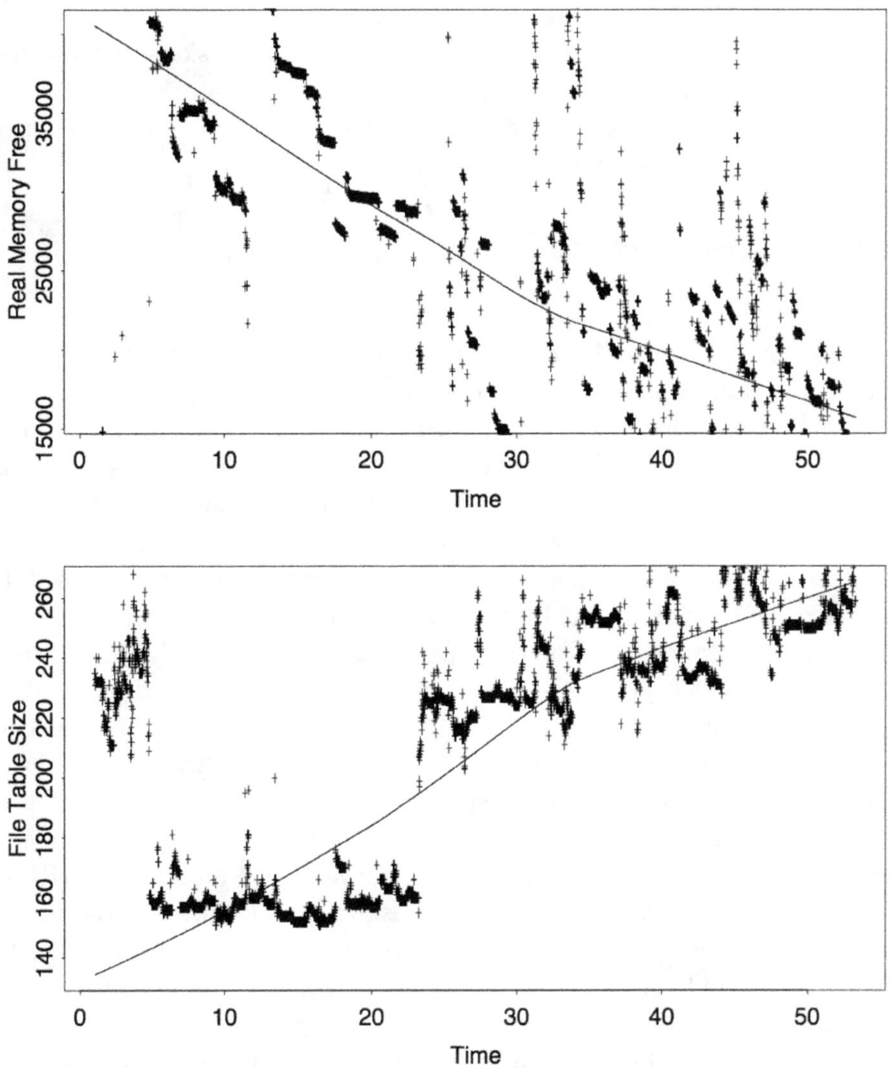

Fig. 11.3. Non-parametric regression smoothing for free memory and file table size, using data from the SNMP-based PFM tool.

The data also enabled a quantitative analysis of software aging problems, including:

- The autocorrelation function of the time series indicates that many of the series exhibit daily and weekly periodicity (due to seasonal usage patterns). Therefore, there is a need to factor out the periodic component when estimating the intensity of the aging trend.
- The Mann-Kendall hypothesis test confirmed that indeed the time series exhibited an increasing or decreasing trend.
- Using the Sen's procedure, the authors estimated the slope of the trends (i.e., the rate of resource consumption), and the *time-to-exhaustion* (TTE) of the resources. They found that physical memory and swap space exhibited the highest trends and the lowest TTE.

11.2.2. *Valgrind and Memcheck*

11.2.2.1. *Overview*

Valgrind [3] is a general framework for building program analysis tools (such as profiles, visualizers, and checkers). The official Valgrind distribution includes a framework core and a toolsuite built on top of this core. These tools serve for debugging (in particular, bugs in memory management and synchronization) and profiling (such as cache utilization and call graphs). *Memcheck* is the most widely-used tool in Valgrind (and often the name Valgrind is used synonymously with Memcheck), and can be used for analyzing memory leak bugs that cause software aging.

Memcheck (and the Valgrind framework) perform *dynamic binary analysis* of C/C++ programs, that is, a program is analyzed at run-time (by exercising it with a workload) and by looking at its machine-code instructions. This is accomplished by running the program on a virtual machine environment, in a manner similar to Java programs running on top of a JVM. The Valgrind VM takes one block at a time of machine-code instructions, and translates them into an *intermediate representation* (IR, see Fig. 11.4). Then, the Valgrind tools (such as Memcheck) introduce additional instructions in the IR for checking or profiling the program. Finally, the block is translated back into machine-code instructions and executed on the physical CPU.

Memcheck uses the Valgrind framework to keep track of memory areas allocated and referenced by the program, in order to detect memory management bugs (such as memory leaks, buffer overruns, double frees, use of

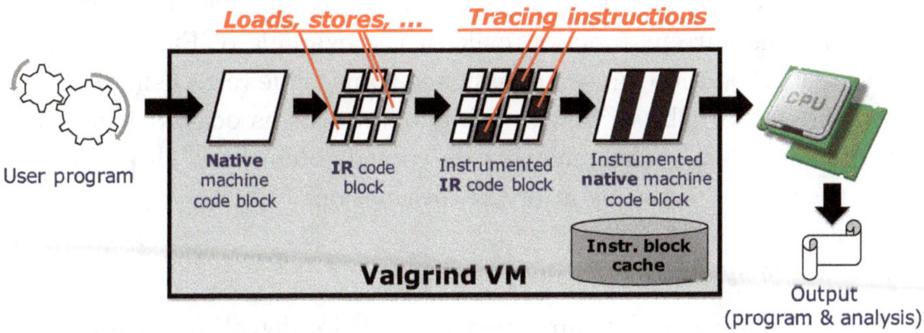

Fig. 11.4. Overview of dynamic binary analysis in Valgrind.

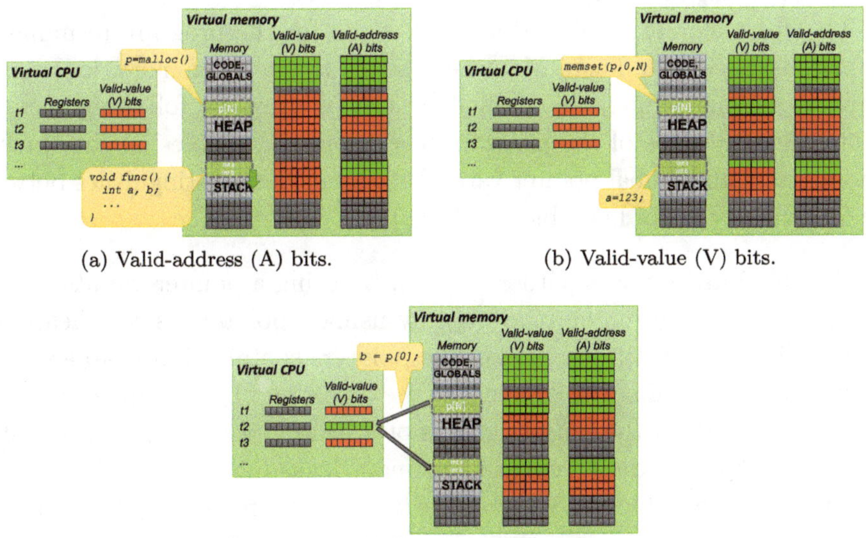

(a) Valid-address (A) bits.

(b) Valid-value (V) bits.

(c) Propagation of valid-value (V) bits.

Fig. 11.5. Tracking memory status in Memcheck.

uninitialized memory, etc.). In Memcheck, every bit of data processed, stored and handled by the program (either in CPU registers or main memory) has an associated *valid-value* (V) bit, which denotes whether or not the accompanying bit has a legitimate value (i.e., the memory has been assigned a value at a given point of execution). In addition, all bytes in memory (but not in the CPU) have an associated *valid-address* (A) bit. This bit indicates whether or not the program can legitimately read or write that location (e.g., the data is in a heap memory area allocated through *malloc*; or the data is within the current stack area). In the example of Fig. 11.5(a), the A bits are set by Memcheck for the area allocated by *malloc* and for the stack frame allocated by the current function call. In the example of Fig. 11.5(b), the V bits are set when these areas are assigned some value (e.g., using *memset*). Finally, Fig. 11.5(c) shows that a V bit follows the associated memory bit across the execution. When memory is copied, Memcheck also copies the V-bit of the source to the V-bit of the destination.

11.2.2.2. *Aging symptoms and use cases*

Memcheck can support software aging analysis by detecting memory leaks, i.e., heap blocks that are not released when they are no longer needed, and that could accumulate over time (thus causing resource exhaustion and performance degradation).

To detect memory leaks, Memcheck waits for the program termination or for a user request. Then, Memcheck scans the heap memory, looking for heap blocks that cannot be reached by the program by following *memory pointers* in the scope of the program (e.g., pointer variables on the stack of the program, and global pointer variables). Memcheck distinguishes between the following types of heap blocks (Fig. 11.6):

- **Still reachable** blocks, either *directly*, by using a pointer variable in the scope of the program, or *indirectly*, by using a pointer inside a heap area which, in turn, is still reachable. The pointers contained in heap areas are detected by scanning the contents of the areas, and by looking for memory words that match the initial address of a heap block. In Memcheck, still-reachable blocks do not represent memory leaks.
- **Definitely lost** blocks, either *directly* (i.e., there is no pointer to the block) or *indirectly* (i.e., there are pointers to the block, but it still cannot be reached by following pointers in the scope of the program). The definitely-lost blocks must be considered memory leaks, since they consume memory but do not contribute in any way to the correct execution of the program (since the program cannot refer to these blocks). Memcheck is also able to report which instruction of the program allocated the leaked block, in order to ease debugging.
- **Possibly lost** blocks. In this case, Memcheck cannot decide whether a heap block is not reachable. These are the cases of heap blocks that are pointed to by *interior pointers* (*i-p*), that is, pointers that contain an address in the middle of the heap block (rather than the initial address of the heap block). Interior pointers can be intentional: for example, in the case of special C++ entities such as the *std::string* class, the first three

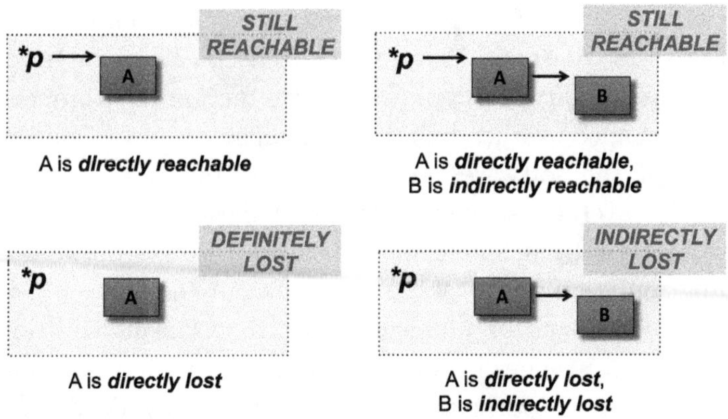

(a) Reachable and lost blocks.

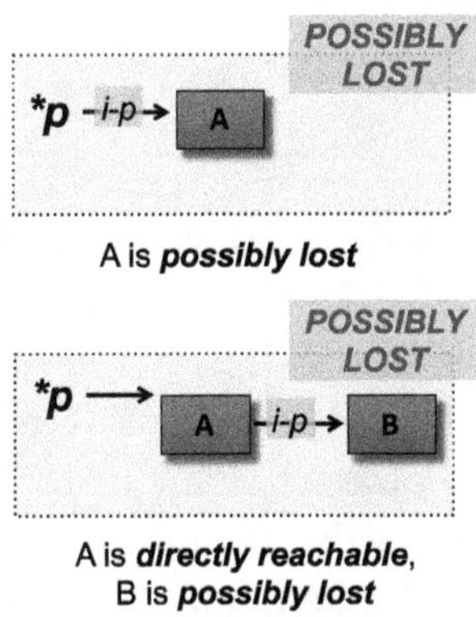

(b) Possibly lost blocks.

Fig. 11.6. Reachability of heap memory areas.

words of the heap area contain the string length, capacity and a reference counter; thus, pointers to the string point to the fourth word in the heap area. However, interior pointers can also be unintentional: for example, a program variable with a random junk value which matches, by chance, a heap memory address. In the case of unintentional interior pointers, the heap block should be considered not reachable. However, Memcheck is unable to distinguish between intentional and unintentional *i-ps*, since it can only analyze machine-code instructions without any information on the source code of the program. Thus, possibly-lost blocks are reported separately from definitely-lost blocks, and need to be further investigated by the programmer.

The main use case of Valgrind/Memcheck is to debug memory leaks in laboratory tests. However, Valgrind/Memcheck cannot be used to detect aging symptoms in software deployed in production environments, due to the high performance overhead that could cause serious inconveniences for the end-users of the software. Performance tests on Valgrind/Memcheck report that the average slowdown of the Valgrind framework (including the Valgrind VM and machine-code translation) ranges between 2x and 9x (i.e., the program takes much more time to execute compared to its original duration); the slowdown for Memcheck (which performs additional checks on memory accesses) ranges between 13x and 47x, with a median slowdown of 26x. However, this overhead is often accepted by developers since it is rewarded by a higher bug-finding power, as shown by the widespread adoption of Valgrind in automated regression test suites in open-source projects [3].

11.2.2.3. *Applications*

An example application of Valgrind for software aging analysis has been presented in an experimental study by Carrozza *et al.* [4]. This experiment evaluated the effects of software aging in the context of a CORBA middleware (CARDAMOM) used in long-running applications for Air Traffic Control. This middleware adopts a modular architecture, in which services can be plugged to applications by including external libraries. Moreover, CARDAMOM is based on Off-The-Shelf (OTS) software, and in particular a third-party Object Request Broker (ORB) named TAO [5].

Valgrind has been used to pinpoint components in CARDAMOM that were responsible for memory consumption trends under stressful conditions. Two versions of CARDAMOM were considered: a public open-source Community Edition (CE) version of the platform, and a Development Version (DV) with improvements added in the course of the project. The tests were performed on a distributed client-server application using CARDAMOM services. Valgrind has been applied to break down the Total Memory Consumption (TMC) of the test application into two contributions: Intentional Memory Consumption (IMC) and Memory Definitely Lost (MDL).

The memory consumption of the client and server on CARDAMOM CE processes are shown in Table 11.2, which points out memory leaks in both processes, but especially in the client since it makes a more extensive usage of CARDAMOM libraries. Moreover, Table 11.3 provides details on the sources of memory leaks for CARDAMOM CE. Most of the leaks were

Table 11.2. Memory consumption (KB) for CARDAMOM CE processes.

	Client				Server		
	1 hour	2 hours	3 hours		1 hour	2 hours	3 hours
TMC	140,120	184,832	229,268	**TMC**	116,280	128,052	139,740
IMC	115,755	136,337	156,635	**IMC**	113,897	123,334	132,694
MDL	24,365	48,495	72,633	**MDL**	2,383	4,718	7,046

Table 11.3. Memory leaks for CARDAMOM CE.

(a) Client process.

Source Object	Leaked Bytes	Errors / Functions
libACE.so.5.4.1	31,826,000	1 / 1
libTAO.so.1.4.1	31,826,262	5 / 2
libcdmwcommon.so	29	1 / 1
libcdmwlbcommon.so	276	3 / 2
libcdmwlogging.so	10,723,932	52 / 1
libxerces-c1_3.so	24	1 / 1

(b) Server process.

Source Object	Leaked Bytes	Errors / Functions
libTAO.so.1.4.1	3,202	1 / 1
libcdmwcommon.so	29	1 / 1
libcdmwlbcommon.so	176	2 / 1
libcdmwlogging.so	7,212,140	16 / 1
libxerces-c1_3.so	24	1 / 1

Table 11.4. Memory consumption (KB) for CARDAMOM DV processes.

	Client				Server		
	1 hour	2 hours	3 hours		1 hour	2 hours	3 hours
TMC	153,108	202,768	252,604	**TMC**	140,336	174,704	210,240
IMC	152,930	202,414	252,074	**IMC**	140,332.8	174,700.8	210,236.8
MDL	178	354	530	**MDL**	3.2	3.2	3.2

due to the Trace service and the TAO ORB. In particular, memory leaks in TAO are affected by the volume of data transferred by the workload. Thus, the study hypothesized that leaks were hidden in the request serialization handling code. Memory usage reports helped to pinpoint the defects in CARDAMOM source code that caused memory leaks, which were reported to the CARDAMOM development team in order to get these bugs fixed.

Tables 11.4 and 11.5 provide the same information for tests on CARDAMOM DV. This version achieved a significant reduction of the MDL. The main source of memory leaks in CARDAMOM CE (i.e., the shared library code of the Trace service) was removed. Nevertheless, the TMC in CARDAMOM DV was even greater, since unused memory was still referenced by CARDAMOM during execution. The study hypothesized that

Table 11.5. Memory leaks for CARDAMOM DV.

(a) Client process.

Source Object	Leaked Bytes	Errors / Functions
libACE.so.5.5.1	362, 082	2 / 1
libTAO.so.1.5.1	181, 276	5 / 2
libcdmwlbcommon.so	276	3 / 2

(b) Server process.

Source Object	Leaked Bytes	Errors / Functions
libcdmwlbcommon.so	3, 321	2 / 1

CARDAMOM developers prevented memory leaks by continuously storing references to the memory allocated (e.g., by means of the C++ "smart pointers" feature or abstract data types such as STL containers), in order to delay deallocation of unnecessary memory. This approach can inadvertently lead to memory exhaustion if deallocation does not occur on time (e.g., elements within an STL container are never deleted), as in the case of CARDAMOM DV. Moreover, the experiment pointed out that memory leaks were still present in the TAO library, since CARDAMOM developers were unable to correct these defects located in a third-party OTS component.

11.2.3. *SystemTap and Kprobes*

11.2.3.1. *Overview*

SystemTap [6] is a tool for the Linux OS that can collect information at run-time from the Linux kernel and user-space processes. This tool takes advantage of *Kprobes* [7], which is a debugging mechanism provided by the Linux kernel. These tools can intercept events that occur in the kernel or in user-space processes, such as the invocation of system calls, an incoming packet from the network, the expiration of a timer, and the allocation of new memory areas, for troubleshooting purposes.

These tools allow the user to easily customize which events to monitor, and which information should be collected when an event occurs. The tools *dynamically* insert new routines in the Linux kernel (i.e., without requiring the modification of the source code of the kernel and its rebuilding and restarting), which are invoked on the occurrence of selected events. These routines are similar to *breakpoint handling* in debuggers, in which the execution of a program is stopped when the execution reaches a user-defined statement of the program, in order to allow the user to inspect the state of the process. In SystemTap and Kprobes, the user can customize both the contents of the routine, and the events that will trigger the routine.

Kprobes is a low-level mechanism for probing the execution of kernel/ user code. Similar to a debugger, it instruments the instruction to be probed

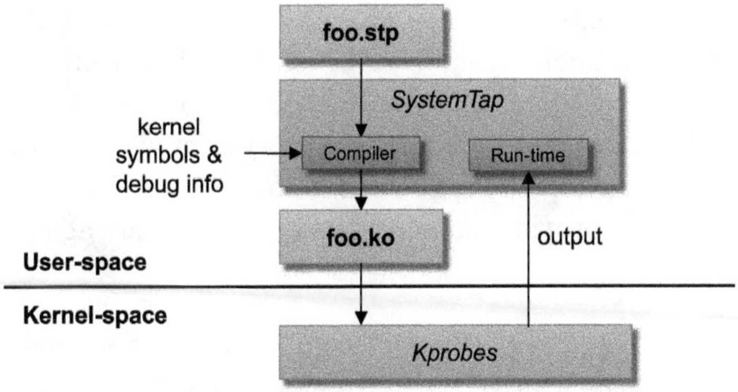

Fig. 11.7. Overview of SystemTap and Kprobes.

(i.e., an instruction that is executed when the event of interest happens, such as the entry point of a system call, or the handler for incoming packets). This instruction is replaced with a breakpoint instruction that will trigger an exception handler when the instruction is executed by the CPU; in turn, the handler will invoke the routine supplied by the user.

SystemTap is a higher-level tool that makes Kprobes easier to use and more powerful. Their relationship is shown in Fig. 11.7. SystemTap provides a custom language, similar to popular scripting languages, to write probing routines (in place of using the C language, as in Kprobes). Moreover, SystemTap provides utilities to automatically translate scripts (*.stp*) into kernel modules (*.ko*), to run them, and to efficiently transfer information (e.g., data logged by the user routines) from kernel-space to user-space. Moreover, SystemTap simplifies the task of writing routines by leveraging input debugging information for the Linux kernel (such as the location of key functions and variables in kernel code) and pre-defined probe points for the Linux kernel and for other popular open-source software, such as the Postgres DBMS and the Python interpreter; and by providing high-level programming constructs for inspecting kernel data structures (e.g., operators for safely de-referencing pointers and structure fields).

11.2.3.2. *Aging symptoms and use cases*

The SystemTap and Kprobes tools only introduce a moderate overhead on execution (e.g., the cost of triggering exceptions, executing the probe routine, and transferring data to user-space). This overhead is considered reasonable for use in production environments for problem diagnosis. This overhead can also be acceptable for live monitoring purposes, assuming that the frequency of the monitored events is not too high. Moreover, these tools can also be useful for testing and debugging in laboratory environments.

These tools can also support the analysis of software aging, at a much finer granularity than other tools that collect system-wide metrics. They can collect performance and resource consumption metrics that are application-specific and that can provide more insights about software aging phenomena. For example:

- Probes can be installed at the service interface of a system, in order to measure the time at which, respectively, the incoming service requests are received and completed. For example, probes can be inserted at the entry and exit points of RPCs and system calls. In turn, these measures allow one to derive useful metrics such as the service rate, latency, etc.
- Probes can be installed at resource allocation/deallocation points, in order to track memory leaks and, in general, suspicious trends in resource utilization.
- Probes can be triggered periodically to sample the contents of selected internal variables, which reflect the health status of the system.

11.2.3.3. *Applications*

Matias *et al.* [8] adopted SystemTap and Kprobes to point out software aging effects inside the Linux kernel. In a first experiment (see Fig. 11.8(a)), they reproduced a memory leak bug in the Linux networking subsystem, in which the kernel leaked "socket buffers" (*SKB*s, which are data structures that hold network packets) when it received malformed multicast packets. They used SystemTap and Kprobes to keep track of SKBs that were being allocated (*__alloc_skb* and *__alloc_clone*) and deallocated (*__kfree_skb*) during the experiment, showing an accumulation of stale SKBs.

In a second round of experiments, they tracked memory fragmentation events reported by the Linux kernel. A memory fragmentation event (*extfrag*) occurs when the kernel tries to allocate a large number of contiguous physical pages of memory, but there is no available group of pages (for example, the free memory space may be fragmented among several small non-contiguous groups of pages), thus requiring page migration. The Linux kernel exposes a trace point (*mm_page_alloc_extfrag*) to which SystemTap connects to, which also provides additional information such as the "allocation order" (i.e., the power-of-two closest to the number of pages that need to be allocated, which is used by the Linux memory allocator). In these experiments, the authors exercised the kernel with

```
global alloc, free

function dump(){
    printf("\nTotal SKB\n")
    printf("---------\n")
    printf("Allocated: %d\n", alloc);
    printf("Freed : %d\n", free);
    printf("Diff : %d\n", alloc - free);
}

probe kernel.function("__alloc_skb"){
    alloc += 1
}
probe kernel.function("__skb_clone"){
    alloc += 1
}
probe kernel.function("__kfree_skb"){
    free += 1
}
probe timer.s(2){
    dump()
}
probe end{
    dump()
}
```

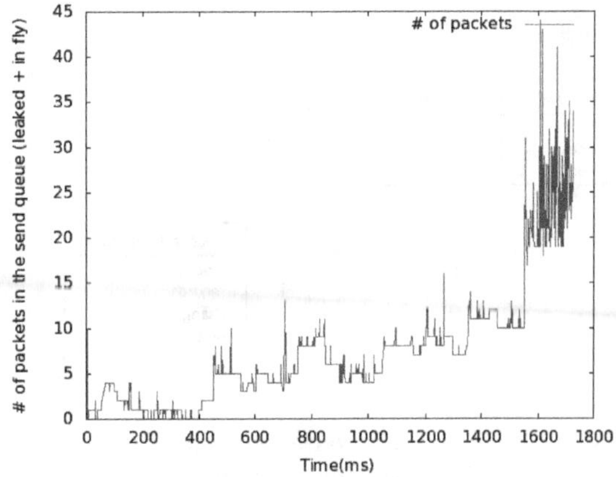

(a) Memory leaks in the Linux networking subsystem.

```
probe kernel.trace("mm_page_alloc_extfrag") {

   printf("Ext. fragmentation event: %d, %d\n",
         $alloc_order, $fallback_order);

}
```

LTP process	# extfrag events
growfiles	1483
mtest01	772
hackbench	67
msgctl10	29
ms3gctl09	3
rm	3
fs_racer_file_l	3
fcntl14_64	1
page01	1
pth_str02	1
msgctl11	1
ls	1

(b) Memory fragmentation events.

Fig. 11.8. Examples of probing software aging symptoms in the Linux kernel.

several test programs from the Linux Test Project [9], and identified the test programs that triggered fragmentation events. This knowledge is useful to reproduce memory fragmentation problems and to devise better memory management algorithms (e.g., to counteract the gradual memory fragmentation).

Cotroneo and Natella [10] also used SystemTap to analyze software aging effects. They studied aging in a user-space application (the MySQL DBMS), by monitoring for trends in integer variables (such as variables representing the table size). In the worst case, integer values can exceed the maximum representable value by their integer type, causing a numerical overflow. They

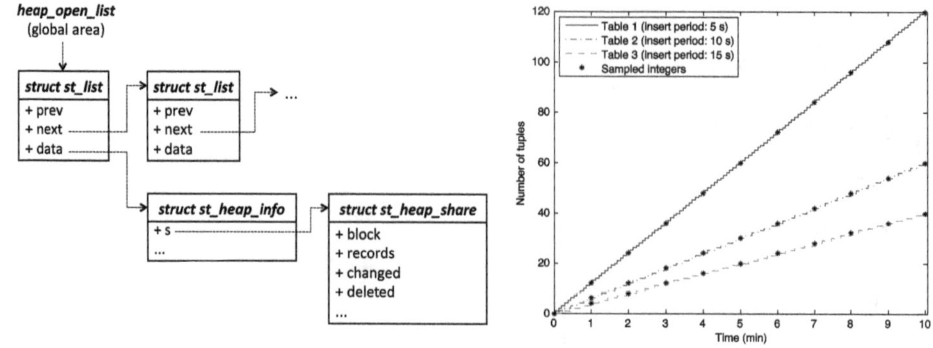

Fig. 11.9. Example of data structures to be monitored for keeping track of table size in the MySQL Memory storage engine.

monitored the size of tables managed by the memory storage engine for MySQL [11], which stores data in RAM memory in order to avoid disk I/O. This storage engine can be exposed to the problem of over-growing tables, since memory is a relatively scarce resource.

Figure 11.9 shows the data structure that was monitored with SystemTap to track the table size. The *heap_open_list* is a global pointer, which references the first element of a linked list; each element in the list, in turn, references a structure that represents a table (*struct st_heap_info*), where *struct st_heap_share* contains information about the table (e.g., the *records* field provides the number of tuples in the table) and its actual data (e.g., the *block* field). Therefore, the monitoring tool can obtain the number of tuples by following pointers, starting from the *heap_open_list* pointer in the global area. This information can be used to identify aging trends that would be invisible or difficult to diagnose with system-wide metrics (such as the total memory consumption of the MySQL process).

11.2.4. *Other Tools*

In this section, we briefly discuss other tools for the software aging analysis of C/C++ software, which could not be presented in this chapter because of space limitations. In particular, it is important to mention the *xSeries Software Rejuvenation Agent (SRA)* [12], which is a proprietary product developed by IBM in cooperation with the authors of the SNMP-based PFM tool (Section 11.2.1). The xSeries SRA uses SNMP to collect resource utilization metrics from a production environment; moreover, the tool embeds additional resource forecasting techniques (such as piecewise regression models) to forecast aging failures, and a user-friendly graphical interface to interpret the model and to schedule rejuvenation at a convenient time. Among the academic solutions, it is worth mentioning the *sysmon SRA* [13], which has been designed to monitor software aging in the Apache HTTPD web-server, and to rejuvenate its worker processes to keep low memory consumption; and the VM-REJUV framework [14–16], which is a distributed architecture for rejuvenating complex web-applications (e.g., based on J2EE) by monitoring not only resource utilization, but also performance (e.g., in terms of service latency, by measuring HTTP response times through a proxy). Related to this approach is the work by Avritzer *et al.* [17] on using customer-affecting metric monitoring to trigger rejuvenation before performance degradation becomes too severe. Finally, the approach VerComp exploits anomaly detection between software versions [18, 19]. In detail, it compares the memory-related behavior of versions of software under development, and identifies anomalies which can indicate potential leaks in a newer software version. The technique is tailored to modern software development processes like integration testing, and can exploit regular software tests. It can perform anomaly detection on the whole application level, as well as on the level of object allocation sites (as support for root-cause analysis and debugging). Research prototypes implementing this method exist for Java [20–22] as well as for C/C++ [18, 19].

In the field of testing and debugging tools, there are several open-source and commercial tools that aim to identify the root causes of memory leaks and other memory management bugs. Among them, it is worth mentioning the well-known commercial tools *Insure++* [23] and *PurifyPlus* [24], and the open-source tools *Dr. Memory* [25] and *AddressSanitizer* (and the related tools *MemorySanitizer* and *LeakSanitizer* from the same family) [26]. These tools adopt different techniques for instrumenting applications at compile-, link-, and run-time, and achieve different trade-offs in terms of the wealth of memory management bugs addressed and execution overhead. Moreover, the commercial tools provide a tight integration with popular IDEs, and support advanced visualizations to ease the identification of memory management bugs.

11.3. Java Applications

Despite language-supported memory management, memory leaks in Java are a serious and widespread issue, plaguing mature open-source software [27], as well as industrial projects [28]. Memory leak detection approaches for Java can be grouped into several categories [29]:

- detection of object and heap growth
- analysis of captured states (typically heap dumps)
- discovery of object staleness
- static analysis of the source code
- methods combining several of the techniques above, for example static and dynamic analysis

In this chapter we focus on tools based on the first two approaches, as those have turned out to strike a good balance between accuracy and practical applicability. In addition to the tools described there are many prototypical implementations discussed in research papers [28]. These differ in their degree of maturity, amount of necessary instrumentation, runtime overhead, and intrusiveness, all being important factors for widespread acceptance of such tools. For example, several approaches [30–32] for staleness detection assume that a research Java Virtual Machine such as Jikes RVM can be used in the diagnosis process, which clearly limits their adoption in industrial scenarios.

11.3.1. *LeakBot*

11.3.1.1. *Overview*

LeakBot is an approach and tool by Mitchell and Sevitsky [33] for memory leak detection based on an analysis of captured states. This technique acquires partial heap dumps, originally via an agent based on the JVMPI profiling interface.[a] These dumps are analyzed in multiple phases, ordered from less to more expensive. Contrary to many other techniques, LeakBot analyses not only individual objects but whole data structures, and analyses their evolution and growth over multiple heap dumps. LeakBot first identifies unique *leak roots*, i.e. objects at the head of a leaking data structure, see Fig. 11.10. Subsequently, so-called *co-evolving regions* under each such leak root are found, in order to distinguish multiple leak problems in the same data structure.

[a]The Java Virtual Machine Profiling Interface (JVMPI) has been deprecated since SDK version 1.5.0 and was replaced by the Java Virtual Machine Tool Interface (JVMTI) in 2004.

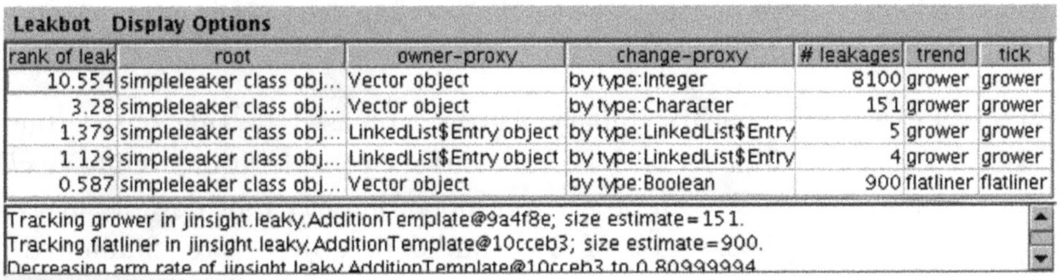

Fig. 11.10. Screenshot of the results stated by the LeakBot tool (taken from [33]). Each row describes a suspicious co-evolving region with its rank, the leak root, and further properties like the growth trend.

Table 11.6. Cumulative filtering effectiveness of the binary metrics used in phase one of the LeakBot approach for five large applications.

		# Objects Remaining After				
Application Name	#Original Objects	$S_1 \dots S_4$	T_1	T_2	T_3	T_4
IDE	350 136	25 653	99	99	29	10
phone company	267 956	16 346	73	73	72	29
brokerage	838 912	26 291	97	82	81	67
brokerage2	1 015 112	12 020	102	102	64	17
finance	1 320 953	106 900	579	519	518	242

11.3.1.2. *Approach details*

LeakBot analysis is performed in three phases: first, potential leak roots are identified and ranked. In phases two and three, the data structures specified by leak roots are further investigated to identify and isolate leak regions. This tool requires multiple heap snapshots (at least one taken early in the run) as runtime data. These snapshots are used to construct a full or partial *reference graph*, i.e. a directed graph constituted by outgoing references of objects. The first two phases require at least two snapshots to construct a full reference graph, while in the last phase, only a part of the reference graph is monitored, namely the objects we need to look at to understand how suspicious regions evolve.

Phase one. At first, objects and data structures featuring growth are identified from a series of the few heap snapshots. These are then filtered and ranked in three substeps described below. In this process, the number of potential leak roots is reduced from millions to a few hundred (see Table 11.6), and the remaining objects are ranked. Each of the steps is computationally more expensive than the previous one, yet it operates on a smaller number of objects.

Step 1. First, eight "cheap" binary metrics are used to rule out certain objects or data structures from further considerations. Only if *all* eight metrics rate an object as a potential leak root does it survive this step (thus, most of the candidate objects are eliminated). Four metrics capture the structural properties of the objects in the reference graph, and four others quantify the temporal properties of the objects in this graph. An example for a structural metric S_2 is an indicator of whether an object is a Java array ("primitive", i.e. not a List container). Since an array has a fixed number of elements at creation, it cannot be a leak root. The temporal metric T_1 filters out all candidates which own either only older objects (such candidates can be pools or other unchanging data structures), *or* which own only new objects (such candidates are likely to be transient data structures, caught by a heap dump during processing).

Step 2. The second step ranks the remaining candidate leak roots by a mixture of nine attributes, which are specific for particular data structures. In addition, each attribute value is *gated*: only if an attribute has a strongly negative value, does the gate assign a negative rank. Otherwise, the attribute "accepts" the object as a leak root candidate without influencing its rank. Examples of the attributes include: G_2, which excludes objects reachable from on-stack roots, or G_8, which strongly discounts objects that transitively reference (or "own") different datatypes in subsequent heap snapshots.

Step 3. In the final step of filtering and ranking leak roots, ranks computed in Step 2 are refined using *iterative fixpoint ranking*. The key observation here is that the rank of an object as computed in Step 2 depends on the rank of other objects. For example, if object A is a unique owner of a leaking data structure B, the high rank of B is likely to imply a high rank for A. However, only A should be identified as a leak root and receive a high rank. In this step, ranks of objects linked by the "is-owner-of" relation (or the so-called domination relation) are adjusted iteratively until the rank values reach fixpoints. In this way, enclosing data structures receive higher ranks then their (suspicious) children (relations in the reference graph).

Phase two. The purpose of this phase is to identify and characterize so-called *co-evolving regions* (CERs), i.e. maximally large groups of objects under one leak root that evolve in a coherent and unique way. The motivation is that one leak root might identify a data structure with multiple leaks. The authors distinguish four types of region evolution: monotonic growth, monotonic shrinkage, bounded-changing constituency, and bounded-fixed constituency [33, Section 11.4].

The details of identifying CERs are rather involved, and so we only outline this process. *Fringe* is a set of edges in the reference graph which define a boundary between older and recently created objects. A path P_m from a leak root m to any recently created object x in m's vicinity must cross the fringe at least once. We can characterize this path from m to x by two important waypoints: the *owner-proxy*, and the *change-proxy*. The earlier is a stable (long-lived) object on the path P_m close to the fringe on the "old" side (i.e. same side as m), and the latter is a stable object on P_m close to the fringe on the "new" side of the fringe (i.e. same side as x). Finally, two objects are in the same region, if they share the same leak root and the same owner-proxy, and if their change-proxies have the same datatype.

For each leak root m ranked above a certain threshold, LeakBot identifies and ranks all co-evolving regions in the data structure owned by m. Essentially, the rank of a CER increases with the rank of its root, with the number of distinct data substructures in the region, and with the growth of the number of such substructures [33, Section 11.4.2].

Phase three. In this optional phase LeakBot monitors the evolution of previously identified co-evolving regions in order to refine the analysis. It traverses online (via separate threads) paths in the reference graph which characterize the suspicious CERs (in particular, owner-proxies and change-proxies of these paths are monitored). In this way, LeakBot can update information on the evolution type of each CER, depending whether objects are added, removed, or replaced. The results of this continuous yet low-overhead analysis are shown to the user as illustrated in Fig. 11.10. The last two columns in this table indicate whether a CER grows, shrinks, or oscillates.

11.3.1.3. *Use cases and applications*

The LeakBot approach is targeted at very large and framework-intensive Java applications, for example server-side e-Business applications using J2EE. Such applications intentionally retain large numbers of objects in caches, making it difficult to detect leaks with traditional tools such as profilers. Contrary to this, LeakBot has been reported to accurately pinpoint leak roots even with very slow growth within a few minutes. The underlying technology was first integrated into IBM Rational Application Developer (IRAD) 6.0 in June 2005, but removed from the software in release 7.0. It is now available as the Memory Dump Diagnostic for Java (MDD4J) tool for IBM Tivoli Composite Application Manager for Application Diagnostics.[b]

In the original paper [33], the LeakBot is evaluated on one internal IBM application (IDE), and four applications of IBM customers, see Table 11.6. As shown in this table, even for a heap dump with more than one million objects, LeakBot can reduce the number of potential leak roots to only a few hundred. Among these, only the highest-ranked objects are considered in phases two and three. This yields a short list of suspicious co-evolving regions as shown in Fig. 11.10.

Another source [34] reports that the IRAD tool saves hours of working time (per case) for experienced software engineers. In the six customer applications considered, the number of objects in the heap dump ranged from 41 700 to more than 8 million. The time required by LeakBoat for leak diagnosis ranged between 39 and 9 100 seconds, respectively.

11.3.2. *Plumbr*

11.3.2.1. *Overview and approach*

The commercial tool Plumbr[c] has been conceived to work under industrial JVM implementations (such as HotSpot of OpenJDK) with little performance penalty and to provide support for automatic end-to-end leak detection. It is based on a growth analysis method introduced by Šor *et al.* [36].

In detail, Plumbr monitors the age of live objects grouped by object allocation site (i.e. a code fragment creating new objects or cloning them). If the live objects created by a specific site feature a wide spectrum of ages, they are likely to constitute leaks. The intuition here is that creating new objects should not be necessary if old objects are still not disposed, and such a pattern neither fits to the behavior of caches nor to sites creating objects temporarily. The authors provide empirical evidence based on data (from 1272 different customers [35]) that leaky allocation sites do indeed instantiate objects with such age distributions.

[b]IBM Tivoli Composite Application Manager for Application Diagnostics, Version 7.1.0.4.
[c]http://plumbr.eu

To formalize, we need to describe a *GenCount*-metric [35]. Let $GC = (gc_1, gc_2, \ldots, gc_n)$ denote the set of consecutive garbage collections, and let A be the set of allocation sites of the application. If an object is created before gc_1, it is said to belong to *generation* 0. If it is created between gc_i and gc_{i+1}, it belongs to *generation* i. We introduce a function G which maps an allocation site $as \in A$ and an integer $j \in \{0, \ldots n\}$ to the set $\{0,1\}^j$ (i.e. $G : (as, j) \to \{0,1\}^j$), such that for $i \in 0, \ldots, j$:

$$G(as, j)_i = \begin{cases} 1 & \text{if after } gc_j \text{ there exists any live object instantiated} \\ & \text{in generation } i \text{ by the allocation site } as \\ 0 & \text{otherwise.} \end{cases}$$

For an allocation site as of the application and an integer $j \in \{0, \ldots n\}$ the *GenCount* metric is then defined as:

$$GenCount(as, j) = \sum_{i=0}^{j} G(as, gc_j)_i$$

In other words, $GenCount(as, j)$ tells us in how many *different* previous generation sites as has created objects that are still not disposed of in the current generation j. It is expected that for a leaky allocation site as, *GenCount* grows in an unbounded manner with larger j, as older objects are not disposed of. Contrary to this, for a non-leaky site *GenCount* is expected to remain bounded. Essentially, if after some execution time some allocation sites show much higher *GenCount*-values than others, they are likely to produce leaks. For this reason, relative *GenCount*-values for all sites of an application are sorted, and the approach tries to find a large increase ("gap") between neighbors, see Fig. 11.11.

An early version of Plumbr was using a simple threshold approach to detect such a gap. A later improvement [37] uses *GenCount* along with other metrics/features (calculated for each allocation site) to train classification models predicting whether an allocation site is leaky, or not (it is not clear whether the current implementation of Plumbr is using this enhancement). As demonstrated by Andrzejak *et al.* [38], this machine learning based extension of *GenCount* can also successfully detect memory leaks in C++.

11.3.2.2. *Implementation*

Plumbr is implemented as two JVM agents: an auxiliary native agent and an orchestrating Java agent. The native agent is responsible for gather-

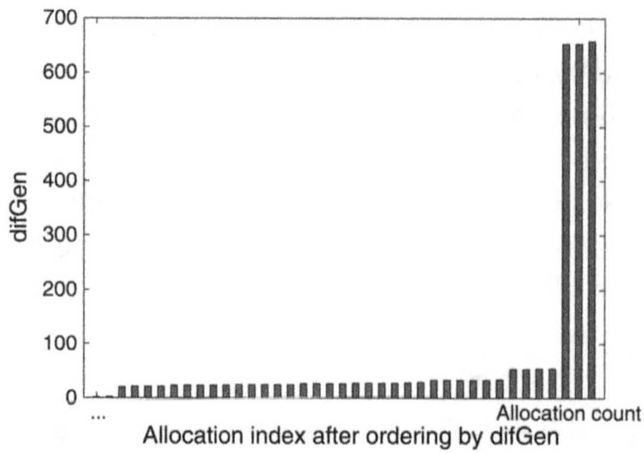

Fig. 11.11. Distribution of the relative differences of the *GenCount*-values over allocation sites in an exemplary application [35]. The three rightmost sites have significantly higher relative *GenCount*-values and are likely to produce leaks.

ing low-level information, for example, obtaining a lightweight reference graph, or receiving *ObjectFree*-events, and for tagging objects using 64-bit JVMTI-tags.

The Java agent is responsible for the overall analysis process, which is executed in the following steps [35]:

(1) Tracking instantiated objects by instrumenting the byte code of each allocation site. In this way, at each object creation a callback method is invoked that stores a weak object reference and the corresponding site ID. When the queue is periodically processed, objects which are still alive are tagged by the native agent, and their meta-data is stored in internal data structures.
(2) After each full garbage collection, the approach described above analyses the *GenCount*-values over all allocation sites.
(3) If the previous step has identified any leak candidates, the lightweight reference graph is computed by the native agent.
(4) Next, the reference graph is analysed to find paths from garbage collection roots to the leaking objects. To this end, objects created by each suspicious site are identified in the graph (via JVMTI-tags) and several graph algorithms are executed (Dijkstra's algorithm and the merging of leak paths).
(5) Finally, a report is generated, with information about the address of each leaky site, and the chain of references preventing the object disposal (from leaky objects to CG roots).

The overhead on the execution performance imposed by Plumbr for Java ranges widely (e.g. from 2% to 127% for applications in the DaCapo Benchmark suite version 9.12) but is on average about 40% [35]. The overhead in terms of additional heap memory is typically below 10%. Similar overheads are observed in the case of the tool for C++ based on *GenCount* [38]. While these overheads are still non-negligible, they are acceptable for diagnosis sessions and in real-world scenarios (compare with the median slowdown imposed by Valgrind/Memcheck of 26x, Section 11.2.2).

11.3.2.3. *Applications*

The memory detection tool is integrated into a product called "Java Agent" from the company Plumbr. The product is reported to be used by 1500+ customers, including NASA, Akamai, VMware, DELL, and HBO. The typical usage scenarios are server-side diagnoses of web applications and services.

While details of customer scenarios are not disclosed, Šor *et al.* [35] discuss multiple case studies of leak detection in large open-source applications. In each case, their study compares the times taken for the system to crash due to the OutOfMemoryError for the original and the instrumented version and the memory usage in both cases, and also states how fast a leak was detected (in each case a leak was detected and there were no false positives). We summarize these results in Table 11.7.

11.3.3. *Eclipse Memory Analyzer*

11.3.3.1. *Overview*

The Eclipse Memory Analyzer (MAT) [39] is a production-quality open-source tool for heap dump exploration and analysis, scaling to dumps with hundreds of millions of objects. Originally developed by SAP under the name *SAP Memory Analyzer*, it has been available for public use since

Table 11.7. Results of case studies for Plumbr on large open-source applications.

	Time to Crash		
Application Name	Original	w/Plumbr	Detection Time
Apache ActiveMQ	1 h 17 min	1 h 15 min	36 min
eHealth Web Portal	2 h 30 min	6 h 0 min	2 h 30 min
HtmlUnit	28 min	26 min	20 sec

at least 2007. It supports the manual identification of memory leaks and the reduction of memory consumption but also offers a "wizard" for the automated discovery of memory anti-patterns. Its main applications are the diagnosis of Out-of-Memory errors (due to leaks or insufficient heap size) and high memory consumption.

In terms of leak detection, the three most important functions of MAT are:

- the estimation and visual analysis of the *retained heap* (size) of all objects, i.e. the amount of reclaimed heap memory if an object and all dependent objects are garbage collected
- the computation and browsing of the *dominator tree* (explained below), for the complete heap, or for each class loader corresponding to a separate application module
- for each object, the computation of the chain(s) of references from the garbage collection root(s) to this object; they essentially show which references prevent the disposal of an object, and where these references originate.

As explained in Section 11.3.3.2, a combination of the above functions allows the effective identification of leaking objects.

In addition to these core elements, MAT provides a collection of further functions that support heap analysis [40]. These include the ability to acquire a heap dump from a running JVM, an inspector which shows detailed information about the currently selected class or object, and tools to investigate threads, stacks, local variables and Strings maintained in the JVM. Moreover, MAT facilitates finding objects in the heap and creating its own reports using a flexible Object Query Language (OQL). It can also export reports in a variety of formats.

11.3.3.2. *Memory leak detection with MAT*

We start by explaining the *dominator tree* of a heap snapshot. Essentially, it is a tree in the object reference graph G (see Section 11.3.1.2) induced by the following relation: object d dominates an object y if every path in G from any of the garbage collection roots to y must go through d (see Fig. 11.12).

This tree is also called a "keep-alive" tree, since every object d dominating y is responsible for the non-disposal of y. Also note that if d is garbage collected (or all its outgoing references are cleared), all objects dominated by d can be disposed of. The set R_d of objects dominated by

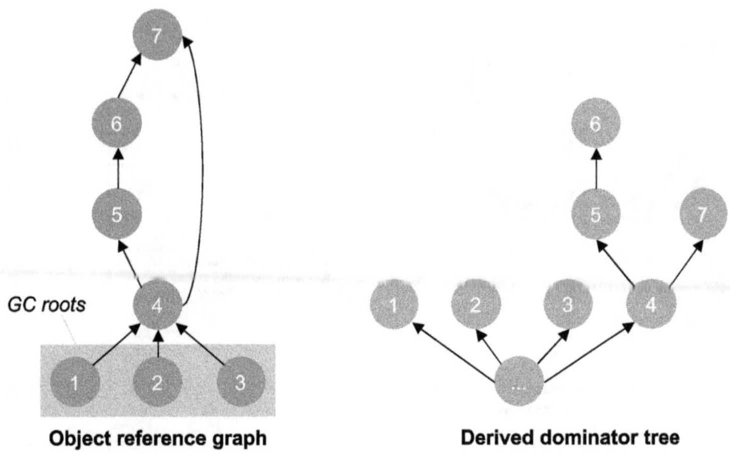

Fig. 11.12. The object reference graph with garbage collection roots 1, 2, 3 (left), and the derived dominator tree (right).

d is called the *retained set*, and the sum of their heap memory is called the *retained size* (of d).

Compared to the object reference graph, the dominator tree has several advantages when detecting memory leaks:

- It allows a quick estimate of how much total heap space would be freed by disposing of a dominating object d, i.e. an estimation of the retained size of d.
- For each object y, it identifies the *immediate dominator*: the closest one responsible for keeping y alive.
- It identifies distinct objects with the largest retained sizes, which allows for easy grouping of object families by class or class loaders (and so by different application components).

MAT computes the dominator tree of a heap dump, and shows the largest dominating objects as a table. It is also possible to drill-down for detailed information, for example to query for paths to garbage collection roots, see Fig. 11.13.

Detection of memory leaks with MAT is executed in several steps. At first one collects a heap dump which exposes a memory leak well. In this step it is advisable to execute the target application with *twice* the usual heap size until an Out-of-Memory error occurs. This ensures that at least half of the objects in the dump are leaks, and facilitates further analysis.

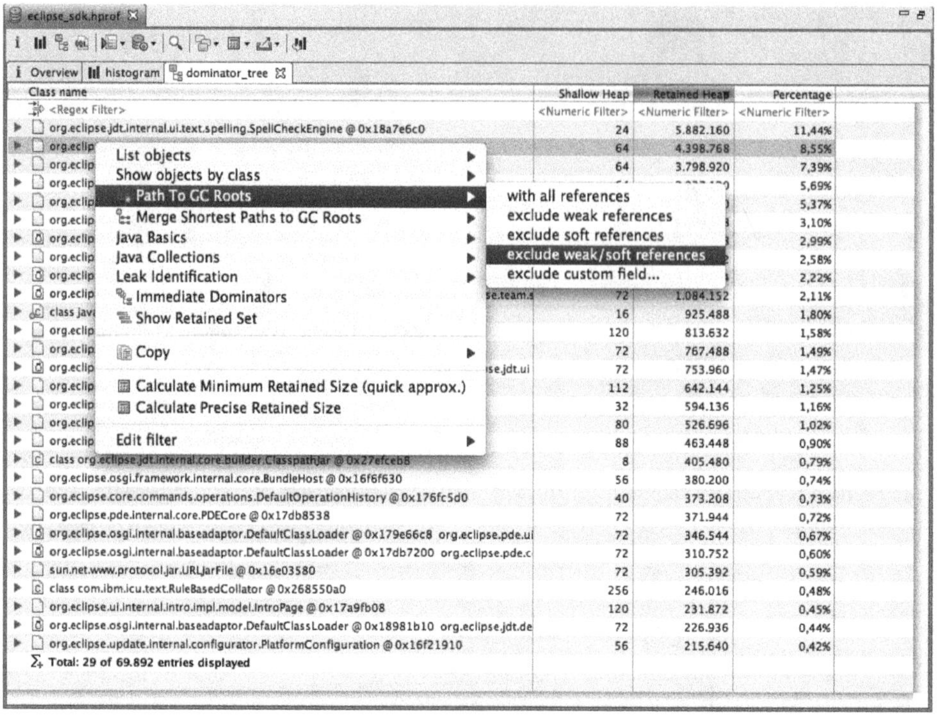

Fig. 11.13. Screenshot of the Eclipse Memory Analyzer displaying the dominator tree of a heap snapshot, and a menu to find paths to garbage collection roots (taken from [39]).

In the subsequent step objects with the largest retained size in the dominator tree are identified with the MAT tool. If there are multiple such objects with comparable sizes, then it is advisable to re-compute the dominator trees with objects grouped by class loaders, and to perform the following analysis for each group (corresponding to an application component).

Let d_0 be an object with the largest retained size (typically a top-level object in the tree). We follow a path from d_0 over dominated objects with similar retained size until the last such "large" object d_1 (i.e. all objects dominated by d_1 have significantly smaller retained size), see Fig. 11.12. Object d_1, called an *accumulation point* (typically a Java collection), is likely to be responsible for a leak by holding (unnecessary) references to many dominated objects. While it is not guaranteed that such a structure in the dominator tree exists, it is frequently encountered as many leaks are related to container (or collection) classes [32, 41].

In the subsequent and final analysis step MAP helps us to understand which references need to be removed to fix the leak-inducing defect. To this end, a user can compute the chain(s) of references from the garbage collection root(s) to d_1, and identify a reference which needs to be removed to make d_1 disposable. An alternative strategy is to ensure that d_1 is cleaning up its references to the dominated objects, e.g. by ensuring that a collection is cleared after its usage.

11.3.3.3. *Applications*

Since its initial version as a proprietary product from SAP, and then as an open-source tool, the Eclipse Memory Analyzer has become a fundamental tool for Java developers. Among its uses, we mention the debugging of J2EE web applications [42], of Android mobile applications [43], and even of a Java-based language interpreter [44].

11.3.4. *JVMMon*

11.3.4.1. *Overview*

JVMMon [45] is a monitoring infrastructure that has been developed to support experiments for the dependability evaluation of JVM implementations under stress (i.e., under intensive workloads and fault injection). In particular, this tool can be used to obtain insights about the conditions under which software aging manifests in the JVM, by profiling the workload of the JVM (e.g., the allocation rate of Java objects, the time and extent of garbage collections, the number of threads waiting on mutexes, etc.), and the state of JVM's subsystems (such as the current state of threads and the current utilization of heap memory).

JVMMon uses the JVM Tool Interface (JVMTI) exposed by the JVM (according to the Java Platform Profiling Architecture [46]), and bytecode instrumentation, to intercept events inside the JVM, and to query the JVM about its state. The architecture of JVMMon is shown in Fig. 11.14. A JVMTI agent inside the *monitored JVM* collects information by handling events raised in the JVM, and by periodically querying the state of the JVM. This information is sent to a *Local Monitor Daemon* deployed on the same host, by communicating through a shared memory, and through a local log file with the events raised inside the JVM. Moreover, the JVMTI agent sends heartbeat messages at a fixed rate, to allow the Local Monitor Daemon to detect JVM failures. The Local Monitor Daemon notifies the *Data Collector*

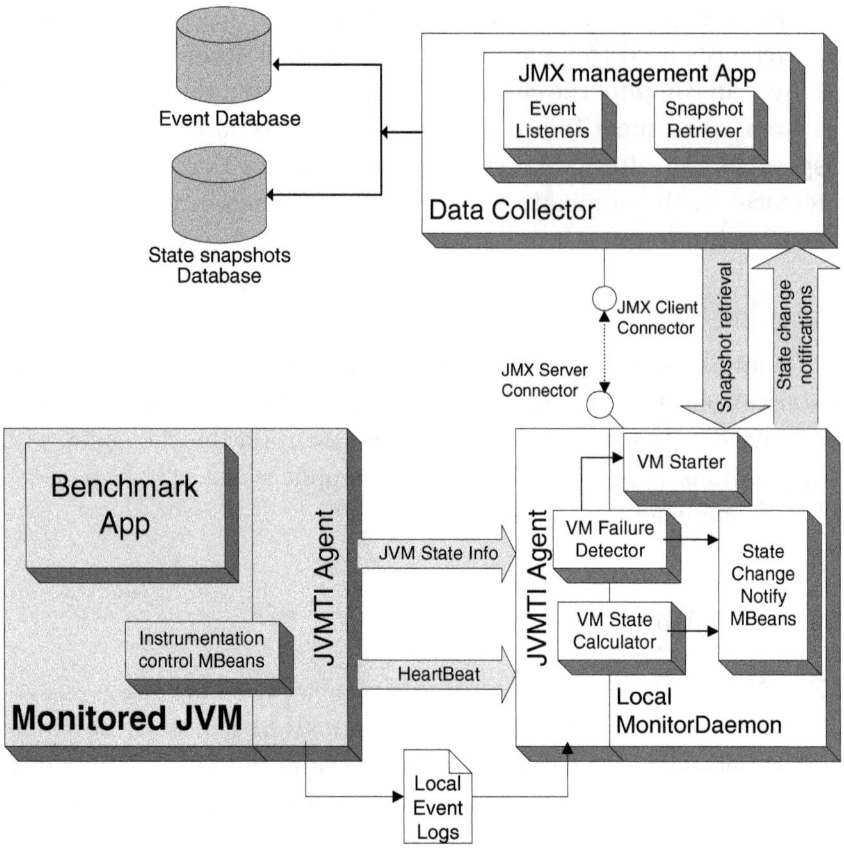

Fig. 11.14. Architecture of JVMMon.

about the failures and relevant state changes of the JVM, which are written in an event database.

11.3.4.2. *Aging symptoms and use cases*

JVMMon is meant to collect a large number of metrics about the state and the workload of the JVM. These metrics make it possible to:

- Obtain a *workload characterization* of the JVM, by identifying which are the relevant states of a workload by *clustering* workload metrics.
- Perform a *correlation analysis* between the workload states and software aging symptoms (such as, trends in application throughput).

Table 11.8 shows the full list of metrics that are collected by JVMMon for workload characterization. They include 5 key subsystems of the JVM:

Table 11.8. Metrics for workload characterization in JVMMon.

Component	Parameter	Description	U.M.
Runtime Unit	MET_INV	Method Invocation Rate	*methods/min*
	OBJ_ALL	Object Allocation Rate	*objects/min*
	ARR_ALL	Array Allocation Rate	*arrays/min*
	CLS_INIT	Time spent in class initialization	*ms*
Class Loader	CLS_VER	Time spent in class verification	*ms*
	CLS_LOAD	Time spent in class loading	*ms*
	INIT_CLS	Number of Initialized Classes	*classes/min*
Memory Management	SM	Object Size Mean	*bytes*
	SV	Object Size Variance	*bytes*
	COLL0_INV	Number of Young Generation Collector (Copying) Invocations	*invocations/min*
	COLL0_TIME	Time spent during Young Generation Collection	*ms*
	COLL0_TIMEPERINV	Young Collection Duration	*ms*
	COLL1_INV	Number of Tenured Generation Collector (Compacting) Invocations	*invocations/min*
	COLL1_TIME	Time spent during Tenured Generation Collection	*ms*
	COLL1_TIMEPERINV	Tenured Collection Duration	*ms*
	SAFEPOINTS	Number of Safepoints (*) reached	*safepoints/min*
JIT Compiler	CI_THR0_EVENTS	compiler thread 0 events	*events/min*
	CI_THR0_TIME	compiler thread 0 time	*ms*
	CI_NATIVE_COMP	native JIT-compilations	*events/min*
	CI_NATIVE_TIME	native JIT-compilation time	*ms*
	CI_OSR_COMPILES	On-Stack-Replacement (OSR) JIT-compilations	*events/min*
	CI_OSR_TIME	OSR JIT-compilation time	*ms*
	CI_STD_COMP	standard JIT-compilations	*events/min*
	CI_STD_TIME	standard JIT-compilation time	*ms*
	CI_TIMEPERCOMP	time per compilation	*ms*

(*Continued*)

Table 11.8. (*Continued*)

Component	Parameter	Description	U.M.
Thread Management Unit	TE	Threading Events	*events/min*
	WM	Waiters (threads waiting on a mutex) Mean	*# of threads*
	WV	Waiters (threads waiting on a mutex) Variance	*# of threads*
	NWM	Notify Waiters (Threads waiting on a condition variable) Mean	*# of threads*
	NWV	Notify Waiters (Threads waiting on a condition variable) Variance	*# of threads*

*The HotSpot JVM uses a safepointing mechanism to halt program execution only when the locations of all objects are known. When a safepoint is reached, each thread stops its execution, enters the VM and stores its current Java Stack Pointer.

the *Runtime Unit*; the *Class Loader*; the *Memory Management*; the *JIT Compiler*; and the *Thread Management Unit*. These collected metrics are obtained from events occurring inside the JVM, and they reflect the intensity of the work and the degree of stress for each of the 5 subsystems. Moreover, since three of these subsystems are stateful, JVMMon performs additional queries to obtain a snapshot of their state:

- *Class Loader*: The list of classes loaded in the "permanent generation" area of the JVM. In turn, each Java Class can be in any of the following states: *loaded*, *prepared*, *initialized*, *unloaded*, or *erroneous* (e.g., an error occurred during preparation or initialization).
- *Thread Management Unit*: The state of this component is given by the combination of current Java threads (not including threads that are internal to the VM). For each thread, JVMMon collects: the current state of the thread (*Running*, *Waiting*, *Blocked*, etc.); the stack trace of the thread; the monitors owned by the thread, and the monitor on which a thread may be blocked; the timestamps at which the thread has been scheduled, and at which it yielded the processor.
- *Memory Management Unit*: JVMMon tracks the amount of memory committed to the application, and the space actually allocated into the heap of the JVM (in order to get more insight on the respective resource usages by the application layer and the JVM layer).

11.3.4.3. *Applications*

Cotroneo *et al.* [47] used JVMMon to perform an extensive analysis of software aging phenomena in the Sun Hotspot Java Virtual Machine [48], version 1.5. The JVM has been exercised with the JAMES mail server, which has been stressed with intensive POP3 and SMTP email workloads. In total, 29 experiments were performed, which differed with respect to the intensity of the workload (emails per minute), in order to point out relevant relationships between aging trends and the workload of the JVM subsystems.

First, the study presented a workload characterization using the data from JVMMon. For each event, the study analyzed the average rate and trends in the occurrences of the event, across the different experiments. Then, a cluster analysis was performed. Interestingly, the execution of the JVM alternates between two main clusters (states): a *normal collection state* (in which there is a high rate of invocations of garbage collections, and a low duration of collections in the "young generation" area of the JVM heap), and a *low collection state* (in which the invocation rate is lower, and the collection times in the "young generation" area are higher). Moreover, the time spent on garbage collection also increased during the experiments, as shown by the trends in Fig. 11.15.

For each experiment, the study performed a trend analysis on the throughput of POP3/SMTP traffic (Fig. 11.16), and on the memory depletion both at the application and at the JVM layers (Fig. 11.17). The experiments showed noticeable trends, which were exacerbated by the intensity of the workload.

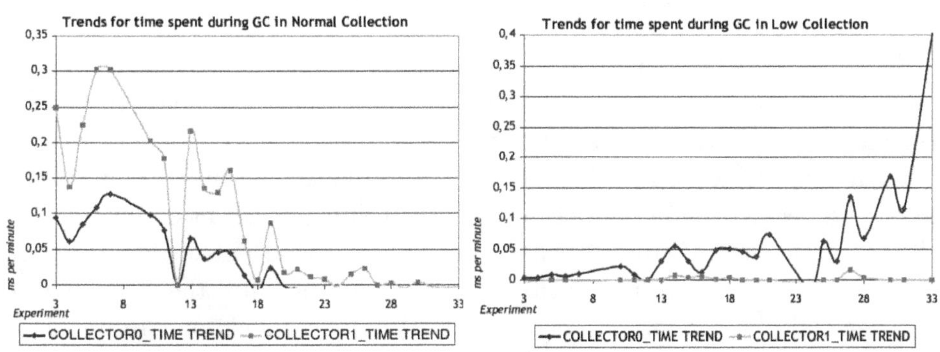

Fig. 11.15. Trends for time spent on garbage collections, respectively in the *normal* and *low collection* states.

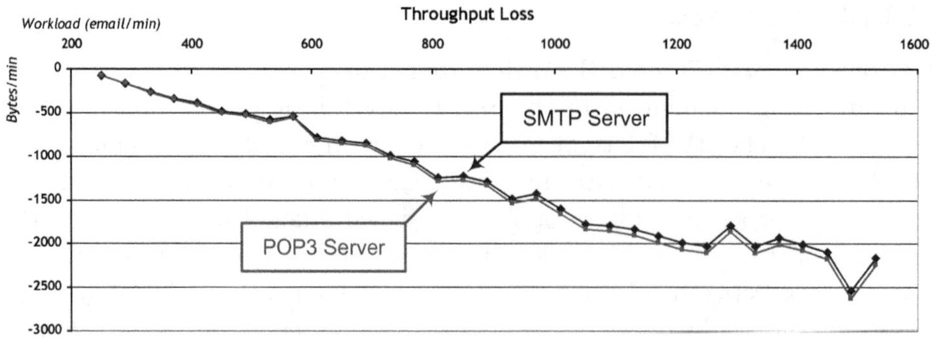

Fig. 11.16. Throughput loss trends.

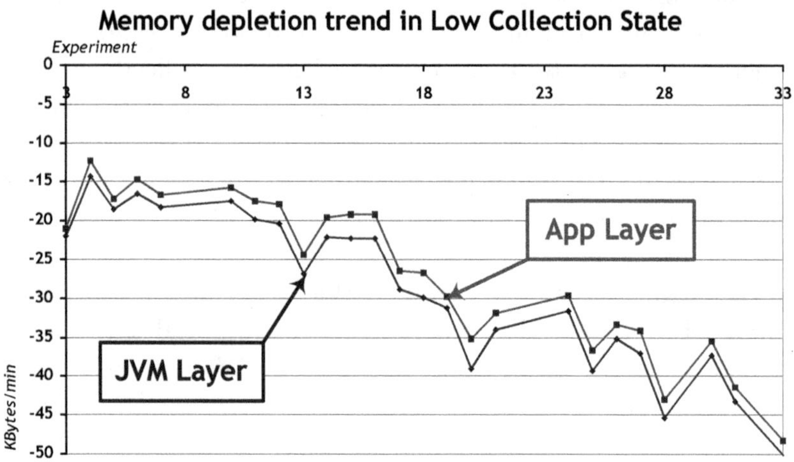

Fig. 11.17. Memory depletion trends.

Finally, the study performed a statistical analysis based on PCA (to reduce the number of workload parameters), and on partial linear regression (to identify dependencies between workload parameters and aging trends). This analysis enabled identification of the workload parameters that most influenced aging trends, and thus the JVM subsystems most involved in the aging phenomena. In particular, the memory management unit seems to be the main subsystem responsible for aging effects, since the frequency of garbage collections couldn't keep up with the high allocation rates of Java objects, in particular under the *low collection* state. Tables 11.9 and 11.10 show the result of partial regression respectively for throughput and memory depletion.

Table 11.9. Throughput loss as a linear function of the most relevant JVM workload parameters.

	SMTP Server		
	OBJ_ALL_AVG	MET_INV_AVG	COLLECTORO_TIMEPERINV
Student's t	−35,84	−25,4	−5,17
Pr > |t|	<.0001	<.0001	<.0001
Est. Slope	−0.055 KB/100KAll**	−0.0047 KB/Minv*	−3.002 KB/ms
95% Conf. Int.	[−0.058; −0.052]	[−0.005; −0.0043]	[−4.195; −1.81]
	POP3 Server		
	OBJ_ALL_AVG	MET_INV_AVG	COLLECTORO_TIMEPERINV
Student's t	−35,91	−25,46	−5,15
Pr > |t|	<.0001	<.0001	<.0001
Est, Slope	−0.057 KB/100KAll**	−0.0048 KB/Minv*	−3.177 KB/ms
95% Conf. Int.	[−0.06; −0.054]	[−0.0052; −0.0044]	[−4.34; −1.866]

**Millions of method invocations per minute*
**Number of object allocation per minute * 100.000*

11.3.5. *Other Tools*

Among recent academic tools, we mention the recent PerfBlower tool [49]. A key feature of PerfBlower is that it provides a domain-specific language (DSL) for allowing developers to describe performance problems, including memory management bugs. PerfBlower uses this description to instrument the JVM; then, the instrumented JVM looks for specific events on objects, and increases/decreases a score for the object, according to the specification.

Among commercial tools, the YourKit Java Profiler [50] represents one of the state-of-the-art solutions in the field. It provides a rich set of utilities for analyzing several types of performance issues, including issues involving memory utilization and garbage collection activity. Moreover, it provides the ability to configure the profiling mechanisms (e.g., by enabling/disabling bytecode instrumentation), in order to provide control on the performance overhead imposed by the profiler.

Table 11.10. Memory depletion as a linear function of the most relevant JVM workload parameters.

	NORMAL COLLECTION STATE - JVM_FREE			
	CI_STD_TIME_AVG	CI_STD_COMPILES_AVG	CI_OSR_TIME_AVG	CI_TIMEPERCOMP_AVG
Student's t	−3,11	−1,3	−0,86	−1,99
Pr > |t|	0,0045	0,2063	0,3977	0,0572
Est. Slope	−0.097 KB/ms	−2.384 KB/comp*	−0.02 KB/ms	−0.0014 KB/ms
95% Conf. Int.	[−0.167; −0.027]	[−6.167; 1.39]	[−0.067; 0.027]	[−0.002; −0.0007]
	LOW COLLECTION STATE - JVM_FREE			
	COLLECTOR0_INV_AVG	COLLECTOR1_TIME_AVG	COLLECTOR1_TIME_TREND	
Student's t	−7,66	−5,95	−0,71	
Pr > |t|	<0.0001	<0.0001	0,4876	
Est. Slope	−2.41 KB/inv**	−3.74 KB/ms	−0.347 KB/(ms/min)	
95% Conf. Int.	[−3.05; −1.76]	[−5.16; −2.44]	[−1.36; 0.67]	
	LOW COLLECTION STATE - APP_FREE			
	COLLECTOR0_INV_AVG	COLLECTOR1_TIME_AVG	COLLECTOR1_TIME_TREND	
Student's t	7,29	−5,85	−0,54	
Pr > |t|	<0.0001	<0.0001	0,5926	
Est. Slope	−2.35 KB/inv**	−3.68 KB/ms	−0.265 KB/(ms/min)	
95% Conf. Int.	[−3.01; −1.68]	[−4.99; −2.38]	[−1.27; 0.747]	

References

1. S. Garg, A. Van Moorsel, K. Vaidyanathan, and K. S. Trivedi. (1998). A methodology for detection and estimation of software aging. In *Proceedings of the Ninth International Symposium on Software Reliability Engineering, Paderborn, Germany, November 4–7*, pp. 283–292.
2. W. Stallings. (1998). *SNMP, SNMPv2, SNMPv3, and RMON 1 and 2*. Boston, Massachusetts, USA: Addison-Wesley Longman Publishing.
3. N. Nethercote and J. Seward. (2007). Valgrind: A framework for heavyweight dynamic binary instrumentation. *ACM Sigplan Notices*, **42**, 89–100.
4. G. Carrozza, D. Cotroneo, R. Natella, A. Pecchia, and S. Russo. (2010). Memory leak analysis of mission-critical middleware. *Journal of Systems and Software*, **83**(9), 1556–1567.
5. D. C. Schmidt, D. L. Levine, and S. Mungee. (1998). The design of the TAO real-time object request broker. *Computer Communications*, **21**(4), 294–324.
6. F. C. Eigler. (2006). Problem solving with SystemTap. In *Proceedings of the Ottawa Linux Symposium, Ottawa, Ontario, Canada, July 19–22*, pp. 261–268.
7. R. Krishnakumar. (2005). Kernel Korner: KProbes–A kernel debugger. *Linux Journal*, **2005**(133), 11.
8. R. Matias, I. Beicker, B. Leitão, and P. R. Maciel. (2010). Measuring software aging effects through OS kernel instrumentation. In *Proceedings of the 2010 IEEE Second International Workshop on Software Aging and Rejuvenation (WoSAR), San Jose, California, USA, November 2*, pp. 1–6.
9. P. Larson. (2002). Testing Linux with the Linux Test Project. In *Proceedings of the Ottawa Linux Symposium, Otttawa, Ontario, Canada, June 26–29*, pp. 265–273.
10. D. Cotroneo and R. Natella. (2012). Monitoring of aging software systems affected by integer overflows. In *Proceedings of the 2012 IEEE 23rd International Symposium on Software Reliability Engineering Workshops (ISSREW), Dallas, Texas, USA, November 27–30*, pp. 265–270.
11. B. Schwartz, P. Zaitsev, V. Tkachenko, J. Zawodny, A. Lentz, and D. Balling. (2008). *High Performance MySQL*. Sebastopol, California, USA: O'Reilly Media.
12. V. Castelli, R. E. Harper, P. Heidelberger, S. W. Hunter, K. S. Trivedi, K. Vaidyanathan, and W. P. Zeggert. (2001). Proactive management of software aging. *IBM Journal of Research and Development*, **45**(2), 311–332.
13. R. Matias and J. P. Filho. (2006). An experimental study on software aging and rejuvenation in web servers. In *Proceedings of the 30th Annual International Computer Software and Applications Conference (COMPSAC), Chicago, Illinois, USA, September 17–21*, vol. 1, pp. 189–196.
14. L. M. Silva, J. Alonso, P. Silva, J. Torres, and A. Andrzejak. (2007). Using virtualization to improve software rejuvenation. In *Proceedings of the Sixth IEEE International Symposium on Network Computing and Applications (NCA 2007), Cambridge, MA, USA, July 12–14*, pp. 33–44. doi: 10.1109/NCA.2007.53.
15. J. Alonso, L. M. Silva, A. Andrzejak, P. Silva, and J. Torres. (2007). High-available grid services through the use of virtualized clustering. In *Proceedings of the 8th IEEE/ACM International Conference on Grid Computing (GRID 2007), Austin, Texas, USA, September 19–21*, pp. 34–41. doi: 10.1109/GRID.2007.4354113.
16. L. M. Silva, J. Alonso, and J. Torres. (2009). Using virtualization to improve software rejuvenation. *IEEE Transactions on Computers*, **58**(11), 1525–1538.
17. A. Avritzer, A. Bondi, M. Grottke, K. S. Trivedi, and E. J. Weyuker. (2006). Performance assurance via software rejuvenation: Monitoring, statistics and algorithms. In

Proceedings of the IEEE/IFIP International Conference on Dependable Systems and Networks (DSN), Philadelphia, Pennsylvania, USA, June 25–28, pp. 435–444.

18. R. Matias, A. Andrzejak, F. Machida, D. Elias, and K. S. Trivedi. (2014). A systematic differential analysis for fast and robust detection of software aging. In *Proceedings of the 33rd IEEE International Symposium on Reliable Distributed Systems, (SRDS 2014), Nara, Japan, October 6–9*, pp. 311–320. doi: 10.1109/SRDS.2014.38.
19. R. Matias, G. O. de Sena, A. Andrzejak, and K. S. Trivedi. (2016). Software aging detection based on differential analysis: An experimental study. In *Proceedings of the 2016 IEEE International Symposium on Software Reliability Engineering Workshops, Ottawa, Ontario, Canada, October 23–27*, pp. 71–77. doi: 10.1109/ISSREW.2016.44.
20. M. Ghanavati and A. Andrzejak. (2015). Automated memory leak diagnosis by regression testing. In *Proceedings of the 15th IEEE International Working Conference on Source Code Analysis and Manipulation, (SCAM 2015), Bremen, Germany, September 27–28*, pp. 191–200. doi: 10.1109/SCAM.2015.7335415.
21. F. Langner and A. Andrzejak. (2013). Detecting software aging in a cloud computing framework by comparing development versions. In *Proceedings of the 2013 IFIP/IEEE International Symposium on Integrated Network Management (IM 2013), Ghent, Belgium, May 27–31*, pp. 896–899.
22. F. Langner and A. Andrzejak. (2013). Detection and root cause analysis of memory-related software aging defects by automated tests. In *Proceedings of the 2013 IEEE 21st International Symposium on Modelling, Analysis and Simulation of Computer and Telecommunication Systems, San Francisco, CA, USA, August 14–16*, pp. 365–369. doi: 10.1109/MASCOTS.2013.53.
23. Parasoft Insure++. https://www.parasoft.com/products/insure. Accessed: 2018-06-26.
24. UNICOM Systems PurifyPlus. http://www.unicomsi.com/purifyplus. Accessed: 2018-06-26.
25. D. Bruening and Q. Zhao. (2011). Practical memory checking with Dr. Memory. In *Proceedings of the 9th Annual IEEE/ACM International Symposium on Code Generation and Optimization, (CGO '11), Chamonix, France, April 2–6*, pp. 213–223, ISBN 978-1-61284-356-8.
26. K. Serebryany, D. Bruening, A. Potapenko, and D. Vyukov. (2012). AddressSanitizer: A fast address sanity checker. In *Proceedings of the USENIX ATC, Boston, Massachusetts, USA, June 13–15*, pp. 309–318.
27. M. Ghanavati, D. Costa, A. Andrzejak, and J. Seboek. (2018). Poster: Memory and resource leak defects in Java projects: An empirical study. In *Proceedings of the 40th International Conference on Software Engineering: Companion Proceeedings (ICSE 2018), Gothenburg, Sweden, May 27–June 3, 2018*, pp. 410–411. doi: 10.1145/3183440.3195032.
28. V. Šor and S. N. Srirama. (2014). Memory leak detection in Java: Taxonomy and classification of approaches. *Journal of Systems and Software*, **96**, 139–151. ISSN 0164-1212. doi: 10.1016/j.jss.2014.06.005.
29. V. Šor. (2014). *Statistical approach for memory leak detection in Java applications.* (PhD thesis, University of Tartu, Estonia, Tartu, Estonia).
30. M. D. Bond and K. S. McKinley. (2006). Bell: Bit-encoding online memory leak detection. In *Proceedings of the 12th International Conference on Architectural Support for Programming Languages and Operating Systems (ASPLOS XII), San Jose, California, USA, October 21–25*, pp. 61–72. ISBN 1-59593-451-0. doi: 10.1145/1168857.1168866.

31. M. Jump and K. S. McKinley. (2007). Cork: Dynamic memory leak detection for garbage-collected languages. In *Proceedings of the 34th Annual ACM SIGPLAN-SIGACT Symposium on Principles of Programming Languages (POPL '07), Nice, France, January 17–19*, pp. 31–38, ISBN 1-59593-575-4. doi: 10.1145/1190216.1190224.
32. G. Xu and A. Rountev. (2008). Precise memory leak detection for java software using container profiling. In *Proceedings of the 30th International Conference on Software Engineering (ICSE '08), Leipzig, Germany, May 10–18*, pp. 151–160. ISBN 978-1-60558-079-1. doi: 10.1145/1368088.1368110.
33. N. Mitchell and G. Sevitsky. (2003). LeakBot: An automated and lightweight tool for diagnosing memory leaks in large Java applications. In Cardelli L. (ed.). *ECOOP 2003 — Object-Oriented Programming*, Lecture Notes in Computer Science, no. 2743. Berlin/Heidelberg, Germany: Springer. ISBN 978-3-540-40531-3 978-3-540-45070-2.
34. S. C. Gupta and R. Palanki. (2005). Java memory leaks – catch me if you can. URL http://www.ibm.com/developerworks/rational/library/05/0816_GuptaPalanki/. Accessed: 2018-07-01.
35. V. Šor, S. N. Srirama, and N. Salnikov-Tarnovski. (2015). Memory leak detection in Plumbr. *Software: Practice and Experience*, **45**(10), 1307–1330. ISSN 1097-024X. doi: 10.1002/spe.2275.
36. V. Šor, N. Salnikov-Tarnovski, and S. N. Srirama. (2011). Automated statistical approach for memory leak detection: Case studies. In *Proceedings of the 2011 Confederated International Conference on On the Move to Meaningful Internet Systems (OTM'11), Hersonissos, Crete, Greece, October 17–21*, Part II, pp. 635–642. ISBN 978-3-642-25105-4.
37. V. Sor, P. Ou, T. Treier, and S. Srirama. (2013). Improving statistical approach for memory leak detection using machine learning. In *Proceedings of the 2013 29th IEEE International Conference on Software Maintenance (ICSM), Eindhoven, The Netherlands, September 22–28*, pp. 544–547. doi: 10.1109/ICSM.2013.92.
38. A. Andrzejak, F. Eichler, and M. Ghanavati. (2017). Detection of memory leaks in C/C++ code via machine learning. In *Proceedings of the 2017 IEEE International Symposium on Software Reliability Engineering Workshops (ISSREW), Toulouse, France, October 23–26*, pp. 252–258. doi: 10.1109/ISSREW.2017.72.
39. Eclipse memory analyzer. URL http://www.eclipse.org/mat/. Accessed: 2018-07-01.
40. I. Bull. (January 21, 2013). 10 tips for using the Eclipse memory analyzer. URL https://eclipsesource.com/de/blogs/2013/01/21/10-tips-for-using-the-eclipse-memory-analyzer. Accessed: 2018-07-01.
41. G. Xu. (2013). Resurrector: A tunable object lifetime profiling technique for optimizing real-world programs. In *Proceedings of the 2013 ACM SIGPLAN International Conference on Object Oriented Programming Systems Languages & Applications (OOPSLA '13), Indianapolis, Indiana, USA, October 26–31*, pp. 111–130. ISBN 978-1-4503-2374-1. doi: 10.1145/2509136.2509512.
42. M. Haller. (November 3, 2011). How to analyze leaky webapps. URL https://blog.bosch-si.com/developer/how-to-analyze-leaky-webapps/. Accessed: 2018-06-26.
43. P. Dubroy. (March 24, 2011). Memory Analysis for Android applications. URL https://android-developers.googleblog.com/2011/03/memory-analysis-for-android.html. Accessed: 2018-06-26.
44. C. O. Nutter. (July 12, 2010). Finding leaks in Ruby apps with Eclipse memory analyzer. URL http://blog.headius.com/2010/07/finding-leaks-in-ruby-apps-with-eclipse.html. Accessed: 2018-06-26.

45. S. Orlando and S. Russo. (2006). Java Virtual Machine monitoring for dependability benchmarking. In *Proceedings of the Ninth IEEE International Symposium on Object and Component-Oriented Real-Time Distributed Computing (ISORC 2006), Gyeoungju, Korea, April 24–26*, pp. 433–440.
46. S. Liang and D. Viswanathan. (1999). Comprehensive profiling support in the Java Virtual Machine. In *Proceedings of the 5th USENIX Conference on Object-Oriented Technologies and Systems (COOTS '99), San Diego, California, USA, May 3–7*, pp. 229–242.
47. D. Cotroneo, S. Orlando, and S. Russo. (2007). Characterizing aging phenomena of the Java Virtual Machine. In *Proceedings of the 26th IEEE International Symposium on Reliable Distributed Systems, (SRDS 2007), Beijing, China, October 10–12*, pp. 127–136.
48. OpenJDK. (2017). The HotSpot Group. URL http://openjdk.java.net/groups/hotspot/. Accessed: 2018-07-01.
49. L. Fang, L. Dou, and G. Xu. (2015). PerfBlower: Quickly detecting memory-related performance problems via amplification. In *Proceedings of the 29th European Conference on Object-Oriented Programming (ECOOP 2015), Prague, Czech Republic, July 5–10*, pp. 296–320. ISBN 978-3-939897-86-6. doi: http://dx.doi.org/10.4230/LIPIcs.ECOOP.2015.296.
50. YourKit Java Profiler. URL https://www.yourkit.com/. Accessed: 2018-06-26.

Chapter 12

Implementation of Micro-rejuvenation with Cooperative Stack Leasing

Sandip HomChaudhuri

Qualcomm Technologies Inc. San Jose, USA

shomchau@qti.qualcomm.com

Stack Overflow [1] continues to be a problem in computing systems despite the presence of many professional and research tools [2, 3] that assist in the analysis and mitigation of the pathology. The uncertain and dynamic nature of a released software, subject to various unpredictable inputs and call flows that were not necessarily envisioned at the time of software design and sizing (of the stacks), makes it particularly tough to eliminate stack overflow. Examples of such unpredictable inputs and call flows are function arguments which bloat the stack frame, intentionally or unintentionally, and function invocations or recursions that go deeper than originally assumed, caused by an aging or a non-aging mandelbug [4]. The problem is exacerbated when libraries are provided to be used by the developer community, but the latter creates new software flows that call into the supposedly "well-tested" libraries triggering an unpredictable growth in stack frame. Stack overflow incidents are typically handled with a complete reboot of the system due to the widespread impact they cause across a collection of threads. To deal with this uncertainty, gross overestimation during the design of the system has been an accepted practice in the industry. A 20 to 30 percent over-estimation per stack is a common practice in the industry [5] and continues to happen today. This approach has multiple issues: (1) it still does not eliminate the problem, though it reduces the probability of the problem occurring, and may still not be acceptable in extremely mission critical systems, (2) it is expensive for cost-sensitive embedded systems, to the point of being prohibitive in many cases, and (3) it is also power inefficient for IoT (Internet of Things) products with embedded memories as these arrays of memory cells lead to significant leakage current in standby modes. In this chapter, we study an approach to the problem of stack overflow in a multithreaded embedded system where the reliability of the system is improved from being a function of the weakest link (i.e., the thread which faulted with overflow) to being a function of a cooperative effort across all the threads and then using the rescue effort as a trigger for an opportunistic micro-rejuvenation of the affected thread and their dependents such that overall reliability of the system is enhanced.

12.1. Introduction

More than a million lines of code run on a typical embedded device of the modern day (e.g., smartphones, laptops, drones, etc.) and over 100+ software threads, from an operating system standpoint, execute on the computer system, each providing a logical functionality. Some threads have higher priority than others when it comes to being processed by a shared Central Processing Unit (CPU). These embedded systems are particularly prone to post-release software faults, the root causes of which are not always attributable to software, but to a mix of software, environment and the underlying hardware. Common root causes seen are race conditions across multiple software threads, buffer overflows, the accumulation of errors due to the narrowing of data types during type conversion, the return of stack addresses, race conditions across software and hardware threads (e.g., in multithreaded CPUs), the memory corruption of software heaps and stacks by hardware bus masters (e.g., DMAs) and more. A comprehensive list of top software errors in the last decade has been well-catalogued [6] and it should not come as a surprise that buffer overflows (of the stack or of the heap) rank as the top third cause of all known software vulnerabilities. While it is not impossible to test for all such faults prior to software release, it is not practical to do so in large and complex systems due to the demands of time-to-market and the cost associated with such an activity. It is, therefore, necessary to design software and hardware with such failures in mind. Either reactive or proactive measures should be put into place to improve the reliability of the overall system.

Towards that, Software Rejuvenation [7] was put forth as a powerful new ideology to manage such elusive faults in post-released software. The motivation behind this approach was to accept the presence of faults in a complex system and to design a method to handle their occurrence in a way that is not detrimental to the end user experience. The first analytic study of rejuvenation [8] was seen in Unix workstation mainframes which demonstrated its practical utility in improving the longevity of such a complex cluster of machines. Since then, rejuvenation has morphed into various forms (micro-rejuvenation, macro-rejuvenation, restart) and has started to be applied to a variety of systems including servers, mission critical designs and virtual systems. Subsequently, researchers have documented an exhaustive summary [9, 10] on the history of rejuvenation and its varied applications in different industries. However, there has not been a focused treatment of stack overflow as a cause of system failure and any recovery techniques around that. This forms the motivation for this chapter where we assume an environment of memory-constrained embedded systems where stack overflow faults are common and put forth a framework that blends in a *just-in-time* recovery technique coupled with the more classical approach of micro-rejuvenation.

We focus specifically on system failures triggered by stack overflow, a condition where the contents of a stack frame of one thread spills and overwrites one or more locations of the adjacent stack belonging to another thread. Many of the infamous bugs in the computing world have been associated with this fault, some with immense financial impact [11–15]. A catalogue of buffer overflow attacks is well maintained by Purdue University [16] and can be perused to gauge the impact of this problem in different applications related to computing. Of the two overflow kinds — heap and stack — the latter is more interesting to attackers as it always easily provides a way to execute malicious code by hijacking a return address of a function. In contrast, the heap is more of a passive container of data and may or may not contain a pointer to a function. This makes detection and avoidance of and recovery from stack overflow a particularly interesting topic in computing. The failure can be systematic (e.g., caught by a watchdog logic in the hardware or in the operating system and raising an exception) or chaotic (e.g., an undetected and corrupted stack leading to malfunctioning function jumps, crashes or even a security breach). As the outcome cannot be predicted, the handling of stack overflow errors, once detected, has always been simple and swift: bring down the entire system and restart.

The approaches to handling stack overflow can be broadly grouped into three categories: techniques to avoid, techniques to mitigate impact and techniques to recover. As an example, an overflow can be avoided by careful estimation of the stack size using innovative tools and system modelling [17, 18]. But the research indicates that all such passive estimation is still fraught with inaccuracies leaving room for overflow, albeit with lesser probability. As a result, the literature is rife with examples of handling an overflow with the intention of mitigating its impact by detecting it at the earliest opportunity. StackGuard [19], StackShield [20], StackGhost [21], and Program Counter (PC) Encoding [21] are a few such well-documented techniques. In one of them, canaries are placed in the stack around the return address pointers and checked for corruption by the kernel prior to its dispatching the return address. In another approach, return address pointers are encoded with an encryption key which is validated prior to their jumping to the return address. Novel micro-architectural techniques have been explored [22] which use Secure Return Address Stack (SRAS) registers to preserve the integrity of a return address while allowing the other contents of a stack to be corrupted via overflow. There are very few instances of research on handling the stack overflow with the aim of recovery without introducing any corruption to the target stack. Two such good examples [23, 24] of recovery are seen where redundant memory units are designed into the system as extension stacks for whenever an overflow is detected in a thread. While this can be a viable solution for mission critical systems, the allocation of unused memory is usually not a preferred route for cost-sensitive embedded systems. It is perhaps a common theme in all the aforementioned techniques to handle the problem of stack overflow within the same stack but none of them provides a framework to handle overgrowth of the stack beyond design estimates due to incorrect estimation, deep (unplanned) recursion or mandelbugs, which is the focus of this chapter. We propose a new approach to handling stack overflow faults in a cooperative manner across all participating threads in an operating system that helps to minimize wastage of memory by over-estimation and that also avoids unused memory, as seen in prior research. The scheme is based on a few key observations drawn from multitudes of crash reports reported in the field from one such complex embedded device [25] that is found in every modern-day smartphone.

- At the time of a buffer overflow crash, the faulted thread usually ran out of its stack memory segment space, and
- Concomitant to the overflow of the faulted thread, most of the other threads had significant memory in their stack segments still unused, the sum total of which was larger than the overall stack size of the faulted thread and, sometimes, more than the largest stack segment in the entire system.

Consequently, this raises some interesting questions:

(1) *Can the Free Stack Space (FSS) of other stacks be used just-in-time to rescue the faulted stack?*
(2) *If so, how do we select the rescuing stack to maximize the probability of a successful recovery?*
(3) *What if the faulted stack overflows again in the rescued stack?*
(4) *How do we minimize the probability of the rescuing stack overflowing?*
(5) *Do we need micro-architectural changes to improve the rescue process?*
(6) *Can we apply directed micro-rejuvenation of the rescued stack to prevent future overflow events?*

The rest of the chapter is organized as follows: Section 12.2 outlines the FSS (Free Stack Space) opportunity as seen during a stack overflow event in any given thread and explains how the FSS can be harvested. Section 12.3 introduces the idea of Joint Defense[a] where the entire system, via its FSS, comes to the rescue of the faulted stack/thread to prevent a system collapse and goes on to elucidate the various trade-offs involved [26]. In the process, it reveals the need for a new processor micro-architecture that can make this stack leasing scheme robust. This section also proffers a sample operating system scheduling algorithm that can help in optimal selection of the rescuing stack[b] and that shows the configurable knobs of the selection process that can be applied with specific weights and distributions for future modeling. Section 12.4 provides a holistic flow of all the individual elements of the Joint Defense from the onset of a stack overflow to its eventual recovery. Section 12.5 ties the concept of Joint Defense to a traditional rejuvenation concept as an opportunistic trigger to further improve the longevity of the system and prevent future stack overflow events from the same stack(s). The chapter is then concluded with remarks on future research areas that can be conducted on various aspects of this framework.

12.2. Free Stack Space (FSS) Opportunity

Handing a stack overflow fault can be broken down into three phases:

(1) *Detection*
(2) *Resolution*
(3) *Avoidance or Deferment until a more appropriate time*

Detection mechanisms can be *preemptive instantaneous* or *delayed* depending on where they are implemented and when they are detected. The former requires assistance from a micro-processor to perform *just-in-time* checking of the stack pointer against the configured boundary of the stack and then alerts the micro-processor with an exception if the stack operation is about to breach the boundary towards an overflow or an underflow. Typically, the boundary of the stack is loaded into one of the micro-processor registers by the operating system as part of context switching the thread to a run state. An example of such a scheme can be seen in the ARM v8 micro-architecture [27] which uses a stack-limit register to compare with the

---

[a]Joint Defense was a concept introduced in 2007 while the author was at Samsung Research & Development, India.

[b]The thread which offers loan of its stack to the faulted thread.

active stack pointer. The latter is a reactive method of detection in which placed markers (*a la* canaries) in the beginning of every stack segment or individual stack frame[c] are checked by the operating system during a context switch or while returning from a procedure to determine if the marker was corrupted. This is also a common, often preferred, practice in the industry and can be seen supported in widely deployed embedded processors [28, 29].

Let us now contrast the two approaches. The former is precise and enables a proactive handling of the stack overflow but comes with an execution overhead as the micro-processor needs to perform a compare concomitant with every stack operation, such as a PUSH or a POP. In this technique, the stack overflow or underflow is avoided entirely if the operating system performs a recovery option immediately in context of the raised exception prior to corrupting the stack by completing the PUSH or POP operation. On the other hand, the latter is imprecise and reactive but very lightweight as the comparative check is performed once per context switch or upon a procedure return, typically by operating system software. The focus of this technique is not as much an avoidance of the error but rather a detection of the error at the earliest opportunity before the corruption leads to unpredictable results or security breaches in the system.

An example of a downwards growing stack (i.e., growing from higher address to lower address) and its overflow is shown in Fig. 12.1. Every

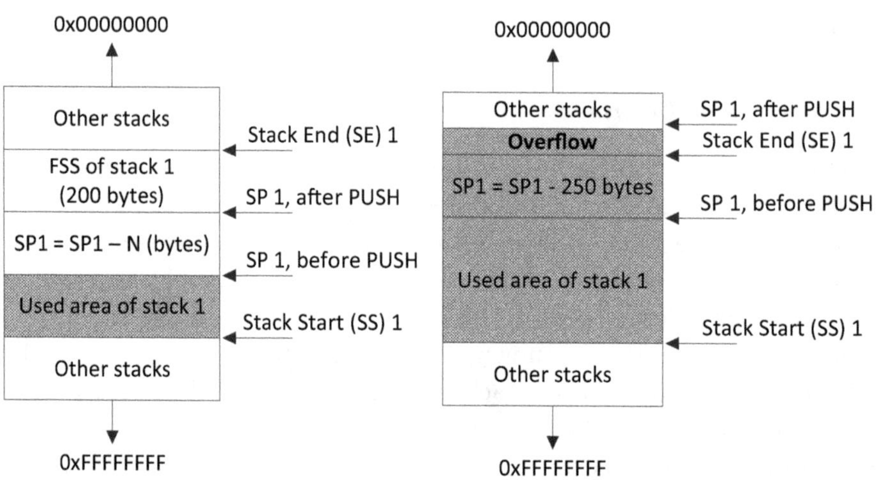

Fig. 12.1. Stack overflow and free stack space.

[c]Blocks of code within a procedure that possess independent stack variables, disjoint from the stack variables of the procedure.

procedure call creates a stack frame which adjusts the stack pointer, referred to as the SP_1, and decrements it by "n" bytes. This also adjusts the FSS of the stack. In the case of an overflow, the SP_1 exceeds the stack end limit, referred to as the SE_1, and corrupts the adjacent stack (or stacks, depending on how big "n" is. A *preemptive instantaneous* scheme catches the event and raises an exception keeping the SP_1 at its previous value as shown in the right hand portion of Fig. 12.1. Whereas in the *delayed* scheme, the adjacent stack (or stacks) would be overflowed and only later would the detection happen. While a stack is commonly identified by three well-known parameters (Stack Start or SS, Stack End or SE and Stack Pointer or SP), we introduce a few more parameters expressly required to elucidate the concepts in this chapter. First, we define *Free Stack Space (FSS)*, the metric which keeps track of the instantaneous available space (in bytes) in the stack and which is updated every time the stack is acted upon with a PUSH or a POP instruction. Second, we define *GAP*, the parameter which tracks the amount of spacing (in bytes) between the stack pointer of the incumbent (rescuing) stack and the stack start of the faulted (rescued) stack within the incumbent's leased stack. Third, we define *GAP_MIN_VALUE*, a parameter which ensures a minimum separation (in bytes, again) between the rescuing and the rescued stacks in the cooperatively leased stack segment. The rest of the chapter assumes a *preemptive instantaneous* scheme as the foundation upon which the rest of the Joint Defense recovery mechanism will be developed.

We go on to show, via an example from a practical embedded system in Table 12.1, the amount of FSS that is typically present when a system faults. It is a reflection of the over-estimation that is still prevalent in the industry

Table 12.1. Stack size and FSS distribution.

Priority	Thread	Stack Size (SE-SS)	FSS (SE-SP)
P0	T0	4000	1000
P1	T1	4000	1000
P2	T2	16,384	4096
P3	T3	8000	2000
P4	T4	25,000	6000
P5	T5	16,000	2000
P6	T6	20,480	5120
P7	T7	12,288	2950
P8	T8	20,480	4096
P9	T9	98,304	24,576

which occurs during the designing of an embedded system. As can be seen in the table, threads of higher priority, such as those processing a frame in the air interface, are latency sensitive with complex interactions with underlying hardware, but they do not usually have deep nesting of functions and usually have smaller stack size to begin with. Whereas threads of lower priority (such as those higher in the layered stack) have more software flows with deeper nesting of functions, but, as they are not as latency sensitive, have much larger stack size. This pattern is quite common and this table directly reflects the extent of the over-estimation of stack size prevalent in the industry. It is also important to note the irony of a system crash due to the depleted stack of one errant thread when the entire system, looked upon as a whole, has an enormous amount of free memory at its disposal scattered across the constituent threads and their stacks.

12.3. Cooperative Stack Leasing Paradigm

The fundamental concept outlined in this chapter is that of a cooperative stack leasing across participating threads at the time of a stack overflow fault of one or more software threads. The chapter goes on to show the algorithm and necessary micro-architecture support needed to effectively execute the procedure. The philosophy is thereby termed *Joint Defense*, as all threads offer their respective resources, in this case the stack, to jointly rescue a single faulted thread in a cooperative sense. The extension of this concept to other resources owned by a thread is certainly a possibility that can be explored further and a brief mention of such resources is made at the end of the chapter.

The concept of coordinated stack leasing is explained below with reference to Fig. 12.2 which depicts the sequence of events at the onset of a stack overflow detected preemptively (i.e., before the PUSH was committed to overflow the stack). Four threads, denoted T_1, T_2, T_3, T_4, are used along with a system Interrupt Service Routine or ISR thread and the kernel that executes in privileged mode when the stack overflow exception is raised. The stack of the kernel exception handler is not shown for brevity. Furthermore, **B** indicates a thread in "BLOCKED" state; **ISR** indicates the occurrence of an interrupt and **Scheduler** indicates the execution of the operating system's scheduling procedure. The column on the extreme right shows the system RAM during this time with a plurality of stack segments growing downwards with their used and FSS regions respectively. The dotted lines indicate a **PUSH** or a **POP** operation on the stack, whereas the dashed lines represent a kernel software execution. The priorities of threads T_1, T_2, T_3, T_4

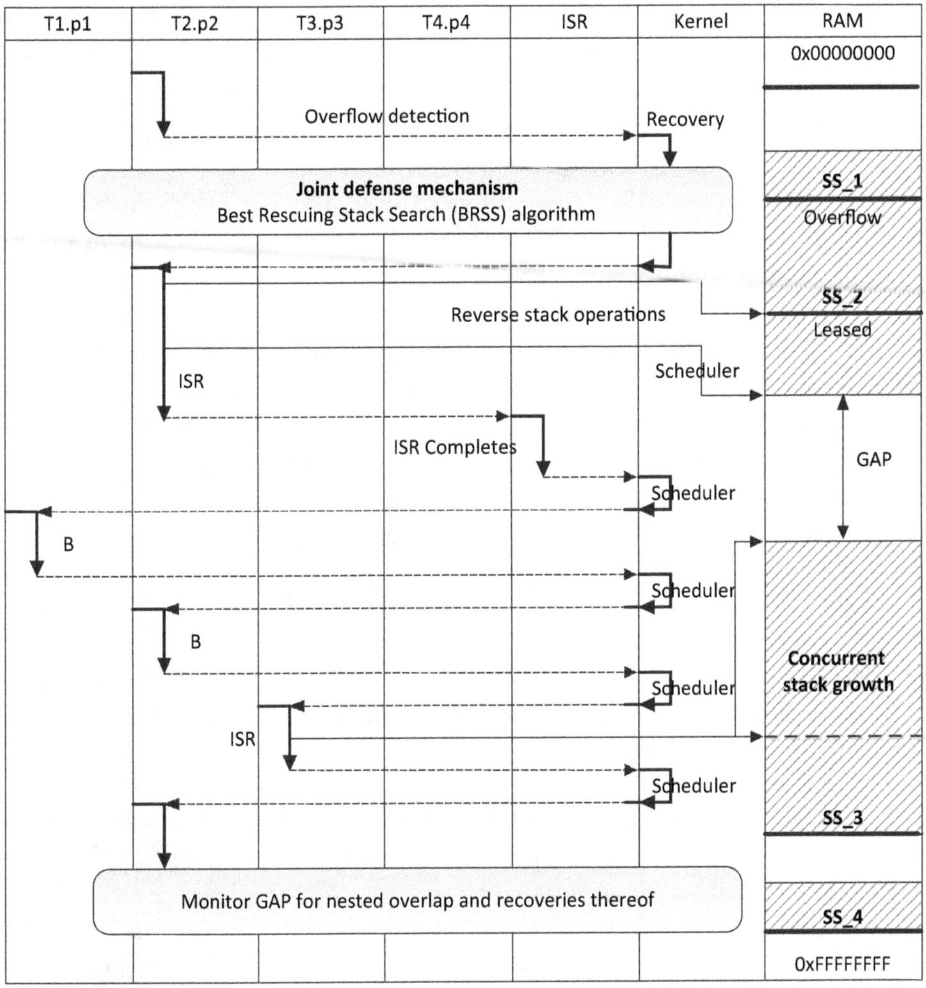

Fig. 12.2. Stack overflow handing via coordinated leasing.

are mapped to P_1, P_2, P_3, P_4 respectively and they are ordered thus:

$$P_1 > P_2 > P_3 > P_4$$

We further assume that the scheduling environment is one that is a preemptive priority in nature where the highest priority READY thread always runs preceding any other lower priority READY threads. Lastly, T_2 is assumed to have encountered a stack overflow at which point the control is transferred to the operating system, via a micro-processor exception. This triggers the search for the best rescuing stack, a concept explored in detail in Section 12.3.4. We assume that the search yielded T_3 to be the rescue stack. All the spillover bytes of the stack frame in the PUSH operation from T_2 are seamlessly diverted into a rescuing stack, offered by T_3. This process is explored in Section 12.3.1. It is important to introduce, at this point, the conflict of resources that can arise from this leasing process. The hitherto BLOCKED rescuing thread T_3, despite being lower in priority to the RUNNING thread T_2, may get activated into a READY state while the coordinated leasing process is still in effect. Such occurrences are quite common in a preemptive priority environment due to a variety of factors. One such cause is priority inversion where the lower priority thread would temporarily assume the priority of a higher priority thread and get scheduled out of turn. Another possibility is parallelism, which is exhibited in multiple core systems or multiple (hardware) threaded systems where several software threads, of different priorities, may run on a plurality of such hardware cores or hardware threads. Such a conflict of resources in the leased region can be addressed by one of the two possible options for the PUSH operation:

- *Allocate the stack frame in the same direction as the regular stack, keeping a gap between the permanent and leased region*
- *Allocate the stack frame to the far end of the leased stack and grow in the opposite direction until a minimum gap develops between the leased stack and the permanent region*

These two approaches are not without reproach, albeit one outmerits the other in certain cases. The first route is prohibitively complicated during the nested execution of the two threads (e.g., T_2 and T_3) as the entire stack will have to be littered with markers to fragment the regions belonging to either participant. Consequently, we avoid discussing this option in this chapter. The second technique has the clear advantage of keeping the two stacks in the same leased stack memory segment as far apart as possible, thereby minimizing the probability of an overlap should the two threads (i.e., T_2 and T_3) simultaneously start running. In fact, the two threads can continue to inter-operate so long as the gap between the downward-growing stack and the upward-growing stack is maintained at a configured minimum. Despite its elegance, this approach does present an unprecedented problem: the **concurrently bidirectional stack**, a topic that is explored further in Section 12.3.2. The solution to this problem is presented with a new micro-architecture that forms the topic of Section 12.3.3.

Going back to Fig. 12.2, let us assume now that an interrupt fired which got handled within an ISR, which are typically of higher priority than any other user threads such as $T_1, \ldots, T_n$. Furthermore, let us assume that the

ISR activates T_1 which is the highest priority user thread in the system. There are two outcomes possible:

- *T_1 runs to completion whereupon the scheduler restarts T_2. T_2 may additionally send an inter-process communication (IPC) message to T_3 and stay blocked until a response is received from T_3.*
- *T_1 acquires a shared resource previously held by T_3, causing a priority inversion that the operating system addresses by elevating the priority of T_3 temporarily, a.k.a. priority inheritance.*

In either case, T_3 would get activated while it is still rescuing T_2 with its leased stack. Keeping a safe separation in stack regions between the permanent resident and the leased resident of the stack is therefore a necessary condition in order to have a meaningful recovery. Furthermore, this brings to the fore the need to have a proper selection algorithm for the rescue stack such that the probability of such a concurrent execution of the rescuing and rescued threads is minimized.

12.3.1. *Re-Entrant and Non-Contiguous Leasing*

The kernel evaluates the FSS of all the constituent threads and selects the most appropriate rescuing stack subject to a search algorithm specific to the scheduling environment. For the overflowing thread, it will be a transparent expansion of its own stack and a normal program execution would ensue; the kernel achieves the stack leasing by managing the stack pointers seamlessly. The process is transparent to the software executing on the faulted thread. This is indicated in Fig. 12.2. While the first overflow is still being handled, the system could encounter a second overflow in the same thread or another thread. In such a case, the operating system invokes a re-entrant stack leasing process, conditioned on a desired re-entrant depth. In the event of not identifying a single rescuing stack to meet the overflowing stack requirement, the system could resort to a non-contiguous stack leasing from multiple rescuing stacks or could trigger a complete system restart — the choice between the two is left as an implementation decision depending on the complexity and cost of restart.

12.3.2. *Reverse Stack Growth — Concurrent Bi-Directionality*

Stack leasing facilitates the relocation of the overflowing data from the faulted stack into the rescuing stack. If the overflowing data is pushed into the leased stack in the same direction, starting from the current stack pointer location of the rescuing thread, tremendous complexity would ensue in managing the multiple stack pointers inside the rescuing stack should the rescuing thread start to run concurrently. To avoid such operational complexities, a new concept of **Reverse Stack Growth** is introduced where the system operates in a unidirectional stack model in regular mode but switches to reverse growth only within the leased stack and only during the leasing process of the faulted thread. The lease process is controlled via a continuously updated metric, GAP, that tracks the distance between the stack pointer of the two participating threads. A separate parameter GAP_MIN_VALUE is maintained and advertised to the kernel by each thread participating in this coordinated stack leasing process. The GAP is always compared against the GAP_MIN_VALUE and in the event of a breach, further usage on the leased stack ceases. The system at this time can either perform a nested recovery by searching yet another stack or it can abort and perform a system restart, should the search for a rescuing stack fail.

12.3.3. *Polymorphic Op-Code Micro-Architecture*

Attaining concurrent bi-directionality of a stack segment is not an easy process and practically impossible with software-only methods. The limitation arises from the fact that computer programs are compiled with *a priori* configuration of a downwards or an upwards growing stack and the microprocessor instructions (e.g., PUSH, POP) are chosen to follow that direction. Altering the behavior of a PUSH or a POP instruction in run-time is not feasible. We propose a new micro-architecture to achieve that goal. The key to such a micro-architecture would be a *Special Hardware Unit (SHU)* inside the execution stage of the microprocessor that could be engaged or disengaged by side-band signals controlled by the operating system at the entry and exit of the stack leasing process respectively. Once engaged, the SHU performs a run-time op-code translation that translates the PUSH (or POP) instructions in-line into a PUSH_R (or a POP_R) instruction prior to routing them to the execution pipeline. Suffice to say, the PUSH_R and the POP_R are exactly the same as PUSH and POP but just operate in the reverse direction as far as updating the stack pointer goes. A concept diagram of SHU is shown in Fig. 12.3. While the scheme is proposed only for two instructions that matter to stack handling, this proposal of polymorphic op-codes can be extended to any scenario for denser code where situation-aware

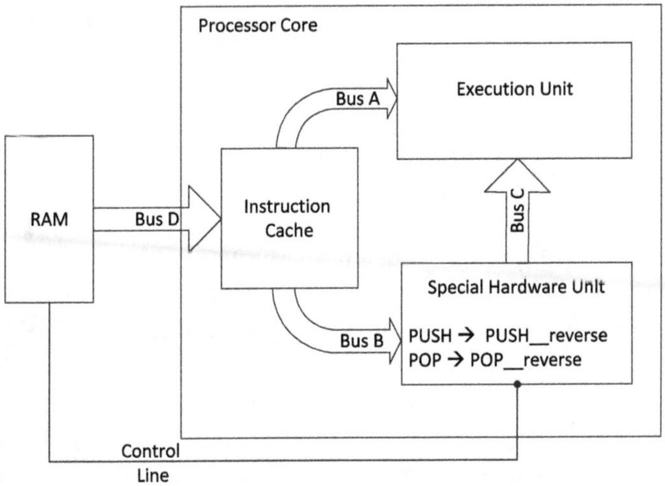

Fig. 12.3. SHU: A Von Neumann architecture with modifications showing a side-band control for activation.

multiplexing can be achieved out of the single instruction. That, however, is not explored in this chapter and is left as a note to the reader for further deliberation.

12.3.4. *Best Rescuing Stack Search (BRSS) Algorithm*

It would be evident by now that an improperly selected rescuing stack would result in sub-optimal system performance owing to frequent overlaps thereby leading to nested leasing and possibly a system restart due to the impracticality of performing too deep a nesting. We now focus our discussion towards one such possible algorithm, operating in a preemptive priority scheduling environment, that can be used to direct the candidate search in a way that minimizes the probability of such overlaps.

Firstly, any candidate rescue thread should have the following two attributes, independent of the underlying scheduling environment of the system, in that specific order:

(1) *Lowest probability of being scheduled in the immediate future*
(2) *Lowest probability of an overlap if it got scheduled while in rescue mode*

For the rest of the discussion, let us assume that the stack overflow fault happened in thread T_1 in a system of N threads $T_1, T_2, T_3, \ldots, T_N$. Note that determining the stack with the highest FSS is a trivial process and can be completed in $\Omega(N)$ time — as part of the *BRSS* algorithm. However, evaluating the probability of any thread, other than T_1, being scheduled in the next δ units of time is rather complicated. The metric to be modelled in this pursuit would be a series of conditional probabilities, defined as follows:

$$P\left(\frac{T_j : waiting \rightarrow ready)}{T_i : active}\right), \quad j \in 1, \ldots, N, \; j \neq i \tag{12.1}$$

The conditional probability can be made more realistic by having not just one, but multiple dependent threads being active, in one particular embodiment. Deriving these conditional probabilities can be done in two ways. In one approach, this metric may be derived *a priori* statically based on the associativity of threads as identified during system design by the architects. Except for the cases of unknown call flows and input triggers, this is a fairly risk-free method that guarantees sufficient accuracy in the model, albeit one that is onerous for the designers. In the other approach, these probabilities are learnt dynamically based on the run-time Markov modelling of the system behavior and identifying the pattern and linkages across the threads in most common use-cases. These explorations are outside the scope of this chapter and are possibilities for future research while a simpler algorithm is presented below to explain the key considerations of the BRSS algorithm. The high-level states of the algorithm are depicted in Fig. 12.4 and comprise an *Identification Stage*, a *Selection Stage* and a *Rescuing Stage*. These are explained in the following steps:

12.3.4.1. *Step 1*

As shown in Fig. 12.4, in this stage we identify the set of candidate threads which have priorities lower than the priority of the thread that faulted. If a non-empty set is obtained, we move to the selection stage, explained in Section 12.3.4.2; if an empty set is obtained, that would generally mean the fault occurred in the lowest priority thread. This leaves open the possibility of every other thread in the system running due to any IPC or externally generated interrupt event while preempting the faulted thread. The selection of a rescuing thread here is one that involves minimizing the probability of imminent execution as much as possible. We explore this further in Section 12.3.4.3.

12.3.4.2. *Step 2*

All candidate threads in this set are of a priority lower than the faulted thread. We sort them in decreasing order of their weighted FSS (FSS^w)

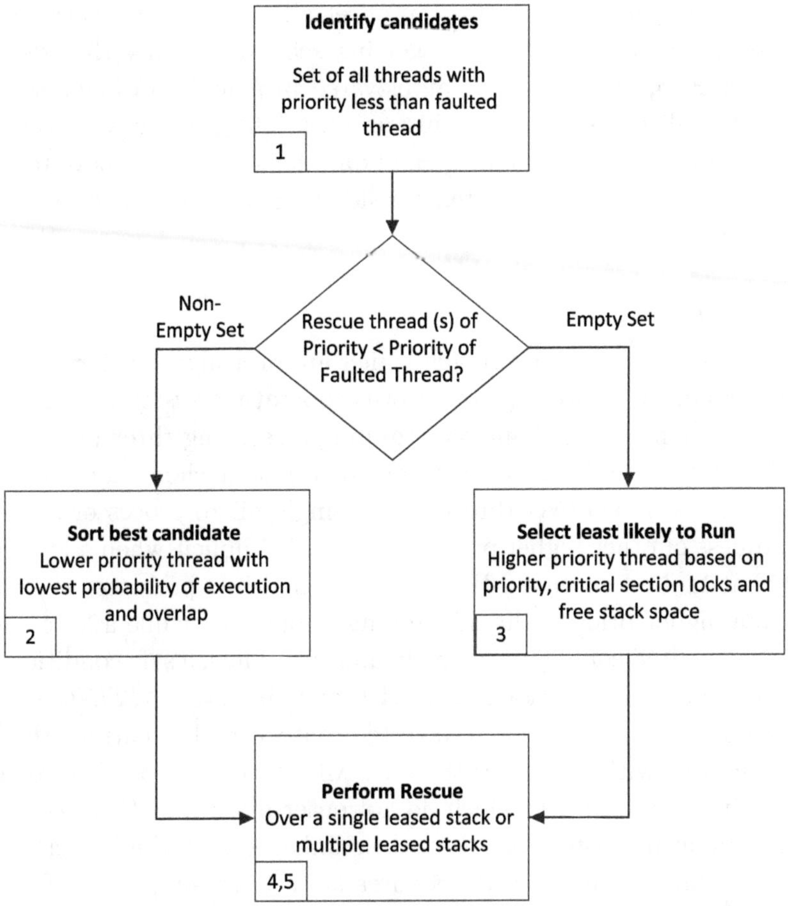

Fig. 12.4. BRSS algorithm flow.

given by the formula:

$$FSS_i^w = FSS_i * PENALTY_i, \forall i \in N \tag{12.2}$$

The penalty factor assumes the value 1 (i.e., no penalty) for a given candidate thread when the concerned thread is in the *WAITING* state of the operating system and takes a fractional value from the set 0.1, 0.2... 0.9 when the concerned thread is in the *READY* state. The absolute value of the penalty factor is dependent on the relative priority of the threads. As an example, a thread with a higher priority will have a higher penalty factor (i.e., smaller fractional value) to lower its weighted FSS. For threads blocked on a semaphore or a mutex, a higher penalty factor is accorded due to the possibility of an unplanned priority inversion and uplifting of its priority.

This factor, thereby, ensures that we offset all those lower priority threads which are higher in probability of getting scheduled. Only threads having a very large FSS, despite having an elevated probability of being scheduled imminently, will get selected in this process. The top entry in the sorted list, t, would therefore be the best candidate for rescue. We move to Section 12.3.4.3 to ascertain if the selected thread is viable given the exact needs of the overflow event.

12.3.4.3. *Step 3*

In this set, we have all the threads which are of a higher priority than the faulted thread. In a preemptive priority operating system, that provides mutual exclusion on the chances of running a rescuing thread should it get into a *READY* state. It is, therefore, obvious that we choose a rescuing stack from one of the *WAITING* threads. In a single micro-processor system the non-readiness of other higher priority threads is implicit when a low priority thread that faulted executes. However, in a multiple processor system, one can have a higher priority thread running in one core while a lower priority thread that faulted could be running in another. Thus, a safe condition would be to select one higher priority thread that is in the *WAITING* state and one which is not in any priority inverted state with the current thread or, for that matter, with any other threads. Alternatively, it is also worthwhile to keep a list of all threads which do not entertain any critical section calls with the operating system based on their linkages with the kernel calls. We now sort this list of higher priority threads in decreasing order of weighted FSS, given by a different formula:

$$FSS_i^w = FSS_i * (1 - PSF_i), \forall i \in N \tag{12.3}$$

The rationale of the PSF (Priority Scaling Factor) is to offset the higher priority threads having a higher probability of getting scheduled. Due to the PSF, the higher priority threads have a slimmer chance of getting selected as the rescuing thread, unless they have an enormous amount of FSS to spare. A simplified implementation of the PSF could be:

$$PSF_i = \frac{Priority_i}{MAX\_Priority + 1}, \forall i \in N \tag{12.4}$$

As an example, the highest priority thread in the system, having a priority value of 100 (MAX_PRIORITY), would have the PSF as 0.99 and the corresponding offset as 0.01. However, the PSF can be learnt dynamically based on various parameters, including a history of mutex operations and the rate of scheduling and interrupt sensitivities, among other things. The candidate that tops this list is deemed the best rescuing thread. We now move to Step 4 of the algorithm.

12.3.4.4. *Step 4*

At this step, the kernel evaluates if the FSS of the rescuing thread, obtained from Section 12.3.4.2 or Section 12.3.4.3, is greater than the overflowing memory need, which was calculated upon entry into any function and before loading the stack frame, by at least a confidence margin. This factor would be registered by each of the constituent threads agreeing to support this Joint Defense paradigm. If the equality shown below is satisfied, the search for the best rescuing thread concludes here and the results of the search are returned with the details of the rescuing thread.

$$FSS_i > (Overflow\_Bytes + mem\_confidence\_factor_i), \forall i \in N \qquad (12.5)$$

If, however, the equality is not satisfied, we perform a recursive search to identify more chunks of stack to attempt a non-contiguous stack leasing

12.3.4.5. *Step 5*

Reaching this step is an indication that there is no single thread which can satisfy the stack memory needs of the faulted thread. The Joint Defense is now achieved by leasing smaller chunks of memory from multiple numbers of candidate threads, subject to the desired amount of multiplicity, yet another parameter of the scheme. In the event no tenable set of rescuing threads is found, classical software rejuvenation techniques are invoked which would lead to a system restart.

12.4. System Architecture

In this section, synergy is brought into the disparate elements of the joint-defense system to explain across hardware and software boundary lines how a stack overflow fault is handled. This section further illustrates the location and functionality of the *SHU* which will be instrumental in performing the op-code translation to achieve the on-demand, simultaneous bi-directionality of the stack growth. The *SHU* and the associated events within the faulted and rescuing stack are depicted in Fig. 12.5. When the system boots up, it registers with the *SHU* the set of instructions which would require monitoring and run-time translation. The registration is done as a 2-tuple such as $PUSH \rightarrow PUSH\_R$ and $POP \rightarrow POP\_R$ respectively. The system

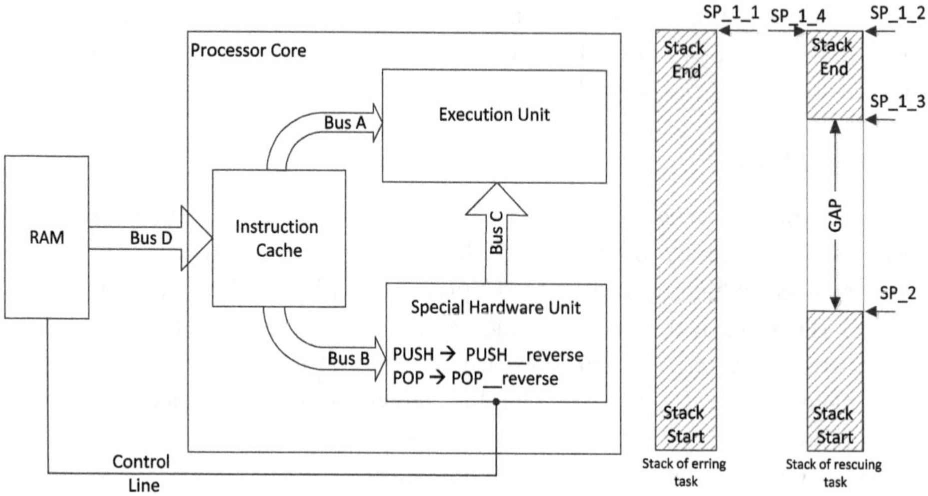

Fig. 12.5. SHU hardware unit (left) and stack flow (right).

also ensures that the *SHU* and the associated data buses **B** and **C** are in their default deactivated state while the data buses **A** and **D** are in their default activated state. This is the configuration where instructions are routed from memory to the micro-processor execution pipeline without any translation. With reference to Fig. 12.5, let us assume now that T_1 was getting executed when its stack pointer (SP_1) reached the STACK_END. The stack pointer is shown by SP_1_1 at the STACK_END of its home stack Stack_1. Upon the detection of a stack overflow, an exception is sent to the kernel which configures the *SHU* to activate data buses **B** and **C** and correspondingly deactivate data buses **A** and **D**. This ensures that all subsequent instructions are routed via the *SHU* while it performs an inline monitoring of the instructions that are required to be translated. The key phases of the procedure are depicted in Fig. 12.6.

The stages are explained below in context of the stack diagram shown in Fig. 12.6 where a stack overflow is preemptively detected in T_1:

(1) The operating system kernel stores the current stack pointer SP_1_1 into the thread control block (TCB) of the faulted T_1 thread.
(2) The kernel invokes the rescue candidate thread algorithm (Section 12.3.4). Assume the search returned a valid rescuing thread T_2; the stack pointer of T_2 is shown by SP_2 in Stack_2 in Fig. 12.5, which is now the rescuing stack and whose parameters GAP and GAP_MIN_VALUE are retrieved from its TCB. If no candidate is found in this step, the system

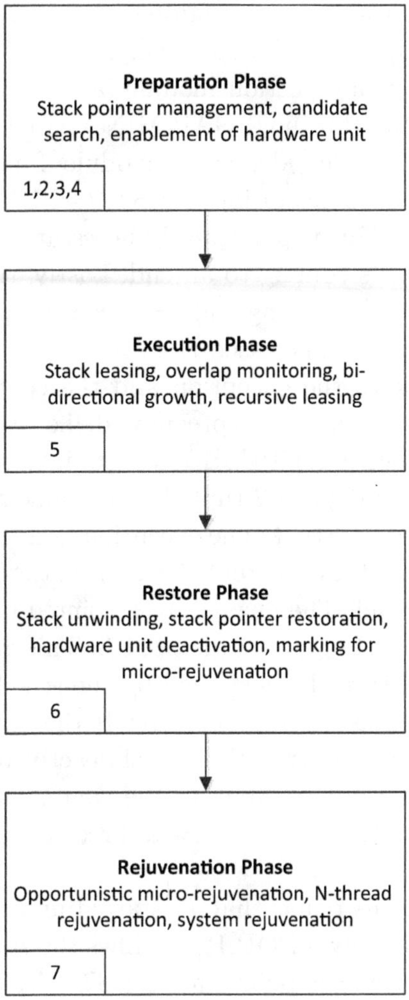

Fig. 12.6. Joint defense phases.

jumps to Phase 7 and performs a complete system rejuvenation, as done in present systems in absence of this paradigm.

(3) The kernel updates the stack pointer of T_1 to the address STACK_END of Stack_2 as shown by SP_1_2. Additionally, the kernel enables the *SHU* to deactivate the data bus **A** and activate the data buses **B** and **C**. All subsequent op-codes are now sent via data bus **B** into the *SHU* for the monitor-translate operation and then forwarded into the execution unit via data bus **C** either transparently or via translation, depending on the configured look-up rules. The kernel starts maintaining the GAP and,

at every stack operation by the faulted thread T_1, the kernel updates (adds or subtracts) the GAP accordingly.

(4) The kernel instructs a detection module (a hardware monitor) to check if GAP breaches the threshold GAP_MIN_VALUE as advertised by the rescuing thread T_2. The detection module further watches out for the stack pointer SP_1 acquiring the STACK_END address Stack_2 of the rescuing stack. This is particularly necessary to catch the condition of the leasing process coming to an end. Lastly, the kernel updates the TCB of T_1 to indicate an ongoing stack leasing process and keeps the list of threads which it has leased from.

(5) The kernel completes the exception and the control goes back to the T_1, at the point where it was preempted, i.e., just before the PUSH operation. The op-code for PUSH now gets into the *SHU* via data bus **B**. The *SHU* finds a defined 2-tuple for the same and translates the op-code from PUSH to PUSH_R. The execution unit thus performs a reverse stack growth on the stack pointer SP_1_2, from the STACK_END address of the rescuing thread. The new address pointed to by the stack pointer of T_1, after the PUSH operation, is SP_1_3. This goes on until the stack overflow ends or a thread is switched by the scheduler. The translation process must not affect any other threads that are not in this faulted state. To handle this scenario, the kernel deactivates the *SHU* again via the control line as the first thing in the context switching process and re-configures the data buses to allow a direct path from memory to the execution unit.

(6) Let us assume, at this point, that T_1 started unwinding the stack frame data. A POP, effectively a POP_R, modifies the stack pointer of T_1 from SP_1_3 to SP_1_4, which points to the STACK_END of the rescuing stack. The detection module, as instructed in the preparation phase, raises an exception to inform the end of stack leasing. The kernel, thereafter, brings SP_1 into its home stack by updating SP_1 with the address that was stored earlier in its TCB (i.e., SP_1_1). Additionally, the kernel deactivates the *SHU* and updates the TCB accordingly to signal the end of the stack leasing process. This marks the end of the cooperative stack leasing process and the recovery of the faulted thread.

(7) The process described above was a *just-in-time* handling of a stack overflow fault that prevented the system from crashing — it, however, did not address the fundamental anomaly in the software or hardware or the environment that led to this fault. This stack overflow fault could have been due to a mandelbug and can repeat if the system

variables are not restored to their pristine state. One of the house-keeping activities of this process is to mark the faulted thread T_1 as a victim of a possible mandelbug and look for opportune times in future to restart or rejuvenate the thread and its dependent threads using the classical techniques of software rejuvenation. It should be apparent to the reader that the coordinated stack leasing process is an instantaneous recovery technique and enables the more traditional rejuvenation framework to have a clear sense of which thread or threads to act on to increase the overall longevity of the system.

12.5. Opportunistic Micro-Rejuvenation

The scheme outlined above addresses the just-in-time need to prevent the system from a fatal crash, providing a sort of micro recovery to the thread. The overflow could be caused by many reasons including, but not limited to,

(1) *Mandelbugs — the aging or non-aging kind*
(2) *Improper stack size estimation*
(3) *Unchecked deep recursion*
(4) *New call flows from an external caller*

While an incorrect estimation or new flow cannot be fixed without updating the software to re-size the stack, the aging-related bugs or the non-aging mandelbugs can be addressed via a precise thread rejuvenation. A stack overflow fault handled via the above Joint Defense paradigm provides a deterministic trigger to the rejuvenation framework which concerns the state of the thread.

It now remains to identify an opportune moment to trigger the rejuvenation of the faulted thread. Such a moment can be, but is not limited to being, the operating state of the thread such as when the thread is in the **WAITING** state. Further qualifications can be applied by observing the associativity of the thread in the system and observing that the states of those associated threads are dormant as well. This association can be maintained statically or can be learnt dynamically via a Markov modelling of the system behavior. In one embodiment, just the affected thread can be rejuvenated, thereby drawing parallels with the classical micro-rejuvenation concepts [30], and further explored in one specific embodiment [31] around a global stack-sharing model. In another embodiment, the affected thread and a set of associated threads can be micro-rejuvenated to improve the reliability of the overall system. And in yet another embodiment, the stack can be re-partitioned across the associated threads to better align the dynamic stack needs of one or more of threads compared to the others in that group of associated threads.

12.6. Conclusion

As can be understood from Fig. 12.6, the four-phase system built with the Joint Defense paradigm would be able to recover from a stack overflow event through an efficient management of the plurality of stacks using the cooperative stack leasing approach while still ensuring a memory-efficient design. This would help in designing embedded systems with higher reliability against the presence of stack overflow faults. The presence of such a mechanism would help system architects reduce the widely prevalent over-estimation of stack segments and thereby reduce the overall memory requirement of the system. This helps with the cost of the system and with the overall size of the Application Specific Integrated Circuits (ASICs). If, for instance, all the threads, $T_1, T_2, \ldots, T_10$ in Table 12.1, allocated stack sizes that were 15% smaller, there would have been a memory saving of almost 35731.2 bytes; enough to fit in 8 more threads of P_0, P_1 priority ranges. The concept outlined also helps in mission critical systems where stack size may not be the reason for an overflow fault, but an unplanned call stack or a mandelbug triggering an unbounded recursion can still trigger an overflow causing a system abort where the aforementioned set of techniques can prevent the system failure and provide a path towards a graceful recovery and a precise trigger for eliminating the anomaly via opportunistic micro-rejuvenation at an opportune time.

We conclude this chapter with a mention of a few possible topics for future research. One area to which the Joint Defense paradigm can be extrapolated would be heap memories which, like stacks, are an immutable property of a thread and often over-estimated to protect against memory depletion. Secondly, even with over-estimation, they tend to overflow due to nefarious buffer overflow attacks caused by array index violations and pointer math errors as commonly seen in practice. Thirdly, the best rescuing stack search algorithm provides a rich area of innovation around the prediction of the next task that will be executed given the dynamic system behavior. Identifying the probabilities of the next task's execution, learnt dynamically via a Markov modelling of the system, provides a clear input to the search criteria that minimizes overlap in the rescuing stack. Lastly, the search algorithm assumed a preemptive priority kernel scheduler, but can be extended to cater to other scheduling algorithms as well.

Acknowledgments

The author expresses gratitude to Kishor Trivedi for his valuable inputs in shaping the contents of this chapter and connecting the steps to the larger system of software rejuvenation. Thanks are due to Douglas Dahlby for his inputs towards improving the chapter with relevant information around practical embedded systems where stack overflow continues to surface as a reliability impacting phenomenon.

References

1. A. Zhiyuan and L. Haiyan. (2010). Realization of buffer overflow. In *Proceedings of the 2010 International Forum on Information Technology and Applications, Kunming, China, July 16–18*, vol. 1, pp. 347–349.
2. IAR Systems. (n.d.). Detecting and avoiding stack overflows in embedded systems. URL https://www.iar.com/support/resources/articles/detecting-and-avoiding-stack-overflow-in-embedded-systems/. Accessed: 2019-11-13.
3. N. Jones. (September 7, 2016). How to prevent and detect stack overflow. URL https://barrgroup.com/Embedded-Systems/How-To/Prevent-Detect-Stack-Overflow. Accessed: 2019-11-13.
4. M. Grottke and K. Trivedi. (2005). A classification of software faults. In *Supplemental Proceedings of the Sixteenth International IEEE Symposium on Software Reliability Engineering, Chicago, Illinois, USA, November 8–11*, pp. 4.19–4.20.
5. Expresslogic. (n.d.). Detecting and avoiding stack overflow in IoT/embedded systems. URL https://rtos.com/wp-content/uploads/2017/10/EL_Detecting_and_Avoiding_Stack_Overflow.pdf. Accessed: 2019-11-13.
6. S. Christey. Top 25 most dangerous software errors. URL https://cwe.mitre.org/top25/archive/2011/2011_cwe_sans_top25.pdf. Accessed: 2019-11-13.
7. Y. Huang, C. Kintala, N. Kolettis, and N. D. Fulton. (1995). Software rejuvenation: Analysis, module and applications. In *Proceedings of the Twenty-Fifth International Symposium on Fault-Tolerant Computing, Pasadena, California, USA, June 27–30*, pp. 381–390.
8. S. Garg, A. van Moorsel, K. Vaidyanathan, and K. S. Trivedi. (1998). A methodology for detection and estimation of software aging. In *Proceedings of the Ninth International Symposium on Software Reliability Engineering, Paderborn, Germany, November 4–7*, pp. 283–292.
9. D. Cotroneo, R. Natella, R. Pietrantuono, and S. Russo. (2011). Software aging and rejuvenation: Where we are and where we are going. In *Proceedings of the 2011 IEEE Third International Workshop on Software Aging and Rejuvenation, Hiroshima, Japan, November 29–December 2*, pp. 1–6. doi: 10.1109/WoSAR.2011.15.
10. D. Cotroneo, R. Natella, R. Pietrantuono, and S. Russo. (2014). A survey of software aging and rejuvenation studies. *Journal of Emerging Technologies in Computing Systems*, **10**(1), 8:1–8:34. ISSN 1550-4832. doi: 10.1145/2539117.

11. H. Orman. (2003). The morris worm: A fifteen-year perspective. *IEEE Security & Privacy*, **99**(5), 35–43. ISSN 1540-7993. doi: 10.1109/MSECP.2003.1236233.
12. C. Shannon and D. Moore. (2004). The spread of the witty worm. *IEEE Security & Privacy*, **2**(4), 46–50. ISSN 1540-7993. doi: 10.1109/MSP.2004.59.
13. M. Bailey, E. Cooke, F. Jahanian, and D. Watson. (2005). The blaster worm: Then and now. *IEEE Security & Privacy*, **3**(4), 26–31. ISSN 1540-7993. doi: 10.1109/MSP.2005.106.
14. D. Moore, V. Paxson, S. Savage, C. Shannon, S. Staniford, and N. Weaver. (2003). Inside the slammer worm. *IEEE Security & Privacy*, **99**(4), 33–39. ISSN 1540-7993. doi: 10.1109/MSECP.2003.1219056.
15. Buffer Overflow Attack. (n.d.). The twilight hack. URL https://sites.google.com/site/bufferattack/history/twilight. Accessed: 2019-11-13.
16. Purdue University. (n.d.). The buffer overflow page. URL https://engineering.purdue.edu/ResearchGroups/SmashGuard/BoF.html. Accessed: 2019-11-13.
17. D. T. V. R. Rao. (2006). Efficient stack sizing for very large software systems. In *Proceedings of the 2006 International Conference on Computing Informatics, Kuala Lumpur, Malaysia, June 6–8*, pp. 1–10. doi: 10.1109/ICOCI.2006.5276453.
18. J. Regehr, A. Reid, and K. Webb. (2005). Eliminating stack overflow by abstract interpretation. *ACM Transactions on Embedded Computing Systems*, **4**(4), 751–778. ISSN 1539-9087. doi: 10.1145/1113830.1113833.
19. C. Cowan, C. Pu, D. Maier, H. Hintony, J. Walpole, P. Bakke, S. Beattie, A. Grier, P. Wagle, and Q. Zhang. (1988). Stackguard: Automatic adaptive detection and prevention of buffer-overflow attacks. In *Proceedings of the 7th USENIX Security Symposium, San Antonio, Texas, USA, January 26–29*, pp. 63–78.
20. T.-C. Chiueh and F.-H. Hsu. (2001). Rad: A compile-time solution to buffer overflow attacks. In *Proceedings of the 21st International Conference on Distributed Computing Systems, Phoenix, Arizona, USA, April 16–19*, pp. 409–417. doi: 10.1109/ICDSC.2001.918971.
21. M. Frantzen and M. Shuey. (2001). Stackghost: Hardware facilitated stack protection. In *Proceedings of the 10th USENIX Security Symposium (SSYM'01), Washington, D.C., USA, August 13–17*, pp. 55–66.
22. Y.-J. Park, Z. Zhang, and G. Lee. (2006). Microarchitectural protection against stack-based buffer overflow attacks. *IEEE Micro*, **26**(4), 62–71. ISSN 0272-1732. doi: 10.1109/MM.2006.76.
23. P. I. Perez-Mendez. (September 20, 1983). Auxiliary memory for microprocessor stack overflow. US Patent 4405983. URL https://patentscope.wipo.int/search/en/detail.jsf?docId=US37369292&tab=NATIONALBIBLIO&maxRec=1000.
24. N. Masayuk and E. Takeshi. (September 18, 2003). Auxiliary memory for microprocessor stack overflow. US Patent 20030177328. URL https://patentscope.wipo.int/search/en/detail.jsf?docId=US40274837&redirectedID=true.
25. Qualcomm. Snapdragon platform. URL https://www.qualcomm.com/products/snapdragon/processors/835. Accessed: 2019-11-13.
26. S. HomChaudhuri. (September 12, 2016). Method for handling crashes in a computer system owing to buffer/stack overflow fatalities. India Patent 275578. URL https://patentscope.wipo.int/search/en/detail.jsf?docId=US40274837&redirectedID=true.
27. ARM. Stack limit checking. URL http://infocenter.arm.com/help/index.jsp?topic=/com.arm.doc.100230_0002_00_en/qws1472393709006.html. Accessed: 2019-11-13.

28. ARM. Arm® v8-m exception handling. URL https://static.docs.arm.com/100701/0100/armv8_m_processor_exception_handling_100701_0100_00_en.pdf. Accessed: 2019-11-13.
29. ARM. Stack protection in arm processors. URL http://infocenter.arm.com/help/index.jsp?topic=/com.arm.doc.dui0491i/BCFGBAIC.html. Accessed: 2019-11-13.
30. G. Candea, S. Kawamoto, Y. Fujiki, G. Friedman, and A. Fox. (2004). Microreboot — a technique for cheap recovery. In *Proceedings of the 6th Symposium on Operating System Design & Implementation (OSDI'04), San Francisco, California, USA, December 6–8*, pp. 31–44.
31. V. Sundaram, S. HomChaudhuri, S. Garg, C. Kintala, and S. Bagchi. (2007). Improving dependability using shared supplementary memory and opportunistic micro rejuvenation in multi-tasking embedded systems. In *Proceedings of the 13th Pacific Rim International Symposium on Dependable Computing (PRDC 2007), Melbourne, Victoria, Australia, December 17–19*, pp. 240–247. doi: 10.1109/PRDC.2007.54.

Part V

Future Directions and Appendix

Chapter 13, Future Directions, presents an overview of promising topics for future research in software aging and rejuvenation.

The Appendix, Stochastic Modeling Techniques in Software Aging and Rejuvenation Phenomena, provides an overview of the methods and analytical solution techniques related to the stochastic processes that are more often encountered in the literature on software aging and rejuvenation. The appendix is particularly addressed to researchers who want to have an initial approach to these topics.

Chapter 13

Future Directions for Software Aging and Rejuvenation Research

Alberto Avritzer*, Roberto Pietrantuono† and Kishor Trivedi‡

eSulabSolutions, Inc., Princeton, USA
Università degli Studi di Napoli Federico II, Italy
Duke University, USA
**beto@esulabsolutions.com*
†roberto.pietrantuono@unina.it
‡ktrivedi@duke.edu

In this chapter we present a summary of some future directions for software aging and rejuvenation research.

13.1. Introduction

This chapter is written to follow the way the book is organized and is divided into four sections: 1) fundamentals, 2) data-driven approaches, 3) model-driven approaches, and, 4) applications.

13.2. Fundamentals

13.2.1. *Control Theory*

Measurements of software aging, followed by the analysis of the measured data and the prediction of the time to exhaustion of OS resources, can allow the execution of a possible rejuvenation action. This MAPE (Measure, Analyze, Predict and Execute) loop is well known in feedback control systems. We expect that researchers in future will take this on-line feedback control view of software aging and rejuvenation [1]. These ideas are also being proposed for cyber security [2, 3]. The essential components of such a control system are the controlled entity, the controller and the feedback loop. Furthermore there is also a goal to achieve.

In our case, the controlled entity would be the software system — e.g., the OS, the VMM, the VM, an application or an application component. The goal could be to maximize the software availability, minimize response time, minimize the total cost of system operation, etc. Alternatively, the goal could be to prevent or postpone software failures caused by aging-related bugs.

If rejuvenation scheduling is time-based then we need the distribution of time to failure as one of the inputs. So a measured sequence of inter-failure times is needed. Once this sequence is available, we can either fit a distribution to this data (such as the Weibull or the hypo-exponential) and then use the 3-state model SMP (as discussed in Chapter 5 of this book) to determine the optimal rejuvenation schedule.

Alternatively we can use the non-parametric method discussed in the work by Dohi *et al.* [4] In the original model, inter-failure time data is assumed to be measured for a system without rejuvenation. But to use this method in an on-line feedback control setting we will need to account for the fact that the data collected is modified, as it is inter-failure time data with rejuvenation included. This requires a considerable amount of future research.

In the case that an inspection-based approach is used for rejuvenation scheduling, the data to be measured/collected is for health indicator performance variables that show the effects of aging. Once the specific performance variables are chosen, we may determine threshold values for these variables to trigger rejuvenation [5] or use prediction methods to determine the time to resource exhaustion and hence trigger rejuvenation. Determining what performance variables to monitor and how to determine threshold values are topics for future research. Though the methods of prediction of individual instances of resource exhaustion are known, further research is needed to predict the overall time to system failure. The on-line measurement of aging will become increasingly important as closed-loop feedback control becomes more prevalent. Finally, software rejuvenation scheduling in the context of multi-granularity software rejuvenation needs a lot of future research [5, 6].

13.3. Data-Driven Approaches

13.3.1. *Data Analysis and Machine Learning*

We expect to see an increased use of machine learning techniques because they represent a hybrid between model-based and measurement-based approaches. Indeed, as systems become more and more complex, several indicators will need to be analyzed to detect software aging.

Moreover, it will become increasingly difficult to distinguish between software aging and the expected fluctuations of system performance, because of inter-relations among multiple parameters.

All this calls for more complex statistical techniques that are able to analyze the cause/effect relations (besides correlations) among multiple indicators and to spot those critical patterns relevant for aging identification in complex systems.

13.3.2. *Experimental Approaches to Detect Aging Root Causes*

Experimental approaches to detect software aging are involved in the detection of the root causes of aging and in approaches to eliminate the causes of aging.

There is a need to research experimental approaches to dealing with aging bugs pre-release detection, removal or prevention. While many studies assume that aging is there, and thus deal with how to "tolerate" aging effects and when/how to rejuvenate the system affected by aging, little effort has been spent to *i)* **prevent** the introduction of aging bugs (e.g., design methodologies), *ii)* **detect** and **remove** the root causes before software delivery (i.e., at development time) by using proper testing and debugging techniques and dynamic analysis tools, *iii)* **predict** aging bugs before they are triggered at runtime and cause aging. These are all open topics which future works can explore.

A few attempts have been made to classify and predict the emergence of aging bugs, which can be a starting point for the aging prediction task. The software aging and rejuvenation repository [7] describes a software aging repository that can be used to support experimental approaches for software aging detection. The data are organized into two separate repositories. The former contains information on aging-related bugs found in two open-source projects (the Linux kernel and the MySQL DBMS). This dataset has been used to investigate defect prediction approaches for aging-related bugs, by using software complexity metrics and machine learning techniques. The associated repository can be accessed at: https://zenodo.org/record/581659#.XFqeR_x7nVo.

The latter contains a list of bugs from four open-source projects (the Linux kernel, the MySQL DBMS, the Apache HTTPD web server, and the Apache AXIS WS framework), classified into Mandelbugs, Bohrbugs, or Aging-Related Bugs, by analyzing the conditions that exercise the bug (i.e., the "fault trigger"). The associated repository can be found at: https://zenodo.org/record/581660#.XFqePfx7nVo.

13.4. Model-Driven Approaches

13.4.1. *Cloud Computing and Virtualized Infrastructures*

There is a need for comprehensive models that are able to account for the costs/benefits of rejuvenation actions at several layers of the cloud stack, and for the increasing complexity of virtualization technologies. In addition, research into new aging indicators for the different layers and components of a cloud-based system and on measuring cause-effect relations across virtualization layers is also needed.

Software rejuvenation research in cloud computing infrastructures may include the following topics:

- Investigating the costs/benefits of (passive/active) replication-based strategies (for the rejuvenation of the VMM, VM, container, or application) not only in relation to the downtime reduction, but also considering the cost of setting up and managing replicas, their energy consumption, and the side-effects on security as well as on scalability,
- Analyzing the overhead of rejuvenation in virtualized systems, e.g., its effect on memory or storage fragmentation,
- Micro-rebooting for parts of the virtualization infrastructure,
- Security and aging in cloud-based systems: aging-related vulnerability/attacks in the cloud (e.g., induced VM leakage),
- Energy consumption as a key factor in cloud-based systems, multi-objective aging detection and multi-objective rejuvenation (considering availability, resource consumption, energy, security),
- SAR in emerging contexts related to the cloud/virtualization, such as edge and fog computing, and network function virtualization/software-defined networks,
- The impact of deployment on several layers and the interactions between those layers. How to define a holistic approach for availability improvements when aging can occur at several layers of the infrastructure, cloud and virtualization?

13.4.2. *Restart Approaches*

Chapter 7 on models for restart, reboot and rejuvenation contains the detailed Section 7.7 describing proposals for future work related to black-box models of restart.

13.5. Applications

13.5.1. *Operating Systems*

Chapter 9 on applications to operating systems contains suggestions for future research related to operating systems.

13.5.2. *Software Architecture*

Monitoring is a key facility in microservice architectures. Therefore monitoring could be exploited for software aging detection.

Identifying architecture patterns that are likely to cause software aging is a topic that is related to research on software performance anti-patterns [8–11]. Research related to software performance anti-patterns includes a characterization of the sub-set of performance anti-patterns that could be defined as software aging anti-patterns. Examples of some software performance anti-patterns that could be related to software aging anti-patterns are:

- Circuitous Treasure Hunt — when database statements are poorly organized, data might be retrieved from several tables in sequence, as if the programmer is engaged in a circuitous treasure hunt. As a consequence, the response times of programs that implement this performance anti-pattern are usually long. As time passes, it is possible that database tables will grow and the software will appear to age.
- Extensive Processing — if a long running process is in control of a resource and a thread is blocked waiting for that resource, the extensive processing anti-pattern will occur. In addition, if the execution time of the long running process is a function of the process restart time, the software might show aging.
- Wrong Cache Strategy — when a cache strategy is wrongly implemented, it might be related to memory leaks and an excessive number of garbage collection events. The accumulation of such events over time can be related to software aging.

13.5.3. *AI Systems*

The resilience requirements of mission-critical systems and the expected ubiquity of AI systems and Robotics will require such systems to be tolerant to software aging. In these systems, a further difficulty is caused by the complex and dynamic interaction with the surrounding environment, which can cause the software aging dynamics to be much harder to model, detect and tolerate.

13.5.4. *Mobile Devices and Embedded Systems*

The software aging and rejuvenation of embedded and mobile systems has been addressed [12–14].

In the work by Kintala [12], memory and stack overflow problems in mobile devices were attributed to the lack of tools to properly configure memory in mobile devices. A technique called micro-rejuvenation was introduced to detect and correct memory and stack overflow problems. Chapter 12 of this book is on the implementation of micro-rejuvenation with cooperative stack leasing. It extends on the research presented by Kintala [12] to propose a collaborative approach among system stacks.

This is a very promising future research direction, as software aging and rejuvenation is a very effective approach to addressing the unreliability issues associated with mobile systems, such as stack and heap overflow problems.

13.5.5. *Anomaly Detection Systems*

Anomaly detection systems based on system performance metrics have been proposed for the detection of security intrusions [15–18]. In addition, software rejuvenation was introduced to counteract worm epidemics in large distributed systems [19].

Related future research on software aging and rejuvenation could address some of the following topics:

- How to define metrics to detect software aging related to security intrusions [16]?
- How to distinguish between software aging related to security intrusions and software aging related to performance and reliability issues [20]?
- How to design and implement an automated approach for software aging and rejuvenation to counteract security intrusions [21]?

13.6. Other Topics for Future Research

Prognostics and Health Management (PHM) could be combined with software aging detection and rejuvenation techniques in the future.

Rejuvenation can also be combined with the Remaining Useful Life (RUL) prediction, in the sense that the rejuvenation schedule could be planned according to RUL-predicted values.

When rejuvenation is implemented, the software system is not shut down. So, under rejuvenation the system can still operate although at reduced capability. Thus, this concept cannot be considered when availability is examined, since in this case the system is considered as "down" when being rejuvenated. Alternative performance measures concerning the capability of the system to provide service (even under rejuvenation) could be defined and examined.

References

1. Y. Hong, D. Chen, L. Li, and K. Trivedi (2002). Closed loop design for software rejuvenation. In *Proceedings of the Workshop on Self-Healing, Adaptive and self-MANaged Systems (SHAMAN), New York City, NY, USA, June 23.*
2. M. Platania, D. Obenshain, T. Tantillo, R. Sharma, and Y. Amir. (2014). Towards a practical survivable intrusion tolerant replication system. In *Proceedings of the 33rd IEEE International Symposium on Reliable Distributed Systems (SRDS 2014), Nara, Japan, October 6–9*, pp. 242–252.
3. R. Romagnoli, B. H. Krogh, and B. Sinopoli. (2018). Design of software rejuvenation for CPS security using invariant sets. *Computing Research Repository*, **abs/1810.10484**.
4. T. Dohi, K. Goševa-Popstojanova, and K. S. Trivedi. (2001). Estimating software rejuvenation schedule in high assurance systems. *The Computer Journal*, **44**(6), 473–485.
5. G. Ning, J. Zhao, Y. Lou, J. Alonso, R. Matias, K. S. Trivedi, B. B. Yin, and K. Y. Cai. (2016). Optimization of two-granularity software rejuvenation policy based on the Markov regenerative process. *IEEE Transactions on Reliability*, **65**(4), 1630–1646.
6. W. Xie, Y. Hong, and K. Trivedi. (2005). Analysis of a two-level software rejuvenation policy. *Reliability Engineering and System Safety*, **87**(1), 13–22.
7. D. Cotroneo, A. K. Iannillo, R. Natella, R. Pietrantuono, and S. Russo. (2015). The software aging and rejuvenation repository: http://openscience.us/repo/software-aging/. In *Proceedings of the 2015 IEEE International Symposium on Software Reliability Engineering Workshops (ISSREW), Gaithersburg, Maryland, USA, November 2–5*, pp. 108–113. doi: 10.1109/ISSREW.2015.7392054.
8. C. U. Smith and L. G. Williams. (2000). Software performance antipatterns. In *Proceedings of the 2nd International Workshop on Software and Performance (WOSP '00), Ottawa, Ontario, Canada, September 17–20*, pp. 127–136. ISBN 1-58113-195-X. doi: 10.1145/350391.350420.

9. C. Trubiani, A. Bran, A. van Hoorn, A. Avritzer, and H. Knoche. (2018). Exploiting load testing and profiling for performance antipattern detection. *Information & Software Technology*, **95**, 329–345. doi: 10.1016/j.infsof.2017.11.016.
10. T.-H. Chen, W. Shang, Z. M. Jiang, A. E. Hassan, M. Nasser, and P. Flora. (2014). Detecting performance anti-patterns for applications developed using object-relational mapping. In *Proceedings of the 36th International Conference on Software Engineering (ICSE 2014), Hyderabad, India, May 31–June 7*, pp. 1001–1012. ISBN 978-1-4503-2756-5. doi: 10.1145/2568225.2568259.
11. A. Wert, M. Oehler, C. Heger, and R. Farahbod. (2014). Automatic detection of performance anti-patterns in inter-component communications. In *Proceedings of the 10th International ACM Sigsoft Conference on Quality of Software Architectures (QoSA '14), Marcq-en-Baroeul, Lille, France, June 30–July 4*, pp. 3–12. ISBN 978-1-4503-2576-9. doi: 10.1145/2602576.2602579.
12. C. M. Kintala. (2009). Software rejuvenation in embedded systems. *Journal of Automata, Languages, and Combinatorics*, **14**(1), 63–73. ISSN 1430-189X.
13. J. Xiang, C. Weng, A. Andrzejak, Z. Dongdong, T. Jing, X. Shengwu, and L. Lin. (2018). A new software rejuvenation model for Android. In *Proceedings of the 10th International Workshop on Software Aging and Rejuvenation (WoSAR 2018), Memphis, Tennessee, USA, October 18, pp. 293-299.* doi: 10.1109/ISSREW.2018.00021.
14. D. Cotroneo, F. Fucci, A. K. Iannillo, R. Natella, and R. Pietrantuono. (2016). Software aging analysis of the Android mobile OS. In *Proceedings of the 27th IEEE International Symposium on Software Reliability Engineering (ISSRE 2016), Ottawa, Ontario, Canada, October 23–27*, pp. 478–489. doi: 10.1109/ISSRE.2016.25.
15. A. Avritzer, R. G. Cole, and E. J. Weyuker. (2007). Using performance signatures and software rejuvenation for worm mitigation in tactical manets. In *Proceedings of the 6th International Workshop on Software and Performance (WOSP 2007), Buenos Aires, Argentina, February 5–8*, pp. 172–180.
16. A. Milenkoski, M. Vieira, S. Kounev, A. Avritzer, and B. D. Payne. (2015). Evaluating computer intrusion detection systems: A survey of common practices. *ACM Computing Surveys*, **48**(1), 12.
17. C. Wang, Z. Zhao, L. Gong, L. Zhu, Z. Liu, and X. Cheng. (2018). A distributed anomaly detection system for in-vehicle network using HTM. *IEEE Access*, **6**, 9091–9098.
18. C. Kruegel and G. Vigna. (2003). Anomaly detection of web-based attacks. In *Proceedings of the 10th ACM Conference on Computer and Communications Security (CCS '03), Washington D. C., USA, October 27–30*, pp. 251–261. ISBN 1-58113-738-9.
19. A. Avritzer, R. G. Cole, and E. J. Weyuker. (2010). Methods and opportunities for rejuvenation in aging distributed software systems. *Journal of Systems and Software*, **83**(9), 1568–1578. doi: 10.1016/j.jss.2010.05.026.
20. A. Avritzer, A. Bondi, and E. J. Weyuker. (2005). Ensuring stable performance for systems that degrade. In *Proceedings of the 5th International Workshop on Software and Performance (WOSP '05), Palma, Illes Balears, Spain, July 12–14*, pp. 43–51. ISBN 1-59593-087-6. doi: 10.1145/1071021.1071026.
21. A. Avritzer, V. Ferme, A. Janes, B. Russo, H. Schulz, and A. van Hoorn. (2018). A quantitative approach for the assessment of microservice architecture deployment alternatives by automated performance testing. In *Proceedings of the 12th European Conference on Software Architecture, (ECSA 2018), Madrid, Spain, September 24–28*, pp. 159–174.

Appendix

Stochastic Modeling Techniques in Software Aging and Rejuvenation Phenomena

Andrea Bobbio*,¶, Antonio Puliafito†,‖, Marco Scarpa†,** and Miklós Telek‡,§,††

*Università del Piemonte Orientale, Italy
†Università di Messina, Italy
‡Budapest University of Technology and Economics, Hungary
§MTA-BME Information Systems Research Group, Hungary
¶andrea.bobbio@uniupo.it
‖antonio.puliafito@unime.it
**mscarpa@unime.it
††telek@bme.hu

Quantitative modeling of software aging and rejuvenation has been the object of a vast literature in the last decades. Due to the probabilistic nature of the phenomena to which these studies are devoted, the models rely on the theory of stochastic processes. The present chapter is intended to provide an overview of the methods and analytical solution techniques related to the stochastic processes that are more often encountered in the literature on software aging and rejuvenation. The chapter is particularly addressed to researchers who want to have an initial approach to these topics.

A.1. Introduction

The phenomenon of software aging has come to light in the last decades as a cause of the degradation of the software performance over time. Although we adopt the phrase software aging, it should be clear that no deterioration of the software system per se is implied but rather, the software appears to age due to the degradation of the operating environment (for example, the gradual depletion of resources) [1]. Software rejuvenation was proposed for the first time in the seminal paper by Huang *et al.* [2] as a proactive maintenance technique to counteract aging. Software rejuvenation involves occasionally stopping the running software, cleaning its internal state or its environment, and restarting it. Like software aging, software rejuvenation actually does not imply any modification of the software but refers to the rejuvenation of the environment in which the software is executing [3].

The aging of the software and the action of rejuvenation can be captured and analyzed through stochastic models that aim to characterize their behavior according to quantitative parameters such as the mean time to a failure condition, the optimal rejuvenation interval, the probability that the software is in a fully working condition and so on.

In their original paper, Huang *et al.* [2] consider the software aging as a two-step process. From a clean state the system jumps into a "degraded" state from which two further actions are possible: rejuvenation (with a return back to the clean state) or transition to the complete failure state. The authors model a three-state process as a *continuous-time Markov chain (CTMC)* for which they derive and discuss only the steady-state behavior.

The problem connected to software rejuvenation has then been investigated by many research groups introducing more refined modeling assumptions by abandoning the exponential assumption in the time evolution of the phenomenon and considering the interaction of the software aging with the workload on the system. Further, rejuvenation can be activated at constant intervals, at random intervals or at time epochs related to the software degradation.

Garg *et al.* [4, 5] consider the effect of the workload by including the arrival and queuing of jobs in the system, and the time dependency of the load and of the service time on the age of the system. With this addition, the arrival and service rates are time-varying and the overall model becomes a three-state non-homogeneous Markov process. Zheng *et al.* [6] investigate workload-based policies where the arrival stream of jobs follows a Markovian arrival process (MAP).

In the analytical approach, different authors have assumed general transition time distributions, and have developed Markov processes, semi-Markov processes (SMPs), and Markov regenerative processes (MRGPs), to compute and optimize system availability or related measures. For instance, semi-Markov models were used in [7] and [8] and Markov regenerative models were considered in [9] and [10].

Stochastic Petri net models and their variants have been often invoked to generate the system model. Examples of this include Markov regenerative stochastic Petri nets (MRSPNs) in [9] or fluid stochastic Petri nets (FSPNs) in [11] and [12].

The present chapter is intended to provide the readers who are not particularly aware of the theory of stochastic modeling with the basic notions, definitions and formulas that are encountered in the chapters of the book. In each section, some relevant references are cited and an example taken from the software rejuvenation literature is described and fully developed and solved.

Section A.2 introduces the renewal theory with particular reference to the Poisson process that is usually used to model the stream of jobs arriving to a software system. A Poisson shock model, utilized in [13] and [14] to characterize a software aging process, is reported. In Section A.3, the homogeneous Markov chain model is introduced and the basic solution equations for both the transient and steady-state cases are discussed. As an example, the rejuvenation model discussed in [2] is presented and analyzed.

Section A.4 reports the transient and steady-state solutions for the non-homogeneous Markov process and illustrates the corresponding rejuvenation example taken from [5].

Sections A.5 and A.6 deal with SMPs and MRGPs respectively, and provide the steady-state and transient solution equations in both cases. An SMP example taken from [15] and an MRGP in [9] are also introduced.

Finally, Section A.7 is devoted to the introduction of Petri net (PN) formalism and focuses its attention on stochastic Petri nets (SPNs) such as generalized Stochastic PNs (GSPNs), Stochastic Reward Nets (SRNs) and non-Markovian SPNs etc. In particular, an MRSPN model derived from [9] is provided to show how an MRGP can be generated from an MRSPN.

A.2. Renewal Process

The stochastic process generated by a sequence of independent identically distributed random variables $(Y_1, Y_2, \ldots, Y_n, \ldots)$ (Fig. A.1) with cumulative distribution function (CDF) $F(t)$, density $f(t)$, $t \geq 0$, and expected value $\mathbf{E}[Y]$ is called a *renewal process* [16].

$$F(t) = \mathbf{P}\{Y \leq t\}, \quad f(t) = \frac{dF(t)}{dt}, \quad \mathbf{E}[Y] = m.$$

The corresponding Laplace transforms (LTs) are denoted by the symbol $*$:

$$F^*(s) = \mathcal{L}[F(t)] = \int_0^\infty e^{-st} F(t)dt, \quad f^*(s) = \mathcal{L}[f(t)] = \int_0^\infty e^{-st} f(t)dt.$$

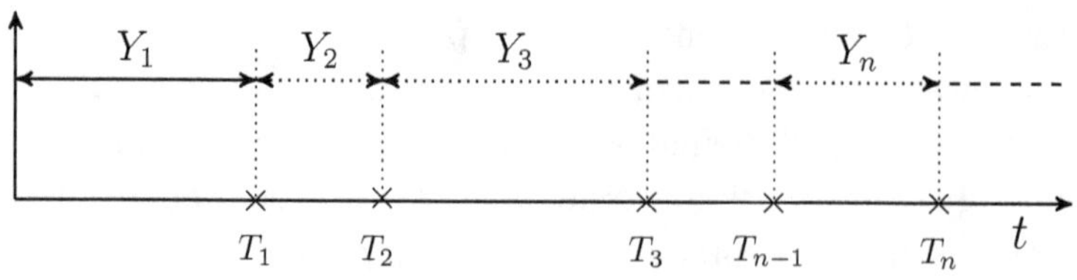

Fig. A.1. A renewal process.

Let $T_k = \sum_{i=1}^{k} Y_i$, with $k \geq 1$, denote the time of the k-th event in the renewal process, and $F_k(t)$ and $f_k(t)$ denote its CDF and density, respectively. We can write:

$$F_k(t) = \mathbf{P}\{T_k \leq t\}, \quad f_k(t) = \frac{d\,F_k(t)}{d\,t}. \tag{A.1}$$

Applying the convolution theorem for LTs, it could be represented as Eq. (A.1) in the Laplace domain:

$$F_k^*(s) = \frac{1}{s}\,[f^*(s)]^k, \quad f_k^*(s) = [f^*(s)]^k. \tag{A.2}$$

If $N(t)$ is the number of renewals in the interval $(0, t]$, then the following relation holds:

$$N(t) < k \quad \text{if and only if} \quad T_k > t$$

from which:

$$\mathbf{P}\{N(t) < k\} = \mathbf{P}\{T_k > t\} = 1 - F_k(t). \tag{A.3}$$

From Eq. (A.3), we obtain:

$$\begin{aligned}\mathbf{P}\{N(t) = k\} &= \mathbf{P}\{N(t) < k+1\} - \mathbf{P}\{N(t) < k\} \\ &= F_k(t) - F_{k+1}(t).\end{aligned} \tag{A.4}$$

A.2.1. *Poisson Process*

A renewal process in which the generating random variable Y is exponentially distributed is called a Poisson Process. Assume that Y is exponentially distributed with rate λ, then:

$$F(t) = 1 - e^{-\lambda t} \quad \Longrightarrow \quad F^*(s) = \frac{\lambda}{s\,(s+\lambda)}$$

$$f(t) = \lambda\, e^{-\lambda t} \quad \Longrightarrow \quad f^*(s) = \frac{\lambda}{s+\lambda}.$$

The CDF and density of the time up to the k-th arrival T_k can be obtained from Eq. (A.2), in the LT domain:

$$F_k^*(s) = \frac{\lambda^k}{s\,(s+\lambda)^k}, \quad f_k^*(s) = \left(\frac{\lambda}{s+\lambda}\right)^k. \tag{A.5}$$

Transforming back to the time domain the LT density (A.5) for $k = 1, 2, \ldots$ we obtain

$$\begin{aligned}
f_1(t) &= \mathcal{L}^{-1}\left[\frac{\lambda}{s+\lambda}\right] = \lambda\, e^{-\lambda t} \\
f_2(t) &= \mathcal{L}^{-1}\left[\frac{\lambda^2}{(s+\lambda)^2}\right] = \lambda^2\, t\, e^{-\lambda t} \\
&\cdots\cdots\cdots \\
f_k(t) &= \mathcal{L}^{-1}\left[\frac{\lambda^k}{(s+\lambda)^k}\right] = \frac{\lambda\,(\lambda\, t)^{k-1}}{(k-1)!}\, e^{-\lambda t}
\end{aligned}$$

and its CDF of order k:

$$F_k(t) = \int_0^t f_k(u)\, du = 1 - \sum_{i=0}^{k-1} \frac{(\lambda\, t)^i}{i\,!}\, e^{-\lambda t}$$

which is actually the CDF of the k-stage Erlang random variable with parameter λ [17, 18].

Denote $P_k(t)$ as the probability of having k renewals in a time duration of length t, then from Eq. (A.4):

$$P_k(t) = \mathbf{P}\{N(t) = k\} = F_k(t) - F_{k+1}(t).$$

Taking LTs:

$$P_k^*(s) = \frac{\lambda^k}{s\,(s+\lambda)^k} - \frac{\lambda^{k+1}}{s\,(s+\lambda)^{k+1}} = \frac{\lambda^k}{(s+\lambda)^{k+1}}.$$

Inverting again to the time domain, we obtain the Poisson probability mass function (pmf):

$$P_k(t) = \mathbf{P}\{N(t) = k\} = \frac{(\lambda\, t)^{\,k}}{k\,!}\; e^{-\lambda\, t} \tag{A.6}$$

or, in a recursive form:

$$P_k(t) = \mathbf{P}\{N(t) = k\} = \frac{\lambda\, t}{k}\; P_{k-1}(t). \tag{A.7}$$

In a Poisson process, the number of renewals at time t follows a Poisson distribution of parameter $\lambda\, t$.

A.2.2. *Poisson Shock Process* [19]

The aging process of a software system consists of a sequence of additive random shocks and is monitored by observing a degradation level of the system performance, whose value at time t is denoted by $S(t)$. The shock events occur according to a Poisson process with rate λ. Each shock increases the degradation level by a positive damage denoted as variable X $(X \geq 0)$ with CDF $F_X(x)$. All damages $X_1, X_2, \ldots$ from successive shocks are mutually independent with the common CDF $F_X(x)$. Damages accumulate additively, and the system survives if the amount of damage accumulated does not exceed a threshold a, representing the maximum tolerated value of the degradation level. We call T_a the random time at which the degradation level reaches the threshold a. The CDF $H_{T_a}(t) = \mathbf{P}\{T_a < t\} = \mathbf{P}\{S(t) > a\}$ is the probability that at time t the degradation level has reached level a and $\overline{H}_{T_a}(t) = 1 - H_{T_a}(t) = \mathbf{P}\{S(t) < a\}$ is the probability that at time t the degradation level is below the threshold a, i.e., the survival probability.

After k shocks, the degradation level will be $S_k = \sum_{i=0}^{k} X_i$, with distribution $F_X^{\dagger k}(x) = \mathbf{P}\{S_k < x\}$ where $F_X^{\dagger k}(x)$ can be obtained from $F_X(x)$ by the k-fold convolution $F_X^{\dagger k}(x) = \int_0^x F_X^{\dagger k-1}(x-y)dF_X(y)$ (or in the Laplace domain as in (A.5)). Since shocks occur according to a Poisson process with rate λ, $N(t)$, the survival probability is given by

$$\begin{aligned}\overline{H}_{T_a}(t) = \mathbf{P}\{S(t) < a\} &= \sum_{i=0}^{\infty} \mathbf{P}\{N(t) = k\}\mathbf{P}\{S_k < a\} \\ &= \sum_{i=0}^{\infty} e^{-\lambda\, t}\, \frac{(\lambda\, t)^k}{k\,!}\, F_X^{\dagger k}(a).\end{aligned}$$

The above equation is essentially a compound Poisson distribution. A software aging model based on a Poisson shock process has been utilized in [13] and [14].

A.3. Homogeneous Continuous-Time Markov Chain

A stochastic process is a family of random variables $X(t)$ on a sample space. The values assumed by $X(t)$ are called *states*, and the set of all the possible states is the *state space*. When the value of $X(t)$ changes, the process undergoes a *state transition*. The state space of a stochastic process can be either discrete or continuous. If the state space is discrete, we call the process a *chain*. The time parameter of a stochastic process can be either discrete or continuous.

A stochastic process can be classified by the dependence of its state at a particular time on the states at previous times. If the state of a stochastic process depends only on the immediately preceding state, we have a *Markov process*. Discrete state Markov processes are known as Markov chains. We distinguish between discrete-time Markov chains (DTMCs) and continuous-time Markov chains, depending on the nature of the time parameter. Let $\mathbf{P}\{X(t_n) = j\}$ be the probability that the process is in the state j at the time t_n. $X(t)$ is a Markov chain if, for any ordered time sequence $t_1 < t_2 < \cdots < t_n$ and all $i_n \in S$, the conditional probability of being in any state j is such that:

$$\begin{aligned}\mathbf{P}\{X(t_n) = j | X(t_{n-1}) = i_{n-1}, X(t_{n-2}) = i_{n-2}, \ldots, X(t_1) = i_1\} = \\ = \mathbf{P}\{X(t_n) = j | X(t_{n-1}) = i_{n-1}\}.\end{aligned} \tag{A.8}$$

The condition in Eq. (A.8) defines what is called the *Markov property* that says that the state of a Markov chain after a transition may (but does not have to) depend on the state immediately before it, but it cannot depend on any states before that. In other words, at the time of a transition, the entire past history is summarized by the current state. If the conditional probability is invariant with respect to the time origin u, the Markov chain is said to be homogeneous. To be more specific, a Markov chain is homogeneous if for any t and u,

$$\mathbf{P}\{X(t) = j | X(u) = i\} = \mathbf{P}\{X(t-u) = j | X(0) = i\}. \tag{A.9}$$

For homogeneous Markov chains, if $X(u) = j$, then the probability of finding the system in state j at time $t > u$ depends on state j but not on the time the system has been in state j before u. The process can therefore be said to be *memoryless*, as regards not only the states it has occupied in the past, but also the amount of time it has already spent in the current state. This implies that the time a homogeneous Markov chain spends in a state (the *sojourn time*) cannot be arbitrarily distributed, but it can only follow a memoryless distribution, which is the geometric distribution for discrete time models and the exponential distribution for continuous time models.

A.3.1. *Basic Equations*

Without loss of generality, the state space of a Markov chain is given by $S = \{0, 1, 2, \ldots\}$. A purpose of the analysis of a Markov chain is to compute the state probabilities $\pi_j(t) = \mathbf{P}\{X(t) = j\}$, for all states j, i.e., the vector of state probabilities is $\boldsymbol{\pi}(t) = [\pi_0(t), \pi_1(t), \ldots]$, both for finite values of t (transient solution) and for $t \to \infty$ (steady-state solution). We define a *transition probability* to be

$$p_{ij}(t-u) = \mathbf{P}\{X(t) = j | X(u) = i\}, \tag{A.10}$$

the probability that the system is in state j at time t, given that it was in state i at time u; most often, we will have $u = 0$. The matrix $\boldsymbol{P}(t)$ is the square matrix of the transition probabilities $p_{ij}(t)$. For the system to be in state j at time t, it must have been in some state i at time u, which we can express as:

$$\boldsymbol{\pi}(t) = \boldsymbol{\pi}(u) \cdot \boldsymbol{P}(t-u) \tag{A.11}$$

This is a form of the *Chapman-Kolmogorov equation* that will be used for calculating $\boldsymbol{\pi}(t)$ for both the discrete and continuous parameter cases.

A.3.2. *Discrete-Time Markov Chains*

Let the points at which a DTMC changes state be $\{0, 1, \ldots\}$. Let us define $\boldsymbol{P} = \boldsymbol{P}(1) = [p_{ij}]$ as the *one-step transition probability* matrix. All the elements of $\boldsymbol{P}$ are probabilities and should lie in the range $[0, 1]$ and the elements of any row must sum to one because they describe the probability of a complete set of events, with respect to the next state of the process.

A matrix with such properties is called a *stochastic* matrix. For a homogeneous DTMC, Eq. (A.11) simplifies to the following recurrence relation:

$$\boldsymbol{\pi}(n+1) = \boldsymbol{\pi}(n) \cdot \boldsymbol{P}. \tag{A.12}$$

The state probability vector after n steps $\boldsymbol{\pi}(n)$ can be computed in terms of the initial probability vector $\boldsymbol{\pi}(0)$, as:

$$\boldsymbol{\pi}(n) = \boldsymbol{\pi}(0) \cdot \boldsymbol{P}^n. \tag{A.13}$$

If $\lim_{n\to\infty} \boldsymbol{\pi}(n)$ exists, taking the limit on both sides of Eq. (A.12) gives the following system of equations for computing the limiting probability vector:

$$\boldsymbol{\pi} = \boldsymbol{\pi} \cdot \boldsymbol{P} \tag{A.14}$$

where we impose the normalization condition,

$$\boldsymbol{\pi} \cdot \boldsymbol{e}^T = 1, \tag{A.15}$$

where $\boldsymbol{e}$ is the row vector with all its elements equal to one.

A.3.3. *Continuous-Time Markov Chains*

If we let $u = t - \Delta t$ and subtract $\boldsymbol{\pi}(t - \Delta t)$ from both sides of (A.11), we get

$$\boldsymbol{\pi}(t) - \boldsymbol{\pi}(t - \Delta t) = \boldsymbol{\pi}(t - \Delta t)[\boldsymbol{P}(\Delta t) - \boldsymbol{I}]. \tag{A.16}$$

If we then divide by Δt and take the limit as $\Delta t \to 0$, we get the following relation:

$$\frac{d\boldsymbol{\pi}(t)}{dt} = \boldsymbol{\pi}(t) \lim_{\Delta t \to 0} \frac{\boldsymbol{P}(\Delta t) - \boldsymbol{I}}{\Delta t}. \tag{A.17}$$

By introducing the Kronecker delta symbol δ_{ij} ($\delta_{ij} = 1$ if $i = j$, zero otherwise), in the homogeneous case, the matrix $\boldsymbol{Q} = [q_{ij}]$ can be written as

$$q_{ij} = \lim_{\Delta t \to 0} \frac{p_{ij}(\Delta t) - \delta_{ij}}{\Delta t}. \tag{A.18}$$

We can rewrite Eq. (A.17) as

$$\frac{d\boldsymbol{\pi}(t)}{dt} = \boldsymbol{\pi}(t)\,\boldsymbol{Q}. \tag{A.19}$$

The above equation is known as the *Kolmogorov differential equation*, whose initial condition is the initial behavior of the Markov chain, $\boldsymbol{\pi}(0)$. The solution of Eq. (A.19) is

$$\boldsymbol{\pi}(t) = \boldsymbol{\pi}(0)e^{\boldsymbol{Q}t} = \boldsymbol{\pi}(0)\sum_{i=0}^{\infty}\frac{t^i}{i!}\boldsymbol{Q}^i. \tag{A.20}$$

The definition of $\boldsymbol{Q}$ implies that, for a small interval Δt, we have

$$\begin{aligned} 1 - p_{ii}(\Delta t) &\approx -q_{ii}\Delta t, \\ p_{ij}(\Delta t) &\approx q_{ij}\Delta t, \quad \forall i \neq j. \end{aligned}$$

Thus, q_{ij} is the rate at which the system goes from state i to j and $-q_{ii}$ is the rate at which the system departs from state i, since we must have

$$\sum_{j\neq i} p_{ij}(\Delta t) + p_{ii}(\Delta t) = 1. \tag{A.21}$$

Because of this interpretation, $\boldsymbol{Q}$ is called the infinitesimal generator matrix of the CTMC. We can apply Eq. (A.21) and take the limit as $\Delta t \to 0$ to get:

$$\sum_{j} q_{ij} = 0. \tag{A.22}$$

This means that all elements in any row of $\boldsymbol{Q}$ must sum to 0, which can be written, in matrix form, as $\boldsymbol{Q}\boldsymbol{e}^T = \boldsymbol{0}^T$. Since the off- diagonal elements must be non negative ($q_{ij}\Delta t$ is a probability), we deduce that the elements along the diagonal of $\boldsymbol{Q}$ must be non-positive. In fact, the diagonal entry equals the negative sum of the off-diagonal entries in any row:

$$q_{ii} = -\sum_{j\neq i} q_{ij}, \tag{A.23}$$

and $q_i = -q_{ii}$ is the net rate out of state i. The average amount of time spent by the CTMC in state i during the interval $(0, t]$ is $L_i(t) = \int_0^t \pi_i(x)dx$. Integrating both sides of Eq. (A.19), we obtain a differential equation for the vector $\boldsymbol{L}(t) = [L_0(t), L_1(t), \ldots]$:

$$\frac{d\boldsymbol{L}(t)}{dt} = \boldsymbol{L}(t)\boldsymbol{Q} + \boldsymbol{\pi}(0), \quad L(0) = 0. \tag{A.24}$$

If the state transition graph of a CTMC is such that every state is reachable from every other state, the CTMC is said to be *irreducible*. For an irreducible CTMC the state probabilities reach an asymptotic value, independent of the initial condition, as the time goes to infinity [20, 21].

We call the asymptotic solution the *steady-state* solution. If the steady-state solution exists, then for any state i:

$$\lim_{t\to\infty} \pi_i(t) = \pi_i, \quad \lim_{t\to\infty} \frac{d\,\pi_i(t)}{dt} = 0, \tag{A.25}$$

and, in vector form, we immediately get

$$\lim_{t\to\infty} \boldsymbol{\pi}(t) = \boldsymbol{\pi}, \quad \lim_{t\to\infty} \frac{d\,\boldsymbol{\pi}(t)}{dt} = \mathbf{0}, \tag{A.26}$$

where $\boldsymbol{\pi}$ is the steady-state value of the state probability vector and $\mathbf{0}$ is the vector of appropriate dimension with all entries equal to 0. Taking into account Eqs. (A.19) and (A.26), we get accordingly

$$\boldsymbol{\pi} \cdot \boldsymbol{Q} = \mathbf{0} \quad \text{with} \quad \boldsymbol{\pi}\,\boldsymbol{e}^{\mathrm{T}} = 1. \tag{A.27}$$

Equation (A.27) is a linear homogeneous set of n equations with constant coefficients. It is easy to verify that $\boldsymbol{\pi} = 0$ is a solution for $\boldsymbol{\pi} \cdot \boldsymbol{Q} = \mathbf{0}$. If a non-zero solution exists, multiplication of the solution by any constant will still be a solution to the equation. But since $\boldsymbol{\pi}$ is a probability vector, it should also satisfy the normalization condition represented in vector form in Eq. (A.27). The normalized steady-state solution is then unique when the Markov chain is irreducible.

A.3.4. *Example*

The paper by Huang *et al.* [2], that initiated the study of software aging and rejuvenation, proposed the CTMC model shown in Fig. A.2, where we have maintained the same symbols of the original figure. The system first starts in a highly robust state S_0 and then goes into a failure-probable state S_p due to software aging with transition rate r_2. From state S_P two actions are possible: a transition to the failure state S_F with rate λ and a transition

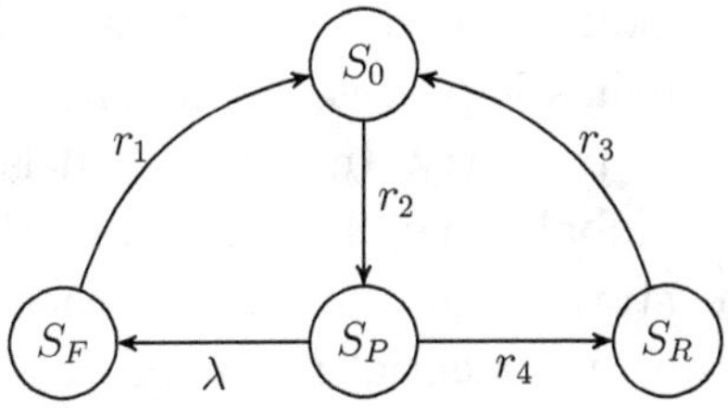

Fig. A.2. The CTMC rejuvenation model in Huang *et al.* [2]

to the rejuvenation state S_R with rate r_4. r_1 is the repair rate that takes back the system from a failure state to the highly robust state, and r_3 is the rejuvenation rate of the transition from rejuvenation state to the highly robust state. In Huang *et al.* [2] the rejuvenation is assumed to be periodic with mean period equal to t so that $r_4 = 1/t$. Applying Eq. (A.27), the steady-state solution is:

$$\pi_P = \frac{1}{1 + \frac{\lambda}{r_1} + \frac{r_4}{r_3} + \frac{\lambda + r_4}{r_2}} \; ; \quad \pi_0 = \frac{\lambda + r_4}{r_2}\pi_P \; ; \quad \pi_F = \frac{\lambda}{r_1}\pi_P \; ; \quad \pi_R = \frac{r_4}{r_3}\pi_P$$

A.3.5. *Markov Reward Model (MRM)*

In a Markov reward model (MRM), we attach to each state of a CTMC with state space S a non-negative real variable, called a *reward rate*, that indicates the level of performance or the cost incurred by the system in that state. In particular, the reward rates are defined based on the system requirements, be it availability-, reliability-, or task-orientedness. If r_i is the reward rate attached to state i, then, a reward $r_i \, \Delta t$ is accumulated when the CTMC spends a time Δt in state i. If $R(t)$ is the instantaneous reward rate of the MRM at time t and $Y_R(t)$ the total accumulated reward up to time t, we have the expected instantaneous reward rate at time t, $E[R(t)]$, and the expected accumulated reward up to time t, $E[Y_R(t)]$, as below:

$$E[R(t)] = \sum_{i \in S} r_i \pi_i(t),$$

$$Y_R(t) = \int_0^t R(u) \, du,$$

$$E[Y_R(t)] = \sum_{i \in S} r_i \int_0^t \pi_i(u) \, du = \sum_{i \in S} r_i \, L_i(t).$$

A.4. Non-Homogeneous Continuous-Time Markov Chains

Non-homogeneous continuous-time Markov chains (NHCTMCs) are discrete-state, continuous-time stochastic processes that satisfy the Markov property, but not the homogeneity property. In these models, the transition rates are dependent on the global time, i.e. the variable taking care of the flow of time since the starting of the whole process. Thus, the sojourn time distributions are not exponential anymore and do not experience the memoryless property. We note here the distinction between the Markov property and the memoryless property: the former is a property of some stochastic processes (e.g., DTMC, CTMC, NHCTMC) while the latter is the property of some distributions (e.g., the exponential and the geometric). To distinguish between homogeneous and non-homogeneous CTMC, we refer in this section to the first type as HCTMC and to the latter as NHCTMC.

A.4.1. *Basic Equations*

Similarly to HCTMCs, the transient behavior of an NHCTMC is defined by the system of Kolmogorov ordinary differential equations (ODE) [17, 18]:

$$\frac{d\boldsymbol{\pi}(t)}{dt} = \boldsymbol{\pi}(t)\boldsymbol{Q}(t) \tag{A.28}$$

whose initial condition is the initial behavior of the Markov chain, $\boldsymbol{\pi}(0)$. Equation (A.28) is very similar to Eq. (A.19), defined for an HCTMC, with one difference: the generator matrix $\boldsymbol{Q}(t) = [q_{ij}(t)]$ is now time-dependent.

The solution of Eq. (A.28) can be computed with various numerical ODE solver methods. Apart from general ODE solver approaches like the Euler method and the Runge-Kutta method [22], specific methods (e.g., TR-BFD2) have been developed for improving the numerical properties of the computation [23, 24].

For special NHCTMC models various alternative methods have been proposed for the transient analysis such as the convolution integration approach, the uniformization approach and the piecewise constant approximation (PCA) approach. Yet another approach is based on using a phase-type (PH) expansion of the non-exponential distributions [18].

A special case of NHCTMC could be considered where the matrix $\boldsymbol{Q}(t)$ can be factored so that $\boldsymbol{Q}(t) = g(t)\,\boldsymbol{W}$, with matrix $\boldsymbol{W}$ having all its entries independent of time. In this case the solution to the NHCTMC can be written down as:

$$\boldsymbol{\pi}(t) = \boldsymbol{\pi}(0)\, e^{(\int_0^t g(\tau)d\tau)\boldsymbol{W}} = \boldsymbol{\pi}(0)\, e^{\boldsymbol{W}g^*t}, \tag{A.29}$$

where $g^* = (\int_0^t g(\tau)d\tau)/t$ and $\boldsymbol{W}\,g^*$ is the generator matrix of an HCTMC. Thus by solving an "equivalent" HCTMC, we can obtain the solution of the original NHCTMC in this special case. We refer to this method of solving an NHCTMC as the *Equivalent-HCTMC method.*

When the above factorization is not possible and the NHCTMC is acyclic, the convolution integration approach can be recommended [17, 25], which is based on the following equation:

$$p_{ij}(t) = \delta_{ij} e^{-\int_0^t q_{ii}(\tau)d\tau} + \int_0^t \sum_k p_{ik}(x) q_{kj}(x) e^{-\int_x^t q_{jj}(\tau)d\tau} dx, \qquad \text{(A.30)}$$

where δ_{ij} is the Kronecker delta function defined by $\delta_{ij} = 1$ if $i = j$ and 0 otherwise. The corresponding equation for unconditional state probability is thus:

$$\pi_i(t) = \pi_i(0) e^{-\int_0^t q_{ii}(\tau)d\tau} + \int_0^t \sum_{k \neq i} \pi_k(x) q_{ki}(x) e^{-\int_x^t q_{ii}(\tau)d\tau} dx. \qquad \text{(A.31)}$$

The PCA method is based on approximating a continuous function of time by a staircase function whose value remains constant in certain intervals. We divide the interval $(0, t]$ over which the original continuous function should be evaluated, into n smaller intervals, such that the function can be considered approximately constant over any of the n small intervals. In this way, computing the value of the original function in the midpoint of each small interval, we can generate the approximating staircase function. The approximation improves as n increases and the length of each small interval decreases.

The PH expansion method consists in replacing the non-exponential distributions present in the model with a PH distribution, which is defined by the probability distribution of the absorbing time in a HCTMC. Since the PH distribution family is dense, the PH distribution can approximate any probability distribution with high precision. In this way, the original non-exponential model can be approximated by an expanded HCTMC that can be solved using the methods of Section A.3.

A.4.2. *Example*

A system consists of a server type software to which transactions arrive according to a Poisson process of rate λ (Section A.2.1) [5]. The software system is subject to aging and hang/crash failures that are assumed to be stochastically independent processes. Rejuvenation (or preventive maintenance) to counteract aging, and recovering to restore from failure, are regenerative actions that take back the system to an *as good as new* state. Each transaction receives service for a random period. The effect of aging may be captured by using a decreasing service rate and an increasing failure rate, where the decrease or the increase, respectively, can be a function of time since the last rejuvenation/recovery action. Assuming that the software

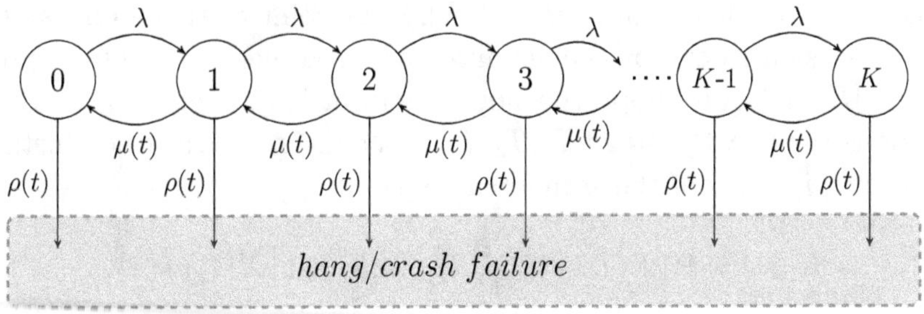

Fig. A.3. An NHCTMC model for a software system with aging and failure.

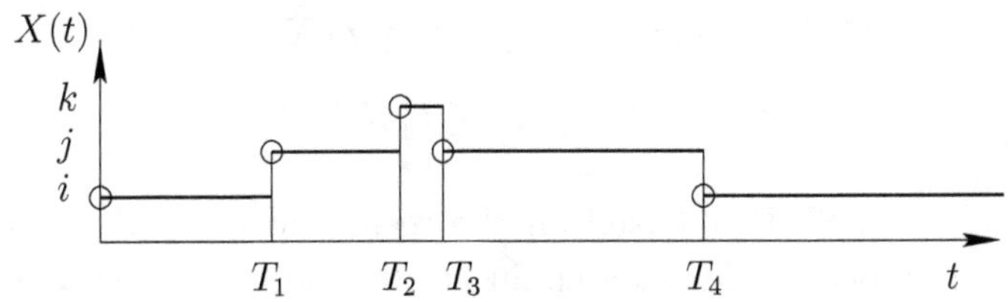

Fig. A.4. A semi-Markov process, which experiences the Markov property at the indicated time points.

queue may allocate up to K transactions, the state transition diagram of the software system is given in Fig. A.3, where t is the time from the last renewal. We have maintained the notation in Garg *et al.* [5].

A.5. Semi-Markov Process (SMP)

The discrete-state continuous-time random process, $X(t)$, is a Semi-Markov process (SMP) if it is time-homogeneous and if it experiences the Markov property at the state transition instances (see Fig. A.4).

The name SMP comes from the fact that an SMP does not always experience the Markov property (during the sojourn in a state), but only at the state transition instances. Specifically, during a sojourn in state i, both the remaining time in that state and the next visited state depend on the elapsed time since the process is in state i. The state transition instances where the Markov property holds are marked with a circle in Fig. A.4.

The most important consequences of the definition of SMP are:

— the sojourn time in a state can be any positive random variable;
— the distribution of the next state and the time spent in a state are not independent.

Consequently, to define an SMP the following joint distribution has to be given. It is usually done by the definition of the kernel matrix of the process $\boldsymbol{K}(t) = [K_{ij}(t)]$ (we adopt the notation from [18]). Let $X(t) \in S$ be a continuous-time SMP, and let $T_1, T_2, T_3, \ldots$ be the state transition instances, then, the (i, j) entry of the kernel matrix is:

$$K_{ij}(t) = \mathbf{P}\{X(T_{i+1}) = j,\ T_{i+1} - T_i \le t \,|\, X(T_i) = i\}.$$

Utilizing the time homogeneity property of the process, we further have for T_i that

$$\begin{aligned} &\mathbf{P}\{X(T_{i+1}) = j, T_{i+1} - T_i \le t \,|\, X(T_i) = i\} \\ &\quad = \mathbf{P}\{X(T_1) = j, T_1 \le t \,|\, X(0) = i\}. \end{aligned}$$

The analysis of an SMP is based on the results of renewal theory and the analysis of an embedded Markov chain (EMC) built on the sequence of the transition instances. The definition of an SMP requires the knowledge of the kernel matrix $\boldsymbol{K}(t) = \{K_{ij}(t)\}$ (for $t \ge 0$) and an initial distribution. It is commonly assumed that $X(t)$ experiences the Markov property at time $t = 0$.

A.5.1. *Analysis Based on State Transitions*

We intend to compute the transient state transition probability $V_{ij}(t) = \mathbf{P}\{X(t) = j \,|\, X(0) = i\}$ assuming that the sojourn in the first state finishes at time h ($T_1 = h$), that is

$$V_{ij}(t|T_1 = h) = \mathbf{P}\{X(t) = j \,|\, X(0) = i, T_1 = h\}.$$

In this case

$$V_{ij}(t|T_1 = h) = \begin{cases} \delta_{ij} & h > t \\ \displaystyle\sum_{k \in S} \mathbf{P}\{X(T_1) = k \,|\, X(0) = i, T_1 = h\}\ V_{kj}(t - h) & h \le t, \end{cases} \tag{A.32}$$

where $\mathbf{P}\{X(T_1) = k \,|\, X(0) = i, T_1 = h\}$ is the probability that the process starts from state i at time $t = 0$ and it is in state k right after the state transition at time T_1 assuming $T_1 = h$. In contrast with CTMCs this probability depends on the sojourn time in state i:

$$\begin{aligned}
&\mathbf{P}\{X(T_1) = k \,|\, X(0) = i, T_1 = h\} \\
&\quad = \lim_{\Delta \to 0} \frac{\mathbf{P}\{X(T_1) = k, h < T_1 \leq h + \Delta \,|\, X(0) = i\}}{\mathbf{P}\{h < T_1 \leq h + \Delta \,|\, X(0) = i\}} \\
&\quad = \lim_{\Delta \to 0} \frac{K_{ik}(h + \Delta) - K_{ik}(h)}{H_i(h + \Delta) - H_i(h)} = \frac{dK_{ik}(h)}{dH_i(h)},
\end{aligned} \tag{A.33}$$

where $H_i(h)$ denotes the distribution of time spent in state i,

$$\begin{aligned}
H_i(t) &= \mathbf{P}\{T_1 \leq t \,|\, X(0) = i\} \\
&= \sum_{k \in S} \mathbf{P}\{X(T_1) = k, T_1 \leq t \,|\, X(0) = i\} = \sum_{k \in S} K_{ik}(t).
\end{aligned} \tag{A.34}$$

It is commonly assumed that the state transitions are real, which means that after staying in state i a state transition moves the process to a different state. It means that $K_{ii}(t) = 0$, $\forall i \in S$. It is also possible to consider virtual state transitions from state i to state i, but it does not expand the set of SMPs and we do not consider this case here. Note that the meaning of the diagonal element of an SMP kernel matrix is completely different from the meaning of the diagonal element of an infinitesimal generator of a CTMC. One of the technical consequences of this difference is the fact that we do not need to exclude the diagonal element from the summations over the set of states.

There are two cases considered in Eq. (A.32):

- If the time point of interest, t, is before the first state transition of the process (i.e. $t < h$), then the conditional state transition probability is either 0 or 1 depending on the initial and the final state. If the initial state i is identical with the final state j then the transition probability is 1, because there is no state transition up to time t, otherwise it is 0.
- If the time point of interest, t, is after the first state transition of the process (i.e. $h \leq t$) then we need to evaluate the distribution of the next state k assuming that the state transition occurs at time h, and after that the state transition probability from the new state k to the final state j during time $t - h$, using the Markov property of the process at time h. The probability that the process moves to state k assuming it occurs at time h is $\frac{dK_{ik}(h)}{dH_i(h)}$ and the probability of it moving from state k to state j during an interval of length $t - h$ is $V_{kj}(t - h)$.

The distribution of the condition of Eq. (A.32) is known. The distribution of the sojourn time in state i is $H_i(h)$. Using the law of total probability we obtain

$$V_{ij}(t) = \int_{h=t}^{\infty} \delta_{ij}\, dH_i(t) + \int_{h=0}^{t} \sum_{k \in S} \frac{dK_{ik}(h)}{dH_i(h)}\, V_{kj}(t-h)\, dH_i(h)$$
$$= \delta_{ij}\,(1 - H_i(t)) + \int_{h=0}^{t} \sum_{k \in S} V_{kj}(t-h)\, dK_{ik}(h). \qquad \text{(A.35)}$$

The analysis of an SMP based on the first state transition resulted in a Volterra integral equation. The transient behaviour of SMPs can be computed using numerical methods for Volterra integral equations [26].

Transform domain description: We take the Laplace-Stieltjes transform (LST) of both sides of the Volterra integral equation (A.35). The only non-trivial term is a convolution integral on the right hand side.

$$V_{ij}^{\sim}(s) = \delta_{ij}\,(1 - H_i^{\sim}(s)) + \sum_{k \in S} K_{ik}^{\sim}(s)\, V_{kj}^{\sim}(s),$$

where the LST functions are defined as $f^{\sim}(s) = \int_0^{\infty} e^{-st} df(t)$.

Introducing the diagonal matrix $\boldsymbol{E}^{\sim}(s)$ composed by the elements $1 - H_i^{\sim}(s)$, that is $\boldsymbol{E}^{\sim}(s) = \mathrm{diag}\langle 1 - H_i^{\sim}(s)\rangle$, the LST of the state transition probabilities are obtained in matrix form:

$$\boldsymbol{V}^{\sim}(s) = \boldsymbol{E}^{\sim}(s) + \boldsymbol{K}^{\sim}(s)\boldsymbol{V}^{\sim}(s),$$

from which

$$\boldsymbol{V}^{\sim}(s) = [\boldsymbol{I} - \boldsymbol{K}^{\sim}(s)]^{-1}\boldsymbol{E}^{\sim}(s).$$

Stationary behaviour: Let the transition probability matrix of the EMC be $\boldsymbol{P} = [p_{ij}]$. It is obtained from the kernel matrix through the following relation

$$p_{ij} = \mathbf{P}\{X(T_1) = j \,|\, X(0) = i\} = \lim_{t \to \infty} \mathbf{P}\{X(T_1) = j, T_1 \le t \,|\, X(0) = i\}$$
$$= \lim_{t \to \infty} K_{ij}(t).$$

The stationary distribution of the EMC $\boldsymbol{\nu} = [\nu_i]$ is the solution of the linear system $\boldsymbol{\nu} = \boldsymbol{\nu}\boldsymbol{P}, \sum_i \nu_i = 1$. The stationary distribution of the SMP is given by

$$\pi_i = \frac{\nu_i\, h_i}{\sum_j \nu_j\, h_j}, \tag{A.36}$$

where h_i is the mean time spent in state i and can be computed from the kernel matrix through $h_i = \int_0^\infty (1 - H_i(t))dt$.

A.5.2. *Example*

The system we study is taken from Chen and Trivedi [15] and consists of a server type software that is available in state $\boldsymbol{U}$. The software can fail, upon which a recovery procedure is started. The state in which the software is recovering and is unavailable for service is denoted as state $\boldsymbol{D}$. The software occasionally undergoes rejuvenation or preventive maintenance (PM). This state is denoted as state $\boldsymbol{R}$. When the system (see Fig. A.5) stays in the available state $\boldsymbol{U}$, it will undergo a rejuvenation and enter state $\boldsymbol{R}$ after a random time with distribution function $F_0(t)$ or fail and enter state $\boldsymbol{D}$ with a general distribution function $F_2(t)$. The distribution function for the duration of preventive maintenance is $F_1(t)$, and the distribution function for the duration of repair is $F_3(t)$. We assume that all the states are regenerative, that is, that any transition instance experiences the Markov property. Hence, the process is an SMP to which we can apply the transient and steady-state analysis of Section A.5. The kernel matrix $\boldsymbol{K}(t)$ has the following structure:

$$\boldsymbol{K}(t) = \begin{bmatrix} 0 & K_{01}(t) & K_{02}(t) \\ K_{10}(t) & 0 & 0 \\ K_{20}(t) & 0 & 0 \end{bmatrix}$$

With

$$\begin{aligned} K_{01}(t) &= \mathbf{P}\{\text{PM occurs before failure within time t}\} \\ &= \int_0^t (1 - F_2(x))\, dF_0(x), \end{aligned}$$

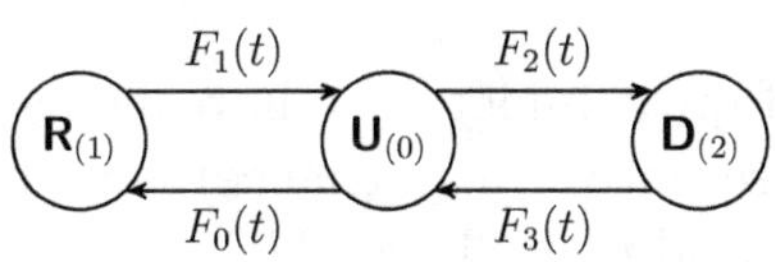

Fig. A.5. An SMP model for a software system with preventive maintenance (rejuvenation) and failure.

$$
\begin{aligned}
K_{02}(t) &= \mathbf{P}\{\text{failure occurs before PM within time t}\} \\
&= \int_0^t (1 - F_0(x))\, dF_2(x), \\
K_{10}(t) &= \mathbf{P}\{\text{PM completes within time t}\} = F_1(t), \\
K_{20}(t) &= \mathbf{P}\{\text{repair completes within time t}\} = F_3(t).
\end{aligned}
$$

It follows that the one-step transition probability matrix of the EMC $\boldsymbol{P} = \lim_{t\to\infty} \boldsymbol{K}(t)$ becomes:

$$
\boldsymbol{P} = \begin{bmatrix} 0 & p_{01} & p_{02} \\ p_{10} & 0 & 0 \\ p_{20} & 0 & 0 \end{bmatrix}
$$

Solving the EMC steady-state equations $\boldsymbol{\nu} = \boldsymbol{\nu}\boldsymbol{P}, \sum_i \nu_i = 1$ we get

$$
\nu_0 = 1/2, \quad \nu_i = p_{0i}/2, \quad i = 1, 2
$$

Further the expected sojourn times in all states are

$$
\begin{aligned}
h_0 = \mathbf{E}[H_0] &= \int_0^\infty (1 - F_0(t))(1 - F_2(t))\, dt, \\
h_1 = \mathbf{E}[H_1] &= \int_0^\infty (1 - F_1(t))\, dt, \\
h_2 = \mathbf{E}[H_2] &= \int_0^\infty (1 - F_3(t))\, dt.
\end{aligned}
$$

Applying Eq. (A.36), we obtain the steady-state availability of the system as:

$$
A = \pi_0 = \frac{h_0}{h_0 + h_1 p_{01} + h_2 p_{02}}. \tag{A.37}
$$

In a special case of great importance in realistic applications where the rejuvenation (or the preventive maintenance) is executed periodically with a deterministic time period t_0, we have $F_0(t) = u(t - t_0)$ (see Fig. A.6), and

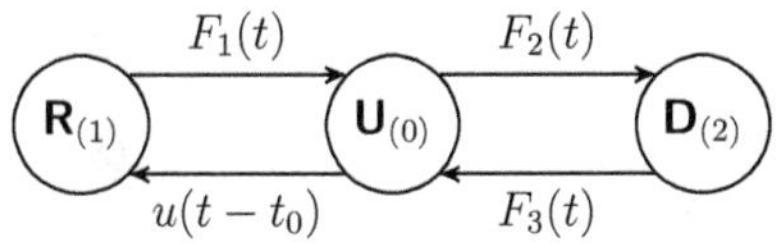

Fig. A.6. An SMP model for a software system with rejuvenation triggered at constant time t_0.

the one-step transition probabilities simplify to

$$p_{01} = \mathbf{P}\{\text{PM triggers before failure occurs}\} = 1 - F_2(t_0),$$

$$p_{02} = \mathbf{P}\{\text{failure occurs before PM triggers}\} = F_2(t_0),$$

$$p_{10} = p_{20} = 1.$$

The mean sojourn times h_1 and h_2 remain unchanged and

$$h_0 = \mathbf{E}[H_0] = \int_0^{t_0} (1 - F_2(t))\, dt.$$

To proceed further and compute the availability in Eq. (A.37), the distribution functions $F_i(t)$, $(i = 1 - 3)$ should be assigned. Examples assuming Weibull, Two-stage Hypoexponential or Log-normal distributions are given in [15] and [18].

A.6. Markov Regenerative Process

The discrete-state, continuous-time, and time-homogeneous stochastic process $X(t)$ is a Markov regenerative process (MRGP) if there exists a random time series $T_0, T_1, T_2, \ldots$ $(T_0 = 0)$ such that the process $X(t)$ experiences the Markov property at time epochs $T_0, T_1, T_2, \ldots$ [21, 27] (see Fig. A.7). The time epochs $T_0, T_1, T_2, \ldots$ that satisfy the Markov property are called *regeneration time points* (RTPs).

An MRGP is a generalization of many stochastic processes [21, 27]. In a CTMC any time epoch t satisfies the Markov property (Eq. A.8), in an SMP the Markov property is satisfied at all the time instances at which the process undergoes a state transition, and in an MRGP the Markov property holds only when the process enters a subset of specific states called *regeneration states*.

Compared to the properties of SMP, where the process experiences the Markov property at all instances of state transition, the definition of MRGPs

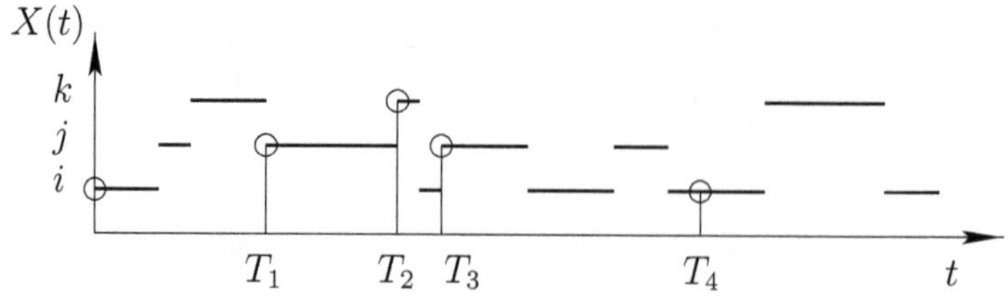

Fig. A.7. Markov regenerative process — the circles denote the points with the Markov property.

is less restrictive since the MRGP experiences the Markov property only at some transition instances, i.e. the RTPs. The analysis of MRGPs is based on the occurrence of the RTPs where the process experiences the Markov property.

The definition of an MRGP does not prescribe how the behaviour of the process between two consecutive RTPs $T_0, T_1, T_2, \ldots$ should be. Hence, MRGPs can be characterized by any kind of stochastic process between two consecutive RTPs. In practice, the use of the renewal theorem for the analysis of these processes is meaningful only when the stochastic behavior between consecutive time points $T_0, T_1, T_2, \ldots$ is analytically tractable. The common analysis method of MRGPs is based on the analysis of the next time point with Markov property (T_1).

We denote by $Y_0, Y_1, Y_2, \ldots$ the series of states reached by the MRGP right after an RTP: i.e. $Y_i = X(T_i)$. The series of random variables $\{Y_n, T_n; n \geq 0\}$ is a time-homogeneous *Markov renewal series* since it satisfies the following relation

$$\begin{aligned}
&\mathbf{P}\{Y_{n+1} = y, T_{n+1} - T_n \leq t \,|\, Y_0, \ldots, Y_n, T_0, \ldots, T_n\} \\
&\quad = \mathbf{P}\{Y_{n+1} = y, T_{n+1} - T_n \leq t \,|\, Y_n\} \\
&\quad = \mathbf{P}\{Y_1 = y, T_1 - T_0 \leq t \,|\, Y_0\}
\end{aligned}$$

for all $n \geq 0$, $y \in \Omega$ and $t \geq 0$. From the definition of Markov renewal series, the sequence of states $Y_0, Y_1, Y_2, \ldots$ forms a DTMC.

The analysis of an MRGP is based on this *embedded* Markov renewal series. To this end the joint distribution of the next RTP and the state in that RTP has to be known, and it is denoted as

$$K_{ij}(t) = \mathbf{P}\{Y_1 = j, T_1 - T_0 \leq t \,|\, Y_0 = i\}, \quad i, j \in S$$

Matrix $\boldsymbol{K}(t) = \{K_{ij}(t)\}$ is referred to as the global kernel of the MRGP and completely characterizes the stochastic properties of the MRGP at the RTPs. The description of the process between RTPs is complex, but for the transient analysis (more precisely for computing transient state probabilities) it is enough to know the transient state probabilities between consecutive RTPs. It is given by the local kernel matrix of the MRGP $\boldsymbol{E}(t) = \{E_{ij}(t)\}$, whose elements are

$$E_{ij}(t) = \mathbf{P}\{X(t) = j,\, T_1 > t,\, | Y_0 = i\}.$$

$E_{ij}(t)$ is the probability that the process starts in state i, that the first RTP is later than t and that the process stays in state j at time t.

A.6.1. *Transient Analysis Based on the Embedded Markov Renewal Series*

Let the transient state transition probability matrix be $\boldsymbol{V}(t)$, whose elements are

$$V_{ij}(t) = \mathbf{P}\{X(t) = j \,|\, X(0) = i\}.$$

Assuming that $T_1 = h$ we can compute the conditional state transition probability as follows

$$V_{ij}(t \,|\, T_1 = h) = \begin{cases} \mathbf{P}\{X(t) = j \,|\, T_1 = h,\, X(0) = i\}, & h > t, \\ \sum\limits_{k \in S} \mathbf{P}\{X(T_1) = k \,|\, X(0) = i, T_1 = h\} \cdot V_{kj}(t-h), & h \le t. \end{cases} \tag{A.38}$$

Similar to the transient analysis of SMPs, the Eq. (A.38) describes two exhaustive and exclusive events $h \le t$ and $h > t$. In case of the SMPs the $h > t$ case resulted in 0 or 1, while in case of the MRGPs the conditional probability for $h > t$ can be different from 0 or 1, because the process can also have state transitions before T_1.

Using the distribution of T_1 and the formula of total probability we obtain

$$\begin{aligned} V_{ij}(t) = &\int_{h=t}^{\infty} \mathbf{P}\{X(t) = j \,|\, T_1 = h,\, X(0) = i\}\, dH_i(h) \\ &+ \int_{h=0}^{t} \sum_{k \in S} \frac{dK_{ik}(h)}{dH_i(h)}\, V_{kj}(t-h)\, dH_i(h), \end{aligned} \tag{A.39}$$

where $H_i(t) = \sum_j K_{ij}(t)$ (see Eq. (A.34)) is the distribution of time spent in state i. Let us consider the first term of the right hand side

$$\begin{aligned}
&\int_{h=t}^{\infty} \mathbf{P}\{X(t) = j \mid T_1 = h,\, X(0) = i\}\, dH_i(h) \\
&\quad = \int_{h=t}^{\infty} \lim_{\Delta\to 0} \mathbf{P}\{X(t) = j \mid h \le T_1 < h + \Delta,\, X(0) = i\}\;\, dH_i(h) \\
&\quad = \int_{h=t}^{\infty} \lim_{\Delta\to 0} \frac{\mathbf{P}\{X(t) = j,\, h \le T_1 < h + \Delta \mid X(0) = i\}}{\mathbf{P}\{h \le T_1 < h + \Delta,\, \mid X(0) = i\}}\; dH_i(h) \\
&\quad = \int_{h=t}^{\infty} \frac{d_h\, \mathbf{P}\{X(t) = j,\, T_1 < h \mid X(0) = i\}}{dH_i(h)}\; dH_i(h) \\
&\quad = \mathbf{P}\{X(t) = j,\, t < T_1 \mid X(0) = i\}
\end{aligned}$$

from which

$$V_{ij}(t) = E_{ij}(t) + \sum_{k\in S} \int_{h=0}^{t} V_{kj}(t - h)\, dK_{ik}(h), \tag{A.40}$$

which is a Volterra integral equation.

Similar to the transient analysis of CTMCs and SMPs, we obtained the above Volterra equation for the transient analysis of MRGPs.

Transform domain description: The LST of Eq. (A.40) is

$$V_{ij}^{\sim}(s) = E_{ij}^{\sim}(s) + \sum_{k\in\Omega} K_{ik}^{\sim}(s)\, V_{kj}^{\sim}(s), \tag{A.41}$$

which can be written in matrix form

$$\boldsymbol{V}^{\sim}(s) = \boldsymbol{E}^{\sim}(s) + \boldsymbol{K}^{\sim}(s)\, \boldsymbol{V}^{\sim}(s). \tag{A.42}$$

The solution of Eq. (A.42) is

$$\boldsymbol{V}^{\sim}(s) = [\boldsymbol{I} - \boldsymbol{K}^{\sim}(s)]^{-1}\, \boldsymbol{E}^{\sim}(s). \tag{A.43}$$

Based on Eq. (A.43), numerical inverse Laplace methods can also be used for the transient analysis of MRGPs.

Stationary behaviour: In spite of the differences between SMP and Markov regenerative processes their stationary analysis goes along the same steps. The state transition probability of the DTMC embedded in the RTPs $\boldsymbol{P} = [p_{ij}]$ is computed from:

$$p_{ij} = \mathbf{P}\{X(T_1) = j \mid X(0) = i\} = \lim_{t\to\infty} \mathbf{P}\{X(T_1) = j, T_1 \le t \mid X(0) = i\}$$
$$= \lim_{t\to\infty} K_{ij}(t).$$

The stationary distribution of the EMC $\boldsymbol{\nu} = [\nu_{ij}]$ is the solution of

$$\boldsymbol{\nu} = \boldsymbol{\nu}\boldsymbol{P}, \qquad \sum_i \nu_i = 1. \tag{A.44}$$

Now we need to compute the mean time spent in different states during the interval (T_0, T_1). Fortunately, the local kernel carries the necessary information. Let α_{ij} be the mean time the process spends in state j during the interval (T_0, T_1) assuming that it starts from state i $(X(T_0) = i)$. Then

$$\alpha_{ij} = \mathbf{E}\left[\int_{t=0}^{\infty} \mathcal{I}_{\{X(t)=j,T_1>t\}} \mid X(T_0) = i \, dt\right] \tag{A.45}$$

where $\mathcal{I}_{\{\bullet\}}$ is the binary indicator variable of event $\bullet$, i.e. $\mathcal{I}_{\{\bullet\}} = 1$ when event $\bullet = true$ and $\mathcal{I}_{\{\bullet\}} = 0$ when event $\bullet = false$. When the process stays in state j at time t and T_1 is greater than t then $\mathcal{I}_{\{X(t)=j,T_1>t\}} = 1$, that is, the integral in (A.45) counts the time the process spends in state j during the interval (T_0, T_1). This is a random time which depends on the evolution of the process and its mean is needed for the stationary analysis. From Eq.(A.45) we derive:

$$\alpha_{ij} = \int_{t=0}^{\infty} \mathbf{E}\big[\mathcal{I}_{\{X(t)=j,T_1>t\}} \mid X(T_0) = i\big] \, dt$$
$$= \int_{t=0}^{\infty} \mathbf{P}\{X(t) = j, T_1 > t \mid X(T_0) = i\} dt$$
$$= \int_{t=0}^{\infty} E_{ij}(t) dt,$$

The mean length of the interval (T_0, T_1) is

$$\alpha_i = \sum_{j\in\Omega} \alpha_{ij}.$$

Finally the stationary distribution of the process can be computed as

$$\pi_i = \frac{\sum_{j\in\Omega} \nu_j \alpha_{ji}}{\sum_{j\in\Omega} \nu_j \alpha_j}. \tag{A.46}$$

A.6.2. *Example*

This example is taken from Garg *et al.* [9] and refers to a client-server type system, where the server software is required to run continuously for very long periods, and is periodically rejuvenated at a constant interval of length δ. In their paper, the system was modeled through a Markov regenerative stochastic Petri net (MRSPN) (see Section A.7.4); however, in this example we utilize the state transition model derived from the MRSPN, reported in Garg *et al.* [9], and shown in Fig. A.8. State 1 models the robust up state. The aging of the software moves the system to the failure-probable state 2. From state 2 a crash failure of the software leads the system to state 4, where a restart is initiated and every other activity is suspended. Rejuvenation is activated at constant intervals of duration δ. The dashed transitions labelled $u(t-\delta)$ indicate that the clock count is not reset by the possible jump from state 1 to state 2, and it is resumed in state 2 from the value it had before the jump. If the system is in state 1 when rejuvenation is triggered the system transits to state 3, while if the system is in the failure-probable state 2, the transition is toward state 5. From both states 3 and 5 the rejuvenation leads back the system to the robust state 1, and every other activity is suspended. It is assumed that rejuvenation and repair are completely regenerative. We assume that all the transition times are exponentially distributed, but the trigger time of rejuvenation is deterministic.

Considering the presence of exponential transitions, it can be seen from Fig. A.8 that the regeneration times exactly correspond to the times of entering either of states 1, 3, 4 or 5. In contrast, when the process transits from state 1 to state 2 the deterministic activity initiated in state 1 goes on. Thus, in order to probabilistically determine future states of the process, the time already spent in state 1 needs to be known apart from the knowledge that the process is in state 2. The process identified in Fig. A.8 is an MRGP.

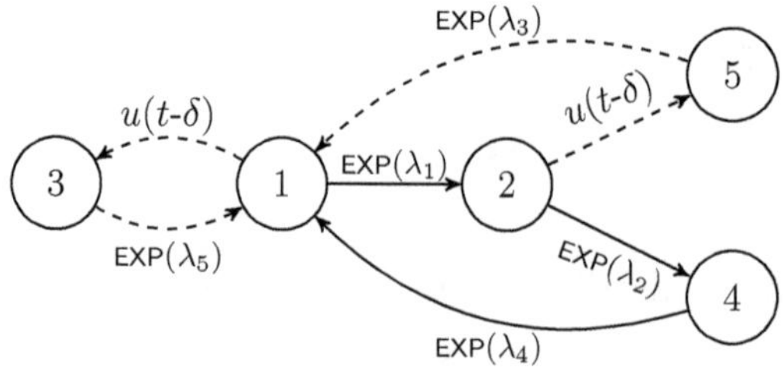

Fig. A.8. Markov regenerative process.

The set of states at regeneration instants is $\Omega = \{1, 3, 4, 5\}$ and the global kernel matrix becomes:

$$\boldsymbol{K}(t) = \begin{bmatrix} 0 & K_{13}(t) & K_{14}(t) & K_{15}(t) \\ K_{31}(t) & 0 & 0 & 0 \\ K_{41}(t) & 0 & 0 & 0 \\ K_{51}(t) & 0 & 0 & 0 \end{bmatrix}$$

Note that the subscripts ij on $K_{ij}(t)$ denote the actual state labels in Fig. A.8. For the non-zero entries, we have

$$K_{13}(t) = e^{-\lambda_1 \delta}\, u(t-\delta),$$

$$K_{14}(t) = \begin{cases} 1 - \dfrac{\lambda_1}{\lambda_1 - \lambda_2} e^{-\lambda_2 t} + \dfrac{\lambda_2}{\lambda_1 - \lambda_2} e^{-\lambda_1 t}, & 0 \le t < \delta \\[2ex] 1 - \dfrac{\lambda_1}{\lambda_1 - \lambda_2} e^{-\lambda_2 \delta} + \dfrac{\lambda_2}{\lambda_1 - \lambda_2} e^{-\lambda_1 \delta}, & t \ge \delta, \end{cases}$$

$$K_{15}(t) = \frac{\lambda_1}{\lambda_1 - \lambda_2}\left[e^{-\lambda_2 \delta} - e^{-\lambda_1 \delta}\right] u(t-\delta),$$

$$K_{i1}(t) = 1 - e^{-\lambda_i t}, \quad i = 3, 4, 5.$$

Since the local kernel $\boldsymbol{E}(t)$ describes the time behavior of the process between two consecutive RTPs, starting from an RTP, hence it is a 4×5 matrix given as:

$$\boldsymbol{E}(t) = \begin{bmatrix} E_{11}(t) & E_{12}(t) & 0 & 0 & 0 \\ 0 & 0 & E_{33}(t) & 0 & 0 \\ 0 & 0 & 0 & E_{44}(t) & 0 \\ 0 & 0 & 0 & 0 & E_{55}(t) \end{bmatrix}$$

Again, the subscripts ij on $E_{ij}(t)$ denote the actual state labels in Fig. A.8. Zero entries in the matrix at the ij-th location indicate that either a transition from i to j is not possible or that it results in a regeneration. The non-zero entries are

$$E_{11}(t) = e^{-\lambda_1 t}\,(u(t) - u(t-\delta)),$$

$$E_{12}(t) = \frac{\lambda_1}{\lambda_1 - \lambda_2}\left[e^{-\lambda_2 t} - e^{-\lambda_1 t}\right](u(t) - u(t-\delta)),$$

$$E_{ii}(t) = e^{-\lambda_i t}, \quad i = 3, 4, 5.$$

$E_{11}(t)$ is the probability that the process starting in state 1 stays in it till time t. Here t lies in the interval $[0, \delta)$ as at time δ, the process transits to state 3 resulting in a regeneration. $E_{12}(t)$ is the probability that at time t the process is in state 2 given that it was in state 1 at $t = 0$. Note that t takes values in $[0, \delta)$. $E_{12}(t)$ is obtained by conditioning on time to enter state 2 and un-conditioning. $E_{ii}(t)$, for $i = 3$, 4, 5 is the probability that the corresponding enabled exponential transition does not fire by time t.

The transient solution is obtained by applying Eq. (A.43) and inverting the related LST. To compute the steady-state distribution the non-zero α_{ij} entrics are

$$\begin{aligned}
\alpha_{11} &= \int_0^\infty E_{11}(t)\,dt = \frac{1}{\lambda_1}[1 - e^{-\lambda_1\delta}],\\
\alpha_{12} &= \int_0^\infty E_{12}(t)\,dt = \frac{1}{\lambda_2} - \frac{\lambda_1}{\lambda_1 - \lambda_2}\left[\frac{e^{-\lambda_2\delta}}{\lambda_2} - \frac{e^{-\lambda_1\delta}}{\lambda_1}\right],\\
\alpha_{ii} &= \int_0^\infty E_{ii}(t)\,dt = \frac{1}{\lambda_i}, \quad i = 3, 4, 5
\end{aligned}$$

and the solution of (A.44) is

$$\begin{aligned}
\nu_1 &= \frac{1}{2},\\
\nu_3 &= \frac{1}{2}e^{-\lambda_1\delta},\\
\nu_4 &= \frac{1}{2} - \frac{\lambda_1}{2(\lambda_1 - \lambda_2)}e^{-\lambda_2\delta} - \frac{\lambda_2}{2(\lambda_1 - \lambda_2)}e^{-\lambda_1\delta},\\
\nu_5 &= \frac{\lambda_1}{2(\lambda_1 - \lambda_2)}\left[e^{-\lambda_2\delta} - e^{-\lambda_1\delta}\right].
\end{aligned}$$

The stationary distribution is obtained from Eq. (A.46) as

$$\begin{aligned}
\pi_i &= \nu_i\alpha_{ii}, \quad i = 1, 3, 4, 5,\\
\pi_2 &= \nu_1\alpha_{12}.
\end{aligned}$$

A.7. Petri Nets

Petri nets (PNs) are a mathematical and graphical tool for describing complex systems with concurrent and conflicting activities. The structure of a standard Petri net (PN) is a bipartite graph that comprises a set of *places*, a set of *transitions*, and a set of *directed arcs* [28].

Formally a PN is defined by a tuple $\mathcal{PN} = (\mathcal{P}, \mathcal{T}, I, O, H, M_0)$, where:

- $\mathcal{P}$ is the set of places with cardinality n_P;
- $\mathcal{T}$ is the set of transitions with cardinality n_T;
- $I, O, H : \mathcal{T} \rightarrow Bag(\mathcal{P})$ are respectively the sets of input, output, and inhibition functions that map transitions to bags[a] of places;
- M_0 is the initial marking of the net, i.e., the initial distribution of tokens among the places in $\mathcal{P}$.

A place p is called (i) an *input* place for a given transition t if there is an input arc that connects p to t; (ii) an *output* place if there is an output arc that connects t to p; (iii) an *inhibitor* place if an inhibitor arc connects p to t. In the following, the symbols $I(t)$, $O(t)$ and $H(t)$ respectively denote the sets of input, output and inhibitor places of transition t.

The marking of a PN is defined by a bag M_i with the number of tokens contained in each of the places. The symbol $M_i(p)$ denotes the numbers of tokens contained in place p in marking M_i. The graphical structure of a PN is a bipartite directed graph where places (drawn as circles) and transitions (drawn as bars) are the nodes, and arcs (drawn as arrows) are the edges. Markings are represented by black dots (called tokens) in the places. An example of the graphical representation of a PN is shown in Fig. A.9(a) with initial marking $M_0 = (1001100)$.

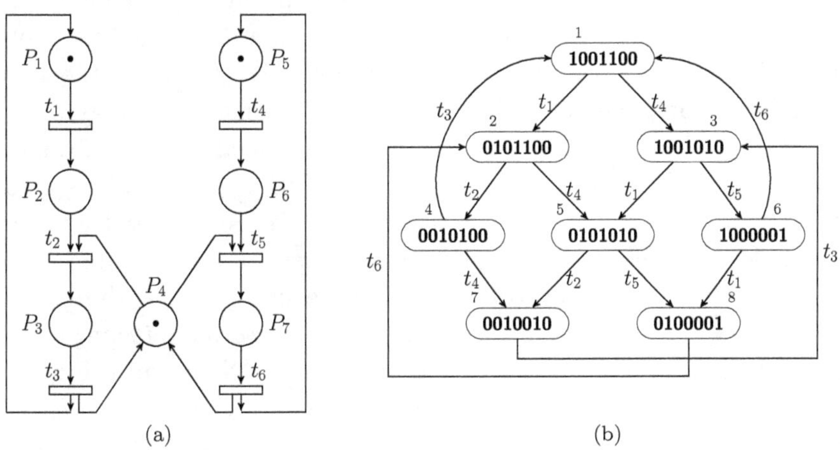

Fig. A.9. A marked PN a) and its reachability graph b).

[a]A bag is a set with duplication of elements allowed; that is, it keeps track of the "occurrence count" of each set element.

The dynamic evolution of a PN is specified by the *enabling* and *firing* rules. A transition $t \in \mathcal{T}$ is *enabled* in marking M_i if

(1) each input place contains at least as many tokens as the multiplicity of the corresponding input arc,
(2) each inhibitor place contains a number of tokens strictly smaller than the multiplicity of the corresponding inhibitor arc.

When a transition t_k is enabled in marking M_i it can *fire*, removing from each input place as many tokens as the multiplicity of the input arcs, and adding in all the output places as many tokens as the multiplicity of the output arcs. The firing of a transition in marking M_i produces a new marking M_j with a token count given by:

$$M_j = M_i - I(t_k) + O(t_k). \tag{A.47}$$

If two transitions are enabled in the same marking and the firing of one does not disable the other one the two transitions are said to be *concurrent*. If the firing of one of the two disables the other one, the two transitions are said to be in *conflict*.

Reachability graph — The firing rules allow us to describe the evolution of a marked PN starting from its initial marking M_0. Every time an enabled transition $t_k \in \mathcal{T}$ fires in marking M_i a new marking M_j is computed; the marking M_j is said to be directly reachable from M_i, and this property is denoted with $M_i - t_k \rightarrow M_j$. Applying the firing rule to the reached marking, it is possible to find a sequence of transition firings and new markings describing the net evolution. The set of all reachable markings starting from an initial marking M_0 is called the *reachability set* and is denoted by $RS(M_0)$. The reachability set can be represented as a graph whose nodes are the markings in $RS(M_0)$ and the arcs connecting the nodes are labelled with the transitions whose firing causes the change of marking $M_i - t_k \rightarrow M_j$. This graph is called a *reachability graph*, and is denoted by $R(M_0)$. The reachability graph of the PN shown in Fig. A.9(a) is represented in Fig. A.9(b). Starting from the initial marking M_0, shown in Fig. A.9(a), and applying the enabling and firing rules, it is possible to derive the structure of Fig. A.9(b).

An *execution sequence* $\mathcal{E}$ in a marked PN, is a sequence of legal markings obtained by firing a sequence of enabled transitions (note that $M_{(0)} = M_0$):

$$\mathcal{E} = \{(M_{(0)}, t_{(0)}); (M_{(1)}, t_{(1)}); \ldots; (M_{(j)}, t_{(j)}); \ldots\}.$$

An execution sequence $\mathcal{E}$ can be viewed as a connected path in the reachability graph $R(M_0)$ of the PN.

A.7.1. *Stochastic Petri Nets (SPNs)*

Original PNs did not carry any notion of time [29]. In order to use the PN formalism for the quantitative analysis of software systems, several extensions have been proposed in the literature, in particular by associating *firing times* with the transitions [30].

A timed execution sequence $\mathcal{S}_E$ of a marked PN starting from an initial marking $M_{(0)}$ is an execution sequence $\mathcal{E}$ augmented by a non-decreasing sequence of real values representing the epochs of firing of each transition, such that consecutive transitions $(t_{(j)}; t_{(j+1)})$ in $\mathcal{E}$ correspond to ordered epochs $\tau_j \leq \tau_{j+1}$ in $\mathcal{S}_E$. Thus formally [31, 32]:

$$\mathcal{S}_E = \{ (M_{(0)}, t_{(0)}, \tau_0); (M_{(1)}, t_{(1)}, \tau_1); \ldots ; (M_{(j)}, t_{(j)}, \tau_j); \ldots \}.$$

The time interval $\tau_{j+1} - \tau_j$ between consecutive epochs represents the period that the PN sojourns in marking $M_{(j)}$. In the sequel we always assume the initial epoch to be $\tau_0 = 0$. The ensemble of all the possible timed execution sequences defines the Marking Process $\mathcal{M}(t)$.

Stochastic Petri nets (SPNs) [31, 33] are PNs in which the firing delays between successive transitions are exponentially distributed random variables. To this end, a transition t_k enabled in marking M_j is associated with a constant, possibly marking-dependent, firing rate $\lambda_k(M_j)$. Molloy [33] has proven that when the random firing times associated with PN transitions are exponentially distributed, the dynamic behavior of the PN can be mapped into a homogeneous continuous-time Markov chain with state space isomorphic to the reachability graph of the PN. The isomorphic CTMC can be automatically generated from the reachability graph $RS(M_0)$ with the following rules:

- at each marking $M_i \in RS(M_0)$ corresponds to a state i in the CTMC,
- an arc between two states i and j of the CTMC has a rate given by the sum of the rates of the transitions whose individual firings produce the change of marking from M_i to M_j.

From the reachability graph of Fig. A.9(b) we can immediately derive the corresponding CTMC, by replacing markings with states, and assigning to each arc the constant transition rate λ_i assigned to the PN transition t_i.

A.7.2. *Generalized Stochastic Petri Nets (GSPNs)*

Activities whose durations differ by orders of magnitude can often be encountered in the modeling processes of software systems. The corresponding CTMC becomes stiff and hard to solve numerically [24].

To overcome this problem, Ajmone *et al.* [34] have introduced two classes of transitions: timed transitions with exponentially distributed firing times and untimed or *immediate* transitions. Immediate transitions fire in zero time and have higher priority over the timed ones. SPNs augmented with immediate transitions are called *generalized* SPNs (GSPNs) [34, 35].

The markings where only timed transitions are enabled are referred to as *tangible* markings, in contrast, markings where at least one single immediate transition is enabled are called *vanishing* markings. Vanishing markings are traversed in zero time and do not contribute to the time evolution of the net but only influence the logic evolution.

In a vanishing marking only immediate transitions can fire since they have higher priority over the timed ones. If in a vanishing marking more than one immediate transition is enabled, a rule to select the one that fires needs to be introduced. The choice is done in a probabilistic way associating a weight w_i to any immediate transition t_i. Given the set of immediate transitions $T_e^{(i)}$ enabled in marking M_i, the probability that transitions $t_k \in T_e^{(i)}$ fire is

$$\mathbf{P}\{t_k \text{ fires}|\text{marking } M_i\} = \frac{w_k}{\sum_{t\in T_e^{(i)}} w_t}. \tag{A.48}$$

These probabilities are called *switching probabilities* in GSPN terminology.

The evolution of a GSPN cannot be described by a CTMC, due to the presence of vanishing markings [36]. However, an automated procedure can be envisaged to progressively eliminate vanishing states from the reachability graph until only tangible states remain. A reachability graph where all the vanishing markings are eliminated is called a *reduced reachability graph* and over the reduced reachability graph an isomorphic CTMC can be built. The reduction procedure, described in [18, 34, 36], can be implemented with software tools so that it becomes completely transparent to the analyst.

The marking process $\mathcal{M}(t)$ after elimination of vanishing states is a CTMC-generated process as explained in Section A.7.1, and can be solved using Eqs. (A.19) and (A.27).

A.7.3. *Stochastic Reward Nets (SRNs)*

GSPNs provide a useful high-level language but their use in the representation of large systems may lead to very intricate structures. To alleviate this problem and make the high level representation more compact and readable, several structural extensions to PNs were introduced in the literature. We refer, in particular, to the *Stochastic Reward Nets* (SRNs) formalism defined in [36] and [37].

The SRN extensions include guard functions, very general marking dependency, variable cardinality arcs and the superposition of a reward structure. From an SRN, a Markov reward model is thus generated, facilitating the specification and computation of important reward-based metrics (see Section A.3.5). Parameters such as the firing rate of the timed transitions, the multiplicities of input/output arcs and the reward rate in a marking can be specified as functions of the number of tokens in any place in the SRN. Another important characteristic of an SRN is the ability to express complex enabling/disabling conditions through guard functions that greatly simplify the graphical representations of complex systems.

To get the performance and reliability/availability measures of a system, appropriate reward rates are assigned to its SRN model. As an SRN is automatically transformed into a Markov reward model (MRM), thence a steady-state and/or transient numerical solution of the MRM produces the required measures of the original SRN. Examples of use of SRN models in rejuvenation problems can be found in [38–40].

A.7.4. *Non-Markovian Stochastic Petri Nets (NMSPNs)*

Non-Markovian stochastic Petri nets (NMSPNs) enrich the formalism of SPNs, by assuming that the firing time associated to a transition can be a generally distributed random variable with known CDF. The inclusion of non-exponential distributions destroys the memoryless property of the associated marking process [41, 42], and further specifications are needed at the PN level for univocally defining the stochastic process underlying an NMSPN, given the topology of the PN and the set of CDFs associated to each timed transition. The set of specifications constitutes the *execution policy* whose semantic was first investigated by Ajmone *et al.* [32].

The execution policy comprises two specifications, the *firing policy* and the *memory policy*. The firing policy specifies how to select the next transition to fire. The standard choice is to adopt a *race policy*: the transition that fires is the one with minimum stochastic delay among the enabled transitions.

The memory policy specifies the way in which the process is conditioned upon its past history. In NMSPN the memory is represented by an age variable a_k associated to each timed transition t_k that increases with the time in which the transition is enabled. The way in which a_k is related to the past history determines the different memory policies. Three alternatives are considered:

— *Age memory* — The age variable a_k accounts for the total time in which t_k has been enabled from its last firing. The distribution of the firing delay in a given marking depends on the residual time needed for the transition to complete given a_k.
— *Enabling memory* — The age variable a_k accounts for the time elapsed from the last epoch in which t_k has been enabled. When transition t_k is disabled (even without firing) the corresponding enabling age variable is reset. The distribution of the firing delay in a given marking depends on the residual time needed for the transition to complete given a_k.
— *Resampling* — The age variable a_k is reset to zero at any change of marking. The firing distribution depends only on the time elapsed in the current marking.

At the entrance in a new tangible marking, the residual firing time is computed for each enabled timed transition given its age variable and memory policy and then the race policy is applied. The marking process $\mathcal{M}(t)$ does not have, in general, an analytically tractable formulation, unless various restrictions are applied [42, 43].

A *Markov regenerative stochastic Petri net (MRSPN)* is an NMSPN whose marking process $\mathcal{M}(t)$ is an MRGP (Section A.6) [44]. In an MRSPN an embedded sequence of RTPs should be present in the marking process, where an RTP occurs when at the entrance in a new tangible marking all the age variables are equal to 0. A sufficient condition for an NMSPN to be an MRSPN is that in each tangible marking at most one single transition with generally distributed firing time is allowed (all the other ones being exponential). Some extensions to the above rule have been studied in the literature [45].

A.7.5. *Example*

The MRGP presented in Example A.6.2 was generated by Garg *et al.* [9] by resorting to the MRSPN of Fig. A.10. The white rectangles represent

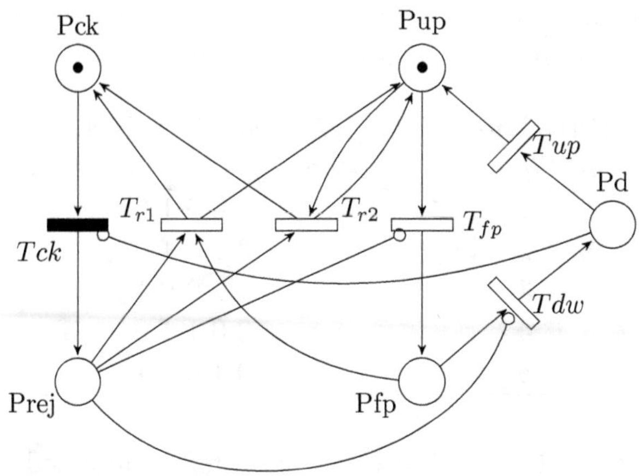

Fig. A.10. The MRSPN generating the MRGP of Example A.6.2.

transitions with exponentially distributed firing time while the black rectangles represent transitions with generally distributed firing time. In the case of Fig. A.10, the black rectangle models the clock with associated deterministic delay, which triggers rejuvenation at constant intervals. Place Pup is the up state. Transition T_{fp} models the aging process of the software. When this transition fires, the software enters the failure-probable state Pfp. The transition Tdw models the crash failure of the software. During the restart of the software, represented by the firing of transition Tup, the clock count Tck is suspended. The transition Tck fires when the clock expires by moving a token in place Prej. The token in Prej starts the action related with software rejuvenation and, at the same time, suspends any other activity by means of inhibitor arcs. Upon the completion of rejuvenation, the net is reinitialized by putting one token again in place Pup and one in place Pck, all the other places being empty. If the software was in state Pup when Tck fired, the rejuvenation action is represented by transition T_{r2}. If the software had reached the failure-probable state Pfp, then T_{r1} fires to complete the rejuvenation. In both cases the net is reinitialized.

As there is only one deterministic transition in the net, the condition for at most one generally distributed transition enabled at any time is automatically satisfied, and the SPN model belongs to the MRSPN class.

The derivation of the MRGP corresponding to the MRSPN of Fig. A.10 starts from the generation of the reachability graph. Assuming as an initial marking the one represented in Fig. A.10 and ordering the places in the sequence (Pup, Pfp, Pd, Pck, Prej), it is easy to check that the reachability graph is isomorphic to the state space of Fig. A.8 with the following correspondence between states and markings [9]:

MRGP States in Fig. A.8	*Markings in Fig. A.10 Pup Pfp Pd Pck Prej*
1	1 0 0 1 0
2	0 1 0 1 0
3	1 0 0 0 1
4	0 0 1 1 0
5	0 1 0 0 1

The MRGP already discussed in Example A.6.2 is obtained by assigning to the PN transitions the following distributions:

$$\begin{array}{lclclcl} T_{fp} & \rightarrow & \mathrm{EXP}(\lambda_1) & \qquad & Tdw & \rightarrow & \mathrm{EXP}(\lambda_2) \\ Tup & \rightarrow & \mathrm{EXP}(\lambda_4) & & T_{r2} & \rightarrow & \mathrm{EXP}(\lambda_5) \\ T_{r1} & \rightarrow & \mathrm{EXP}(\lambda_3) & & Tck & \rightarrow & u(t-\delta) \end{array}$$

A.8. Conclusions

We have provided an overview on the theory of stochastic processes and Petri nets that are mainly used in the literature on quantitative modeling of software aging and rejuvenation. We hope that the reader not particularly accustomed with this matter can find material useful to pursuing his/her investigation and research about the topics on which this book is centered.

Acknowledgements

A.B. received a financial support for this original work from the Università del Piemonte Orientale. M.T. was partially supported by the OTKA K-123914 project.

References

1. Y. Bao, X. Sun, and K. S. Trivedi. (2003). Adaptive software rejuvenation: Degradation model and rejuvenation scheme. In *Proceedings of the 2003 International Conference on Dependable Systems and Networks, San Francisco, California, USA, June 22–25*, pp. 241–248.
2. Y. Huang, C. Kintala, N. Kolettis, and N. D. Fulton. (1995). Software rejuvenation: Analysis, module and applications. In *Proceedings of the 25th Fault Tolerant Computing Symposium (FTCS-25), Pasadena, California, USA, June 27–30*, pp. 381–390.

3. K. Vaidyanathan and K. Trivedi. (2005). A comprehensive model for software rejuvenation. *IEEE Transactions on Dependable and Secure Computing*, **2**(2), 124–137. ISSN 1545-5971.
4. S. Garg, A. Pfening, A. Puliafito, M. Telek, and K. Trivedi. (1996). Modeling and analysis of load and time dependent software rejuvenation policies. In *Proceedings of the 3rd International Workshop on Performability Modeling of Computer and Communication Systems (PMCCS3), Bloomingdale, Illinois, USA, September 6–8*, pp. 35–39.
5. S. Garg, A. Puliafito, M. Telek, and T. Trivedi. (1998). Analysis of preventive maintenance in transactions based software systems. *IEEE Transactions on Computers*, **47**(1), 96–107.
6. J. Zheng, H. Okamura, L. Li, and T. Dohi. (2017). A comprehensive evaluation of software rejuvenation policies for transaction systems with Markovian arrivals. *IEEE Transactions on Reliability*, **66**(4), 1157–1177.
7. T. Dohi, K. Goseva-Popstojanova, and K. S. Trivedi. (2000). Analysis of software cost models with rejuvenation. In *Proceedings of the Fifth IEEE International Symposium on High Assurance Systems Engineering (HASE 2000), Albuquerque, New Mexico, USA, 15–17 November*, pp. 25–34.
8. W. Xie, Y. Hong, and K. Trivedi. (2005). Analysis of a two-level software rejuvenation policy. *Reliability Engineering & System Safety*, **87**(1), 13–22.
9. S. Garg, A. Puliafito, M. Telek, and K. Trivedi. (1995). Analysis of software rejuvenation using Markov Regenerative Stochastic Petri Nets. In *Proceedings of the 6th International Symposium on Software Reliability Engineering, Toulouse, France, October 24–27*, pp. 180–187.
10. G. Ning, J. Zhao, Y. Lou, J. Alonso, R. Matias, K. S. Trivedi, B. B. Yin, and K. Y. Cai. (2016). Optimization of two-granularity software rejuvenation policy based on the Markov Regenerative Process. *IEEE Transactions on Reliability*, **65**(4), 1630–1646. ISSN 0018-9529. doi: 10.1109/TR.2016.2570539.
11. A. Bobbio, S. Garg, M. Gribaudo, A. Horváth, M. Sereno, and M. Telek. (1999). Modeling software systems with rejuvenation, restoration and checkpointing through Fluid Stochastic Petri Nets. In *Proceedings of the 8th International Conference on Petri Nets and Performance Models (PNPM99), Zaragoza, Spain, September 8–10*, pp. 83–92.
12. A. Bobbio, S. Garg, M. Gribaudo, A. Horváth, M. Sereno, and M. Telek. (2008). Compositional fluid stochastic petri net model for operational software system performance. In *2008 IEEE International Conference on Software Reliability Engineering Workshops (ISSRE WOSAR08), Seattle, Washington, USA, November 11*, pp. 1–6.
13. H. Fujio, H. Okamura, and T. Dohi. (2003). Fine-grained shock models to rejuvenate software systems. *IEICE Transactions Information & Systems*, **E-86D**(10), 2165–2171.
14. A. Bobbio, M. Sereno, and C. Anglano. (2001). Fine grained software degradation models for optimal rejuvenation policies. *Performance Evaluation*, **46**, 45–62.
15. D. Chen and K. Trivedi. (2001). Analysis of periodic preventive maintenance with general system failure distribution. In *Proceedings of the Pacific Rim International Symposium on Dependable Computing (PRDC), Seoul, Korea, December 17–19*, pp. 103–107.
16. D. R. Cox. (1962). *Renewal Theory*. London, UK: Chapman & Hall.
17. K. Trivedi. (2016). *Probability & Statistics with Reliability, Queuing & Computer Science Applications* (2nd ed.). Hoboken, New Jersey, USA: John Wiley & Sons.

18. K. Trivedi and A. Bobbio. (2017). *Reliability and Availability Engineering: Modeling, Analysis, and Applications.* Cambridge, UK: Cambridge University Press.
19. J. D. Esary, A. W. Marshall, and F. Proschan. (1973). Shock models and wear processes. *The Annals of Probability*, **1**, 627–649.
20. D. Cox and H. Miller. (1965). *The Theory of Stochastic Processes.* London, UK: Chapman & Hall.
21. V. G. Kulkarni. (1995). *Modeling and Analysis of Stochastic Systems.* London, UK: Chapman & Hall.
22. J. Lambert. (1973). *Computational Methods in Ordinary Differential Equations.* New York City, New York, USA: John Wiley & Sons.
23. A. Reibman and K. S. Trivedi. (1988). Numerical transient analysis of Markov models. *Computers and Operations Research*, **15**, 19–36.
24. M. Malhotra, J. K. Muppala, and K. S. Trivedi. (1994). Stiffness-tolerant methods for transient analysis of stiff Markov chains. *Journal of Microelectronics and Reliability*, **34**, 1825–1841.
25. W. Feller. (1968). *An Introduction to Probability Theory and Its Applications — Vol. I and II.* New York City, New York, USA: John Wiley & Sons.
26. G. Gripenberg, S. O. Londen, and O. Staffans. (1990). *Volterra Integral and Functional Equations.* Encyclopedia of Mathematics and its Applications. Cambridge, UK: Cambridge University Press. doi: 10.1017/CBO9780511662805.
27. E. Cinlar. (1975). *Introduction to Stochastic Processes.* Englewood Cliffs, New Jersey, USA: Prentice-Hall.
28. J. L. Peterson. (1981). *Petri Net Theory and the Modeling of Systems.* Englewood Cliffs, New Jersey, USA: Prentice-Hall.
29. T. Murata. (1989). Petri nets: Properties, analysis and applications. *Proceedings of the IEEE*, **77**, 541–580.
30. A. Bobbio. (1990). System modelling with Petri nets. In Colombo A. and de Bustamante A. S. (eds.). *System Reliability Assessment.* Dordrecht, The Netherlands: Kluwer Academic Publishers Group.
31. G. Florin and S. Natkin. (1985). Les reseaux de Petri stochastiques. *Technique et Science Informatique*, **4**, 143–160.
32. M. A. Marsan, G. Balbo, A. Bobbio, G. Chiola, G. Conte, and A. Cumani. (1989). The effect of execution policies on the semantics and analysis of stochastic Petri nets. *IEEE Transactions on Software Engineering*, **SE-15**, 832–846.
33. M. K. Molloy. (1982). Performance analysis using stochastic Petri nets. *IEEE Transactions on Computers*, **C-31**, 913–917.
34. M. A. Marsan, G. Balbo, and G. Conte. (1984). A class of generalized stochastic Petri nets for the performance evaluation of multiprocessor systems. *ACM Transactions on Computer Systems*, **2**, 93–122.
35. M. A. Marsan, G. Balbo, G. Chiola, and G. Conte. (1993). Generalized stochastic Petri nets: A definition at the net level and its implications. *IEEE Transactions on Software Engineering*, **19**, 89–107.
36. G. Ciardo, J. Muppala, and K. Trivedi. (1991). On the solution of GSPN reward models. *Performance Evaluation*, **12**, 237–253.
37. G. Ciardo, A. Blakemore, P. F. Chimento, J. K. Muppala, and K. Trivedi. (1993). Automated generation and analysis of Markov reward models using stochastic reward nets. In Meyer C. D. and Plemmons R. J. (eds.). *Linear Algebra, Markov Chains, and Queueing Models.* The IMA Volumes in Mathematics and Its Applications, vol. 48. New York City, New York, USA: Springer. ISBN 978-1-4613-8353-6.

38. D. Wang, W. Xie, and K. S. Trivedi. (2007). Performability analysis of clustered systems with rejuvenation under varying workload. *Performance Evaluation*, **64**(3), 247–265.
39. F. Machida, D. S. Kim, and K. S. Trivedi. (2013). Modeling and analysis of software rejuvenation in a server virtualized system with live VM migration. *Performance Evaluation*, **70**(3), 212–230.
40. J. Xu, X. Li, Y. Zhong, and H. Zhang. (2014). Availability modeling and analysis of a single-server virtualized system with rejuvenation. *Journal of Software*, **9**, 129–139.
41. A. Bobbio and M. Telek. (1998). Non-exponential stochastic Petri nets: An overview of methods and techniques. *Computer Systems: Science & Engineering*, **13**(6), 339–351.
42. A. Bobbio, A. Puliafito, M. Telek, and K. Trivedi. (1998). Recent developments in non-Markovian stochastic Petri nets. *Journal of Systems Circuits and Computers*, **8**(1), 119–158.
43. A. Bobbio and M. Telek. (1994). Computational restrictions for SPN with generally distributed transition times. In *Proceedings of the First European Dependable Computing Conference (EDCC-1), Berlin, Germany, October 4–6*, pp. 131–148.
44. H. Choi, V. Kulkarni, and K. Trivedi. (1993). Markov regenerative stochastic Petri nets. In *Proceedings of the International Symposium on Computer Performance, Modeling, Measurement and Evaluation, Rome, Italy, September 27–October 1*, pp. 337–357.
45. A. Puliafito, M. Scarpa, and K. Trivedi. (1998). Petri nets with K simultaneously enabled generally distributed timed transitions. *Performance Evaluation*, **32**(1), 1–34.

Index

Accelerated Life Testing (ALT), 11, 105
Accelerated Degradation Testing (ADT), 11
accumulation of errors, 328
active stack pointer, 332
adaptivity metrics, 183
agile, 197, 200
aging, 73, 83, 262
  estimation, 262
  software, 73
aging analysis, 264
  hybrid, 263, 273
  measurement-based, 262, 264, 268
  model-based, 262, 264
  threshold-based, 270
aging effects, 21, 23, 26
aging failure, 264
aging forecasting, 270, 285
aging indicators, 23, 33, 265
aging phenomena, 270
aging symptoms, 290
aging trends, 23
aging-related bug, 9, 21, 23 202, 266, 271, 357, 358
aging-related failure, 21, 23, 25, 278, 290
Android, 315
Android operating system, 13
anomaly detection, 360
ANOVA, 80
Apache, 27, 75, 80
Apache HTTPD, 303
Apache web server, 27, 150
approaches, 42, 73
  statistical, 73
  threshold-based, 73
ARIMA, 79
ARM v8 micro-architecture, 331
ARMA, 79
ARX, 79
assignment errors, 244
attachment pipelining, 247, 249
attacks, 85
  flood, 85
  security, 85
autocorrelation function, 292
availability, 42, 44, 45, 52, 78, 254, 265
avoidance of stack overflow, 331

background boot, 247, 248
best rescuing stack, 335
Black-Box Models, 155, 181
block policy, 146
BLOCKED state, 334, 336
Bohrbugs, 9, 358
breakpoint, 298
BRSS algorithm, 339
buffer overflow attacks, 329
buffer overflows, 328
burst arrival, 146

cache consistency, 241
cache hit ratio, 240
cache management, 241
cache misses, 239, 240
cache pages, 241
callback method, 310
canaries, 329
capacity degradation, 6
cause-effect, 86
central limit theorem, 76
chapters, 109
checkpointed state, 26

checkpointing, 111
chunk, 28, 29
Circuitous Treasure Hunt, 359
Cisco Security Advisory, 230
classification, 73, 81
classifier, 82
closed-loop feedback, 356
cloud, 80
  Eucalyptus, 80
cloud applications, 271
cloud computing, 11, 184, 261
cloud-based software, 268
cloud-based system, 358
clustering method, 104
cold-VM reboot, 254
Cold-VM rejuvenation, 107, 275
completion time
  optimal restart strategy, 167
completion time distribution, 156, 157, 185
  exponential distribution, 159
  heavy-tailed distribution, 161
  hyper-exponential distribition, 159
  hypo-exponential distribution, 160
  moments of completion time, 158, 162
  probability to meet deadline, 158, 167, 172
complex system, 73
computing, 80
concurrently bidirectional stack, 336
condition-based software rejuvenation, 122, 285
condition-triggered policy, 129
conditions, 75
  aging, 75
confidence interval (CI), 105
consistency mechanism, 240
consolidation, 239
constant failure rate (CFR), 100
consumption, 83
  memory, 83
containers, 298
continuous time Markov chain, 91, 95
cooperative stack leasing, 334, 346
CORBA, 296
correlation analysis, 316
correlations, 86
Cox-Stuart test, 79
CPU, 74
CTMC, 95
  homogeneous, 95
cumulative reward, 143

data corruption, 22
data corruption buildup, 26
data-driven, 42
data-driven approach, 43
debugger, 298
decreasing failure rate (DFR), 100
degradation, 76, 83
  performance, 76
delayed detection mechanism, 331
delayed scheme, 333
dependability, 271
design of experiment, 80
detection of failure-prone state, 85
detection of stack overflow, 331
detection of software aging, 285
detector, 75
  aging, 75
deterministic and stochastic Petri nets (DSPNs), 91, 115
deterministic transition, 113
devops methodology, 197, 199, 204, 210
discrete-time Markov chain (DTMC), 133
DoE, 80
dominator tree, 312–314
downtime, 251
downtime costs, 107
downwards growing stack, 332
DSPN, 129
Dwarf, 245
Dwarf-based rejuvenation, 245
dynamic page, 75
dynamic binary analysis, 292

Eclipse Memory Analyzer, 311
effect, 74
  aging, 74
embedded, 360
embedded Markov chain, 133, 142
embedded system, 333
  over-estimation, 333
energy consumption, 267, 269
entropy, 81
equilibrium distribution, 107
Erlang distribution, 105, 114

error accumulation, 21–23
Ethernet, 187
Eucalyptus, 28
execution state, 253
experiment, 75
ext3 file system, 244
Extensive Processing, 359
extfrag, 300

fail-stop, 236
failed rejuvenation, 55
failure, 73
  aging-related failure, 206, 211, 220
  complete failures, 206
  non-aging-related failure, 212
  partial failure, 206, 212
failure classification, 205
failure detectors, 178
failure model, 197
failure rate, 21, 131
failure-probable state, 25, 95
fault injection tool, 244
fault-error-failure chain, 23
faulted stack, 337
feedback control, 355
file blocks, 240
file descriptor, 30, 33
file locks, 22
file table, 289, 291
firmware, 29
flow shop scheduling, 183
fluid stochastic Petri nets (FSPNs), 91, 111
forecasting, 85
forest, 82
  random, 82
fragmentation, 26, 29, 85, 300, 301
framework, 80
free memory, 239, 291
Free Stack Space (FSS), 330, 333, 337

GAP, 333, 338, 344–346
GAP_MIN_VALUE, 333, 338, 344, 346
garbage collection, 319, 320
generation, 309
granularity, 45
granularity level, 41, 44
  application granularity rejuvenation, 51
  application level, 43
  application-level granularity, 47
  Application-level rejuvenation, 48
  multi-granularity rejuvenation, 44
  operating system (OS) level, 43
  OS-level rejuvenation, 47, 48
  physical node level, 43
  single-granularity rejuvenation, 44, 45, 48, 50
  virtualization level, 43
  virtualization level granularity, 46
  VMM rejuvenation granularity, 46
granularity levels, 43
  OS granularity, 47
  VM rejuvenation granularity, 46
GSPN, 129
guard functions, 114
guest boot, 236
guest reboot, 236

hardware reset, 241
Hazard Rates, 185
heap, 29, 286, 295
heap growth, 304
hibernation, 234
hierarchical model, 91, 102
high-availability system, 197, 198, 209, 212, 215, 225
  testing, 201
Hodrick-Prescott filter, 79
Holt-Winters, 79
HTTP, 79, 185
hyper-exponential distribution, 105
hypervisor, 29
hypo-exponential distribution, 95

IBM Director, 231
IDE, 308
Identification Stage, 340
immediate transitions, 115
improper stack size estimation, 347
in-memory DB, 244
increasing failure rate (IFR), 95
indicators, 75
information leakage, 241
inspection-based, 7, 9, 11, 356
instrumentation, 288
inter-process communication (IPC) message, 337

intermediate representation, 292
Inverse Power Law (IPL) Weibull distribution, 105
IPL lognormal distribution, 105

J2EE, 303, 307, 315
J48, 82
Java, 286, 303, 306
Java virtual machine, 13, 184, 262, 271
Jikes, 304
Job completion time, 107
Joint Defense, 331, 343
Joint Defense recovery mechanism, 333
just-in-time recovery technique, 329
JVM, 286, 318, 319
JVMMon, 315, 316
JVMPI, 304

k-armed bandit, 181
Kexec, 248
knowledge, 74
  prior, 74
Kolmogorov's forward equation, 136
Kprobes, 298, 299

Laplace-Stieltjes transform (LST), 108
Las Vegas algorithms, 177, 183, 187
latency, 83
LDA, 82
leak, 83
  memory, 83
  resource, 84
leak detection, 272
leak root, 304–306
LeakBot, 305
learning, 73
  machine, 73
Linux, 299
Linux kernel, 230
Linux operating system, 13
live VM migration, 119
load sensitive faults, 36
load testing, 35
logistic, 80
  Pearl-Reed, 80
loss probability of transactions, 133, 134

$M/M/i/m+i$ queue, 115
$M/M_t/1/K$ queueing model, 128
$M/M_t/1/K$ queueing system, 131
$M/M_t/m/K$ queueing system, 143
machine learning, 183, 269, 356
main memory, 238
maintenance, 268
malloc, 29, 293, 294
Mandelbugs, 9, 203, 330, 347, 358
Mann-Kendall hypothesis test, 292
Mann-Kendall test, 77, 268, 274
manufacturing systems, 183
Markov chain, 210, 223, 225
Markov decision process (MDP), 8, 129
Markov model, 5, 181, 201, 206, 207, 224
Markov modulated Poisson process (MMPP), 146
Markov regenerative process (MRGP), 7, 110, 147
Markov regenerative stochastic Petri net (MRSPN), 91, 110
Markov renewal reward process, 142
Markov-chain-based testing, 6
Markovian arrival process (MAP), 107, 147
Markovian property, 200
mean response time on transactions, 133, 135
measurement-based, 356
measurements, 85
memcached, 244
Memcheck, 292, 294–296
memory consumption, 13, 272, 297
memory corruption of software heaps, 328
memory fragmentation, 278
memory images, 252
memory leak, 102, 230, 272, 297, 303
memory leakage, 22
memory pointers, 294
memory protection, 242
memory-constrained embedded systems, 329
memset, 294
Mercury, 121
metrics, 73, 83
micro-reboot, 251, 257, 277
micro-rejuvenation, 328
microservice architectures, 359
Migrate-VM rejuvenation, 117, 275

MMPP (Markov modulated Poisson process), 130
MMSE, 81
mobile devices, 13
mobile offloading, 181
mobile systems, 360
model-based approaches, 356
model-based aging analysis, 264
model-driven approach, 42, 43
monitored system metrics, 76
monitoring a system's health indicators, 264
monitoring tool for aging analysis, 272
monitoring in microservice architectures, 359
monitoring the software aging, 5
MP5, 82
MRGP (Markov regenerative process), 129
multi-granularity software rejuvenation, 54–56, 356
  three-level software rejuvenation, 54
multiple (hardware) threaded systems, 336
multiple core systems, 336
multithreaded embedded system, 327
multithreading, 32
MySQL, 301, 302

N-policy, 139
N-policy II, 139
narrowing of data types, 328
Network Effect, 186
new call flows from an external caller, 347
new processor micro-architecture, 331, 338
non-aging-related bug, 202, 220, 221
non-contiguous stack leasing, 337
non-homogeneous continuous time Markov chains (NHCTMCs), 374
non-homogeneous Markov chains (NHMCs), 102, 136
non-parametric statistical techniques, 11
non-parametric method, 356
non-stable state, 81
nonlinear, 80
  multivariate, 80
numerical error accrual, 26
numerical experiments, 214

Object Query Language, 312
Object Request Broker (ORB), 296
observations, 76
off-line estimation, 152
Off-The-Shelf (OTS), 296
OLTP, 81
on-line estimation, 152
on-line feedback control, 356
on-memory resume, 252
on-memory suspend, 252
op-code translation, 343
open-source projects, 357
operating system, 24, 359
opportunistic micro-rejuvenation, 327
opportunity time-triggered rejuvenation, 106
optimal rejuvenation time, 73
optimal rejuvenation schedule, 8, 79, 98
OS, 77
OS level, 44
OS rejuvenation, 254
OTS, 298

page cache, 238
parametric time-series, 11
PCA, 80
PerfBlower, 321
performability, 45, 114, 265
performance, 83, 94
performance degradation, 21, 36, 243, 261
performance engineering, 21, 34
performance recovery, 239
performance testing, 34
periodic rollback, 5
periodically, 76
Petri nets (PNs), 109, 182
PH-expansion, 121
phase-based reboot, 232
phenomenon, 73
piecewise regression, 302
planning, 85
Plumbr, 308
polymorphic op-codes, 338
POP, 332–334
POP3, 319
Postgres, 299
power efficiency, 182
prediction of failure, 73
prediction-based methods, 11

prediction-based rejuvenation, 271
preemptive instantaneous, 331, 333
preemptive priority environment, 336
preemptive priority scheduling environment, 339
preemptive-repeat (*prt*), 107
preemptive-resume (*prs*), 108
preventive maintenance, 22, 100
Principal Component Analysis, 80
priority inversion, 336, 337
privileged VMs, 251
proactive/reactive fault tolerance, 263
Probes, 300
process, 31, 73, 302
Process Control Block, 31
process state inheritance, 245
process states, 244
Prognostics and Health Management, 361
Program Counter (PC) Encoding, 329
protection mode, 242
ps, 31
PSF (Priority Scaling Factor), 342
Purdue University, 329
PUSH, 332–334, 336
Python, 299

QDA, 82
quasi-birth-and-death (QBD), 147
queueing model, 128, 182
quick reload, 252

race conditions, 328
Randomised Algorithms, 177
rate, 83
    transaction, 83
re-entrant stack leasing process, 337
reachability, 295
READY threads, 335, 336
real memory, 289
reboot, 155
reboot-based recovery, 232
recovery, 270
recovery rate, 211, 212
Redis, 244
reference graph, 305, 310
regression, 81, 82
    Linear, 82
regression smoothing, 291
reinforcement learning algorithm, 152
rejuvenating the virtual machine monitors, 251
rejuvenation, 73, 74, 155, 197, 261
    software, 73
rejuvenation events, 75, 220
rejuvenation model, 254
rejuvenation schedule, 25
rejuvenation techniques, 274
reliability, 42, 45, 78
reliability block diagram (RBD), 119
Remaining Useful Life, 361
renewal process, 107
renewal reward process, 133
repairable system, 182
replication, 277
requests, 79
rescued stack, 330
rescuing stack, 330, 331, 336, 337
Rescuing Stage, 340
resident memory, 32
resiliency, 121
resolution, 331
resource consumption, 271
resource contention, 252
resource exhaustion, 43, 52
resource leakage, 24, 26, 30
resources, 84
    application-specific, 84
    concurrency-related, 84
    filesystem-related, 84
    network-related, 84
response, 83
response time, 34
restart, 155
restart strategies, 167
    optimal expected completion time, 168
    optimal moments of completion time, 170
    optimal probability to meet deadline, 172
    real-time adaptive schemes for restarts, 184
    uncertainty and risk, 187
    universal strategy, 177
restartable candidates, 233
restartable image, 234
restartable points, 233
restarts, 156

resume policy, 141
retries, 155
return address pointers, 329
return of stack addresses, 328
reusability, 243
Reverse Stack Growth, 338
reward function, 78
reward rates, 105
Rio file cache, 244
robust state, 25
run-time op-code translation, 338, 343
Runge-Kutta method, 137
RUNNING, 336

SAT solvers, 183
sbrk, 29
scalability, 109
Scheduler, 334
seasonal Kendall test, 77
second overflow, 337
Secure Return Address Stack, 330
security intrusions, 360
Selection Stage, 340
self-management, 185
semi-Markov, 78
semi-Markov models, 91, 182
semi-Markov process (SMP), 7, 96
semi-Markov reward, 10
Sen's non-parametric method, 78
Sen's procedure, 292
sensitive information, 241
series, 73
    time, 73
server farms, 186
server virtualization, 117
server-virtualized system, 107
Service-Oriented Systems, 184
SHARPE, 121
SHU, 343, 346
Simple Network Management Protocol, 288
single-level rejuvenation, 98
SLA, 83
smart pointers, 298
SMO, 82
smoothly degrading systems, 6
SMP
    semi-Markov reward model, 104
SMTP, 319
snapshot, 234, 235
SNMP, 77, 288, 291, 302
socket buffers, 300
socket handle, 30, 33
software, 83
software aging, 21, 41–43, 45, 46, 48, 251, 261
software aging analysis, 285, 287
software aging and rejuvenation modeling, 198
software aging and rejuvenation repository, 357
software bugs, 22
software capacity restoration, 4
software failure, 41, 42, 48
    aging-related failures, 42
software life extension, 273
software performance anti-patterns, 359
software rejuvenation, 22, 41–46, 48, 51, 52, 54, 55, 127, 235, 251, 328
    application component rejuvenation, 50
    application-level rejuvenation, 49, 50
    component level rejuvenation, 51
    failed rejuvenation, 54
    full rejuvenation, 51
    multi-granularity rejuvenation, 43, 44
    multi-level rejuvenation, 53
    node-level rejuvenation, 45, 48
    partial rejuvenation, 51
    single-granularity level, 43
    single-granularity rejuvenation, 51, 52
    two-granularity software rejuvenation, 51, 53
    two-level software rejuvenation, 52
    VM rejuvenation, 46, 47
    VM-level rejuvenation, 53
    VMM rejuvenation, 47
    VMM-level rejuvenation, 53
Software Rejuvenation Agent, 302
Special Hardware Unit (SHU), 338
split–merge system, 181
stack overflow, 327–329, 331, 335, 343, 346
    avoidance, 329
    detection, 329
    faults, 330
    just-in-time handling, 346

new approach to handling faults, 330
recovery, 329
techniques to avoid, 329
techniques to mitigate impact, 329
techniques to recover, 329
stack segment, 338
concurrent bi-directionality, 338
stack-limit register, 331
StackGhost, 329
StackGuard, 329
StackShield, 329
state reward, 210, 212
state-less approach, 231
state-retaining approach, 231
stateless applications, 244
static, 75
statistical clustering, 78
statistical models, 104
steady-state availability, 133, 134
steady-state probability vector, 133
steady-state system availability, 103
STL, 298
Stochastic Petri Net Package (SPNP), 114
stochastic Petri nets (SPNs), 91, 109
stochastic reward nets (SRNs), 9, 91, 113, 182
storage, 84
stress testing, 35
Support Vector Machines, 82
survivability, 265
survivability assessment, 197
survivability metrics, 202, 210
survivability model, 216
swap space, 289
sysmon, 303
system, 73
system availability, 94
system call, 299
Systems Modeling Language (SysML), 121
SystemTap, 298, 299, 301

3-state model SMP, 356
T-policy, 131
T-policy I, 132
T-policy II, 132
TAO, 296
TCP retransmission, 157, 175
test case generation, 200
think-time, 35
thrashing, 28
thread, 31
thread control block (TCB), 31, 344
threshold, 74
threshold values, 356
threshold-based, 11
threshold-values based, 12
throughput, 34, 83
accumulated throughput, 219, 220
baseline throughput, 212
degraded throughput, 212
instantaneous throughput, 219
throughput loss, 272
time, 74, 83
response, 74
time series analysis, 268
time to (resource) exhaustion, 23, 104, 270
time-based, 11, 12
time-based software rejuvenation, 7, 97, 122, 267
time-series, 76
time-to-aging-failure, 85
time-to-exhaustion, 292
TimeNET, 121
timestamps, 77
top software errors, 328
Total Time On Test, 186
trade-off, 76
transient bugs, 231
transient performability, 197
transient solution, 214, 225, 226
transients, 76
transition probability matrix, 133
Trees, 82
Decision, 82
trend detection, 268
trend estimation, 77, 268
trigger, 85
TTE, 81, 83
two-level software rejuvenation, 98

unavailability, 96
unchecked deep recursion, 347
Unified Modeling Language (UML), 121
UNIX, 78, 288
UNIX operating system, 104
utilization, 76

Valgrind, 292, 296
valid-address, 293
variability, 76
virtual machine monitor, 182, 234, 262
virtual machines (VMs), 117, 183, 232, 261
virtual memory, 32
virtualization, 46, 261, 358
virtualization technology, 262
virtualized environment, 239, 261
virtualized server, 10
virtualized system, 265
VM, 84
VM Failover, 277
VM migration, 273
VM rejuvenation, 266
VMM rejuvenation, 107, 254, 275
VoltDB, 245

warm-cache reboot, 239, 240
warm-VM reboot, 252
Warm-VM rejuvenation, 108, 275
weighted FSS, 340, 341
working set, 240
workload, 23, 297
workload characterization, 316
workload-based, 78
workload-based analysis, 274
workload-based policy, 130
worm epidemics, 360
Wrong Cache Strategy, 359

zero-copy process migration, 247
ZeroR, 82

CPSIA information can be obtained
at www.ICGtesting.com
Printed in the USA
BVHW092039031021
618070BV00003B/199

9 789811 214561